W9-AAQ-923

George Bush
THE UNAUTHORIZED BIOGRAPHY

George Bush
THE UNAUTHORIZED BIOGRAPHY

by Webster Griffin Tarpley
and
Anton Chaitkin

Executive Intelligence Review
Washington, D.C.
1992

© 1992 Executive Intelligence Review
ISBN: 0–943235–05–7
Library of Congress Catalogue Card Number: 91–78005
EIB 92–002

Front cover photo: EIRNS/Stuart Lewis

cover design: World Composition, Inc.
book design: World Composition, Inc.
project editors: Marianna Wertz, Christina Huth

Please direct all inquiries to the publisher:

Executive Intelligence Review
P.O. Box 17390
Washington, D.C. 20041–0390

TABLE OF CONTENTS

Introduction: American Caligula   1
I.   The House of Bush: Born in a Bank   13
II.   The Hitler Project   26
III.   Race Hygiene: Three Bush Family Alliances   45
IV.   'The Center of Power is in Washington'   63
V.   Poppy and Mommy   83
VI.   Bush in World War Two   101
VII.   Skull and Bones: The Racist Nightmare
        at Yale   115
VIII.   The Permian Basin Gang   138
IX.   Bush Challenges Yarborough for the Senate   155
X.   Rubbers Goes to Congress   186
XI.   United Nations Ambassador, Kissinger Clone   214
XII.   Chairman George in Watergate   238
XIII.   Bush in Beijing   272
XIV.   CIA Director   289
XV.   Campaign 1980   327
XVI.   The Attempted Coup d'Etat of
        March 30, 1981   363
XVII.   Iran-Contra   385
XVIII. The Leveraged Buyout Mob   439
XIX.   The Phony War on Drugs   460
XX.   Omaha   469
XXI.   Bush Takes the Presidency   479
XXII.   The End of History   499
XXIII. The New World Order   541
XXIV.   Thyroid Storm   601
        Index   635
Illustrations follow pages 114, 237, 384, and 540.

ACKNOWLEDGMENTS

We wish to thank Mrs. Helga Zepp-LaRouche for providing, in the dark days after the Persian Gulf war of 1991, the initial impetus that led to this study. We also wish to thank Lyndon H. LaRouche, to whom the authors owe much more than could be hinted at here, for his generous help.

We express our gratitude to Senator Ralph Webster Yarborough of Texas, who kindly granted us access to his 1964 campaign files and, in several interviews, guided us through the political battles of those years as no one else could have.

The authors wish further to express their gratitude to the following persons:

• Kathleen Klenetsky, who led the way with the groundbreaking research and writing on Bush's record in the House of Representatives;

• Herb Quinde, who provided vital insights and writing on the Omaha story, Iran-Contra, and other topics;

• Raynald Rouleau, Carl Osgood, and Bill Jones, who labored mightily in the Library of Congress to assemble the documentation on which all else was based;

• Harley Schlanger, who led us through the thickets of Texas politics as well as offering valuable insights on Bush's links with the leveraged buyout gang;

• Joseph Brewda, who shared his knowledge of the invisible government;

• Linda de Hoyos, who was our touchstone for everything impinging on Asia;

• Michael Liebig, for the European dimension;

• Sylvia Brewda, Susan Schlanger, Steve Carr, John McCarthy, and Martha Quinde, for hospitality and assistance;

• Nancy Spannaus and Christina Huth, for unstinting editorial assistance;

• Marianna Wertz, for infinite patience; and

• Leah and Chloe Peltier, for being there when it mattered.

We wish to thank the staffs of the following libraries and archives:
• The Library of Congress, Washington, D.C.
• The Gerald Ford Presidential Library, Ann Arbor, Michigan
• The Barker Library of the University of Texas, Austin
• The Texas Historical Society, Houston
• The Austin History Center, Austin, Texas
• The Assassination Archives and Research Center, Washington, D.C.
• The Arlington Central Library, Arlington, Virginia
We extend our heartfelt thanks to the many who have helped us, but who prefer to remain anonymous.

INTRODUCTION
AMERICAN CALIGULA

The necessity of writing this book became overwhelming in the minds of the authors in the wake of the ghastly slaughter of the Iraq war of January–February 1991. That war was an act of savage and premeditated genocide on the part of President George Bush, undertaken in connivance with a clique in London which has, in its historical continuity, represented both the worst enemy of the long-term interests of the American people, and the most implacable adversary of the progress of the human species.

The authors observed George Bush as the Gulf crisis and the war unfolded, and had no doubt that his enraged public outbursts constituted real psychotic episodes, indicative of a deranged mental state that was full of ominous portent for humanity. The authors were also horrified by the degree to which their fellow citizens willfully ignored the shocking reality of these public fits. A majority of the American people proved more than willing to lend its support to a despicable enterprise of killing.

By their roll-call votes of January 12, 1991, the Senate and the House of Representatives authorized Bush's planned war measures to restore the Emir of Kuwait, who owns and holds chattel slaves. That vote was a crime against God's justice.

This book is part of an attempt to help the American people to survive this terrible crime, both for the sake of the world and for our own sake. It is intended as a contribution to a process of education that might help to save the American people from the awesome destruction of a second Bush presidency.

As this book goes to press, public awareness of the long-term

1

depression of the American economy is rapidly growing. In a second term, Bush would view himself as beyond the reach of the American electorate; with the federal deficit rising over a billion dollars a day, a second Bush administration would dictate such crushing austerity as to bring the country to the brink of civil war.

Why do we fight the Bush power cartel with a mere book? We have no illusions of easy success, but we were encouraged in our work by the hope that a biography might stimulate opposition to Bush and his policies. And, although Bush is now what journalists call a world leader, no accurate account of his actual career exists in the public domain.

The volume which we submit to the court of world public opinion is, to the best of our knowledge, the first book-length, unauthorized biography of George Bush. It is the first approximation of the truth about his life. This is the first biography worthy of the name, a fact that says a great deal about the sinister and obsessive secrecy of this personage. None of the other biographies (including Bush's campaign autobiography) can be taken seriously; each of these books is a pastiche of lies, distortions and banalities that run the gamut from campaign panegyric, to the Goebbels Big Lie, to fake but edifying stories for credulous children. Almost without exception, the available Bush literature is worthless as a portrait of the subject.

Bush's family pedigree establishes him as a network asset of Brown Brothers Harriman, one of the most powerful political forces in the United States during much of the twentieth century, and for many years the largest private bank in the world. It suffices in this context to think of Averell Harriman negotiating during World War II in the name of the United States with Churchill and Stalin, or of the role of Brown Brothers Harriman partner Robert Lovett in guiding John F. Kennedy's choice of his cabinet, to begin to see the implications of Senator Prescott Bush's post as managing partner of this bank. Brown Brothers Harriman networks pervade government and the mass media. Again and again in the course of the following pages we will see stories embarrassing to George Bush refused publication, documents embarrassing to Bush suspiciously disappear, and witnesses inculpatory to Bush overtaken by mysterious and conveniently timed deaths. The few relevant facts which have found their way into the public domain have necessarily been filtered by this gigantic apparatus. This problem has been compounded by the corruption and servility of authors, journalists, news executives and publishers who have functioned more and more as kept advocates for a governmental regime of which Bush has been a prominent part for a quarter-century.

The Red Studebaker Myth

George Bush wants key aspects of his life to remain covert. At the same time, he senses that his need for coverup is a vulnerability. The need to protect this weak flank accounts for the steady stream of fake biographical material concerning George, as well as the spin given to many studies that may never mention George directly. Over the past several months, we have seen a new book about Watergate that pretends to tell the public something new by fingering Al Haig as Deep Throat, but ignoring the central role of George Bush and his business partners in the Watergate affair. We have a new book by Lt. Col. Oliver North which alleges that Reagan knew everything about the Iran-Contra affair, but that George Bush was not part of North's chain of command. The latter point merely paraphrases Bush's own lame excuse that he was "out of the loop" during all those illegal transactions. During the hearings on the nomination of Robert Gates to become Director of Central Intelligence, nobody had anything new to add about the role of George Bush, the boss of the National Security Council's Special Situation Group crisis staff that was a command center for the whole affair. These charades are peddled to a very credulous public by operatives whose task goes beyond mere damage control to mind control—the "MK" in the government's MK-Ultra operation.

Part of the free ride enjoyed by George Bush during the 1988 elections is reflected in the fact that at no point in the campaign was there any serious effort by any of the news organizations to provide the public with an accurate and complete account of his political career. At least two biographies of Dukakis appeared, which, although hardly critical, were not uniformly laudatory either. But in the case of Bush, all the public could turn to was Bush's old 1980 campaign biography and a newer campaign autobiography, both of them a tissue of lies.

Early in the course of our research for the present volume it became apparent that all books and most longer articles dealing with the life of George Bush had been generated from a single print-out of thoroughly approved "facts" about Bush and his family. We learned that during 1979–80, Bush aide Pete Roussel attempted to recruit biographers to prepare a life of Bush based on a collection of press releases, news summaries, and similar pre-digested material.

Most biographical writing about Bush consists merely of the points from this printout, strung out chronologically and made into a narrative through the interpretation of comments, anecdotes, embellishments, or special stylistic devices.

The canonical Bush-approved printout is readily identified. One dead giveaway is the inevitability with which the hacks out to cover up the substance of Bush's life refer to a 1947 red Studebaker which George Bush allegedly drove into Odessa, Texas in 1948. This is the sort of detail which has been introduced into Bush's real life in a deliberate and deceptive attempt to humanize his image. It has been our experience that any text that features a reference to Bush's red Studebaker has probably been derived from Bush's list of approved facts, and is therefore practically worthless for serious research into Bush's life. We therefore assign such texts to the "red Studebaker school" of coverup and falsification.

Some examples? This is from Bush's campaign autobiography, *Looking Forward*, ghost-written by his aide Vic Gold: "Heading into Texas in my Studebaker, all I knew about the state's landscape was what I'd seen from the cockpit of a Vultee Vibrator during my training days in the Navy."[1]

Here is the same moment as recaptured by Bush's crony Fitzhugh Green, a friend of the Malthusian financier Russell Train, in his *George Bush: An Intimate Portrait*, published after Bush had won the presidency: "He (Bush) gassed up his 1948 Studebaker, arranged for his wife and son to follow, and headed for Odessa, Texas."[2]

Harry Hurt III wrote the following lines in a 1983 Texas magazine article that was even decorated with a drawing of what apparently is supposed to be a Studebaker, but which does not look like a Studebaker of that vintage at all: "When George Herbert Walker Bush drove his battered red Studebaker into Odessa in the summer of 1948, the town's population, though constantly increasing with newly-arrived oil field hands, was still under 30,000."[3]

We see that Harry Hurt has more imagination than many Bush biographers, and his article does provide a few useful facts. More degraded is the version offered by Richard Ben Cramer, whose biography of Bush is expected to be published during 1992. Cramer was given the unenviable task of breathing life once more into the same tired old printout. But the very fact that the Bush team feels that it requires another biography indicates that it still feels that it has a potential vulnerability here. Cramer has attempted to solve his problem by recasting the same old garbage into a frenetic and hyperkinetic, we would almost say *hyperthyroid* style. The following is from an excerpt of this forthcoming book that was published in

Esquire in June 1991: "In June, after the College World Series and graduation day in New Haven, Poppy packed up his new red Studebaker (a graduation gift from Pres), and started driving south."[4]

Was that Studebaker shiny and new, or old and battered? Perhaps the printout is not specific on this point; in any case, as we see, our authorities diverge.

Joe Hyams's 1991 romance of Bush at war, the *Flight of the Avenger*,[5] does not include the obligatory "red Studebaker" reference, but this is more than compensated for by the most elaborate fawning over other details of our hero's war service. The publication of *Flight of the Avenger*, which concentrates on a heroic retelling of Bush's war record, and ignores all evidence that might tend to puncture this myth, was timed to coincide with Bush's war with Iraq. This is a vile tract written with the open assistance of Bush, Barbara Bush, and the White House staff. *Flight of the Avenger* recalls the practice of totalitarian states according to which a war waged by the regime should be accompanied by propaganda which depicts the regime's strong man in a martial posture. In any case, this book deals with Bush's life up to the end of World War II; we never reach Odessa.

Only one of the full-length accounts produced by the Bush propaganda machine neglects the red Studebaker story. This is Nicholas King's *George Bush: A Biography,* the first book-length version of Bush's life, produced as a result of Pete Roussel's efforts for the 1980 campaign. Nicholas King had served as Bush's spokesman when he was U.S. ambassador to the United Nations. King admits in his preface that he can be impugned for writing a work of the most transparent apologetics: "In retrospect," he says , "this book may seem open to the charge of puffery, for the view of its subject is favorable all around."[6] Indeed.

Books about Barbara Bush slavishly rehearse the same details from the same printout. Here is the relevant excerpt from the warmly admiring *Simply Barbara Bush: A Portrait of America's Candid First Lady*, written by Donnie Radcliffe and published after Bush's 1988 election victory: "With $3,000 left over after he graduated in June, 1948, he headed for Texas in the 1947 red Studebaker his father had given him for graduation after George's car died on the highway."[7]

Even foreign journalists attempting to inform their publics about conditions in the United States have fallen victim to the same old Bush printout. The German author and reporter Rainer Bonhorst, the former Washington correspondent of the *Westdeutsche Allge-*

meine Zeitung, in his 1988 book *George Bush: The New Man in the White House,* named a chapter of this Bush political biography "To Texas in the Red Studebaker." Bonhorst writes as follows: "Then there was still the matter of the red Studebaker. It plays— right after the world war effort—a central role in the life history of George Bush. It is the history of his rebellion. The step which made a careless Texan out of a stiff New Englander, a self-made man out of a patrician's son, born into wealth. . . ."

We see that Bonhorst is acutely aware of the symbolic importance assumed by the red Studebaker in these hagiographic accounts of Bush's life.

What is finally the truth of the matter? There is good reason to believe that George Bush did not first come to Odessa, Texas, in a red Studebaker. One knowledgeable source is the well-known Texas oil man and Bush campaign contributor Oscar Wyatt of Houston. In a recent letter to the *Texas Monthly,* Wyatt specifies that "when people speak of Mr. Bush's humble beginnings in the oil industry, it should be noted that he rode down to Texas on Dresser's private aircraft. He was accompanied by his father, who at that time was one of the directors of Dresser Industries. . . . I hate it when people make statements about Mr. Bush's humble beginnings in the oil industry. It just didn't happen that way," writes Mr. Wyatt.[8] Dresser was a Harriman company, and Bush got his start working for one of its subsidiaries. One history of Dresser Industries contains a photograph of George Bush with his parents, wife and infant son "in front of a Dresser company airplane in West Texas" (see picture section).[9] Can this be a photo of Bush's arrival in Odessa during the summer of 1948? In any case, this most cherished myth of the Bush biographers is very much open to doubt.

The Roman Propaganda Machine

Fawning biographies of bloodthirsty tyrants are nothing new in world literature. The red Studebaker school goes back a long way; these writers of today can be usefully compared with a certain Gaius Velleius Paterculus, who lived in the Roman Empire under the Emperors Augustus and Tiberius, and who was thus an approximate contemporary of Jesus Christ. Velleius Paterculus was a historian and biographer who is known today, if at all, for his biographical notes on the Emperor Tiberius, which are contained within Paterculus's history of Rome.

Paterculus, writing under Tiberius, gave a very favorable treatment of Julius Caesar, and became fulsome when he came to write of Augustus. But the worst excesses of flattery came in Velleius Paterculus's treatment of Tiberius himself.

But why bring up Rome? Some readers may be scandalized by the things that truth obliges us to record about a sitting President of the United States. Are we not disrespectful to this high office? No.

One of the reasons for glancing back at Imperial Rome is to remind ourselves that in times of moral and cultural degradation like our own, rulers of great evil have inflicted incalculable suffering on humanity. In our modern time of war and depression, this is once again the case. If Tiberius and Caligula were possible then, who could claim that the America of the New World Order should be exempt?

In order to find Roman writers who tell us anything reliable about the first dozen emperors, we must wait until the infamous Julio-Claudian dynasty of Julius Caesar, Augustus, Tiberius, Caligula, Claudius, Nero and the rest had entirely passed from the scene, to be supplanted by new ruling houses. Tiberius reigned from 14 to 37 A.D.; Caligula, his designated successor, from 37 to 41 A.D.; and Nero from 54 to 68 A.D. But the first accurate account of the crimes of some of these emperors comes from Publius Cornelius Tacitus in about 115-17 A.D., late in the reign of the Emperor Trajan. It was feasible for Tacitus to write and publish a more realistic account of the Julio-Claudian emperors because one of the constant themes of Trajan's propaganda was to glorify himself as an enlightened emperor through comparison with the earlier series of bloody tyrants.

Tacitus manages to convey how the destructiveness of these emperors in their personal lives correlated with their mass executions and their genocidal economic policies. Tacitus was familiar with the machinery of Roman Imperial power: He was of senatorial rank, served as consul in Italy in 97 A.D., and was the governor of the important province of western Anatolia (today's Turkey) which the Romans referred to simply as Asia. Tacitus writes of Tiberius: ". . . his criminal lusts shamed him. Their uncontrollable activity was worthy of an oriental tyrant. Free-born children were his victims. He was fascinated by beauty, youthful innocence, and aristocratic birth. New names for types of perversions were invented. Slaves were charged to locate and procure his requirements. . . . It was like the sack of a captured city."

Because of lacunae in the manuscripts of Tacitus's work[10] that have come down to us, much of what we know of the rule of Caligula (Gaius Caesar, in power from 37 to 41 A.D.) derives from *The Lives of the Twelve Caesars*, a book by Gaius Suetonius Tranquillus. The character and administration of Caligula present some striking parallels with the subject of the present book.

As a stoic, Caligula was a great admirer of his own "immovable rigor." His motto was "Remember that I have the right to do anything to anybody." He made no secret of his bloodthirsty vindictiveness. Caligula was a fan of the green team in the Roman arena, and when the crowd applauded a charioteer who wore a different color, Caligula cried out, "I wish the Roman people had but a single neck." At one of his state dinners Caligula burst into a fit of uncontrollable laughter, and when a consul asked him what was so funny, he replied that it was the thought that as Emperor, Caligula had the power to have the throats of the top officials cut at any time he chose. Caligula carried this same attitude into his personal life: Whenever he kissed or caressed the neck of his wife or one of his mistresses, he liked to remark: "Off comes this beautiful head whenever I give the word."

Above all, Caligula was vindictive. After his death, two notebooks were found among his personal papers, one labeled "The Sword" and the other "The Dagger." These were lists of the persons he had proscribed and liquidated, and were the forerunners of the enemies lists and discrediting committee of today. Suetonius frankly calls Caligula "a monster," and speculates on the psychological roots of his criminal disposition: "I think I may attribute to mental weakness the existence of two exactly opposite faults in the same person, extreme assurance and, on the other hand, excessive timorousness." Caligula was "full of threats" against "the barbarians," but at the same time prone to precipitous retreats and flights of panic. Caligula worked on his "body language" by "practicing all kinds of terrible and fearsome expressions before a mirror."

Caligula kept his wife, Caesonia (described by Suetonius as "neither beautiful nor young") with him until the very end. But his greatest devotion was to his horse, whom he made consul of the Roman state. Ultimately Caligula fell victim to a conspiracy of the Praetorian Guard, led by the tribune Gaius Chaerea, a man whom Caligula had taken special delight in humiliating.[11]

The authors of the present study are convinced that these references to the depravity of the Roman emperors, and to the records of that depravity provided by such authors as Tacitus and Suetonius, are directly germane to our present task of following the career of a member of the senatorial class of the Anglo-American elite through the various stages of his formation and ultimate ascent to imperial power. The Roman Imperial model is germane because the American ruling elite of today is far closer to the world of Tiberius and Caligula than it is to the world of the American Revolution or the Constitutional Convention of 1789. The leitmotif of modern American presidential politics is unquestionably an imperial theme, most blatantly expressed by Bush in his slogan for 1990, the "New World Order," and for 1991, the "pax universalis." The central project of the Bush presidency is the creation and consolidation of a single, universal Anglo-American (or Anglo-Saxon) empire very directly modeled on the various phases of the Roman Empire.

The Olympian Delusion

There is one other aspect of the biographical-historical method of the Graeco-Roman world which we have sought to borrow. Ever since Thucydides composed his monumental work on the Peloponnesian War, those who have sought to imitate his style—with the Roman historian Titus Livius prominent among them—have employed the device of attributing long speeches to historical personages, even when it appears very unlikely that such lengthy orations could have been made by the protagonists at the time. This has nothing to do with the synthetic dialogue of current American political writing, which attempts to present historical events as a series of trivial and banal soap-opera exchanges, which carry on for such interminable lengths as to suggest that the authors are getting paid by the word. Our idea of fidelity to the classical style has simply been to let George Bush speak for himself wherever possible, through direct quotation. We are convinced that by letting Bush express himself directly in this way, we afford the reader a more faithful—and damning—account of Bush's actions.

George Bush might agree that "history is biography," although we suspect that he would not agree with any of our other conclusions. There may be a few peculiarities of the present work as biography that are worthy of explanation at the outset.

One of our basic theses is that George Bush is, and considers himself to be, an oligarch. The notion of oligarchy includes first of all the idea of a patrician and wealthy family capable of introducing its offspring into such elite institutions as Andover, Yale, and Skull and Bones. Oligarchy also subsumes the self-conception of the oligarch as belonging to a special, exalted breed of mankind, one that is superior to the common run of mankind as a matter of hereditary, genetic superiority. This mentality generally goes together with a fascination for eugenics, race science and just plain racism as a means of building a case that one's own family tree and racial stock are indeed superior. These notions of "breeding" are a constant in the history of the titled feudal aristocracy of Europe, especially Britain, toward inclusion in which an individual like Bush must necessarily strive. At the very least, oligarchs like Bush see themselves as demigods occupying a middle ground between the immortals above and the *hoi polloi* below. The culmination of this insane delusion, which Bush has demonstrably long since attained, is the obsessive belief that the principal families of the Anglo-American elite, assembled in their freemasonic orders, by themselves directly constitute an Olympian Pantheon of living deities who have the capability of abrogating and disregarding the laws of the universe according to their own irrational caprice. If we do not take into account this element of fatal and megalomaniac hubris, the lunatic Anglo-American policies in regard to the Gulf war, international finance, or the AIDS epidemic must defy all comprehension.

Part of the ethos of oligarchism as practiced by George Bush is the emphasis on one's own family pedigree. This accounts for the attention we dedicate in the opening chapters of this book to Bush's family tree, reaching back to the nineteenth century and beyond. It is impossible to gain insight into Bush's mentality unless we realize that it is important for him to be considered a cousin, however distant, of Queen Elizabeth II of the House of Mountbatten-Windsor and for his wife Barbara to be viewed in some sense a descendant of President Franklin Pierce.

The Family Firm

For related reasons, it is our special duty to illustrate the role played in the formation of George Bush as a personality by his maternal grandfather and uncle, George Herbert Walker and George Herbert Walker, Jr., and by George H.W. Bush's father, the late Senator Prescott Bush. In the course of this task, we must speak at length about the institution to which George Bush owes the most, the Wall Street international investment bank of Brown Brothers Harriman, the political and financial powerhouse mentioned above. For George Bush, Brown Brothers Harriman was and remains the family firm in the deepest sense. The formidable power of this bank and its ubiquitous network, wielded by Senator Prescott Bush up through the time of his death in 1972, and still active on George's behalf down to the present day, is the single most important key to every step of George's business, covert operations, and political career.

In the case of George Bush, as many who have known him

personally have noted, the network looms much larger than George's own character and will. The reader will search in vain for strong, principled commitments in George Bush's personality; the most that will be found is a series of characteristic obsessions, of which the most durable are race, vanity, personal ambition, and settling scores with adversaries. What emerges by contrast is the decisive importance of Bush's network of connections. His response to the Gulf crisis of 1991 will be largely predetermined, not by any great flashes of geopolitical insight, but rather by his connections to the British oligarchy, to Kissinger, to Israeli and Zionist circles, to Texas oilmen in his fundraising base, to the Saudi Arabian and Kuwaiti royal houses. If the question is one of finance, then the opinions of J. Hugh Liedtke, Henry Kravis, Robert Mosbacher, T. Boone Pickens, Nicholas Brady, James Baker III and the City of London will be decisive. If covert operations and dirty tricks are on the agenda, then there is a whole stable of CIA old boys with whom he will consult, and so on down the line. During much of 1989, despite his control over the presidency, Bush appeared as a weak and passive executive, waiting for his networks to show him what it was he was supposed to do. When German reunification and the crumbling of the Soviet empire spurred those—primarily British—networks into action, Bush was suddenly capable of violent and daring adventures. As his battle for a second term approaches, Bush may be showing increasing signs of a rage-driven self-starter capability, especially when it comes to starting new wars designed to secure his reelection.

The United States in Decline

Biography has its own inherent discipline: It must be concerned with the life of its protagonist, and cannot stray too far away. In no way has it been our intention to offer an account of American history during the lifetime of George Bush. The present study nevertheless reflects many aspects of that recent history of U.S. decline. It will be noted that Bush has succeeded in proportion as the country has failed, and that Bush's advancement has proceeded *pari passu* with the degradation of the national stage upon which he has operated and which he has come to dominate. At various phases in his career, Bush has come into conflict with persons who were intellectually and morally superior to him. Exemplary is Bush's long-standing personal vendetta against Lyndon LaRouche, his most consistent and capable adversary. LaRouche was jailed seven days after Bush's inauguration in the most infamous political frameup of recent U.S.

history. As our study will document, at critical moments in Bush's career, LaRouche's political interventions have frustrated some of Bush's best-laid political plans: A very clear example is LaRouche's role in defeating Bush's 1980 presidential bid in the New Hampshire primary. Over the intervening years, LaRouche has become George Bush's "man in the iron mask," the principled political adversary whom Bush seeks to jail and silence at all costs. The restoration of justice in this country must include the freeing of Lyndon LaRouche, LaRouche's political associates, and all the other political prisoners of the Bush regime.

The authors have been at some pains to make this work intelligible to readers around the world. We offer this book to those who share our aversion to the imperialist-colonialist New World Order, and our profound horror at the concept of a return to a single, worldwide Roman Empire as suggested by Bush's "pax universalis" slogan. This work is tangible evidence that there is an opposition to Bush inside the United States, and that the new Caligula is very vulnerable indeed on the level of the exposure of his own misdeeds.

We do not delude ourselves that we have said the last word about George Bush. But we have for the first time sketched out at least some of the most salient features and gathered them into a comprehensible whole. We encourage an aroused citizenry, as well as specialized researchers, to improve upon what we have been able to accomplish. In so doing, we recall the words of the Florentine Giovanni Boccaccio when he reluctantly accepted the order of a powerful king to produce an account of the old Roman Pantheon: "If I don't succeed completely in this exposition, at least I will provide a stimulus for the better work of others who are wiser."—Boccaccio, *Genealogy of the National Gods*

Notes for Introduction

1. George Bush and Victor Gold, *Looking Forward* (New York: Doubleday, 1987), p. 47.

2. Fitzhugh Green, *George Bush: An Intimate Portrait* (New York: Hippocrene, 1989), p. 53.

3. Harry Hurt III, "George Bush, Plucky Lad," *Texas Monthly*, June, 1983, p. 142.

4. Richard Ben Cramer, "How He Got Here," *Esquire*, June, 1991, p. 84.

5. Joe Hyams, *Flight of the Avenger: George Bush at War* (New York: Harcourt, Brace, Jovanovitch, 1991).

6. Nicholas King, *George Bush: A Biography* (New York: Dodd, Mead, 1980), p. xi.

7. Donnie Radcliffe, *Simply Barbara Bush* (New York: Warner, 1989), p. 103.

8. See "The Roar of the Crowd," *Texas Monthly*, Nov. 1991. See also Jan Jarboe, "Meaner Than a Junkyard Dog," *Texas Monthly*, April 1991, pp. 122 ff. Here Wyatt observes: "I knew from the beginning George Bush came to Texas only because he was politically ambitious. He flew out here on an airplane owned by Dresser Industries. His daddy was a member of the board of Dresser."

9. Darwin Payne, *Initiative in Energy* (New York: Simon and Schuster, 1979), p. 233.

10. Cornelius Tacitus, *The Annals of Imperial Rome* (New York: Penguin, 1962).

11. Gaius Suetonius Tranquillus, *The Lives of the Twelve Caesars* (New York: Modern Library, 1931), pp. 165–204 passim.

I

THE HOUSE OF BUSH: BORN IN A BANK

Who is George Bush? How did he become the 41st U.S. President?

He is said to be a man of the "old establishment," who "chose to seek his fortune as an independent oilman. . . ."[1]

In fact, Bush was never "independent." Every career step in his upward climb relied on his family's powerful associations. The Bush family joined the Eastern Establishment comparatively recently, and only as servitors. Their wealth and influence resulted from their loyalty to another, more powerful family, and their willingness to do *anything* to get ahead.

For what they did, Bush's forebears should have become very famous, or infamous. They remained obscure figures, managers from behind the scenes. But their actions—including his father's role as banker for Adolf Hitler—had tragic effects for the whole planet.

It was these services to his family's benefactors, which propelled George Bush to the top.

Prescott Goes to War

President George Herbert Walker Bush was born in 1924, the son of Prescott S. Bush and Dorothy Walker Bush. We will begin the George Bush story about a decade before his birth, on the eve of World War I. We will follow the career of his father, Prescott Bush, through his marriage with Dorothy Walker, on the path to fortune, elegance and power.

Prescott Bush entered Yale University in 1913. A native of Columbus, Ohio, Prescott had spent the last five years before college in St. George's Episcopal preparatory school in Newport, Rhode Island.

Prescott Bush's first college year, 1913, was also the freshman year at Yale for E. Roland "Bunny" Harriman, whose older brother (Wm.) Averell Harriman had just graduated from Yale. This is the Averell Harriman who went on to fame as the U.S. ambassador to the Soviet Union during World War II, as a governor of New York State, and as a presidential advisor who was greatly responsible for starting the Vietnam War.

The Harrimans would become the sponsors of the Bushes, to lift them onto the stage of world history.

In the spring of 1916, Prescott Bush and "Bunny" Harriman were chosen for membership in an elite Yale senior-year secret society known as Skull and Bones. This unusually morbid, death-celebrating group helped Wall Street financiers find active young men of "good birth" to form a kind of imitation British aristocracy in America.

World War I was then raging in Europe. With the prospect that the U.S.A. would soon join the war, two Skull and Bones "Patriarchs," Averell Harriman (class of 1913) and Percy A. Rockefeller (class of 1900), paid special attention to Prescott's class of 1917. They wanted reliable cadres to help them play the Great Game, in the lucrative new imperial era that the war was opening up for London and New York moneycrats. Prescott Bush, by then a close friend of "Bunny" Harriman, and several other Bonesmen from their class of 1917 would later comprise the core partners in Brown Brothers Harriman, the world's largest private investment bank.

World War I did make an immense amount of money for the clan of stock speculators and British bankers who had just taken over U.S. industry. The Harrimans were stars of this new Anglo-American elite.

Averell's father, stockbroker E.H. Harriman, had gained control of the Union Pacific Railroad in 1898 with credit arranged by William Rockefeller, Percy's father, and by Kuhn Loeb and Co.'s British-affiliated private bankers, Otto Kahn, Jacob Schiff and Felix Warburg.

William Rockefeller, treasurer of Standard Oil and brother of Standard founder John D. Rockefeller, owned National City Bank (later "Citibank") together with Texas-based James Stillman. In return for their backing, E.H. Harriman deposited in City Bank the vast receipts from his railroad lines. When he issued tens of millions of dollars of "watered" (fraudulent) railroad stock, Harriman sold most of the shares through the Kuhn Loeb company.

The First World War elevated Prescott Bush and his father, Samuel P. Bush, into the lower ranks of the Eastern Establishment.

As war loomed in 1914, National City Bank began reorganizing the U.S. arms industry. Percy A. Rockefeller took direct control of the Remington Arms company, appointing his own man, Samuel F. Pryor, as the new chief executive of Remington.

The U.S entered World War I in 1917. In the spring of 1918, Prescott's father, Samuel P. Bush, became chief of the Ordnance, Small Arms and Ammunition Section of the War Industries Board.[2] The senior Bush took national responsibility for government assistance to and relations with Remington and other weapons companies.

This was an unusual appointment, as Prescott's father seemed to have no background in munitions. Samuel Bush had been president of the Buckeye Steel Castings Co. in Columbus, Ohio, makers of railcar parts. His entire career had been in the railroad business—supplying equipment to the Wall Street-owned railroad systems.

The War Industries Board was run by Bernard Baruch, a Wall Street speculator with close personal and business ties to old E.H. Harriman. Baruch's brokerage firm had handled Harriman speculations of all kinds.[3]

In 1918, Samuel Bush became director of the Facilities Division of the War Industries Board. Prescott's father reported to the Board's Chairman, Bernard Baruch, and to Baruch's assistant, Wall Street private banker Clarence Dillon.

Robert S. Lovett, President of Union Pacific Railroad, chief counsel to E.H. Harriman and executor of his will, was in charge of national production and purchase "priorities" for Baruch's board.

With the war mobilization conducted under the supervision of the War Industries Board, U.S. consumers and taxpayers showered unprecedented fortunes on war producers and certain holders of raw materials and patents. Hearings in 1934 by the committee of U.S. Senator Gerald Nye attacked the "Merchants of Death"—war profiteers such as Remington Arms and the British Vickers company—whose salesmen had manipulated many nations into wars, and then supplied all sides with the weapons to fight them.

Percy Rockefeller and Samuel Pryor's Remington Arms supplied machine guns and Colt automatic pistols; millions of rifles to Czarist Russia; over half of the small-arms ammunition used by the Anglo-American allies in World War I; and 69 percent of the rifles used by the United States in that conflict.[4]

Samuel Bush's wartime relationship to these businessmen would continue after the war, and would especially aid his son Prescott's career of service to the Harrimans.

Most of the records and correspondence of Samuel Bush's arms-related section of the government have been burned, "to save space" in the National Archives. This matter of destroyed or misplaced records should be of concern to citizens of a constitutional republic. Unfortunately, it is a rather constant impediment with regard to researching George Bush's background: He is certainly the most "covert" American chief executive.

Now, arms production in wartime is by necessity carried on with great security precautions. The public need not know details of the private lives of the government or industry executives involved, and a broad interrelationship between government and private-sector personnel is normal and useful.

But during the period preceding World War I, and in the war years 1914–1917 when the U.S. was still neutral, interlocking Wall Street financiers subservient to British strategy lobbied heavily, and twisted U.S. government and domestic police functions. Led by the J.P. Morgan concern, Britain's overall purchasing agent in America, these financiers wanted a world war and they wanted the United States in it as Britain's ally. The U.S. and British arms companies, owned by these international financiers, poured out weapons abroad in deals not subject to the scrutiny of any electorate back home. The same gentlemen, as we shall see, later supplied weapons and money to Hitler's Nazis.

That this problem persists today, is in some respect due to the "control" over the documentation and the history of the arms traffickers.

World War I was a disaster for civilized humanity. It had terrible, unprecedented casualties, and shattering effects on the moral philosophy of Europeans and Americans.

But for a brief period, the war treated Prescott Bush rather well.

In June, 1918, just as his father took over responsibility for relations of the government with the private arms producers, Prescott went to Europe with the U.S. Army. **His unit did not come near any fire until September.** But on August 8, 1918, the following item appeared on the front page of Bush's home-town newspaper:

3 High Military Honors Conferred on Capt. Bush
For Notable Gallantry, When Leading Allied Commanders Were Endangered, Local Man is Awarded French, English and U.S. Crosses.

International Honors, perhaps unprecedented in the life of an

American soldier, have been conferred upon Captain Prescott Sheldon Bush, son of Mr. and Mrs. S.P. Bush of Columbus.

Upon young Bush ... were conferred: Cross of the Legion of Honor, ... Victoria Cross, ... Distinguished Service Cross. ...

Conferring of the three decorations upon one man at one time implies recognition of a deed of rare valor and probably of great military importance as well.

From word which has reached Columbus during the last few days, it appears as if the achievement of Captain Bush well measures up to these requirements.

The incident occurred on the western front about the time the Germans were launching their great offensive of July 15. ... The history of the remarkable victory scored later by the allies might have been written in another vein, but for the heroic and quick action of Captain Bush.

The ... three allied leaders, Gen. [Ferdinand] Foch, Sir Douglas Haig and Gen. [John J.] Pershing ... were making an inspection of American positions. Gen. Pershing had sent for Captain Bush to guide them about one sector. ...

Suddenly Captain Bush noticed a shell coming directly for them. He shouted a warning, suddenly drew his bolo knife, stuck it up as he would a ball bat, and parried the blow, causing the shell to glance off to the right. ...

Within 24 hours young Bush was notified ... [that] the three allied commanders had recommended him for practically the highest honors within their gift. ...

Captain Bush is 23 years old, a graduate of Yale in the class of 1917. He was one of Yale's best-known athletes ... was leader of the glee club ... and in his senior year was elected to the famous Skull and Bones Society. ...[5]

The day after this astonishing story appeared, there was a large cartoon on the editorial page. It depicted Prescott Bush as a small boy, reading a story-book about military heroism, and saying: "Gee! I wonder if anything like that could ever truly happen to a boy." The caption below was a rehash of the batting-away-the-deadly-shell exploit, written in storybook style.[6]

Local excitement about the military "Babe Ruth" lasted just four weeks. Then this somber little box appeared on the front page:

Editor State Journal:

A cable received from my son, Prescott S. Bush, brings word that he has not been decorated, as published in the papers a month ago. He feels dreadfully troubled that a letter, written in a spirit of fun, should have been misinterpreted. He says he is no hero and asks me to make explanations. I will appreciate your kindness in publishing this letter. . . .

Flora Sheldon Bush.
Columbus, Sept. 5.[7]

Prescott Bush later claimed that he spent "about 10 or 11 weeks" in the area of combat in France. "We were under fire there. . . . It was quite exciting, and of course a wonderful experience."[8]

Prescott Bush was discharged in mid-1919, and returned for a short time to Columbus, Ohio. But his humiliation in his home town was so intense that he could no longer live there. The "war hero" story was henceforth not spoken of in his presence. Decades later, when he was an important, rich U.S. Senator, the story was whispered and puzzled over among the Congressmen.

Looking to be rescued from this ugly situation, Captain Bush went to the 1919 reunion of his Yale class in New Haven, Connecticut. Skull and Bones Patriarch Wallace Simmons, closely tied to the arms manufacturers, offered Prescott Bush a job in his St. Louis railroad equipment company. Bush took the offer and moved to St. Louis—and his destiny.

A Thoroughbred Marriage

Prescott Bush went to St. Louis to repair his troubled life. Sometime that same year, Averell Harriman made a trip there on a project which would have great consequences for Prescott. The 28-year-old Harriman, until then something of a playboy, wanted to bring his inherited money and contacts into action in the arena of world affairs.

President Theodore Roosevelt had denounced Harriman's father for "cynicism and deep-seated corruption" and called him an "undesirable citizen."[9] For the still-smarting Averell to take his place among the makers and breakers of nations, he needed a financial and intelligence-gathering organization of his own. The man Harriman sought to create such an institution for him was Bert Walker, a Missouri stock broker and corporate wheeler-dealer.

George Herbert ("Bert") Walker, for whom President George H.W. Bush was named, did not immediately accept Harriman's proposal. Would Walker leave his little St. Louis empire, to try his influence in New York and Europe?

Bert was the son of a dry goods wholesaler who had thrived on imports from England.[10] The British connection had paid for Walker summer houses in Santa Barbara, California, and in Maine—"Walker's Point" at Kennebunkport. Bert Walker had been sent to England for his prep school and college education.

By 1919 Bert Walker had strong ties to the Guaranty Trust Company in New York and to the British-American banking house J.P. Morgan and Co. These Wall Street concerns represented all the important owners of American railroads: the Morgan partners and their associates or cousins in the intermarried Rockefeller, Whitney, Harriman and Vanderbilt families.

Bert Walker was known as the midwest's premier deal-arranger, awarding the investment capital of his international-banker contacts to the many railroads, utilities and other midwestern industries of which he and his St. Louis friends were executives or board members.

Walker's operations were always quiet, or mysterious, whether in local or global affairs. He had long been the "power behind the throne" in the St. Louis Democratic Party, along with his crony, former Missouri Governor David R. Francis. Walker and Francis together had sufficient influence to select the party's candidates.[11]

Back in 1904, Bert Walker, David Francis, Washington University President Robert Brookings and their banker/broker circle had organized a world's fair in St. Louis, the Louisiana Purchase Exposition. In line with the old Southern Confederacy family backgrounds of many of these sponsors, the fair featured a "Human Zoo": live natives from backward jungle regions were exhibited in special cages under the supervision of anthropologist William J. McGee.

So Averell Harriman was a natural patron for Bert Walker. Bert shared Averell's passion for horse breeding and horse racing, and easily accommodated the Harriman family's related social philosophy. They believed that the horses and racing stables they owned showed the way toward a sharp upgrading of the human stock— just select and mate thoroughbreds, and spurn or eliminate inferior animals.

The First World War had brought the little St. Louis oligarchy into the Confederate-slaveowner-oriented administration of President Woodrow Wilson and his advisors, Col. Edward House and Bernard Baruch.

Walker's friend Robert Brookings got into Bernard Baruch's War Industries Board as director of national Price Fixing (sic). David R. Francis became U.S. ambassador to Russia in 1916. As the Bolshevik Revolution broke out, we find Bert Walker busy appointing people to Francis's staff in Petrograd.[12]

Walker's earliest activities in relation to the Soviet state are of significant interest to historians, given the activist role he was to play there together with Harriman. But Walker's life is as covert as the rest of the Bush clan's, and the surviving public record is extremely thin.

The 1919 Versailles peace conference brought together British imperial strategists and their American friends to make postwar global arrangements. For his own intended international adventures, Harriman needed Bert Walker the seasoned intriguer, who quietly represented many of the British-designated rulers of American politics and finance.

After two persuasion trips west by Harriman,[13] Walker at length agreed to move to New York. But he kept his father's summer house in Kennebunkport, Maine.

Bert Walker formally organized the W.A. Harriman & Co. private bank in November 1919. Walker became the bank's president and chief executive; Averell Harriman was chairman and controlling co-owner with his brother Roland ("Bunny"), Prescott Bush's close friend from Yale; and Percy Rockefeller was a director and a founding financial sponsor.

In the autumn of 1919, Prescott Bush made the acquaintance of Bert Walker's daughter Dorothy. They were engaged the following year, and were married in August, 1921.[14] Among the ushers and grooms at the elaborate wedding were Ellery S. James, Knight Woolley and four other fellow Skull and Bonesmen from the Yale Class of 1917.[15]

The Bush-Walker extended family has gathered each summer at the "Walker country home" in Kennebunkport, from this marriage of President Bush's parents down to the present day.

When Prescott married Dorothy, he was only a minor executive of the Simmons Co., railroad equipment suppliers, while his wife's father was building one of the most gigantic businesses in the world. The following year the couple tried to move back to Columbus, Ohio; there Prescott worked for a short time in a rubber products company owned by his father. But they soon moved again to Milton, Mass., after outsiders bought the little family business and moved it near there.

Thus Prescott Bush was going nowhere fast, when his son George Herbert Walker Bush—the future U.S. President—was born in Milton, Mass., on June 12, 1924.

Perhaps it was as a birthday gift for George, that "Bunny" Harriman stepped in to rescue his father Prescott from oblivion, bringing him into the Harriman-controlled U.S. Rubber Co. in New York City. In 1925 the young family moved to the town where George was to grow up: Greenwich, Connecticut, a suburb both of New York and of New Haven/Yale.

Then on May 1, 1926, Prescott Bush joined W.A. Harriman & Co. as its vice president, under the bank's president, Bert Walker, his father-in-law and George's maternal grandfather—the head of the family.[16]

The Great Game

Prescott Bush would demonstrate strong loyalty to the firm he joined in 1926. And the bank, with the scope and power of many ordinary nations, could amply reward its agents. George Bush's Grandfather Walker had put the enterprise together, quietly, secretly, using all the international connections at his disposal. Let us briefly look back at the beginning of the Harriman firm—the Bush family enterprise—and follow its course into one of history's darkest projects.

The firm's first global lever was its successful arrangement to get into Germany by dominating that country's shipping. Averell Harriman announced in 1920 that he would re-start Germany's Hamburg-Amerika Line, after many months of scheming and arm-twisting. Hamburg-Amerika's commercial steamships had been confiscated by the United States at the end of the First World War. These ships had then become the property of the Harriman enterprise, by some arrangements with the U.S. authorities that were never made public.

The deal was breathtaking; it would create the world's largest private shipping line. Hamburg-Amerika Line regained its confiscated vessels for a heavy price. The Harriman enterprise took "the right to participate in 50 percent of all business originated in Hamburg"; and for the next twenty years (1920–1940), the Harriman enterprise had "complete control of all activities of the Hamburg line in the United States." [17]

Harriman became co-owner of Hamburg-Amerika. The Harriman-Walker firm gained a tight hold on its management, with the not-so-subtle backing of the post-World War I occupation of Germany by the armies of England and America.

Just after Harriman's public statement, the St. Louis press celebrated Bert Walker's role in assembling the money to consummate the deal:

"Ex-St. Louisan Forms Giant Ship Merger"

"G. H. Walker is Moving Power Behind Harriman-Morton Shipping Combine. . . ."

The story celebrated a "merger of two big financial houses in New York, which will place practically unlimited capital at the disposal of the new American-German shipping combine. . . ."[18]

Bert Walker had arranged a "marriage" of J.P. Morgan credit and Harriman family inherited wealth.

W.A. Harriman & Co., of which Walker was president and founder, was merging with the Morton & Co. private bank—and Walker was "[p]rominent in the affairs of Morton & Co.," which was interlocked with the Morgan-controlled Guaranty Trust Co.

The Hamburg-Amerika takeover created an effective instrument for the manipulation and fatal subversion of Germany. One of the great "merchants of death," Samuel Pryor, was in it from the beginning. Pryor, then chairman of the executive committee of Remington Arms, helped arrange the deal and served with Walker on the board of Harriman's shipping front organization, the American Ship and Commerce Co.

Walker and Harriman took the next giant step in 1922, setting up their European headquarters office in Berlin. With the aid of the Hamburg-based Warburg bank, W.A. Harriman & Co. began spreading an investment net over German industry and raw materials.

From the Berlin base, Walker and Harriman then plunged into deals with the new dictatorship of the Soviet Union. They led a select group of Wall Street and British Empire speculators who restarted the Russian oil industry, which had been devastated by the Bolshevik Revolution. They contracted to mine Soviet manganese, an element essential to modern steelmaking. These concessions were arranged directly with Leon Trotsky, then with Feliks Dzerzhinsky, founder of the Soviet dictatorship's secret intelligence service (KGB), whose huge statue was finally pulled down by pro-democracy demonstrators in 1991.

These speculations created both channels of communication, and the style of accomodation, with the communist dictatorship, that have continued in the family down to President Bush.

With the bank launched, Bert Walker found New York the ideal place to satisfy his passion for sports, games and gambling. Walker was elected president of the U.S. Golf Association in 1920. He negotiated new international rules for the game with the Royal and Ancient Golf Club of St. Andrews, Scotland. After these talks he contributed the three-foot-high silver Walker Cup, for which British and American teams have since competed every two years.

Bert's son-in-law Prescott Bush was later secretary of the U.S. Golf Association, during the grave political and economic crises of the early 1930s. Prescott became USGA President in 1935, while he was otherwise embroiled in the family firm's work with Nazi Germany.

When George was one year old, in 1925, Bert Walker and Averell Harriman headed a syndicate which rebuilt Madison Square Garden as the modern Palace of Sport. Walker was at the center of New York's gambling scene in its heyday, in that Prohibition era of colorful and bloody gangsters. The Garden bloomed with million-dollar prize fights; bookies and their clients pooled more millions, trying to match the pace of the speculation-crazed stock and bond men. This was the era of "organized" crime—the national gambling and bootleg syndicate structured on the New York corporate model.

By 1930, when George was a boy of six, Grandpa Walker was New York State Racing Commissioner. The vivid colors and sounds of the racing scene must have impressed little George as much as his grandfather. Bert Walker bred race horses at his own stable, the Log Cabin Stud. He was president of the Belmont Park race track. Bert also personally managed most aspects of Averell's racing interests—down to picking the colors and fabrics for the Harriman racing gear.[19]

From 1926, George's father Prescott Bush showed a fierce loyalty to the Harrimans and a dogged determination to advance himself; he gradually came to run the day-to-day operations of W.A. Harriman & Co. After the firm's 1931 merger with the British-American banking house Brown Brothers, Prescott Bush became managing partner of the resulting company: Brown Brothers Harriman. This was ultimately the largest and politically the most important private banking house in America.

Financial collapse, world depression and social upheaval followed the fevered speculation of the 1920s. The 1929–31 crash of securities values wiped out the small fortune Prescott Bush had gained since 1926. But because of his devotion to the Harrimans, they "did a very generous thing," as Bush later put it. They staked him to what he had lost and put him back on his feet.

Prescott Bush described his own role, from 1931 through the 1940s, in a confidential interview:

I emphasize ... that the Harrimans showed great courage and loyalty and confidence in us, because three or four of us were really running the business, the day to day business. Averell was all over the place in those days ... and Roland was involved in a lot of directorships, and he didn't get down into the "lift-up-and-bear-down" activity of the bank, you see—the day-to-day decisions ...

we were really running the business, the day to day business, all the administrative decisions and the executive decisions. We were the ones that did it. We were the managing partners, let's say.[20]

But of the "three or four" partners in charge, Prescott was effectively at the head of the firm, because he had taken over management of the gigantic *personal investment funds* of Averell and E. Roland "Bunny" Harriman.

In those interwar years, Prescott Bush made the family fortune which George Bush inherited. He piled up the money from an international project which continued until a new world war, and the action of the U.S. government, intervened to stop him.

Notes for Chapter I

1. *Washington Post,* Aug. 16, 1991, p. A1.

2. Gen. Hugh S. Johnson to Major J.H.K. Davis, June 6, 1918, file no. 334.8/168 or 334.8/451 in U.S. National Archives, Suitland, Maryland.

3. Bernard M. Baruch, *My Own Story* (New York: Henry Holt and Co., 1957), pp. 138–39. Baruch related that "our firm did a large business for Mr. Harriman. . . . In 1906 Harriman had [us] place heavy bets on Charles Evans Hughes in his race for Governor of New York against William Randolph Hearst. After several hundred thousand dollars had been wagered, [our firm] stopped. Hearing of this, Harriman called . . . up. 'Didn't I tell you to bet?' he demanded. 'Now go on.' "

4. Alden Hatch, *Remington Arms: An American History,* 1956, copyright by the Remington Arms Co., pp. 224–25.

5. *The Ohio State Journal,* Columbus, Ohio, Thursday, Aug. 8, 1918.

6. *The Ohio State Journal,* Friday, Aug. 9, 1918.

7. *The Ohio State Journal,* Friday, Sept. 6, 1918.

8. Interview with Prescott Bush in the Oral History Research Project conducted by Columbia University in 1966, Eisenhower Administration Part II; pp. 5–6. The interview was supposed to be kept confidential and was never published, but Columbia later sold microfilms of the transcript to certain libraries, including Arizona State University.

9. Theodore Roosevelt to James S. Sherman, Oct. 6, 1906, made public by Roosevelt at a press conference April 2, 1907. Quoted in Henry F. Pringle, *Theodore Roosevelt* (New York: Harcourt, Brace and Company, 1931), p. 452. Roosevelt later confided to Harriman lawyer Robert S. Lovett that his views on Harriman were based on what J.P. Morgan had told him.

10. See *The Industries of St. Louis,* published 1885 by J.M. Elstner & Co., pp. 61–62 for Crow, Hagardine & Co., David Walker's first business; and p. 86 for Ely & Walker.

11. See Letter of G.H. Walker to D.R. Francis, March 20, 1905, in the Francis collection of the Missouri Historical Society, St. Louis, Missouri, on the organization of the Republicans and Democrats to run the election of the mayor, a Democrat acceptable to the socially prominent. The next day Walker became the treasurer and Francis the president of this "Committee of 1000." See also George H. Walker obituary, *St. Louis Globe-Democrat,* June 25, 1953.

12. Letter of Perry Francis to his father, Ambassador David R. Francis, Oct. 15, 1917, Francis collection of the Missouri Historical Society. ". . . Joe Miller left for San Francisco last Tuesday night, where he will receive orders to continue to Petrograd. I was told by Mildred Kotany [Walker's sister-in-law] that Bert Walker got him his appointment through Breck Long. I didn't know Joe was after it, or could have helped him myself. He will be good company for you when he gets there. . . ."

13. Private interview with a Walker family member, cousin of President Bush.

14. Prescott Bush, Columbia University, *op. cit.,* p. 7.

15. *St. Louis Globe Democrat,* Aug. 7, 1921.

16. This is the sequence of events, from Simmons to U.S. Rubber, which Prescott Bush gave in his Columbia University interview, *op. cit.,) pp.* 7–8.

17. *Public statement of Averell Harriman, New York Times,* Oct. 6, 1920, p. 1.

18. *St. Louis Globe-Democrat,* Oct. 12, 1920, p. 1.

19. Sports-as-business has continued in the family up through George Bush's adult life. Bert's

son George Walker, Jr.—President Bush's uncle and financial angel in Texas—co-founded the New York Mets and was the baseball club's vice president and treasurer for 17 years until his death in 1977. The President's son, George Walker Bush, was co-owner of the Texas Rangers baseball club during his father's presidency.

20. Prescott Bush, Columbia University, *op. cit.,* pp. 16–22.

II

THE HITLER PROJECT

Bush Property Seized—Trading with the Enemy

In October 1942, ten months after entering World War II, America was preparing its first assault against Nazi military forces. Prescott Bush was managing partner of Brown Brothers Harriman. His 18-year-old son George, the future U.S. President, had just begun training to become a naval pilot.

On Oct. 20, 1942, the U.S. government ordered the seizure of Nazi German banking operations in New York City which were being conducted by Prescott Bush.

Under the *Trading with the Enemy Act*, the government took over the **Union Banking Corporation,** in which Bush was a director. The U.S. Alien Property Custodian seized Union Banking Corp.'s stock shares, all of which were owned by Prescott Bush, E. Roland "Bunny" Harriman, three Nazi executives, and two other associates of Bush.[1]

The order seizing the bank "vests" (seizes) "all of the capital stock of Union Banking Corporation, a New York corporation," and names the holders of its shares as:

"E. Roland Harriman—3991 shares"

[chairman and director of Union Banking Corp. (UBC); this is "Bunny" Harriman, described by Prescott Bush as a place holder who didn't get much into banking affairs; Prescott managed his personal investments]

"Cornelis Lievense—4 shares"
[president and director of UBC; New York resident banking functionary for the Nazis]

"Harold D. Pennington—1 share"
[treasurer and director of UBC; an office manager employed by Bush at Brown Brothers Harriman]

"Ray Morris—1 share"
[director of UBC; partner of Bush and the Harrimans]

"Prescott S. Bush—1 share"
[director of UBC, which was co-founded and sponsored by his father-in-law George Walker; senior managing partner for E. Roland Harriman and Averell Harriman]

"H.J. Kouwenhoven—1 share"
[director of UBC; organized UBC as the emissary of Fritz Thyssen in negotiations with George Walker and Averell Harriman; managing director of UBC's Netherlands affiliate under Nazi occupation; industrial executive in Nazi Germany; director and chief foreign financial executive of the German Steel Trust]

"Johann G. Groeninger—1 share"
[director of UBC and of its Netherlands affiliate; industrial executive in Nazi Germany]

"all of which shares are held for the benefit of . . . members of the Thyssen family, [and] is property of nationals . . . of a designated enemy country. . . ."

By Oct. 26, 1942, U.S. troops were under way for North Africa. On Oct. 28, the government issued orders seizing two Nazi front organizations run by the Bush-Harriman bank: the **Holland-American Trading Corporation** and the **Seamless Steel Equipment Corporation.**[2]

U.S. forces landed under fire near Algiers on Nov. 8, 1942; heavy combat raged throughout November. Nazi interests in the **Silesian-American Corporation,** long managed by Prescott Bush and his father-in-law George Herbert Walker, were seized under the Trading with the Enemy Act on Nov. 17, 1942. In this action, the government announced that it was seizing only the Nazi interests, leaving the Nazis' U.S. partners to carry on the business.[3]

These and other actions taken by the U.S. government in wartime were, tragically, too little and too late. President Bush's family had already played a central role in financing and arming Adolf Hitler for his takeover of Germany; in financing and managing the buildup of Nazi war industries for the conquest of Europe and war against the U.S.A.; and in the development of Nazi genocide theories and racial propaganda, with their well-known results.

The facts presented here must be known, and their implications reflected upon, for a proper understanding of President George Herbert Walker Bush and of the danger to mankind that he represents. The President's family fortune was largely a result of the Hitler project. The powerful Anglo-American family associations, which later boosted him into the Central Intelligence Agency and up to the White House, were his father's partners in the Hitler project.

President Franklin Roosevelt's Alien Property Custodian, Leo T. Crowley, signed Vesting Order Number 248 seizing the property of Prescott Bush under the Trading with the Enemy Act. The order, published in obscure government record books and kept out of the news,[4] explained nothing about the Nazis involved; only that the Union Banking Corporation was run for the "Thyssen family" of "Germany and/or Hungary"—"nationals . . . of a designated enemy country."

By deciding that Prescott Bush and the other directors of the Union Banking Corp. were legally *front men for the Nazis,* the government avoided the more important historical issue: In what way *were Hitler's Nazis themselves hired, armed and instructed by* the New York and London clique of which Prescott Bush was an executive manager? Let us examine the Harriman-Bush Hitler project from the 1920s until it was partially broken up, to seek an answer for that question.

Origin and Extent of the Project

Fritz Thyssen and his business partners are universally recognized as the most important German financiers of Adolf Hitler's takeover of Germany. At the time of the order seizing the Thyssen family's Union Banking Corp., Mr. Fritz Thyssen had already published his famous book, *I Paid Hitler,*[5] admitting that he had financed Adolf Hitler and the Nazi movement since October 1923. Thyssen's role as the leading early backer of Hitler's grab for power in Germany had been noted by U.S. diplomats in Berlin in 1932.[6] The order seizing the Bush-Thyssen bank was curiously quiet and modest about the identity of the perpetrators who had been nailed.

But two weeks before the official order, government investigators had reported secretly that "W. Averell Harriman was in Europe sometime prior to 1924 and at that time became acquainted with Fritz Thyssen, the German industrialist." Harriman and Thyssen agreed to set up a bank for Thyssen in New York. "[C]ertain of [Harriman's] associates would serve as directors. . . ." Thyssen agent "H. J. Kouwenhoven . . . came to the United States . . . prior to 1924 for conferences with the Harriman Company in this connection. . . ."[7]

When exactly was "Harriman in Europe sometime prior to 1924"? In fact, he was in Berlin in 1922 to set up the Berlin branch of W.A. Harriman & Co. under George Walker's presidency.

The Union Banking Corporation was established formally in 1924, as a unit in the Manhattan offices of W.A. Harriman & Co., interlocking with the Thyssen-owned *Bank voor Handel en Scheepvaart* (BHS) in the Netherlands. The investigators concluded that "the Union Banking Corporation has since its inception handled funds chiefly supplied to it through the Dutch bank by the Thyssen interests for American investment."

Thus by personal agreement between Averell Harriman and Fritz Thyssen in 1922, W.A. Harriman & Co. (alias Union Banking Corporation) would be transferring funds back and forth between New York and the "Thyssen interests" in Germany. By putting up about $400,000, the Harriman organization would be joint owner and manager of Thyssen's banking operations outside of Germany.

How important was the Nazi enterprise for which President Bush's father was the New York banker?

The 1942 U.S. government investigative report said that Bush's Nazi-front bank was an interlocking concern with the *Vereinigte Stahlwerke* (United Steel Works Corporation or **German Steel Trust**) led by Fritz Thyssen and his two brothers. After the war, congressional investigators probed the Thyssen interests, Union Banking Corp. and related Nazi units. The investigation showed that the *Vereinigte Stahlwerke* had produced the following approximate proportions of total German national output:

50.8% of Nazi Germany's pig iron
41.4% of Nazi Germany's universal plate
36.0% of Nazi Germany's heavy plate
38.5% of Nazi Germany's galvanized sheet
45.5% of Nazi Germany's pipes and tubes
22.1% of Nazi Germany's wire
35.0% of Nazi Germany's explosives.[8]

Prescott Bush became vice president of W.A. Harriman & Co. in 1926. That same year, a friend of Harriman and Bush set up a giant new organization for their client Fritz Thyssen, prime sponsor of politician Adolf Hitler. The new **German Steel Trust,** Germany's largest industrial corporation, was organized in 1926 by Wall Street banker Clarence Dillon. Dillon was the old comrade of Prescott Bush's father Sam Bush from the "Merchants of Death" bureau in World War I.

In return for putting up $70 million to create his organization, majority owner Thyssen gave the Dillon Read company two or more representatives on the board of the new Steel Trust.[9]

Thus there is a division of labor: Thyssen's own confidential accounts, for political and related purposes, were run through the Walker-Bush organization; the German Steel Trust did its corporate banking through Dillon Read.

The Walker-Bush firm's banking activities were not just politically neutral money-making ventures which happened to coincide with the aims of German Nazis. All of the firm's European business in those days was organized around anti-democratic political forces.

In 1927, criticism of their support for totalitarianism drew this retort from Bert Walker, written from Kennebunkport to Averell Harriman: "It seems to me that the suggestion in connection with Lord Bearsted's views that we withdraw from Russia smacks somewhat of the impertinent. . . . I think that we have drawn our line and should hew to it."[10]

Averell Harriman met with Italy's fascist dictator, Benito Mussolini. A representative of the firm subsequently telegraphed good news back to his chief executive Bert Walker: ". . . During these last days . . . Mussolini . . . has examined and approved our c[o]ntract 15 June."[11]

The great financial collapse of 1929–31 shook America, Germany and Britain, weakening all governments. It also made the hard-pressed Prescott Bush even more willing to do whatever was necessary to retain his new place in the world. It was in this crisis that certain Anglo-Americans determined on the installation of a Hitler regime in Germany.

W.A. Harriman & Co., well-positioned for this enterprise and rich in assets from their German and Russian business, merged with the British-American investment house, Brown Brothers, on January 1, 1931. Bert Walker retired to his own G.H. Walker & Co. This left the Harriman brothers, Prescott Bush and Thatcher M. Brown as the senior partners of the new Brown Brothers Harriman firm.

(The London, England branch of the Brown family firm continued operating under its historic name—Brown, Shipley.)

Robert A. Lovett also came over as a partner from Brown Brothers. His father, E.H. Harriman's lawyer and railroad chief, had been on the War Industries Board with Prescott's father. Though he remained a partner in Brown Brothers Harriman, the junior Lovett soon replaced his father as chief executive of Union Pacific Railroad.

Brown Brothers had a racial tradition that fitted it well for the Hitler project! American patriots had cursed its name back in U.S. Civil War days. Brown Brothers, with offices in the U.S.A. and in England, had carried on their ships fully 75 percent of the slave cotton from the American South over to British mill owners.

Now in 1931, the virtual dictator of world finance, Bank of England Governor Montagu Collet Norman, was a former Brown Brothers partner, whose grandfather had been boss of Brown Brothers during the U.S. Civil War. Montagu Norman was known as the most avid of Hitler's supporters within British ruling circles, and Norman's intimacy with this firm was essential to his management of the Hitler project.

In 1931, while Prescott Bush ran the New York office of Brown Brothers Harriman, Prescott's partner was Montagu Norman's intimate friend Thatcher Brown. The Bank of England chief always stayed at the home of Prescott's partner on his hush-hush trips to New York. Prescott Bush concentrated on the firm's German activities, and Thatcher Brown saw to their business in old England, under the guidance of his mentor Montagu Norman.[12]

Hitler's Ladder to Power

Adolf Hitler became Chancellor of Germany January 30, 1933, and absolute dictator in March 1933, after two years of expensive and violent lobbying and electioneering. Two affiliates of the Bush-Harriman organization played great parts in this criminal undertaking: Thyssen's German Steel Trust; and the Hamburg-Amerika Line and several of its executives.[13]

Let us look more closely at the Bush family's German partners.

Fritz Thyssen told Allied interrogators after the war about some of his financial support for the Nazi Party: "In 1930 or 1931 . . . I told [Hitler's deputy Rudolph] Hess . . . I would arrange a credit for him with a Dutch bank in Rotterdam, the Bank für Handel und Schiff [i.e. Bank voor Handel en Scheepvaart (BHS), the Harriman-Bush affiliate]. I arranged the credit . . . he would pay it back in three years. .... I chose a Dutch bank because I did not want to be mixed up with German banks in my position, and because I thought it was better to do business with a Dutch bank, and I thought I would have the Nazis a little more in my hands. ...

"The credit was about 250–300,000 [gold] marks—about the sum I had given before. The loan has been repaid in part to the Dutch bank, but I think some money is still owing on it. ...."[14]

The overall total of Thyssen's political donations and loans to the Nazis was well over a million dollars, including funds he raised from others—in a period of terrible money shortage in Germany.

Friedrich Flick was the major co-owner of the German Steel Trust with Fritz Thyssen, Thyssen's long-time collaborator and occasional competitor. In preparation for the war crimes tribunal at Nuremberg, the U.S. government said that Flick was "one of leading financiers and industrialists who from 1932 contributed large sums to the Nazi Party ... [a] member of 'Circle of Friends' of Himmler who contributed large sums to the SS."[15]

Flick, like Thyssen, financed the Nazis to maintain their private armies called *Schutzstaffel* (S.S. or Black Shirts) and *Sturmabteilung* (S.A., storm troops or Brown Shirts).

The Flick-Harriman partnership was directly supervised by Prescott Bush, President Bush's father, and by George Walker, President Bush's grandfather.

The Harriman-Walker Union Banking Corp. arrangements for the German Steel Trust had made them bankers for Flick and his vast operations in Germany by no later than 1926.

The **Harriman Fifteen Corporation** (George Walker, president, Prescott Bush and Averell Harriman, sole directors) held a substantial stake in the Silesian Holding Co. at the time of the merger with Brown Brothers, Jan. 1, 1931. This holding correlated to Averell Harriman's chairmanship of the **Consolidated Silesian Steel Corporation,** the American group owning one-third of a complex of steel-making, coal-mining and zinc-mining activities in Germany and Poland, in which Friedrich Flick owned two-thirds.[16]

The Nuremberg prosecutor characterized Flick as follows:

"Proprietor and head of a large group of industrial enterprises (coal and iron mines, steel producing and fabricating plants) ... *'Wehrwirtschaftsfuhrer',* 1938 [title awarded to prominent industrialists for merit in armaments drive—'Military Economy Leader']. ...."[17]

For this buildup of the Hitler war machine with coal, steel and arms production, using slave laborers, the Nazi Flick was condemned to seven years in prison at the Nuremberg trials; he served three years. With friends in New York and London, however, Flick lived into the 1970s and died a billionaire.

On March 19, 1934, Prescott Bush—then director of the German Steel Trust's Union Banking Corporation—initiated an alert to the absent Averell Harriman about a problem which had developed in the Flick partnership.[18] Bush sent Harriman a clipping from the *New York Times* of that day, which reported that the Polish government was fighting back against American and German stockholders who controlled "Poland's largest industrial unit, the Upper Silesian Coal and Steel Company. . . ."

The *Times* article continued: "The company has long been accused of mismanagement, excessive borrowing, fictitious bookkeeping and gambling in securities. Warrants were issued in December for several directors accused of tax evasions. They were German citizens and they fled. They were replaced by Poles. Herr Flick, regarding this as an attempt to make the company's board entirely Polish, retaliated by restricting credits until the new Polish directors were unable to pay the workmen regularly."

The *Times* noted that the company's mines and mills "employ 25,000 men and account for 45 percent of Poland's total steel output and 12 percent of her coal production. Two-thirds of the company's stock is owned by Friedrich Flick, a leading German steel industrialist, and the remainder is owned by interests in the United States."

In view of the fact that a great deal of Polish output was being exported to Hitler Germany under depression conditions, the Polish government thought that Prescott Bush, Harriman and their Nazi partners should at least pay full taxes on their Polish holdings. The U.S. and Nazi owners responded with a lockout. The letter to Harriman in Washington reported a cable from their European representative: "Have undertaken new steps London Berlin . . . please establish friendly relations with Polish Ambassador [in Washington]."

A 1935 Harriman Fifteen Corporation memo from George Walker announced an agreement had been made "in Berlin" to sell an 8,000 block of their shares in Consolidated Silesian Steel.[19] But the dispute with Poland did not deter the Bush family from continuing its partnership with Flick.

Nazi tanks and bombs "settled" this dispute in September, 1939 with the invasion of Poland, beginning World War II. The Nazi army had been equipped by Flick, Harriman, Walker and Bush, with materials essentially stolen from Poland.

There were probably few people at the time who could appreciate the irony, that when the Soviets also attacked and invaded Poland from the East, their vehicles were fueled by oil pumped from Baku wells revived by the Harriman/Walker/Bush enterprise.

Three years later, nearly a year after the Japanese attack on Pearl Harbor, the U.S. government ordered the seizure of the Nazis' share in the Silesian-American Corporation under the Trading with the Enemy Act. Enemy nationals were said to own 49 percent of the common stock and 41.67 percent of the preferred stock of the company.

The order characterized the company as a "business enterprise within the United States, owned by [a front company in] Zurich, Switzerland, and held for the benefit of Bergwerksgesellschaft George von Giesche's Erben, a German corporation. . . ."[20]

Bert Walker was still the senior director of the company, which he had founded back in 1926 simultaneously with the creation of the German Steel Trust. Ray Morris, Prescott's partner from Union Banking Corp. and Brown Brothers Harriman, was also a director.

The investigative report prior to the government crackdown explained the "NATURE OF BUSINESS: The subject corporation is an American holding company for German and Polish subsidiaries, which own large and valuable coal and zinc mines in Silesia, Poland and Germany. Since September 1939, these properties have been in the possession of and have been operated by the German government and have undoubtedly been of considerable assistance to that country in its war effort."[21]

The report noted that the American stockholders hoped to regain control of the European properties after the war.

Control of Nazi Commerce

Bert Walker had arranged the credits Harriman needed to take control of the Hamburg-Amerika Line back in 1920. Walker had organized the **American Ship and Commerce Corp.** as a unit of the W.A. Harriman & Co., with contractual power over Hamburg-Amerika's affairs.

As the Hitler project went into high gear, Harriman-Bush shares in American Ship and Commerce Corp. were held by the Harriman Fifteen Corp., run by Prescott Bush and Bert Walker.[22]

It was a convenient stroll for the well-tanned, athletic, handsome Prescott Bush: From the Brown Brothers Harriman skyscraper at 59 Wall Street—where he was senior managing partner, confidential investments manager and adviser to Averell and his brother

"Bunny"—he walked across to the Harriman Fifteen Corporation at One Wall Street, otherwise known as G.H. Walker & Co.—and around the corner to his subsidiary offices at 39 Broadway, former home of the old W.A. Harriman & Co., and still the offices for American Ship and Commerce Corp., and of the Union Banking Corporation.

In many ways, Bush's Hamburg-Amerika Line was the pivot for the entire Hitler project.

Averell Harriman and Bert Walker had gained control over the steamship company in 1920 in negotiations with its post-World War I chief executive, **Wilhelm Cuno,** and with the line's bankers, M.M. Warburg. Cuno was thereafter completely dependent on the Anglo-Americans, and became a member of the Anglo-German Friendship Society. In the 1930–32 drive for a Hitler dictatorship, Wilhelm Cuno contributed important sums to the Nazi Party.[23]

Albert Voegler was chief executive of the Thyssen-Flick German Steel Trust for which Bush's Union Banking Corp. was the New York office. He was a director of the Bush-affiliate BHS Bank in Rotterdam, and a director of the Harriman-Bush Hamburg-Amerika Line. Voegler joined Thyssen and Flick in their heavy 1930–33 Nazi contributions, and helped organize the final Nazi leap into national power.[24]

The **Schroeder** family of bankers was a linchpin for the Nazi activities of Harriman and Prescott Bush, closely tied to their lawyers Allen and John Foster Dulles.

Baron Kurt von Schroeder was co-director of the massive Thyssen-Hütte foundry along with Johann Groeninger, Prescott Bush's New York bank partner. Kurt von Schroeder was treasurer of the support organization for the Nazi Party's private armies, to which Friedrich Flick contributed. Kurt von Schroeder and Montagu Norman's protégé Hjalmar Schacht together made the final arrangements for Hitler to enter the government.[25]

Baron Rudolph von Schroeder was vice president and director of the Hamburg-Amerika Line. Long an intimate contact of Averell Harriman's in Germany, Baron Rudolph sent his grandson Baron Johann Rudolph for a tour of Prescott Bush's Brown Brothers Harriman offices in New York City in December 1932—on the eve of their Hitler-triumph.[26]

Certain actions taken directly by the Harriman-Bush shipping line in 1932 must be ranked among the gravest acts of treason in this century.

The U.S. embassy in Berlin reported back to Washington that the "costly election campaigns" and "the cost of maintaining a private army of 300,000 to 400,000 men" had raised questions as to the Nazis' financial backers. The constitutional government of the German republic moved to defend national freedom by ordering the Nazi Party private armies disbanded. The U.S. embassy reported that the **Hamburg-Amerika Line was purchasing and distributing propaganda attacks against the German government, for attempting this last-minute crackdown on Hitler's forces.**[27]

Thousands of German opponents of Hitlerism were shot or intimidated by privately armed Nazi Brown Shirts. In this connection we note that the original "Merchant of Death," Samuel Pryor, was a founding director of both the Union Banking Corp. and the American Ship and Commerce Corp. Since Mr. Pryor was executive committee chairman of Remington Arms and a central figure in the world's private arms traffic, his use to the Hitler project was enhanced as the Bush family's partner in Nazi Party banking and trans-Atlantic shipping.

The U.S. Senate arms-traffic investigators probed Remington after it was joined in a cartel agreement on explosives to the Nazi firm I.G. Farben. Looking at the period leading up to Hitler's seizure of power, the Senators found that "German political associations, like the Nazi and others, are nearly all armed with American . . . guns. . . . Arms of all kinds coming from America are transshipped in the Scheldt to river barges before the vessels arrive in Antwerp. They then can be carried through Holland without police inspection or interference. The Hitlerists and Communists are presumed to get arms in this manner. The principal arms coming from America are Thompson submachine guns and revolvers. The number is great."[28]

The beginning of the Hitler regime brought some bizarre changes to the Hamburg-Amerika Line—and more betrayals.

Prescott Bush's American Ship and Commerce Corp. notified Max Warburg of Hamburg, Germany, on March 7, 1933, that Warburg was to be the corporation's official, designated representative on the board of Hamburg-Amerika.[29]

Max Warburg replied on March 27, 1933, assuring his American sponsors that the Hitler government was good for Germany: "For the last few years business was considerably better than we had anticipated, but a reaction is making itself felt for some months. We are actually suffering also under the very active propaganda against Germany, caused by some unpleasant circumstances. These occurrences were the natural consequence of the very excited election campaign, but were extraordinarily exaggerated in the foreign press. The Government is firmly resolved to maintain public peace and order in Germany, and I feel perfectly convinced in this respect that there is no cause for any alarm whatsoever."[30]

This seal of approval for Hitler, coming from a famous Jew, was just what Harriman and Bush required, for they anticipated rather serious "alarm" inside the U.S.A. against their Nazi operations.

On March 29, 1933, two days after Max's letter to Harriman, Max's son, Erich Warburg, sent a cable to his cousin, Frederick M. Warburg, a director of the Harriman railroad system. He asked Frederick to "use all your influence" to stop all anti-Nazi activity in America, including "atrocity news and unfriendly propaganda in foreign press, mass meetings, etc." Frederick cabled back to Erich: "No responsible groups here [are] urging [a] boycott [of] German goods[,] merely excited individuals." Two days after that, on March 31, 1933, the **American Jewish Committee,** controlled by the War-burgs, and the **B'nai B'rith,** heavily influenced by the Sulzbergers (*New York Times*), issued a formal, official joint statement of the two organizations, counseling "that no American boycott against Germany be encouraged," and advising "that no further mass meet-ings be held or similar forms of agitation be employed."[31]

The American Jewish Committee and the B'nai B'rith (mother of the "Anti-Defamation League") continued with this hardline, no-attack-on-Hitler stance all through the 1930s, blunting the fight mounted by many Jews and other anti-fascists.

Thus the decisive interchange reproduced above, taking place entirely within the orbit of the Harriman/Bush firm, may explain something of the relationship of George Bush to American Jewish and Zionist leaders. Some of them, in close cooperation with his family, played an ugly part in the drama of Naziism. Is this why "professional Nazi-hunters" have never discovered how the Bush family made its money?

The executive board of the **Hamburg Amerika Line (Hapag)** met jointly with the North German Lloyd Company board in Hamburg on Sept. 5, 1933. Under official Nazi supervision, the two firms were merged. Prescott Bush's American Ship and Commerce Corp. installed Christian J. Beck, a long-time Harriman executive, as man-ager of freight and operations in North America for the new joint Nazi shipping lines (**Hapag-Lloyd**) on Nov. 4, 1933.

According to testimony of officials of the companies before Con-gress in 1934, a supervisor from the **Nazi Labor Front** rode with every ship of the Harriman-Bush line; employees of the New York offices were directly organized into the Nazi Labor Front organization; Hamburg-Amerika provided free passage to individuals going abroad for Nazi propaganda purposes; and the line subsidized pro-Nazi newspapers in the U.S.A., as it had done in Germany against the constitutional German government.[32]

In mid-1936, Prescott Bush's American Ship and Commerce Corp. cabled M.M. Warburg, asking Warburg to represent the company's heavy share interest at the forthcoming Hamburg-Amerika stockholders meeting. The Warburg office replied with the information that "we represented you" at the stockholders meeting and "exercised on your behalf your voting power for Rm [gold marks] 3,509,600 Hapag stock deposited with us."

The Warburgs transmitted a letter received from Emil Helfferich, German chief executive of both Hapag-Lloyd and of the Standard Oil subsidiary in Nazi Germany: "It is the intention to continue the relations with Mr. Harriman on the same basis as heretofore. . . ." In a colorful gesture, Hapag's Nazi chairman Helfferich sent the line's president across the Atlantic on a Zeppelin to confer with their New York string-pullers.

After the meeting with the Zeppelin passenger, the Harriman-Bush office replied: "I am glad to learn that Mr. Hellferich [sic] has stated that relations between the Hamburg American Line and ourselves will be continued on the same basis as heretofore."[33]

Two months before moving against Prescott Bush's Union Banking Corporation, the U. S. government ordered the seizure of all property of the Hamburg-Amerika Line and North German Lloyd, under the Trading with the Enemy Act. The investigators noted in the pre-seizure report that Christian J. Beck was still acting as an attorney representing the Nazi firm.[34]

In May 1933, just after the Hitler regime was consolidated, an agreement was reached in Berlin for the coordination of all Nazi commerce with the U.S.A. The **Harriman International Co.,** led by Averell Harriman's first cousin Oliver, was to head a syndicate of 150 firms and individuals, to conduct *all exports from Hitler Germany to the United States.*[35]

This pact had been negotiated in Berlin between Hitler's economics minister, Hjalmar Schacht, and John Foster Dulles, international attorney for dozens of Nazi enterprises, with the counsel of Max Warburg and Kurt von Schroeder.

John Foster Dulles would later be U.S. Secretary of State, and the great power in the Republican Party of the 1950s. Foster's friendship and that of his brother Allen (head of the Central Intelligence Agency), greatly aided Prescott Bush to become the Republican U.S. Senator from Connecticut. And it was to be of inestimable value to

George Bush, in his ascent to the heights of "covert action government," that both of these Dulles brothers were the lawyers for the Bush family's far-flung enterprise.

Throughout the 1930s, John Foster Dulles arranged debt restructuring for German firms under a series of decrees issued by Adolf Hitler. In these deals, Dulles struck a balance between the interest owed to selected, larger investors, and the needs of the growing Nazi war-making apparatus for producing tanks, poison gas, etc.

Dulles wrote to Prescott Bush in 1937 concerning one such arrangement. The German Atlantic Cable Company, owning Nazi Germany's only telegraph channel to the United States, had made debt and management agreements with the Walker-Harriman bank during the 1920s. A new decree would now void those agreements, which had originally been reached with non-Nazi corporate officials. Dulles asked Bush, who managed these affairs for Averell Harriman, to get Averell's signature on a letter to Nazi officials, agreeing to the changes. Dulles wrote:

Sept. 22, 1937
Mr. Prescott S. Bush
59 Wall Street, New York, N.Y.

Dear Press,
   I have looked over the letter of the German-American [sic] Cable Company to Averell Harriman. . . . It would appear that the only rights in the matter are those which inure in the bankers and that no legal embarrassment would result, so far as the bondholders are concerned, by your acquiescence in the modification of the bankers' agreement.
   Sincerely yours,
   John Foster Dulles

Dulles enclosed a proposed draft reply, Bush got Harriman's signature, and the changes went through.[36]

In conjunction with these arrangements, the German Atlantic Cable Company attempted to stop payment on its debts to smaller American bondholders. The money was to be used instead for arming the Nazi state, under a decree of the Hitler government.

Despite the busy efforts of Bush and Dulles, a New York court decided that this particular Hitler "law" was invalid in the United States; small bondholders, not parties to deals between the bankers and the Nazis, were entitled to get paid.[37]

In this and a few other of the attempted swindles, the intended victims came out with their money. But the Nazi financial and political reorganization went ahead to its tragic climax.

For his part in the Hitler revolution, Prescott Bush was paid a fortune.

This is the legacy he left to his son, President George Bush.

An Important Historical Note: How the Harrimans Hired Hitler

It was not inevitable that millions would be slaughtered under fascism and in World War II. At certain moments of crisis, crucial pro-Nazi decisions were made outside of Germany. These decisions for pro-Nazi actions were more aggressive than the mere "appeasement" which Anglo-American historians later preferred to discuss.

Private armies of 300,000 to 400,000 terrorists aided the Nazis' rise to power. W.A. Harriman's Hamburg-Amerika Line intervened against Germany's 1932 attempt to break them up.

The 1929–31 economic collapse bankrupted the Wall-Street-backed German Steel Trust. When the German government took over the Trust's stock shares, interests associated with Konrad Adenauer and the anti-Nazi Catholic Center Party attempted to acquire the shares. But the Anglo-Americans—Montagu Norman and the Harriman-Bush bank—made sure that their Nazi puppet Fritz Thyssen regained control over the shares and the Trust. Thyssen's bankrolling of Hitler could then continue unhindered.

Unpayable debts crushed Germany in the 1920s, reparations required by the Versailles agreements. Germany was looted by the London-New York banking system, and Hitler's propaganda exploited this German debt burden.

But immediately *after* Germany came under Hitler's dictatorship, the Anglo-American financiers granted debt relief, which freed funds to be used for arming the Nazi state.

The North German Lloyd steamship line, which was merged with Hamburg-Amerika Line, was one of the companies which stopped debt payments under a Hitler decree arranged by John Foster Dulles and Hjalmar Schacht.

Kuhn Loeb and Co.'s Felix Warburg carried out the Hitler finance plan in New York. Kuhn Loeb asked North German Lloyd bondholders to accept new lower interest steamship bonds, issued by Kuhn Loeb, in place of the better pre-Hitler bonds.

New York attorney Jacob Chaitkin, father of coauthor Anton Chaitkin, took the cases of many different bondholders who rejected the swindle by Harriman, Bush, Warburg, and Hitler. Representing a women who was owed $30 on an old steamship bond—and opposing John Foster Dulles in New York municipal court—Chaitkin threatened a writ from the sheriff, tying up the 30,000 ton transatlantic liner *Europa* until the client received her $30. (*New York Times*, January 10, 1934, p. 31 col. 3).

The American Jewish Congress hired Jacob Chaitkin as the legal director of the boycott against Nazi Germany. The American Federation of Labor cooperated with Jewish and other groups in the anti-import boycott. On the other side, virtually all the Nazi trade with the United States was under the supervision of the Harriman interests and functionaries such as Prescott Bush, father of President George Bush.

Meanwhile, the Warburgs demanded that American Jews not "agitate" against the Hitler government, or join the organized boycott. The Warburgs' decision was carried out by the American Jewish Committee and the B'nai B'rith, who opposed the boycott as the Nazi military state grew increasingly powerful.

The historical coverup on these events is so tight that virtually the only exposé of the Warburgs came in journalist John L. Spivak's "Wall Street's Fascist Conspiracy," in the pro-communist *New Masses* periodical (Jan. 29 and Feb. 5, 1934). Spivak pointed out that the Warburgs controlled the American Jewish Committee, which opposed the anti-Nazi boycott, while their Kuhn Loeb and Co. had underwritten Nazi shipping; and he exposed the financing of pro-fascist political activities by the Warburgs and their partners and allies, many of whom were bigwigs in the American Jewish Committee and B'nai B'rith.

Given where the Spivak piece appeared, it is not surprising that Spivak called Warburg an ally of the Morgan Bank, but made no mention of Averell Harriman. Mr. Harriman, after all, was a permanent hero of the Soviet Union.

John L. Spivak later underwent a curious transformation, himself joining the coverup. In 1967, he wrote an autobiography (*A Man in His Time*, New York: Horizon Press), which praises the American Jewish Committee. The pro-fascism of the Warburgs does not appear in the book. The former "rebel" Spivak also praises the action arm of the B'nai B'rith, the Anti-Defamation League. Pathetically, he comments favorably that the League has spy files on the American populace which it shares with government agencies.

Thus is history erased; and those decisions, which direct history into one course or another, are lost to the knowledge of the current generation.

Notes for Chapter II

1. Office of Alien Property Custodian, Vesting Order No. 248. The order was signed by Leo T. Crowley, Alien Property Custodian, executed October 20, 1942; F.R. Doc. 42–11568; Filed, November 6, 1942, 11:31 A.M.; 7 Fed. Reg. 9097 (Nov. 7, 1942). See also the *New York City Directory of Directors* (available at the Library of Congress). The volumes for the 1930s and 1940s list Prescott Bush as a director of Union Banking Corporation for the years 1934 through 1943.

2. Alien Property Custodian Vesting Order No. 259: Seamless Steel Equipment Corporation; Vesting Order No. 261: Holland-American Trading Corp.

3. Alien Property Custodian Vesting Order No. 370: Silesian-American Corp.

4. The *New York Times* on December 16, 1944, ran a five-paragraph page 25 article on actions of the New York State Banking Department. Only the last sentence refers to the Nazi bank, as follows: "The Union Banking Corporation, 39 Broadway, New York, has received authority to change its principal place of business to 120 Broadway."
The *Times* omitted the fact that the Union Banking Corporation had been seized by the government for trading with the enemy, and even the fact that 120 Broadway was the address of the government's Alien Property Custodian.

5. Fritz Thyssen, *I Paid Hitler,* 1941, reprinted in (Port Washington, N.Y.: Kennikat Press, 1972), p. 133. Thyssen says his contributions began with 100,000 marks given in October 1923, for Hitler's attempted "putsch" against the constitutional government.

6. Confidential memorandum from U.S. embassy, Berlin, to the U.S. Secretary of State, April 20, 1932, on microfilm in *Confidential Reports of U.S. State Dept., 1930s, Germany,* at major U.S. libraries.

7. Oct. 5, 1942, Memorandum to the Executive Committee of the Office of Alien Property Custodian, stamped CONFIDENTIAL, from the Division of Investigation and Research, Homer Jones, Chief. Now declassified in United States National Archives, Suitland, Maryland annex. See Record Group 131, Alien Property Custodian, investigative reports, in file box relating to Vesting Order No. 248.

8. *Elimination of German Resources for War:* Hearings Before a Subcommittee of the Committee on Military Affairs, United States Senate, Seventy-Ninth Congress; Part 5, Testimony of [the United States] Treasury Department, July 2, 1945. P. 507: Table of *Vereinigte Stahlwerke* output, figures are percent of German total as of 1938; Thyssen organization including Union Banking Corporation pp. 727–31.

9. Robert Sobel, *The Life and Times of Dillon Read* (New York: Dutton-Penguin, 1991), pp. 92–111. The Dillon Read firm cooperated in the development of Sobel's book.

10. George Walker to Averell Harriman, Aug. 11, 1927, in the W. Averell Harriman papers at the Library of Congress (designated hereafter WAH papers).

11. "Iaccarino" to G. H. Walker, RCA Radiogram Sept. 12, 1927. The specific nature of their business with Mussolini is not explained in correspondence available for public access.

12. Andrew Boyle, *Montagu Norman* (London: Cassell, 1967).
Sir Henry Clay, *Lord Norman* (London, MacMillan & Co., 1957), pp. 18, 57, 70–71.
John A. Kouwenhouven, *Partners in Banking . . . Brown Brothers Harriman* (Garden City: Doubleday & Co., 1969).

13. Coordination of much of the Hitler project took place at a single New York address. The Union Banking Corporation had been set up by George Walker at 39 Broadway. Management of the Hamburg-Amerika Line, carried out through Harriman's American Ship and Commerce Corp., was also set up by George Walker at 39 Broadway.

14. Interrogation of Fritz Thyssen, EF/Me/1 of Sept. 4, 1945 in U.S. Control Council records, photostat on page 167 in Anthony Sutton, *An Introduction to The Order* (Billings, Mt.: Liberty House Press, 1986).

15. *Nazi Conspiracy and Aggression—Supplement B,* by the Office of United States Chief of Counsel for Prosecution of Axis Criminality, United States Government Printing Office, (Washington: 1948), pp. 1597, 1686.

16. "Consolidated Silesian Steel Corporation - [minutes of the] Meeting of Board of Directors," Oct. 31, 1930 (Harriman papers, Library of Congress), shows Averell Harriman as Chairman of the Board.
Prescott Bush to W.A. Harriman, Memorandum Dec. 19, 1930 on their Harriman Fifteen Corp.
Annual Report of United Konigs and Laura Steel and Iron Works for the year 1930 (Harriman papers, Library of Congress) lists "Dr. Friedrich Flick . . . Berlin" and "William Averell Harriman . . . New York" on the Board of Directors.
"Harriman Fifteen Corporation Securities Position February 28, 1931," Harriman papers, Library of Congress. This report shows Harriman Fifteen Corporation holding 32,576 shares in

Silesian Holding Co. V.T.C. worth (in scarce depression dollars) $1,628,800, just over half the value of the Harriman Fifteen Corporation's total holdings.

The *New York City Directory of Directors* volumes for the 1930s (available at the Library of Congress) show Prescott Sheldon Bush and W. Averell Harriman as the directors of Harriman Fifteen Corp.

"Appointments," (three typed pages) marked "Noted May 18 1931 W.A.H.," (among the papers from Prescott Bush's New York Office of Brown Brothers Harriman, Harriman papers, Library of Congress), lists a meeting between Averell Harriman and Friedrich Flick in Berlin at 4:00 P.M., Wednesday April 22, 1931. This was followed immediately by a meeting with Wilhelm Cuno, chief executive of the Hamburg-Amerika Line.

The "Report To the Stockholders of the Harriman Fifteen Corporation," Oct. 19, 1933 (in the Harriman papers, Library of Congress) names G.H. Walker as president of the corporation. It shows the Harriman Fifteen Corporation's address as 1 Wall Street—the location of G.H. Walker and Co.

17. *Nazi Conspiracy and Aggression—Supplement B, op. cit.*, p. 1686.

18. Jim Flaherty (a BBH manager, Prescott Bush's employee), March 19, 1934 to W.A. Harriman.

"Dear Averell:
   In Roland's absence Pres[cott] thought it advisable for me to let you know that we received the following cable from [our European representative] Rossi dated March 17th [relating to conflict with the Polish government]. . . ."

19. Harriman Fifteen Corporation notice to stockholders Jan. 7, 1935, under the name of George Walker, President.

20. Order No. 370: Silesian-American Corp. Executed Nov. 17, 1942. Signed by Leo T. Crowley, Alien Property Custodian. F.R. Doc. 42–14183; Filed Dec. 31, 1942, 11:28 A.M.; 8 Fed. Reg. 33 (Jan. 1, 1943).

The order confiscated the Nazis' holdings of 98,000 shares of common and 50,000 shares of preferred stock in Silesian-American.

The Nazi parent company in Breslau, Germany wrote directly to Averell Harriman at 59 Wall St. on Aug. 5, 1940, with "an invitation to take part in the regular meeting of the members of the Bergwerksgesellsc[h]aft Georg von Giesche's Erben. . . ." WAH papers.

21. Sept. 25, 1942, Memorandum To the Executive Committee of the Office of Alien Property Custodian, stamped CONFIDENTIAL, from the Division of Investigation and Research, Homer Jones, Chief. Now declassified in United States National Archives, Suitland, Maryland annex. See Record Group 131, Alien Property Custodian, investigative reports, in file box relating to Vesting Order No. 370.

22. George Walker was a director of American Ship and Commerce from its organization through 1928. Consult *New York City Directory of Directors*.

"Harriman Fifteen Corporation Securities Position February 28, 1931," *op. cit.* The report lists 46,861 shares in the American Ship & Commerce Corp.

See "Message from Mr. Bullfin," Aug. 30, 1934 (Harriman Fifteen section, Harriman papers, Library of Congress) for the joint supervision of Bush and Walker, respectively director and president of the corporation.

23. Cuno was later exposed by Walter Funk, Third Reich Press Chief and Under Secretary of Propaganda, in Funk's postwar jail cell at Nuremberg; but Cuno had died just as Hitler was taking power. William L. Shirer, *The Rise and Fall of the Third Reich* (New York: Simon and Schuster, 1960), p. 144. *Nazi Conspiracy and Aggression—Supplement B, op. cit.*, p. 1688.

24. See "Elimination of German Resources for War," *op. cit.*, pp. 881–82 on Voegler.

See Annual Report of the (Hamburg-Amerikanische-Packetfahrt-Aktien-Gesellschaft (Hapag or Hamburg-Amerika Line), March 1931, for the board of directors. A copy is in the New York Public Library Annex at 11th Avenue, Manhattan.

25. *Nazi Conspiracy and Aggression—Supplement B, op. cit.*, pp. 1178, 1453–54, 1597, 1599.

See "Elimination of German Resources for War," *op. cit.*, pp. 870–72 on Schroeder; p. 730 on Groeninger.

26. Annual Report of Hamburg-Amerika, *op. cit.*

Baron Rudolph Schroeder, Sr. to Averell Harriman, Nov. 14, 1932. K[night] W[ooley] handwritten note and draft reply letter, Dec. 9, 1932.

In his letter, Baron Rudolph refers to the family's American affiliate, J. Henry Schroder [name anglicized], of which Allen Dulles was a director, and his brother John Foster Dulles was the principal attorney.

Baron Bruno Schroder of the British branch was adviser to Bank of England Governor Montagu Norman, and Baron Bruno's partner Frank Cyril Tiarks was Norman's co-director of the Bank of England throughout Norman's career. Kurt von Schroeder was Hjalmar Schacht's delegate to the Bank for International Settlements in Geneva, where many of the financial arrangements for the Nazi regime were made by Montagu Norman, Schacht and the Schroeders for several years of the Hitler regime right up to the outbreak of World War II.

27. Confidential memorandum from U.S. embassy, Berlin, *op. cit.*

28. U.S. Senate "Nye Committee" hearings, Sept. 14, 1934, pp. 1197–98, extracts from letters of Col. William N. Taylor, dated June 27, 1932 and Jan. 9, 1933.

29. American Ship and Commerce Corporation to Dr. Max Warburg, March 7, 1933.

Max Warburg had brokered the sale of Hamburg-Amerika to Harriman and Walker in 1920. Max's brothers controlled the Kuhn Loeb investment banking house in New York, the firm which had staked old E.H. Harriman to his 1890s buyout of the giant Union Pacific Railroad.

Max Warburg had long worked with Lord Milner and others of the racialist British Round Table concerning joint projects in Africa and Eastern Europe. He was an advisor to Hjalmar Schacht for several decades and was a top executive of Hitler's Reichsbank. The reader may consult David Farrer, *The Warburgs: The Story of A Family* (New York: Stein and Day, 1975).

30. Max Warburg, at M.M. Warburg and Co., Hamburg, to Averill [sic] Harriman, c/o Messrs. Brown Brothers Harriman & Co., 59 Wall Street, New York, N.Y., March 27, 1933.

31. This correspondence, and the joint statement of the Jewish organizations, are reproduced in Moshe R. Gottlieb, *American Anti-Nazi Resistance, 1933–41: An Historical Analysis* (New York: Ktav Publishing House, 1982).

32. *Investigation of Nazi Propaganda Activities and Investigation of Certain Other Propaganda Activities:* Public Hearings before A Subcommittee of the Special Committee on Un-American Activities, United States House of Representatives, Seventy Third Congress, New York City, July 9–12, 1934—Hearings No. 73-NY-7 (Washington: U.S. Govt. Printing Office, 1934). See testimony of Capt. Frederick C. Mensing, John Schroeder, Paul von Lilienfeld-Toal, and summaries by Committee members.

See *New York Times,* July 16, 1933, p. 12, for organizing of Nazi Labor Front at North German Lloyd, leading to Hamburg-Amerika after merger.

33. American Ship and Commerce Corporation telegram to Rudolph Brinckmann at M.M. Warburg, June 12, 1936.

Rudolph Brinckmann to Averell Harriman at 59 Wall St., June 20, 1936, with enclosed note transmitting Helfferich's letter.

Reply to Dr. Rudolph Brinckmann c/o M.M. Warburg and Co, July 6, 1936, in the Harriman papers at the Library of Congress. The file copy of this letter carries no signature, but is presumably from Averell Harriman.

34. Office of Alien Property Custodian, Vesting Order No. 126. Signed by Leo T. Crowley, Alien Property Custodian, executed August 28, 1942. F.R. Doc. 42–8774; Filed September 4, 1942, 10:55 A.M.; 7 F.R. 7061 (No. 176, Sept. 5, 1942.)

July 18, 1942, Memorandum To the Executive Committee of the Office of Alien Property Custodian, stamped CONFIDENTIAL, from the Division of Investigation and Research, Homer Jones, Chief. Now declassified in United States National Archives, Suitland, Maryland annex. See Record Group 131, Alien Property Custodian, investigative reports, in file box relating to Vesting Order No. 126.

35. *New York Times,* May 20, 1933. Leading up to this agreement is a telegram which somehow escaped the shredder and may be seen in the Harriman papers in the Library of Congress. It is addressed to Nazi official Hjalmar Schacht at the Mayflower Hotel, Washington, dated May 11, 1933: "Much disappointed to have missed seeing you Tuesday afternoon. . . . I hope to see you either in Washington or New York before you sail.

with my regards W.A. Harriman"

36. Dulles to Bush letter and draft reply in WAH papers.

37. *New York Times,* Jan. 19, 1938.

III

RACE HYGIENE: THREE BUSH FAMILY ALLIANCES

"The [government] must put the most modern medical means in the service of this knowledge.... Those who are physically and mentally unhealthy and unworthy must not perpetuate their suffering in the body of their children. ... The prevention of the faculty and opportunity to procreate on the part of the physically degenerate and mentally sick, over a period of only 600 years, would ... free humanity from an immeasurable misfortune."

"The per capita income gap between the developed and the developing countries is increasing, in large part the result of higher birth rates in the poorer countries.... Famine in India, unwanted babies in the United States, poverty that seemed to form an unbreakable chain for millions of people—how should we tackle these problems? ... It is quite clear that one of the major challenges of the 1970s ... will be to curb the world's fertility."

These two quotations are alike in their mock show of concern for human suffering, and in their cynical remedy for it: Big Brother must prevent the "unworthy" or "unwanted" people from living.

Let us now further inquire into the family background of our President, so as to help illustrate how the second quoted author, **George Bush**[1] came to share the outlook of the first, **Adolf Hitler**.[2]

We shall examine here the alliance of the Bush family with three other families: **Farish, Draper** and **Gray.**

The private associations among these families have led to the President's relationship to his closest, most confidential advisers.

45

These alliances were forged in the earlier Hitler project and its immediate aftermath. Understanding them will help us to explain George Bush's obsession with the supposed overpopulation of the world's non-Anglo-Saxons, and the dangerous means he has adopted to deal with this "problem."

Bush and Farish

When George Bush was elected Vice President in 1980, Texas mystery man William ("Will") Stamps Farish III took over management of all of George Bush's personal wealth in a "blind trust." Known as one of the richest men in Texas, Will Farish keeps his business affairs under the most intense secrecy. Only the source of his immense wealth is known, not its employment.[3]

Will Farish has long been Bush's closest friend and confidante. He is also the unique private host to Britain's Queen Elizabeth II: Farish owns and boards the studs which mate with the Queen's mares. That is her public rationale when she comes to America and stays in Farish's house. It is a vital link in the mind of our Anglophile President.

President Bush can count on Will Farish not to betray the violent secrets surrounding the Bush family money. For Farish's own family fortune was made in the same Hitler project, in a nightmarish partnership with George Bush's father.

On March 25, 1942, U.S. Assistant Attorney General Thurman Arnold announced that William Stamps Farish (grandfather of the President's money manager) had pled "no contest" to charges of criminal conspiracy with the Nazis. Farish was the principal manager of a worldwide cartel between Standard Oil Co. of New Jersey and the I.G. Farben concern. The merged enterprise had opened the Auschwitz slave labor camp on June 14, 1940, to produce artificial rubber and gasoline from coal. The Hitler government supplied political opponents and Jews as the slaves, who were worked to near death and then murdered.

Arnold disclosed that Standard Oil of N.J. (later known as Exxon), of which Farish was president and chief executive, had agreed to stop hiding from the United States patents for artificial rubber which the company had provided to the Nazis.[4]

A Senate investigating committee under Senator (later U.S. President) Harry Truman of Missouri had called Arnold to testify at hearings on U.S. corporations' collaboration with the Nazis. The Senators expressed outrage at the cynical way Farish was continuing an alliance with the Hitler regime that had begun back in 1933, when Farish became chief of Jersey Standard. Didn't he know there was a war on?

The Justice Department laid before the committee a letter, written to Standard president Farish by his vice president, shortly after the beginning of World War II (Sept. 1, 1939) in Europe. The letter concerned a renewal of their earlier agreements with the Nazis:

Report on European Trip
Oct. 12, 1939
Mr. W.S. Farish
30 Rockefeller Plaza
  Dear Mr. Farish: ... I stayed in France until Sept. 17th. ... In England I met by appointment the Royal Dutch [Shell Oil Co.] gentlemen from Holland, and ... a general agreement was reached on the necessary changes in our relations with the I.G. [Farben], in view of the state of war. ... [T]he Royal Dutch Shell group is essentially British. ... I also had several meetings with ... the [British] Air Ministry. ...
  I required help to obtain the necessary permission to go to Holland. ... After discussions with the [American] Ambassador [Joseph Kennedy] ... the situation was cleared completely. ... The gentlemen in the Air Ministry ... very kindly offered to assist me [later] in reentering England. ...
  Pursuant to these arrangements, I was able to keep my appointments in Holland [having flown there on a British Royal Air Force bomber], where I had three days of discussion with the representatives of I.G. They delivered to me assignments of some 2,000 foreign patents and *we did our best to work out complete plans for a modus vivendi which could operate through the term of the war, whether or not the U.S. came in.* ... [emphasis added]
  Very truly yours, F[rank] A. Howard[5]

Here are some cold realities behind the tragedy of World War II, which help explain the Bush-Farish family alliance—and their peculiar closeness to the Queen of England:

• Shell Oil is principally owned by the British royal family. Shell's chairman, Sir Henri Deterding, helped sponsor Hitler's rise to power,[6] by arrangement with the royal family's Bank of England Governor, Montagu Norman. Their ally Standard Oil would take part in the Hitler project right up to the bloody, gruesome end.

• When grandfather Farish signed the Justice Department's consent decree in March 1942, the government had already started picking its way through the tangled web of world-monopoly oil and chemical agreements between Standard Oil and the Nazis. Many patents and other Nazi-owned aspects of the partnership had been seized by the U.S. Alien Property Custodian.

Uncle Sam would not seize Prescott Bush's Union Banking Corporation for another seven months.

The Bush-Farish axis had begun back in 1929. In that year the Harriman bank bought Dresser Industries, supplier of oil-pipeline couplers to Standard and other companies. Prescott Bush became a director and financial czar of Dresser, installing his Yale classmate Neil Mallon as chairman.[7] George Bush would later name one of his sons after the Dresser executive.

William S. Farish was the main organizer of the Humble Oil Co. of Texas, which Farish merged into the Standard Oil Company of New Jersey. Farish built up the Humble-Standard empire of pipelines and refineries in Texas.[8]

The stock market crashed just after the Bush family got into the oil business. The world financial crisis led to the merger of the Walker-Harriman bank with Brown Brothers in 1931. Former Brown partner Montagu Norman and his protégé Hjalmar Schacht paid frantic visits to New York that year and the next, preparing the new Hitler regime for Germany.

The most important American political event in those preparations for Hitler was the infamous "Third International Congress on Eugenics," held at New York's American Museum of Natural History August 21–23, 1932, supervised by the International Federation of Eugenics Societies.[9] This meeting took up the stubborn persistence of African-Americans and other allegedly "inferior" and "socially inadequate" groups in reproducing, expanding their numbers, and amalgamating with others. It was recommended that these "dangers" to the "better" ethnic groups and to the "well-born," could be dealt with by sterilization or "cutting off the bad stock" of the "unfit."

Italy's fascist government sent an official representative. Averell Harriman's sister Mary, director of "Entertainment" for the Congress, lived down in Virginia fox-hunting country; her state supplied the speaker on "racial purity," W.A. Plecker, Virginia commissioner of vital statistics. Plecker reportedly held the delegates spellbound with his account of the struggle to stop race-mixing and inter-racial sex in Virginia.

The Congress proceedings were dedicated to Averell Harriman's mother; she had paid for the founding of the race-science movement in America back in 1910, building the Eugenics Record Office as a branch of the Galton National Laboratory in London. She and other Harrimans were usually escorted to the horse races by old George

Herbert Walker—they shared with the Bushes and the Farishes a fascination with "breeding thoroughbreds" among horses and humans.[10]

Averell Harriman personally arranged with the Walker/Bush Hamburg-Amerika Line to transport Nazi ideologues from Germany to New York for this meeting.[11] The most famous among those transported was Dr. Ernst Rüdin, psychiatrist at the Kaiser Wilhelm Institute for Genealogy and Demography in Berlin, where the Rockefeller family paid for Dr. Rüdin to occupy an entire floor with his eugenics "research." Dr. Rüdin had addressed the International Federation's 1928 Munich meeting, speaking on "Mental Aberration and Race Hygiene," while others (Germans and Americans) spoke on race-mixing and sterilization of the unfit. Rüdin had also led the German delegation to the 1930 Mental Hygiene Congress in Washington, D.C.

At the Harrimans' 1932 New York Eugenics Congress, Ernst Rüdin was unanimously elected president of the International Federation of Eugenics Societies. This was recognition of Rüdin as founder of the German Society for Race Hygiene, with his co-founder, Eugenics Federation vice president Alfred Plötz.

As depression-maddened financiers schemed in Berlin and New York, Rüdin was now official leader of the world eugenics movement. Components of his movement included groups with overlapping leadership, dedicated to:

• sterilization of mental patients ("mental hygiene societies");
• execution of the insane, criminals and the terminally ill ("euthanasia societies"); and
• eugenical race-purification by prevention of births to parents from "inferior" blood stocks ("birth control societies").

Before the Auschwitz death camp became a household word, these British-American-European groups called openly for the elimination of the "unfit" by means including force and violence.[12]

Ten months later, in June 1933, Hitler's interior minister Wilhelm Frick spoke to a eugenics meeting in the new Third Reich. Frick called the Germans a "degenerate" race, denouncing one-fifth of Germany's parents for producing "feeble-minded" and "defective" children. The following month, on a commission by Frick, Dr. Ernst Rüdin wrote the "Law for the Prevention of Hereditary Diseases in Posterity," the sterilization law modeled on previous U.S. statutes in Virginia and other states.

Special courts were soon established for the sterilization of German mental patients, the blind, the deaf and alcoholics. A quarter million people in these categories were sterilized. Rüdin, Plötz and their colleagues trained a whole generation of physicians and psychiatrists—as sterilizers and as killers.

When the war started, the eugenicists, doctors and psychiatrists staffed the new "T4" agency, which planned and supervised the mass killings: first at "euthanasia centers," where the same categories which had first been subject to sterilization were now to be murdered, their brains sent in lots of 200 to experimental psychiatrists; then at slave camps such as Auschwitz; and finally, for Jews and other race victims, at straight extermination camps in Poland, such as Treblinka and Belsen.[13]

In 1933, as what Hitler called his "New Order" appeared, John D. Rockefeller, Jr. appointed William S. Farish the chairman of Standard Oil Co. of New Jersey (in 1937 he was made president and chief executive). Farish moved his offices to Rockefeller Center, New York, where he spent a good deal of time with Hermann Schmitz, chairman of I.G. Farben; his company paid a publicity man, Ivy Lee, to write pro-I.G. Farben and pro-Nazi propaganda and get it into the U.S. press.

Now that he was outside of Texas, Farish found himself in the shipping business—like the Bush family. He hired Nazi German crews for Standard Oil tankers. And he hired **Emil Helfferich,** chairman of the Walker/Bush/Harriman Hamburg-Amerika Line, as chairman also of the Standard Oil Company subsidiary in Germany. Karl Lindemann, board member of Hamburg-Amerika, also became a top Farish-Standard executive in Germany.[14]

This interlock between their Nazi German operations put Farish together with Prescott Bush in a small, select group of men operating from abroad through Hitler's "revolution," and calculating that they would never be punished.

In 1939, Farish's daughter Martha married Averell Harriman's nephew, Edward Harriman Gerry, and Farish in-laws became Prescott Bush's partners at 59 Broadway.[15]

Both Emil Helfferich and Karl Lindemann were authorized to write checks to Heinrich Himmler, chief of the Nazi S.S., on a special Standard Oil account. This account was managed by the German-British-American banker, Kurt von Schroeder. According to U.S. intelligence documents reviewed by author Anthony Sutton, Emil Helfferich continued his payments to the S.S. into 1944, when the S.S. was supervising the mass murder at the Standard-I.G. Farben Auschwitz and other death camps. Helfferich told Allied interrogators after the war that these were not his personal contributions—they were corporate Standard Oil funds.[16]

After pleading "no contest" to charges of criminal conspiracy with the Nazis, William Stamps Farish was fined $5,000. (Similar fines were levied against Standard Oil—$5,000 each for the parent company and for several subsidiaries.) This of course did not interfere with the millions of dollars that Farish had acquired in conjunction with Hitler's New Order, as a large stockholder, chairman and president of Standard Oil. All the government sought was the use of patents which his company had given to the Nazis—the Auschwitz patents—but had withheld from the U.S. military and industry.

But a war was on, and if young men were to be asked to die fighting Hitler . . . something more was needed. Farish was hauled before the Senate committee investigating the national defense program. The committee chairman, Senator Harry Truman, told newsmen before Farish testified: "I think this approaches treason."[17]

Farish began breaking apart at these hearings. He shouted his "indignation" at the Senators, and claimed he was not "disloyal."

After the March–April hearings ended, more dirt came gushing out of the Justice Department and the Congress on Farish and Standard Oil. Farish had deceived the U.S. Navy to prevent the Navy from acquiring certain patents, while supplying them to the Nazi war machine; meanwhile, he was supplying gasoline and tetra-ethyl lead to Germany's submarines and air force. Communications between Standard and I.G. Farben from the outbreak of World War II were released to the Senate, showing that Farish's organization had arranged to deceive the U.S. government into passing over Nazi-owned assets: They would nominally buy I.G.'s share in certain patents because "in the event of war between ourselves and Germany . . . it would certainly be very undesirable to have this 20 percent Standard-I.G. pass to an alien property custodian of the U.S. who might sell it to an unfriendly interest."[18]

John D. Rockefeller, Jr. (father of David, Nelson and John D. Rockefeller III), controlling owner of Standard Oil, told the Roosevelt administration that he knew nothing of the day-to-day affairs of his company, that all these matters were handled by Farish and other executives.[19]

In August, Farish was brought back for more testimony. He was now frequently accused of lying. Farish was crushed under the intense, public grilling; he became morose, ashen. While Prescott Bush escaped publicity when the government seized his Nazi banking organization in October, Farish had been nailed. He collapsed and died of a heart attack on Nov. 29, 1942.

The Farish family was devastated by the exposure. Son William

Stamps Farish, Jr., a lieutenant in the Army Air Force, was humiliated by the public knowledge that his father was fueling the enemy's aircraft; he died in a training accident in Texas six months later.[20]

With this double death, the fortune comprising much of Standard Oil's profits from Texas and Nazi Germany was now to be settled upon the little four-year-old grandson, William ("Will") Stamps Farish III. Will Farish grew up a recluse, the most secretive multimillionaire in Texas, with investments of "that money" in a multitude of foreign countries, and a host of exotic contacts overlapping the intelligence and financial worlds—particularly in Britain.

The Bush-Farish axis started George Bush's career. After his 1948 graduation from Yale (and Skull and Bones), George Bush flew down to Texas on a corporate airplane and was employed by his father's Dresser Industries. In a couple of years he got help from his uncle, George Walker, Jr., and Farish's British banker friends, to set him up in the oil property speculation business. Soon thereafter, George Bush founded the Zapata Oil Company, which put oil drilling rigs into certain locations of great strategic interest to the Anglo-American intelligence community.

Will Farish at 25 years old was a personal aide to Zapata chairman George Bush in Bush's unsuccessful 1964 campaign for Senate. Will Farish used "that Auschwitz money" to back George Bush financially, investing in Zapata. When Bush was elected to Congress in 1966, Farish joined the Zapata board.[21]

When George Bush became U.S. Vice President in 1980, the Farish and Bush family fortunes were again completely, secretly commingled. As we shall see, the old projects were now being revived on a breathtaking scale.

Bush and Draper

Twenty years before he was U.S. President, George Bush brought two "race-science" professors in front of the Republican Task Force on Earth Resources and Population. As chairman of the Task Force, then-Congressman Bush invited Professors William Shockley and Arthur Jensen to explain to the committee how allegedly runaway birth-rates for African-Americans were "down-breeding" the American population.

Afterwards Bush personally summed up for the Congress the testimony his black-inferiority advocates had given to the Task Force.[22] George Bush held his hearings on the threat posed by black babies on August 5, 1969, while much of the world was in a better frame of mind—celebrating mankind's progress from the first moon landing 16 days earlier. Bush's obsessive thinking on this subject was guided by his family's friend, Gen. William H. Draper, Jr., the founder and chairman of the Population Crisis Committee, and vice chairman of the Planned Parenthood Federation. Draper had long been steering U.S. public discussion about the so-called "population bomb" in the non-white areas of the world.

If Congressman Bush had explained to his colleagues *how his family had come to know General Draper,* they would perhaps have felt some alarm, or even panic, and paid more healthy attention to Bush's presentation. Unfortunately, the Draper-Bush population doctrine is now official U.S. foreign policy.

William H. Draper, Jr. had joined the Bush team in 1927, when he was hired by Dillon Read & Co., New York investment bankers. Draper was put into a new job slot at the firm: handling the Thyssen account.

We recall that in 1924, Fritz Thyssen set up his Union Banking Corporation in George Herbert Walker's bank at 39 Broadway, Manhattan. Dillon Read & Co.'s boss, Clarence Dillon, had begun working with Fritz Thyssen sometime after Averell Harriman first met with Thyssen—at about the time Thyssen began financing Adolf Hitler's political career.

In January 1926, Dillon Read created the **German Credit and Investment Corporation** in Newark, New Jersey and Berlin, Germany, as Thyssen's short-term banker. That same year Dillon Read created the *Vereinigte Stahlwerke* (German Steel Trust), incorporating the Thyssen family interests under the direction of New York and London finance.[23]

William H. Draper, Jr. was made director, vice president and assistant treasurer of the German Credit and Investment Corp. His business was short-term loans and financial management tricks for Thyssen and the German Steel Trust. Draper's clients sponsored Hitler's terroristic takeover; his clients led the buildup of the Nazi war industry; his clients made war against the United States. The Nazis were Draper's direct partners in Berlin and New Jersey: Alexander Kreuter, residing in Berlin, was president; Frederic Brandi, whose father was a top coal executive in the German Steel Trust, moved to the U.S. in 1926 and served as Draper's co-director in Newark.

Draper's role was crucial for Dillon Read & Co., for whom Draper was a partner and eventually vice president. The German Credit and Investment Corp. (GCI) was a "front" for Dillon Read: It had the same New Jersey address as U.S. & International Securities Corp. (USIS), and the same man served as treasurer of both firms.[24]

Clarence Dillon and his son C. Douglas Dillon were directors of USIS, which was spotlighted when Clarence Dillon was hauled before the Senate Banking Committee's famous "Pecora" hearings in 1933. USIS was shown to be one of the great speculative pyramid schemes which had swindled stockholders of hundreds of millions of dollars. These investment policies had rotted the U.S. economy to the core, and led to the Great Depression of the 1930s.

But William H. Draper, Jr.'s GCI "front" was not *apparently* affiliated with the USIS "front" or with Dillon, and the GCI escaped the Congressmen's limited scrutiny. This oversight was to prove most unfortunate, particularly to the 50 million people who subsequently died in World War II.

Dillon Read hired public relations man Ivy Lee to prepare their executives for their testimony and to confuse and further baffle the Congressmen.[25] Lee apparently took enough time out from his duties as image-maker for William S. Farish and the Nazi I.G. Farben Co.; he managed the congressional thinking so that the Congressmen did not disturb the Draper operation in Germany—and did not meddle with Thyssen, or interfere with Hitler's U.S. moneymen.

Thus in 1932, William H. Draper, Jr. was free to finance the International Eugenics Congress as a "Supporting Member".[26] Was he using his own income as a Thyssen trust banker? Or did the funds come from Dillon Read corporate accounts, perhaps to be written off income tax as "expenses for German project: race purification"? Draper helped select Ernst Rüdin as chief of the world eugenics movement, who used his office to promote what he called Adolf Hitler's "holy, national and international racial hygienic mission."[27]

W.S. Farish, as we have seen, was publicly exposed in 1942, humiliated and destroyed. Just before Farish died, Prescott Bush's Nazi banking office was quietly seized and shut down. But Prescott's close friend and partner in the Thyssen-Hitler business, William H. Draper, Jr., *neither died nor moved out of German affairs*. Draper listed himself as a director of the German Credit and Investment Corp. through 1942, and the firm was not liquidated until November 1943.[28] But a war was on; Draper, a colonel from previous military service, went off to the Pacific theater and became a general.

General Draper apparently had a hobby: magic—illusions, sleight of hand, etc.—and he was a member of the Society of American Magicians. This is not irrelevant to his subsequent career.

The Nazi regime surrendered in May 1945. In July 1945, General Draper was called to Europe by the American military government authorities in Germany. Draper was appointed head of the Economics Division of the U.S. Control Commission. He was assigned to take apart the Nazi corporate cartels. There is an astonishing but perfectly logical rationale to this—Draper knew a lot about the subject! General Draper, who had spent about 15 years financing and managing the dirtiest of the Nazi enterprises, was now authorized to decide *who was exposed, who lost and who kept his business, and in practical effect, who was prosecuted for war crimes.*[29]

(Draper was not unique within the postwar occupation government. Consider the case of John J. McCloy, U.S. Military Governor and High Commissioner of Germany, 1949–1952. Under instructions from his Wall Street law firm, McCloy had lived for a year in Italy, serving as an advisor to the fascist government of Benito Mussolini. An intimate collaborator of the Harriman/Bush bank, McCloy had sat in Adolf Hitler's box at the 1936 Olympic games in Berlin, at the invitation of Nazi chieftains Rudolf Hess and Hermann Göring.)[30]

William H. Draper, Jr., as a "conservative," was paired with the "liberal" U.S. Treasury Secretary Henry Morgenthau in a vicious game. Morgenthau demanded that Germany be utterly destroyed as a nation, that its industry be dismantled and it be reduced to a purely rural country. As the economic boss in 1945 and 1946, Draper "protected" Germany from the Morgenthau Plan—but at a price.

Draper and his colleagues demanded that Germany and the world accept the *collective guilt of the German people* as *the* explanation for the rise of Hitler's New Order, and the Nazi war crimes. This, of course, was rather convenient for General Draper himself, as it was for the Bush family. It is still convenient decades later, allowing Prescott's son, President Bush, to lecture Germany on the danger of Hitlerism. Germans are too slow, it seems, to accept his New World Order.

After several years of government service (often working directly for Averell Harriman in the North Atlantic Alliance), General Draper was appointed in 1958 chairman of a committee which was to advise President Dwight Eisenhower on the proper course for U.S. military aid to other countries. At that time, Prescott Bush was a U.S. Senator from Connecticut, a confidential friend and golf partner with National Security Director Gordon Gray, and an important golf partner with Dwight Eisenhower as well. Prescott's old lawyer from the Nazi days, John Foster Dulles, was Secretary of State, and his brother Allen Dulles, formerly of the Schroder bank, was head of the CIA.

This friendly environment emboldened General Draper to pull off a stunt with his military aid advisory committee. He changed the subject under study. The following year the Draper committee recommended that the U.S. government react to the supposed threat of the "population explosion" by formulating plans to depopulate the poorer countries. The growth of the world's non-white population, he proposed, should be regarded as dangerous to the national security of the United States![31]

President Eisenhower rejected the recommendation. But in the next decade, General Draper founded the "Population Crisis Committee" and the "Draper Fund," joining with the Rockefeller and DuPont families to promote eugenics as "population control." The administration of President Lyndon Johnson, advised by General Draper on the subject, began financing birth control in the tropical countries through the U.S. Agency for International Development (USAID).

General Draper was George Bush's guru on the population question.[32] But there was also Draper's money—from that uniquely horrible source—and Draper's connections on Wall Street and abroad. Draper's son and heir, William H. Draper III, was co-chairman for finance (chief of fundraising) of the Bush-for-President national campaign organization in 1980. With George Bush in the White House, the younger Draper heads up the depopulation activities of the United Nations throughout the world.

General Draper was vice president of Dillon Read until 1953. During the 1950s and 1960s, the chief executive there was Frederic Brandi, the German who was Draper's co-director for the Nazi investments and his personal contact man with the Nazi German Steel Trust. Nicholas Brady was Brandi's partner from 1954, and replaced him as the firm's chief executive in 1971. Nicholas Brady, who knows where all the bodies are buried, was chairman of his friend George Bush's 1980 election campaign in New Jersey, and has been United States Treasury Secretary throughout Bush's presidency.[33]

Bush and Gray

The U.S. Agency for International Development says that surgical sterilization is the Bush administration's "first choice" method of population reduction in the Third World.[34]

The United Nations Population Fund claims that 37 percent of contraception users in Ibero-America and the Caribbean have already been surgically sterilized. In a 1991 report, William H. Draper III's agency asserts that 254 million couples will be surgically sterilized over the course of the 1990s; and that if present trends continue, 80 percent of the women in Puerto Rico and Panama will be surgically sterilized.[35]

The U.S. government pays directly for these sterilizations.

Mexico is first among targeted nations, on a list which was drawn up in July 1991, at a USAID strategy session. India and Brazil are second and third priorities, respectively.

On contract with the Bush administration, U.S. personnel are working from bases in Mexico to perform surgery on millions of Mexican men and women. The acknowledged strategy in this program is to sterilize those young adults who have not already completed their families.

George Bush has a rather deep-seated personal feeling about this project, in particular as it pits him against Pope John Paul II in Catholic countries such as Mexico. (See Chapter 4 below, on the origin of a Bush family grudge in this regard.)

The spending for birth control in the non-white countries is one of the few items that is headed upwards in the Bush administration budget. As its 1992 budget was being set, USAID said its Population Account would receive $300 million, a 20 percent increase over the previous year. Within this project, a significant sum is spent on political and psychological manipulations of target nations, and rather blatant subversion of their religions and governments.[36]

These activities might be expected to cause serious objections from the victimized nationalities, or from U.S. taxpayers, especially if the program is somehow given widespread publicity.

Quite aside from moral considerations, *legal* questions would naturally arise, which could be summed up: **How does George Bush think he can get away with this?**

In this matter the President has expert advice. Mr. (Clayland) Boyden Gray has been counsel to George Bush since the 1980 election. As chief legal officer in the White House, Boyden Gray can walk the President through the dangers and complexities of waging such unusual warfare against Third World populations. Gray knows how these things are done.

When Boyden Gray was four and five years old, his father organized the pilot project for the present worldwide sterilization program, from the Gray family household in North Carolina.

It started in 1946. The eugenics movement was looking for a way to begin again in America.

Nazi death camps such as Auschwitz had just then seared the conscience of the world. The Sterilization League of America, which had changed its name during the war to "Birthright, Inc.," wanted to start up again. First they had to overcome public nervousness about crackpots proposing to eliminate "inferior" and "defective" people. The League tried to surface in Iowa, but had to back off because of negative publicity: A little boy had recently been sterilized there and had died from the operation.

They decided on North Carolina, where the Gray family could play the perfect host. Through British imperial contacts, Boyden Gray's grandfather, Bowman Gray, had become principal owner of the R.J. Reynolds Tobacco Co. Boyden's father, Gordon Gray, had recently founded the Bowman Gray (memorial) Medical School in Winston-Salem, using his inherited cigarette stock shares. The medical school was already a eugenics center.

As the experiment began, Gordon Gray's great aunt, Alice Shelton Gray, who had raised him from childhood, was living in his household. Aunt Alice had founded the "Human Betterment League," the North Carolina branch of the national eugenical sterilization movement.

Aunt Alice was the official supervisor of the 1946–47 experiment. Working under Miss Gray was Dr. Claude Nash Herndon, whom Gordon Gray had made assistant professor of "medical genetics" at Bowman Gray Medical School.

Dr. Clarence Gamble, heir to the Proctor and Gamble soap fortune, was the sterilizers' national field operations chief.

The experiment worked as follows. *All children enrolled in the school district of Winston-Salem, N.C., were given a special "intelligence test." Those children who scored below a certain arbitrary low mark were then cut open and surgically sterilized.*

We quote now from the official story of the project[37]:

In Winston-Salem and in [nearby] Orange County, North Carolina, the [Sterilization League's] field committee had participated in testing projects to identify school age children who should be considered for sterilization. The project in Orange County was conducted by the University of North Carolina and was financed by a 'Mr. Hanes,' a friend of Clarence Gamble and supporter of the field work project in North Carolina. The Winston-Salem project was also financed by Hanes." ["Hanes" was underwear mogul James Gordon Hanes, a trustee of Bowman Gray Medical School and treasurer of Alice Gray's group]. . . .

The medical school had a long history of interest in eugenics and had compiled extensive histories of families carrying inheritable disease. In 1946, Dr. C. Nash Herndon . . . made a statement to the press on the use of sterilization to prevent the spread of inheritable diseases. . . .

The first step after giving the mental tests to grade school children was to interpret and make public the results. In Orange County the results indicated that three percent of the school age children were either insane or feebleminded. . . . [Then] the field committee hired a social worker to review each case . . . and to present any cases in which sterilization was indicated to the State Eugenics Board, which under North Carolina law had the authority to order sterilization. . . .

Race science experimenter Dr. Claude Nash Herndon provided more details in an interview in 1990.[38]

> Alice Gray was the general supervisor of the project. She and Hanes sent out letters promoting the program to the commissioners of all 100 counties in North Carolina. . . . What did I do? Nothing besides riding herd on the whole thing! The social workers operated out of my office. I was at the time also director of outpatient services at North Carolina Baptist Hospital. We would see the [targeted] parents and children there. . . . I.Q. tests were run on all the children in the Winston-Salem public school system. Only the ones who scored really low [were targeted for sterilization], the real bottom of the barrel, like below 70.
> Did we do sterilizations on young children? Yes. This was a relatively minor operation. . . . It was usually not until the child was eight or ten years old. For the boys, you just make an incision and tie the tube. . . . We more often performed the operation on girls than with boys. Of course, you have to cut open the abdomen, but again, it is relatively minor.

Dr. Herndon remarked coolly that "we had a very good relationship with the press" for the project. This is not surprising, since Gordon Gray owned the *Winston-Salem Journal*, the *Twin City Sentinel* and radio station WSJS.

In 1950 and 1951, John Foster Dulles, then chairman of the Rockefeller Foundation, led John D. Rockefeller III on a series of world tours, focusing on the need to stop the expansion of the non-white populations. In November 1952, Dulles and Rockefeller set up the Population Council, with tens of millions of dollars from the Rockefeller family.

At that point, the American Eugenics Society, still cautious from the recent bad publicity vis-a-vis Hitler, left its old headquarters at Yale University. The Society moved its headquarters into the office of the Population Council, and the two groups melded together. The long-time secretary of the American Eugenics Society, Frederick Osborne, became the first president of the Population Council. The Gray family's child-sterilizer, Dr. Claude Nash Herndon, became president of the American Eugenics Society in 1953, as its work expanded under Rockefeller patronage.

Meanwhile, the International Planned Parenthood Federation was founded in London, in the offices of the British Eugenics Society.

The undead enemy from World War II, renamed "Population Control," had now been revived.

George Bush was U.S. ambassador to the United Nations in 1972, when with prodding from Bush and his friends, the U.S. Agency for International Development first made an official contract with the old Sterilization League of America. The League had changed its name twice again, and was now called the "Association for Voluntary Surgical Contraception." The U.S. government began paying the old fascist group to sterilize non-whites in foreign countries.

The Gray family experiment had succeeded.

In 1988, the U.S. Agency for International Development signed its latest contract with the old Sterilization League (a.k.a. Association for Voluntary Surgical Contraception), committing the U.S. government to spend $80 million over five years.

Having gotten away with sterilizing several hundred North Carolina school children, "not usually less than eight to ten years old," the identical group is now authorized by President Bush to do it to 58 countries in Asia, Africa and Ibero-America. The group modestly claims it has directly sterilized "only" two million people, with 87 percent of the bill paid by U.S. taxpayers.

Meanwhile, Dr. Clarence Gamble, Boyden Gray's favorite soap manufacturer, formed his own "Pathfinder Fund" as a split-off from the Sterilization League. Gamble's Pathfinder Fund, with additional millions from USAID, concentrates on penetration of local social groups in the non-white countries, to break down psychological resistance to the surgical sterilization teams.

Notes for Chapter III

1. Phyllis Tilson Piotrow, *World Population Crisis: The United States Response* (New York: Praeger Publishers, 1973), "Forward" by George H.W. Bush, pp. vii-viii.

2. Adolf Hitler, *Mein Kampf* (Boston, Houghton Mifflin Company, 1971), p. 404.

3. "The Ten Richest People in Houston," in *Houston Post Magazine*, March 11, 1984. "$150 million to $250 million from . . . inheritance, plus subsequent investments . . . chief heir to a family fortune in oil stock. . . . As to his financial interests, he is . . . coy. He once described one of his businesses as a company that 'invests in and oversees a lot of smaller companies . . . in a lot of foreign countries.' "

4. The announcements were made in testimony before a Special Committee of the U.S. Senate Investigating the National Defense Program. The hearings on Standard Oil were held March 5, 24, 26, 27, and 31, and April 1, 2, 3 and 7, 1942. Available on microfiche, law section, Library of Congress. See also *New York Times*, March 26 and March 27, 1942, and *Washington Evening Star*, March 26 and March 27, 1942.

5. *Ibid.*, Exhibit No. 368, printed on pp. 4584–87 of the hearing record. See also Charles Higham, *Trading With The Enemy* (New York: Delacorte Press, 1983), p. 36.

6. Confidential memorandum from U.S. embassy, Berlin, *op. cit.*, chapter 2. Sir Henri Deterding was among the most notorious pro-Nazis of the early war period.

7. See sections on Prescott Bush in Darwin Payne, *Initiative in Energy: Dresser Industries, Inc.* (New York: Distributed by Simon and Schuster, 1979) (published by the Dresser Company).

8. William Stamps Farish obituary, *New York Times*, Nov. 30, 1942.

9. *A Decade of Progress in Eugenics: Scientific Papers of the Third International Congress of Eugenics held at American Museum of Natural History New York, Aug. 21–23, 1932.* (Baltimore: Williams & Wilkins Company, Sept., 1934).

The term "eugenics" is taken from the Greek to signify "good birth" or "well-born," as in aristocrat. Its basic assumption is that those who are not "well-born" should not exist.

10. See among other such letters, George Herbert Walker, 39 Broadway, N.Y., to W. A. Harriman, London, Feb. 21, 1925, in WAH papers.

11. Averell Harriman to Dr. Charles B. Davenport, President, The International Congress of Eugenics, Cold Spring Harbor, L.I., N.Y.

January 21, 1932

Dear Dr. Davenport:
I will be only too glad to put you in touch with the Hamburg-American Line ... they may be able to co-operate in making suggestions which will keep the expenses to a minimum. I have referred your letter to Mr. Emil Lederer [of the Hamburg-Amerika executive board in New York] with the request that he communicate with you.

Davenport to Mr. W.A. Harriman,
59 Wall Street, New York, N.Y.
January 23, 1932

Dear Mr. Harriman:
Thank you very much for your kind letter of January 21st and the action you took which has resulted at once in a letter from Mr. Emil Lederer. This letter will serve as a starting point for correspondence, which I hope will enable more of our German colleagues to come to America on the occasion of the congresses of eugenics and genetics, than otherwise.

Congressional hearings in 1934 established that Hamburg-Amerika routinely provided free transatlantic passage for those carrying out Nazi propaganda chores. See *Investigation of Nazi Propaganda Activities and Investigation of Certain Other Propaganda Activities, op. cit.*, chapter 2.

12. Alexis Carrel, *Man the Unknown* (New York: Halcyon House, published by arrangement with Harper & Brothers, 1935), pp. 318–19.

The battle cry of the New Order was sounded in 1935 with the publication of *Man the Unknown*, by Dr. Alexis Carrel of the Rockefeller Institute in New York. This Nobel Prizewinner said "enormous sums are now required to maintain prisons and insane asylums. ... Why do we preserve these useless and harmful beings? This fact must be squarely faced. Why should society not dispose of the criminals and the insane in a more economical manner? ... The community must be protected against troublesome and dangerous elements. ... Perhaps prisons should be abolished. ... The conditioning of the petty criminal with the whip, or some more scientific procedure, followed by a short stay in hospital, would probably suffice to insure order. [Criminals including those] who have ... misled the public on important matters, should be humanely and economically disposed of in small euthanasic institutions supplied with proper gases. A similar treatment could be advantageously applied to the insane, guilty of criminal acts."

Carrel claimed to have transplanted the head of a dog to another dog and kept it alive for quite some time.

13. Bernhard Schreiber, *The Men Behind Hitler: A German Warning to the World*, France: La Hay-Mureaux, ca. 1975), English language edition supplied by H & P. Tadeusz, 369 Edgewere Road, London W2. A copy of this book is now held by Union College Library, Syracuse, N.Y.

14. Higham, *op. cit.*, p. 35.

15. Engagement announced Feb. 10, 1939, *New York Times*, p. 20. See also *Directory of Directors* for New York City, 1930s and 1940s.

16. Higham, *op. cit.*, pp. 20, 22 and other references to Schroeder and Lindemann.

Anthony Sutton, *Wall Street and the Rise of Hitler* (Seal Beach: '76 Press, 1976). Sutton is also a good source on the Harrimans.

17. *Washington Evening Star*, March 27, 1942, p. 1.

18. Higham, *op. cit.* p. 50.

19. *Ibid.*, p. 48.

20. *Washington Post*, April 29, 1990, p. F4. Higham, *op. cit.*, pp. 52–53.

21. Zapata annual reports, 1950s–60s, Library of Congress microforms.

22. See Congressional Record for Bush speech in the House of Representatives, Sept. 4, 1969. Bush inserted in the record the testimony given before his Task Force on Aug. 5, 1969.

23. Sobel, *op. cit.*, pp. 92–111. See also Boyle, *op. cit.*, chapter 1, concerning the Morgan-led Dawes Committee of Germany's foreign creditors.

Like Harriman, Dillon used the Schroeder and Warburg banks to strike his German bargains. All Dillon Read & Co. affairs in Germany were supervised by J.P. Morgan & Co. partner Thomas Lamont, and were authorized by Bank of England Governor Montagu Norman.

24. See *Poor's Register of Directors and Executives,* (New York: Poor's Publishing Company, late 1920s, '30s and '40s). See also *Standard Corporation Records* (New York: Standard & Poor), 1935 edition pp. 2571–25, and 1938 edition pp. 7436–38, for description and history of the German Credit and Investment Corporation. For Frederic Brandi, See also Sobel, *op. cit.*, pp. 213–14.

25. Sobel, *op. cit.*, pp. 180, 186. Ivy Lee had been hired to improve the Rockefeller family image, particularly difficult after their 1914 massacre of striking miners and pregnant women in Ludlow, Colorado. Lee got old John D. Rockefeller to pass out dimes to poor people lined up at his porch.

26. Third International Eugenics Congress papers *op. cit.*, footnote 7, p. 512, "Supporting Members."

27. Schreiber, *op. cit.*, p. 160. The Third Int. Eugenics Congress papers, p. 526, lists the officers of the International Federation as of publication date in September, 1934. Rüdin is listed as president—a year after he has written the sterilization law for Hitler.

28. *Directory of Directors for New York City, 1942.* Interview with Nancy Bowles, librarian of Dillon Read & Co.

29. Higham, *op. cit.*, p. 129, 212–15, 219–23.

30. Walter Isaacson and Evan Thomas, *The Wise Men: Six Friends and the World They Made—Acheson, Bohlen, Harriman, Kennan, Lovett, McCloy* (New York: Simon and Schuster, 1986), pp. 122, 305.

31. Piotrow, *op. cit.*, pp. 36–42.

32. *Ibid.*, p. viii. "As chairman of the special Republican Task Force on Population and Earth Resources, I was impressed by the arguments of William H. Draper, Jr. . . . Gen. Draper continues to lead through his tireless work for the U.N. Population Fund."

33. Sobel, *op. cit.*, pp. 298, 354.

34. Interview July 16, 1991, with Joanne Grossi, an official with the USAID's Population Office.

35. Dr. Nafis Sadik, "The State of World Population," 1991, New York, United Nations Population Fund.

36. See *User's Guide to the Office of Population,* 1991, Office of Population, Bureau for Science and Technology, United States Agency for International Development. Available from S&T/POP, Room 811 SA–18, USAID, Washington D.C. 20523–1819.

37. "History of the Association for Voluntary Sterilization [formerly Sterilization League of America], 1935–64," thesis submitted to the faculty of the graduate school of the University of Minnesota by William Ray Van Essendelft, March, 1978, available on microfilm, Library of Congress. This is the official history, written with full cooperation of the Sterilization League.

38. Interview with Dr. C. Nash Herndon, June 20, 1990.

IV

'THE CENTER OF POWER IS IN WASHINGTON'

Brown Brothers Harriman & Co.
59 Wall Street, New York
Cable Address "Shipley-New York"
Business Established 1818
Private Bankers

September 5, 1944

The Honorable W.A. Harriman
American Ambassador to the U.S.S.R.
American Embassy,
Moscow, Russia

Dear Averell:
    Thinking that possibly Bullitt's article in the recent issue of "LIFE" may not have come to your attention, I have clipped it and am sending it to you, feeling that it will interest you.
    At present writing all is well here.
    With warm regards, I am,
    Sincerely yours,
    Pres—

"At present writing all is well here." Thus the ambassador to Russia was reassured by the managing partner of his firm, Prescott Bush. Only 22–1/2 months before, the U.S. government had seized and shut down the Union Banking Corp., which had been operated on behalf of Nazi Germany by Bush and the Harrimans (see Chapter 2). But that was behind them now and they were safe. There would be no publicity on the Harriman-Bush sponsorship of Hitlerism.

Prescott's son George, the future U.S. President, was also safe. Three days before this note to Moscow was written, George Bush had parachuted from a Navy bomber airplane over the Pacific Ocean, killing his two crew members when the unpiloted plane crashed.

Five months later, in February 1945, Prescott's boss, Averell Harriman, escorted President Franklin Roosevelt to the fateful summit meeting with Soviet leader Joseph Stalin at Yalta. In April Roosevelt died. The agreement reached at Yalta, calling for free elections in Poland once the war ended, was never enforced.

Over the next eight years (1945 through 1952), Prescott Bush was Harriman's anchor in the New York financial world. The increasingly powerful Mr. Harriman and his allies gave Eastern Europe over to Soviet dictatorship. A Cold War was then undertaken, to "counterbalance" the Soviets.

This British-inspired strategy paid several nightmarish dividends. Eastern Europe was to remain enslaved. Germany was "permanently" divided. Anglo-American power was jointly exercised over the non-Soviet "Free World." The confidential functions of the British and American governments were merged. The Harriman clique took possession of the U.S. national security apparatus, and in doing so, they opened the gate and let the Bush family in.

Following his services to Germany's Nazi Party, Averell Harriman spent several years mediating between the British, American and Soviet governments in the war to stop the Nazis. He was ambassador to Moscow from 1943 to 1946.

President Harry Truman, whom Harriman and his friends held in amused contempt, appointed Harriman U.S. ambassador to Britain in 1946.

Harriman was at lunch with former British Prime Minister Winston Churchill one day in 1946, when Truman telephoned. Harriman asked Churchill if he should accept Truman's offer to come back to the U.S. as Secretary of Commerce. According to Harriman's account, Churchill told him: "Absolutely. The center of power is in Washington."[1]

Jupiter Island

The reorganization of the American government after World War II—the creation of the U.S. Central Intelligence Agency along British lines, for example—had devastating consequences. We are concerned here with only certain aspects of that overall transformation, those matters of policy and family which gave shape to the life and mind of George Bush, and gave him access to power.

It was in these postwar years that George Bush attended Yale University, and was inducted into the Skull and Bones society. The Bush family's home at that time was in Greenwich, Connecticut. But it was just then that George's parents, Prescott and Dorothy Walker Bush, were wintering in a peculiar spot in Florida, a place that is excluded from mention in literature originating from Bush circles.

Certain national news accounts early in 1991 featured the observations on President Bush's childhood by his elderly mother Dorothy. She was said to be a resident of Hobe Sound, Florida. More precisely, the President's mother lived in a hyper-security arrangement created a half-century earlier by Averell Harriman, adjacent to Hobe Sound. Its correct name is Jupiter Island.

During his political career, George Bush has claimed many different "home" states, including Texas, Maine, Massachusetts and Connecticut. It has not been expedient for him to claim Florida, though that state has a vital link to his role in the world, as we shall see. And George Bush's home base in Florida, throughout his adult life, has been Jupiter Island.

The unique, bizarre setup on Jupiter Island began in 1931, following the merger of W.A. Harriman & Co. with the British-American firm Brown Brothers.

The reader will recall Mr. Samuel Pryor, the "Merchant of Death." A partner with the Harrimans, Prescott Bush, George Walker and Nazi boss Fritz Thyssen in banking and shipping enterprises, Sam Pryor remained executive committee chairman of Remington Arms. In this period, the Nazi private armies (S.A. and S.S.) were supplied with American arms—most likely by Pryor and his company—as they moved to overthrow the German republic. Such gun-running as an instrument of national policy would later become notorious in the "Iran-Contra" affair.

Samuel Pryor's daughter Permelia married Yale graduate Joseph V. Reed on the last day of 1927. Reed immediately went to work for Prescott Bush and George Walker as an apprentice at W.A. Harriman & Co.

During World War II, Joseph V. Reed had served in the "special services" section of the U.S. Army Signal Corps. A specialist in security, codes and espionage, Reed later wrote a book entitled *Fun with Cryptograms*.[2]

Now, Sam Pryor had had property around Hobe Sound, Florida, for some time. In 1931, Joseph and Permelia Pryor Reed bought the entirety of Jupiter Island.

This is a typically beautiful Atlantic coast "barrier island," a half-mile wide and nine miles long. The middle of Jupiter Island lies just off Hobe Sound. The south bridge connects the island with the town of Jupiter, to the north of Palm Beach. It is about 90 minutes by auto from Miami—today, a few minutes by helicopter.

Early in 1991, a newspaper reporter asked a friend of the Bush family about security arrangements on Jupiter Island. He responded, "If you called up the White House, would they tell you how many security people they had? It's not that Jupiter Island is the White House, although he [George Bush] does come down frequently."

But for several decades before Bush was President, Jupiter Island had an ordinance requiring the registration and fingerprinting of all housekeepers, gardeners and other non-residents working on the island. The Jupiter Island police department says that there are sensors in the two main roads that can track every automobile on the island. If a car stops in the street, the police will be there within one or two minutes. Surveillance is a duty of all employees of the town of Jupiter Island. News reporters are to be prevented from visiting the island.[3]

To create this astonishing private club, Joseph and Permelia Pryor Reed sold land only to those who would fit in. Permelia Reed was still the grande dame of the island when George Bush was inaugurated President in 1989. In recognition of the fact that the Reeds know where *all* the bodies are buried, President Bush appointed Permelia's son, Joseph V. Reed, Jr., chief of protocol for the U.S. State Department, in charge of private arrangements with foreign dignitaries.

Averell Harriman made Jupiter Island a staging ground for his 1940s takeover of the U.S. national security apparatus. It was in that connection that the island became possibly the most secretive private place in America.

Let us briefly survey the neighborhood, back then in 1946–48, to see some of the uses various of the residents had for the Harriman clique.

Residents on Jupiter Island

• Jupiter Islander **Robert A. Lovett**,[4] Prescott Bush's partner at Brown Brothers Harriman, had been Assistant Secretary of War for Air from 1941 to 1945. Lovett was the leading American advocate of the policy of terror-bombing of civilians. He organized the Strategic Bombing Survey, carried out for the American and British governments by the staff of the Prudential Insurance Company, guided by London's Tavistock Psychiatric Clinic.

In the postwar period, Prescott Bush was associated with Prudential Insurance, one of Lovett's intelligence channels to the British secret services. Prescott was listed by Prudential as a director of the company for about two years in the early 1950s.

Their Strategic Bombing Survey failed to demonstrate any real military advantage accruing from such outrages as the fire-bombing of Dresden, Germany. But the Harrimanites nevertheless persisted in the advocacy of terror from the air. They glorified this as "psychological warfare," a part of the utopian military doctrine opposed to the views of military traditionalists such as Gen. Douglas MacArthur.

Robert Lovett later advised President Lyndon Johnson to terror-bomb Vietnam. President George Bush revived the doctrine with the bombing of civilian areas in Panama, and the destruction of Baghdad.

On Oct. 22, 1945, Secretary of War Robert Patterson created the Lovett Committee, chaired by Robert A. Lovett, to advise the government on the post-World War II organization of U.S. intelligence activities. The existence of this committee was unknown to the public until an official CIA history was released from secrecy in 1989. But the CIA's author (who was President Bush's prep school history teacher; see chapter 5) gives no real details of the Lovett Committee's functioning, claiming: "The record of the testimony of the Lovett Committee, unfortunately, was not in the archives of the agency when this account was written."[5]

The CIA's self-history does inform us of the advice that Lovett provided to the Truman cabinet, as the official War Department intelligence proposal.

Lovett decided that there should be a separate Central Intelligence Agency. The new agency would "consult" with the armed forces, but it must be the sole collecting agency in the field of foreign espionage and counterespionage. The new agency should have an independent budget, and its appropriations should be granted by Congress without public hearings.

Lovett appeared before the Secretaries of State, War and Navy on November 14, 1945. He spoke highly of the FBI's work because it had "the best personality file in the world." Lovett said the FBI was expert at producing false documents, an art "which we developed so successfully during the war and at which we became outstandingly adept." Lovett pressed for a virtual resumption of the wartime Office of Strategic Services (OSS) in a new CIA.

U.S. military traditionalists centered around Gen. Douglas Mac-Arthur opposed Lovett's proposal.

The continuation of the OSS had been attacked at the end of the war on the grounds that the OSS was entirely under British control, and that it would constitute an American Gestapo.[6]

But the CIA was established in 1947 according to the prescription of Robert Lovett, of Jupiter Island.

• **Charles Payson** and his wife, **Joan Whitney Payson,** were extended family members of Harriman's and business associates of the Bush family.

Joan's aunt, Gertrude Vanderbilt Whitney, was a relative of the Harrimans. Gertrude's son, Cornelius Vanderbilt ("Sonny") Whitney, long-time chairman of Pan American Airways (Prescott was a Pan Am director), became Assistant Secretary of the U.S. Air Force in 1947. Sonny's wife Marie had divorced him and married Averell Harriman in 1930. Joan and Sonny's uncle, Air Marshall Sir Thomas Elmhirst, was director of intelligence for the British Air Force from 1945 to 1947.

Joan's brother, John Hay ("Jock") Whitney, was to be ambassador to Great Britain from 1955 to 1961—when it would be vital for Prescott and George Bush to have such a friend. Joan's father, grandfather and uncle were members of the Skull and Bones secret society.

Charles Payson organized a uranium refinery in 1948. Later he was chairman of Vitro Corp., makers of parts for submarine-launched ballistic missiles, equipment for frequency surveillance and torpedo guidance, and other subsurface weaponry.

Naval warfare has long been a preoccupation of the British Empire. British penetration of the U.S. Naval Intelligence service has been particularly heavy since the tenure of Joan's Anglophile grandfather, William C. Whitney, as Secretary of the Navy for President Grover Cleveland. This traditional covert British orientation in the U.S. Navy, Naval Intelligence and the Navy's included service, the Marine Corps, forms a backdrop to the career of George Bush—and to the whole neighborhood on Jupiter Island. Naval Intelligence maintained direct relations with gangster boss Meyer Lansky for Anglo-American political operations in Cuba during World War II, well before the establishment of the CIA. Lansky officially moved to Florida in 1953.[7]

• **George Herbert Walker, Jr.** (Skull and Bones 1927), was extremely close to his nephew George Bush, helping to sponsor his entry into the oil business in the 1950s. "Uncle Herbie" was also a partner of Joan Whitney Payson when they co-founded the New York Mets baseball team in 1960. His son, G.H. Walker III, was a Yale classmate of Nicholas Brady and Moreau D. Brown (Thatcher Brown's grandson), forming what was called the "Yale Mafia" on Wall Street.

• **Walter S. Carpenter, Jr.** had been chairman of the finance committee of the Du Pont Corporation (1930–40). In 1933, Carpenter oversaw Du Pont's purchase of Remington Arms from Sam Pryor and the Rockefellers, and led Du Pont into partnership with the Nazi I.G. Farben Company for the manufacture of explosives. Carpenter became Du Pont's president in 1940. His cartel with the Nazis was broken up by the U.S. government. Nevertheless, Carpenter remained Du Pont's president as the company's technicians participated massively in the Manhattan Project to produce the first atomic bomb. He was chairman of Du Pont from 1948 to 1962, retaining high-level access to U.S. strategic activities.

Walter Carpenter and Prescott Bush were fellow activists in the Mental Hygiene Society. Originating at Yale University in 1908, the movement had been organized into the World Federation of Mental Health by Montagu Norman, himself a frequent mental patient, former Brown Brothers partner and Bank of England Governor. Norman had appointed as the federation's chairman, Brigadier John Rawlings Rees, director of the Tavistock Psychiatric Clinic, chief psychiatrist and psychological warfare expert for the British intelligence services. Prescott was a director of the society in Connecticut; Carpenter was a director in Delaware.

• **Paul Mellon** was the leading heir to the Mellon fortune, and a long-time neighbor of Averell Harriman's in Middleburg, Virginia, as well as Jupiter Island, Florida. Paul's father, Andrew Mellon, U.S. Treasury Secretary 1921–32, had approved the transactions of Harriman, Pryor and Bush with the Warburgs and the Nazis. Paul Mellon's son-in-law, **David K.E. Bruce,** worked in Prescott Bush's W.A. Harriman & Co. during the late 1920s; was head of the London branch of U.S. intelligence during World War II; and was Averell Harriman's Assistant Secretary of Commerce in 1947–48. Mellon family money and participation would be instrumental in many domestic U.S. projects of the new Central Intelligence Agency.

• **Carll Tucker** manufactured electronic guidance equipment for the Navy. With the Mellons, Tucker was an owner of South American oil properties. Mrs. Tucker was the great aunt of Nicholas Brady, later George Bush's Iran-Contra partner and U.S. Treasury

Secretary. Their son Carll Tucker, Jr. (Skull and Bones 1947), was among the 15 Bonesmen who selected George Bush for induction in the class of 1948.

• **C. Douglas Dillon** was the boss of William H. Draper, Jr. in the Draper-Prescott Bush-Fritz Thyssen Nazi banking scheme of the 1930s and 40s. His father, Clarence Dillon, created the *Vereinigte Stahlwerke* (Thyssen's German Steel Trust) in 1926. C. Douglas Dillon made Nicholas Brady the chairman of the Dillon Read firm in 1971 and himself continued as chairman of the executive committee. C. Douglas Dillon would be a vital ally of his neighbor Prescott Bush during the Eisenhower administration.

• Publisher **Nelson Doubleday** headed his family's publishing firm, founded under the auspices of J.P. Morgan and other British Empire representatives. When George Bush's "Uncle Herbie" died, Doubleday took over as majority owner and chief executive of the New York Mets baseball team.

• **George W. Merck,** chairman of Merck & Co., drug and chemical manufacturers, was director of the War Research Service: Merck was the official chief of all U.S. research into biological warfare from 1942 until at least the end of World War II. After 1944, Merck's organization was placed under the U.S. Chemical Warfare Service. His family firm in Germany and the U.S. was famous for its manufacture of morphine.

• **A.L. Cole** was useful to the Jupiter Islanders as an executive of *Reader's Digest*. In 1965, just after performing a rather dirty favor for George Bush (see Chapter 9), Cole became chairman of the executive committee of the *Digest,* the world's largest-circulation periodical.

From the late 1940s, Jupiter Island has served as a center for the direction of covert action by the U.S. government and, indeed, for the covert management of the government. Jupiter Island will reappear later on, in our account of George Bush in the Iran-Contra affair.

Target: Washington

George Bush graduated from Yale in 1948. He soon entered the family's Dresser oil supply concern in Texas. We shall now briefly describe the forces that descended on Washington, D.C. during those years when Bush, with the assistance of family and powerful friends, was becoming "established in business on his own."

From 1948 to 1950, Prescott Bush's boss Averell Harriman was U.S. "ambassador-at-large" to Europe. He was a non-military "theater commander," the administrator of the multi-billion-dollar Marshall Plan, participating in all military/strategic decision-making by the Anglo-American alliance.

The U.S. Secretary of Defense, James Forrestal, had become a problem to the Harrimanites. Forrestal had long been an executive at Dillon Read on Wall Street. But in recent years he had gone astray. As Secretary of the Navy in 1944, Forrestal proposed the racial integration of the Navy. As Defense Secretary he pressed for integration in the armed forces and this eventually became the U.S. policy.

Forrestal opposed the utopians' strategy of appeasement coupled with brinkmanship. He was simply opposed to communism. On March 28, 1949, Forrestal was forced out of office and flown on an Air Force plane to Florida. He was taken to "Hobe Sound" (Jupiter Island), where Robert Lovett and an army psychiatrist dealt with him.[8]

He was flown back to Washington, locked in Walter Reed Army Hospital and given insulin shock treatments for alleged "mental exhaustion." He was denied all visitors except his estranged wife and children—his son had been Averell Harriman's aide in Moscow. On May 22, James Forrestal's body was found, his bathrobe cord tied tightly around his neck, after he had plunged from a sixteenth-story hospital window. The chief psychiatrist called the death a suicide even before any investigation was started. The results of the Army's inquest were kept secret. Forrestal's diaries were published, 80 percent deleted, after a year of direct government censorship and rewriting.

North Korean troops invaded South Korea in June 1950, after U.S. Secretary of State Dean Acheson (Harriman's very close friend) publicly specified that Korea would not be defended. With a new war on, Harriman came back to serve as President Truman's adviser, to "oversee national security affairs."

Harriman replaced Clark Clifford, who had been special counsel to Truman. Clifford, however, remained close to Harriman and his partners as they gained more and more power. Clifford later wrote about his cordial relations with Prescott Bush:

> Prescott Bush . . . had become one of my frequent golfing partners in the fifties, and I had both liked and respected him. . . . Bush had a splendid singing voice, and particularly loved quartet singing. In the fifties, he organized a quartet that included my daughter Joyce. . . . They would sing in Washington, and, on occasion, he invited the group to Hobe Sound in Florida to perform. His son [George],

though, had never struck me as a strong or forceful person. In 1988, he presented himself successfully to the voters as an outsider—no small trick for a man whose roots wound through Connecticut, Yale, Texas oil, the CIA, a patrician background, wealth, and the Vice-Presidency.[9]

With James Forrestal out of the way, Averell Harriman and Dean Acheson drove to Leesburg, Virginia, on July 1, 1950, to hire the British-backed U.S. Gen. George C. Marshall as Secretary of Defense. At the same time, Prescott's partner, Robert Lovett, himself became Assistant Secretary of Defense.

Lovett, Marshall, Harriman and Acheson went to work to un-horse Gen. Douglas MacArthur, commander of U.S. forces in Asia. MacArthur kept Wall Street's intelligence agencies away from his command, and favored real independence for the non-white nations. Lovett called for MacArthur's firing on March 23, 1951, citing MacArthur's insistence on defeating the Communist Chinese invaders in Korea. MacArthur's famous message, that there was "no substitute for victory," was read in Congress on April 5; MacArthur was fired on April 10, 1951.

That September, Robert Lovett replaced Marshall as Secretary of Defense. Meanwhile, Harriman was named director of the Mutual Security Agency, making him the U.S. chief of the Anglo-American military alliance. By now, Brown Brothers Harriman was everything but Commander-in-Chief.

These were, of course exciting times for the Bush family, whose wagon was hitched to the financial gods of Olympus—to Jupiter, that is.

Brown Brothers Harriman & Co.
59 Wall Street, New York 5, N.Y.
Business Established 1818
Cable Address "Shipley-New York"
Private Bankers
April 2, 1951

The Honorable W.A. Harriman,
The White House, Washington, D.C.

Dear Averell:
   I was sorry to miss you in Washington but appreciate your cordial note. I shall hope for better luck another time.

I hope you had a good rest at Hobe Sound.
With affectionate regard, I am,
Sincerely yours,
Pres [signed]
Prescott S. Bush.

A central focus of the Harriman security regime in Washington (1950–53) was the organization of covert operations, and "psychological warfare." Harriman, together with his lawyers and business partners, Allen Dulles and John Foster Dulles, wanted the government's secret services to conduct extensive propaganda campaigns and mass-psychology experiments within the U.S.A., and paramilitary campaigns abroad. This would supposedly ensure a stable world-wide environment favorable to Anglo-American financial and political interests.

The Harriman security regime created the Psychological Strategy Board (PSB) in 1951. The man appointed director of the PSB, Gordon Gray, is familiar to the reader as the sponsor of the child sterilization experiments, carried out by the Harrimanite eugenics movement in North Carolina following World War II (see Chapter 3).

Gordon Gray was an avid Anglophile, whose father had gotten controlling ownership of the R.J. Reynolds Tobacco Company through alliance with the British Imperial Tobacco cartel's U.S. representatives, the Duke family of North Carolina. Gordon's brother, R.J. Reynolds chairman Bowman Gray, Jr., was also a Naval Intelligence officer, known around Washington as the "founder of operational intelligence." Gordon Gray became a close friend and political ally of Prescott Bush; and Gray's son became for Prescott's son, George, his lawyer and the shield of his covert policy.

But President Harry Truman, as malleable as he was, constituted an obstacle to the covert warriors. An insular Missouri politician vaguely favorable to the U.S. Constitution, he remained skeptical about secret service activities that reminded him of the Nazi Gestapo.

So, "covert operations" could not fully take off without a change of the Washington regime. And it was with the Republican Party that Prescott Bush was to get his turn.

Prescott had made his first attempt to enter national politics in 1950, as his partners took control of the levers of governmental power. Remaining in charge of Brown Brothers Harriman, he ran against Connecticut's William Benton for a seat in the U.S. Senate. (The race was for a two-year unexpired term, left empty by the death of the previous Senator.)

In those days, Wisconsin's drunken Senator Joseph R. McCarthy was making a circus-like crusade against communist influence in Washington. McCarthy attacked liberals and leftists, State Department personnel, politicians and Hollywood figures. He generally left unscathed the Wall Street and London strategists who donated Eastern Europe and China to communist dictatorship—like George Bush, their geopolitics was beyond left and right.

Prescott Bush had no public ties to the notorious Joe McCarthy, and appeared to be neutral about his crusade. But the Wisconsin Senator had his uses. Joe McCarthy came into Connecticut three times that year to campaign for Bush and against the Democrats. Bush himself made charges of "Korea, Communism and Corruption" into a slick campaign phrase against Benton, which then turned up as a national Republican slogan.

The response was disappointing. Only small crowds turned out to hear Joe McCarthy, and Benton was not hurt. McCarthy's pro-Bush rally in New Haven, in a hall that seated 6,000, drew only 376 people. Benton joked on the radio that "200 of them were my spies."

Prescott Bush resigned from the Yale Board of Fellows for his campaign, and the board published a statement to the effect that the "Yale vote" should support Bush—despite the fact that William Benton was a Yale man, and in many ways identical in outlook to Bush. Yale's Whiffenpoof singers appeared regularly for Prescott's campaign. None of this was particularly effective, however, with the voting population.[10]

Then Prescott Bush ran into a completely unexpected problem. At that time, the old Harriman eugenics movement was centered at Yale University. Prescott Bush was a Yale trustee, and his former Brown Brothers Harriman partner, Lawrence Tighe, was Yale's treasurer. In that connection, a slight glimmer of the truth about the Bush-Harriman firm's Nazi activities now made its way into the campaign.

Not only was the American Eugenics Society itself headquartered at Yale, but all parts of this undead fascist movement had a busy home at Yale. The coercive psychiatry and sterilization advocates had made the Yale/New Haven Hospital and Yale Medical School their laboratories for hands-on practice in brain surgery and psychological experimentation. And the Birth Control League was there, which had long trumpeted the need for eugenical births—fewer births for parents with "inferior" bloodlines. Prescott's partner

Tighe was a Connecticut director of the league, and the Connecticut league's medical advisor was eugenics advocate Dr. Winternitz of Yale Medical School.

Now in 1950, people who knew something about Prescott Bush knew that he had very unsavory roots in the eugenics movement. There were then, just after the anti-Hitler war, few open advocates of sterilization of "unfit" or "unnecessary" people. (That would be revived later, with the help of General Draper and his friend George Bush.) But the Birth Control League was public—just about then it was changing its name to the euphemistic "Planned Parenthood."

Then, very late in the 1950 senatorial campaign, Prescott Bush was publicly exposed for being an activist in that section of the old fascist eugenics movement. Prescott Bush lost the election by about 1,000 out of 862,000 votes. He and his family blamed the defeat on the exposé. The defeat was burned into the family's memory, leaving a bitterness and perhaps a desire for revenge.

In his foreword to a population control propaganda book, George Bush wrote about that 1950 election: "My own first awareness of birth control as a public policy issue came with a jolt in 1950 when my father was running for United States Senate in Connecticut. Drew Pearson, on the Sunday before Election day, 'revealed' that my father was involved with Planned Parenthood. . . . Many political observers felt a sufficient number of voters were swayed by his alleged contacts with the birth controllers to cost him the election. . . . "[11]

Prescott Bush was defeated, while the other Republican candidates fared well in Connecticut. When he tried again, Prescott Bush would not leave the outcome to the blind whims of the public.

Prescott Bush moved into action again in 1952 as a national leader of the push to give the Republican presidential nomination to Gen. Dwight D. ("Ike") Eisenhower. Among the other team members were Bush's Hitler-era lawyer John Foster Dulles, and Jupiter Islander C. Douglas Dillon.

Dillon and his father were the pivots as the Harriman-Dulles combination readied Ike for the presidency. As a friend put it: "When the Dillons . . . invited [Eisenhower] to dinner it was to introduce him to Wall Street bankers and lawyers."[12]

Ike's higher-level backers believed, correctly, that Ike would not interfere with even the dirtiest of their covert action programs. The bland, pleasant Prescott Bush was in from the beginning: a friend to Ike, and an original backer of his presidency.

On July 28, 1952, as the election approached, Connecticut's

senior U.S. Senator, James O'Brien McMahon, died at the age of 48.*

This was *extremely* convenient for Prescott. He got the Republican nomination for U.S. Senator at a special delegated meeting, with backing by the Yale-dominated state party leadership. Now he would run in a special election for the suddenly vacant Senate seat. He could expect to be swept into office, since he would be on the same electoral ticket as the popular war hero, General Ike. By a technicality, he would instantly become Connecticut's senior Senator, with extra power in Congress. And the next regularly scheduled senatorial race would be in 1956 (when McMahon's term would have ended), so Prescott could run again in that presidential election year—once again on Ike's coattails!

With this arrangement, things worked out very smoothly. In Eisenhower's 1952 election victory, Ike won Connecticut by a margin of 129,507 votes out of 1,092,471. Prescott Bush came in last among the statewide Republicans, but managed to win by 30,373 out of 1,088,799 votes case, his margin nearly 100,000 behind Eisenhower. He took the traditionally Republican towns.

In Eisenhower's 1956 reelection, Ike won Connecticut by 303,036 out of 1,114,954 votes, the largest presidential margin in Connecticut's history. Prescott Bush managed to win again, by 129,544 votes out of 1,085,206—his margin this time 290,082 smaller than Eisenhower's.[13]

In January 1963, when this electoral strategy had been played out and his second term expired, Prescott Bush retired from government and returned to Brown Brothers Harriman.

The 1952 Eisenhower victory made John Foster Dulles Secretary of State, and his brother Allen Dulles head of the CIA. The reigning Dulles brothers were the "Republican" replacements for their client and business partner, "Democrat" Averell Harriman. Occasional public posturings aside, their strategic commitments were identical to his.

Undoubtedly the most important work accomplished by Prescott Bush in the new regime was on the golf links, where he was Ike's favorite partner.

Toward the "National Security State"

Prescott Bush was a most elusive, secretive Senator. By diligent research, his views on some issues may be traced: He was opposed

---

*McMahon had been Assistant U.S. Attorney General, in charge of the Criminal Division, from 1935 to 1939. Was there a chance he might someday speak out about the unpunished Nazi-era crimes of the wealthy and powerful?

to the development of public power projects like the Tennessee Valley Authority; he opposed the constitutional amendment introduced by Ohio Senator John W. Bricker, which would have required congressional approval of international agreements by the executive branch.

But Prescott Bush was essentially a covert operative in Washington.

On June 10, 1954, Bush received a letter from Connecticut resident H. Smith Richardson, owner of Vick Chemical Company (cough drops, Vapo-Rub):

". . . At some time before Fall, Senator, I want to get your advice and counsel on a [new] subject—namely what should be done with the income from a foundation which my brother and I set up, and which will begin its operation in 1956. . . ."[14]

This letter presages the establishment of the **H. Smith Richardson Foundation,** a Bush family-dictated private slush fund which was to be utilized by the Central Intelligence Agency, and by Vice President Bush, for the conduct of his Iran-Contra adventures.

The Bush family knew Richardson and his wife through their mutual friendship with Sears Roebuck's chairman, Gen. Robert E. Wood. General Wood had been president of the America First organization, which had lobbied against war with Hitler Germany. H. Smith Richardson had contributed the start-up money for America First and had spoken out against the U.S. "joining the Communists" by fighting Hitler. Richardson's wife was a proud relative of Nancy Langehorne from Virginia, who married Lord Astor and backed the Nazis from their Cliveden Estate.

General Wood's daughter Mary had married the son of Standard Oil president William Stamps Farish. The Bushes had stuck with the Farishes through their disastrous exposure during World War II (see Chapter 3). Young George Bush and his bride Barbara were especially close to Mary Farish, and to her son W.S. Farish III, who would be the great confidante of George's presidency.[15]

The H. Smith Richardson Foundation was organized by Eugene Stetson, Jr., Richardson's son-in-law. Stetson (Skull and Bones, 1934) had worked for Prescott Bush as assistant manager of the New York branch of Brown Brothers Harriman.

In the late 1950s, the H. Smith Richardson Foundation took part in the "psychological warfare" of the CIA. This was not a foreign, but a domestic, covert operation, carried out mainly against unwitting U.S. citizens. CIA Director Allen Dulles and his British allies organized "MK-Ultra," the testing of psychotropic drugs including LSD on a very large scale, allegedly to evaluate "chemical warfare" possibilities. In this period, the Richardson Foundation helped finance experiments at Bridgewater Hospital in Massachusetts, the center of some of the most brutal MK-Ultra tortures. These outrages have been graphically portrayed in the movie *Titticut Follies*.

During 1990, an investigator for this book toured H. Smith Richardson's **Center for Creative Leadership** just north of Greensboro, North Carolina. The tour guide said that in these rooms, agents of the Central Intelligence Agency and the Secret Service are trained. He demonstrated the two-way mirrors through which the government employees are watched, while they are put through mind-bending psychodramas. The guide explained that "virtually everyone who becomes a general" in the U.S. armed forces also goes through this "training" at the Richardson Center.

Another office of the Center for Creative Leadership is in Langley, Virginia, at the headquarters of the Central Intelligence Agency. Here also, Richardson's Center trains leaders of the CIA.

Prescott Bush worked throughout the Eisenhower years as a confidential ally of the Dulles brothers. In July 1956, Egypt's President Gamel Abdul Nasser announced he would accept the U.S. offer of a loan for the construction of the Aswan Dam project. John Foster Dulles then prepared a statement telling the Egyptian ambassador that the U.S.A. had decided to retract its offer. Dulles gave the explosive statement in advance to Prescott Bush for his approval. Dulles also gave the statement to President Eisenhower, and to the British government.[16]

Nasser reacted to the Dulles brush-off by nationalizing the Suez Canal to pay for the dam. Israel, then Britain and France, invaded Egypt to try to overthrow Nasser, leader of the anti-imperial Arab nationalists. However, Eisenhower refused (for once) to play the Dulles-British game, and the invaders had to leave Egypt when Britain was threatened with U.S. economic sanctions.

During 1956, Senator Prescott Bush's value to the Harriman-Dulles political group increased when he was put on the Senate Armed Services Committee. Bush toured U.S. and allied military bases throughout the world, and had increased access to the national security decision-making process.

In the later years of the Eisenhower presidency, Gordon Gray rejoined the government. As an intimate friend and golfing partner of Prescott Bush, Gray complemented the Bush influence on Ike. The Bush-Gray family partnership in the "secret government" continues up through the George Bush presidency.

Gordon Gray had been appointed head of the new Psychological Strategy Board in 1951 under Averell Harriman's rule as assistant to President Truman for national security affairs. From 1958 to 1961, Gordon Gray was national security chief under President Eisenhower. Gray acted as Ike's intermediary, strategist and handholder, in the President's relations with the CIA and the U.S. and allied military forces.

Eisenhower did not oppose the CIA's covert action projects; he only wanted to be protected from the consequences of their failure or exposure. Gray's primary task, in the guise of "oversight" on all U.S. covert action, was to protect and hide the growing mass of CIA and related secret government activities.

It was not only covert *projects* which were developed by the Gray-Bush-Dulles combination; it was also new, hidden *structures* of the United States government.

Senator Henry Jackson (D.-Wash.) challenged these arrangements in 1959 and 1960. Jackson created a Subcommittee on National Policy Machinery of the Senate Committee on Governmental Operations, which investigated Gordon Gray's reign at the National Security Council. On January 26, 1960, Gordon Gray warned President Eisenhower that a document revealing the existence of a secret part of the U.S. government had somehow gotten into the bibliography being used by Senator Jackson. The unit was Gray's "5412 Group" within the administration, officially but secretly in charge of approving covert action. Under Gray's guidance, Ike " 'was clear and firm in his response' that Jackson's staff *not* be informed of the existence of this unit [emphasis in the original]."[17]

Several figures of the Eisenhower administration must be considered the fathers of this permanent covert action monolith, men who continued shepherding the monster after its birth in the Eisenhower era:

• **Gordon Gray,** the shadowy assistant to the President for national security affairs, Prescott Bush's closest executive branch crony and golf partner along with Eisenhower. By 1959–60, Gray had Ike's total confidence and served as the Harrimanites' monitor on all U.S. military and non-military projects.

British intelligence agent Kim Philby defected to the Russians in 1963. Philby had gained virtually total access to U.S. intelligence activities beginning in 1949, as the British secret services' liaison to the Harriman-dominated CIA. After Philby's defection, it seemed obvious that the aristocratic British intelligence service was in fact a menace to the western cause. In the 1960s, a small team of U.S. counterintelligence specialists went to England to investigate the situation. They reported back that the British secret service could be thoroughly trusted. The leader of this "expert" team, Gordon

Gray, was the head of the counterespionage section of the President's Foreign Intelligence Advisory Board for Presidents John Kennedy through Gerald Ford.

• **Robert Lovett,** Bush's Jupiter Island neighbor and Brown Brothers Harriman partner, from 1956 on a member of the President's Foreign Intelligence Advisory Board. Lovett later claimed to have criticized—from the "inside"—the plan to invade Cuba at the Bay of Pigs. Lovett was asked to choose the cabinet for John Kennedy in 1961.

• **CIA Director Allen Dulles,** Bush's former international attorney. Kennedy fired Dulles after the Bay of Pigs invasion, but Dulles served on the Warren Commission, which whitewashed President Kennedy's murder.

• **C. Douglas Dillon,** neighbor of Bush on Jupiter Island, became Undersecretary of State in 1958 after the death of John Foster Dulles. Dillon had been John Foster Dulles's ambassador to France (1953–57), coordinating the original U.S. covert backing for the French imperial effort in Vietnam, with catastrophic results for the world. Dillon was Treasury Secretary for both John Kennedy and Lyndon Johnson.

• **Ambassador to Britain Jock Whitney,** extended family member of the Harrimans and neighbor of Prescott Bush on Jupiter Island. Whitney set up a press service in London called Forum World Features, which published propaganda furnished directly by the CIA and the British intelligence services. Beginning in 1961, Whitney was chairman of the British Empire's "English Speaking Union."

• **Senator Prescott Bush,** friend and counselor of President Eisenhower.

Bush's term continued on in the Senate after the Eisenhower years, throughout most of the aborted Kennedy presidency.

In 1962, the National Strategy Information Center was founded by Prescott Bush and his son Prescott, Jr., William Casey (the future CIA chief) and Leo Cherne. The center came to be directed by Frank Barnett, former program officer of the Bush family's H. Smith Richardson Foundation. The center conduited funds to the London-Based Forum World Features, for the circulation of CIA-authored "news stories" to some 300 newspapers internationally.[18]

"Democrat" Averell Harriman rotated back into official government in the Kennedy administration. As Assistant Secretary and Undersecretary of State, Harriman helped push the United States into the Vietnam War. Harriman had no post in the Eisenhower administration. Yet he was perhaps more than anyone the leader and the glue for the incredible evil that was hatched by the CIA in the final Eisenhower years: a half-public, half-private Harrimanite army, never since demobilized, and increasingly associated with the name of Bush.

Following the rise of Castro, the U.S. Central Intelligence Agency contracted with the organization of Mafia boss Meyer Lansky to organize and train assassination squads for use against the Cuban government. Among those employed were John Rosselli, Santos Trafficante and Sam Giancana. Uncontested public documentation of these facts has been published by congressional bodies and by leading Establishment academics.[19]

But the disturbing implications and later consequences of this engagement are a crucial matter for further study by the citizens of every nation. This much is established:

On Aug. 18, 1960, President Eisenhower approved a $13 million official budget for a secret CIA-run guerrilla war against Castro. It is known that Vice President Richard M. Nixon took a hand in the promotion of this initiative. The U.S. military was kept out of the covert action plans until very late in the game.

The first of eight admitted assassination attempts against Castro took place in 1960.

The program was, of course, a failure, if not a circus. The invasion of Cuba by the CIA's anti-Castro exiles was put off until after John Kennedy took over the presidency. The invasion at the Bay of Pigs was a fiasco, and Castro's forces easily prevailed. But the program continued.

In 1960, Felix Rodriguez, Luis Posada Carriles, Rafael "Chi Chi" Quintero, Frank Sturgis (or "Frank Fiorini") and other Florida-based Cuban exiles were trained as killers and drug-traffickers in the Cuban initiative; their supervisor was E. Howard Hunt. Their overall CIA boss was Miami Station Chief Theodore G. Shackley, seconded by Thomas Clines. In later chapters we will follow the subsequent careers of these characters—increasingly identified with George Bush—through the Watergate coup, and the Iran-Contra scandal.

Notes for Chapter IV

1. Walter Isaacson and Evan Thomas, *The Wise Men: Six Friends and the World They Made—Acheson, Bohlen, Harriman, Kennan, Lovett, McCloy* (New York: Simon and Schuster, 1986), p. 377.

2. Reed was better known in high society as a minor diplomat, the founder of the Triton Press and the president of the American Shakespeare Theater.

3. *Palm Beach Post*, Jan. 13, 1991.

4. For Lovett's residency there see Isaacson and Thomas, *op. cit.*, p. 417. Some Jupiter Island residencies were verified by their inclusion in the 1947 membership list of the Hobe Sound Yacht Club, in the Harriman papers, Library of Congress; others were established from interviews with long-time Jupiter Islanders.

5. Arthur Burr Darling, *The Central Intelligence Agency: An Instrument of Government, to 1950* (College Station: Pennsylvania State University, 1990), p. 59.

6. The *Chicago Tribune,* Feb. 9, 1945, for example, warned of "Creation of an all-powerful intelligence service to spy on the postwar world and to pry into the lives of citizens at home." Cf. Anthony Cave Brown, *Wild Bill Donovan: The Last Hero* (New York: Times Books, 1982), p. 625, on warnings to FDR about the British control of U.S. intelligence.

7. Dennis Eisenberg, Uri Dan, Eli Landau, *Meyer Lansky: Mogul of the Mob* (New York: Paddington Press, 1979) pp. 227–28.

8. See John Ranelagh, *The Agency: The Rise and Decline of the CIA* (New York: Simon and Schuster, 1987), pp. 131–32.

9. Clark Clifford, *Counsel to the President* (New York: Random House, 1991).

10. Sidney Hyman, *The Lives of William Benton* (Chicago: The University of Chicago Press, 1969), pp. 438–41.

11. Phyllis Tilson Piotrow, *World Population Crisis: The United States Response* (New York: Praeger Publishers, 1973), "Foreward," by George H.W. Bush, p. vii.

12. Herbert S. Parmet, *Eisenhower and the American Crusades* (New York: The Macmillan Company, 1972), p. 14.

13. *New York Times,* Sept. 6, 1952, Nov. 5, 1952, Nov. 7, 1956.

14. Richardson to Prescott Bush, H. Smith Richardson Papers, University of North Carolina, Chapel Hill.

15. Wayne S. Cole, *America First: The Battle Against Intervention, 1940–1941* (Madison: the University of Wisconsin Press, 1953); interviews with Richardson family employees; H. Smith Richardson Foundation annual reports; Richardson to Prescott Bush, March 26, 1954, Richardson Papers. *Washington Post,* April 29, 1990.

16. Parmet, *op. cit.,* p. 481.

17. John Prados, *Keepers of the Keys: A History of the National Security Council from Truman to Bush* (New York: William Morrow, 1991) pp. 92–95.

18. Robert Callaghan in *Covert Action,* No. 33, Winter 1990. Prescott, Jr. was a board member of the National Strategy Information Center as of 1991. Both Prescott Sr. and Jr. were deeply involved along with Casey in the circles of Pan American Airlines, Pan Am's owners the Grace family, and the CIA's Latin American affairs. The center, based in Washington, D.C., declines public inquiries about its founding.

See also *EIR Special Report:* "American Leviathan: Administrative Fascism under the Bush Regime" (Wiesbaden, Germany: Executive Intelligence Review Nachrichtenagentur, April 1990), p. 192.

19. For example, see Trumbull Higgins, *The Perfect Failure: Kennedy, Eisenhower, and the CIA at the Bay of Pigs* (New York: W.W. Norton and Co., 1987), pp. 55–56, 89–90.

Unverified information on the squads is provided in the affidavit of Daniel P. Sheehan, attorney for the Christic Institute, reproduced in *EIR Special Report:,* "Project Democracy: The 'Parallel Government' behind the Iran-Contra Affair" (Washington, D.C.: Executive Intelligence Review, 1987), pp. 249–50.

Some of the hired assassins have published their memoirs. See, for example, Felix Rodriguez and John Weisman, *Secret Warrior* (New York: Simon and Schuster, 1989); and E. Howard Hunt, *Undercover: Memoirs of an American Secret Agent* (New York: G.P. Putnam's Sons, 1974).

V

POPPY AND MOMMY

"Oh Mother, Mother! What have you done? Behold! the heavens do ope. The gods look down, and this unnatural scene they laugh at."
Coriolanus, Shakespeare.

The Silver Spoon

George Herbert Walker Bush was born in Milton, Massachusetts, on June 12, 1924. During the next year the family moved to Greenwich, Connecticut, and established their permanent residency.

Prescott and Dorothy Walker Bush had had a son, Prescott, Jr., before George. Later there was a little sister, Nancy, and another brother, Jonathan; a fourth son, William ("Bucky"), was born 14 years after George, in 1939.

George was named after his grandfather, George Herbert Walker. Since George's mother called Grandfather Walker "Pop," she began calling her son, his namesake, "little Pop," or "Poppy." Hence, Poppy Bush is the name the President's family friends have called him since his youth.

Prescott, Sr. joined W.A. Harriman & Co. May 1, 1926. With his family's lucrative totalitarian projects, George Bush's childhood began in comfort and advanced dramatically to luxury and elegance.

The Bushes had a large, dark-shingled house with "broad verandas and a portecochere" (originally a roofed structure extending out to the driveway to protect the gentry who arrived in coaches) on Grove Lane in the Deer Park section of Greenwich.[1]

Here they were attended by four servants—three maids (one of whom cooked) and a chauffeur.

The U.S.A. was plunged into the Great Depression beginning with the 1929–31 financial collapse. But George Bush and his family were totally insulated from this crisis. Before and after the crash, their lives were a frolic, sealed off from the concerns of the population at large.

During the summers, the Bushes stayed in a second home on the family's ten-acre spread at Walker's Point at Kennebunkport, Maine. Flush from the Soviet oil deals and the Thyssen-Nazi Party arrangements, Grandfather Walker had built a house there for Prescott and Dorothy. They and other well-to-do summer colonists used Kennebunkport's River Club for tennis and yachting.

In the winter season, they took the train to Grandfather Walker's plantation, called "Duncannon," near Barnwell, South Carolina. The novices were instructed in skeet shooting, then went out on horseback, following the hounds in pursuit of quail and dove. George's sister Nancy recalled "the care taken" by the servants "over the slightest things, like the trimmed edges of the grapefruit. We were waited on by the most wonderful black servants who would come into the bedrooms early in the morning and light those crackling pine-wood fires. . . ."[2]

The money poured in from the Hamburg-Amerika steamship line, its workforce crisply regulated by the Nazi Labor Front. The family took yet another house at Aiken, South Carolina. There the Bush children had socially acceptable "tennis and riding partners. Aiken was a Southern capital of polo in those days, a winter resort of considerable distinction and serenity that attracted many Northerners, especially the equestrian oriented. The Bush children naturally rode there, too. . . ."[3] Averell Harriman, a world-class polo player, also frequented Aiken.

Poppy Bush's father and mother anxiously promoted the family's distinguished lineage, and its growing importance in the world. Prescott Bush claimed that he "could trace his family's roots back to England's King Henry III, making George a thirteenth cousin, twice removed of Queen Elizabeth."[4]

This particular conceit may be a bad omen for President Bush. The cowardly, acid-tongued Henry III was defeated by France's Louis IX (Saint Louis) in Henry's grab for power over France and much of Europe. Henry's own barons at length revolted against his blundering arrogance, and his power was curbed.

As the 1930s economic crisis deepened, Americans experienced unprecedented hardship and fear. The Bush children were taught that those who suffered these problems had no one to blame but themselves.

A hack writer, hired to puff President Bush's "heroic military background," wrote these lines from material supplied by the White House:

"Prescott Bush was a thrifty man. . . . He had no sympathy for the nouveau riches who flaunted their wealth—they were without class, he said. As a sage and strictly honest businessman, he had often turned failing companies around, making them profitable again, and he had scorn for people who went bankrupt because they mismanaged their money. Prescott's lessons were absorbed by young George. . . ."[5]

When he reached the age of five, George Bush joined his older brother Pres in attending the Greenwich Country Day School. The brothers' "lives were charted from birth. Their father had determined that his sons would be . . . educated and trained to be members of America's elite. . . . Greenwich Country Day School [was] an exclusive all-male academy for youngsters slated for private secondary schools. . . .

"Alec, the family chauffeur, drove the two boys to school every morning after dropping Prescott, Sr. at the railroad station for the morning commute to Manhattan. The Depression was nowhere in evidence as the boys glided in the family's black Oldsmobile past the stone fences, stables, and swimming pools of one of the wealthiest communities in America."[6]

But though the young George Bush had no concerns about his material existence, one must not overlook the important, private anxiety gnawing at him from the direction of his mother.

The President's wife, Barbara, has put most succinctly the question of Dorothy Bush and her effect on George: *"His mother was the most competitive living human."*[7]

If we look here in his mother's shadow, we may find something beyond the routine medical explanations for President Bush's "driven" states of rage, or hyperactivity.

Mother Bush was the best athlete in the family, the fastest runner. She was hard. She expected others to be hard. They must win, but they must always *appear* not to care about winning.

This is put politely, delicately, in a "biography" written by an admiring friend of the President: "She was with them day after day, . . . often curbing their egos as only a marine drill instructor can. Once when . . . George lost a tennis match, he explained to her that he had been off his game that morning. She retorted, 'You don't have a game.' "[8]

According to this account, Barbara was fascinated by her mother-in-law's continuing ferocity:

> George, playing mixed doubles with Barbara on the Kennebunkport court, ran into a porch and injured his right shoulder blade. "His mother said it was my ball to hit, and it happened because I didn't run for it. She was probably right," Barbara told [an interviewer]. . . . When a discussion of someone's game came up, as Barbara described it, "if Mrs. Bush would say, 'She had some good shots,' it meant she stank. That's just the way she got the message across. When one of the grandchildren brought this girl home, everybody said, 'We think he's going to marry her,' and she said, 'Oh, no, she won't play net.' "[9]

A goad to *rapid motion* became embedded in his personality. It is observable throughout George Bush's life.

A companion trait was Poppy's uncanny urge, his master obsession with the need to "kiss up," to propitiate those who might in any way advance his interests. A life of such efforts could at some point reach a climax of released rage, where the triumphant one may finally say, "Now it is only I who must be feared."

This dangerous cycle began very early, a response to his mother's prodding and intimidation; it intensified as George became more able to calculate his advantage.

His mother says: "George was a most unselfish child. When he was only a little more than two years old . . . we bought him one of those pedal cars you climb into and work with your feet.

"[His brother] Pres knew just how to work it, and George came running over and grabbed the wheel and told Pres he should 'have half,' meaning half of his new possession. 'Have half, have half,' he kept repeating, and for a while around the house we called him 'Have half.' "[10]

George "learned to ask for no more than what was due him. Although not the school's leading student, his report card was always good, and his mother was particularly pleased that he was always graded 'excellent' in one category she thought of great importance: 'Claims no more than his fair share of time and attention.' This consistent ranking led to a little family joke—George always did best in 'Claims no more.'

"He was not a selfish child, did not even display the innocent possessiveness common to most children. . . ."[11]

Andover

George Bush left Greenwich Country Day School in 1936. He joined his older brother at Phillips Academy in Andover, Massachusetts, 20 miles north of Boston. "Poppy" was 12 years old, handsome and rich. Though the U.S. economy took a savage turn for the worse the following year, George's father was piling up a fortune, arranging bond swindles for the Nazis with John Foster Dulles.

Only about one in 14 U.S. secondary school students could afford to be in private schools during George Bush's stay at Andover (1936–42). The New England preparatory or "prep" schools were the most exclusive. Their students were almost all rich white boys, many of them Episcopalians. And Andover was, in certain strange ways, the most exclusive of them all.

A 1980 campaign biography prepared by Bush's own staff concedes that "it was to New England that they returned to be educated at select schools that produce leaders with a patrician or aristocratic stamp—adjectives, incidentally, which cause a collective wince among the Bushes. . . . At the close of the 1930s . . . these schools . . . brought the famous 'old-boy networks' to the peak of their power."[12]

These American institutions have been consciously modeled on England's elite private schools (confusingly called "public" schools because they were open to all English boys with sufficient money). The philosophy inculcated into the son of a British Lord Admiral or South African police chief, was to be imbibed by sons of the American republic.

George made some decisive moral choices about himself in these first years away from home. The institution which guided these choices, and helped shape the peculiar obsessions of the 41st President, was a pit of Anglophile aristocratic racialism when George Bush came on the scene.

"Andover was . . . less dedicated to 'elitism' than some [schools]. . . . There were even a couple of blacks in the classes, tokens of course, but this at a time when a black student at almost any other Northeastern prep school would have been unthinkable."[13]

Andover had a vaunted "tradition," intermingled with the proud bloodlines of its students and alumni, that was supposed to reach back to the school's founding in 1778. But a closer examination reveals this "tradition" to be a fraud. It is part of a larger, highly significant historical fallacy perpetrated by the Anglo-Americans— and curiously stressed by Bush's agents in foreign countries.

Thomas Cochran, a partner of the J.P. Morgan banking firm, donated considerable sums to construct swanky new Andover buildings in the 1920s. Among these were George Washington Hall and Paul Revere Hall, named for leaders of the American Revolution against the British Empire. These and similar "patriotic" trappings, with the alumni's old school-affiliated genealogies, might seem to indicate an unbroken line of racial imperialists like Cochran and his circle, reaching back to the heroes of the Revolution!

Let us briefly tour Andover's history, and then ponder whether General Washington would want to be identified with Poppy Bush's school.

Thirty years after Samuel Phillips founded the Academy at Andover, Massachusetts, the quiet little school became embroiled in a violent controversy. On one side were certain diehard pro-British families, known as Boston Brahmins, who had prospered in the ship transportation of rum and black slaves. They had regained power in Boston since their allies had lost the 1775–83 American Revolution.

In 1805 these cynical, neo-pagan, "Tory" families succeeded in placing their representative in the Hollis chair of Philosophy at Harvard College. The Tories, parading publicly as liberal religionists called Unitarians, were opposed by American nationalists led by the geographer-historian Rev. Jedidiah Morse (1761–1826). The nationalists rallied the Christian churches of the northeastern states behind a plan to establish, at Andover, a new religious institution which would counter the British spies, atheists and criminals who had taken over Harvard.

British Empire political operatives Stephen Higginson, Jr. and John Lowell, Jr. published counterattacks against Rev. Morse, claiming he was trying to rouse the lower classes of citizens to hatred against the wealthy merchant families. Then the Tories played the "conservative" card. Ultra-orthodox Calvinists, actually business partners to the Harvard liberals, threatened to set up their own religious institution in Tory-dominated Newburyport. Their assertion, that Morse was not conservative enough, split the resources of the region's Christians, until the Morse group reluctantly brought the Newburyport ultras as partners into the management of the Andover Theological Seminary in 1808.

The new theological seminary and the adjacent boys academy were now governed together under a common board of trustees (balanced between the Morse nationalists and the Newburyport anti-nationalists, the opposing wings of the old Federalist Party).

Jedidiah Morse made Andover the headquarters of a rather heroic, anti-racist, Christian missionary movement, bringing literacy, printing presses, medicine and technological education to Southeast Asia and American Indians, notably the Georgia Cherokees. This activist Andover doctrine of racial equality and American Revolutionary spirit was despised and feared by British opium pushers in East Asia and by Boston's blue-blooded Anglophiles. Andover missionaries were eventually jailed in Georgia; their too-modern Cherokee allies were murdered and driven into exile by pro-slavery mobs.

When Jedidiah Morse's generation died out, the Andover missionary movement was crushed by New England's elite families— who were then Britain's partners in the booming opium traffic. Andover was still formally Christian after 1840; Boston's cynical Brahmins used Andover's orthodox Protestant board to prosecute various of their opponents as "heretics."

Neo-paganism and occult movements bloomed after the Civil War with Darwin's new materialist doctrines. In the 1870s the death-worshipping Skull and Bones Society sent its alumni members back from Yale University, to organize aristocratic secret satanic societies for the teenagers at the Andover prep school. But these cults did not yet quite flourish. National power was still precariously balanced between the imperial Anglo-American financiers, and the old-line nationalists who built America's railroads, steel and electrical industries.

The New Age aristocrats proclaimed their victory under Theodore Roosevelt's presidency (1901–09). The Andover Theological Seminary wound up its affairs and moved out of town, to be merged with the Harvard Divinity School! Andover prep school was now largely free of the annoyance of religion, or any connection whatsoever with the American spirit. Secret societies for the school's children, modeled on the barbarian orders at Yale, were now established in permanent, incorporated headquarters buildings just off campus at Andover. Official school advisers were assigned to each secret society, and participated in their cruel and literally insane rituals.

When J.P. Morgan partner Thomas Cochran built Andover's luxurious modern campus for boys like Poppy Bush, the usurpers of America's name had cause to celebrate. Under their supervision, fascism was rising in Europe. The new campus library was named for Oliver Wendell Holmes, Andover class of 1825. This dreadful poet of the "leisure class," a tower of Boston blue-blooded conceit, was famous as the father of the twentieth century U.S. Supreme Court justice. His son, Oliver Wendell Holmes, Jr., symbolized the arbitrary rule of the racial purity advocates, the usurpers, over American society.

Andover installed a new headmaster in 1933. Claude Moore Fuess (rhymes with fleece) replaced veteran headmaster Alfred E. Stearns, whom the Brahmins saw as a dyed-in-the-wool reactionary. Stearns was forced out over a "scandal": a widower, he had married his housekeeper, who was beneath his social class.

The new headmaster was considered forward-looking and flexible, ready to meet the challenges of the world political crisis: For example, Fuess favored psychiatry for the boys, something Stearns wouldn't tolerate.

Claude Fuess had been an Andover history teacher since 1908, and gained fame as a historian. He was one of the most skillful liars of the modern age.

Fuess had married into the Boston Cushing family. He had written the family-authorized whitewash biography of his wife's relative, Caleb Cushing, a pro-slavery politician of the middle nineteenth century. The outlandish, widely known corruption of Cushing's career was matched by Fuess's bold, outrageous coverup.[14]

During George Bush's years at Andover, Fuess, his headmaster, wrote an authorized biography of Calvin Coolidge, the late U.S. President. This work was celebrated in jest as a champion specimen of unwholesome flattery. In other books, also about the blue bloods, Fuess was simply given the family papers and designated the chief liar for the "Bostonian Race."

Both the Cushing and Coolidge families had made their fortunes in opium trafficking. Bush's headmaster named his son John Cushing Fuess, perhaps after the fabled nineteenth-century dope kingpin who had made the Cushings rich. [15]

Headmaster Fuess used to say to his staff, "I came to power with Hitler and Mussolini."[16] This was not merely a pleasantry, referring to his appointment the year Hitler took over Germany.

In his 1939 memoirs, Headmaster Fuess expressed the philosophy which must guide the education of the well-born young gentlemen under his care:

> Our declining birth rate . . . may perhaps indicate a step towards national deterioration. Among the so-called upper and leisure classes, noticeably among the university group, the present birth rate is strikingly low. Among the Slavonic and Latin immigrants, on the other hand, it is relatively high. We seem thus to be letting the best blood thin out and disappear; while at the same time our humanitarian efforts for the preservation of the less fit, those who for some reason are crippled and incapacitated, are being greatly stimulated. The effect on the race will not become apparent for some generations and certainly cannot now be accurately predicted; but the phenomenon must be mentioned if you are to have a true picture of what is going on in the United States.[17]

Would George Bush adopt this anti-Christian outlook as his own? One can never know for sure how a young person will respond to the doctrines of his elders, no matter how cleverly presented. There is a much higher degree of certainty that he will conform to criminal expectations, however, if the student is brought to practice cruelty against other youngsters, and to degrade himself in order to get ahead. At Andover, this was where the Secret Societies came in.

The Secret Societies

Nothing like Andover's secret societies existed at any other American school. What were they all about?

Bush's friend Fitzhugh Green wrote in 1989:

> Robert L. "Tim" Ireland, Bush's longtime supporter [and Brown Brothers Harriman partner], who later served on the Andover board of trustees with him, said he believed [Bush] had been in AUV. "What's that? I asked. "Can't tell you," laughed Ireland. "It's secret!" Both at Andover and Yale, such groups only bring in a small percentage of the total enrollment in any class. "That's a bit cruel to those who don't make AU[V] or 'Bones,' " conceded Ireland.[18]

A retired teacher, who was an adviser to one of the groups, cautiously disclosed in his bicentennial history of Andover, some aspects of the secret societies. The reader should keep in mind that this account was published by the school, to celebrate itself:

> A charming account of the early days of K.O.A, the oldest of the Societies, was prepared by Jack [i.e. Claude Moore] Fuess, a member of the organization, on the occasion of their Fiftieth Anniversary. The Society was founded in . . . 1874. . . .
> [A] major concern of the membership was the initiation ceremony. In K.O.A. the ceremony involved visiting one of the local cemeteries at midnight, various kinds of tortures, running the gauntlet—though the novice was apparently punched rather than paddled, being baptized in a water tank, being hoisted in the air by a pulley, and finally being placed in a coffin, where he was cross-examined by the members. . . . K.O.A. was able to hold the loyalty of its members over the years to become a powerful institution at Phillips Academy and to erect a handsome pillared Society house on School Street.
> The second Society of the seven that would survive until 1950 was A.U.V. [George Bush's group]. The letters stood for Auctoritas, Unitas, Veritas. [Authority, Unity, Truth.] This organization resulted from a merger of two . . . earlier Societies . . . in 1877. A new constitution was drawn up . . . providing for four chief officers—Imperator [commander], Vice Imperator [vice-commander], Scriptor [secretary], and Quaestor [magistrate or inquisitor]. . . .

Like K.O.A, A.U.V. had an elaborate initiation ceremony. Once a pledge had been approved by the Faculty, he was given a letter with a list of rules he was to follow. He was to be in the cemetery every night from 12:30 to 5:00, deliver a morning paper to each member of the Society each morning, must not comb or brush his hair nor wash his face or hands, smoke nothing but a clay pipe with Lucky Strike tobacco, and not speak to any student except members of A.U.V.

After the pledge had memorized these rules, his letter of instruction was burned. The pledge had now become a "scut" and was compelled to learn many mottoes and incantations. On Friday night of initiation week the scut was taken to Hartigan's drugstore downtown and given a "scut sundae," which consisted of pepper, ice cream, oysters, and raw liver. Later that night he reported to the South Church cemetery, where he had to wait for two hours for the members to arrive. There followed the usual horseplay—the scut was used as a tackling dummy, threats were made to lock him in a tomb, and various other ceremonies observed. On Saturday afternoon the scut was taken on a long walk around town, being forced to stop at some houses and ask for food, to urinate on a few porches, and generally to make a fool of himself. On Saturday night came the initiation proper. The scut was prepared by reporting to the cellar in his underwear and having dirt and flour smeared all over his body. He was finally cleaned up and brought to the initiation room, where a solemn ceremony followed, ending with the longed-for words "Let him have light," at which point his blindfold was removed, some oaths were administered, and the boy was finally a member. . . .

Shortly after 1915 the present [A.U.V.] house was constructed. From then until the Society crisis of the 1940s, A.U.V. continued strong and successful. There were, to be sure, some problems. In the mid-1920s, the scholarship average of the Society dropped abysmally. The members had also been pledging students illegally—without the approval of the Faculty guardian. In one initiation a boy had been so battered that he was unable to run in the Andover-Exeter track meet. . . . Yet the Society managed to overcome these problems and well deserved its position as one of the big three among the school's Societies. . . .[19]

From all available evidence, at Andover prep George Bush was completely obsessed with status, with seeming to be important. His 1980 campaign biography boasts that he achieved this goal:

"There was, as there always is at any institution, an elitism in terms of the group that ran things, the power group among the boys who recognized each other as peers. George was among this group, but for him it was natural. . . ."[20]

The A.U.V. roster, 32 members including George Bush, is given in the Andover Class of 1942 yearbook. Why was it "natural" for George to be "among this group"?

The hierarchical top banana of the A.U.V. in George's class was Godfrey Anderson ("Rocky") Rockefeller. In the yearbook just above the A.U.V. roster is a photograph of "Rocky Rockefeller" and "Lem [Lehman F.] Beardsley"; Rockefeller stands imperiously without a shirt, Beardsley scowls from behind sunglasses. Certainly the real monarch of George Bush's Andover secret society, and George's sponsor, was this Rocky's father, **Godfrey S. Rockefeller.**

The latter gentleman had been on the staff of the Yale University establishment in China in 1921–22. Yale and the Rockefellers were breeding a grotesque communist insurgency with British Empire ideology; another Yale staffer there was Mao Zedong, later the communist dictator and mass murderer. While he was over in China, Papa Godfrey's cousin Isabel had been the bridesmaid at the wedding of George Bush's parents. His Uncle Percy had co-founded the Harriman bank with George Walker, and backed George Bush's father in several Nazi German enterprises. His grandfather had been the founding treasurer of the Standard Oil Company, and had made the Harrimans (and thus, ultimately, George Bush) rich.

Faculty adviser to A.U.V. in those days was Norwood Penrose Hallowell; his father by the same name was chairman of Lee, Higginson & Co. private bankers, the chief financiers of Boston's extreme racialist political movements. The elder Hallowell was based in London throughout the 1930s, on intimate terms with Montagu Norman and his pro-Hitler American banking friends.

But this kind of backing, by itself, cannot ensure that a person will rise to the top, to authentic "big-shot" status. You have to want it very, very badly.

One of Poppy Bush's teachers at Andover, now in retirement, offered to an interviewer for this book, a striking picture of his former pupil. How was the President as a student?

"He never said a word in class. He was bored to death. And other teachers told me Bush was the worst English student ever in the school."

But was this teenager simply slow, or dull? On the contrary.

"He was the classic 'BMOC' (Big Man On Campus). A great glad-hander. Always smiling."[21]

Leaving academic studies aside, George Bush was the most insistent self-promoter on the campus. He was able to pursue this career, being fortunately spared from the more mundane chores some other students had to do. For example, he mailed his dirty laundry home each week, to be done by the servants. It was mailed back to him clean and folded.[22]

Student records show a massive list of offices and titles for Poppy, perhaps more than for any other student:

- A.U.V.
- President of Senior Class (1 term)
- Secretary of Student Council (1 term)
- Student Council (1941–42) (surveillance of students during tests, keeping order in the movies, investigating student thieves)
- President of Society of Inquiry (1941–42)
- Senior Prom Committee
- Chairman of Student Deacons (1941–42)
- Advisory Board (management of sports, choosing of P.A. Police to control student body, choosing of cheerleaders)
- President of Greeks (1940–42)
- Captain of Baseball (1942)
- Captain of Soccer (1941)
- Manager of Basketball (1941)
- Society of Inquiry (1940–42) (formerly a Christian mission group, now management of extra-curricular activities)
- Student Deacon (1940–42)
- Editorial Board of the *Phillipian* (1938–39)
- All-club Soccer (1938)
- Business Board of the *Pot Pourri* (1940–42)
- Deputy Housemaster
- Varsity Soccer Squad (1939–41)
- Varsity Basketball Team (1941–42)
- Junior Varsity Baseball Team (1939)
- Varsity Baseball Squad (1940)
- Varsity Baseball Team (1941–42)
- Johns Hopkins Prize (1938)
- Treasurer of Student Council (1 term)

The Class of 1942 was officially polled, to see who had the most status among the students themselves.

For "Best All-Around Fellow," Poppy Bush was third.

Bush did not show up in the "Most Intelligent" category.

Interestingly, Bush came in second on "Most Faculty Drag"— the teachers' pets—even though Bush did not appear at all on the school's Scholastic Honors list. In fact, no member of the Rockefeller-Bush A.U.V. was on the Honors list—despite chanting incantations, being smeared with filth and urinating on porches.

Barbara Pierce's Tradition

The Japanese attacked the U.S. naval base at Pearl Harbor, Hawaii on Dec. 7, 1941, bringing America into World War II. Because of his family's involvement with the Nazis, this would later pose a very different problem for Andover senior Poppy Bush than for the ordinary young man his age.

Meanwhile, the social whirl went on. A couple of weeks after Pearl Harbor, during Christmas vacation, George went to a "cotillion at the Round Hill Country Club in Greenwich, Connecticut. It was a social affair attended by upcoming debutantes and acceptable young men."[23]

Here George Bush met his future wife, Barbara Pierce, whose family was in the High Society set in nearby Rye, New York. Barbara was an attractive 16-year-old girl, athletic like George's mother. She was home for the holidays from her exclusive boarding school, Ashley Hall, in Charleston, South Carolina. Her breeding was acceptable:

"Barbara's background, though not quite so aristocratic as George's, was also socially impressive in a day when Society was defined by breeding rather than wealth. Her father, Marvin Pierce, was a distant nephew of President Franklin Pierce (1853–57). . . . Barbara's mother, Pauline Robinson . . . was [the daughter of] an Ohio Supreme Court justice."[24]

Barbara's father, Marvin Pierce, was then vice president of McCall Corporation, publisher of Redbook and McCall's magazines. After his daughter joined the banking oligarchy by marrying into the Bush family (1945), Pierce became McCall's chief executive. Pierce and his magazine's theme of "Togetherness"—stressing family social existence divorced from political, scientific, artistic or creative activities—played a role in the cult of conformity and mediocrity which crushed U.S. mental life in the 1950s.

A great deal is made about Barbara Pierce Bush's family connection to U.S. President Franklin Pierce. It is inserted in books written by Bush friends and staff members. Barbara Bush's gossip-column biographer says: "Her own great-great-great uncle President Franklin Pierce had his [White House] office in the Treaty Room. . . ." In fact, President Pierce was a distant cousin of Barbara Pierce's great-great grandfather, not his brother, as this claim would imply.*

Like the Henry III ancestral claim, Franklin Pierce may be a

*Established through consultation with the New Hampshire Historical Society and Pierce family experts in Pennsylvania, this fact is acknowledged by Mrs. Bush's White House staff.

bad omen for George Bush. The catastrophic Pierce was refused renomination by his own political party. Pierce backed schemes to spread slavery by having mercenaries, called "filibusters," invade Mexico, Central America and the Caribbean islands. During the Civil War, he attacked the Emancipation Proclamation that outlawed black slavery in the rebel states. His former backers among the wealthy New England families abandoned him and treated him like dirt. He died unmourned in 1869.

One may ask, in what way are President Bush and his backers conscious of an oligarchical tradition? For a clue, let us look at the case of Arthur Burr Darling, George Bush's prep school history teacher.

Just after Claude Fuess "came into power with Hitler and Mussolini" in 1933, Fuess brought Darling in to teach. Dr. Darling was head of the Andover history department from 1937 to 1956, and Faculty Guardian of one of the secret societies. His *Political Changes in Massachusetts, 1824 to 1848* covered the period of Andover's eclipse by Boston's aristocratic opium lords. Darling's book attacks Andover's greatest humanitarian, Jedidiah Morse, as a dangerous lunatic, because Morse warned about international criminal conspiracies involving these respectable Bostonians. The same book attacks President John Quincy Adams as a misguided troublemaker, responsible with Morse for the anti-freemasonic movement in the 1820s–30s.

Arthur Burr Darling, while still head of Andover's history department, was chosen by the Harrimanites to organize the historical files of the new Central Intelligence Agency, and to write the CIA's own official account of its creation and first years. Since this cynical project was secret, Darling's 1971 obituary did not reflect his CIA employment.[25]

Darling's *The Central Intelligence Agency: An Instrument of Government, to 1950* was classified Secret on its completion in December 1953. For 36 years it was only to be consulted for self-justification by the Harrimanites. This mercenary work was finally declassified in 1989 and was published by Pennsylvania State University in 1990. Subsequent editions of *Who Was Who in America* were changed, in the fashion of Joe Stalin's "history revisers," to tell the latest, official version of what George Bush's history teacher had done with his life.

Crisis

Having met his future wife Barbara, Poppy Bush returned from the Christmas holidays after New Year's Day, 1942, for his final months at Andover. The U.S. entry into World War II made things rather awkward for Bush and some of his schoolmates, and cast a dark shadow on his future.

Since early 1941, the Justice Department had been investigating the Nazi support apparatus among U.S. firms. This probe centered on the Harriman, Rockefeller, DuPont and related enterprises, implicating George's father Prescott, his partners, and the Bushes' close family friends.

On March 5, 1942—at about the time Poppy Bush and Rocky Rockefeller were contemplating the tortures they would inflict on the Class of 1943 A.U.V. recruits—the Special Committee of the U.S. Senate Investigating the National Defense Program began explosive public hearings in Washington, D.C. The subject: cartel agreements between U.S. and Nazi firms that should be hit with anti-trust actions. Pearl Harbor, the draft of American boys, and these sensational hearings were causing a popular attitude quite dangerous for the higher-level Nazi collaborators.

But on March 20, 1942, Henry L. Stimson, U.S. Secretary of War and *president of Andover prep's Board of Trustees,* sent a memorandum to President Franklin Roosevelt recommending *stopping* the investigations of the U.S.-Nazi trusts: The resulting lawsuits would "unavoidably consume the time of executives and employees of those corporations which are engaged in war work." Stimson got Navy Secretary Frank Knox and Assistant Attorney General Thurman Arnold to co-sign the memo. President Roosevelt agreed to Stimson's request, but conceded to Arnold and his antitrust staff that he would press for extended statutes of limitation to make postwar prosecutions possible.[26]

Stimson's intervention for his friends could not, however, entirely cancel the already ongoing exposure and prosecution of Rockefeller's Standard Oil of New Jersey. After Farish's death, the prosecutions were suspended, but the seizures of Nazi corporate assets continued, and this would soon lead to Prescott Bush and to Grandfather Walker. Could aristocratic friends be relied upon to prevent scandal or legal trouble from smashing up Poppy's world, and wrecking his carefully prepackaged golden future?

As George wound up his Andover career, and paid court to Barbara, U.S. government investigators sifted through the affairs of the Hitler-Harriman-Bush steamship lines, Hamburg-Amerika and North German Lloyd. Their final report, issued under confidential seal on July 18, 1942, would show that long-time Harriman-Bush executive Christian J. Beck was still the New York attorney for the merged Nazi firms. (See Chapters 2 and 3 for details and description of sources.)

Seizure orders on the shipping lines would be issued in August. The government would seize other Nazi assets, still managed by the Bush family, in the autumn. Prescott Bush, legally responsible for Nazi German banking operations in New York, would have to be named in a seizure order. Could friends in high places keep all this out of the public eye?

Along about this time, *something* was going very wrong with the secret societies at Andover prep school.

Andover's historian, as quoted above, affirmed that "until the Society crisis of the 1940s, A.U.V. continued strong and successful." But a few months after Poppy Bush and Rocky Rockefeller left the school, Headmaster Fuess and his trustees announced they were closing and banning the secret societies forever. This set off a storm of controversy.

Bush's A.U.V. had been humiliating students and teaching anti-Christian rituals since 1877. Fuess was himself a member of one of the Societies. What had happened, to precipitate this drastic decision?

The great Society crisis at Andover was highly charged, because so many of the alumni and parents of current students were leaders of government and finance. An ugly scandal there would reverberate around the world. Whatever really prompted the close-down decision was kept a tight secret, and remains wrapped in mystery today, a half-century later.

Headmaster Fuess claimed that an event which happened nine years earlier had moved him to the decision. This event was duly recorded in the Andover history book:

> In 1934 one undergraduate had been killed during the course of a Society initiation. A group of alumni had joined the undergraduates for part of the ceremonies that were held in a barn on the outskirts of Andover. On the way back the initiate rode on the running board of a car driven by one of the alumni. The roads were slippery, and the car crashed into a telegraph pole, crushing the boy, who died in Dr. Fuess's presence in the hospital a few hours later.[27]

But this tragedy had been brushed off by the school administration, with no suggestion of interfering with the satanic Societies. Was there another, significantly worse disaster, that happened to Class of 1943 secret society recruits?

When the alumni heard about the decision, they exploded into action. They accused Fuess of "fascism" and attacked his "star-chamber proceedings." A Boston newspaper headline proclaimed, "10,000 Andover Alumni Battle Trustees on Abolishing Secret Societies." The headmaster, releasing no specifics to back up his proposal, said, "the purpose for which the secret societies were founded no longer seems apparent." His allies said, quite vaguely, that the Societies "promoted exclusiveness," operated "on a special privilege basis," and created "social cleavage."[28]

The stealthy shut-down decision, having now become loudly public, had to be squelched. Andover's Board of Trustees president, Secretary of War Stimson, settled the matter and kept a lid on things with his familiar refrain that the war effort should not be disturbed. Whatever had pushed Fuess and the trustees to act, was never disclosed. The Societies were quietly closed down in 1950.

Secretary of War Stimson made a famous speech in June 1942, to Poppy Bush and the other graduating Andover boys. Stimson told them the war would be long, and they, the elite, should go on to college.

But George Bush had some very complicated problems. The decision had already been made that he would join the service and get quite far away from where he had been. For reasons of family (which will be discussed in Chapter 7), there was a very special niche waiting for him in naval aviation.

There was one serious hitch in this plan. It was illegal. Though he would be 18 years old on June 12, he would not have the two years of college the Navy required for its aviators.

Well, if you had an *urgent* problem, perhaps the law could be simply *set aside, for you and you alone,* ahead of all the five million poor slobs who had to go in the mud with the infantry or swab some stinking deck—especially if your private school's president was currently Secretary of War (Henry Stimson), if your father's banking partner was currently Assistant Secretary of War for Air (Robert Lovett), and if your father had launched the career of the current Assistant Navy Secretary for Air (Artemus Gates).

And it was done.

As a Bush-authorized version puts it, "One wonders why the Navy relaxed its two years of college requirement for flight training in George Bush's case. He had built an outstanding record at school as a scholar [sic], athlete and campus leader, but so had countless thousands of other youths.

"Yet it was George Bush who appeared to be the only beneficiary of this rule-waiving, and thus he eventually emerged as the youngest pilot in the Navy—a fact that he can still boast about and because of which he enjoyed a certain celebrity during the war."[29]

Notes for Chapter V

1. Nicholas King, *George Bush: A Biography* (New York: Dodd, Mead & Company, 1980), pp. 13–14.
2. *Ibid.*, p. 19.
3. *Ibid.*
4. Joe Hyams, *Flight of the Avenger: George Bush at War* (New York: Harcourt, Brace, Jovanovitch, 1991), p. 14.
5. *Ibid.*, p. 17.
6. *Ibid.*, pp. 16–17.
7. Donnie Radcliffe, *Simply Barbara Bush* (New York: Warner Books, 1989), p. 132.
8. Fitzhugh Green, *George Bush: An Intimate Portrait* (New York: Hippocrene Books, 1989), p. 16.
9. Radcliffe, *op. cit.*, p. 133.
10. King, *op. cit,* p. 14.
11. Hyams, *op. cit.*, pp. 17–19.
12. King, *op. cit.*, pp. 10, 20.
13. *Ibid.*, p. 21.
14. Claude M. Fuess, *The Life of Caleb Cushing,* 2 vols. (New York: Harcourt, Brace and Company, 1923).
15. John Perkins Cushing was a multi-millionaire opium smuggler who retired to Watertown, Massachusetts with servants dressed as in a Canton gangster carnival. See Vernon L. Briggs, *History and Genealogy of the Cabot Family, 1475–1927* (Boston: privately printed, 1927), vol. II, p. 558–559. John Murray Forbes, *Letters and Recollections* (reprinted New York: Arno Press, 1981), Vol I, p. 62–63. Mary Caroline Crawford, *Famous Families of Massachusetts* (Boston: Little, Brown & Co., 1930), 2 vols.
16. Interview with a retired Andover teacher.
17. Claude M. Fuess, *Creed of a Schoolmaster* (reprinted Freeport, New York: Books for Libraries Press, 1970), pp. 192–93.
18. Green, *op. cit.*, p. 49.
19. Frederick S. Allis, *Youth from Every Quarter: A Bicentennial History of Phillips Academy, Andover* (Andover, Mass.: Phillips Academy, 1979), distributed by the University Press of New England, Hanover, N.H.), pp. 505–7.
20. King, *op. cit.*, p. 21.
21. Spoke on condition of non-attribution.
22. Hyams, *op. cit.*, pp. 23–24.
23. *Ibid.*, p. 24.
24. *Ibid.*, p. 27.
25. See *New York Times*, Nov. 29, 1971.
26. Joseph Borkin, *The Crime and Punishment of I.G. Farben* (New York: Macmillan Publishing Co., 1978), p. 89.
27. Allis, *op. cit.*, p. 512.
28. *Newsweek*, August 9, 1943; *Boston Globe*, July 22, 1943.
29. Green, *op. cit.*, page 28.

VI
BUSH IN WORLD WAR II

Plut aux dieux que ce fut le dernier de ses crimes! *
—Racine, *Britannicus*

George Bush has always traded shamelessly on his alleged record as a naval aviator during the Second World War in the Pacific theatre. During the 1964 Senate campaign in Texas against Senator Ralph Yarborough, Bush televised a grainy old film which depicted young George being rescued at sea by the crew of the submarine U.S.S. *Finnback* after his Avenger torpedo bomber was hit by Japanese anti-aircraft fire during a bombing raid on the island of Chichi Jima on September 2, 1944. That film, retrieved from the Navy archives, backfired when it was put on the air too many times, eventually becoming something of a maladroit cliché.

Bush's campaign literature has always celebrated his alleged military exploits and the Distinguished Flying Cross he received. As we become increasingly familiar with the power of the Brown Brothers Harriman/Skull and Bones network working for Senator Prescott Bush, we will learn to become increasingly skeptical of such official accolades and of the official accounts on which they are premised.

During Bush's Gulf war adventure of 1990–91, the adulation of Bush's ostensible warrior prowess reached levels that were previously considered characteristic of openly totalitarian and militaristic regimes. Late in 1990, after Bush had committed himself irrevocably to his campaign of bombing and savagery against Iraq, hack

*Would the gods that this were the last of his crimes!

writer Joe Hyams completed an authorized account of George Bush at war. This was entitled *Flight of the Avenger*, and appeared during the time of the Middle East conflagration that was the product of Bush's obsessions.

Hyams's work had the unmistakable imprimatur of the regime: Not just George, but also Barbara had been interviewed during its preparation, and its adulatory tone placed this squalid text squarely within the "red Studebaker" school of political hagiography.

The appearance of such a book at such a time is suggestive of the practice of the most infamous twentieth-century dictatorships, in which the figure of the strong man, fuhrer, duce, or vozhd, as he might be called, has been used for the transmission of symbolic-allegorical directives to the subject population. Was fascist Italy seeking to assert its economic autarky in food production in the face of trade sanctions by the League of Nations? Then a film would be produced by the MINCULPOP (the Ministry of Popular Culture, or propaganda) depicting Mussolini indefatigably harvesting grain. Was Nazi Germany in the final stages of preparation of a military campaign against a neighboring state? If so, Goebbels would orchestrate a cascade of magazine articles and best-selling pulp evoking the glories of Hitler in the trenches of 1914–18. Closer to our own time, Leonid Brezhnev sought to aliment his own personality cult with a little book called *Malaya Zemlya*, an account of his war experiences which was used by his propagandists to motivate his promotion to Marshal of the U.S.S.R. and the erection of a statue in his honor during his own lifetime. This is the tradition to which *Flight of the Avenger* belongs.

Bush tells us in his campaign autobiography that he decided to enlist in the armed forces, specifically naval aviation, shortly after he heard of the Japanese attack on Pearl Harbor. About six months later, Bush graduated from Phillips Academy at Andover, and the commencement speaker was Secretary of War Henry Stimson, éminence grise of the U.S. ruling elite. Stimson was possibly mindful of the hecatomb of young members of the British ruling classes which had occurred in the trenches of World War I on the western front. In any event, Stimson's advice to the Andover graduates was that the war would go on for a long time, and that the best way of serving the country was to continue one's education in college. Prescott Bush supposedly asked his son if Stimson's recommendation had altered his plan to enlist. Young Bush answered that he was still committed to join the Navy.

Henry L. Stimson was certainly an authoritative spokesman for the Eastern Liberal Establishment, and Bushman propaganda has lately exalted him as one of the seminal influences on Bush's political outlook. Stimson had been educated at both Yale (where he had been tapped by Skull and Bones) and Harvard Law School. He became the law partner of Elihu Root, who was Theodore Roosevelt's Secretary of State. Stimson had been Theodore Roosevelt's anti-corruption, trust-busting U.S. Attorney in New York City during the first years of the FBI, then Taft's Secretary of War, a colonel of artillery in World War I, Governor General of the Philippines for Coolidge, Secretary of State for Hoover, and enunciator of the "Stimson doctrine." This last was a piece of hypocritical posturing directed against Japan, asserting that changes in the international order brought about by force of arms (and thus in contravention of the Kellogg-Briand Pact of 1928) should not be given diplomatic recognition. This amounted to a U.S. commitment to uphold the Versailles system, the same policy upheld by James Baker, Eagleburger and Kissinger in the Serbian war on Slovenia and Croatia during 1991. Stimson, though a Republican, was brought into Franklin Roosevelt's war cabinet in 1940 in token of bipartisan intentions.

But in 1942, Bush was not buying Stimson's advice. It is doubtless significant that in the mind of young George Bush, World War II meant exclusively the war in the Pacific, against the Japanese. In the Bush-approved accounts of this period of his life, there is scarcely a mention of the European theater, despite the fact that Roosevelt and the entire Anglo-American establishment had accorded strategic priority to the "Germany first" scenario. Young George, it would appear, had his heart set on becoming a Navy flier.

Normally the Navy required two years of college from volunteers wishing to become naval aviators. But as we said, for reasons which have never been satisfactorily explained, young George was exempted from this requirement.

On June 12, 1942, his eighteenth birthday, Bush joined the Navy in Boston as a seaman second class.[1] He was ordered to report for active duty as an aviation cadet on August 6, 1942. After a last date with Barbara, George was taken to Penn Station in New York City by father Prescott to board a troop train headed for Chapel Hill, North Carolina. At Chapel Hill Naval Air Station, one of Bush's fellow cadets was the well-known Boston Red Sox hitter Ted Williams, who would later join Bush on the campaign trail in his desperate fight in the New Hampshire primary in February 1988.

After preflight training at Chapel Hill, Bush moved on to Wold-Chamberlain Naval Airfield in Minneapolis, Minnesota, where he flew solo for the first time, in November 1942. In February 1943,

Bush moved on to Corpus Christi, Texas for further training. Bush received his commission as an ensign at Corpus Christi on June 9, 1943.

After this Bush moved through a number of naval air bases over a period of almost a year for various types of advanced training. In mid-June 1943 he was learning to fly the Grumman TBF Avenger torpedo-bomber at Fort Lauderdale, Florida. In August he made landings on the U.S.S. *Sable,* a paddle-wheel ship that was used as an aircraft carrier for training purposes. During the summer of 1943, Bush spent a couple of weeks of leave with Barbara at Walker's Point in Kennebunkport; their engagement was announced in the *New York Times* of December 12, 1943.

Later in the summer of 1943, Bush moved on to the Naval Air Base at Norfolk, Virginia. In September 1943 Bush's new squadron, called VT–51, moved on to the Naval Air Station at Chincoteague, Virginia, located on the Delmarva peninsula. On December 14, 1943 Bush and his squadron were brought to Philadelphia to attend the commissioning of the U.S.S. *San Jacinto* (CVL30), a light attack carrier built on a cruiser hull. Since the name of the ship recalled Sam Houston's defeat of the Mexican leader Santa Anna in 1836, and since the ship flew a Lone Star flag, Bushman propaganda has made much of these artifacts in an attempt to buttress "carpetbag" Bush's tenuous connections to the state of Texas. Bush's VF–51 squadron reported on board this ship for a shakedown cruise on February 6, 1944, and on March 25, 1944 the *San Jacinto* left for San Diego by way of the Panama Canal. The *San Jacinto* reached Pearl Harbor on April 20, 1944, and was assigned to Admiral Marc A. Mitscher's Task Force 58/38, a group of fast carriers, on May 2, 1944.

In June Bush's ship joined battle with Japanese forces in the Marianas archipelago. Here Bush flew his first combat missions. On June 17, a loss of oil pressure forced Bush to make an emergency landing at sea. Bush, along with his two crew members, gunner Leo Nadeau and radioman-tail gunner John L. Delaney, were picked up by a U.S. destroyer after some hours in the water. Bush's first Avenger, named by him the "Barbara," was lost.

During July 1944 Bush took part in 13 air strikes, many in connection with the U.S. Marines' landing on Guam. In August Bush's ship proceeded to the area of Iwo Jima and Chichi Jima in the Bonin Islands for a new round of sorties.

On September 2, 1944 Bush and three other Avenger pilots, escorted by Hellcat fighter planes, were directed to attack a radio transmitter on Chichi Jima. Planes from the U.S.S. *Enterprise* would also join in the attack. On this mission Bush's rear-seat gunner would not be the usual Leo Nadeau, but rather Lt. junior grade William Gardner "Ted" White, the squadron ordnance officer of VT–51, already a Yale graduate, and already a member of Skull and Bones. White's father had been a classmate of Prescott Bush. White took his place in the rear-facing machine-gun turret of Bush's TBM Avenger, the Barbara II. The radioman-gunner was John L. Delaney, a regular member of Bush's crew.

What happened in the skies of Chichi Jima that day is a matter of lively controversy. Bush has presented several differing versions of his own story. In his campaign autobiography published in 1987, Bush gives the following account:

> The flak was the heaviest I'd ever flown into. The Japanese were ready and waiting: their antiaircraft guns were set up to nail us as we pushed into our dives. By the time VT–51 was ready to go in, the sky was thick with angry black clouds of exploding antiaircraft fire.
>
> Don Melvin led the way, scoring hits on a radio tower. I followed, going into a thirty-five degree dive, an angle of attack that sounds shallow but in an Avenger felt as if you were headed straight down. The target map was strapped to my knee, and as I started into my dive, I'd already spotted the target area. Coming in, I was aware of black splotches of gunfire all around.
>
> Suddenly there was a jolt, as if a massive fist had crunched into the belly of the plane. Smoke poured into the cockpit, and I could see flames rippling across the crease of the wing, edging towards the fuel tanks. I stayed with the dive, homed in on the target, unloaded our four 500-pound bombs, and pulled away, heading for the sea. Once over water, I leveled off and told Delaney and White to bail out, turning the plane to starboard to take the slipstream off the door near Delaney's station.
>
> Up to that point, except for the sting of dense smoke blurring my vision, I was in fair shape. But when I went to make my jump, trouble came in pairs.[2]

In this account, there is no more mention of White and Delaney until Bush hit the water and began looking around for them. Bush says that it was only after having been rescued by the U.S.S. *Finnback*, a submarine, that he "learned that neither Jack Delaney nor Ted White had survived. One went down with the plane; the other was seen jumping, but his parachute failed to open." The Hyams account of 1991 was written after an August 1988 interview with Chester Mierzejewski, another member of Bush's squadron, had raised important questions about the haste with which Bush bailed out, rather than attempting a water landing. Mierzejewski's account, which is summarized below, contradicted Bush's own version of these events, and hinted that Bush might have abandoned his two crew members to a horrible and needless death. The Hyams account, which is partly intended to refute Mierzejewski, develops as follows:

> . . . Bush was piloting the third plane over the target, with Moore flying on his wing. He nosed over into a thirty-degree glide, heading straight for the radio tower. Determined to finally destroy the tower, he used no evasive tactics and held the plane directly on target. His vision ahead was occasionally canceled by bursts of black smoke from the Japanese antiaircraft guns. The plane was descending through thickening clouds of flak pierced by the flaming arc of tracers.
>
> There was a sudden flash of light followed by an explosion. "The plane was lifted forward, and we were enveloped in flames," Bush recalls. "I saw the flames running along the wings where the fuel tanks were and where the wings fold. I thought, This is really bad! It's hard to remember the details, but I looked at the instruments and couldn't see them for the smoke."
>
> Don Melvin, circling above the action while waiting for his pilots to drop their bombs and get out, thought the Japanese shell had hit an oil line on Bush's Avenger. "You could have seen that smoke for a hundred miles."

Perhaps so, but it is difficult to understand why the smoke from Bush's plane was so distinctly visible in such a smoke-filled environment. Hyams goes on to describe Bush's completion of his bombing run. His account continues:

> By then the wings were covered in flames and smoke, and the engine was blazing. He considered making a water landing but realized it would not be possible. Bailing out was absolutely the last choice, but he had no other option. He got on the radio and notified squadron leader Melvin of his decision. Melvin radioed back, "Received your message. Got you in sight. Will follow."
>
> . . . Milt Moore, flying directly behind Bush, saw the Avenger going down smoking. "I pulled up to him; then he lost power and I went sailing by him."
>
> As soon as he was back over water, Bush shouted on the intercom for White and Delaney to "hit the silk!" . . . Dick Gorman, Moore's radioman-gunner, remembers hearing someone on the intercom shout, "Hit the silk!" and asking Moore, "Is that you, Red?"
>
> "No," Moore replied. "It's Bush, he's hit!"
>
> Other squadron members heard Bush repeating the command to bail out, over and over, on the radio.

There was no response from either of Bush's crewmen and no way he could see them; a shield of armor plate between him and Lt. White blocked his view behind. He was certain that White and Delaney had bailed out the moment they got the order.[3]

Hyams quotes a later entry by Melvin in the squadron log as to the fate of Bush's two crewmen: "At a point approximately nine miles bearing 045'T (degrees) from Minami Jima, Bush and one other person were seen to bail out from about 3,000 feet. Bush's chute opened and he landed safely in the water, inflated his raft, and paddled farther away from Chichi Jima. The chute of the other person who bailed out did not open. Bush has not yet been returned to the squadron . . . so this information is incomplete. While Lt. junior grade White and J.L. Delaney are reported missing in action, it is believed that both were killed as a result of the above described action."[4] But it is interesting to note that this report, contrary to usual standard Navy practice, has no date. This should alert us to that tampering with public records, such as Bush's filings at the Securities and Exchange Commission during the 1960s, which appears to be a specialty of the Brown Brothers Harriman/Skull and Bones network.

For comparison, let us now cite the cursory account of this same incident provided by Bush's authorized biographer in the candidate's 1980 presidential campaign biography:

> On a run toward the island, Bush's plane was struck by Japanese antiaircraft shells. One of his two crewmen was killed instantly and the aircraft was set on fire. Bush was able to score hits on the enemy installations with a couple of five-hundred pound bombs before he wriggled out of the smoking cockpit and floated towards the water. The other crewman also bailed out but died almost immediately thereafter because, as the fighter pilot behind Bush's plane was later to report, his parachute failed to open properly. Bush's own parachute became momentarily fouled on the tail of the plane after he hit the water.[5]

King's account is interesting for its omission of any mention of Bush's injury in bailing out, a gashed forehead he got when he struck the tail assembly of the plane. This had to have occurred long before Bush had hit the water, so this account is garbled indeed.

Let us also cite parts of the account provided by Fitzhugh Green in his 1989 authorized biography. Green has Bush making his attack "at a 60-degree angle." "For his two crew members," notes Green, "life was about to end." His version goes on:

Halfway through Bush's dive, the enemy found his range with one or more shells. Smoke filled his cabin; his plane controls weakened; the engine began coughing, and still he wasn't close enough to the target. He presumed the TBM to be terminally damaged. Fighting to stay on course, eyes smarting, Bush managed to launch his bombs at the last possible moment. He couldn't discern the result through black fumes. But a companion pilot affirmed later that the installation blew up, along with two other buildings. The Navy would decorate Bush for literally sticking to his guns until he completed his mission under ferocious enemy fire.

Good! Now the trick was to keep the plane aloft long enough to accomplish two objectives: first, get far enough away from the island to allow rescue from the sea before capture or killing by the enemy; second, give his planemates time to parachute out of the burning aircraft.

The TBM sputtered on its last few hundred yards. Unbeknownst to Bush, one man freed himself. Neither fellow squadron pilots nor Bush ever were sure which crew member this was. As he jumped, however, his parachute snarled and failed to open.[6]

Green writes that when Bush was swimming in the water, he realized that "his crew had disappeared" and "the loss of the two men numbed Bush."

For the 1992 presidential campaign, the Bushmen have readied yet another rehash of the adulatory "red Studebaker" printout in the form of a new biography by Richard Ben Cramer. This is distinguished as a literary effort above all by the artificial verbal pyrotechnics with which the author attempts to breathe new life into the dog-eared Bush canonical printout. For these, Cramer relies on a hyperkinetic style with non-verbal syntax, which to some degree echoes Bush's own disjointed manner of speaking. The resulting text may have found favor with Bush when he was gripped by his hyperthyroid rages during the buildup for the Gulf war. A part of this text has appeared in *Esquire* magazine.[7] Here is Cramer's description of the critical phase of the incident:

He felt a jarring lurch, a crunch, and his plane leaped forward, like a giant had struck it from below with a fist. Smoke started to fill the cockpit. He saw a tongue of flame streaming down the right wing toward the crease. Christ! The fuel tanks!

He called to Delaney and White—We've been hit! He was diving. Melvin hit the tower dead-on—four five hundred pounders. West was on the same beam. Bush could have pulled out. Have to get rid of these bombs. Keep the dive. . . . A few seconds. . . .

He dropped on the target and let 'em fly. The bombs spun down,

the plane shrugged with release, and Bush banked away hard to the
east. No way he'd get to the rendezvous point with Melvin. The
smoke was so bad he couldn't see the gauges. Was he climbing? Have
to get to the water. They were dead if they bailed out over land. The
Japs killed pilots. Gonna have to bail out. Bush radioed the skipper,
called his crew. No answer. Does White know how to get to his
chute? Bush looked back for an instant. God, was White hit? He was
yelling the order to bail out, turning right rudder to take the slipstream
off their hatch . . . had to get himself out. He leveled off over water,
only a few miles from the island . . . more, ought to get out farther
. . . that's it, got to be now. . . . He flicked the red toggle switch on
the dash—the IFF, Identification Friend or Foe—supposed to alert
any U.S. ship, send a special frequency back to his own carrier . . .
no other way to communicate, had to get out now, had to be . . .
NOW.

It will be seen that these versions contain numerous internal
contradictions, but that the hallmark of "red Studebaker" orthodoxy, especially after the appearance of the Mierzejewski account,
is that Bush's plane was on fire, with visible smoke and flames. The
Bush propaganda machine needs the fire on board the Avenger in
order to justify Bush's precipitous decision to bail out, leaving his
two crew members to their fate, rather than attempting the water
landing which might have saved them.

The only person who has ever claimed to have seen Bush's plane
get hit, and to have seen it hit the water, is Chester Mierzejewski,
who was the rear turret gunner in the aircraft flown by Squadron
Commander Douglas Melvin. During 1987–88, Mierzejewski became increasingly indignant as he watched Bush repeat his canonical
account of how he was shot down. Shortly before the Republican
National Convention in 1988, Mierzejewski, by then a 68-year-old
retired aircraft foreman living in Cheshire, Connecticut, decided to
tell his story to Allan Wolper and Al Ellenberg of the *New York
Post,* which printed it as a copyrighted article.[8]

"That guy is not telling the truth," Mierzejewski said of Bush.

As the rear-looking turret gunner on Commander Melvin's plane,
Mierzejewski had the most advantageous position for observing the
events in question here. Since Melvin's plane flew directly ahead of
Bush's, he had a direct and unobstructed view of what was happening aft of his own plane. When the *New York Post* reporters asked
former Lt. Legare Hole, the executive officer of Bush's squadron,
about who might have best observed the last minutes of the Barbara
II, Hole replied: "The turret gunner in Melvin's plane would have

had a good view. If the plane was on fire, there is a very good chance he would be able to see that. The pilot can't see everything that the gunner can, and he'd miss an awful lot," Hole told the *New York Post.*

Gunner Lawrence Mueller of Milwaukee, another former member of Bush's squadron who flew on the Chichi Jima mission, when asked who would have had the best view, replied: "The turret gunner of Melvin's plane." Mierzejewski for his part said that his plane was flying about 100 feet ahead of Bush's plane during the incident—so close that he could see into Bush's cockpit.

Mierzejewski, who is also a recipient of the Distinguished Flying Cross, told the *New York Post* that he saw "a puff of smoke" come out of Bush's plane and quickly dissipate. He asserted that after that there was no more smoke visible, that Bush's "plane was never on fire" and that "no smoke came out of his cockpit when he opened his canopy to bail out." Mierzejewski stated that only one man ever got out of the Barbara II, and that was Bush himself. "I was hoping I would see some other parachutes. I never did. I saw the plane go down. I knew the guys were still in it. It was a helpless feeling."

Mierzejewski has long been troubled by the notion that Bush's decision to parachute from his damaged aircraft might have cost the lives of radioman second class John Delaney, a close friend of Mierzejewski, as well as gunner Lt. junior grade William White. "I think [Bush] could have saved those lives, if they were alive. I don't know that they were, but at least they had a chance if he had attempted a water landing," Mierzejewski told the *New York Post.*

Former executive officer Legare Hole summed up the question for the *New York Post* reporters as follows: "If the plane is on fire, it hastens your decision to bail out. If it is not on fire, you make a water landing." The point is that a water landing held out more hope for all members of the crew. The Avenger had been designed to float for approximately two minutes, giving the tailgunner enough time to inflate a raft and giving everyone an extra margin of time to get free of the plane before it sank. Bush had carried out a water landing back in June when his plane had lost oil pressure.

The official—but undated—report on the incident among the squadron records was signed by Commander Melvin and an intelligence officer named Lt. Martin E. Kilpatrick. Kilpatrick is deceased, and Melvin in 1988 was hospitalized with Parkinson's disease and could not be interviewed. Mierzejewski in early August 1988 had never seen the undated intelligence report in question. "Kilpatrick was the first person I spoke to when we got back to the ship," he said. "I told him what I saw. I don't understand why it's not in the report."

Gunner Lawrence Mueller tended to corroborate Mierzejewski's account. Mueller had kept a log book of his own in which he made notations as the squadron was debriefed in the ready room after each mission. For September 2, 1944, Mueller's personal log had the following entry: "White and Delaney presumed to have gone down with plane." Mueller told the *New York Post* that "no parachute was sighted except Bush's when the plane went down." The *New York Post* reporters were specific that, according to Mueller, no one in the *San Jacinto* ready room during the debriefing had said anything about a fire on board Bush's plane. Mueller said, "I would have put it in my log book if I had heard it."

According to this *New York Post* article, the report of Bush's debriefing aboard the submarine *Finnback* after his rescue makes no mention of any fire aboard the plane. When the *New York Post* reporters interviewed Thomas R. Keene, an airman from another carrier, who had been picked up by the *Finnback* a few days after Bush, they referred to the alleged fire on board Bush's plane and "Keene was surprised to hear" it. "Did he say that?" Keene asked.

Leo Nadeau, Bush's usual rear turret gunner, who had been in contact with Bush during the 1980s, attempted to undercut Mierzejewski's credibility by stating that "Ski," as Mierzejewski was called, would have been "too busy shooting" to have been able to focus on the events involving Bush's plane. But even the pro-Bush accounts agree that the reason that White had been allowed to come aloft in the first place was the expectation that there would be no Japanese aircraft over the target, making a thoroughly trained and experienced gunner superfluous. Indeed, no account alleges that any Japanese aircraft appeared over Chichi Jima.

Bush and Mierzejewski met again on board the *San Jacinto* after the downed pilot was returned from the *Finnback* about a month after the loss of the Barbara II. According to the *New York Post* account, about a month after all these events, Bush, clad in Red Cross pajamas, returned to the *San Jacinto*. "He came into the ready room and sat down next to me," Mierzejewski recounted. "He [Bush] knew I saw the whole thing. He said, 'Ski, I'm sure those two men were dead. I called them on the radio three times. They were dead.' When he told me they were dead, I couldn't prove they weren't. He seemed distraught. He was trying to assure me he did the best he could. I'm thinking what am I going to say to him," Mierzejewski commented in 1988.

Mierzejewski began to become concerned about Bush's presentation of his war record while watching Bush's December 1987 interview with David Frost, which was one of the candidate's most sanctimonious performances. In March 1988, Mierzejewski wrote to Bush and told him that his recollections were very different from the Vice President's story. Mierzejewski's letter was not hostile in tone, but voiced concern that political opponents might come forward to dispute Bush. There was no reply to this letter, and Chester Mierzejewski ultimately elected to tell his own unique eye-witness version of the facts to the *New York Post*. Certainly his authoritative, first-hand account places a large question mark over the events of September 2, 1944, which Bush has so often sought to exploit for political gain.

Several days after Mierzejewski's interview was published, Bush's office obtained and released to the press a copy of the (undated) squadron log report. One Donald Rhodes of Bush's office called Mierzejewski to offer him a copy of the report.

It is typical of Joe Hyams's hack work for Bush in *Flight of the Avenger* that he never mentions Mierzejewski's critical account, although he is obviously acutely aware of the objections raised by Mierzejewski and wants very much to discredit those objections. Indeed, Hyams totally ignores Mierzejewski as a source, and also studiously ignores the other witness who would have supported Mierzejewski, that is to say, Mueller. Hyams had the support of Bush's White House staff in arranging interviews for his book, but somehow he never got around to talking to Mierzejewski and Mueller. This must increase our suspicion that Bush has some damning circumstance he wishes to hide.

Bush himself admits that he was in a big hurry to get out of his cockpit: "The wind was playing tricks, or more likely, I pulled the rip cord too soon."[9] This caused his gashed forehead and damaged his parachute.

Concerning the ability of Brown Brothers Harriman to fix a combat report in naval aviation, it is clear that this could be accomplished as easily as fixing a parking ticket. Artemus Gates is someone who could have helped out. Other Brown Brothers Harriman assets in powerful posts included Secretary of War Stimson, Secretary of War for Air Robert Lovett, Special Envoy W. Averell Harriman, and even President Franklin Roosevelt's confidant and virtual alter ego, Harry Hopkins, an asset of the Harriman family.

Bush was very upset about what had happened to his two crewmen. Later, during one of his Skull and Bones "Life History" self-exposures, Bush referred to Lt. White, the Skull and Bones member who had gone to his death with the Barbara II: "I wish I hadn't let him go," said Bush, according to former Congressman Thomas W.L. (Lud) Ashley, a fellow Skull and Bones member, and during 1991 one of the administrators of the Neil Bush legal defense fund. According to Ashley, "Bush was heartbroken. He had gone over it in his mind 100,000 times and concluded he couldn't have done anything. . . . He didn't feel guilty about anything that happened. . . . But the incident was a source of real grief to him. It tore him up, real anguish. It was so fresh in his mind. He had a real friendship with this man," said Ashley.[10]

Bush later wrote letters to the families of the men who had died on his plane. He received a reply from Delaney's sister, Mary Jane Delaney. The letter read in part:

"You mention in your letter that you would like to help me in some way. There is a way, and that is to stop thinking you are in any way responsible for your plane accident and what has happened to your men. I might have thought you were if my brother Jack had not always spoken of you as the best pilot in the squadron."[11]

Bush also wrote a letter to his parents in which he talked about White and Delaney: "I try to think about it as little as possible, yet I cannot get the thought of those two out of my mind. Oh, I'm OK—I want to fly again and I won't be scared of it, but I know I won't be able to shake the memory of this incident and I don't believe I want to completely."[12]

As Bush himself looked back on all these events from the threshold of his genocidal assault on Iraq, he complacently concluded that the pagan fates had preserved his life for some future purpose. He told Hyams:

"There wasn't a sudden revelation of what I wanted to do with the rest of my life, but there was an awakening. There's no question that underlying all that were my own religious beliefs. In my own view there's got to be some kind of destiny and I was being spared for something on earth."[13]

After having deliberately ignored the relevant dissenting views about the heroism of his patron, Hyams chooses to conclude his book on the following disturbing note:

"When flying his Avenger off the deck of the San Jac, Bush was responsible for his own fate as well as his crewmen's. As president he is responsible for the fate of all Americans as well as that of much of the world."

And that is precisely the problem.

Notes for Chapter VI

1. For details of Bush's Navy career, see Joe Hyams, *Flight of the Avenger: George Bush at War* (New York: Harcourt, Brace, Jovanovitch, 1991), *passim.*

2. George Bush and Victor Gold, *Looking Forward* (New York: Doubleday, 1987), p. 36.

3. Hyams, *op. cit.*, pp. 106–7.

4. *Ibid.*, p. 111.

5. Nicholas King, *George Bush: A Biography* (New York: Dodd, Mead & Company, 1980), pp. 30–31.

6. Fitzhugh Green, *George Bush: An Intimate Portrait* (New York: Hippocrene Books, 1989), pp. 36–37.

7. Richard Ben Cramer, "George Bush: How He Got Here," *Esquire,* June 1991.

8. Allan Wolper and Al Ellenberg, "The Day Bush Bailed Out," *New York Post,* Aug. 12, 1988, pp. 1 ff.

9. Bush and Gold, *op. cit.*, p. 36.

10. *Washington Post,* Aug. 7, 1988. For the Skull and Bones Society and its "life history" self-exposure, see Chapter 7.

11. Hyams, *op. cit.*, p. 143.

12. Bush and Gold, *op. cit.*, pp. 40–41.

13. Hyams, *op. cit.*, p. 134.

Library of Congress/Harriman Papers

E.H. Harriman: railroad "robber baron" whose millions spawned son Averell's world-spanning intrigues.

EIRNS/Philip Ulanowsky

Averell Harriman: banker, New York governor, famous Yalta diplomat, he hired the Bush family and sponsored Hitler's Nazis.

Percy A. Rockefeller: stock manipulator, co-founder W.A. Harriman & Company.

Samuel P. Bush: Harriman-linked railroad supplier, government armaments executive, father of Prescott Bush.

Prescott Bush: President Bush's father, director of Harriman's Nazi-front Union Banking Corporation.

Washington Star photo, ©Washington Post, courtesy Washington D.C. Public Library

Washington Star photo, ©Washington Post, courtesy Washington D.C. Public Library

Dorothy Walker Bush: mother of the President, wealthy, athletic, terrifyingly competitive.

U.S. National Archives

Owner Averell Harriman (center) with Hamburg-Amerika employees. This photo was seized in 1942 by the U.S. government from Nazi publicity files of Hamburg-Amerika.

SA.-Verbot in Berlin
Räumung des Büros in der Hedemannstraße. 13. April 1932

Library of Congress/Nazi Party Archives

German government workers shut down offices of Hitler's S.A. private army, Berlin, 1932. The Harriman-Bush Hamburg-Amerika Line put out propaganda attacking the German republic for this move against the Nazis.

WERKZEUG IN GOTTES HAND?
SPIELZEUG IN THYSSENS HAND!

Harriman-Bush client Fritz Thyssen with Adolf Hitler as his puppet, in a German anti-Nazi cartoon of the 1930s.

Nazi banking and shipping businesses run by Prescott Bush and George H. Walker were seized here at 39 Broadway by U.S. government in 1942.

Anton Chaitkin

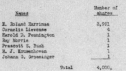

OFFICE OF ALIEN PROPERTY CUSTODIAN
Washington

Vesting Order Number 248

Re: All of the capital stock of Union
Banking Corporation and certain indebtedness owing by it

Under the authority of the Trading with the enemy Act, as amended, and
Executive Order No. 9095, as amended, and pursuant to law, the undersigned,
after investigation, finding:

(a) That the property described as follows:

All of the capital stock of Union Banking Corporation, a New York corporation, New York, New York,
which is a business enterprise within the United
States, consisting of 4,000 shares of $100 par value
common capital stock, the names of the registered
owners of which, and the number of shares owned by
them respectively, are as follows:

Names	Number of shares
E. Roland Harriman	3,991
Cornelis Lievense	4
Harold D. Pennington	1
Ray Morris	1
Prescott S. Bush	1
H. J. Kouwenhoven	1
Johann G. Groeninger	1
Total	4,000,

all of which shares are held for the benefit of Bank
voor Handel en Scheepvaart, N. V., Rotterdam, The
Netherlands, which bank is owned or controlled by
members of the Thyssen family, nationals of Germany
and/or Hungary,

is property of nationals, and represents ownership of said business
enterprise which is a national, of a designated enemy country or
countries (Germany and/or Hungary);

(b) That the property described as follows:

All right, title, interest and claim of any name or
nature whatsoever of the aforesaid Bank voor Handel
en Scheepvaart, and August Thyssen-Bank, Berlin,
Germany, and each of them, in and to all indebtedness,
contingent or otherwise and whether or not matured,
owing to them, or each of them, by said Union Banking
Corporation, including but not limited to all security

The U.S. government World War II "vesting order" #248 seizing the Union Banking Corp. as a front for Fritz Thyssen and his Nazi Steel Trust.

Library of Congress/Law Department

Library of Congress/Harriman Papers

E. Roland ("Bunny") Harriman (left), who brought Prescott Bush into Skull and Bones, and his brother Averell. Roland chaired Thyssen's Union Banking Corp.

Library of Congress/Harriman papers

Averell Harriman (right) with Soviet officials, on a 1926 manganese mining venture for the Walker-Bush-Harriman bank.

Bush campaign financier William H. Draper III, son of the Nazi banker, is current head of all United Nations population programs.

United Nations Development Program

C. Boyden Gray, chief counsel to President Bush. His family sterilized North Carolina school children, a pilot project for the current worldwide program.

EIRNS/Stuart Lewis

THE TWO CHILD FAMILY – AN AMERICAN SOCIAL & FAMILY IDEAL FOR THE 70'S

VOLUNTARY STERILIZATION, THE BEST, MOST RELIABLE METHOD OF BIRTH CONTROL FOR THAT LARGE PERCENTAGE OF COUPLES WHO WANT NO MORE CHILDREN.

Poster of the Association for Voluntary Sterilization. The U.S. government now pays this group from the Nazi era to sterilize nonwhites overseas.

Brown Brothers Harriman headquarters at 59 Wall Street. Prescott Bush was senior partner from 1931 to 1950 and from 1963 to 1972.

Anton Chaitkin

Robert Lovett, Prescott Bush's partner, helped arrange the demise of James Forrestal, and planned the founding of the British-modeled CIA.

Library of Congress/Biography photo file USZ62-77269

Standard Oil president William Stamps Farish, exposed by the U.S. Senate for cartel with the Nazis. George Bush's closest friend, financial counselor W.S. Farish III, inherited his grandfather's Auschwitz fortune.

Vicks Vapo-Rub's H. Smith Richardson, Prescott Bush crony whose fund bankrolled secret police projects of the U.S. "parallel government."

Library of Congress/U.S. News and World Report Collection

Prescott Bush (left) with President Eisenhower at the 1956 Republican convention.

Webster Griffin Tarpley

A.U.V., Bush's secret society at Andover prep school, celebrated death, sadism, and humiliation. Inset: The number "321" on A.U.V.'s seal boasts of its affiliation with Yale's Skull and Bones, which bills itself as "322."

Andover Headmaster Claude M. Fuess, historian for the Boston Brahmins.

courtesy Phillips Academy, Andover, Mass.

Arthur Burr Darling, George Bush's history teacher, who perfected the art of coverup. He wrote the CIA's official history.

courtesy Phillips Academy, Andover, Mass.

The New York Post, *August 12, 1988, quoted eyewitness Chester Mierzejewski debunking Bush's fiery crash story.*

Flight of the Avenger, *the book commissioned by George Bush to glorify his wartime bravery.*

VII

SKULL AND BONES: THE RACIST NIGHTMARE AT YALE

"Wise statesmen . . . established these great self-evident truths, that when in the distant future some man, some faction, some interest, should set up the doctrine that none but rich men, or none but white men, were entitled to life, liberty and the pursuit of happiness, their posterity should look up again at the Declaration of Independence and take courage to renew the battle which their fathers began. . . ."[1]

—Abraham Lincoln

Honeymoon

The U.S. Navy delivered George Bush back home for good on Christmas Eve, 1944; the war in the Pacific raged on over the next half year, with Allied forces taking Southeast Asia, the Netherlands East Indies (Indonesia), and islands such as Iwo Jima and Okinawa.

Barbara Pierce quit Smith College in her sophomore year to marry George. Prescott and Mother Bush gave a splendid prenuptial dinner at the Greenwich Field Club. The wedding took place January 6, 1945, in the Rye, New York Presbyterian Church, as the U.S. Third Fleet bombarded the main Philippine island of Luzon in preparation for invasion. Afterwards there was a glamorous reception for 300 at Appawamis Country Club. The newlyweds honeymooned at The Cloisters, a five-star hotel on Sea Island, Georgia, with swimming, tennis and golf.

George's next assignment was to train pilots at Norfolk, Virginia Naval Air Station. "George's duty . . . was light. As for other young marrieds, whose husbands were between warzone tours, this was kind of an extended (and paid) honeymoon."[2]

Japan surrendered in August. That fall, George and Barbara Bush moved to New Haven where Bush entered Yale University. He and Barbara moved into an apartment at 37 Hillhouse Avenue, across the street from Yale President Charles Seymour.

College life was good to George, what he saw of it. A college career usually occupies four years. But we know that George Bush is a rapidly moving man. Thus he was pleased with the special arrangement made for veterans, by which Yale allowed him to get his degree after attending classes for only two and a half years.

Bush and his friends remember it all fondly, as representatives of the Fashionable Set: "[M]embers of [Bush's] class have since sighed with nostalgia for those days of the late 1940s. . . . Trolley cars still rumbled along the New Haven streets. On autumn afternoons they would be crowded with students going out to football games at the Yale Bowl, *scattering pennies along the way and shouting 'scramble' to the street kids diving for them"* [emphasis added].[3]

In 1947, Barbara gave birth to George W. Bush, the President's namesake.

By the time of his 1948 graduation, he had been elected to Phi Beta Kappa, an honor traditionally associated with academic achievement. A great deal is known about George Bush's career at Yale, except the part about books and studies. Unfortunately for those who would wish to consider his intellectual accomplishment, everything about *that* has been sealed shut and is top secret. The Yale administration says they have turned over to the FBI custody of all of Bush's academic records, allegedly because the FBI needs such access to check the resumés of important office holders.

From all available testimony, his mental life before college was anything but outstanding. His campaign literature claims that, as a veteran, Bush was "serious" at Yale. But we cannot check exactly how he achieved election to Phi Beta Kappa, in his abbreviated college experience. Without top secret clearance, we cannot consult his test results, read his essays, or learn much about his performance in class. We know that his father was a trustee of the university, in charge of "developmental" fundraising. And his family friends were in control of the U.S. secret services.

A great deal is known, however, about George Bush's *status* at Yale.

His fellow student John H. Chafee, later a U.S. Senator from Rhode Island and Secretary of the Navy, declared: "We didn't see much of him because he was married, but I guess my first impression

was that he was—and I don't mean this in a derogatory fashion—
in the inner set, the movers and shakers, the establishment. I don't
mean he put on airs or anything, but . . . just everybody knew him."

Chafee, like Bush, and Dan Quayle, was in the important national
fraternity, Delta Kappa Epsilon (DKE or the "Dekes"). But Chafee
says, "I never remember seeing him there. He wasn't one to hang
around with the fellows."[4]

The Tomb

George Bush, in fact, passed his most important days and nights
at Yale in the strange companionship of the senior-year Skull and
Bones Society.[5]

Out of those few who were chosen for Bones membership, George
was the last one to be notified of his selection—this honor is traditionally reserved for the highest of the high and mighty.

His father, Prescott Bush, several other relatives and partners,
and Roland and Averell Harriman, who sponsored the Bush family,
were also members of this secret society.

The undoubted political and financial power associated with
Skull and Bones has given rise to many popular questions about the
nature and origin of the group. Its members have fed the mystery
with false leads and silly speculations.

The order was incorporated in 1856 under the name "Russell
Trust Association." By special act of the state legislature in 1943,
its trustees are exempted from the normal requirement of filing
corporate reports with the Connecticut Secretary of State.

As of 1978, all business of the Russell Trust was handled by its
lone trustee, Brown Brothers Harriman partner John B. Madden,
Jr. Madden started with Brown Brothers Harriman in 1946, under
senior partner Prescott Bush, George Bush's father.

Each year, Skull and Bones members select ("tap") 15 third-year
Yale students to replace them in the senior group the following year.
Graduating members are given a sizeable cash bonus to help them
get started in life. Older graduate members, the so-called "Patriarchs," give special backing in business, politics, espionage and legal
careers to graduate Bonesmen who exhibit talent or usefulness.

The home of Skull and Bones on the Yale campus is a stone
building resembling a mausoleum, and known as "the Tomb." Initi-
ations take place on Deer Island in the St. Lawrence River (an island
owned by the Russell Trust Association), with regular reunions on
Deer Island and at Yale. Initiation rites reportedly include strenuous
and traumatic activities of the new member, while immersed naked

in mud, and in a coffin. More important is the "sexual autobiography": The initiate tells the Order all the sex secrets of his young life. Weakened mental defenses against manipulation, and the blackmail potential of such information, have obvious permanent uses in enforcing loyalty among members.

The loyalty is intense. One of Bush's former teachers, whose own father was a Skull and Bones member, told our interviewer that his father used to stab his little Skull and Bones pin into his skin to keep it in place when he took a bath.

Members continue throughout their lives to unburden themselves on their psycho-sexual thoughts to their Bones Brothers, even if they are no longer sitting in a coffin. This has been the case with President George Bush, for whom these ties are reported to have a deep personal meaning. Beyond the psychological manipulation associated with freemasonic mummery, there are very solid political reasons for Bush's strong identification with this cult.

Observers of Skull and Bones, apologists and critics alike, have accepted various deceptive notions about the order. There are two outstanding, among these falsehoods:

1) that it is essentially an *American* group, an assembly of wealthy, elite "patriots"; it is in fact, an agency for British Empire penetration and subversion of the American republic; and

2) that it is somehow *the* unique center of conspiratorial control over the United States. This misconception is certainly understandable, given the rather astonishing number of powerful, historically important and grotesquely anti-human individuals, who have come out of Skull and Bones. But there are in fact congruent organizations at other Ivy League colleges, which reflect, as does Skull and Bones, the over-arching oligarchical power of several heavily intermarried financier families.

The mistaken, speculative notions may be corrected by examining the history of Skull and Bones, viewed within the reality of the American Eastern Establishment.

Skull and Bones—the Russell Trust Association—was first established among the class graduating from Yale in 1833. Its founder was William Huntington Russell of Middletown, Connecticut. The Russell family was the master of incalculable wealth derived from the largest U.S. criminal organization of the nineteenth century: Russell and Company, the great opium syndicate.

There was at that time a deep suspicion of, and national revulsion against, freemasonry and secret organizations in the United States, fostered in particular by the anti-masonic writings of former U.S. President John Quincy Adams. Adams stressed that those who take oaths to politically powerful international secret societies cannot be depended on for loyalty to a democratic republic.

But the Russells were protected as part of the multiply-intermarried grouping of families then ruling Connecticut (see accompanying chart). The blood-proud members of the Russell, Pierpont, Edwards, Burr, Griswold, Day, Alsop and Hubbard families were prominent in the pro-British party within the state. Many of their sons would be among the members chosen for the Skull and Bones Society over the years.

The background to Skull and Bones is a story of Opium and Empire, and a bitter struggle for political control over the new U.S. republic.

Samuel Russell, second cousin to Bones founder William H., established Russell and Company in 1823. Its business was to acquire opium from Turkey and smuggle it into China, where it was strictly prohibited, under the armed protection of the British Empire.

The prior, predominant American gang in this field had been the syndicate created by Thomas Handasyd Perkins of Newburyport, Massachusetts, an aggregation of the self-styled "blue bloods" or Brahmins of Boston's north shore. Forced out of the lucrative African slave trade by U.S. law and Caribbean slave revolts, leaders of the Cabot, Lowell, Higginson, Forbes, Cushing and Sturgis families had married Perkins siblings and children. The Perkins opium syndicate made the fortune and established the power of these families. By the 1830s, the Russells had bought out the Perkins syndicate and made Connecticut the primary center of the U.S. opium racket. Massachusetts families (Coolidge, Sturgis, Forbes and Delano) joined Connecticut (Alsop) and New York (Low) smuggler-millionaires under the Russell auspices.*

John Quincy Adams and other patriots had fought these men for a quarter century by the time the Russell Trust Association was set up with its open pirate emblem—Skull and Bones.

With British ties of family, shipping and merchant banking, the old New England Tories had continued their hostility to American independence after the Revolutionary War of 1775–83. These pretended conservative patriots proclaimed Thomas Jefferson's 1801 presidential inauguration "radical usurpation."

The Massachusetts Tories ("Essex Junto") joined with Vice-President Aaron Burr, Jr. (a member of the Connecticut Edwards and Pierpont families) and Burr's cousin and law partner Theodore

---

*Certain of the prominent Boston opium families, such as Cabot and Weld, did not affiliate directly with Russell, Connecticut and Yale, but were identified instead with Harvard.

Dwight, in political moves designed to break up the United States and return it to British allegiance.

The U.S. nationalist leader, former Treasury Secretary Alexander Hamilton, exposed the plan in 1804. Burr shot him to death in a duel, then led a famous abortive conspiracy to form a new empire in the Southwest, with territory to be torn from the U.S.A. and Spanish Mexico. For the "blue bloods," the romantic figure of Aaron Burr was ever afterwards the symbol of British feudal revenge against the American republic.

The Connecticut Tory families hosted the infamous Hartford Convention in 1815, toward the end of the second war between the U.S. and Britain (the War of 1812). Their secessionist propaganda was rendered impotent by America's defensive military victory. This faction then retired from the open political arena, pursuing instead entirely private and covert alliances with the British Empire. The incestuously intermarried Massachusetts and Connecticut families associated themselves with the British East India Company in the criminal opium traffic into China. These families made increased profits as partners and surrogates for the British during the bloody 1839–42 Opium War, the race war of British forces against Chinese defenders.

Samuel and William Huntington Russell were quiet, wary builders of their faction's power. An intimate colleague of opium gangster Samuel Russell wrote this about him:

> While he lived no friend of his would venture to mention his name in print. While in China, he lived for about twenty-five years almost as a hermit, hardly known outside of his factory [the Canton warehouse compound] except by the chosen few who enjoyed his intimacy, and by his good friend, Hoqua [Chinese security director for the British East India Company], but studying commerce in its broadest sense, as well as its minutest details. Returning home with well-earned wealth he lived hospitably in the midst of his family, and a small circle of intimates. Scorning words and pretensions from the bottom of his heart, he was the truest and staunchest of friends; hating notoriety, he could always be absolutely counted on for every good work which did not involve publicity.

The Russells' Skull and Bones Society was the most important of their domestic projects "which did not involve publicity."

A police-blotter type review of Russell's organization will show why the secret order, though powerful, was not the unique organ of "conspiracy" for the U.S. Eastern Establishment. The following gentlemen were among Russells' partners:

• Augustine Heard (1785–1868): ship captain and pioneer U.S. opium smuggler.

• John Cleve Green (1800–75): married to Sarah Griswold; gave a fortune in opium profits to Princeton University, financing three Princeton buildings and four professorships; trustee of the Princeton Theological Seminary for 25 years.

• Abiel Abbott Low (1811–93): his opium fortune financed the construction of the Columbia University New York City campus; father of Columbia's president Seth Low.

• John Murray Forbes (1813–98): his opium millions financed the career of author Ralph Waldo Emerson, who married Forbes's daughter, and bankrolled the establishment of the Bell Telephone Company, whose first president was Forbes's son.

• Joseph Coolidge: his Augustine Heard agency got $10 million yearly as surrogates for the Scottish dope-runners Jardine Matheson during the fighting in China; his son organized the United Fruit Company; his grandson, Archibald Cary Coolidge, was the founding executive officer of the Anglo-Americans' Council on Foreign Relations.

• Warren Delano, Jr.: chief of Russell and Co. in Canton; grandfather of U.S. President Franklin Delano Roosevelt.

• Russell Sturgis: his grandson by the same name was chairman of the Baring Bank in England, financiers of the Far East opium trade.

Such persons as John C. Green and A.A. Low, whose names adorn various buildings at Princeton and Columbia Universities, made little attempt to hide the criminal origin of their influential money. Similarly with the Cabots, the Higginsons and the Welds for Harvard. The secret groups at other colleges are analogous and closely related to Yale's Skull and Bones.

Princeton has its "eating clubs," especially Ivy Club and Cottage Club, whose oligarchical tradition runs from Jonathan Edwards and Aaron Burr through the Dulles brothers. At Harvard there is the ultra-blue-blooded Porcelian (known also as the Porc or Pig club); Theodore Roosevelt bragged to the German Kaiser of his membership there; Franklin Roosevelt was a member of the slightly "lower" Fly Club.

A few of the early initiates in Skull and Bones went on to careers in obvious defiance of the order's oligarchical character; two such were the scientists Benjamin Silliman, Jr. (Skull and Bones 1837), and William Chauvenet (Skull and Bones 1840). This reflects the continued importance of republican factions at Yale, Harvard and other colleges during the middle three decades of the nineteenth century. Silliman and Chauvenet became enemies of everything Skull and Bones stood for, while the Yale secret group rapidly conformed to the Russells' expectations.

Yale was the northern college favored by southern slaveowning would-be aristocrats. Among Yale's southern students were John C. Calhoun, later the famous South Carolina defender of slavery against nationalism, and Judah P. Benjamin, later Secretary of State for the slaveowners' Confederacy.

Young South Carolinian Joseph Heatly Dulles, whose family bought their slaves with the money from contract-security work for the British conquerors in India, was in a previous secret Yale group, the "Society of Brothers in Unity." At Yale Dulles worked with the Northern secessionists and attached himself to Daniel Lord; their two families clove together in the fashion of a gang. The Lords became powerful Anglo-American Wall Street lawyers, and J.H. Dulles's grandson was the father of Allen Dulles and John Foster Dulles.

In 1832–33 Skull and Bones was launched under the Russell pirate flag.

Among the early initiates of the order were Henry Rootes Jackson (S&B 1839), a leader of the 1861 **Georgia** Secession Convention and post-Civil War president of the Georgia Historical Society (thus the false accounts of the "good old slavery days" and the "bad northern invaders"); John Perkins, Jr. (S&B 1840), chairman of the 1861 **Louisiana** Secession Convention, who fled abroad for 13 years after the Civil War; and William Taylor Sullivan Barry (S&B 1841), a national leader of the secessionist wing of the Democratic Party during the 1850s, and chairman of the 1861 **Mississippi** Secession Convention.

Alphonso Taft was a Bonesman alongside William H. Russell in the Class of 1833. As U.S. Attorney General in 1876–77, Alphonso Taft helped organize the backroom settlement of the deadlocked 1876 presidential election. The bargain gave Rutherford B. Hayes the presidency (1877–81) and withdrew the U.S. troops from the South, where they had been enforcing blacks' rights.

Alphonso's son, William Howard Taft (S&B 1878), was U.S. President from 1909 to 1913. President Taft's son, Robert Alphonso Taft (S&B 1910), was a leading U.S. Senator after World War II; his family's Anglo-Saxon racial/ancestral preoccupation was the disease which crippled Robert Taft's leadership of American nationalist "conservatives."

Other pre-Civil War Bonesmen were:
• William M. Evarts (S&B 1837): Wall Street attorney for British and southern slaveowner projects, collaborator of Taft in the 1876 bargain, U.S. Secretary of State 1877–81;
• Morris R. Waite (S&B 1837): Chief Justice of the U.S. Supreme Court 1874–88, whose rulings destroyed many rights of African-Americans gained in the Civil War; he helped his cohorts Taft and Evarts arrange the 1876 presidential settlement scheme to pull the rights-enforcing U.S. troops out of the South;
• Daniel Coit Gilman (S&B 1852): co-incorporator of the Russell Trust; founding president of Johns Hopkins University as a great center for the racialist eugenics movement;
• Andrew D. White (S&B 1853): founding president of Cornell University; psychic researcher; and diplomatic cohort of the Venetian, Russian and British oligarchies;
• Chauncey M. Depew (S&B 1856): general counsel for the Vanderbilt railroads, he helped the Harriman family to enter into high society.

By about the mid-1880s, the Skull and Bones membership roster began to change from its earlier, often "scholarly," coloration; the change reflected the degradation of American political and economic life by imperialist, neo-pagan and racialist ideology.

Irving Fisher (S&B 1888) became the racialist high priest of the economics faculty (Yale professor 1896–1946), and a famous merchant of British Empire propaganda for free trade and reduction of the non-white population. Fisher was founding president of the American Eugenics Society under the financial largesse of Averell Harriman's mother.

Gifford Pinchot (S&B 1889) invented the aristocrats' "conservation" movement. He was President Theodore Roosevelt's chief forester, substituting federal land-control in place of Abraham Lincoln's free-land-to-families farm creation program. Pinchot's British Empire activism included the Psychical Research Society and his vice-presidency of the first International Eugenics Congress in 1912.

Helping Pinchot initiate this century's racialist environmentalism were his cohorts George W. Woodruff (S&B 1889), Teddy Roosevelt's Assistant Attorney General and Acting Interior Secretary; and Henry Solon Graves (S&B 1892), chief U.S. forester 1910–20. Frederick E. Weyerhauser (S&B 1896), owner of vast tracts of American forest, was a follower of Pinchot's movement, while the

Weyerhauser family were active collaborators of British-South African super-racist Cecil Rhodes. This family's friendship with President George Bush is a vital factor in the present environmentalist movement.

With **Henry L. Stimson** (S&B 1888) we come to the Eastern Liberal Establishment which has ruled America during the twentieth century. Stimson was President Taft's Secretary of War (1911–13), and President Herbert Hoover's Secretary of State (1929–33). As Secretary of War (1940–45), this time under President Harry Truman, Stimson pressed Truman to drop the atomic bomb on the Japanese. This decision involved much more than merely "pragmatic" military considerations. These Anglophiles, up through George Bush, have opposed the American republic's tradition of alliance with national aspirations in Asia; and they worried that the invention of nuclear energy would too powerfully unsettle the world's toleration for poverty and misery. Both the U.S. and the Atom had better be dreaded, they thought.

The present century owes much of its record of horrors to the influential Anglophile American families which came to dominate and employ the Skull and Bones Society as a political recruiting agency, particularly the Harrimans, Whitneys, Vanderbilts, Rockefellers and their lawyers, the Lords and Tafts and Bundys.

The politically aggressive Guaranty Trust Company, run almost entirely by Skull and Bones initiates, was a financial vehicle of these families in the early 1900s. Guaranty Trust's support for the Bolshevik and Nazi revolutions overlapped the more intense endeavors in these fields by the Harrimans, George Walker and Prescott Bush a few blocks away, and in Berlin.

Skull and Bones was dominated from 1913 onward by the circles of Averell Harriman. They displaced remaining traditionalists such as Douglas MacArthur from power in the United States.

For George Bush, the Skull and Bones Society is more than simply the British, as opposed to the American, strategic tradition. It is merged in the family and personal network within which his whole life has been, in a sense, handed to him prepackaged.

Britain's Yale Flying Unit

During Prescott Bush's student days, the Harriman set at Yale decided that World War I was sufficiently amusing that they ought to get into it as recreation. They formed a special Yale Unit of the Naval Reserve Flying Corps, at the instigation of **F. Trubee Davison.** Since the United States was not at war, and the Yale students were going to serve Britain, the Yale Unit was privately and lavishly financed by F. Trubee's father, Henry Davison, the senior managing partner at J.P. Morgan and Co. At that time, the Morgan bank was the official financial agency for the British government in the United States. The Yale Unit's leader was amateur pilot Robert A. Lovett. They were based first on Long Island, New York, then in Palm Beach, Florida.

The Yale Unit has been described by Lovett's family and friends in a collective biography of the Harriman set:

> Training for the Yale Flying Unit was not exactly boot camp. Davison's father . . . helped finance them royally, and newspapers of the day dubbed them "the millionaires' unit." They cut rakish figures, and knew it; though some dismissed them as dilettantes, the hearts of young Long Island belles fluttered at the sight. . . .
>
> [In] Palm Beach . . . they ostentatiously pursued a relaxed style. "They were rolled about in wheel chairs by African slaves amid tropical gardens and coconut palms," wrote the unit's historian. . . . "For light exercise, they learned to glance at their new wristwatches with an air of easy nonchalance". . . . [Lovett] was made chief of the unit's private club, the Wags, whose members started their sentences, "Being a Wag and therefore a superman". . . .
>
> Despite the snide comments of those who dismissed them as frivolous rich boys, Lovett's unit proved to be daring and imaginative warriors when they were dispatched for active duty in 1917 with Britain's Royal Naval Air Service.[6]

Lovett was transferred to the U.S. Navy after the U.S. joined Britain in World War I.

The Yale Flying Unit was the glory of Skull and Bones. Roland Harriman, Prescott Bush and their 1917 Bonesmates selected for 1918 membership in the secret order these Yale Flying Unit leaders: **Robert Lovett, F. Trubee Davison, Artemus Lamb Gates, and John Martin Vorys.** Unit flyers **David Sinton Ingalls** and F. Trubee's brother, **Harry P. Davison** (who became Morgan vice chairman), were tapped for the 1920 Skull and Bones.

Lovett did not actually have a senior year at Yale: "He was tapped for Skull and Bones not on the Old Campus but at a naval station in West Palm Beach; his initiation, instead of being conducted in the 'tomb' on High Street, occurred at the headquarters of the Navy's Northern Bombing Group between Dunkirk and Calais."[7]

Some years later, Averell Harriman gathered Lovett, Prescott Bush and other pets into the utopian oligarchs' community a few miles to the north of Palm Beach, called Jupiter Island (see Chapter 4).

British Empire loyalists flew right from the Yale Unit into U.S. strategymaking positions:

• F. Trubee Davison was Assistant U.S. Secretary of War for Air from 1926 to 1933. David S. Ingalls (on the board of Jupiter Island's Pan American Airways) was meanwhile Assistant Secretary of the Navy for Aviation (1929–32). Following the American Museum of Natural History's Hitlerite 1932 eugenics congress, Davison resigned his government Air post to become the Museum's president. Then, under the Harriman-Lovett national security regime of the early 1950s, F. Trubee Davison became Director of Personnel for the new Central Intelligence Agency.

• Robert Lovett was Assistant Secretary of War for Air from 1941–45.

• Lovett's 1918 Bonesmate Artemus Gates (chosen by Prescott and his fellows) became Assistant Secretary of the Navy for Air in 1941. Gates retained this post throughout the Second World War until 1945. Having a man like Gates up there, who owed his position to Averell, Bob, Prescott and their set, was quite reassuring to young naval aviator George Bush; especially so, when Bush would have to worry about the record being correct concerning his controversial fatal crash.

Other Important Bonesmen
• **Richard M. Bissell, Jr.** was a very important man to the denizens of Jupiter Island.

He graduated from Yale in 1932, the year after the Harrimanites bought the island. Though not in Skull and Bones, Bissell was the younger brother of William Truesdale Bissell, a Bonesman from the class of 1925. Their father, Connecticut insurance executive Richard M. Bissell, Sr., had put the U.S. insurance industry's inside knowledge of all fire-insured industrial plants at the disposal of government planners during World War I.

The senior Bissell, a powerful Yale alumnus, was also the director of the Neuro-Psychiatric Institute of the Hartford Retreat for the Insane; there, in 1904, Yale graduate Clifford Beers underwent mind-destroying treatment which led this mental patient to found the Mental Hygiene Society, a major Yale-based Skull and Bones project. This would evolve into the CIA's cultural engineering effort of the 1950s, the drugs and brainwashing adventure known as "MK-Ultra."

Richard M. Bissell, Jr. studied at the London School of Economics in 1932 and 1933, and taught at Yale from 1935 to 1941. He then joined Harriman's entourage in the U.S. government. Bissell was an economist for the Combined Shipping Adjustment Board in 1942–43, while Averell Harriman was the U.S. leader of that board in London.

In 1947 and 1948, Bissell was executive secretary of the "Harriman Commission," otherwise known as the President's Commission on Foreign Aid. When Harriman was the administrator of the Marshall Plan, Bissell was assistant administrator.

Harriman was director of Mutual Security (1951–53), while Bissell was consultant to the director of Mutual Security 1952.

Bissell then joined F. Trubee Davison at the Central Intelligence Agency. When Allen Dulles became CIA Director, Bissell was one of his three aides.

Why could this be of interest to our Floridians? We saw in Chapter 4, that the great anti-Castro covert initiative of 1959–61 was supervised by an awesome array of Harriman agents. We need now add to that assessment only the fact that the detailed management of the invasion of Cuba, and of the assassination planning, and the training of the squads for these jobs, was given into the hands of Richard M. Bissell, Jr.

This 1961 invasion failed. Fidel Castro survived the widely-discussed assassination plots against him. But the initiative succeeded in what was probably its core purpose: to organize a force of multiuse professional assassins.

The Florida-trained killers stayed in business under the leadership of Ted Shackley. They were all around the assassination of President Kennedy in 1963. They kept going with the Operation Phoenix mass murder of Vietnamese civilians, with Middle East drug and terrorist programs, and with George Bush's Contra wars in Central America.

• **Harvey Hollister Bundy** (S&B 1909) was Henry L. Stimson's Assistant Secretary of State (1931–33); then he was Stimson's Special Assistant Secretary of War, alongside Assistant Secretary Robert Lovett of Skull and Bones and Brown Brothers Harriman.

Harvey's son **William P. Bundy** (S&B 1939) was a CIA officer from 1951 to 1961; as a 1960s defense official, he pushed the Harriman-Dulles scheme for a Vietnam war. Harvey's other son, **McGeorge Bundy** (S&B 1940), co-authored Stimson's memoirs in 1948. As President John Kennedy's Director of National Security, McGeorge Bundy organized the whitewash of the Kennedy assassination, and immediately switched the U.S. policy away from the Kennedy pullout and back toward war in Vietnam.

• There was also **Henry Luce,** a Bonesman of 1920 with David S.

Ingalls and Harry Pomeroy. Luce published *Time* magazine, where his ironically-named "American Century" blustering was straight British Empire doctrine: Bury the republics, hail the Anglo-Saxon conquerors.

• **William Sloane Coffin,** tapped for 1949 Skull and Bones by George Bush and his Bone companions, was from a long line of Skull and Bones Coffins. William Sloane Coffin was famous in the Vietnam War protest days as a leader of the left protest against the war. Was the fact that he was an agent of the Central Intelligence Agency embarrassing to William Sloane?

This was no contradiction. His uncle, the Reverend Henry Sloane Coffin (S&B 1897), had also been a "peace" agitator, and an oligarchical agent. Uncle Henry was for 20 years president of the Union Theological Seminary, whose board chairman was Prescott Bush's partner Thatcher Brown. In 1937, Henry Coffin and John Foster Dulles led the U.S. delegation to England to found the **World Council of Churches,** as a "peace movement" guided by the pro-Hitler faction in England.

The Coffins have been mainstays of the liberal death lobby, for euthanasia and eugenics. The Coffins outlasted Hitler, arriving into the CIA in the 1950s.

• **Amory Howe Bradford** (S&B 1934) married Carol Warburg Rothschild in 1941. Carol's mother, Carola, was the acknowledged head of the Warburg family in America after World War II. This family had assisted the Harrimans' rise in the world in the nineteenth and early twentieth centuries; in concert with the Sulzbergers at the *New York Times*, they had used their American Jewish Committee and B'nai B'rith to protect the Harriman-Bush deals with Hitler.

This made it nice for Averell Harriman, just like family, when Amory Howe Bradford worked on the Planning Group of Harriman's NATO secretariat in London, 1951–52. Bradford was meanwhile assistant to the publisher of the *New York Times*, and went on to become general manager of the *Times*.

Other modern Bonesmen have been closely tied to George Bush's career.

• **George Herbert Walker, Jr.** (S&B 1927) was the President's uncle and financial angel. In the 1970s he sold G.H. Walker & Co. to White, Weld & Co. and became a director of White, Weld; company heir William Weld, the original federal prosecutor of Lyndon LaRouche and current Massachusetts governor, is an active Bush Republican.

• Publisher **William F. Buckley** (S&B 1950) had a family oil business in Mexico. There Buckley was a close ally to CIA covert operations manager E. Howard Hunt, whose lethal antics were performed under the eyes of Miami Station and Jupiter Island.

• **David Lyle Boren** (S&B 1963) was assistant to the director of the Office of Civil and Defense Mobilization, and a propaganda analyst for the U.S. Information Agency, before graduating from Yale. Thus while he was imbibing the British view at Oxford University (1963–65), Boren was already an Anglo-American intelligence operative, listed in the "speakers bureau" of the American embassy in London. David Boren was elected to the U.S. Senate in 1979 and became chairman of the Senate Intelligence Committee.

Though a Democrat (who spoke knowingly of the "parallel government" operating in Iran-Contra), Boren's Intelligence Committee rulings have been (not unexpectedly) more and more favorable to his "Patriarch" in the White House.

Bush's Own Bones

Among the traditional artifacts collected and maintained within the High Street Tomb are human remains of various derivations. The following concerns one such set of Skull and Bones.

Geronimo, an Apache faction leader and warrior, led a party of warriors on a raid in 1876, after Apaches were moved to the San Carlos Reservation in Arizona territory. He led other raids against U.S. and Mexican forces well into the 1880s; he was captured and escaped many times.

Geronimo was finally interned at Fort Sill, Oklahoma. He became a farmer and joined a Christian congregation. He died at the age of 79 years in 1909, and was buried at Fort Sill. Three-quarters of a century later, his tribesmen raised the question of getting their famous warrior reinterred back in Arizona.

Ned Anderson was Tribal Chairman of the San Carlos Apache Tribe from 1978 to 1986. This is the story he tells[8]:

Around the fall of 1983, the leader of an Apache group in another section of Arizona said he was interested in having the remains of Geronimo returned to his tribe's custody. Taking up this idea, Anderson said that the remains properly belonged to his group as much as to the other Apaches. After much discussion, several Apache groups met at a kind of summit meeting held at Fort Sill, Oklahoma. The army authorities were not favorable to the meeting, and it only occurred through the intervention of the office of the Governor of Oklahoma.

As a result of this meeting, Ned Anderson was written up in the newspapers as an articulate Apache activist. Soon afterwards, in late 1983 or early 1984, a Skull and Bones member contacted Anderson and leaked evidence that Geronimo's remains had long ago been pilfered—by Prescott Bush, George's father. The informant said that in May of 1918, Prescott Bush and five other officers at Fort Sill desecrated the grave of Geronimo. They took turns watching while they robbed the grave, taking items including a skull, some other bones, a horse bit and straps. These prizes were taken back to the Tomb, the home of the Skull and Bones Society at Yale in New Haven, Connecticut. They were put into a display case, which members and visitors could easily view upon entry to the building.

The informant provided Anderson with photographs of the stolen remains, and a copy of a Skull and Bones log book in which the 1918 grave robbery had been recorded. The informant said that Skull and Bones members used the pilfered remains in performing some of their Thursday and Sunday night rituals, with Geronimo's skull sitting out on a table in front of them.

Outraged, Anderson traveled to New Haven. He did some investigation on the Yale campus and held numerous discussions, to learn what the Apaches would be up against when they took action, and what type of action would be most fruitful.

Through an attorney, Ned Anderson asked the FBI to move into the case. The attorney conveyed to him the Bureau's response: If he would turn over every scrap of evidence to the FBI, and completely remove himself from the case, they would get involved. He rejected this bargain, since it did not seem likely to lead toward recovery of Geronimo's remains.

Due to his persistence, he was able to arrange a September 1986 Manhattan meeting with Jonathan Bush, George Bush's brother. Jonathan Bush vaguely assured Anderson that he would get what he had come after, and set a followup meeting for the next day. But Bush stalled—Anderson believes this was to gain time to hide and secure the stolen remains against any possible rescue action.

The Skull and Bones attorney representing the Bush family and managing the case was Endicott Peabody Davison. His father was the F. Trubee Davison mentioned above, who had been president of New York's American Museum of Natural History, and personnel director for the Central Intelligence Agency. The general attitude of this Museum crowd has long been that "Natives" should be stuffed and mounted for display to the Fashionable Set.

Finally, after about 11 days, another meeting occurred. A display case was produced, which did in fact match the one in the photograph the informant had given to Ned Anderson. But the skull he was shown was that of a ten-year-old child, and Anderson refused to receive it or to sign a legal document promising to shut up about the matter.

Anderson took his complaint to Arizona Congressmen Morris Udahl and John McCain III, but with no results. George Bush refused Congressman McCain's request that he meet with Anderson.

Anderson wrote to Udahl, enclosing a photograph of the wall case and skull at the "Tomb," showing a black and white photograph of the living Geronimo, which members of the Order had boastfully posted next to their display of his skull. Anderson quoted from a Skull and Bones Society internal history, entitled *Continuation of the History of Our Order for the Century Celebration, 17 June 1933, by The Little Devil of D'121.*

> From the war days [W.W. I] also sprang the mad expedition from the School of Fire at Fort Sill, Oklahoma, that brought to the T[omb] its most spectacular "crook," the skull of Geronimo the terrible, the Indian Chief who had taken forty-nine white scalps. An expedition in late May, 1918, by members of four Clubs [i.e. four graduating-class years of the Society], Xit D.114, Barebones, Caliban and Dingbat, D.115, S'Mike D.116, and Hellbender D.117, planned with great caution since in the words of one of them: "Six army captains robbing a grave wouldn't look good in the papers." The stirring climax was recorded by Hellbender in the Black Book of D.117: ". . . The ring of pick on stone and thud of earth on earth alone disturbs the peace of the prairie. An axe pried open the iron door of the tomb, and Pat[riarch] Bush entered and started to dig. We dug in turn, each on relief taking a turn on the road as guards. . . . Finally Pat[riarch] Ellery James turned up a bridle, soon a saddle horn and rotten leathers followed, then wood and then, at the exact bottom of the small round hole, Pat[riarch] James dug deep and pried out the trophy itself. . . . We quickly closed the grave, shut the door and sped home to Pat[riarch] Mallon's room, where we cleaned the Bones. Pat[riarch] Mallon sat on the floor liberally applying carbolic acid. The Skull was fairly clean, having only some flesh inside and a little hair. I showered and hit the hay . . . a happy man. . . ."[9]

The other grave robber whose name is given, Ellery James, we encountered in Chapter 1—he was to be an usher at Prescott's wedding three years later. And the fellow who applied acid to the stolen skull, burning off the flesh and hair, was **Neil Mallon.** Years later, Prescott Bush and his partners chose Mallon as chairman of Dresser Industries; Mallon hired Prescott's son, George Bush, for George's first job; and George Bush named his son, **Neil Mallon Bush,** after the flesh-picker.

In 1988, the *Washington Post* ran an article, originating from the Establishment-line *Arizona Republic*, entitled "Skull for Scandal: Did Bush's Father Rob Geronimo's Grave?" The article included a small quote from the 1933 Skull and Bones *History of Our Order*: "An axe pried open the iron door of the tomb, and . . . Bush entered and started to dig. . . ." and so forth, but neglected to include other names beside Bush.

According to the *Washington Post*, the document which Bush attorney Endicott Davison tried to get the Apache leader to sign, stipulated that Ned Anderson agreed it would be "inappropriate for you, me [Jonathan Bush] or anyone in association with us to make or permit any publication in connection with this transaction." Anderson called the document "very insulting to Indians." Davison claimed later that the Order's own history book is a hoax, but during the negotiations with Anderson, Bush's attorney demanded Anderson give up his copy of the book.[10]

Bush crony Fitzhugh Green gives the view of the President's backers on this affair, and conveys the arrogant racial attitude typical of Skull and Bones:

> Prescott Bush had a colorful side. In 1988 the press revealed the complaint of an Apache leader about Bush. This was Ned Anderson of San Carlos, Oklahoma [sic], who charged that as a young army officer Bush stole the skull of Indian Chief [sic] Geronimo and had it hung on the wall of Yale's Skull and Bones Club. After exposure of "true facts" by Anderson, and consideration by some representatives in Congress, the issue faded from public sight. Whether or not this alleged skullduggery actually occurred, *the mere idea casts the senior Bush in an adventurous light*[11][emphasis added].

George Bush's crowning as a Bonesman was intensely, personally important to him. These men were tapped for the Class of 1948:

Thomas William Ludlow Ashley
Lucius Horatio Biglow, Jr.
George Herbert Walker Bush
John Erwin Caulkins
William Judkins Clark
William James Connelly, Jr.
George Cook III
David Charles Grimes
Richard Elwood Jenkins
Richard Gerstle Mack
Thomas Wilder Moseley

George Harold Pfau, Jr.
Samuel Sloane Walker, Jr.
Howard Sayre Weaver
Valleau Wilkie, Jr.

Survivors of this 1948 Bones group were interviewed for a 1988 *Washington Post* campaign profile of George Bush. The members described their continuing intimacy with and financial support for Bush up through his 1980s vice-presidency. Their original sexual togetherness at Yale is stressed:

> The relationships that were formed in the "Tomb" . . . where the Society's meetings took place each Thursday and Sunday night during the academic year, have had a strong place in Bush's life, according to all 11 of his fellow Bonesmen who are still alive.
>
> Several described in detail the ritual in the organization that builds the bonds. Before giving his life history, each member had to spend a Sunday night reviewing his sex life in a talk known in the Tomb as CB, or "connubial bliss". . . .
>
> "The first time you review your sex life. . . . We went all the way around among the 15," said Lucius H. Biglow Jr., a retired Seattle attorney. "That way you get everybody committed to a certain extent. . . . It was a gradual way of building confidence."
>
> The sexual histories helped break down the normal defenses of the members, according to several of the members from his class. William J. Connelly, Jr. . . . said, "In Skull and Bones we all stand together, 15 brothers under the skin. [It is] the greatest allegiance in the world."[12]

Here is our future U.S. President with the other wealthy, amoral young men, excited about their future unlimited power over the ignorant common people, sharing their sex secrets in a mausoleum surrounded by human remains. The excited young men are entirely directed by the "Patriarchs," the cynical alumni financiers who are the legal owners of the Order.

The Yale Tories Who Made Skull and Bones

The accompanying chart depicts family relationships which were vital to the persons appearing on the chart. At less exalted levels of society, one is supposed to be praised or blamed only according to one's own actions. But in these Yale circles, "family"—genealogy— is an overwhelming consideration when evaluating individuals. Thus what we present here is more than simply a system of associations. It is a tradition which has operated powerfully on the emotions and

The Yale Tories Who Made Skull and Bones

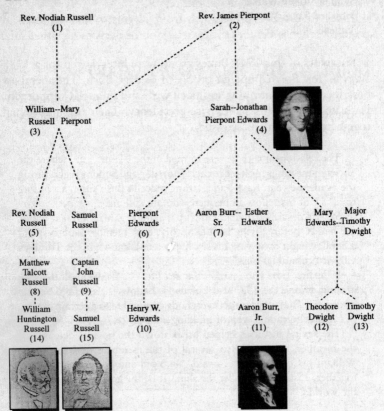

Rev. Nodiah Russell
(1)

Rev. James Pierpont
(2)

William--Mary
Russell Pierpont
(3)

Sarah--Jonathan
Pierpont Edwards
(4)

Rev. Nodiah
Russell
(5)

Samuel
Russell

Pierpont
Edwards
(6)

Aaron Burr-- Esther
Sr.   Edwards
(7)

Mary Major
Edwards--Timothy
        Dwight

Matthew
Talcott
Russell
(8)

Captain
John
Russell
(9)

William
Huntington
Russell
(14)

Samuel
Russell
(15)

Henry W.
Edwards
(10)

Aaron Burr,
Jr.
(11)

Theodore Timothy
Dwight   Dwight
(12)   (13)

judgment of the leaders of Yale University; they have merged their own identities into this tradition.

Lines are directed downwards from parents to their children. A double hyphen—signifies the marriage of the persons on either side.

GUIDE TO THE YALE FAMILY CHART

1) Rev. Nodiah Russell: One of 10 or 12 men who founded Yale University in 1701. Yale Trustee 1701–13. Pastor, First Congregational Church, Middletown, Ct. ca. 1691–1716.

2) Rev. James Pierpont: Most celebrated of the Yale founders. Yale Trustee, 1701–14.

3) William Russell: Yale Trustee 1745–61. Pastor, First Congregational Church, Middletown, Ct. 1716–61.

4) Jonathan Edwards: Graduated Yale 1720. Ultra-Calvinist theologian, president of Princeton University (called then "College of New Jersey").

5) Rev. Nodiah Russell: Graduated Yale 1750.

6) Pierpont Edwards (1750–1826): Made Master of Connecticut Masons by the British Army occupying New York in 1783; he administered the estate of the traitor Benedict Arnold.

7) Aaron Burr, Sr.: Graduated yale 1735. President of Princeton University ("College of New Jersey").

8) Matthew Talcott Russell: Graduated Yale 1769. Deacon of First Congregational Church, Middletown, Ct. for 30 years. Lawyer for the Middletown Russell family. Died ca. 1817.

9) Captain John Russell. Died 1801 or 1802.

10) Henry W. Edwards: Governor of Connecticut 1833, 1835–38. Protector of Samuel Russell's opium-financed enterprises, patron of William Huntington Russell's new secret society, Skull and Bones.

11) Aaron Burr, Jr.: U.S. Vice President 1801–05. Killed Alexander Hamilton in a duel in 1804. Secession conspirator. Acquitted of treason in 1807, but wanted for murder, he fled to England. Returned to U.S.A. in 1812. Wall Street lawyer, 1812–36. Hero of imperial Anglo-Americans.

12) Theodore Dwight (1764–1846): Law partner of his cousin Aaron Burr, Jr. Secretary of the secessionist Hartford Convention, 1815. He united the Connecticut pro-British party with Massachusetts "Essex Junto."

13) Timothy Dwight: Secessionist. President of Yale, 1795–1817.

14) William Huntington Russell (1809–85): Graduated Yale 1833. Founder of Skull and Bones Society (or Russell Trust Association), which came to dominate Yale. Founded prep school for boys,

1836. His secret organization spread in the 1870s to Phillips Academy, the Andover, Massachusetts prep school.

15) Samuel Russell: Born in 1789 in the main ancestral house of the Russell family of Middletown. This house had been owned by the co-founder of Yale, Nodiah Russell (1), and by William Russell (3) and his wife Mary, sister-in-law to Jonathan Edwards.

He became head of the Middletown Russells. He established Russell and Co. in 1823, which by the 1830s superseded Perkins syndicate as largest American opium smuggling organization. His partners included leading Boston families.

He founded the Russell Manufacturing Company, Middletown, in 1837; he was president of Middlesex County Bank. During the formative years of Skull and Bones, the fabulously wealthy Samuel Russell was undisputed king of Middletown.

Note to Reader:
For the sake of clarity, we have omitted from this chart the ancestral line from Rev. James Pierpont (2) to his great grandson Rev. John Pierpont.

Rev. John Pierpont wrote poetry for the pro-British secessionists; he denounced President Thomas Jefferson for saying that Pierpont's New England relatives were "under the influence of the whore of England." Rev. John was an employee of Aaron Burr's family during Burr's western conspiracy. Rev. John's daughter Juliet married Connecticut-born British banker Junius Morgan and gave birth to U.S. financial kingpin **John Pierpont Morgan,** named for his grandfather Rev. John.

Notes for Chapter VII

1. Speech at Lewistown, Illinois, August 17, 1858; quoted in James Mellon (editor), *The Face of Lincoln* (New York: Viking Press, 1979), p. 35.

2. Fitzhugh Green, *George Bush: An Intimate Portrait* (New York: Hippocrene Books, 1989), p. 41.

3. Nicholas King, *George Bush: A Biography* (New York: Dodd, Mead & Company, 1980), p. 38.

4. Green, *op. cit.,* p. 48.

5. Among the sources used for this section are:

Skull and Bones membership list, 1833–1950, printed 1949 by the Russell Trust Association, New Haven, Connecticut, available through the Yale University Library, New Haven.

Biographies of the Russells and related families, in the Yale University Library, New Haven, and in the Russell Library, Middletown, Connecticut.

Ron Chernow, *The House of Morgan: An American Banking Dynasty and the Rise of Modern Finance* (New York: Atlantic Monthly Press, 1990).

Anthony C. Sutton, *How the Order Creates War and Revolution,* (Phoenix: Research Publications, Inc., 1984).

Anthony C. Sutton, *America's Secret Establishment: An Introduction to the Order of Skull and Bones,* (Billings, Mt.: Liberty House Press, 1986).

Anton Chaitkin, *Treason in America: From Aaron Burr to Averell Harriman,* second edition (New York: New Benjamin Franklin House, 1985).

Anton Chaitkin, "Station Identification: Morgan, Hitler, NBC," *New Solidarity*, Oct. 8, 1984.

Interviews with Bones members and their families.

6. Walter Isaacson and Evan Thomas, *The Wise Men: Six Friends and the World They Made—Acheson, Bohlen, Harriman, Kennan, Lovett, McCloy* (New York: Simon and Schuster, 1986), pp. 90–91.

7. *Ibid.,* p. 93.

8. Interview with Ned Anderson, Nov. 6, 1991.

9. Quoted in Ned Anderson to Anton Chaitkin, Dec. 2, 1991, in possession of the authors.

10. Article by Paul Brinkley-Rogers of the *Arizona Republic,* in the *Washington Post,* Oct. 1, 1988.

11. Green, *op. cit.,* p. 50.

12. Bob Woodward and Walter Pincus, "Bush Opened Up To Secret Yale Society," *Washington Post,* Aug. 7, 1988.

VIII

THE PERMIAN BASIN GANG, 1948–59

*Pecunia non olet.**
—Vespasian

During the years following the Second World War, the patrician families of the Eastern Anglophile Liberal Establishment sent numbers of their offspring to colonize those geographic regions of the United States which, the families estimated, were likely to prosper in the postwar period. On the surface, this appears as a simple reflex of greed: Cadet sons were dispatched to those areas of the provinces where their instinctive methods of speculation and usury could be employed to parasitize emerging wealth. More fundamentally, this migration of young patrician bankers answered the necessity of political control.

The Eastern Establishment, understood as an agglomeration of financier factions headquartered in Wall Street, had been the dominant force in American politics since J.P. Morgan had bailed out the Grover Cleveland regime in the 1890s. Since the assassination of William McKinley and the advent of Theodore Roosevelt, the power of the Wall Street group had grown continuously. The Eastern Establishment may have had its earliest roots north of Boston and in the Connecticut River Valley, but it was determined to be, not a mere regional financier faction, but the undisputed ruling elite of the United States as a whole, from Boston to Bohemian Grove and from Palm Beach to the Pacific Northwest. It was thus imperative

*Money has no smell.

that the constant tendency toward the formation of regional factions be preempted by the pervasive presence of men bound by blood loyalty to the dominant cliques of Washington, New York, and the "mother country," the City of London.

If the Eastern Liberal Establishment were thought of as a cancer, then after 1945 that cancer went into a new phase of malignant metastasis, infecting every part of the American body politic. George Bush was one of those motile, malignant cells. He was not alone; Robert Mosbacher also made the journey from New York to Texas, in Mosbacher's case, directly to Houston.

The various sycophant mythographers who have spun their yarns about the life of George Bush have always attempted to present this phase of Bush's life as the case of a fiercely independent young man who could have gone straight to the top in Wall Street by trading on father Prescott's name and connections, but who chose instead to strike out for the new frontier among the wildcatters and rough-necks of the west Texas oil fields and become a self-made man.

As George Bush himself recounted in a 1983 interview, "If I were a psychoanalyzer, I might conclude that I was trying to, not compete with my father, but do something on my own. My stay in Texas was no Horatio Alger thing, but moving from New Haven to Odessa just about the day I graduated was quite a shift in lifestyle."[1]

These fairy tales from the "red Studebaker" school seek to obscure the facts: that Bush's transfer to Texas was arranged from the top by Prescott's Brown Brothers Harriman cronies, and that every step forward made by Bush in the oil business was assisted by the capital resources of our hero's maternal uncle, George Herbert Walker, Jr., "Uncle Herbie," the boss of G.H. Walker & Co. investment firm of Wall Street. Uncle Herbie had graduated from Yale in 1927, where he had been a member of Skull and Bones. This is the Uncle Herbie who will show up as lead investor and member of the board of Bush-Overbey oil, of Zapata Petroleum, and of Zapata Offshore after 1959. If we assume that the Bush-Walker clan as an extended oligarchical family decided to send cadet son George Bush into the Texas and Oklahoma oilfields, we will not be far wrong.

Father Prescott procured George not one job, but two, in each case contacting cronies who depended at least partially on Brown Brothers Harriman for business.

One crony contacted by father Prescott was **Ray Kravis,** who was in the oil business in Tulsa, Oklahoma. Oklahoma had experienced a colossal oil boom between the two world wars, and Ray Kravis had cashed in, building up a personal fortune of some $25 million. Ray was the son of a British tailor whose father had come to America and set up a haberdashery in Atlantic City, New Jersey. Young Ray Kravis had arrived in Tulsa in 1925, in the midst of the oil boom that was making the colossal fortunes of men like J. Paul Getty. Ray Kravis was primarily a tax accountant, and he had invented a very special tax shelter which allowed oil properties to be "packaged" and sold in such a way as to reduce the tax on profits earned from the normal oil property rate of 81 percent to a mere 15 percent. This meant that the national tax base was eroded, and each individual taxpayer bilked, in order to subsidize the formation of immense private fortunes; this will be found to be a constant theme among George Bush's business associates down to the present day.

Ray Kravis's dexterity in setting up these tax shelters attracted the attention of Joseph P. Kennedy, the buccaneering bootlegger, entrepreneur, political boss and patriarch of the Massachusetts Kennedy clan. For many years Ray Kravis functioned as the manager of the Kennedy family fortune (or fondo), the same job that later devolved to Stephen Smith. Ray Kravis and Joe Kennedy both wintered in Palm Beach, where they were sometimes golf partners.[2]

In 1948–49, father Prescott was the managing partner of Brown Brothers Harriman. Prescott knew Ray Kravis as a local Tulsa finance mogul and wheeler-dealer, who was often called upon by Wall Street investment houses as a consultant to evaluate the oil reserves of various companies. The estimates that Ray Kravis provided often involved the amount of oil in the ground that these firms possessed, and these estimates went to the heart of the oil business, as a ground-rent exploitation in which current oil production was far less important than the reserves still beneath the soil.

Such activity imparted the kind of primitive-accumulation mentality that was later seen to animate Ray Kravis's son Henry. During the 1980s, as we will see, **Henry Kravis** personally generated some $58 billion in debt for the purpose of acquiring 36 companies and assembling the largest corporate empire, in paper terms, of all time. Henry Kravis would be one of the leaders of the leveraged buyout gang which became a mainstay of the political machine of George Bush. But in 1948, these events were all far in the future.

So father Prescott asked Ray if he had a job for young George. The answer was, of course he did.

But in the meantime, Prescott Bush had also been talking with another crony beholden to him, **Henry Neil Mallon,** who was the president and chairman of the board of Dresser Industries, a leading manufacturer of drill bits and related oil well drilling equipment. Dresser had been incorporated in 1905 by Solomon R. Dresser, but had been bought up and reorganized by W.A. Harriman & Co. in 1928–29.

Henry Neil Mallon, for whom the infamous Neil Mallon Bush of Hinckley and Silverado fame is named, came from a Cincinnati family who were traditional retainers for the Taft clan, in the same way that the Bush-Walker family were retainers for the Harrimans. As a child, Neil Mallon had gone with his family to visit their close friends, President William Howard Taft and his family, at the White House. Mallon had then attended the Taft School in Watertown, Connecticut, and had gone on to Yale University in the fall of 1913, where he met Bunny Harriman, Prescott Bush, Knight Woolley and the other Bonesmen.

After graduation from Yale, Mallon went into the army with several fellow Skull and Bones members. As we recall from the previous chapter, the society's internal history boasted that in 1918, Mallon burned the flesh and hair off the skull of Geronimo, which Prescott Bush and his friends stole from the despoiled grave at Fort Sill, Oklahoma.

One day in December 1928, Bunny Harriman, father Prescott and Knight Wooley were sitting around the Harriman counting house discussing their reorganization of Dresser Industries. Mallon, who was returning to Ohio after six months spent mountaineering in the Alps, came by to visit. At a certain point in the conversation, Bunny pointed to Mallon and exclaimed, "Dresser! Dresser!" Mallon was subsequently interviewed by George Herbert Walker, the president of W.A. Harriman & Co. As a result of this interview, Mallon was immediately made president of Dresser, although he had no experience in the oil business. Mallon clearly owed the Walker-Bush clan some favors.[3]

Prescott Bush had become a member of the board of directors of Dresser Industries in 1930, in the wake of the reorganization of the company, which he had personally helped to direct. Prescott Bush was destined to remain on the Dresser board for 22 years, until 1952, when he entered the United States Senate. Father Prescott was thus calling in a chit which procured George a second job offer, this time with Dresser Industries or one of its subsidiaries.

George Bush knew that the oil boom in Oklahoma had passed its peak, and that Tulsa would no longer offer the sterling opportunities for a fast buck it had presented 20 years earlier. Dresser, by contrast, was a vast international corporation, ideally suited to gaining a rapid overview of the oil industry and its looting practices. George Bush accordingly called Ray Kravis and, in the ingratiating tones he was wont to use as he clawed his way toward the top, said that he wished respectfully to decline the job that Kravis had offered him in Tulsa. His first preference was to go to work for Dresser Industries. Ray Kravis, who looked to Prescott for business, released him at once. "I know George Bush well," said Ray Kravis years later. "I've known him since he got out of school. His father was a very good friend of mine."[4]

This is the magic moment in which all the official Bush biographies show our hero riding into Odessa, Texas in the legendary red Studebaker, to take up a post as an equipment clerk and trainee for the Dresser subsidiary IDECO (International Derrick and Equipment Company).

But the red Studebaker myth, as already noted, misrepresents the facts. According to the semi-official history of Dresser Industries, George Bush was first employed by Dresser at their corporate headquarters in Cleveland, Ohio, where he worked for Dresser executive R.E. Reimer, an ally of Mallon.[5] This stint in Cleveland is hardly mentioned by the pro-Bush biographers, making us wonder what is being covered up. On the same page that relates these interesting facts, there is a picture that shows father Prescott, Dorothy, Barbara Bush, and George holding his infant son George Walker Bush. Young George W. is wearing cowboy boots. They are all standing in front of a Dresser Industries executive airplane, apparently a DC–3. Could this be the way George really arrived in Odessa?

The Dresser history also has George Bush working for Pacific Pumps, another Dresser subsidiary, before finally joining IDECO. According to Bush's campaign autobiography, he had been with IDECO for a year in Odessa, Texas before being transferred to work for Pacific Pumps in Huntington Park and Bakersfield, California. Bush says he worked at Huntington Park as an assemblyman, and it was here that he claims to have joined the United Steelworkers Union, obtaining a union card that he will still pull out when confronted for his long history of union-busting, as for example when he was heckled at a shipyard in Portland, Oregon during the 1988 campaign. Other accounts place Bush in Ventura, Compton and "Richard Nixon's home town of Whittier" during this same period.[6]

If Bush actually went to California first and only later to Odessa, he may be lying in order to stress that he chose Texas as his first choice, a distortion that may have been concocted very early in his political career to defend himself against the constant charge that he was a carpetbagger.

Odessa, Texas and the nearby city of Midland were both located in the geological formation known as the **Permian Basin,** the scene of an oil boom that developed in the years after the Second World War. Odessa at this time was a complex of yards and warehouses, where oil drilling equipment was brought for distribution to the oil rigs that were drilling all over the landscape.

According to the official Bush version of events, George and "Bar" peregrinated during 1949 far from their beloved Texas to various towns in California where Dresser Industries had subsidiaries. Bush claims that he drove a thousand miles a week through the Carrizo Plains and the Cuyama Valley. Some months later they moved to Midland, another tumbleweed town in west Texas. Midland offered the advantage of being the location of the west Texas headquarters of many of the oil companies that operated in Odessa and the surrounding area. In Midland, George and Bar first stayed at a motel, while he commuted by car each day to the IDECO warehouse in Odessa, 20 miles to the southwest. Then, for $7,500, they bought a home on Maple Street in a postwar mini-Levittown development called Easter Egg Row.

Reality was somewhat more complex. The Bush social circle in Odessa was hardly composed of oil field roughnecks. Rather, their peer group was composed more of the sorts of people they had known in New Haven: a clique of well-heeled recent graduates of prestigious eastern colleges who had been attracted to the Permian Basin in the same way that Stanford, Hopkins, Crocker and their ilk were attracted to San Francisco during the gold rush. Here were Toby Hilliard, John Ashmun, and Pomeroy Smith, all from Princeton. Earle Craig had been at Yale. Midland thus boasted a Yale Club and a Harvard Club and a Princeton Club. The natives referred to this clique as "the Yalies." Also present on the scene in Midland were J. Hugh Liedtke and William Liedtke, who had grown up in Oklahoma, but who had attended college at Amherst in Massachusetts.

Many of these individuals had access to patrician fortunes back east for the venture capital they mobilized behind their various deals. Toby Hilliard's full name was **Harry Talbot Hilliard** of Fox Chapel near Pittsburgh, where the Mellons had their palatial residence. **Earle Craig** was also hooked up to big money in the same area. The **Liedtke brothers,** as we will see, had connections to the big oil money that had emerged around Tulsa. Many of these "Yalies" also lived in the Easter Egg Row neighborhood. A few houses away from George Bush there lived a certain **John Overbey.** According to Overbey, the "people from the East and the people from Texas or

Oklahoma all seemed to have two things in common. They all had a chance to be stockbrokers or investment bankers. And they all wanted to learn the oil business instead."[7]

The Landman

Overbey made his living as a landman. Since George Bush would shortly also become a landman, it is worth investigating what this occupation actually entails; in doing so, we will gain a permanent insight into Bush's character. The role of the landman in the Texas oil industry was to try to identify properties where oil might be found, sometimes on the basis of leaked geological information, sometimes after observing that one of the major oil companies was drilling in the same locale. The landman would scout the property, and then attempt to get the owner of the land to sign away the mineral rights to the property in the form of a lease. If the property owner were well informed about the possibility that oil might in fact be found on his land, the price of the lease would obviously go up, because signing away the mineral rights meant that the income (or "royalties") from any oil that might be found would never go to the owner of the land.

A cunning landman would try to gather as much insider information as he could and keep the rancher as much in the dark as possible. In rural Texas in the 1940s, the role of the landman could rather easily degenerate into that of the ruthless, money-grubbing con artist.

Once the farmer or rancher had signed away his right to future oil royalties, the landman would turn around and attempt to "broker" the lease by selling it at an inflated price to a major oil company that might be interested in drilling, or to some other buyer. Sometimes, if a landman were forced to sell a lease to the mineral rights of land where he really thought there might be oil, he would seek to retain an override, perhaps amounting to a sixteenth or a thirty-second of the royalties from future production. But that would mean less cash or even no cash received now, and small-time operators like Overbey, who had no capital resources of their own, were always strapped for cash. Overbey was lucky if he could realize a profit of a few hundred dollars on the sale of a lease.

This form of activity clearly appealed to the mean-spirited and the greedy, to those who enjoyed rooking their fellow man. It was one thing for Overbey, who may have had no alternative to support his family. It was quite another thing for George Herbert Walker Bush, a young plutocrat out slumming. But Bush was drawn to the landman and royalty game, so much so that he offered to raise capital back east if Overbey would join him in a partnership.[8]

Overbey accepted Bush's proposition that they capitalize a company that would trade in the vanished hopes of the ranchers and farmers of northwest Texas. Bush and Overbey flew back east to talk with Uncle Herbie in the oak-paneled board room of G.H. Walker & Co. in Wall Street. According to *Newsweek*, "Bush's partner, John Overbey, still remembers the dizzying whirl of a money-raising trip to the East with George and Uncle Herbie: lunch at New York's 21 Club, weekends at Kennebunkport where a bracing Sunday dip in the Atlantic off Walker's Point ended with a servant wrapping you in a large terry towel and handing you a martini."[9]

The result of the odyssey back east was a capital of $300,000, much of it gathered from Uncle Herbie's clients in the City of London, who were of course delighted at the prospect of parasitizing Texas ranchers. One of those eager to cash in was **James Gammell** of Edinburgh, Scotland, whose Ivory and Sime counting house put up $50,000 from its Atlantic Asset Trust. Gammell's father had been head of the British military mission in Moscow in 1945, part of the Anglo-American core group there with U.S. Ambassador Averell Harriman. Jimmy Gammell is today the éminence grise of the Scottish investment community, and he has retained a close personal relation to Bush over the years. Mark this Gammell well; he will return to our narrative shortly.

Eugene Meyer, the owner of the *Washington Post* and the father of that paper's present owner, Katharine Meyer Graham, anted up an investment of $50,000 on the basis of the tax-shelter capabilities promised by Bush-Overbey. Meyer, a president of the World Bank, also procured an investment from his son-in-law Phil Graham for the Bush venture. Father Prescott Bush was also counted in, to the tune of about $50,000. In the days of real money, these were considerable sums. The London investors got shares of stock in the new company, called Bush-Overbey, as well as Bush-Overbey bonded debt. Bush and Overbey moved into an office on the ground floor of the Petroleum Building in Midland.

There had been a boom in Scurry County, but that was subsiding. Bush drove to Pyote, to Snyder, to Sterling City, to Monahans, with Rattlesnake Air Force Base just outside of town. How many Texas ranchers can remember selling their mineral rights for a pittance to smiling George Bush, and then having oil discovered on the land, oil from which their family would never earn a penny?

Across the street from Bush-Overbey were the offices of Liedtke & Liedtke, Attorneys-at-law. **J. Hugh Liedtke** and **William Liedtke** were from Tulsa, Oklahoma, where they, like Bush, had grown up rich, as the sons of a local judge who had become one of the top corporate lawyers for Gulf Oil. The Liedtkes' grandfather had come from Prussia, but had served in the Confederate Army. J. Hugh Liedtke had found time along the way to acquire the notorious Harvard Master of Business Administration degree in one year. After service in the Navy during World War II, the Liedtkes obtained law degrees of the University of Texas law school, where they rented the servants' quarters of the home of U.S. Senator Lyndon B. Johnson, who was away in Washington most of the time. During those years, Johnson's home was usually occupied by his protégé, John Connally.

The Liedtkes combined the raw, uncouth primitive-accumulation mentality of the oil boom town with the refined arts of usury and speculation as Harvard taught them. Their law practice was such in name only; their primary and almost exclusive activity was buying up royalty leases on behalf of a moneybags in Tulsa who was a friend of their family; the Liedtkes got a five percent commission on every deal they handled.

Hugh Liedtke was always on the lookout for the Main Chance. Following in the footsteps of his fellow Tulsan Ray Kravis, Hugh Liedtke schemed and schemed until he had found a way to go beyond hustling for royalty leases: He concocted a method of trading oil-producing properties in such a way as to permit the eventual owner to defer all tax liabilities until the field was depleted. Sometimes Hugh Liedtke would commute between Midland and Tulsa on an almost daily basis. He would spend the daylight hours prowling the Permian Basin for a land deal, make the 13-hour drive to Tulsa overnight to convince his backers to ante up the cash, and then race back to Midland to close the deal before the sucker got away. It was during this phase that it occurred to Liedtke that he could save himself a lot of marathon commuter driving if he could put together a million dollars in venture capital and "inventory" the deals he was otherwise forced to make on a piecemeal, ad hoc basis.[10]

Zapata Petroleum

The Liedtke brothers now wanted to go beyond royalty leases and land sale tax dodges, and begin large-scale drilling and production of oil. George Bush, by now well versed in the alphas and omegas of oil as ground rent, was thinking along the same lines. In a convergence that was full of ominous portent for the U.S. economy of the

1980s, the Liedtke brothers and George Bush decided to pool their capital and their rapacious talents by going into business together. Overbey was on board initially, but would soon fall away.

The year was 1953, and Uncle Herbie's G.H. Walker & Co. became the principal underwriter of the stock and convertible debentures that were to be offered to the public. Uncle Herbie would also purchase a large portion of the stock himself. When the new company required further infusions of capital, Uncle Herbie would float the necessary bonds. Jimmy Gammell remained a key participant and would find a seat on the board of directors of the new company. Another of the key investors was the Clark Family Estate, meaning the trustees who managed the Singer sewing machine fortune.[11] Some other money came from various pension funds and endowments, sources that would become very popular during the leveraged buyout orgy Bush presided over in the 1980s. Of the capital of the new Bush-Liedtke concern, about $500,000 would come from Tulsa cronies of the Liedtke brothers, and the other $500,000 from the circles of Uncle Herbie. The latter were referred to by Hugh Liedtke as "the New York guys."

The name chosen for the new concern was **Zapata Petroleum**. According to Hugh Liedtke, the new entrepreneurs were attracted to the name when they saw it on a movie marquee, where the new release *Viva Zapata!*, starring Marlon Brando as the Mexican revolutionary, was playing. Liedtke characteristically explains that part of the appeal of the name was the confusion as to whether Zapata had been a patriot or a bandit.[12]

The Bush-Liedtke combination concentrated its attention on an oil property in Coke County called Jameson field, a barren expanse of prairie and sagebrush where six widely separated wells had been producing oil for some years. Hugh Liedtke was convinced that these six oil wells were tapping into a single underground pool of oil, and that dozens or even hundreds of new oil wells drilled into the same field would all prove to be gushers. The wells *were* connected, and 127 wells were drilled without encountering a single dry hole. As a result, the price of a share of stock in Zapata went up from seven cents a share to $23.

During 1955 and 1956, Zapata was able to report a small profit. In 1957, the year of the incipient Eisenhower recession, this turned into a loss of $155,183, as the oil from the Jameson field began to slow down. In 1958, the loss was $427,752, and in 1959, there was $207,742 of red ink. 1960 (after Bush had departed from the scene) brought another loss, this time of $372,258. It was not until 1961 that Zapata was able to post a small profit of $50,482.[13] Despite the fact that Bush and the Liedtkes all became millionaires through the increased value of their shares, it was not exactly an enviable record; without the deep pockets of Bush's Uncle Herbie Walker and his British backers, the entire venture might have foundered at an early date.

Bush and the Liedtkes had been very lucky with the Jameson field, but they could hardly expect such results to be repeated indefinitely. In addition, they were now posting losses, and the value of Zapata stock had gone into a decline. Bush and the Liedtke brothers now concluded that the epoch in which large oil fields could be discovered within the continental United States was over. Mammoth new oil fields, they believed, could only be found offshore, located under hundreds of feet of water on the continental shelves, or in shallow seas like the Gulf of Mexico and the Caribbean.

By a happy coincidence, in 1954 the U.S. federal government was just beginning to auction the mineral rights for these offshore areas. With father Prescott Bush directing his potent Brown Brothers Harriman/Skull and Bones network from the U.S. Senate while regularly hob-nobbing with President Eisenhower on the golf links, George Bush could be confident of receiving special privileged treatment when it came to these mineral rights. Bush and his partners therefore judged the moment ripe for launching a for-hire drilling company, Zapata Offshore, a Delaware corporation that would offer its services to the companies making up the Seven Sisters international oil cartel in drilling underwater wells. Forty percent of the offshore company's stock would be owned by the original Zapata firm. The new company would also be a buyer of offshore royalty leases. Uncle Herbie helped arrange a new issue of stock for this Zapata offshoot. The shares were easy to unload because of the 1954 boom in the New York stock market. "The stock market lent itself to speculation," Bush would explain years later, "and you could get equity capital for new ventures."[14]

1954 was also the year that the CIA overthrew the government of Jacobo Arbenz in Guatemala. This was the beginning of a dense flurry of U.S. covert operations in Central America and the Caribbean, featuring especially Cuba, just where Zapata Offshore's drilling platforms would be located. In fact, Zapata's first asset, the SCORPION, leased by Gulf Oil during 1958, was drilling on the Cay Sal Bank, 131 miles south of Miami, Florida, and just 54 miles north of Isabela, Cuba. In Cuba, the U.S.-backed insurgency of Fidel Castro was rapidly undermining the older U.S.-imposed regime of Fulgencio Batista. We also note that Allen Dulles, then director of the CIA, had previously been legal counsel to Gulf Oil for Latin

American operations, and counsel to Prescott Bush at Brown Brothers Harriman.

During 1956, the Zapata Petroleum officers included J. Hugh Liedtke as president (and board member), George H.W. Bush as vice president (and board member), and William Brumley of Midland, Texas as treasurer. The board of directors also included:

• J.G.S. Gammell, Edinburgh, Scotland, Manager of British Assets Trust, Ltd.;

• William C. Liedtke, independent oil operator, Midland, Texas;

• G.H. Walker, Jr. (Uncle Herbie); and

• Eugene F. Williams, Jr., secretary of the St. Louis Union Trust Company, and fellow member with Bush in the class of 1942 A.U.V. secret society at Andover, later chairman of the Andover board.

Counsel were listed as Baker, Botts, Andrews & Shepherd of Houston, Texas.[15]

George Bush personally was much more involved with the financial management of the company than with its actual oil-field operations. His main activity was not finding oil or drilling wells but, as he himself put it, "stretching paper"—rolling over debt and making new financial arrangements with the creditors.[16]

During 1957 a certain divergence began to appear between Uncle Herbie Walker, Bush, and the "New York guys" on the one hand, and the Liedtke brothers and their Tulsa backers on the other. As the annual report for that year noted, "There is no doubt that the drilling business in the Gulf of Mexico has become far more competitive in the last six months than it has been at any time in the past." Despite that, Bush, Walker and the New York investors wanted to push forward into the offshore drilling and drilling services business, while the Liedtkes and the Tulsa group wanted to concentrate on acquiring oil in the ground and natural gas deposits.

The 1958 annual report notes that, with no major discoveries made, 1958 had been "a difficult year." It was, of course, the year of the brutal Eisenhower recession. SCORPION, VINEGAROON, and NOLA I, the offshore company's three drilling rigs, could not be kept fully occupied in the Gulf of Mexico during the whole year, and so Zapata Offshore had lost $524,441, more than Zapata Petroleum's own loss of $427,752 for that year.

By 1959, there were reports of increasing personal tensions between the domineering and abrasive J. Hugh Liedtke, on the one hand, and Bush's Uncle Herbie Walker on the other. Liedtke was obsessed with his plan for creating a new major oil company, the boundless ambition that would propel him down a path littered with asset-stripped corporations into the devastating Pennzoil-Getty-Texaco wars of a quarter-century later. During the course of this year, the two groups of investors arrived at a separation that was billed as "amicable," and which in any case never interrupted the close cooperation among Bush and the Liedtke brothers. The solution was that the ever-present Uncle Herbie would buy out the Liedtke-Tulsa 40 percent stake in Zapata Offshore, while the Liedtke backers would buy out the Bush-Walker interest in Zapata Petroleum.

For this to be accomplished, George Bush would require yet another large infusion of capital. Uncle Herbie now raised yet another tranche for George, this time over $800,000. The money allegedly came from Bush-Walker friends and relatives.[17] Even if the faithful efforts of Uncle Herbie are taken into account, it is still puzzling to see a series of large infusions of cash into a poorly managed small company that had posted a series of substantial losses and whose future prospects were anything but rosy.

At this point it is therefore legitimate to pose the question: Was Zapata Offshore an intelligence community front at its foundation in 1954, or did it become one in 1959, or perhaps at some later point?

George Bush was now the president of his own company, the undisputed boss of Zapata Offshore. Although the company was falling behind the rest of the offshore drilling industry, Bush made a desultory attempt at expansion through diversification, investing in a plastics machinery company in New Jersey, a Texas pipe lining company, and a gas transmission company; none of these investments proved to be remunerative.

Zapata Offshore

In 1959–60, George Bush was operating out of his new corporate base in Houston, Texas, where Zapata Offshore had transferred upon separating from the Liedtkes. Economic conditions were slowly improving, and Uncle Herbie's ability to mobilize capital permitted George to move toward expanding his fleet of offshore drilling equipment. By 1963, Zapata Offshore had four operational rigs: SIDEWINDER, VINEGAROON, SCORPION/NOLA I, and NOLA III. Bush's interest was attracted down to the Gulf at Galveston, east to New Orleans, then further east and south to Miami, and still further south to Cuba. That island was the target of the immense covert action operation which the Eisenhower administration, advised by father Prescott Bush, was assembling in south Florida and in Guatemala under the code name of JM/WAVE, which in the spring of 1961 would become manifest to the world in the form of the Bay of Pigs attempted invasion of Cuba.

To survive in the cutthroat world of offshore oil rigs, the most important factor for Zapata Offshore was contracts from the big oil companies of the Seven Sisters Anglo-American cartel, the world oil oligopoly, which during these years defended its domination of the world oil market with, among other things, the assassination of Enrico Mattei, the President of the Ente Nazionale Idrocarburi (the Italian State Oil Company), who had dared to undercut the arrogant looting methods of the Seven Sisters and challenge the oligopoly in north Africa and the Arab world.

In the early years of Zapata Offshore, contracts had come from Gulf Oil and Standard Oil of California. During the early 1960s, more and more contracts came from components of Royal Dutch Shell, the Anglo-Dutch heart of the Seven Sisters cartel, the dominant strategic force in the oligopoly. Zapata Offshore soon had British insurance, British contracts, British investors, a British director, and drilling sites in British Commonwealth oil fields in many parts of the world. This should come as no surprise: after all, Prescott Bush's partner, Averell Harriman, had been Franklin D. Roosevelt's special envoy to Churchill during the first years of World War II, and Averell later married the divorced former wife of Churchill's son Randolph.

Although Zapata Offshore was a company of modest dimensions, Bush nevertheless created a network of subsidiaries which was suspiciously complex. This topic is difficult to research because of the very convenient disappearance of the Zapata Offshore filings with the Securities and Exchange Commission in Washington for the years 1960–66, which were "inadvertently" destroyed by a federal warehouse. This is the kind of convenient tampering with official records from which Bush has benefitted again and again over his career, from the combat report on the *San Jacinto* in 1944 to the disappearance of the Hashemi-Pottinger tapes and the shredding of Iran-Contra documents more recently.

Some illumination is provided by a short profile of the Zapata Offshore corporate substructure researched by a Mr. Allan Mandel and submitted to Texas Senator Ralph Yarborough on October 13, 1964, in the midst of Bush's attempt to unseat the Senator.[18] This report was based on "Standard and Poors, oil industry publications, [and] personal interviews with Interior Department officials."

At this time, Mr. Mandel found, Zapata Offshore owned 50

percent of Seacat-Zapata Offshore Company, which operated the drilling rig NOLA III in the Persian Gulf. In addition, Mandel identified the following Zapata Offshore subsidiaries:

A. Zapata de Mexico
B. Zapata International Corporation
C. Zapata Lining Corporation
D. Zavala Oil Company
E. Zapata Overseas Corporation
F. Zapata owns 41 percent of Amata Gas Corporation.

Zapata Lining was the pipe lining concern; it was divested in 1964. Ownership of Amata Gas was shared with the American Research and Development Corporation of Boston. The Zapata annual report for 1964 is strangely silent about the other companies, with the exception of Seacat Zapata.

George Bush has always loved secrecy, and this appears to have extended to the business activities—or alleged business activities— of Zapata Offshore. A small window on a whole range of secret and semi-secret activities and transactions during these years is provided by recently published information about Bush's shady business relations with **Jorge Diaz Serrano** of Mexico, the former head (1976–81) of the Mexican national oil company Pemex, who was convicted and jailed for defrauding the Mexican government of $58 million. During 1960, Bush and Diaz Serrano secretly worked together to set up a Mexican drilling company called Perforaciones Marinas del Golfo, or Permargo. At that time Diaz Serrano had been working as a salesman for Dresser Industries, Bush's old firm. Diaz Serrano came into contact with an American oilman who wanted to drill in Mexico; a new Mexican law stipulated that drilling contracts could be awarded only to Mexican nationals. The American oilman was Edwin Pauley of Pan American Petroleum Corp. When Diaz Serrano wanted to buy drilling equipment from Dresser Industries, Dresser demanded that Diaz take on Bush as a co-owner in the venture. Bush's spokesman Peter Hart conceded in 1988 that Bush and Zapata had been partners with Diaz Serrano, but alleged that the partnership had lasted for only seven months.

Diaz Serrano is very open about being a personal friend of Bush. "One remembers a man that one likes and appreciates," says Diaz, who wanted to become the President of Mexico, before he was sentenced to five years in jail for appropriating government monies; the business dealings spawned "a friendship of which I am most proud." In 1982, Diaz Serrano was made Mexican ambassador to Moscow, and he stopped off to talk with Bush in the White House on his way to his new assignment.

Bush reciprocates the friendship: "I have high regard for Jorge," Bush told *People* magazine in 1981; "I consider him a friend."

One of Jorge Diaz Serrano's associates in the drilling deal was his long-time partner, Jorge Escalante, who has also remained in contact with Bush over the intervening years, a fact that Bush's office also confirms.

Bush was clearly dishonest, in that the annual reports of Zapata Offshore do not mention this deal with Permargo, which created a company that was in direct competition with Zapata Offshore itself, much to the detriment of that "shareholder value" which Bush professed to hold sacred whenever his clique of cronies was on the track of a new leveraged buyout. Bush may also have illegally concealed his dealings from the government. The Zapata Offshore filings with the SEC between 1955 and 1959 are cryptic, and the SEC files on Zapata Offshore between 1960 and 1966, when Bush had exclusive control of the company, were destroyed by the SEC either in 1981, when Bush had just become Vice President, or somewhat later, in October 1983, according to various SEC officials.

Perhaps these files were removed not just to protect Bush, but also to protect Zapata Offshore as a front operation for the U.S. intelligence community. The 1964 Zapata Offshore annual report does note that the drilling barge NOLA I was sold "to a subsidiary of a Mexican drilling company" because it had become "a marginal operation," in that it could only be used in the summer because of a lack of seaworthiness in bad weather, but even this annual report does not name Permargo, which appears to be the Mexican company that bought NOLA I.[19]

Diaz recalls that Bush was a highly political businessman back in 1960: "In those days, I remember very clearly, he was a very young chap and when we were talking business with him at his office he spent more time on the telephone talking about politics than paying attention to the drilling affairs. He was a born politician."

Bush's business dealings had brought him into direct contact with a number of the corporate raiders who would later act out the paroxysm of speculation, looting and usury that would mark the Reagan-Bush years. The Permian Basin of the 1940s and 1950s had attracted all those who would be the leading practitioners of the leveraged buyouts, hostile takeovers, greenmail, mergers and acquisitions of the 1980s. Bush's main business success was in assembling this legion of greed as a base of political support for later on.

Notes for Chapter VIII

1. Harry Hurt III, "George Bush, Plucky Lad," *Texas Monthly,* June 1983.

2. See Sarah Bartlett, *The Money Machine: How KKR Manufactured Power and Profits* (New York, 1991), pp. 9–12.

3. Darwin Payne, *Initiative in Energy: Dresser Industries, Inc., 1880–1978* (New York: Simon and Schuster, 1979), pp. 232 ff.

4. Bartlett, *op. cit.,* p. 268.

5. Payne, *op. cit.,* pp. 232–33.

6. Hurt, *op. cit.*

7. *Ibid.*

8. See Richard Ben Kramer, "How He Got Here," *Esquire,* June 1991.

9. "Bush Battles the 'Wimp Factor'," *Newsweek,* Oct. 19, 1987.

10. See Thomas Petzinger, Jr., *Oil and Honor: The Texaco-Pennzoil Wars* (New York: Putnam Publishing Group, 1987), pp. 37 ff.

11. *Ibid.,* p. 93.

12. *Ibid.,* p. 40.

13. See Zapata Petroleum annual reports, Library of Congress Microform Reading Room.

14. Petzinger, *op. cit.,* p. 41.

15. See Zapata Petroleum Corporation Annual Report for 1956, Library of Congress, Microform Reading Room.

16. Hurt, *op. cit.,* p. 194.

17. Walter Pincus and Bob Woodward, "Doing Well With Help From Family, Friends," *Washington Post,* Aug. 11, 1988.

18. See Bush folder, Yarborough Papers, Eugene C. Barker Texas History Center, University of Texas, Austin.

19. See Jonathan Kwitny, "The Mexican Connection of George Bush," *Barron's,* Sept. 19, 1988.

IX

BUSH CHALLENGES YARBOROUGH FOR THE SENATE

Bush's unsuccessful attempt in 1964 to unseat Texas Democratic Senator Ralph Webster Yarborough is a matter of fundamental interest to anyone seeking to probe the wellsprings of Bush's actual political thinking. In a society which knows nothing of its own recent history, the events of a quarter-century ago might be classed as remote and irrelevant. But as we review the profile of the Bush Senate campaign of 1964, what we see coming alive is the characteristic mentality that rules the Oval Office today. The main traits are all there: the overriding obsession with the race issue, exemplified in Bush's bitter rejection of the civil rights bill before the Congress during those months; the genocidal bluster in foreign affairs, with proposals for nuclear bombardment of Vietnam, an invasion of Cuba, and a rejection of negotiations for the return of the Panama Canal; the autonomic reflex for union-busting expressed in the rhetoric of "right to work"; the paean to free enterprise at the expense of farmers and the disadvantaged, with all of this packaged in a slick, demagogic television and advertising effort.

We now alert the reader that our investigation of this, George Bush's first public political act, has been thorough and intense: We intend the voluminous material presented here to be of use to jurists, historians and others seeking serious explanations for the U.S.A.'s political and moral crisis.

During this Senate race, Bush assumed the coloration of a Goldwater Republican. It remains highly significant that Bush began his public political career in the ideological guise of a southern

Republican, specifically in Texas. The Republican Party in Texas had been in total eclipse since the time of Reconstruction, with the state GOPers complaining that they were living in a one-party state. During the 1950s, the personal popularity of Eisenhower and the increasing visibility of ultra-left Wall Street investment bankers in the circle of Adlai Stevenson's backers began to offer the Texas Republicans some openings. In 1952 and 1956, Texas Democratic Governor Allan Shivers supported Eisenhower, who carried Texas with a substantial majority both times. In 1960, Texas had given its electoral votes to Kennedy, although the margin of Democratic victory was so thin as to constitute an embarrassment to Kennedy's running mate, Texas Senator and Democratic Majority Leader Lyndon B. Johnson ("LBJ").

But Nixon had carried the city of Houston and Harris County, which turned out to be the largest metropolitan area to go for the Nixon-Lodge ticket that year. In 1961, Texas Republicans scored their greatest success in a century by electing John Tower to the U.S. Senate on a platform that was a harbinger of the Goldwater movement. Tower was once asked if there were a single domestic legislative program of John F. Kennedy that he could support, and his answer was that he could not think of a single one. This is the same Tower who would join with Edmund Muskie and Brent Scowcroft in early 1987 to concoct the absurd whitewash of the Iran-Contra affair that would exonerate Bush and attribute the central responsibility to White House Chief of Staff Don Regan, forcing his ouster. This was the same Tower whose nomination by Bush to the post of Secretary of Defense would be derailed by accusation of alcoholism and womanizing, followed by Tower's death in a mysterious airplane crash in early 1991.

The Texas Democratic Party was divided in those days into two wings which fought each other in the Democratic primaries; winning the primary was often tantamount to election to office. One of these wings was called liberal and was identified above all with Bush's opponent, Senator Ralph Yarborough. The "liberal" here is largely a misnomer; more accurate would be populist, but populist ennobled by the revival of the classic nineteenth-century American System that occurred in Texas during Franklin D. Roosevelt's World War II mobilization, when dirigist recovery policies pulled the Texas economy out of a stagnation that had its roots in the failure of post-1865 Reconstruction. The strong suits of these populist Democrats were education and infrastructure—a good first approximation of the actual business of government.

The other wing was called conservative, and was grouped around figures like Allan Shivers and LBJ's protégé, John Connally, with whom Bush has had a history of alternating stretches of conflict and moments of rapprochement. LBJ himself was close to the Shivers-Connally group. The typical figure here is Connally, the governor who was wounded in Dealey Plaza in Dallas the day that Kennedy was killed, and who later went on to join the Nixon administration as the Secretary of the Treasury, who approved the abolition of the post-1944 Bretton Woods gold reserve standard in Camp David on August 15, 1971. Connally subsequently played out the logic of becoming not just a Republican, but indeed a Republican presidential candidate, and of clashing with George Bush once or twice in the snows of New Hampshire in 1979–80.

The Texas Democratic Party also contained an array of personalities of national importance, whose positive traits are part of what has been lost in the descent into today's crisis: Call them populists, call them the post-New Deal or the post-Fair Deal, but do not mistake the fact that they were better for the country than their successors. These were politicians like the legendary Speaker of the House, Sam Rayburn; Congressman Wright Patman of the House Banking Committee, who was a source of continuing populist irritation to the New York banking community; and Tom Clark, who was Attorney General under Truman and who later went on to the U.S. Supreme Court, and whose son, Ramsey Clark, has been distinguished by his denunciation of the war crimes of the Bush regime in the Gulf war of 1991. A later generation of this same circle was represented by former Speaker of the House Jim Wright, who was hounded from office during the first year of George Bush's presidential tenure; and by Congressman Henry Gonzalez.

Gonzalez stands out as one of the very few of the old Texas populist Democrats left in elected office today. Gonzalez has put new luster on the time-honored maverick tradition by offering a bill of impeachment for Ronald Reagan in the wake of the Iran-Contra revelations of 1986; more recently by submitting a bill for the impeachment of George Bush for his illegal conduct of Operation Desert Shield; and by raising his voice as first in the Congress for the cause of humanity against genocide, with a call for the lifting of the economic sanctions against Iraq to prevent the needless slaughter of hundreds of thousands of children after the bombing campaign had ended. And even today there are still others of this tradition left in positions of key influence: for example, Congressman Jack Brooks of the ninth district of Texas, the salty chairman of the House Judiciary Committee, who dared to subpoena Attorney General Richard Thornburgh to appear before his committee with a *ducis tecum* of the documents of the Department of Justice theft of computer software in the Inslaw case.

One of the continuing projects of George Bush's life has been the extirpation of precisely this populist and sometimes dirigist group of Democrats, and their replacement with "free enterprise" Republican ideologues, or financier Democrats of the Lloyd Bentsen variety.

The Texas and Oklahoma populist Democrats must be distinguished from their colleagues of the Old South—of Georgia, Alabama, and Mississippi. But for the Eastern Liberal Establishment, it has proven more convenient to lump them all together under the purveyed image of the racist, bourbon-swilling southern congressional committee chairman, conspiring in cigar-clouded rooms to defy the popular will as expressed by the television networks. All southern Democrats of the old school tended to have crippling weaknesses on the race issue and on the question of union-busting. But on the other side of the ledger, many southern Democrats had an excellent grasp of infrastructure in the broadest sense: internal improvements like highways, canals, water projects, rural electrification, quality accessible public education, health services and electric power generation.

The nascent southern Republicans of the fifties and sixties, by contrast, were generally as bad as, or worse than, the Democrats on race and labor relations, and were at the same time such fanatics of Adam Smith's "free market" mystification that all government commitment to maintaining infrastructure, health care and education went by the boards. The only positive point left for some of these emerging southern Republicans, such as those who followed Barry Goldwater in 1964, was a patriotic rejection of the machinations of the Eastern Liberal Establishment, as embodied most graphically in the figure of New York Governor Nelson Rockefeller. Bush was indeed a Goldwater man in those days, as we will see. But since Bush was himself an organ of that same hated Eastern Liberal Establishment, he stood utterly bereft of redeeming grace.

The enterprise in which we now find Bush engaged, the creation of a Republican Party in the southern states during the 1960s, has proven to be a historical catastrophe. In order to create a Republican Party in the South, it was first necessary to smash the old FDR New Deal constituent coalition of labor, the cities, farmers, blacks and the "solid South." As Bush complains in his campaign autobiography:

"The state was solidly Democratic, and the allegiance of Texans to the 'party of our fathers' became even stronger during the lean years of the Depression. The Democratic campaign line in the 1930s was that the 'Hoover Republicans' were responsible for unemployment and farm foreclosures; Franklin D. Roosevelt and the Democratic Party were said to be the only friends the people had."[1]

But as far as George Bush was concerned, all this was of no consequence: "Philosophically, I was a Republican. . . ."[2] After Bush had declared his candidacy for Yarborough's seat, the veteran political writers at the state capital in Austin shook their heads: Bush had "two crosses to bear—running as a Republican and not a native Texan."[3]

The method that the southern Republicans devised to breach this solid front was the one theorized years later by Lee Atwater, the manager of Bush's 1988 presidential campaign. This was the technique of the "wedge issues," so called precisely because they were chosen to split up the old New Deal coalition using the chisels of ideology. The wedge issues are also known as the "hot-button social issues," and the most explosive among them has always tended to be race. The Republicans could win in the South by portraying the Democratic Party as pro-black. Atwater had learned to be a cunning and vicious practitioner of the "wedge issue" method in the school of Strom Thurmond of South Carolina, after the latter had switched over to the Republicans in the sixties. Racial invective, anti-union demagogy, jingoistic chauvinism, the smearing of opponents for their alleged fealty to "special interests"—none of this began in the Baker-Atwater effort of 1988. These were the stock in trade of the Southern Strategy,[4] and these were all leitmotivs of Bush's 1964 effort against Yarborough.

The Southern Strategy

From the vantage point of the police-state conditions of the early 1990s, we can discern a further implication of the southern Republican project of which Bush was in several moments of the 1960s a leading operative. As the southern GOP emerged out of the play of gang and countergang between McGovernite left liberal investment bankers and Nixon-Reagan right liberal investment bankers (and Bush has been both), it made possible that Southern Strategy which elected Nixon in 1968 and which has given the Republicans a virtual lock on the electoral college ever since. The Watergate-Carter anomaly of 1976 confirms rather than alters this overall picture.

The Southern Strategy that Bush turns out to have been serving in the sixties was not called to the attention of the public until somewhat after the 1964 election, in which Goldwater had garnered electoral votes exclusively in the South. As William Rusher wrote in the *National Review*: "The Democrats had for years begun each race with an assured batch of delegates from the South. . . . The Republican Party strategy," argued Rusher, needs refiguring, given a chance to break into this bloc once denied them. . . ." His conclusion was that "Republicans can put themselves in the position of having the Southern bloc as a starting handicap; after that, they can compete for the rest of the country, needing only that 50 per cent minus (say) 111 [of the electoral college votes]." Doing all this, Rusher contended, would allow Republican presidential candidates to ignore the "traditional centers of urban liberalism," especially in the Northeast. These ideas were further refined in Richard Nixon's brain trust, presided over by Wall Street bond lawyer John Mitchell at 445 Park Avenue, and received their definitive elaboration from Kevin Phillips, who in those years advanced the thesis that the "whole secret of politics" is in "knowing who hates who," which is of course another way of speaking of wedge issues.

The result of the successful application of the Southern Strategy in 1968 and in the following years has been a period of more than two decades of virtual one-party Republican control over the executive branch, of which George Bush personally has been the leading beneficiary, first through his multiple appointments, then through the vice-presidency, and now through the possession of the White House itself. This has had the decisive structural consequence of making possible the kind of continuous, entrenched bureaucratic power that we see in the Bush regime and its leading functionaries.

As we will see, such administrators of the corporate state as James Baker and Brent Scowcroft, for whom the exercise of executive power has long since become a way of life, appear to themselves and to others as immune to the popular reckoning. The democratic republic requires the moment of catharsis, of throwing the bums out, if the arrogance of the powerful is ever to be chastened. If there is no prospect for the White House changing hands, this amounts to a one-party state. The southern Republican Party, including two-party Texas, has provided the Republican lock on the White House, which has proven a mighty stimulus to those tendencies toward authoritarian and even totalitarian rule which have culminated in the administrative fascism of the current Bush regime.

Ralph Webster Yarborough

Bush's opponent in that Goldwater year of 1964 was Senator Ralph Webster Yarborough. Yarborough had been born in Chandler, Texas in 1903 as the seventh of 11 children. He attended public schools in Chandler and Tyler, worked on a farm and went on to attend Sam Houston State Teachers College and, for one year, the U.S. Military Academy at West Point. After World War I, he worked a passage to Europe on board a freighter, and found a job in Germany working in the offices of the American Chamber of Commerce in Berlin. He also pursued studies in Stendahl, Germany. He returned to the United States to earn a law degree at the University of Texas in 1927, and worked as a lawyer in El Paso. At one point he found a job as a harvest hand in the Oklahoma dust bowl of the late 1920s, and also served a stint as a roughneck in the oil fields. Yarborough entered public service as an assistant attorney general of Texas from 1931 to 1934. After that, he was a founding director of the Lower Colorado River Authority, a major water project in central Texas, and was then elected as a district judge in Austin. He was also a member of the 36th Division of the Texas National Guard, in which he advanced from private to sergeant.

Yarborough served in the U.S. Army ground forces during World War II, and was a member of the only division which took part in the postwar occupation of Germany as well as in MacArthur's administration of Japan. When he left the military in 1946, he had attained the rank of lieutenant colonel. It is clear from an overview of Yarborough's career that his victories and defeats were essentially his own, that for him there was no Prescott Bush to secure lines of credit or to procure important posts by telephone calls to bigwigs in Skull and Bones freemasonic networks.

Yarborough had challenged Allan Shivers in the governor's contest of 1952, and had gone down to defeat. Successive bids for the state house in Austin by Yarborough were turned back in 1954 and 1956. Then, when Senator (and former Governor) Price Daniel resigned his seat, Yarborough was finally victorious in a special election. He had then been reelected to the Senate for a full term in 1958.

Yarborough was distinguished first of all for his voting record on civil rights. Just months after he had entered the Senate, he was one of only five southern Senators (including LBJ) to vote for the watershed Civil Rights Act of 1957. In 1960, Yarborough was one of four southern senators—again including LBJ—who cast votes in favor of the Civil Rights Act of 1960. Yarborough would be the lone senator from the 11 states formerly comprising the Confederate States of America to vote for the 1964 Civil Rights bill, the most sweeping since Reconstruction. This is the bill which, as we will see, provided Bush with the ammunition for one of the principal themes of his 1964 election attacks. Later, Yarborough would be one of only three southern senators supporting the Voting Rights Act of 1965, and one of four supporting the 1968 open housing bill.[5]

After Yarborough had left the Senate, his bitter enemies at the *Dallas Morning News* felt obliged to concede that "his name is probably attached to more legislation than that of any other senator in Texas history." Yarborough had become the chairman of the Senate Committee on Labor and Public Welfare. Here his lodestar was infrastructure: infrastructure in the form of education and infrastructure in the form of physical improvements.

In education, Yarborough was either the author or a leading supporter of virtually every important piece of legislation to become law between 1958 and 1971, including some nine major bills.

As chairman of the veterans subcommittee, Yarborough authored the Cold War G.I. Bill, which sought to extend the benefits accorded veterans of World War II and Korea, and which was to apply to servicemen on duty between January 1955 and July 1, 1965. Yarborough was also instrumental in obtaining a five-year extension of the Hill-Burton Act, which provided 4,000 additional beds in Veterans Administration hospitals.

In physical improvements, Yarborough supported appropriations for coastal navigation. He fought for $29 million for the Rural Electrification Administration for counties in the Corpus Christi area alone. In 11 counties in that part of Texas, Yarborough had helped obtain federal grants of $4.5 million and loans of $640,000 under the Kennedy administration accelerated public works projects program, to provide clean water and sewage for towns and cities which could not otherwise afford them.[6]

In short, Ralph Yarborough had a real commitment to racial and economic justice, and was, all in all, among the best that the post-New Deal Democratic Party had to offer. Certainly there were weaknesses: One of the principal ones was to veer in the direction of environmentalism. Here Yarborough was the prime mover behind the Endangered Species Act.

Climbing the Republican Ladder

Bush moved to Houston in 1959, bringing the corporate head-quarters of Zapata Offshore with him. Houston was by far the biggest city in Texas, a center of the corporate bureaucracies of firms doing business in the oil patch. There was also the Baker and Botts law firm, which would function in effect as part of the Bush family network, since Baker and Botts were the lawyers who had been handling the affairs of the Harriman railroad interests in the Southwest.

One prominent lawyer in Houston at the time was James Baker III, a scion of the family enshrined in the Baker and Botts name, but himself a partner in another, satellite firm, because of the so-called anti-nepotism rule that prevented the children of Baker and Botts partners from joining the firm themselves. Soon Bush would be hob-nobbing with Baker and other representatives of the Houston oligarchy, of the Hobby and Cullen families, at the Petroleum Club and at garden parties in the hot, humid, subtropical summers. George, Barbara and their children moved into a new home on Briar Drive.

Before long, Bush became active in the Harris County Republican Party, which was in the process of becoming one of the GOP strong-points in the statewide apparatus then being assembled by Peter O'Donnell, the Republican state chairman, and his associate Thad Hutcheson. By now George Bush claimed to have become a million-aire in his own right, and given his impeccable Wall Street connec-tions, it was not surprising to find him on the Harris County GOP finance committee, a function that he had undertaken in Midland for the Eisenhower-Nixon tickets in 1952 and 1956. He was also a member of the candidates committee.

In 1962 the Democrats were preparing to nominate John Con-nally for governor, and the Texas GOP under O'Donnell was able to mount a more formidable bid than previously for the state house in Austin. The Republican candidate was Jack Cox, a party activist with a right-wing profile. Bush agreed to serve as the Harris County co-chairman of the Jack Cox for Governor finance committee. In the gubernatorial election of 1962, Cox received 710,000 votes, a surprisingly large result. Connally won the governorship, and it was in that capacity that he was present in the Kennedy motorcade in Dallas on November 22, 1963.

During these years, a significant influence was exercised in the Texas GOP by the John Birch Society, which had grown up during the 1950s through the leadership and financing of Robert Welch. Grist for the Birch mill was abundantly provided by the liberal Republicanism of the Eisenhower administration, which counted Prescott Bush, Nelson Rockefeller, Gordon Gray and Robert Keith Gray among its most influential figures. In reaction against this Wall Street liberalism, the Birchers offered an ideology of impotent negative protest based on self-righteous chauvinism in foreign affairs and the mystifications of the free market at home. But they were highly suspicious of the financier cliques of lower Manhattan, and to that extent they had George Bush's number.

Bush is still complaining about the indignities he suffered at the hands of these Birchers, with whom he was straining to have as much as possible in common. But he met with repeated frustration, because his Eastern Liberal Establishment pedigree was always there. In his campaign autobiography, Bush laments that many Texans thought that *Redbook Magazine*, published by his father-in-law, Marvin Pierce of the McCall Corporation, was an official publication of the Communist Party.

Bush recounts a campaign trip with his aide Roy Goodearle to the Texas panhandle, during which he was working a crowd at one of his typical free food, free beer "political barbecues." Bush gave one of his palm cards to a man who conceded that he had heard of Bush, but quickly added that he could never support him. Bush thought this was because he was running as a Republican. "But," [Bush] then realized, "my being a Republican wasn't the thing bothering the guy. It was something worse than that." Bush's interlocutor was upset over the fact that Zapata Offshore had eastern investors. When Bush whined that all oil companies had eastern investors, for such was the nature of the business, his tormentor pointed out that one of Bush's main campaign contributors, a prominent Houston attorney, was not just a "sonofabitch," but also a member of the New York Council on Foreign Relations.

Bush explains, with the whine in his larynx in overdrive: "The lesson was that in the minds of some voters the Council on Foreign Relations was nothing more than a One World tool of the Communist-Wall Street internationalist conspiracy, and to make matters worse, the Houston lawyer had also worked for President Eisenhower—a known tool of the Communists, in the eyes of some John Birch members." Further elucidation is then added in a footnote: "A decade and a half later, running for President, I ran into some of the same political types on the campaign trail. By then, they'd uncovered an international conspiracy even more sinister than the Council on Foreign Relations—the Trilateral Commission, a group that President Reagan received at the White House in 1981."[7]

This, as we shall see, is a reference to Lyndon LaRouche's New Hampshire primary campaign of 1979–80, which included the exposure of Bush's membership not just in David Rockefeller's Trilateral Commission, but also in Skull and Bones, about which Bush always refuses to comment. When Ronald Reagan and other candidates took up this issue, Bush ended up losing the New Hampshire primary, and with it, his best hope of capturing the presidency in 1980. Bush, in short, has been aware since the early sixties that serious attention to his oligarchical pedigree causes him to lose elections. His response has been to seek to declare these very relevant matters off limits, and to order dirty tricks and covert operations against those who persist in making this an issue, most clearly in the case of LaRouche.

Part of the influence of the John Birch Society in those days was due to the support and financing afforded by the Hunt dynasty of Dallas. In particular, the fabulously wealthy oilman H.L. Hunt, one of the richest men in the world, was an avid sponsor of right-wing propaganda which he put out under the name of LIFE LINE. On at least one occasion, Hunt called Bush to Dallas for a meeting during one of the latter's Texas political campaigns. "There's something I'd like to give you," Hunt told Bush. Bush appeared with remarkable alacrity, and Hunt engaged him in a long conversation about many things, but mentioned neither politics nor money. Finally, as Bush was getting ready to leave, Hunt handed him a thick brown envelope. Bush eagerly opened the envelope in the firm expectation that it would contain a large sum in cash. What he found instead was a thick wad of LIFE LINE literature for his ideological reformation.[8]

It was in this context that George Bush, mediocre oilman, fortified by his Wall Street and Skull and Bones connections, but with almost no visible qualifications, and scarcely known in Texas outside of Odessa, Midland and Houston, decided that he had attained senatorial caliber. In the Roman Empire, membership in the Senate was a hereditary attribute of patrician family rank. Prescott Bush had left the Senate in early January of 1963. Before the year was out, George Bush would make his claim. As Senator Yarborough later commented, it would turn out to be an act of temerity.

Harris County Chairman

During the spring of 1963, Bush set about assembling an institutional base for his campaign. The chosen vehicle would be the Republican chairmanship of Harris County, the area around Houston, a bulwark of the Texas GOP. Bush had been participating in the Harris County organization since 1960.

One Sunday morning, Bush invited some county Republican activists to his home on Briar Drive. Present were Roy Goodearle, a young independent oil man who, before Barbara Bush appropriated it, was given the nickname of "the Silver Fox" in the Washington scene. Also present were Jack Steel, Tom and Nancy Thawley, and some others.

Goodearle, presumably acting as the lawyer for the Bush faction, addressed the meeting on the dangers posed by the sectarians of the John Birch Society to the prospects of the GOP in Houston and elsewhere. Over lunch prepared by Barbara Bush, Goodearle outlined the tactical situation in the Harris County organization: A Birchite faction under the leadership of state senator Walter Mengdon, although still a minority, was emerging as a powerful innerparty opposition against the liberals and moderates. In the last vote for GOP county leader, the Birch candidate had been narrowly defeated. Now, after three years in office, the more moderate county chairman, James A. Bertron, would announce on February 8, 1963 that he could no longer serve as chairman of the Harris County Republican Executive Committee. His resignation, he would state, was "necessitated by neglect of my personal business due to my political activities."[9] This was doubtless very convenient in the light of what Bush had been planning.

Bertron was quitting to move to Florida. In 1961, Bertron had been attending a Republican fundraising gathering in Washington, D.C., when he was accosted by none other than Senator Prescott Bush. Bush took Bertron aside and demanded: "Jimmy, when are you going to get George involved?" "Senator, I'm trying," Bertron replied, evidently with some vexation. "We're all trying."[10] In 1961 or at any other time, it is doubtful that George Bush could have found his way to the men's room without the help of a paid informant sent by Senator Prescott Bush.

Roy Goodearle went on to tell the assembled Republicans that unless a "strong candidate" now entered the race, a Bircher was likely to win the post of county chairman. But in order to defeat the well-organized and zealous Birchers, said Goodearle, an anti-Bircher would have to undertake a grueling campaign, touring the county and making speeches to the Republican faithful every night for several weeks. Then, under the urging of Goodearle, the assembled group turned to Bush: Could he be prevailed on to put his hat in the ring? Bush, by his own account, needed no time to think it over, and accepted on the spot.

With that, George and Barbara were on the road in their first campaign in what Bush later called "another apprenticeship." While Barbara busied herself with needlepoint in order to stay awake through a speech she had heard repeatedly, George churned out a pitch on the virtues of the two-party system and the advantages of having a Republican alternative to the entrenched Houston establishment. In effect, his platform was the Southern Strategy *avant la lettre*. Local observers soon noticed that Barbara Bush was able to gain acceptance as a campaign comrade for Republican volunteers, in addition to being esteemed as the wealthy candidate's wife.

When the vote for county chairman came, the candidate opposing

Bush, Russell Prior, pulled out of the race for reasons that have not been satisfactorily explained, thus permitting Bush to be elected unanimously by the executive committee. Henceforth, winning unopposed has been Bush's taste in elections: This is how he was returned to the House for his second term in 1968, and Bush propagandists flirted with a similar approach to the 1992 presidential contest.

At the time of his election, 38-year-old George was not exactly a household word, not even in Houston. In announcing his victory, the *Houston Chronicle* printed the picture of a totally different person, captioned as "George Bush," the man who wanted to "hone the party to a fine edge for the important job ahead in 1964"—that is to say, for the Goldwater for President campaign.[11]

As chairman, Bush was free to appoint the officers of the county GOP. Some of these choices are not without relevance for the future course of world history. For the post of party counsel, Bush appointed William B. Cassin of Baker and Botts, Shepherd and Coates law firm. For his assistant county chairmen, Bush tapped Anthony Farris, Gene Crossman and Roy Goodearle; and for executive director, William R. Simmons.

On March 21, Bush told the *Houston Chronicle* that the Harris County GOP is "conservative," and not "extremist": "The Republican party in the past—and sometimes with justification—has been connected in the mind of the public with extremism," said Bush. "We're not, or at least most of us are not, extremists. We're just responsible people." Bush pledged that his message would be the same all over the county, and that he would "say the same things in River Oaks as in the East End, or in Pasadena."

At the same time that he was inveighing against extremism, Bush was dragooning his party apparatus to mount the Houston Draft Goldwater drive. The goal of this effort was to procure 100,000 signatures for Goldwater, with each signer also plunking down a dollar to fill the GOP coffers.

But Bush's pro-Goldwater efforts were not universally appreciated. In early July, Craig Peper, the current chairman of the party finance committee, stood up in a party gathering and attacked the leaders of the Draft Goldwater movement, including Bush, as "right wing extremists." Bush had not been purging any John Birchers, but he was not willing to permit such attacks from his left. Bush accordingly purged Peper, demanding his resignation after a pro-Goldwater meeting at which Bush had boasted that he was "100 percent for the draft Goldwater move."

Before announcing his bid for the Senate, Bush decided to take out what would appear in retrospect to be a very important insurance policy for his future political career. On April 22, Bush, with the support of Republican state chairman Peter O'Donnell, filed a suit in federal court, calling for the reapportionment of the congressional districts in the Houston area. The suit argued that the urban voters of Harris County were being partially disenfranchised by a system that favored rural voters, and demanded as a remedy that a new congressional district be drawn in the area. "This is not a partisan matter," commented the civic-minded Bush. "This is something of concern to all Harris County citizens." Bush would later win this suit, and that would lead to a court-ordered redistricting, which would create the Seventh Congressional District, primarily out of those precincts which Bush managed to carry in the 1964 Senate race. Was this the invisible hand of Skull and Bones? This would also mean that there would be no entrenched incumbent, no incumbent of any kind in that Seventh District, when Bush got around to making his bid there in 1966. But for now, this was all still in the future.

The Senate Race

On September 10, 1963, Bush announced his campaign for the U.S. Senate. He was fully endorsed by the state Republican organization and its chairman, Peter O'Donnell, who, according to some accounts, had encouraged Bush to run. By December 5, Bush had further announced that he was planning to step down as Harris County chairman and devote himself to full-time, statewide campaigning starting early in 1964.

At this point, Bush's foremost strategic concern appears to have been money—big money. On October 19, the *Houston Chronicle* carried his comment that ousting Yarborough would require nearly $2 million, "if you want to do it right." Much of this would go to the Brown and Snyder advertising agency in Houston for television and billboards. In 1963, this was a considerable sum, but Bush's crony C. Fred Chambers, also an oilman, was committed to raising it. During these years, Chambers appears to have been one of Bush's closest friends, and he received the ultimate apotheosis of having one of the Bush family dogs named in his honor.[12]

It is impossible to establish in retrospect how much Bush spent in this campaign. State campaign finance filings do exist, but they are fragmentary and grossly underestimate the money that was actually committed.

In terms of the tradeoffs of the campaign, Bush and his handlers were confronted with the following configuration: There were three competitors for the Republican senatorial nomination. The most formidable competition came from Jack Cox, the Houston oilman who had run for governor against Connally in 1962, and whose statewide recognition was much higher than Bush's. Cox would position himself to the right of Bush, and would receive the endorsement of Gen. Edwin Walker, who had been forced to resign his infantry command in Germany because of his radical speeches to the troops. A former Democrat, Cox was reported to have financial backing from the Hunts of Dallas. Cox campaigned against medicare, federal aid to education, the war on poverty, and the loss of U.S. sovereignty to the U.N.

Competing with Cox was Dr. Milton Davis, a thoracic surgeon from Dallas, who was expected to be the weakest candidate but whose positions were perhaps the most distinctive: Morris was for "no treaties with Russia," the repeal of the federal income tax, and the "selling off of excess government industrial property such as TVA and REA"—what the Reagan-Bush administrations would later call privatization.

Competing with Bush for the less militant conservatives was Dallas lawyer Robert Morris, who recommended depriving the U.S. Supreme Court of appellate jurisdiction in school prayer cases.[13] In order to avoid a humiliating second-round runoff in the primary, Bush would need to score an absolute majority the first time around. To do that he would have to first compete with Cox on a right-wing terrain, and then move to the center after the primary, in order to take votes from Yarborough there.

But there was also primary competition on the Democratic side for Yarborough. This was Gordon McLendon, the owner of a radio network, the Liberty Broadcasting System, that was loaded with debt. Liberty Broadcasting's top creditor was Houston banker Roy Cullen, a Bush crony. Roy Cullen's name appears, for example, along with such died-in-the wool Bushmen as W.S. Farish III, James A. Baker III, C. Fred Chambers, Robert Mosbacher, William C. Liedtke, Jr., Joseph R. Neuhaus and William B. Cassin, in a Bush campaign ad in the *Houston Chronicle* of late April, 1964. When McLendon finally went bankrupt, it was found that he owed Roy Cullen more than a million dollars. So perhaps it is not surprising that McLendon's campaign functioned as an auxiliary to Bush's own efforts. McLendon specialized in smearing Yarborough with the Billie Sol Estes issue, and it was to this that McLendon devoted most of his speaking time and media budget.

Billie Sol Estes in those days was notorious for his conviction for defrauding the U.S. government of large sums of money in a scam involving the storage of chemicals that turned out not to exist. Billie Sol was part of the LBJ political milieu. As the Estes scandal developed, a report emerged that he had given Yarborough a payment of $50,000 on Nov. 6, 1960. But later, after a thorough investigation, the Department of Justice had issued a statement declaring that the charges involving Yarborough were "without any foundation in fact and unsupported by credible testimony." "The case is closed," said the Justice Department. But this did not stop Bush from using the issue to the hilt: "I don't intend to mud-sling with [Yarborough] about such matters as the Billie Sol Estes case since Yarborough's connections with Estes are a simple matter of record which any one can check," said Bush. "[Yarborough is] going to have to prove to the Texas voters that his connections with Billie Sol Estes were as casual as he claims they were."[14] In a release issued on April 24, Bush "said he welcomes the assistance of Gordon McLendon, Yarborough's primary opponent, in trying to force the incumbent Senator to answer." Bush added that he planned to "hammer at Yarborough every step of the way . . . until I get some sort of answer."

The other accusation that was used against Yarborough during the campaign was advanced most notably in an article published in the September 1964 issue of *Reader's Digest*. The story was that Yarborough had facilitated backing and subsidies through the Texas Area Reconstruction Administration for an industrial development project in Crockett, Texas, only to have the project fail owing to the inability of the company involved to build the factory that was planned. The accusation was that Audio Electronics, the prospective factory builders, had received a state loan of $383,000 to build the plant, while townspeople had raised some $60,000 to buy the plant site, before the entire deal fell through.

The *Reader's Digest* told disapprovingly of Yarborough addressing a group of 35 Crockett residents on a telephone squawk box in March, 1963, telling them that he was authorized by the White House to announce "that you are going to gain a fine new industry—one that will provide new jobs for 180 people, add new strength to your area."

The *Reader's Digest* article left the distinct impression that the $60,000 invested by local residents had been lost. "Because people believed that their Senator's 'White House announcement' of the ARA loan to Audio guaranteed the firm's soundness, several Texans invested in it and lost all. One man dropped $40,000. A retired Air Force officer plowed in $7000." It turned out in reality that those who had invested in the real estate for the plant site had lost nothing, but had rather been made an offer for their land that represented a profit of one-third on the original investment, and thus stood to gain substantially.

Bush campaign headquarters immediately got into the act with a statement that "it is a shame" that Texans had to pick up the *Reader's Digest* and find their Senator "holding the hand of scandal. . . . The citizens of the area raised $60,000 in cash, invested it in the company, and lost it because the project was a fraud and never started."

Yarborough shot back with a statement of his own, pointing out that Bush's claims were "basely false," and adding that the "reckless, irresponsible, false charges by my opponent further demonstrate his untruthfulness and unfitness for the office of U.S. Senator." Most telling was Yarborough's charge on how the *Reader's Digest* got interested in Crockett, Texas, in the first place: "The fact that my opponent's multi-millionaire father's Wall Street investment banking connections enable the planting of false and libelous articles about me in a national magazine like the *Reader's Digest* will not enable the Connecticut candidate to buy a Texas seat in the U.S. Senate." (This was not mere rhetoric: *Reader's Digest* General Manager Albert Cole was Prescott Bush's neighbor and fellow member of the Harrimans' secret enclave on Jupiter Island, Florida.) Yarborough's shot was on target, it hurt. Bush whined in response that it was Yarborough's statement which was "false, libelous, and hogwash," and challenged the Senator to prove it or retract it.[15]

Racism and War

Beyond these attempts to smear Yarborough, it is once again characteristic that the principal issue around which Bush built his campaign was racism, expressed this time as opposition to the Civil Rights bill that was before the Congress during 1964. Bush did this certainly in order to conform to his pro-Goldwater ideological profile, and in order to garner votes (especially in the Republican primary) using racist and states' rights backlash, but most of all in order to express the deepest tenets of the philosophical world-outlook of himself and his oligarchical family.

Very early in the campaign, Bush issued a statement saying: "I am opposed to the Civil Rights bill now before the Senate." Not content with that, Bush proceeded immediately to tap the wellsprings of nullification and interposition: "Texas has a comparably good record in civil rights," he argued, "and I'm opposed to the

Federal Government intervening further into State affairs and individual rights." At this point, Bush claimed that his quarrel was not with the entire bill, but rather with two specific provisions, which he claimed had not been a part of the original draft, but which he hinted had been added to placate violent black extremists. According to his statement of March 17, "Bush pointed out that the original Kennedy Civil Rights bill in 1962 did not contain provisions either for a public accommodations section or a Fair Employment Practices Commission (FEPC) section." "Then, after the hot, turbulent summer of 1962, when it became apparent that in order to get the Civil Rights leaders' support and votes in the 1964 election something more must be done, these two bad sections were added to the bill," according to Bush. "I suggest that these two provisions of the bill—which I most heatedly oppose—were politically motivated and are cynical in their approach to a most serious problem."

But Bush soon abandoned this hair-splitting approach, and on March 25 he told the Jaycees of Tyler, "I oppose the entire bill." Bush explained later that beyond the public accommodations section and the Fair Employment Practices Commission, he found that "the most dangerous portions of the bill are those which make the Department of Justice the most powerful police force in the Nation and the Attorney General the Nation's most powerful police chief." Bush also said "the Civil Rights problem is basically a local problem, best left to the States to handle." Here surely was a respectable-sounding racism for the era of Selma and Bull Connor.

Bush was provided with new rhetorical ammunition when Alabama Governor George Wallace ventured into the presidential primaries of that year and demonstrated unexpected vote-getting power in certain northern states, using a pitch that included overtly racist appeals. In the wake of one such result in Wisconsin, the Bush campaign issued a release quoting the candidate as being "sure that a majority of Americans are opposed to the Civil Rights bill now being debated in the Senate. . . . Bush called attention to the surprising 25 percent of the Wisconsin primary vote received by Governor George C. Wallace of Alabama," said the release. In Bush's view, "you can be sure this big vote was not cast for Wallace himself, but was used as a means of showing public opposition to the Civil Rights Bill. . . . If a flamboyant Governor Wallace can get that kind of a vote in a northern state such as Wisconsin, it indicates to me that there must be general concern from many responsible people over the Civil Rights bill all over the nation," Bush said in Houston. "If I were a member of the Senate today, I would vote against this bill in its entirety."

As could be expected from the man who had so recently challenged John F. Kennedy to "muster the courage" to attack Cuba, some of Bush's most vehement pronouncements concerned Castro and Havana, and were doubtless much appreciated by the survivors of Brigade 2506 and the Miami Cubans in the Bay of Pigs fiasco. Bush started off with what passed for a moderate position in Texas Goldwater circles: "I advocate recognition of a Cuban government in exile and would encourage this government every way to reclaim its country. This means financial and military assistance. . . . I think we should not be found wanting in courage to help them liberate their country." Candidate Morris had a similar position, but both Cox and Davis called for an immediate restoration of the naval blockade of Cuba.

Bush therefore went them one up, and endorsed a new invasion of Cuba. A Bush for Senate campaign brochure depicted a number of newspaper articles about the candidate. The headline of one of these, from an unidentified newspaper, reads as follows: "Cuba Invasion Urged by GOP Candidate." The subtitle reads: "George Bush, Houston oilman, campaigning for the Republican nomination to the U.S. Senate called for a new government-in-exile invasion of Cuba, no negotiation of the Panama Canal treaty, and a freedom package in Austin."

What Bush was proposing would have amounted to a vast and well-funded program for arming and financing anti-Castro Cuban exiles in Miami, and putting the United States government at the service of their adventures—presumably far in excess of the substantial programs that were already being funded. Beneficiaries would have included Theodore Shackley, who was by now the station chief at CIA Miami Station, Felix Rodriguez, Chi Chi Quintero, and the rest of the boys from The Enterprise.

In the middle of April, a Republican policy forum held in Miami heard a report from a Cuban exile leader that the Soviets had positioned missiles on the ocean floor off Cuba, with the missiles pointed at the United States, and that this had been confirmed by diplomatic sources in Havana. This would appear in retrospect to have been a planted story. For Bush it was obvious grist for his campaign mill. Bush, speaking in Amarillo, called the report "the most alarming news in this hemisphere in two years." He called for efforts to "drive the Communists out of Cuba."

But, in keeping with the times, Bush's most genocidal campaign statements were made in regard to Vietnam. Here Bush managed to identify himself with the war, with its escalation, and with the use of nuclear weapons.

Senator Goldwater had recently raised the possibility of using tactical nuclear weapons as the most effective defoliants to strip away the triple canopy jungle of Vietnam. In a response to this, an Associated Press story quoted Bush as saying that he was in favor of anything that could be done safely toward finishing the fighting in Southeast Asia. "Bush said he favors a limited extension of the war in Viet Nam, including restricted use of nuclear weapons if 'militarily prudent,' " according to the AP release.[16] A Bush campaign release of June 1 has him saying he favors a "cautious, judicious, and militarily sound extension of the war in Vietnam." This was all before the Gulf of Tonkin incident and well before U.S. ground troops were committed to Vietnam.

Bush pugnaciously took issue with those who wanted to disengage from the Vietnam quagmire before the bulk of the war's human losses had occurred. He made this part of his "Freedom Package," which was a kind of manifesto for a worldwide U.S. imperialist and colonialist offensive—a precursor of the new world order *ante litteram*. A March 30 campaign release proclaims the "Freedom Package" in these terms: " 'I do not want to continue to live in a world where there is no hope for a real and lasting peace,' Bush said. He decried 'withdrawal symptoms' propounded by U.N. Ambassador Adlai Stevenson and Senators J. William Fulbright and Mike Mansfield. 'Adlai has proposed we [inter]nationalize the Panama Canal,' Bush pointed out, 'Fulbright asks us to accommodate Red Cuba and renegotiate our Panama treaty, and Mansfield suggests we withdraw from the Viet Nam struggle. This is the kind of retreatism we have grown accustomed to among our supposed world leaders and it is just what the Kremlin ordered.' "

Nor did Bush's obsession with Panama and the Panama Canal begin with Noriega. In his campaign literature, Bush printed his basic position that the "Panama Canal . . . is ours by right of treaty and historical circumstance. The Canal is critical to our domestic security and U.S. sovereignty over the Canal must be maintained." What is meant by the right of historical circumstance? "I am opposed to further negotiation in Panama," Bush stated repeatedly in his campaign speeches and releases.

Unbridled Free Enterprise

In economic policy, Bush's starting point was always "unbridled free enterprise," as he stressed in a statement on unemployment on March 16: "Only unbridled free enterprise can cure unemployment. But, I don't believe the federal government has given the private sector of our economy a genuine opportunity to relieve this unemployment. For example, the [Johnson war on poverty program] contains a new version of the CCC, a Domestic Peace Corps, and various and sundry half-baked pies in the sky." Bush's printed campaign literature stated, under the heading of "federal economy," that "the free enterprise system must be unfettered. A strong economy means jobs, opportunity, and prosperity. A controlled economy means loss of freedom and bureaucratic bungling." On April 21, Bush told the voters: "We must begin a phase of re-emphasizing the private sector of our economy, instead of the public sector."

By April 15, Bush had been informed that there were some 33 million Americans living in poverty, to which he replied: "I cannot see how draping a socialistic medi-care program around the sagging neck of our social security program will be a blow to poverty. And I can see only one answer to [the problem of poverty]: Let us turn our free enterprise system loose from government control." Otherwise, Bush held it "the responsibility of the local government first to assume the burden of relieving poverty wherever it exists, and I know of many communities that are more than capable of working with this problem."

Bush's approach to farm policy was along similar lines, combining the rhetoric of Adam Smith with intransigent defense of the food cartels. In his campaign brochure he opined that "Agriculture . . . must be restored to a free market economy, subject to the basic laws of supply and demand." On April 9 in Waco, Bush assailed the wheat-cotton price support bill which had just received the approval of the House. "If I am elected to the Senate," said Bush, I will judge each agricultural measure on the basis of whether it gets the Government further into, or out of, private business." Bush added that farm subsidies are among "our most expensive federal programs."

Another of Bush's recurrent obsessions was his desire to break the labor movement. During the 1960s, he expressed this in the context of campaigns to prevent the repeal of section 14 (b) of the Taft-Hartley law, which permitted the states to outlaw the closed shop and union shop, and thus to protect state laws guaranteeing the so-called open shop or "right to work," a device which in practice prevented the organization of large sectors of the working population of these states into unions. Bush's editorializing takes him back to the era when the Sherman Antitrust Act was still being used against labor unions.

"I believe in the right-to-work laws," said Bush to a group of prominent Austin businessmen at a luncheon in the Commodore

Perry Hotel on March 5. "At every opportunity, I urge union members to resist payment of political assessments. If there's only one in 100 who thinks for himself and votes for himself, then he should not be assessed by COPE."

On Labor Day, Bush spoke to a rally in the courthouse square of Quanah, and called for "protection of the rights of the individual laborer through the state rather than the federal government. The individual laboring man is being forgotten by the Walter Reuthers and Ralph Yarboroughs, and it's up to the business community to protect our country's valuable labor resources from exploitation by these left-wing labor leaders," said Bush, who might just as well have suggested that the fox be allowed to guard the chicken coop.

Back in February, Yarborough had remarked in his typical populist vein that his legislative approach was to "put the jam on the lower shelf so the little man can get his hand in." This scandalized Bush, who countered on February 27 that "it's a cynical attitude and one that tends to set the so-called little man apart from the rest of his countrymen." For Bush, the jam would always remain under lock and key, except for the chosen few of Wall Street.

A few days later, on March 5, Bush elaborated that he was "opposed to special interest legislation because it tends to hyphenate Americans. I don't think we can afford to have veteran-Americans, Negro-Americans, Latin-Americans and labor-Americans these days." Here is Bush as political philosopher, maintaining that the power of the authoritarian state must confront its citizens in a wholly atomized form, not organized into interest groups capable of defending themselves.

Bush was especially irate about Yarborough's Cold War G.I. Bill, which he branded the Senator's "pet project." "Fortunately," said Bush, "he has been unable to cram his Cold War G.I. Bill down Congress' throat. It's bad legislation and special interest legislation which will erode our American way of life. I have four sons, and I'd sure hate to think that any of them would measure their devotion and service to their country by what special benefits Uncle Sam could give them." Neil Bush would certainly never do that!

The Oil Cartel's Candidate

There was a soft spot in Bush's heart for at least a few special interests, however. He was a devoted supporter of the "time-proven" 27.5 percent oil depletion allowance, a tax write-off which allowed the Seven Sisters oil cartel to escape a significant portion of what they otherwise would have paid in taxes. Public pressure to reduce this allowance was increasing, and the oil cartel was preparing to concede a minor adjustment, in the hope that this would neutralize attempts to get the depletion allowance abolished entirely. Bush also called for what he described as a "meaningful oil import program, one which would restrict imports at a level that will not be harmful to our domestic oil industry." "I know what it is to earn a paycheck in the oil business," he boasted.

Yarborough's counterattack on this issue is of great relevance to understanding why Bush was so fanatically committed to wage war in the Gulf to restore the degenerate, slaveholding Emir of Kuwait. Yarborough pointed out that Bush's company, Zapata Offshore, was drilling for oil in Kuwait, the Persian Gulf, Borneo, and Trinidad. "Every producing oil well drilled in foreign countries by American companies means more cheap foreign oil in American ports, fewer acres of Texas land under oil and gas lease, less income to Texas farmers and ranchers," Yarborough stated. "This issue is clear-cut in this campaign—a Democratic senator who is fighting for the life of the free enterprise system as exemplified by the independent oil and gas producers in Texas, and a Republican candidate who is the contractual driller for the international oil cartel."

Later in the campaign, Yarborough visited the town of Gladewater in East Texas. There, standing in view of the oil derricks, Yarborough talked about Bush's ownership of Pennzoil stock, and about Pennzoil's quota of 1,690 barrels per day of imported oil, charging that Bush was undermining the Texas producers by importing cheap foreign oil.

Then, according to a newspaper account, "the senator spiced his charge with a reference to the 'Sheik of Kuwait and his four wives and 100 concubines,' who, he said, are living in luxury off the oil from Bush-drilled wells in the Persian Gulf and sold at cut-rate prices in the United States. He said that imported oil sells for $1.25 a barrel while Texas oil, selling at $3, pays school, city, county, and federal taxes and keeps payrolls going. Yarborough began his day of campaigning at a breakfast with supporters in Longview. Later, in Gladewater, he said he had seen a 'Bush for Senator' bumper sticker on a car in Longview. 'Isn't that a come-down for an East Texan to be a strap-hanger for a carpetbagger from Connecticut who is drilling oil for the Sheik of Kuwait to help keep that harem going?' "[17]

Yarborough challenged Bush repeatedly to release more details about his overseas drilling and producing interests. He spoke of Bush's "S.A. corporations drilling in the Persian Gulf in Asia." He charged that Bush had "gone to Latin America to incorporate two of his companies to drill in the Far East, instead of incorporating them in the United States." That in turn, thought Yarborough, "raises questions of tax avoidance." "Tell them, George," he jeered, "what your 'S.A.' companies, financed with American dollars, American capital, American resources, are doing about American income taxes." Bush protested that "every single tax dollar due by any company that I own an interest in has been paid."[18]

The status of the Rural Electrification Administration was also a campaign issue. Goldwater had said in Denver, Colorado on May 3, 1963, that the time had come "to dissolve the Rural Electrification Administration." Wishing to appear as an orthodox Goldwater clone in every respect, Bush had failed to distance himself from this demand. The REA was justly popular for its efforts to bring electric power to impoverished sectors of the countryside. Yarborough noted first of all that Bush "wouldn't know a cotton boll from a corn shuck," but he insisted on leveling "so un-Texan a blow at the farmers and ranchers of Texas. To sell the REA's in Texas to the private power monopoly would be carrying out the demands of the big Eastern power structure and the wishes of the New York investment bankers who handle the private power monopoly financing. My opponent is in line to inherit his share of that New York investment banking structure," Yarborough told a gathering of Texas REA officials.

Following in Prescott Bush's footsteps, George Bush was implacably hostile to government-sponsored infrastructure projects. Such projects are of course the essence of the American System of political economy as understood by Franklin, Hamilton, Lincoln and FDR. One ongoing water project in Texas in 1964 was the Trinity River project. Early in the campaign, Bush said that he could not support this project because it was exacerbating a federal budget deficit that was already too high. But this stance proved so unpopular in the Texas electorate that Bush later flip-flopped, saying that he had been sympathetic to the Trinity River project all along, and that maybe there was a way to get it done without adding to the deficit.

On other issues. Bush's hypocrisy knew no limits:

On Red China: Beijing, said Bush in 1964, "must never be admitted to the U.N. In the event this does occur, then I advocate withdrawal from the United Nations." Bush was the man who later cast his vote for the admission of Red China to the world body in 1971.

On the U.N.: The United Nations "as presently constituted is gravely deficient and has been a failure in preserving peace. The United States has taken the responsibility for the freedom of the western world. This responsibility we must not relinquish to the

General Assembly. All nations should pay their dues or lose their vote."

Forced into a Runoff

As the Republican senatorial primary approached, Bush declared that he was confident that he could win an absolute majority and avoid a runoff. On April 30, he predicted that Hill Rise would win the Kentucky Derby without a runoff, and that he would also carry the day on the first round. There was no runoff in the Kentucky Derby, but Bush fell short of his goal. Bush did come in first with about 44 percent of the vote or 62,579 votes, while Jack Cox was second with 44,079, with Morris third and Milton Davis fourth. The total number of votes cast was 142,961, so a second round was required.

Cox, who had attracted 710,000 votes in his 1962 race against Connally for the governorship, was at this point far better known around the state than Bush. Cox had the backing of Gen. Edwin Walker, who had made a bid for the Democratic gubernatorial nomination in 1962 himself and gotten some 138,000 votes. Cox also had the backing of H.L. Hunt.

Morris had carried Dallas County, and he urged his supporters to vote against Bush. Morris told the *Dallas Morning News* of May 5 that Bush was "too liberal" and that Bush's strength in the primary was due to "liberal" Republican support.

Between early May and the runoff election of June 6, Cox mounted a vigorous campaign of denunciation and exposure of Bush as a creature of the Eastern Liberal Establishment, Wall Street banking interests, and of Goldwater's principal antagonist for the GOP presidential nomination, the hated Gov. Nelson Rockefeller of New York. According to a story filed by Stuart Long of the Long News Service in Austin on May 25, and preserved among the Yarborough papers in the Barker Texas History Center in Austin, Cox's supporters circulated letters pointing to Prescott Bush's role as a partner in Brown Brothers Harriman as the basis for the charge that George Bush was the tool of "Liberal Eastern Kingmakers." According to Long, the letters also include references to the New York Council on Foreign Relations, which he described as a "black-tie dinner group."[19] The pro-Cox letters also asserted that Bush's Zapata Offshore Company had a history of bidding on drilling contracts for Rockefeller's Standard Oil of New Jersey.

One anti-Bush brochure, preserved among the Yarborough papers at the Barker Center in Austin, is entitled "Who's Behind the

Bush?" published by the Coalition of Conservatives to Beat the Bushes, with one Harold Deyo of Dallas listed as chairman. The attack on Bush here centers on the Council on Foreign Relations, of which Bush was not at that time a public member. The brochure lists a number of Bush campaign contributors and then identifies these as members of the CFR. These include Dillon Anderson and J.C. Hutcheson III of Baker, Botts, Andrews and Shepherd; Leland Anderson of Anderson, Clayton and Company; Lawrence S. Reed of Texas Gulf Producing; Frank Michaux; and W.A. Kirkland of the board of First City National Bank. The brochure then focuses on Prescott Bush, identified as a "partner with Averell Harriman in Brown Brothers, Harriman, and Company." Averell Harriman is listed as a member of the Council on Foreign Relations. "Could it be that Prescott S. Bush, in concert with his Eastern CFR friends, is raising all those 'Yankee Dollars' that are flowing into George's campaign? It is reliably reported that Mr. George Bush has contracted for extensive and expensive television time for the last week of the Runoff." The brochure also targets Paul Kayser of Anderson, Clayton, Bush's Harris County campaign chairman. Five officers of this company, named as W.L. Clayton, L. Fleming, Maurice McAshan, Leland Anderson and Sydnor Oden, are said to be members of the CFR.

On the CFR itself, the brochure quotes from Helen P. Lasell's study, entitled "Power Behind Government Today," which found that the CFR "from its inception has had an important part in planning the whole diabolical scheme of creating a ONE WORLD FEDERATION of socialist states under the United Nations. . . . These carefully worked out, detailed plans, in connection with the WORLD BANK and the use of billions of tax-exempt foundation dollars, were carried out secretively over a period of years. Their fruition could mean not only the absolute destruction of our form of government, national independence and sovereignty, but to a degree at least, that of every nation in the world." The New World Order, we see, is really nothing new.

As the runoff vote approached, Cox focused especially on the eastern financing that Bush was receiving. On May 25 in Abilene, Cox assailed Bush for having mounted "one of the greatest spending sprees ever seen in any political campaign." Cox said that he could not hope to match this funding, "because Jack Cox is not, nor will ever be, connected in any manner with the Eastern kingmakers who seek to control political candidates. Conservatives of Texas will serve notice on June 6 that just as surely as Rockefeller's millions can't buy presidential nomination, the millions at George Bush's disposal can't buy him a senate nomination." Cox claimed that all of his contributions had come from inside Texas.

O'Donnell's Texas Republican organization was overwhelmingly mobilized in favor of Bush. Bush had the endorsement of the state's leading newspapers. When the runoff finally came, Bush was the winner with some 62 percent of the votes cast. Yarborough commented that Bush "smothered Jack Cox in greenbacks."

Gordon McLendon, true to form, had used his own pre-primary television broadcast to rehash the Billie Sol Estes charges against Yarborough. Yarborough nevertheless defeated McLendon in the Democratic senatorial primary with almost 57 percent of the vote. Given the lopsided Texas Democratic advantage in registered voters, and given LBJ's imposing lead over Goldwater at the top of the Democratic ticket, it might have appeared that Yarborough's victory was now a foregone conclusion. That this was not so was due to the internal divisions within the Texas Democratic ranks.

Senate Seat Couldn't Be Bought

First were the Democrats who came out openly for Bush. The vehicle for this defection was called Conservative Democrats for Bush, chaired by Ed Drake, the former leader of the state's Democrats for Eisenhower in 1952. Drake was joined by former Governor Allan Shivers, who had also backed Ike and Dick in 1952 and 1956. Then there was the "East Texas Democrats for George Bush Committee," chaired by E.B. Germany, the former state Democratic leader, a leader of Scottish Rite Freemasons in Texas and in 1964 the chairman of the board of Lone Star Steel.

Then there were various forms of covert support for Bush. Millionaire Houston oilman Lloyd Bentsen, who had been in Congress back in the late 1940s, had been in discussion as a possible Senate candidate. Bush's basic contention was that LBJ had interfered in Texas politics to tell Bentsen to stay out of the Senate race, thus avoiding a more formidable primary challenge to Yarborough. On April 24, Bush stated that Bentsen was a "good conservative" who had been kept out of the race by "Yarborough's bleeding heart act." This and other indications point to a covert political entente between Bush and Bentsen, which re-appeared during the 1988 presidential campaign.

Then there were the forces associated with Governor Big John Connally. Yarborough later confided that Connally had done everything in his power to wreck his campaign, subject only to certain restraints imposed by LBJ. Even these limitations did not amount to real support for Yarborough on the part of LBJ, but were rather attributable to LBJ's desire to avoid the embarrassment of seeing his native state represented by two Republican Senators during his own tenure in the White House. But Connally still sabotaged Yarborough as much as LBJ would let him get away with.[20]

In public, LBJ was for Yarborough, although he could not wholly pass over the frictions between the two. Speaking at Stonewall after the Democratic national convention, LBJ had commented: "You have heard and you have read that Sen. Yarborough and I have had differences at times. I have read a good deal more about them than I was ever aware of. But I do want to say this, that I don't think that Texas has had a senator during my lifetime whose record I am more familiar with than Sen. Yarborough's. And I don't think Texas has had a senator that voted for the people more than Sen. Yarborough has voted for them. And no member of the U.S. Senate has stood up and fought for me or fought for the people more since I became President than Ralph Yarborough." For his part, Bush, years later, quoted a *Time* magazine analysis of the 1964 Senate race which concluded that "if Lyndon would stay out of it, Republican Bush would have a chance. But Johnson is not about to stay out of it, which makes Bush the underdog."[21]

Yarborough's strategy in the November election centered on identifying Bush with Goldwater in the minds of voters, since the Arizona Republican's warlike rhetoric was now dragging him down to certain defeat. Yarborough's first instinct had been to run a substantive campaign, stressing issues and his own legislative accomplishments. Yarborough in 1988 told Bush biographer Fitzhugh Green: "When I started my campaign for re-election I was touting my record of six years in the Senate. But my speech advisers said, all you have to do is quote Bush, who had already called himself 100 per cent for Goldwater and the Vietnam war. So that's what I did, and it worked very well."[22]

Campaigning in Port Arthur on October 30, a part of the state where his labor support loomed large, Yarborough repeatedly attacked Bush as "more extreme than Barry Goldwater." According to Yarborough, even after Barry Goldwater had repudiated the support of the John Birch Society, Bush said that he "welcomed support of the Birch Society and embraced it." "Let's you elect a senator from Texas, and not the Connecticut investment bankers with their $2,500,000," Yarborough urged the voters.[23]

These attacks were highly effective, and Bush's response was to mobilize his media budget for more screenings of his World War II "Flight of the Avenger" television spot, while he prepared a last-minute television dirty trick. There was to be no debate between Bush and Yarborough, but this did not prevent Bush from staging a televised "empty chair" debate, which was aired on more than a dozen stations around the state on October 27. The Bush campaign staff scripted a debate in which Bush answered doctored quotes from audio tapes of Yarborough speaking, with the sentences often cut in half, taken out of context, and otherwise distorted. Yarborough responded by saying: "The sneaky trick my opponent is trying to pull on me tonight of pulling sentences of mine out of context with my recorded voice and playing my voice as a part of his broadcast is illegal under the law, and a discredit to anyone who aspires to be a U.S. Senator. I intend to protest this illegal trick to the Federal Communications Commission." Bush's method was to "cut my statements in half, then let his Madison Avenue speech writers answer those single sentences. . . . My opponent is an exponent of extremism, peddling smear and fear wherever he goes. . . . His conduct looks more like John Birch Society conduct than United States Senate conduct," Yarborough added. Bush also distorted the sound of Yarborough's voice almost beyond recognition.

Yarborough protested to the FCC in Washington, alleging that Bush had violated section 315 of the Federal Communications Act as it then stood, because Yarborough's remarks were pre-censored and used without his permission. Yarborough also accused Bush of violation of section 325 of the same act, since it appeared that parts of the "empty chair" broadcast were material that had been previously broadcast elsewhere, and which could not be re-used without permission. The FCC responded by saying that the tapes used had been made in halls where Yarborough was speaking.

Bush was also smarting under Yarborough's repeated references to his New England birth and background. Bush claimed that he was no carpetbagger, but a Texan by choice, and compared himself in that regard to Sam Rayburn, Sam Houston, Stephen Austin, Colonel Bill Travis, Davy Crockett, Jim Bowie and other heroes of the Alamo. Bush was not hobbled by any false modesty.

In the last days of the campaign, Allan Duckworth of the pro-Bush *Dallas Morning News* was trying to convince his readers that the race was heading for a "photo finish." But in the end, Prescott's networks, the millions of dollars, the recordings, and the endorsements of 36 newspapers were of no avail for Bush. Yarborough defeated Bush by a margin of 1,463,958 to 1,134,337. Within the context of the LBJ landslide victory over Goldwater, Bush had done somewhat better than his party's standard bearer: LBJ beat Goldwater in Texas by 1,663,185 to 958,566. Yarborough, thanks in part to his vote in favor of the Civil Rights Act, won a strong majority of the black districts, and also ran well ahead among Latinos. Bush won the usual Republican counties, including the pockets of GOP support in the Houston area.

Yarborough would continue for one more term in the Senate, vocally opposing the war in Vietnam. In the closing days of the campaign he had spoken of Bush and his retinue as harbingers of a "time and society when nobody speaks for the working man." George Bush, defeated though he was, would now redouble his struggle to make such a world a reality. Yarborough, although victorious, appears in retrospect as the fading rearguard of an imperfect but better America that would disappear during the late sixties and seventies.

Notes for Chapter IX

1. George Bush and Victor Gold, *Looking Forward* (New York: Doubleday, 1987), p. 84.
2. *Ibid.*
3. John R. Knaggs, *Two-Party Texas* (Austin: Eakin Press, 1985), p. 34.
4. For a summary of the Southern Strategy, see Garry Wills, *Nixon Agonistes* (Boston: Houghton Mifflin, 1970), pp. 262 ff.
5. For a profile of Yarborough's voting record on this and other issues, see Chandler Davidson, *Race and Class in Texas Politics* (Princeton: Princeton University Press, 1990), pp. 29 ff.
6. For Yarborough's Senate achievements up to 1964, see Ronnie Dugger, "The Substance of the Senate Contest," in *The Texas Observor*, Sept. 18, 1964.
7. Bush and Gold, *op. cit.*, p. 77 ff.
8. See Harry Hurt III, *Texas Rich* (New York: W.W. Norton, 1981), p. 191; and also Thomas Petzinger, Jr., *Oil and Honor* (New York: Putnam, 1987), passim.
9. On Bush's drive to become Harris County chairman, it is instructive to compare his *Looking Forward* with the clippings from the *Houston Chronicle* of those days, preserved on microfiche in the Texas Historical Society in Houston. Bush says that he decided to run for the post in the spring of 1962, but the Houston press clearly situates the campaign in the spring of 1963. Bush also claims to have been county chairman for two years, whereas the Houston papers show that he served from February 20, 1963 to around December 5, 1963, less than one year.
10. Harry Hurt III, "George Bush, Plucky Lad," *Texas Monthly*, June 1983, p. 196.
11. *Houston Chronicle*, Feb. 21, 1963.
12. See Barbara Bush, *C. Fred's Story* (New York: Doubleday, 1984), p. 2.
13. See Ronnie Dugger, "The Four Republicans," in *The Texas Observer*, April 17, 1964.
14. Quotations from Bush and Yarborough campaign material, except as otherwise indicated, are from Senator Yarborough's papers on deposit in the Eugene C. Barker Texas History Center at the University of Texas in Austin.
15. See Ronnie Dugger, "The Substance of the Senate Contest," in *The Texas Observer*, Sept. 18, 1964.
16. Cited in Ronnie Dugger, *ibid.*
17. *Dallas News,* Oct. 24, 1964.
18. *Dallas News,* Oct. 3, 1964.
19. An untitled report among the Yarborough papers in the Barker Texas History Center refers to "Senator Bush's affiliation in a New York knife-and-fork-club type of organization called, 'The Council on Foreign Relations.' In a general smear—mainly via the 'I happen to know' letter chain of communication—the elder Bush was frequently attacked, and the younger Bushes were greatly relieved when Barry Goldwater volunteered words of affectionate praise for his former colleague during a $100-a-plate Dallas dinner."
20. Just how far these efforts might have gone is a matter of speculation. See Douglas Caddy, *The Hundred Million Dollar Payoff* (New Rochelle: Arlington House, 1974), p. 300.
21. See Bush and Gold, *op. cit.,* p. 87.

22. Fitzhugh Green, *George Bush: An Intimate Portrait* (New York: Hippocrene Books, 1989), p. 85.

23. *Dallas News,* Oct. 31, 1964.

29. Ronnie Dugger, "Goldwater's Policies, Kennedy's Style" in *Texas Observer,* Oct. 30, 1964.

X

RUBBERS GOES
TO CONGRESS

During the heat of the Senate campaign, Bush's redistricting lawsuit had progressed in a way that must have provided him much solace amidst the bitterness of his defeat. First Bush won his suit in the Houston federal district court. Then during Bush's primary campaign, a three-judge panel of the federal circuit court of appeals also ruled that the state of Texas must be redistricted. Bush called that result "a real victory for all the people of Texas." By March, Bush's redistricting suit had received favorable action by the U.S. Supreme Court. This meant that the way was clear to create a no-incumbent, designer district for George in a masterpiece of gerrymandering that would make him an elected official, the first Republican Congressman in the recent history of the Houston area.

The new Seventh District was drawn to create a liberal Republican seat, carefully taking into account which areas Bush had succeeded in carrying in the Senate race. What emerged was for the most part a lily-white, silk-stocking district of the affluent upper-middle class and upper crust. There were also small black and Hispanic enclaves. In the precinct boxes of the new district, Bush had rolled up an eight-to-five margin over Yarborough.[1]

But before gearing up a congressional campaign in the Seventh District in 1966, Bush first had to jettison some of the useless ideological ballast he had taken on for his 1964 Goldwater profile. During the 1964 campaign, Bush had spoken out more frankly and more bluntly on a series of political issues than ever before or since. Apart from the Goldwater coloration, one comes away with the impression that much of the time the speeches were not just inventions, but often reflected his own oligarchical instincts and deeply-rooted obsessions. In late 1964 and early 1965, Bush was afflicted by a hangover induced by what for him had been an unprecedented orgy of self-revelation.

The 1965–66 model George Bush would become a moderate, abandoning the shrillest notes of the 1964 conservative crusade.

As Bush's admirer Fitzhugh Green reports, "one of his first steps was to shuck off a bothersome trace from his 1964 campaign. He had espoused some conservative ideas that didn't jibe with his own moderate attitude." Previous statements were becoming inoperative, one gathers, when Bush discussed the matter with his Anglican pastor, John Stevens. "You know, John," said Bush, "I took some of the far right positions to get elected. I hope I never do it again. I regret it." His radical stance on the civil rights bill was allegedly a big part of his "regret." Stevens later commented: "I suspect that his goal on civil rights was the same as mine: It's just that he wanted to go through the existing authorities to attain it. In that way nothing would get done. Still, he represents about the best of noblesse oblige."[2]

It was characteristically through an attempted purge in the Harris County GOP organization that Bush signaled that he was reversing his field. His gambit here was to call on party activists to take an "anti-extremist and anti-intolerance pledge," as the Houston Chronicle reported on May 26, 1965.[3] Bush attacked unnamed apostles of "guilt by association" and "far-out fear psychology," and his pronouncements touched off a bitter and protracted row in the Houston GOP. Bush made clear that he was targeting the John Birch Society, whose activists he had been eager to lure into his own 1964 effort. Now Bush beat up on the Birchers as a way to correct his right-wing profile from the year before. Bush said, with his usual tortured syntax, that Birch members claim to "abhor smear and slander and guilt by association, but how many of them speak out against it publicly?"

This was soon followed by a Bush-inspired move to oust Bob Gilbert, who had been Bush's successor as the GOP county chairman during the Goldwater period. Bush's retainers put out the line that the "extremists" had been gaining too much power under Gilbert, and that he therefore must go. By June 12, 1965, the Bush faction had enough clout to oust Gilbert. The éminence grise of the right-wing faction, state Senator Walter Mengdon, told the press that the ouster of Gilbert had been dictated by Bush. Bush whined in response that he was very disappointed with Mengdon. "I have stayed out of county politics. I believed all Republicans had backed my campaign," Bush told the *Houston Chronicle* on the day Gilbert fell.

On July 1, the Houston papers reported the election of a new, "anti-extremist" Republican county leader. This was James M. Mayor, who defeated James Bowers by a margin of 95 votes against 80 in the county executive committee. Mayor was endorsed by Bush, as well as by Senator Tower. Bowers was an auctioneer, who called for a return to the Goldwater "magic." GOP state chair O'Donnell hoped that the new chairman would be able to put an end to "the great deal of dissension within the party in Harris County for several years." Despite this pious wish, acrimonious faction fighting tore the county organization to pieces over the next several years.

Congress in his Sights

In 1966 George Bush left his position as president of Zapata Offshore to devote himself full-time to his climb up the ladder of political power.

As the 1966 congressional election approached, Bush was optimistic about his chances of finally getting elected. This time, instead of swimming against the tide of the Goldwater cataclysm, Bush would be favored by the classic mid-term election reflex which almost always helps the congressional candidates of the party out of power. And LBJ in the White House was vulnerable on a number of points, from the escalation of the Vietnam War to "stagflation" (stagnation + inflation). The designer gerrymandering of the new Houston congressional district had functioned perfectly, and so had his demagogic shift toward the "vital center" of moderate conservatism. Because the district was newly drawn, there would be no well-known incumbent to contend with. And now, by one of the convenient coincidences that seem to be strewn through Bush's life, the only obstacle between him and election was a troglodyte Democratic conservative of an ugly and vindictive type, the sort of figure who would make even Bush look reasonable.

The Democrat in question was Frank Briscoe, a former district attorney. According to the *Texas Observer*, "Frank Briscoe was one of the most vicious prosecutors in Houston's history. He actually maintained a 'ten most wanted convictions list' by which he kept the public advised of how much luck he had getting convictions against his chosen defendants then being held in custody. Now, as a candidate for Congress, Briscoe is running red-eyed for the right-wing in Houston. He is anti-Democratic; anti-civil rights; anti-foreign aid; anti-war on poverty. The fact that he calls himself a Democrat is utterly irrelevant." By contrast, from the point of view of the *Texas Observer*: "His opponent, George Bush, is a conservative man. He favors the war in Vietnam; he was for Goldwater, although probably reluctantly; he is nobody's firebrand. Yet Bush is simply civilized in race relations, and he is now openly rejecting the support of the John Birch Society. This is one case where electing a Republican to Congress would help preserve the two-party balance of the country and at the same time spare Texas the embarrassment" of having somebody like Briscoe go to Washington.[4] Bush's ideological face-lifting was working. "I want conservatism to be sensitive and dynamic, not scared and reactionary," Bush told the *Wall Street Journal*.

Frank Briscoe appears in retrospect as a candidate made to order for Bush's new moderate profile, and there are indications that is just what he was. Sources in Houston recall that in 1966 there was another Democratic candidate for the new congressional seat, a moderate and attractive Democrat named Wildenthal. These sources say that Bush's backers provided large-scale financial support for Briscoe in the Democratic primary campaign, with the result that Wildenthal lost out to Briscoe, setting up the race that Bush found to his advantage. A designer district was not enough for George; he also required a designer opponent if he were to prevail—a fact which may be relevant to the final evaluation of what happened in 1988.

One of the key points of differentiation between Bush and Briscoe was on race. The district had about 15 percent black population, but making some inroads here among registered Democrats would be of decisive importance for the GOP side. Bush made sure that he was seen sponsoring a black baseball team, and talked a lot about his work for the United Negro College Fund when he had been at Yale. He told the press that "black power" agitators were not a problem among the more responsible blacks in Houston. "I think the day is past," Bush noted, "when we can afford to have a lily white district. I will not attempt to appeal to the white backlash. I am in step with the 1960's." Bush even took up a position in the Office of Economic Opportunity anti-poverty apparatus in the city. He supported Project Head Start. By contrast, Frank Briscoe "accused" Bush of courting black support, and reminded Bush that other Texas Congressmen had been voting against civil rights legislation when it came up in Congress. Briscoe had antagonized parts of the black community by his relentless pursuit of the death penalty in cases involving black capital defendants. According to the *New York Times*, "Negro leaders have mounted a quiet campaign to get Negroes to vote for [Bush]."

Briscoe's campaign ads stressed that he was a right-winger and a Texan, and accused Bush of being "the darling of the Lindsey [sic] - Javits crowd," endorsed by labor unions, liberal professors, liberal Republicans and liberal syndicated columnists. Briscoe was proud of his endorsements from Gov. John Connally and the Conservative Action Committee, a local right-wing group. One endorsement for Bush that caused Briscoe some difficulty was that of Bush mentor Richard M. Nixon. By 1966, Nixon was on the comeback trail, having withstood the virtual nervous breakdown he had undergone after losing his bid for the governorship of California in 1962. Nixon was now in the course of assembling the delegates that would give him the GOP presidential nomination in Miami in 1968. Nixon came to Houston and made campaign appearances for Bush, as he had in 1964.

Bush had brought in a new group of handlers and image-mongers for this 1966 race. His campaign manager was Jim Allison from Midland. Harry Treleaven was brought in to design Bush's propaganda.

Treleaven had been working at the J. Walter Thompson Advertising Agency in New York City, but he took a leave of absence from J. Walter to come to work for Bush in Texas. At J. Walter Thompson, Treleaven had sold the products of Pan American, RCA, Ford, and Lark cigarettes. He was attracted to Bush because Bush had plenty of money and was willing to spend it liberally. After the campaign was over, Treleaven wrote a long memo about what he had done. He called it "Upset: The Story of a Modern Political Campaign." One of the basic points in Treleaven's selling of Bush was that issues would play no role. "Most national issues today are so complicated, so difficult to understand, and have opinions on[,] that they either intimidate or, more often, bore the average voter. . . . Few politicians recognize this fact." In his memo, Treleaven describes how he walked around Houston in the hot August of 1966 and asked people what they thought of George Bush. He found that many considered Bush to be "an extremely likeable person," but that "there was a haziness about exactly where he stood politically."

For Treleaven, this was an ideal situation. "There'll be few opportunities for logical persuasion, which is all right—because probably more people vote for irrational, emotional reasons than professional politicians suspect." Treleaven's approach was that "politicians are celebrities." Treleaven put 85 percent of Bush's hefty campaign budget into advertising, and 59 percent of that was for television. Newspaper ads got 3 percent. Treleaven knew that Bush was behind in the polls. "We can turn this into an advantage," he wrote, "by creating a 'fighting underdog' image. Bush must convince voters that he really wants to be elected and is working hard to earn their vote. People sympathize with a man who tries hard: they are also flattered that anyone would really exert himself to get their vote. Bush, therefore, must be shown as a man who's working his heart out to win."

As Joe McGinnis summed up the television ads that resulted: "Over and over, on every television set in Houston, George Bush was seen with his coat slung over a shoulder; his sleeves rolled up; walking the streets of his district; grinning, gripping, sweating, letting the voter know he cared. About what, was never made clear."[5]

Coached by these professional spin doctors, Bush was acting as mainstream, fair and conciliatory as could be.

In Bush's campaign ads he invited the voters to "take a couple of minutes and see if you don't agree with me on six important points," including Vietnam, inflation, civil disobedience, jobs, voting rights and "extremism" (Bush was against the far right and the far left). And there was George, billed as "successful businessman . . . civic leader . . . world traveler . . . war hero," bareheaded in a white shirt and tie, with his jacket slung over his shoulder in the post-Kennedy fashion.

In the context of a pro-GOP trend that brought 59 freshmen Republican Congressmen into the House, the biggest influx in two decades, Bush's calculated approach worked. Bush got about 35 percent of the black vote, 44 percent of the usually yellow-dog Democrat rural vote, and 70 percent in the exclusive River Oaks suburb. Still, his margin was not large: Bush got 58 percent of the votes in the district. Bob Gray, the candidate of the Constitution Party, got less than 1 percent.

Despite the role of black voters in his narrow victory, Bush could not refrain from whining. "If there was a disappointing aspect in the vote, it was my being swamped in the black precincts, despite our making an all-out effort to attract black voters. It was both puzzling and frustrating," Bush observed in his 1987 campaign autobiography.[6] Many black voters had not been prepared to reward Bush's noblesse oblige, and that threw him into a rage state, whether or not his thyroid was already working overtime in 1966.

Rubbers in Congress

When Bush got to Washington in January 1967, the Brown Brothers Harriman networks delivered: Bush became the first freshman member of the House of either party since 1904 to be given a seat on the Ways and Means Committee. And he did this, it must be recalled, as a member of the minority party, and in an era when the freshman Congressman was supposed to be seen and not heard. The Ways and Means Committee in those years was still a real center of power, one of the most strategic points in the House along with the Rules Committee and a few others. By constitutional provision, all tax legislation had to originate in the House of Representatives, and given the traditions of committee organization, all tax bills had to originate in the Ways and Means Committee. In addition to the national importance of such a committee assignment, Ways and Means oversaw the legislation touching such vital Texas and district concerns as oil and gas depletion allowances and the like.

Later writers have marveled at Bush's achievement in getting a seat on Ways and Means. For John R. Knaggs, this reflected "the great potential national Republicans held for George Bush." The *Houston Chronicle*, which had supported Briscoe in the election, found that with this appointment, "the GOP was able to point up to the state one benefit of a two-party system."[7]

In this case, unlike so many others, we are able to establish how the invisible hand of Skull and Bones actually worked to procure Bush this important political plum. This is due to the indiscretion of the man who was chairman of Ways and Means for many years, Democratic Congressman Wilbur D. Mills of Arkansas. Mills was hounded out of office because of an alcoholism problem, and later found work as an attorney for a tax law firm. Asked about the Bush appointment to the committee he controlled back in 1967, Mills said: "I put him on. I got a phone call from his father telling me how much it mattered to him. I told him I was a Democrat and the Republicans had to decide; and he said the Republicans would do it if I just asked Gerry Ford." Mills said that he had asked Ford and John W. Byrnes of Wisconsin, who was the ranking Republican on Ways and Means, and Bush was in, thanks once again to Daddy Warbucks, Prescott Bush.[8]

Wilbur Mills may have let himself in for a lot of trouble in later years by not always treating George with due respect. Because of Bush's obsession with birth control for the lower orders, Mills gave Bush the nickname "Rubbers," which stuck with him during his years in Congress.[9] Poppy Bush was not amused. One day Mills might ponder in retrospect, as so many others have, on Bush's vindictiveness.

Wilbur Mills's career in public life was destroyed during the Ford presidency, when he was found cavorting drunk in public with the dancer Fanny Foxe. This came in an era when the Church and Pike congressional committees had been pounding the CIA, and when George Bush was about to take over as CIA Director. The fall of Wilbur Mills, together with the Koreagate scandal of alleged congressional influence peddling, appeared at the time as retaliation designed to knock the Congress on the defensive.

Population Control Champion

With a will informed by the ideas about population, race and economic development that we have seen current in Prescott Bush's circles at Brown Brothers Harriman, George Bush's principal role in Congress would now become protagonist of a series of institutional changes which would contribute to that overall degradation of the cultural paradigm of Western civilization which was emergent at the end of the 1960s.

In 1969, Bush told the House of Representatives that, unless the menace of human population growth were "recognized and made manageable, starvation, pestilence and war will solve it for us." Bush repeatedly compared population growth to a disease.[10] In remarks to the House July 30, 1969, he likened the fight against the polio virus to the crusade to reduce the world's population. Urging the federal government to step up population control efforts, he said: "We have a clear precedent: When the Salk vaccine was discovered, large-scale programs were undertaken to distribute it. I see no reason why similar programs of education and family planning assistance should not be instituted in the United States on a massive scope."

As Jessica Mathews, vice president of one of Washington's most influential zero-growth outfits, the World Resources Institute, later wrote of Bush in those years: "In the 1960s and '70s, Bush had not only embraced the cause of domestic and international family planning, he had aggressively sought to be its champion. . . . As a member of the Ways and Means Committee, Rep. Bush shepherded the first major breakthrough in domestic family planning legislation in 1967," and "later co-authored the legislation commonly known as Title X, which created the first federal family planning program. . . . On the international front," Mathews wrote, Bush "recommended that the U.S. support the United Nations Population Fund.

. . . He urged, in the strongest words, that the U.S. and European countries make modern contraceptives available 'on a massive scale,' to all those around the world who wanted them."

Bush belonged to a small group of Congressmen who successfully conspired to force a profound shift in the official U.S. attitude and policy toward population expansion. Embracing the "limits to growth" ideology with a vengeance, Bush and his coterie, which included such ultraliberal Democrats as then-Senator Walter Mondale (Minn.) and Rep. James Scheuer (N.Y.), labored to enact legislation which institutionalized population control as U.S. domestic and foreign policy.

Bush began his Malthusian activism in the House in 1968, the year that Pope Paul VI issued his encyclical *Humanae Vitae*, with its prophetic warning of the danger of coercion by governments for the purpose of population control. The Pope wrote: "Let it be considered also that a dangerous weapon would be placed in the hands of those public authorities who place no heed of moral exigencies. . . . Who will stop rulers from favoring, from even imposing upon their people, the method of contraception which they judge to be most efficacious?" For poorer countries with a high population rate, the encyclical identified the only rational and humane policy: "No solution to these difficulties is acceptable which does violence to man's essential dignity. . . . The only possible solution . . . is one which envisages the social and economic progress both of individuals and of the whole of human society. . . ."

This was a direct challenge to the cultural paradigm transformation which Bush and other exponents of the oligarchical world outlook were promoting. Not for the first time nor for the last, Bush issued a direct attack on the Holy See. Just days after *Humanae Vitae* was issued, Bush declared: "I have decided to give my vigorous support for population control in both the United States and the world." He continued, "For those of us who feel so strongly on this issue, the recent encyclical was most discouraging."

During his four years in Congress, Bush not only introduced key pieces of legislation to enforce population control both at home and abroad. He also continuously introduced into the congressional debate reams of propaganda about the threat of population growth and the "inferiority" of blacks, and he set up a special Republican task force which functioned as a forum for the most rabid Malthusian ideologues.

Bush's open, public advocacy of government measures tending toward zero population growth was a radical departure from the policies built into the federal bureaucracy up until that time. The climate of opinion just a few years earlier, in December 1959, is illustrated by the comments of President Eisenhower, who had said, "birth control is not our business. I cannot imagine anything more emphatically a subject that is not a proper political or governmental activity . . . or responsibility."

As a Congressman, Bush played an absolutely pivotal role in this shift. Shortly after arriving in Washington, he teamed up with fellow Republican Herman Schneebeli to offer a series of amendments to the Social Security Act to place priority emphasis on what was euphemistically called "family planning services." The avowed goal was to reduce the number of children born to women on welfare.

Bush's and Schneebeli's amendments reflected the Malthusian-genocidalist views of Dr. Alan Guttmacher, then president of Planned Parenthood, and a protégé of its founder, Margaret Sanger. In the years before the grisly outcome of the Nazi cult of race science and eugenics had inhibited public calls for defense of the "gene pool," Sanger had demanded the weeding out of the "unfit" and the "inferior races," and had campaigned vigorously for sterilization, infanticide and abortion, in the name of "race betterment."

Although Planned Parenthood was forced, during the fascist era and immediately thereafter, to tone down Sanger's racist rhetoric from "race betterment" to "family planning" for the benefit of the poor and racial minorities, the organization's basic goal of curbing the population growth rate among "undesirables" never really changed. Bush publicly asserted that he agreed "1,000 percent" with Planned Parenthood.

During hearings on the Social Security amendments, Bush and witness Dr. Alan Guttmacher had the following colloquy:

Bush: Is there any [opposition to Planned Parenthood] from any other organizations or groups, civil rights groups?

Guttmacher: We do have problems. We are in a sensitive area in regard particularly to the Negro. There are some elements in the Negro group that feel we are trying to keep down the numbers. We are very sensitive to this. We have a community relations department headed by a most capable Negro social worker to try to handle that part of the problem. This does, of course, cause us a good bit of concern.

Bush: I appreciate that. For the record, I would like to say I am 1,000 percent in accord with the goals of your organization. I think perhaps more than any other type of organization you can do more in the field of poverty and mental health and everything else than any other group that I can think of. I commend you.

Like his father before him, Bush supported Planned Parenthood at every opportunity. Time after time, he rose on the floor of the House to praise Planned Parenthood's work. In 1967, Bush called for "having the government agencies work even more closely with going private agencies such as Planned Parenthood." A year later, he urged those interested in "advancing the cause of family planning," to "call your local Planned Parenthood Center" to offer "help and support."

The Bush-Schneebeli amendments were aimed at reducing the number of children born to blacks and poor whites. The legislation required all welfare recipients, including mothers of young children, to seek work, and barred increases in federal aid to states where the proportion of dependent children on welfare increased.

Reducing the welfare rolls was a prime Bush concern. He frequently motivated his population-control crusade with thinly veiled appeals to racism, as in his infamous Willie Horton ads during the 1988 presidential campaign. Talking about the rise in the welfare rolls in a July 1968 statement, Bush lamented that "our national welfare costs are rising phenomenally." Worse, he warned, there were far too many children being born to welfare mothers: "The fastest-growing part of the relief rolls everywhere is Aid For Dependent Children [sic]—AFDC [Aid to Families with Dependent Children]. At the end of the 1968 fiscal year, a little over $2 billion will be spent for AFDC, but by fiscal 1972 this will increase by over 75 percent."

Bush emphasized that more children are born into non-white poor families than to white ones. Blacks must recognize, he said, "that they cannot hope to acquire a larger share of American prosperity without cutting down on births. . . ."

Forcing mothers on welfare to work was believed to be an effective means of reducing the number of black children born, and Bush sponsored a number of measures to do just that. In 1970, he helped lead the fight on the Hill for President Nixon's notorious welfare bill, the Family Assistance Program, known as FAP. Billed as a boon to the poor because it provided an income floor, the measure called on every able-bodied welfare recipient, except mothers with children under six, to take a job. This soon became known as Nixon's "workfare" slave-labor bill. Monetarist theoreticians of economic austerity were quick to see that forced labor by welfare recipients could be used to break the unions where they existed, while lowering wages and worsening working conditions for the entire labor force. Welfare recipients could even be hired as scabs to replace workers being paid according to normal pay scales. Those workers, after they had been fired, would themselves end up destitute and on welfare, and could then be forced to take workfare for even lower wages than those who had been on welfare at the outset of the process. This was known as "recycling."

Critics of the Nixon workfare bill pointed out that it contained no minimum standards regarding the kinds of jobs or the level of wages which would be forced upon welfare recipients, and that it contradicted the original purpose of welfare, which was to allow mothers to stay home with their children. Further, it would set up a pool of virtual slave labor, which could be used to replace workers earning higher wages.

But Bush thought these tough measures were exactly what the explosion of the welfare rolls demanded. During House debate on the measure April 15, 1970, Bush said he favored FAP because it would force the lazy to work: "The family assistance plan . . . is oriented toward work," he said. "The present federal-state welfare system encourages idleness by making it more profitable to be on welfare than to work, and provides no method by which the State may limit the number of individuals added to the rolls."

Bush had only "one major worry, and that is that the work incentive provisions will not be enforced. . . . [It] is essential that the program be administered as visualized by the Ways and Means Committee; namely, if an individual does not work, he will not receive funds." The Manchester School's Iron Law of Wages as expounded by George Bush, self-styled expert in the dismal science.

In 1967, Bush joined with Rep. James Scheuer (D-N.Y.), to successfully sponsor legislation that removed prohibitions against mailing and importing contraceptive devices. More than opening the door to French-made condoms, Bush's goal here was a kind of ideological *succes de scandale*. The zero-growth lobby deemed this a major breakthrough in making the paraphernalia for domestic population control accessible.

In rapid succession, Bush introduced legislation to create a National Center for Population and Family Planning and Welfare, and to redesignate the Department of the Interior as the Department of Resources, Environment and Population.

On the foreign policy front, he helped shift U.S. foreign assistance away from funding development projects to grapple with the problem of hunger in the world, to underwriting population control. "I propose that we totally revamp our foreign aid program to give primary emphasis to population control," he stated in the summer of 1968, adding: "In my opinion, we have made a mistake in our foreign aid by concentrating on building huge steel mills and concrete plants in underdeveloped nations. . . ."

One of Bush's more important initiatives on the domestic side was his sponsorship of the Family Planning Services and Population Research Act of 1970, brainchild of Sen. Joseph Tydings of Maryland. Signed into law by President Nixon on December 24, 1970, the Tydings-Bush bill drastically increased the federal financial commitment to population control, authorizing an initial $382 million for family planning services, population research, population education and information through 1973. Much of this money was funnelled through private institutions, particularly local clinics run by Bush's beloved Planned Parenthood. The Tydings-Bush measure mandated the notorious Title X, which explicitly provided "family planning assistance" to the poor. Bush and his zero-growth cohorts talked constantly about the importance of disseminating birth control to the poor. They claimed that there were over five million poor women who wanted to limit their families, but could not afford to do so.

On October 23, 1969, Bush praised the Office of Economic Opportunity for carrying out some of the "most successful" family planning projects, and said he was "pleased" that the Nixon administration "is giving them additional financial muscle by increasing their funds 50 percent—from $15 million to $22 million."

This increased effort he attributed to the Nixon administration's "goal to reach in the next five years the 5 million women in need of these services"—all of them poor, many of them from racial or ethnic minorities. He added: "One needs only to look quickly at the report prepared by the Planned Parenthood-World Population Research Department to see how ineffective federal, state, and local governments have been in providing such necessary services. There is certainly nothing new about the fact that unwanted pregnancies of our poor and near-poor women keep the incidence of infant mortality and mental retardation in America at one of the highest levels of all the developed countries."

The rates of infant mortality and mental retardation Bush was so concerned about, could have been significantly reduced, had the government provided sufficient financing to pre-natal care, nutrition, and other factors contributing to the health of infants and children. On the same day he signed the Tydings-Bush bill, Nixon vetoed—with Bush's support—legislation that would have set up a three-year, $225 million program to train family doctors.

Bush seemed to be convinced that mental retardation, in particular, was a matter of heredity. The eugenicists of the 1920s had spun their pseudoscientific theories around "hereditary feeble-mindedness," and claimed that the "Kallikaks and the Jukes," by reproducing successive "feeble-minded" generations, had cost New York state tens of millions of dollars over decades. But what about learning disorders like dyslexia, which has been known to afflict oligarchical families Bush would consider wealthy, well-bred and able? Nelson Rockefeller had dyslexia, a reading disorder, and Bush's friend Nicholas Brady, and Bush's own son Neil Bush both suffer from it. But these oligarchs are not likely to fall victim to the involuntary sterilization as "mental defectives" which they wish to inflict on those they term the lower orders.

In introducing the House version of the Tydings bill on behalf of himself and Bush, Rep. James Scheuer (D-N.Y.) ranted that while middle-class women "have been limiting the number of offspring for years . . . women of low-income families" did not. "If poverty and family size are so closely related we ask, 'Why don't poor women stop having babies?' " The Bush-Tydings bill took a giant step toward forcing them to do so.

Population Task Force

Among Bush's most important contributions to the neo-Malthusian cause while in Congress was his role in the Republican Task Force on Earth Resources and Population. The task force, which Bush helped found and then chaired, churned out a steady stream of propaganda claiming that the world was already seriously overpopulated; that there was a fixed limit to natural resources and that this limit was rapidly being reached; and that the environment and natural species were being sacrificed to human progress. Bush's task force sought to accredit the idea that the human race was being "down bred," or reduced in genetic qualities by the population growth among non-white, and hence allegedly inferior, races at a time when the Anglo-Saxons were hardly able to prevent their numbers from shrinking.

Comprised of over 20 Republican Congressmen, Bush's task force was a kind of Malthusian vanguard organization, which heard testimony from assorted "race scientists," sponsored legislation, and otherwise propagandized the zero-growth outlook. In its 50-odd hearings during these years, the task force provided a public forum to nearly every well-known zero-growth fanatic, from Paul Ehrlich, founder of Zero Population Growth (ZPG), to race scientist William

Shockley, to the key zero-growth advocates infesting the federal bureaucracy.

Giving a prestigious congressional platform to a discredited racist charlatan like William Shockley in the year after the assassination of Dr. Martin Luther King points up the arrogance of Bush's commitment to eugenics. Shockley, like his co-thinker Arthur Jensen, had caused a furor during the 1960s by advancing his thesis, already repeatedly disproven, that blacks were genetically inferior to whites in cognitive faculties and intelligence. In the same year in which Bush invited him to appear before the GOP task force, Shockley had written: "Our nobly intended welfare programs may be encouraging dysgenics—retrogressive evolution through disproportionate reproduction of the genetically disadvantaged. . . . We fear that 'fatuous beliefs' in the power of welfare money, unaided by eugenic foresight, may contribute to a decline of human quality for all segments of society."

To halt what he saw as pervasive down-breeding of the quality of the U.S. gene pool, Shockley advocated a program of mass sterilization of the unfit and mentally defective, which he called his "Bonus Sterilization Plan." Money bonuses for allowing oneself to be sterilized would be paid to any person not paying income tax who had a genetic deficiency or chronic disease, such as diabetes or epilepsy, or who could be shown to be a drug addict. "If [the government paid] a bonus rate of $1,000 for each point below 100 IQ, $30,000 put in trust for some 70 IQ moron of 20-child potential, it might return $250,000 to taxpayers in reduced cost of mental retardation care," Shockley said.

The special target of Shockley's prescriptions for mass sterilizations were African-Americans, whom he saw as reproducing too fast. "If those blacks with the least amount of Caucasian genes are in fact the most prolific and the least intelligent, then genetic enslavement will be the destiny of their next generation," he wrote. Looking at the recent past, Shockley said in 1967: "The lesson to be drawn from Nazi history is the value of free speech, not that eugenics is intolerable."

As for Paul Ehrlich, his program for genocide included a call to the U.S. government to prepare "the addition of . . . mass sterilization agents" to the U.S. food and water supply, and a "tough foreign policy" including termination of food aid to starving nations. As radical as Ehrlich might have sounded then, this latter point has become a de facto staple of foreign policy under the Bush administration (witness Iraq and Haiti).

On July 24, 1969, the task force heard from Gen. William H.

Draper, Jr., then national chairman of the Population Crisis Committee. General Draper was a close friend of Bush's father, having served with the elder Bush as banker to Thyssen and the Nazi German Steel Trust (see Chapter 3). According to Bush's resumé of his family friend's testimony, Draper warned that the population explosion was like a "rising tide," and asserted that "our strivings for the individual good will become a scourge to the community unless we use our God-given brain power to bring back a balance between the birth rate and the death rate." Draper lashed out at the Catholic Church, charging that its opposition to contraception and sterilization was frustrating population-control efforts in Latin America.

A week later, Bush invited Oscar Harkavy, chief of the Ford Foundation's population program, to testify. In summarizing Harkavy's remarks for the August 4 *Congressional Record,* Bush commented: "The population explosion is commonly recognized as one of the most serious problems now facing the nation and the world. Mr. Harkavy suggested, therefore, that we more adequately fund population research. It seems inconsistent that cancer research funds total $250–275 million annually, more than eight times the amount spent on reproductive biology research."

In reporting on testimony by Dr. William McElroy of the National Science Foundation, Bush stressed that "One of the crises the world will face as a result of present population growth rates is that, assuming the world population increases 2 percent annually, urban population will increase by 6 percent, and ghetto population will increase by 12 percent."

In February 1969, Bush and other members proposed legislation to establish a Select Joint Committee on Population and Family Planning, that would, Bush said, "seek to focus national attention on the domestic and foreign need for family planning. We need to make population and family planning household words," Bush told his House colleagues. "We need to take the sensationalism out of this topic so that it can no longer be used by militants who have no real knowledge of the voluntary nature of the program but, rather, are using it as a political stepping-stone. . . . A thorough investigation into birth control and a collection of data which would give the Congress the criteria to determine the effectiveness of its programs must come swiftly to stave off the number of future mouths which will feed on an ever-decreasing proportion of food," Bush continued. "We need an emphasis on this critical problem . . . we need a massive program in Congress with hearings to emphasize the problem, and earmarked appropriations to do something about it.

We need massive cooperation from the White House like we have never had before and we need a determination by the executive branch that these funds will be spent as earmarked."

On August 6, 1969, Bush's GOP task force introduced a bill to create a Commission on Population and the American Future which, Bush said, would "allow the leadership of this country to properly establish criteria which can be the basis for a national policy on population." The move came in response to President Nixon's call of July 18 to create a blue-ribbon commission to draft a U.S. population policy. Bush was triumphant over this development, having repeatedly urged such a step at various points in the preceding few years. On July 21, he made a statement on the floor of the House to "commend the President" for his action. "We now know," he intoned, "that the fantastic rate of population growth we have witnessed these past 20 years continues with no letup in sight. If this growth rate is not checked now—in this next decade—we face a danger that is as defenseless as nuclear war."

Headed by John D. Rockefeller III, the commission represented a radical, government-sanctioned attack on human life. Its final report, issued in 1972, asserted that "the time has come to challenge the tradition that population growth is desirable: What was unintended may turn out to be unwanted, in the society as in the family." Not only did the commission demand an end to population growth and economic progress, it also attacked the foundations of Western civilization by insisting that man's reason had become a major impediment to right living. "Mass urban industrialism is based on science and technology, efficiency, acquisition, and domination through rationality," the commission's report stated accurately. Then it raved, "The exercise of these same values now contain [sic] the potential for the destruction of our humanity. Man is losing that balance with nature which is an essential condition of human existence."

The commission's principal conclusion was that "there are no substantial benefits to be gained from continued population growth," Chairman Rockefeller explained to the Senate Appropriations Committee. The commission made a host of recommendations to curb both population expansion and economic growth. These included: liberalizing laws restricting abortion and sterilization; having the government fund abortions; and providing birth control to teenagers. The commission had a profound impact on American attitudes toward the population issue, and helped accelerate the plunge into outright genocide. Commission Executive Director Charles Westoff wrote in 1975 that the group "represented an important effort by an advanced country to develop a national population policy—the basic thrust of which was to slow growth in order to maximize the 'quality of life.' "

The collapse of the traditional family-centered form of society during the 1970s and 1980s was but one consequence of such recommendations. It also is widely acknowledged that the commission Bush fought so long and so hard to create broke down the last barriers to legalized abortion on demand. Indeed, just one year after the commission's final report was issued, the Supreme Court delivered the *Roe v. Wade* decision which did just that.

Aware that many blacks and other minorities had noticed that the population control movement was a genocide program aimed at reducing their numbers, the commission went out of its way to cover its real intent by stipulating that all races should cut back on their birth rates. But the racist animus of their conclusions could not be hidden. Commission Executive Director Westoff, who owed his job and his funding to Bush, gave a hint of this in a book he had written in 1966, before joining the commission staff, which was entitled *From Now to Zero*, and in which he bemoaned the fact that the black fertility rate was so much higher than the white.

The population control or zero population growth movement, which grew rapidly in the late 1960s thanks to free media exposure and foundation grants for a stream of pseudoscientific propaganda about the alleged "population bomb" and the "limits to growth," was a continuation of the old prewar, protofascist eugenics movement, which had been forced to go into temporary eclipse when the world recoiled in horror at the atrocities committed by the Nazis in the name of eugenics. By the mid-1960s, the same old crackpot eugenicists had resurrected themselves as the population-control and environmentalist movement. Planned Parenthood was a perfect example of the transmogrification. Now, instead of demanding the sterilization of the inferior races, the newly packaged eugenicists talked about the population bomb, giving the poor "equal access" to birth control, and "freedom of choice."

But nothing had substantively changed—including the use of coercion. While Bush and other advocates of government "family planning" programs insisted these were strictly voluntary, the reality was far different. By the mid-1970s, the number of involuntary sterilizations carried out by programs which Bush helped bring into being, had reached huge proportions. Within the minority communities, where most of the sterilizations were being done, protests arose which culminated in litigation at the federal level.

In his 1974 ruling on this suit, Federal District Judge Gerhard

Gesell found that, "Over the last few years, an estimated 100,000 to 150,000 low-income persons have been sterilized annually under federally funded programs. Although Congress has been insistent that all family planning programs function on a purely voluntary basis," Judge Gesell wrote, "there is uncontroverted evidence . . . that an indefinite number of poor people have been improperly coerced into accepting a sterilization operation under the threat that various federally supported welfare benefits would be withdrawn unless they submitted to irreversible sterilization." Gesell concluded from the evidence that the "dividing line between family planning and eugenics is murky."

Bush and Draper

As we saw in Chapter 3, Gen. William H. Draper, Jr. had been director and vice president of the German Credit and Investment Corp., serving short-term credit to the Nazi Party's financiers from offices in the U.S.A and Berlin. Draper became one of the most influential crusaders for radical population control measures. He campaigned endlessly for zero population growth, and praised the Chinese Communists for their "innovative" methods of achieving that goal. Draper's most influential outlet was the Population Crisis Committee (PCC)-Draper Fund, which he founded in the 1960s.

In 1967–68, a PCC-Draper Fund offshoot, the Campaign to Check the Population Explosion, ran a nationwide advertising campaign hyping the population explosion fraud, and attacking those— particularly the Vatican—who stood in the way of radical population control.

In a 1971 article, Draper likened the developing nations to an "animal reserve," where, when the animals become too numerous, the park rangers "arbitrarily reduce one or another species as necessary to preserve the balanced environment for all other animals." "But who will be the park ranger for the human race?" he asked. "Who will cull out the surplus in this country or that country when the pressure of too many people and too few resources increases beyond endurance? Will the death-dealing Horsemen of the Apocalypse—war in its modern nuclear dress, hunger haunting half the human race, and disease—will the gaunt and forbidding Horsemen become Park Ranger for the two-legged animal called man?"

Draper collaborated closely with George Bush during the latter's congressional career. As noted above, Bush invited Draper to testify to his Republican Task Force on Earth Resources and Population; reportedly, Draper helped draft the Bush-Tydings bill.

Bush felt an overwhelming affinity for the bestial and degraded image of man reflected in the raving statements of Draper. In September 1969, Bush gave a glowing tribute to Draper that was published in the *Congressional Record*. "I wish to pay tribute to a great American," said Bush. "I am very much aware of the significant leadership that General Draper has executed throughout the world in assisting governments in their efforts to solve the awesome problems of rapid population growth. No other person in the past five years has shown more initiative in creating the awareness of the world's leaders in recognizing the economic consequences of our population explosion."

In a 1973 publication, Bush praised the Population Crisis Committee itself for having played a "major role in assisting government policy makers and in mobilizing the United States' response to the world population challenge. . . ." The PCC made no bones about its admiration for Bush; its newsletters from the late 1960s-early 1970s feature numerous articles highlighting Bush's role in the congressional population-control campaign. In a 1979 report assessing the history of congressional action on population control, the PCC/Draper Fund placed Bush squarely with the "most conspicuous activists" on population-control issues, and lauded him for "proposing all of the major or controversial recommendations" in this arena which came before the U.S. Congress in the late 1960s.

Draper's son, William Draper III, has enthusiastically carried out his father's genocidal legacy—frequently with the help of Bush. In 1980, Draper, an enthusiastic backer of the Carter administration's notorious *Global 2000* report, served as national chairman of the Bush presidential campaign's finance committee; in early 1981, Bush convinced Reagan to appoint Draper to head the U.S. Export-Import Bank. At the time, a Draper aide, Sharon Camp, disclosed that Draper intended to reorient the bank's functions toward emphasizing population control projects.

In 1987, again at Bush's behest, Draper was named by Reagan as administrator of the United Nations Development Program, which functions as an adjunct of the World Bank, and has historically pushed population reduction among Third World nations. In late January of 1991, Draper gave a speech to a conference in Washington, in which he stated that the core of Bush's "new world order" should be population reduction.

Helping the Oil Cartel

But we shall not conclude that Bush devoted the entirety of his congressional career to the promotion of race science and global depopulation. He was also concerned with providing "constituent service." This service came in the form of Bush's central role in the implementation of a sophisticated strategy by the oil cartel to maintain its ground-rent tax privileges at the highest rate that the climate of public opinion would permit. Within this strategy, Bush worked to protect the oil depletion allowance as the principal tax giveaway enjoyed by the cartel.

The oil depletion allowance was a 27.5 percent tax write-off for oil producers that had been introduced in 1926, allegedly to strengthen the U.S. petroleum industry. The impact of a 27.5 percent depletion allowance was that many of the largest oil companies, including some of the wealthiest corporate giants, paid a very low rate of corporate income tax. On July 10, 1969, Congressman Bertram Podell of New York wrote an open letter to House Ways and Means Chairman Wilbur Mills in which he pointed out that, primarily as a result of the high oil depletion allowance, Gulf Oil had paid an effective tax rate of only 0.81 percent on more than a billion dollars of 1968 income, while Mobil had paid 3.3 percent, and Atlantic Richfield had paid 1.2 percent. In his letter, Podell paid ironic tribute to the oil cartel's "passionate devotion to old-fashioned virtues, such as greed" to the point that the "oil industry makes the mafia look like a pushcart operation" while "through our various tax loopholes, professional tax evaders like the oil industry churn like panzers over foot soldiers."[11]

In 1950, President Truman had declared that no tax loophole was "so inequitable" as the depletion allowance, and cited the example of one oilman who enjoyed a tax-free income of almost $5 million thanks to this provision. Truman claimed that he wanted to cut the depletion allowance to 15 percent, but Congressmen opposed to the high depletion allowance later claimed that he had done very little to carry out this pledge. Senators of the stripe of Humphrey, Douglas, Williams of Delaware and others offered amendments to reduce the depletion allowance to 15 percent, or to restrict the 27.5 percent to oil producers with incomes below a certain level, but these efforts were defeated in 1951, 1954, 1958, 1962, 1964 and 1967. But in 1969, the issue was back in the form of a clamor for tax reform as the economy deteriorated, and a great deal of public heat was focused on the 27.5 percent for Rockefeller's oil cartel.

Congressman Charles Vanick of Ohio, who was profiling himself as a leading tax reformer, calculated that the oil depletion allowance had resulted in the loss of over $140 billion in tax revenues since the time it was instituted.

In response to this public hue and cry against the 27.5 percent, the public relations men of the oil cartel devised an elaborate public charade, with the depletion allowance to be cut slightly in order to turn off the public pressure and save the bulk of the write-off. In May of 1969, Chairman Wilbur Mills said that the 27.5 percent was a "symbolic" figure and could be slightly trimmed.

In July, the Ways and Means Committee reported out a measure to cut the depletion allowance to 20 percent. Congressman Vanick was happy to have something to show for his efforts: "We've really got a reform bill now," he told the press. Bush was going along with the 20 percent, but defended the principle of a substantial depletion allowance. According to Bush, "unrefuted" expert testimony had proven that a tax incentive was necessary for oil and gas exploration "due to the serious gas reserve shortages in this country." "Depletion," said Bush, "has become a symbol to some people and without examining the reasons for its existence or its fundamental importance to this country, some want to slug away at it."[12]

On August 28, 1969, Congressman George Bush and Texas Senator John Tower flew to San Clemente to meet with President Nixon on this issue. Nixon had said during the 1968 campaign that he favored the 27.5 percent allowance, but he was willing to play ball with the oil cartel. Nixon, Bush and Tower were joined in San Clemente by Treasury Secretary David Kennedy, who was preparing to testify on oil taxes before Russell Long's Senate Finance Committee. Tower and Bush instructed Nixon that the oil cartel was willing to accept some reduction of the depletion allowance, and that the administration should merely state that it was willing to accept whatever the Congress approved. According to one historian of the oil industry, "This was the first step in preparation for the 'sting.' But there was one slight stumble before the con men got their signals worked out perfectly."[13]

Treasury Secretary David Kennedy got confused by the 20 percent figure that had been bandied about in the public debate. He told the Senate that while Nixon would prefer to keep the 27.5 percent figure, he was also willing to come down to 20 percent. This was more than the token concession that the oil cartel had been prepared to make. On October 7, the House passed the 20 percent figure by a vote of 394 to 30, with Bush voting for the cut. This entailed very little risk, since Senator Russell Long of the Senate Finance Committee, himself an oil producer through his participation in the Long family Win or Lose Corporation, was unwilling to reduce the depletion allowance below 23 percent. Nixon's deputy White House counsel, Harry S. Dent, wrote a letter to a county judge in Midland, Texas, of all places, which stated that Treasury Secretary Kennedy had been in error about Nixon seeing two alternatives, 27.5 percent or 20 percent, and that "the President will abide by the judgment of Congress." An aide of Senator Proxmire complained: "If the committee cuts back the depletion allowance by a modest amount— say to 23 percent—it may represent a low enough profile that Senate liberals will have a more difficult time cutting it further." The 23 percent figure was the one that was ultimately accepted, and the reduction in the depletion allowance thus accomplished was calculated to have increased the tax bill of the domestic U.S. oil and gas companies by the trifling sum of $175 million per year. The issue had been defused, and the cartel could resume its normal operations, thanks in part to the stewardship of George Bush.

By the time of the House Ways and Means Committee vote of July 1969, referenced above, the *New York Times* was already touting Bush as a likely Senate candidate, and Bush was indeed to be a candidate for the Senate from Texas in 1970. In Bush's campaign autobiography, he attempts to portray his decision to run for the Senate a second time as a decision assisted by former President Lyndon B. Johnson. That, we should say, is already bad enough. But in reality, the decisive encouragement, funds, and the promise of future advancement that moved Bush to attempt the leap into the Senate once again came from one Richard Milhous Nixon, and the money involved came from the circles of Nixon's Committee to Reelect the President (CREEP).

The Nixon Touch

Nixon, it will be recalled, had campaigned for Bush in 1964 and 1966, and would do so also in 1970. During these years, Bush's positions came to be almost perfectly aligned with the line of the Imperial Presidency. And, thanks in large part to the workings of his father's Brown Brothers Harriman networks—Prescott had been a fixture in the Eisenhower White House where Nixon worked, and in the Senate over which Nixon from time to time presided—Bush became a Nixon ally and crony. Bush's Nixon connection, which pro-Bush propaganda tends to minimize, was in fact the key to Bush's career choices in the late 1960s and early 1970s.

Bush's intimate relations with Nixon are best illustrated in Bush's close brush with the 1968 GOP vice-presidential nomination at the Miami convention of that year. According to a well-informed, but favorable, short biography of Bush published as he was about to take over the presidency, "at the 1968 GOP convention that nominated Nixon for President, Bush was said to be on the four-name short list for Vice President. He attributed that to the campaigning of his friends, but the seriousness of Nixon's consideration was widely attested. Certainly Nixon wanted to promote Bush in one way or another."[14]

Later in August, Bush traveled to Nixon's beachfront motel suite at Mission Bay, California to discuss campaign strategy. It was decided that Bush, Howard Baker, Rep. Clark MacGregor of Minnesota and Gov. Volpe would all function as "surrogate candidates," campaigning and standing in for Nixon at engagements Nixon could not fill. And there is George, in a picture on the top of the front page of the *New York Times* of August 17, 1968, joining with the other three to slap a grinning and euphoric Nixon on the back and shake his hand before they went forth to the hustings.

Bush had no problems of his own with the 1968 election, since he was running unopposed—a neat trick for a Republican in Houston, even taking the designer gerrymandering into account. Running unopposed seems to be Bush's idea of an ideal election.

Bush had great hopes that he could help deliver the Texas electoral votes into the Nixon column. The GOP was counting on further open warfare between Yarborough and Connally, but these divisions proved to be insufficient to prevent Hubert Humphrey, the Democratic nominee, from carrying Texas as he went down to defeat. Winning a second term was no problem; Bush was, however, mightily embarrassed by his inability to deliver Texas for Nixon. "I don't know what went wrong," Bush muttered when interviewed in December. "There was a hell of a lot of money spent," much of it coming from the predecessor organizations to the CREEP.[15] As usual, Bush had a *post festum* theory of what had gone wrong: He blamed it on the black voters. In Houston, Bush found, there were 58,000 black voters, and Nixon only got 800 of them. "You'd think," said Bush, "that there would have been more people just come in there and make a mistake!"[16]

When in 1974 Bush briefly appeared to be the front-runner to be chosen for the vice-presidency by the new President Gerald Ford, the *Washington Post* pointed out that although Bush was making a serious bid, he had almost no qualifications for the post. That criticism applied even more in 1968: For most people, Bush was a rather obscure Texas pol, and he had lost one statewide race previous to the election that got him into Congress. The fact that he made it into the final round at the Miami Hilton was another tribute to the network mobilizing power of Prescott Bush, Brown Brothers Harriman, and Skull and Bones.

As the 1970 election approached, Nixon made Bush an attractive offer. If Bush were willing to give up his apparently safe congressional seat and his place on the Ways and Means Committee, Nixon would be happy to help finance the Senate race. If Bush won a Senate seat, he would be a front-runner to replace Spiro Agnew in the vice-presidential spot for 1972. If Bush were to lose the election, he would then be in line for an appointment to an important post in the executive branch, most likely a cabinet position. This deal was enough of an open secret to be discussed in the Texas press during the fall of 1970: At the time, the *Houston Post* quoted Bush in response to persistent Washington newspaper reports that Bush would replace Agnew on the 1972 ticket. Bush said that was "the most wildly speculative piece I've seen in a long time." "I hate to waste time talking about such wild speculation," Bush said in Austin. "I ought to be out there shaking hands with those people who stood in the rain to support me."[17]

At this time Bush calculated that a second challenge to Yarborough would have a greater chance for success than his first attempt. True, 1970 was another off-year election in which Democrats running against the Republican Nixon White House would have a certain statistical advantage. But 1970 was also the great year of the Silent Majority, Middle America backlash against the Vietnam War protesters.

In an obvious sleight-of-hand, Bush uses his campaign autobiography to make it look like it was LBJ, not Nixon, who urged him to run. But Bush's account is ultimately, as is typical of him, a calculated deception. No, no, George: LBJ resented Yarborough for having opposed him on Vietnam, but LBJ was a has-been in 1970, and it was Nixon who told you to make your Senate bid in 1970, and who sweetened the pot with big bucks and the promise of prestigious posts if you failed.

In September, the *New York Times* reported that Nixon was actively recruiting Republican candidates for the Senate. "Implies He Will Participate in Their Campaigns and Offer Jobs to Losers"; "Financial Aid is Hinted," said the subtitles[18]. It was more than hinted, and the article listed George Bush as first on the list. As it turned out, Bush's Senate race was the single most important focus of Nixon's efforts in the entire country, with both the President and Agnew actively engaged on the ground. Bush would receive money from a Nixon slush fund called the "Townhouse" fund, an operation in the CREEP orbit. Bush was also the recipient of the largesse of W. Clement Stone, a Chicago insurance tycoon who had donated heavily to Nixon's 1968 campaign. Bush's friend John Tower was the chairman of the GOP Senatorial Campaign Committee, and

Bush's former campaign aide, Jim Allison, was now the deputy chairman of the Republican National Committee.

Losing Again

Bush himself was ensconced in the coils of the GOP fundraising bureaucracy. When in May 1969, Nixon's crony Robert Finch, the Secretary of Health, Education and Welfare, met with members of the Republican Boosters Club 1969, Bush was with him, along with John Tower, Rogers Morton and Congressman Bob Wilson of California. The Boosters alone were estimated to be good for about $1 million in funding for GOP candidates in 1970.[19]

By December of 1969, it was clear to all that Bush would get almost all of the cash in the Texas GOP coffers, and that Eggers, the party's candidate for governor, would get short shrift indeed. On December 29, the *Houston Chronicle* front page opined: "GOP Money To Back Bush, Not Eggers." The Democratic Senate candidate would later accuse Nixon's crowd of "trying to buy" the Senate election for Bush: "Washington has been shovelling so much money into the George Bush campaign that now other Republican candidates around the country are demanding an accounting," said Bush's opponent.[20]

But that opponent was Lloyd Bentsen, not Ralph Yarborough. All calculations about the 1970 Senate race had been upset when, at a relatively late hour, Bentsen, urged on by John Connally, announced his candidacy in the Democratic primary. Yarborough, busy with his work as Chairman of the Senate Labor Committee, started his campaigning late. Bentsen's pitch was to attack anti-war protesters and radicals, portraying Yarborough as being a ringleader of the extremists.

Yarborough had lost some of his vim over the years since 1964, and had veered into support for more ecological legislation and even for some of the anti-human "population planning" measures that Bush and his circles had been proposing. But he fought back gamely against Bentsen.

But, on May 2, Bentsen defeated Yarborough, and an era came to an end in Texas politics. Bush's 10-to-1 win in his own primary over his old rival from 1964, Robert Morris, was scant consolation. Whereas it had been clear how Bush would have run against Yarborough, it was not at all clear how he could differentiate himself from Bentsen. Indeed, to many people the two seemed to be twins: Each was a plutocrat oilman from Houston, each was aggressively Anglo-Saxon, each had been in the House of Representatives, each flaunted a record as a World War II airman. In fact, all Bentsen needed to do for the rest of the race was to appear plausible and polite, and let the overwhelming Democratic advantage in registered voters, especially in the yellow-dog Democrat rural areas, do his work for him. This Bentsen posture was punctuated from time to time by appeals to conservatives who thought that Bush was too liberal for their tastes.

Bush hoped for a time that his slick television packaging could save him. His man Harry Treleaven was once more brought in. Bush paid more than half a million dollars, a tidy sum at that time, to Glenn Advertising for a series of Kennedyesque "natural look" campaign spots. Soon Bush was cavorting on the tube in all of his arid vapidity, jogging across the street, trotting down the steps, bounding around Washington and playing touch football, always filled with youth, vigor, action and thyroxin. Although Bentsen's spots were said to give him "all the animation of a cadaver," he was more substantive than Bush, and he was moving ahead.

Were there issues that could help George? His ads put his opposition to school busing to achieve racial balance at the top of the list, but this wedge-mongering got him nowhere. Because of his servility to Nixon, Bush had to support the buzz-word of a "guaranteed annual income," which was the label under which Nixon was marketing the workfare slave-labor program already described; but to many in Texas that sounded like a new give-away, and Bentsen was quick to take advantage. Bush bragged that he had been one of the original sponsors of the bill that had just semi-privatized the U.S. Post Office Department as the Postal Service—not exactly a success story in retrospect. Bush came on as a "fiscal conservative," but this also was of little help against Bentsen.

In an interview on women's issues, Bush first joked that there really was no consensus among women—"the concept of a women's movement is unreal—you can't get two women to agree on anything." On abortion he commented: "I realize this is a politically sensitive area. But I believe in a woman's right to choose. It should be an individual matter. I think ultimately it will be a constitutional question. I don't favor a federal abortion law as such." After 1980, for those who choose to believe him, this changed to strong opposition to abortion.

Could Nixon himself help Bush? Nixon did campaign in the state. Bentsen then told a group of "Anglo-American" businessmen: Texans want "a man who can stand alone without being propped up by the White House."

In the end, Bentsen defeated Bush by a vote of 1,197,726 to

Bush's 1,035,794, about 53 percent to 47 percent. On the night of the election, Bush said that he "felt like Gen. Custer. They asked him why he had lost and he said 'There were too many Indians.' All I can say at this point is that there were too many Democrats," said the fresh two-time loser. Bentsen suggested that it was time for Bush to be appointed to a high position in the government.[21]

Bush's other consolation was a telegram dated November 5, 1970:

> From personal experience I know the disappointment that you and your family must feel at this time. I am sure, however, that you will not allow this defeat to discourage you in your efforts to continue to provide leadership for our party and the nation. Richard Nixon.

This was Nixon's euphemistic way of reassuring Bush that they still had a deal.[22]

Notes for Chapter X

1. See Fitzhugh Green, *George Bush: A Biography* (New York: Dodd, Mead & Company, 1980), p. 92, and George Bush and Victor Gold, *Looking Forward* (New York: Doubleday, 1987), p. 90.

2. Stevens's remarks were part of a Public Broadcasting System "Frontline" documentary program entitled "Campaign: The Choice," Nov. 24, 1988. Cited by Fitzhugh Green, *op. cit.*, p. 91.

3. For the chronicles of the Harris County GOP, see local press articles available on microfiche at the Texas Historical Society in Houston. Observer, July 23, 1965.

4. *Texas Observer*, Oct. 14, 1966.

5. Joe McGinniss, *The Selling of the President 1968* (New York: Penguin Books, 1968), pp. 42–45.

6. Bush and Gold, *op. cit.*, p. 91.

7. See John R. Knaggs, *Two-Party Texas* (Austin: Eakin Press, 1985), p. 111.

8. *Congressional Quarterly*, "President Bush: The Challenge Ahead" (Washington, 1989), p. 94.

9. Harry Hurt III, "George Bush, Plucky Lad," in *Texas Monthly*, June 1983.

10. The following account of Bush's congressional record on population and related issues is derived from the ground-breaking research of Kathleen Klenetsky, to whom the authors acknowledge their indebtedness. The material that follows incorporates sections of Kathleen Klenetsky, "Bush Backed Nazi 'Race Science,' " *Executive Intelligence Review*, May 3, 1991 and *New Federalist*, Vol. 5, No. 16, April 29, 1991.

11. See Robert Sherrill, *The Oil Follies of 1970–1980* (New York: Anchor Press/Doubleday, 1983), pp. 61–65.

12. *New York Times*, July 22, 1969.

13. Sherrill, *op. cit.*, p. 64.

14. *Congressional Quarterly*, *op. cit.*, p. 94.

15. Lewis Chester et al., *An American Melodrama: The Presidential Campaign of 1968* (London: Deutch, 1969), p. 622.

16. *Ibid.*, p. 763.

17. *Houston Post*, Oct. 29, 1970.

18. *New York Times*, Sept, 27, 1969.

19. *New York Times*, May 13, 1969.

20. *Houston Chronicle*, Oct. 6, 1970.

21. *Houston Post*, Nov. 5, 1970.

22. Bush and Gold, *op. cit.*, p. 102.

XI

UNITED NATIONS AMBASSADOR, KISSINGER CLONE

At this point in his career, George Bush entered into a phase of close association with both Richard Nixon and Henry Kissinger. As we will see, Bush was a member of the Nixon cabinet from the spring of 1971 until the day that Nixon resigned. We will see Bush on a number of important occasions literally acting as Nixon's speaking tube, especially in international crisis situations. During these years, Nixon was Bush's patron, providing him with appointments and urging him to look forward to bigger things in the future. On certain occasions, however, Bush was upstaged by others in his quest for Nixon's favor. Then there was Kissinger, far and away the most powerful figure in the Washington regime of those days, who became Bush's boss when the latter became the U.S. ambassador to the United Nations in New York City. Later, on the campaign trail in 1980, Bush would offer to make Kissinger Secretary of State in his administration.

Bush was now listing a net worth of over $1.3 million[1], but the fact is that he was now unemployed, but anxious to assume the next official post, to take the next step of what in the career of a Roman Senator was called the *cursus honorum,* the patrician career, for this is what he felt the world owed him.

Nixon had promised Bush an attractive and prestigious political plum in the executive branch, and it was now time for Nixon to deliver. Bush's problem was that in late 1970 Nixon was more interested in what another Texan could contribute to his administration. That other Texan was John Connally, who had played the role of Bush's nemesis in the elections just concluded, by virtue of the encouragement and decisive support which Connally had given to the candidacy of Lloyd Bentsen. Nixon was now fascinated by the prospect of including the right-wing Democrat Connally in his cabinet in order to provide himself with a patina of bipartisanship, while emphasizing the dissension among the Democrats, strengthening Nixon's chances of successfully executing his Southern Strategy a second time during the 1972 elections.

The word among Nixon's inner circle of this period was "The Boss is in love," and the object of his affections was Big Jawn. Nixon claimed that he was not happy with the stature of his current cabinet, telling his domestic policy advisor John Ehrlichman in the fall of 1970 that "Every cabinet should have at least one potential President in it. Mine doesn't." Nixon had tried to recruit leading Democrats before, asking Senator Henry Jackson to be Secretary of Defense and offering the post of United Nations ambassador to Hubert Humphrey.

Within hours after the polls had closed in the Texas Senate race, Bush received a call from Charles Bartlett, a Washington columnist who was part of the Prescott Bush network. Bartlett tipped Bush to the fact that Treasury Secretary David Kennedy was leaving, and urged him to make a grab for the job. Bush called Nixon and put in his request. After that, he waited by the telephone. But it soon became clear that Nixon was about to recruit John Connally and with him, perhaps, the important Texas electoral votes in 1972. Secretary of the Treasury! One of the three or four top posts in the cabinet! And that before Bush had been given anything for all of his useless slogging through the 1970 campaign! But the job was about to go to Connally. Over two decades, one can almost hear Bush's whining complaint.

This move was not totally unprepared. During the fall of 1970, when Connally was campaigning for Bentsen against Bush, Connally had been invited to participate in the Ash Commission, a study group on government re-organization chaired by Roy Ash. "This White House access was dangerously undermining George Bush," complained Texas GOP chairman Peter O'Donnell. A personal friend of Bush on the White House staff, named Peter Flanigan, generated a memo to White House Chief of Staff H.R. Haldeman with the notation: "Connally is an implacable enemy of the Republican party in Texas, and, therefore, attractive as he may be to the President, we should avoid using him again." Nixon found Connally an attractive political property, and had soon appointed him to the main White House panel for intelligence evaluations:

On November 30, when Connally's appointment to the Foreign
Intelligence Advisory Board was announced, the senior Senator from
Texas, John Tower, and George Bush were instantly in touch with
the White House to express their 'extreme' distress over the appointment.[2] Tower was indignant because he had been promised by Ehrlichman some time before that Connally was not going to receive an
important post. Bush's personal plight was even more poignant: "He
was out of work, and he wanted a job. As a defeated senatorial
candidate, he hoped and fully expected to get a major job in the
administration. Yet the administration seemed to be paying more
attention to the very Democrat who had put him on the job market.
What gives? Bush was justified in asking."[3]

The appointment of Connally to replace David Kennedy as Secretary of the Treasury was concluded during the first week of December, 1970. But it could not be announced without causing an upheaval among the Texas Republicans until something had been
done for lame duck George. On December 7, Nixon retainer H.R.
Haldeman was writing memos to himself in the White House. The
first was: "Connally set." Then came: "Have to do something for
Bush right away." Could Bush become the director of NASA? How
about the Small Business Administration? Or the Republican National Committee? Or then again, he might like to be White House
congressional liaison, or perhaps Undersecretary of Commerce. As
one account puts it, "since no job immediately came to mind, Bush
was assured that he would come to the White House as a top
presidential adviser on something or other, until another fitting job
opened up."

Bush was called to the White House on December 9, 1970 to
meet with Nixon and talk about a post as Assistant to the President
"with a wide range of unspecified general responsibilities," according to a White House memo initialed by H.R. Haldeman. Bush
accepted such a post at one point in his haggling with the Nixon
White House. But Bush also sought the U.N. job, arguing that there
"was a dirth [sic] of Nixon advocacy in New York City and the
general New York area that he could fill that need in the New York
social circles he would be moving in as ambassador."[4] Nixon's U.N.
ambassador had been Charles Yost, a Democrat who was now
leaving. But the White House had already offered that job to Daniel
Patrick Moynihan, who had accepted.

But then Moynihan decided that he did not want the U.N. ambassador post after all, and, with a sigh of relief, the White House
offered it to Bush. Bush's appointment was announced on December
11, Connally's on December 14.[5] In offering the post to Bush,

Haldeman had been brutally frank, telling him that the job, although of cabinet rank, would have no power attached to it. Bush, Haldeman stressed, would be taking orders directly from Kissinger. But Bush says he replied, "even if somebody who took the job didn't understand that, Henry Kissinger would give him a twenty-four hour crash course on the subject."[6]

Nixon told his cabinet and the Republican congressional leadership on December 14, 1970 what had been in the works for some time: that Connally was "coming not only as a Democrat but as Secretary of the Treasury for the next two full years." Even more humiliating for Bush was the fact that our hero had been on the receiving end of Connally's assistance. As Nixon told the cabinet: "Connally said he wouldn't take it until George Bush got whatever he was entitled to. I don't know why George wanted the U.N. appointment, but he wanted it so he got it." Only this precondition from Connally, by implication, had finally prompted Nixon to take care of poor George.[7]

Bush appeared before the Senate Foreign Relations Committee for his *pro forma* and perfunctory confirmation hearings on February 8, 1971. It was a free ride. Many of the Senators had known Prescott Bush, and several were still Prescott's friends. Acting like friends of the family, they gave Bush friendly advice with a tone that was congratulatory and warm, and avoided any tough questions. Stuart Symington warned Bush that he would have to deal with the "duality of authority" between his nominal boss, Secretary of State William Rogers, and his real boss, NSC chief Kissinger. There was only passing reference to Bush's service of the oil cartel during his time in the House, and Bush vehemently denied that he had ever tried to "placate" the "oil interests." Claiborne Pell said that Bush would enhance the luster of the U.N. post.

On policy matters, Bush said that it would "make sense" for the U.N. Security Council to conduct a debate on the wars in Laos and Cambodia, which was something that the U.S. had been attempting to procure for some time. Bush thought that such a debate could be used as a forum to expose the aggressive activities of the North Vietnamese. No Senator asked Bush about China, but Bush told journalists waiting in the hall that the question of China was now under intensive study. The *Washington Post* was impressed by Bush's "lithe and youthful good looks." Bush was easily confirmed and presented his credentials on March 1.

Then Bush, "handsome and trim" at 47, moved into a suite at the Waldorf-Astoria Hotel in Manhattan, and settled into his usual hyperkinetic, thyroid-driven lifestyle. For Bush, a 16-hour work day was more the rule than the exception. His days were packed with one appointment after another, luncheon engagements, receptions, formal dinners—at least one reception and one dinner per day. Sometimes there were three receptions per day—quite an opportunity for networking with like-minded freemasons from all over the world. Bush also traveled to Washington for cabinet meetings, and still did speaking engagements around the country, especially for Republican candidates.

Soon after taking up his U.N. posting, Bush received a phone call from Assistant Secretary of State for Middle Eastern Affairs Joseph Sisco, one of Kissinger's principal henchmen. Sisco had been angered by some comments Bush had made about the Middle East situation in a press conference after presenting his credentials. Despite the fact that Bush, as a cabinet officer, ranked several levels above Sisco, Sisco was in effect the voice of Kissinger. Sisco told Bush that it was Sisco who spoke for the United States government on the Middle East, and that he would do both the on-the-record talking and the leaking about that area. Bush knuckled under, for these were the realities of the Kissinger years.

Kissinger's Clone

Henry Kissinger was now Bush's boss even more than Nixon was, and later, as the Watergate scandal progressed into 1973, the dominion of Kissinger would become even more absolute. During these years Bush, serving his apprenticeship in diplomacy and world strategy under Kissinger, became a virtual Kissinger clone, in two senses. First, to a significant degree, Kissinger's networks and connections merged together with Bush's own, foreshadowing a 1989 administration in which the NSC Director and the number two man in the State Department were both Kissinger's business partners from his consulting and influence-peddling firm, Kissinger Associates. Secondly, Bush assimilated Kissinger's characteristic British-style geopolitical mentality and approach to problems, and this is now the epistemology that dictates Bush's own dealing with the main questions of world politics.

The most essential level of Kissinger was the British one.[8] This meant that U.S. foreign policy was to be guided by British imperial geopolitics, in particular the notion of the balance of power: The United States must always ally with the second strongest land power in the world (Red China) against the strongest land power (the Soviet Union) in order to preserve the balance of power. This was expressed in the 1971–72 Nixon-Kissinger opening to Beijing, to which Bush would contribute from his U.N. post. The balance of power, since it rules out a positive engagement for the economic progress of the international community as a whole, has always been a recipe for new wars. Kissinger was in constant contact with British foreign policy operatives like Sir Eric Roll of S.G. Warburg in London, Lord Victor Rothschild, the Barings bank and others.

On May 10, 1982, in a speech entitled "Reflections on a Partnership" given at the Royal Institute of International Affairs at Chatham House in London, Henry Kissinger openly expounded his role and philosophy as a British agent-of-influence within the U.S. government during the Nixon and Ford years:

> The British were so matter-of-factly helpful that they became a participant in internal American deliberations, to a degree probably never before practiced between sovereign nations. In my period in office, the British played a seminal part in certain American bilateral negotiations with the Soviet Union—indeed, they helped draft the key document. In my White House incarnation then, I kept the British Foreign Office better informed and more closely engaged than I did the American State Department. . . . In my negotiations over Rhodesia I worked from a British draft with British spelling even when I did not fully grasp the distinction between a working paper and a Cabinet-approved document.[9]

Kissinger was also careful to point out that the United States must support colonial and neo-colonial strategies against the developing sector:

> Americans from Franklin Roosevelt onward believed that the United States, with its "revolutionary" heritage, was the natural ally of people struggling against colonialism; we could win the allegiance of these new nations by opposing and occasionally undermining our European allies in the areas of their colonial dominance. Churchill, of course, resisted these American pressures. . . . In this context, the experience of Suez is instructive. . . . Our humiliation of Britain and France over Suez was a shattering blow to these countries' role as world powers. It accelerated their shedding of international responsibilities, some of the consequences of which we saw in succeeding decades when reality forced us to step into their shoes—in the Persian Gulf, to take one notable example. Suez thus added enormously to America's burdens.

Kissinger was the high priest of imperialism and neocolonialism, animated by an instinctive hatred for Indira Gandhi, Aldo Moro, Zulfikar Ali Bhutto and other nationalist world leaders. Kissinger's

British geopolitics simply accentuated Bush's own fanatically Anglo-phile point of view, which he had acquired from father Prescott and imbibed from the atmosphere of the family firm, Brown Brothers Harriman, originally the U.S. branch of a British counting house.

Kissinger was also a Zionist, dedicated to economic, diplomatic and military support of Israeli aggression and expansionism to keep the Middle East in turmoil, so as to prevent Arab unity and Arab economic development while using the region to mount challenges to the Soviets. In this he was a follower of British Prime Minister Benjamin Disraeli and Lord Balfour. In the 1973 Middle East war which he had connived to unleash, Kissinger would mastermind the U.S. resupply of Israel and would declare a U.S.-worldwide thermonuclear alert. In later years, Kissinger would enrich himself through speculative real estate purchases on the west bank of the Jordan, buying up land and buildings that had been virtually confiscated from defenseless Palestinian Arabs.

Kissinger was also Soviet in a sense that went far beyond his sponsorship of the 1970s detente, SALT I, and the ABM treaty with Moscow. Polish KGB agent Michael Goleniewski is widely reported to have told the British government in 1972 that he had seen KGB documents in Poland before his 1959 defection which established that Kissinger was a Soviet asset. According to Goleniewski, Kissinger had been recruited by the Soviets during his Army service in Germany after the end of World War II, when he had worked as a humble chauffeur. Kissinger had allegedly been recruited to an espionage cell called ODRA, where he received the code name of "BOR" or "COLONEL BOR." Some versions of this story also specify that this cell had been largely composed of homosexuals, and that homosexuality had been an important part of the way that Kissinger had been picked up by the KGB. These reports were reportedly partly supported by Golitsyn, another Soviet defector. The late James Jesus Angleton, the CIA counterintelligence director for 20 years up to 1973, was said to have been the U.S. official who was handed Goleniewski's report by the British. Angleton later talked a lot about Kissinger being "objectively a Soviet agent." It has not been established that Angleton ever ordered an active investigation of Kissinger or ever assigned his case a codename.[10]

Kissinger's Chinese side was very much in evidence during 1971–73 and beyond; during these years he was obsessed with anything remotely connected with China and sought to monopolize decisions and contacts with the highest levels of the Chinese leadership. This attitude was dictated most of all by the British mentality and geopolitical considerations indicated above, but it is also unquestionable that Kissinger felt a strong personal affinity for Zhou Enlai, Mao Zedong and the other Chinese leaders, who had been responsible for the genocide of 100 million of their own people after 1949.

Kissinger possessed other dimensions in addition to these, including close links to the Zionist underworld. These will also loom large in George Bush's career.

For all of these Kissingerian enormities, Bush now became the principal spokesman. In the process, he was to become a Kissinger clone.

China Card

The defining events in the first year of Bush's U.N. tenure reflected Kissinger's geopolitical obsession with his China card. Remember that in his 1964 campaign, Bush had stated that Red China must never be admitted to the U.N. and that if Beijing ever obtained the Chinese seat on the Security Council, the U.S. must depart forthwith from the world body. This statement came back to haunt him once or twice. His stock answer went like this: "That was 1964, a long time ago. There's been an awful lot changed since. . . . A person who is unwilling to admit that changes have taken place is out of things these days. President Nixon is not being naive in his China policy. He is recognizing the realities of today, not the realities of seven years ago."

One of the realities of 1971 was that the bankrupt British had declared themselves to be financially unable to maintain their military presence in the Indian Ocean and the Far East, in the area "East of Suez." Part of the timing of the Kissinger China card was dictated by the British desire to acquire China as a counterweight to India in this vast area of the world, and also to insure a U.S. military presence in the Indian Ocean, as seen later in the U.S. development of an important base on the island of Diego Garcia.

On a world tour during 1969, Nixon had told President Yahya Khan, the dictator of Pakistan, that his administration wanted to normalize relations with Red China and wanted the help of the Pakistani government in exchanging messages. Regular meetings between the U.S. and Beijing had gone on for many years in Warsaw, but what Nixon was talking about was a total reversal of U.S. China policy. Up until 1971, the U.S. had recognized the government of the Republic of China on Taiwan as the sole sovereign and legitimate authority over China. The U.S., unlike Britain, France and many other Western countries, had no diplomatic relations with the Beijing Communist regime.

The Chinese seat among the five permanent members of the United Nations Security Council was held by the government in Taipei. Every year in the early autumn there was an attempt by the non-aligned bloc to oust Taipei from the Security Council and replace them with Beijing, but so far this vote had always failed because of U.S. arm-twisting in Latin America and the rest of the Third World. One of the reasons that this arrangement had endured so long was the immense prestige of R.O.C. President Chiang Kai-Shek and the sentimental popularity of the Kuomintang in the United States electorate. There still was a very powerful China lobby, which was especially strong among right-wing Republicans of what had been the Taft and Knowland factions of the party, and which Goldwater continued. Now, in the midst of the Vietnam War, with U.S. strategic and economic power in decline, the Anglo-American elite decided in favor of a geopolitical alliance with Red China against the Soviets for the foreseeable future. This meant that the honor of U.S. commitments to the Republic of China had to be dumped overboard as so much useless ballast, whatever the domestic political consequences might be. This was the task given to Kissinger, Nixon, and George Bush.

The maneuver on the agenda for 1971 was to oust the Republic of China from the U.N. Security Council and assign their seat to Beijing. Kissinger and Nixon calculated that duplicity would insulate them from domestic political damage: While they were opening to Beijing, they would call for a "two Chinas" policy, under which both Beijing and Taipei would be represented at the U.N., at least in the General Assembly, despite the fact that this was an alternative that both Chinese governments vehemently rejected. The U.S. would pretend to be fighting to keep Taipei in the U.N., with George Bush leading the fake charge, but this effort would be defeated. Then the Nixon administration could claim that the vote in the U.N. was beyond its control, comfortably resign itself to Beijing in the Security Council, and pursue the China card. What was called for was a cynical, duplicitous diplomatic charade in which Bush would have the leading part.

This scenario was complicated by the rivalry between Secretary of State Rogers and NSC boss Kissinger. Rogers was an old friend of Nixon, but it was of course Kissinger who made foreign policy for Nixon and the rest of the government, and Kissinger who was incomparably the greater evil. Between Rogers and Kissinger, Bush was unhesitatingly on the side of Kissinger. In later congressional testimony, former CIA official Ray Cline tried to argue that Rogers and Bush were kept in the dark by Nixon and Kissinger about the real nature of the U.S. China policy. The implication is that Bush's efforts to keep Taiwan at the U.N. were in good faith. According to Cline's fantastic account, "Nixon and Kissinger actually 'undermined' the department's efforts in 1971 to save Taiwan."[11] Rogers may have believed that helping Taiwan was U.S. policy, but Bush did not. Cline's version of these events is an insult to the intelligence of any serious person.

The Nixon-era China card took shape during July 1971 with Kissinger's "Operation Marco Polo I," his secret first trip to Beijing. Kissinger says in his memoirs that Bush was considered a candidate to make this journey, along with David Bruce, Elliot Richardson, Nelson Rockefeller and Al Haig.[12] Kissinger first journeyed to India, and then to Pakistan. From there, with the help of Yahya Khan, Kissinger went on to Beijing for meetings with Zhou Enlai and other Chinese officials. He returned by way of Paris, where he met with North Vietnamese negotiator Le Duc Tho at the Paris talks on Indo-China. Returning to Washington, Kissinger briefed Nixon on his understanding with Zhou. On July 15, 1971 Nixon announced to a huge television and radio audience that he had accepted "with pleasure" an invitation to visit China at some occasion before May of 1972. He lamely assured "old friends" (meaning Chiang Kai-Shek and the R.O.C. government on Taiwan) that their interests would not be sacrificed. Later in the same year, between October 16th and 26th, Kissinger undertook operation "Polo II," a second, public visit with Zhou in Beijing to decide the details of Nixon's visit and hammer out what was to become the U.S.-P.R.C. Shanghai Communiqué, the joint statement issued during Nixon's stay. During this visit, Zhou Enlai cautioned Kissinger not to be disoriented by the hostile Beijing propaganda line against the U.S., manifestations of which were everywhere to be seen. Anti-U.S. slogans on the walls, said Zhou, were meaningless, like "firing an empty cannon." Nixon and Kissinger eventually journeyed to Beijing in February 1972.

It was before this backdrop that Bush waged his farcical campaign to keep Taiwan in the U.N. The State Department had stated through the mouth of Rogers on August 2 that the U.S. would support the admission of Red China to the U.N., but would oppose the expulsion of Taiwan. This was the so-called "two Chinas" policy. In an August 12 interview, Bush told the *Washington Post* that he was working hard to line up the votes to keep Taiwan as a U.N. member when the time to vote came in the fall. Responding to the obvious impression that this was a fraud for domestic political purposes only, Bush pledged his honor on Nixon's commitment to "two Chinas." "I know for a fact that the President wants to see the policy implemented," said Bush, apparently with a straight face, adding that he had discussed the matter with Nixon and Kissinger at the White House only a few days before. Bush said that he and other members of his mission had lobbied 66 countries so far, and that this figure was likely to rise to 80 by the following week. Ultimately Bush would claim to have talked personally with 94 delegations to get them to let Taiwan stay, which a fellow diplomat called "a quantitative track record."

Diplomatic observers noted that the U.S. activity was entirely confined to the high-profile "glass palace" of the U.N., and that virtually nothing was being done by U.S. ambassadors in capitals around the world. But Bush countered that if it were just a question of going through the motions as a gesture for Taiwan, he would not be devoting so much of his time and energy to the cause. The main effort was at the U.N. because "this is what the U.N. is for," he commented. Bush said that his optimism about keeping the Taiwan membership had increased over the past three weeks.[13]

By late September, Bush was saying that he saw a better than 50–50 chance that the U.N. General Assembly would seat both Chinese governments. By this time, the official U.S. position as enunciated by Bush was that the Security Council seat should go to Beijing, but that Taipei ought to be allowed to remain in the General Assembly. Since 1961, the U.S. strategy for blocking the admission of Beijing had depended on a procedural defense, obtaining a simple majority of the General Assembly for a resolution defining the seating of Beijing as an Important Question, which required a two-thirds majority in order to be implemented. Thus, if the U.S. could get a simple majority on the procedural vote, one-third plus one would suffice to defeat Beijing on the second vote.

The U.N. debate on the China seat was scheduled to open on October 18; on October 12, Nixon gave a press conference in which he totally ignored the subject, and made no appeal for support for Taiwan. On October 16, Kissinger departed with great fanfare for Beijing. Kissinger says in his memoirs that he had been encouraged to go to Beijing by Bush, who assured him that a highly publicized Kissinger trip to Beijing would have no impact whatever on the U.N. vote. On October 25, the General Assembly defeated the U.S. resolution to make the China seat an Important Question by a vote of 59 to 54, with 15 abstentions. Ninety minutes later came the vote on the Albanian resolution to seat Beijing and expel Taipei, which passed by a vote of 76 to 35. Bush then cast the U.S. vote to seat Beijing, and then hurried to escort the R.O.C. delegate, Liu Chieh, out of the hall for the last time. The General Assembly was the scene of a jubilant demonstration led by Third World delegates over the fact that Red China had been admitted, and even more so that the U.S. had been defeated. The Tanzanian delegate danced a jig in the aisle. Henry Kissinger, flying back from Beijing, got the news on his teletype and praised Bush's "valiant efforts."

Having connived in selling Taiwan down the river, it was now an easy matter for the Nixon regime to fake a great deal of indignation for domestic political consumption about what had happened. Nixon's spokesman Ron Ziegler declared that Nixon had been outraged by the "spectacle" of the "cheering, handclapping, and dancing" delegates after the vote, which Nixon had seen as a "shocking demonstration" of "undisguised glee" and "personal animosity." Notice that Ziegler had nothing to say against the vote, or against Beijing, but concentrated the fire on the Third World delegates, who were also threatened with a cutoff of U.S. foreign aid.

This was the line that Bush would slavishly follow. On the last day of October, the papers quoted him saying that the demonstration after the vote was "something ugly, something harsh that transcended normal disappointment or elation. . . . I really thought we were going to win," said Bush, still with a straight face. "I'm so . . . disappointed." "There wasn't just clapping and enthusiasm" after the vote, he whined. "When I went up to speak I was hissed and booed. I don't think it's good for the United Nations and that's the point I feel very strongly about." In the view of a *Washington Post* staff writer, "the boyish looking U.S. ambassador to the United Nations looked considerably the worse for wear. But he still conveys the impression of an earnest fellow trying to be the class valedictorian, as he once was described."[14]

Bush expected the Beijing delegation to arrive in New York soon, because they probably wanted to take over the presidency of the Security Council, which rotated on a monthly basis. "But why anybody would want an early case of chicken pox, I don't know," said Bush.

When the Beijing delegation did arrive, Chinese Deputy Foreign Minister Ch'aio Kuan-hua delivered a maiden speech full of ideological bombast along the lines of passages Kissinger had convinced Zhou to cut out of the draft text of the Shanghai Communiqué some days before. Kissinger then telephoned Bush to say in his own speech that the U.S. regretted that the Chinese had elected to inaugurate their participation in the U.N. by "firing these empty cannons of rhetoric." Bush, like a ventriloquist's dummy, obediently mouthed Kissinger's one-liner as a kind of coded message to Beijing that all the public bluster meant nothing between the two secret and increasingly public allies.

To the Brink of War in the Subcontinent

The farce of Bush's pantomime in support of the Kissinger China card very nearly turned into the tragedy of general war later in 1971. This involved the December 1971 war between India and Pakistan, which led to the creation of an independent state of Bangladesh, and which must be counted as one of the least-known thermonuclear confrontations of the United States and Soviet Union. For Kissinger and Bush, what was at stake in this crisis was the consolidation of the China card.

In 1970, Yahya Khan, the British-connected, Sandhurst-educated dictator of Pakistan, was forced to announce that elections would be held in the entire country. It will be recalled that Pakistan was at that time two separate regions, east and west, with India in between. In East Pakistan or Bengal, the Awami League of Sheik Mujibur Rahman campaigned on a platform of autonomy for Bengal, accusing the central government in far-off Islamabad of ineptitude and exploitation. The resentment in East Pakistan was made more acute by the fact that Bengal had just been hit by a typhoon, which had caused extensive flooding and devastation, and by the failure of the government in West Pakistan to organize an effective relief effort. In the elections, the Awami League won 167 out of 169 seats in the East. Yahya Khan delayed the seating of the new national assembly and on the evening of March 25 ordered the Pakistani Army to arrest Mujibur and to wipe out his organization in East Pakistan.

The army proceeded to launch a campaign of political genocide in East Pakistan. Estimates of the number of victims range from 500,000 to three million dead. All members of the Awami League, all Hindus, and all students and intellectuals were in danger of execution by roving army patrols. A senior U.S. Foreign Service officer sent home a dispatch in which he told of West Pakistani soldiers setting fire to a women's dormitory at the University of Dacca and then machine-gunning the women when they were forced by the flames to run out. This campaign of killing went on until December, and it generated an estimated ten million refugees, most of whom fled across the nearby borders to India, which had territory all around East Pakistan. The arrival of ten million refugees caused indescribable chaos in India, whose government was unable to prevent untold numbers from starving to death.[15]

From the very beginning of this monumental genocide, Kissinger and Nixon made it clear that they would not condemn Yahya Khan, whom Nixon considered a personal friend. Kissinger referred merely to the "strong-arm tactics of the Pakistani military," and Nixon circulated a memo in his own handwriting saying, "To all hands. Don't squeeze Yahya at this time. RN." Nixon stressed repeatedly that he wanted to "tilt" in favor of Pakistan in the crisis.

One level of explanation for this active complicity in genocide was that Kissinger and Nixon regarded Yahya Khan as their indispensable back channel to Beijing. But Kissinger could soon go to Beijing any time he wanted, and soon he could talk to the Chinese U.N. delegate in a New York safe house. The essence of the support for the butcher Yahya Khan was this: In 1962, India and China had engaged in a brief border war, and the Beijing leaders regarded India as their geopolitical enemy. In order to ingratiate himself with Zhou and Mao, Kissinger wanted to take a position in favor of Pakistan, and therefore of Pakistan's ally China, and against India and against India's ally, the Soviet Union. (Shortly after Kissinger's trip to China had taken place and Nixon had announced his intention to go to Beijing, India and the Soviet Union had signed a 20-year friendship treaty.)

In Kissinger's view, the Indo-Pakistani conflict over Bengal was sure to become a Sino-Soviet clash by proxy, and he wanted the United States aligned with China in order to impress Beijing with the vast benefits to be derived from the U.S.-P.R.C. strategic alliance under the heading of the "China card."

Kissinger and Nixon were isolated within the Washington bureaucracy on this issue. Secretary of State Rogers was very reluctant to go on supporting Pakistan, and this was the prevalent view in Foggy Bottom and in the embassies around the world. Nixon and Kissinger were isolated from the vast majority of congressional opinion, which expressed horror and outrage over the extent of the carnage being carried out week after week, month after month, by Yahya Khan's armed forces. Even the media and U.S. public opinion could not find any reason for the friendly "tilt" in favor of Yahya Khan. On July 31, Kissinger exploded at a meeting of the Senior Review Group when a proposal was made that the Pakistani army could be removed from Bengal. "Why is it our business how they govern themselves?" Kissinger raged. "The President always says to tilt to Pakistan, but every proposal I get [from inside the U.S. government] is in the opposite direction. Sometimes I think I am in a nut house." This went on for months. On December 3, at a meeting of Kissinger's Washington Special Action Group, Kissinger exploded again, exclaiming, "I've been catching unshirted hell every half-hour from the president who says we're not tough enough. He really doesn't believe we're carrying out his wishes. He wants to tilt toward Pakistan and he believes that every briefing or statement is going the other way."[16]

But no matter what Rogers, the State Department and the rest of the Washington bureaucracy might do, Kissinger knew that George Bush at the U.N. would play along with the pro-Pakistan tilt. "And I knew that George Bush, our able U.N. ambassador, would carry out the President's policy," wrote Kissinger in his memoirs, in describing his decision to drop U.S. opposition to a Security Council debate on the subcontinent.[17] This made Bush one of the most degraded and servile U.S. officials of the era.

Indira Gandhi had come to Washington in November to attempt a peaceful settlement to the crisis, but was crudely snubbed by Nixon and Kissinger. The chronology of the acute final phase of the crisis can be summed up as follows:

In December the crisis heated to the brink of thermonuclear confrontation. On December 4, at the U.N. Security Council, George Bush delivered a speech in which his main thrust was to accuse India of repeated incursions into East Pakistan, and challenging the legitimacy of India's resort to arms, in spite of the plain evidence that Pakistan had struck first. Bush introduced a draft resolution which called on India and Pakistan immediately to cease all hostilities. Bush's resolution also mandated the immediate withdrawal of all Indian and Pakistani armed forces back to their own territory, meaning in effect that India should pull back from East Pakistan and let Yahya Khan's forces there get back to their mission of genocide against the local population. Observers were to be placed along the Indo-Pakistani borders by the U.N. Secretary General. Bush's resolution also contained a grotesque call on India and Pakistan to "exert their best efforts toward the creation of a climate conducive to the voluntary return of refugees to East Pakistan." The resolution was out of touch with the two realities: that Yahya Khan had started the genocide in East Pakistan back in March, and that Yahya had now launched aggression against India with his air raids. Bush's resolution was vetoed by the Soviet representative, Yakov Malik.

On December 6, the Indian government extended diplomatic recognition to the independent state of Bangladesh. Indian troops made continued progress against the Pakistani army in Bengal.

The next day, George Bush at the U.N. made a further step forward toward global confrontation by branding India as the aggressor in the crisis, as Kissinger approvingly notes in his memoirs. Bush's draft resolution, described above, which had been vetoed by Malik in the Security Council, was approved by the General Assembly by a non-binding vote of 104 to 11, which Kissinger considered a triumph for Bush.

By December 8 the Soviet Navy had some 21 ships either in or approaching the Indian Ocean, in contrast to a pre-crisis level of three ships. At this point, with the Vietnam War raging unabated, the U.S. had a total of three ships in the Indian Ocean—two old destroyers and a seaplane tender. The last squadron of the British Navy was departing from the region in the framework of the British pullout from east of Suez.

In the evening, Nixon suggested to Kissinger that the scheduled Moscow summit might be canceled. Kissinger raved that India wanted to detach not just Bengal, but Kashmir also, leading to the further secession of Baluchistan and the total dismemberment of Pakistan. "Fundamentally," wrote Kissinger of this moment, "our only card left was to raise the risks for the Soviets to a level where Moscow would see larger interests jeopardized" by its support of India, which had been lukewarm so far.

On December 10 Kissinger ordered the U.S. Navy to create Task Force 74, consisting of the nuclear aircraft carrier *Enterprise* with escort and supply ships, and to have these ships proceed from their post at Yankee Station in the Gulf of Tonkin off Vietnam to Singapore.[18]

In Dacca, East Pakistan, Maj. Gen. Rao Farman Ali Khan, the commander of Pakistani forces in Bengal, asked the United Nations representative to help arrange a cease-fire, followed by the transfer of power in East Pakistan to the elected representatives of the Awami League and the "repatriation with honor" of his forces back to West Pakistan. At first it appeared that this de facto surrender had been approved by Yahya Khan. But when Yahya Khan heard that the U.S. fleet had been ordered into the Indian Ocean, he was so encouraged that he junked the idea of a surrender and ordered Gen. Ali Khan to resume fighting, which he did.

On December 12, Nixon, Kissinger and Haig met in the Oval Office early Sunday morning in a council of war. Kissinger later described this as a crucial meeting, where, as it turned out, "the first decision to risk war in the triangular Soviet-Chinese-American" relationship was taken."[19]

During Nixon's 1975 secret grand jury testimony to the Watergate Special Prosecution Force, the former President insisted that the United States had come "close to nuclear war" during the Indo-

Pakistani conflict. According to one attorney who heard Nixon's testimony in 1975, Nixon had stated that "we had threatened to go to nuclear war with the Russians."[20] These remarks most probably refer to this December 12 meeting, and the actions it set into motion.

Navy Task Force 74 was ordered to proceed through the Straits of Malacca and into the Indian Ocean, and it attracted the attention of the world media in so doing the following day. Task Force 74 was now on wartime alert.

At 11:30 A.M. local time, Kissinger and Haig sent the Kremlin a message over the Hot Line. This was the first use of the Hot Line during the Nixon administration, and apparently the only time it was used during the Nixon years, with the exception of the October 1973 Middle East war. According to Kissinger, this Hot Line message contained the ultimatum that the Soviets respond to earlier American demands; otherwise Nixon would order Bush to "set in train certain moves" in the U.N. Security Council that would be irreversible. But is this all the message said? Kissinger comments in his memoirs a few pages later:

Our fleet passed through the Strait of Malacca into the Bay of Bengal and attracted much media attention. Were we threatening India? Were we seeking to defend East Pakistan? Had we lost our minds? It was in fact sober calculation. We had some seventy-two hours to bring the war to a conclusion before West Pakistan would be swept into the maelstrom. It would take India that long to shift its forces and mount an assault. Once Pakistan's air force and army were destroyed, its impotence would guarantee the country's eventual disintegration. . . . We had to give the Soviets a warning that matters might get out of control on our side too. We had to be ready to back up the Chinese if at the last moment they came in after all, our U.N. initiative having failed. . . . However unlikely an American military move against India, the other side could not be sure; it might not be willing to accept even the minor risk that we might act irrationally.[21]

These comments by Kissinger lead to the conclusion that the Hot Line message of December 12 was part of a calculated exercise in thermonuclear blackmail and brinksmanship. Kissinger's reference to acting irrationally recalls the infamous RAND Corporation theories of thermonuclear confrontations as chicken games in which it is useful to hint to the opposition that one is insane. If your adversary thinks you are crazy, then he is more likely to back down, the argument goes. Whatever threats were made by Kissinger and Haig that day in their Hot Line message are likely to have been of that variety. All evidence points to the conclusion that on December 12,

1971, the world was indeed close to the brink of thermonuclear confrontation.

And where was George? He was acting as the willing mouthpiece for madmen. Late in the evening of December 12, Bush delivered the following remarks to the Security Council, which are recorded in Kissinger's memoirs:

> The question now arises as to India's further intentions. For example, does India intend to use the present situation to destroy the Pakistan army in the West? Does India intend to use as a pretext the Pakistani counterattacks in the West to annex territory in West Pakistan? Is its aim to take parts of Pakistan-controlled Kashmir contrary to the Security Council resolutions of 1948, 1949, and 1950? If this is not India's intention, then a prompt disavowal is required. The world has a right to know: What are India's intentions? Pakistan's aims have become clear: It has accepted the General Assembly's resolution passed by a vote of 104 to 11. My government has asked this question of the Indian Government several times in the last week. I regret to inform the Council that India's replies have been unsatisfactory and not reassuring.
>
> In view of India's defiance of world opinion expressed by such an overwhelming majority, the United States is now returning the issue to the Security Council. With East Pakistan virtually occupied by Indian troops, a continuation of the war would take on increasingly the character of armed attack on the very existence of a Member State of the United Nations.[22]

Bush introduced another draft resolution of pro-Pakistan tilt, which called on the governments of India and Pakistan to take measures for an immediate cease-fire and withdrawal of troops, and for measures to help the refugees. This resolution was also vetoed by the Soviet Union.

On December 16 Indira Gandhi offered an unconditional cease-fire in the west, which Pakistan immediately accepted. Kissinger opined that this decision to end all fighting had been "reluctant" on the part of India, and had been made possible through Soviet pressure generated by U.S. threats. Zhou Enlai also said later that the U.S. had saved West Pakistan. Kissinger praised Nixon's "courage and patriotism" and his commitment to "preserve the balance of power for the ultimate safety of all free people." Apprentice geopolitician George Bush had carried out yeoman service in that immoral cause.

In their stubborn pursuit of an alliance with the second strongest land power at the expense of all other considerations, Kissinger,

Nixon and Bush were following the dictates of classic geopolitics. This is the school in which Bush was trained, and this is how he has reacted to every international crisis down through the Gulf war, which was originally conceived in London as a "geopolitical" adjustment in favor of the Anglo-Saxons against Germany, Japan, the Arabs, the developing sector and the rest of the world.

Genocide in Vietnam

1972 was the second year of Bush's U.N. tenure, and it was during this time that he distinguished himself as a shameless apologist for the genocidal and vindictive Kissinger policy of prolonging and escalating the war in Vietnam. During most of his first term, Nixon pursued a policy he called the "Vietnamization" of the war. This meant that U.S. land forces were progressively withdrawn while the South Vietnamese Army was ostensibly built up so that it could bear the battle against the Viet Cong and the North Vietnamese regulars. This policy went into crisis in March 1972, when the North Vietnamese launched a 12-division assault across the Demilitarized Zone against the south. On May 8, 1972, Nixon announced that the full-scale bombing of the north, which had been suspended since the spring of 1968, would be resumed with a vengeance: Nixon ordered the bombing of Hanoi and the mining of Haiphong harbor, and the savaging of transportation lines and military installations all over the country. This mining had always been rejected as a tactic during the previous conduct of the war because of the possibility that bombing and mining the harbors might hit Soviet, Chinese and other foreign ships, killing the crews and creating the risk of retaliation by these countries against the U.S. Now, before the 1972 elections, Kissinger and Nixon were determined to "go ape," discarding their previous limits on offensive action and risking whatever China and the Soviet Union might do. It was another gesture of reckless confrontation, fraught with incalculable consequences. Later in the same year, in December, Nixon would respond to a breakdown in the Paris talks with the Hanoi government by ordering the infamous Christmastide B–52 attacks on the north.

It was George Bush who officially informed the international diplomatic community of Nixon's March decisions. Bush addressed a letter to the presidency of the U.N. Security Council in which he outlined what Nixon had set into motion:

"The President directed that the entrances to the ports of North Vietnam be mined and that the delivery of seaborne supplies to North Vietnam be prevented. These measures of collective self-defense are hereby being reported to the United Nations Security Council as required by Article 51 of the United Nations Charter."

The guts of Bush's message, the part that was read with greatest attention in Moscow, Beijing and elsewhere, was contained in the following summary of the way in which Haiphong and the other harbors had been mined:

"Accordingly, as the minimum actions necessary to meet this threat, the Republic of Vietnam and the United States of America have jointly decided to take the following measures of collective self-defense: The entrances to the ports of North Vietnam are being mined, commencing 0900 Saigon time May 9, and the mines are set to activate automatically beginning 1900 hours Saigon time May 11. This will permit vessels of other countries presently in North Vietnamese ports three daylight periods to depart safely." In a long circumlocution, Bush also conveyed that all shipping might also be the target of indiscriminate bombing. Bush called these measures "restricted in extent and purpose." The U.S. was willing to sign a cease-fire ending all acts of war in Indochina (thus including Cambodia, which had been invaded in 1970, and Laos, which had been invaded in 1971, as well as the Vietnams) and bring all U.S. troops home within four months.

There was no bipartisan support for the bombing and mining policy Bush announced. Senator Mike Mansfield pointed out that the decision would only protract the war. Senator William Proxmire called it "reckless and wrong." Four Soviet ships were damaged by these U.S. actions. There was a lively debate within the Soviet Politburo on how to respond to this, with a faction around Shelest demanding that Nixon's invitation to the upcoming Moscow superpower summit be rescinded. But Shelest was ousted by Brezhnev, and the summit went forward at the end of May. The "China card" theoreticians congratulated themselves that the Soviets had been paralyzed by fear of what Beijing might do if Moscow became embroiled with Beijing's new de facto ally, the U.S.

In July 1972, reports emerged in the international press of charges by Hanoi that the U.S. had been deliberately bombing the dams and dikes, which were the irrigation and flood control system around Vietnam's Red River. Once again it was Bush who came forward as the apologist for Nixon's "mad bomber" foreign policy. Bush appeared on the NBC Televison "Today" show to assure the U.S. public that the U.S. bombing had created only "the most incidental and minor impact" on North Vietnam's dike system. This, of course, amounted to a backhanded confirmation that such bombing had been done, and damage wrought in the process.

According to North Vietnamese statistics, more than half of the north's 20 million people lived in areas near the Red River that would be flooded if the dike system were breached. An article which appeared in a Hanoi publication had stated that at flood crest many rivers rise to "six or seven meters above the surrounding fields" and that because of this situation "any dike break, especially in the Red River delta, is a disaster with incalculable consequences."

Bush responded in typical diplomatic jargon to cover up genocidal intentions: "I believe we are being set up by a massive propaganda campaign by the North Vietnamese in the event that there is the same kind of flooding this year—to attribute it to bombs whereas last year it happened just out of lack of maintenance. . . . There's been a study made that I hope will be released shortly that will clarify this whole question." The study "would be very helpful because I think it will show what the North Vietnamese are up to in where they place strategic targets." What Bush was driving at here was an allegation that Hanoi customarily placed strategic assets near the dikes in order to be able to accuse the U.S. of genocide if air attacks breached the dikes and caused flooding. Bush's military spokesmen used similar arguments during the Gulf war, when Iraq was accused of placing military equipment in the midst of civilian residential areas.

"I think you would have to recognize," retorted Bush, "that if there was any intention" of breaching the dikes, "it would be very, very simple to do exactly what we are accused of—and that is what we are not doing."[23]

The bombing of the north continued and reached a final paroxysm at Christmas, when B–52s made unrestricted terror bombing raids against Hanoi and other cities. The Christmas bombing was widely condemned, even by the U.S. press.

Bush and Zionism

Bush's activity at the U.N. also coincided with Kissinger's preparation of the October 1973 Middle East war. During the 1980s, Bush attempted to cultivate a public image as a U.S. politician who, although oriented toward close relations with Israel, would not slavishly appease every demand of the Israelis and the Zionist lobby in the United States, but would take an independent position designed to foster U.S. national interests. From time to time, Bush snubbed the Israelis by hinting that they held hostages of their own, and that the Israeli annexation of Jerusalem would not be accepted by the United States. For some, these delusions have survived even a refutation so categoric as the events of the Kuwait crisis of 1990–91.

Bush would be more accurately designated as a Zionist, whose differences with an Israeli leader like Shamir are less significant than the differences between Shamir and other Israeli politicians. Bush's fanatically pro-Israeli ideological-political track record was already massive during the U.N. years.

In September 1972, Palestinian terrorists describing themselves as the "Black September" organization attacked the quarters of the Israeli Olympic team present in Munich for the Olympic games of that year, killing a number of the Israeli athletes. The Israeli government seized on these events as carte blanche to launch a series of air attacks against Syria and Lebanon, arguing that these countries could be held responsible for what had happened in Munich. Somalia, Greece, and Guinea came forward with a resolution in the Security Council which simply called for the immediate cessation of "all military operations." The Arab states argued that the Israeli air attacks were totally without provocation or justification, and had killed numerous civilians who had nothing whatever to do with the terrorist actions in Munich.

The Nixon regime, with one eye on the autumn 1972 elections and the need to mobilize the Zionist lobby in support of a second term, wanted to find a way to oppose this resolution, since it did not sufficiently acknowledge the unique righteousness of the Israeli cause and Israel's inherent right to commit acts of war against its neighbors. It was Bush who authored a competing resolution, which called on all interested parties "to take all measures for the immediate cessation and prevention of all military operations and terrorist activities." It was Bush who dished up the rationalizations for U.S. rejection of the first resolution. That resolution was no good, Bush argued, because it did not reflect the fact that "the fabric of violence in the Middle East is inextricably interwoven with the massacre in Munich." "By our silence on the terror in Munich are we indeed inviting more Munichs?" he asked. Justifying the Israeli air raids on Syria and Lebanon, Bush maintained that certain governments "cannot be absolved of responsibility for the cycle of violence" because of their words and deeds, or because of their tacit acquiescence. Slightly later, after the vote had taken place, Bush argued that "by adopting this resolution, the council would have ignored reality, would have spoken to one form of violence but not another, would have looked to the effect but not the cause."

When the resolution was put to a vote, Bush made front-page headlines around the world by casting the U.S. veto, a veto that had been cast only once before in the entire history of the U.N. The vote was 13 to 1, with the U.S. casting the sole negative vote. Panama was the lone abstention. The only other time the U.S. veto had been used had been in 1970, on a resolution involving Rhodesia.

The Israeli U.N. ambassador, Yosef Tekoah, did not attend the debate because of the Jewish holiday of Rosh Hashanah. But Israel's cause was well defended—by Bush. According to an Israeli journalist observing the proceedings who was quoted by the *Washington Post*, "Bush sounds more pro-Israeli than Tekoah would have."[24]

Later in 1972, attempts were made by non-aligned states and the U.N. Secretariat to arrange the indispensable basis for a Middle East peace settlement—the withdrawal of Israel from the territories occupied during the 1967 war.

In February of 1972, the U.N.'s Middle East mediator, Gunnar Jarring of Norway, had asked that the Security Council reaffirm the original contents of Resolution 242 of 1967 by reiterating that Israel should surrender Arab territory seized in 1967. "Land for peace" was anathema to the Israeli government then as now. Bush undertook to blunt this non-aligned peace bid.

Late in 1972, the non-aligned group proposed a resolution in the General Assembly which called for "immediate and unconditional" Israeli withdrawal from the occupied territories while inviting other countries to withhold assistance that would help Israel to sustain its occupation of the Arab land. Bush quickly rose to assail this text.

In a speech to the General Assembly in December 1972, Bush warned the assembly that the original text of Resolution 242 was "the essential agreed basis for U.N. peace efforts and this body and all its members should be mindful of the need to preserve the negotiating asset that it represents. The assembly," Bush went on, "cannot seek to impose courses of action on the countries directly concerned, either by making new demands or favoring the proposals or positions of one side over the other." Never, never would George Bush take sides or accept a double standard of this type!

A series of machinations followed, finally yielding a resolution that passed, with the United States abstaining and Israel opposed. At the same time, the U.S. promised Israel a continuing supply of Phantom jets, and there was war in the Middle East before the year was out, just as Kissinger had planned.

Bush spent just under two years at the U.N. His tenure coincided with some of the most monstrous crimes against humanity of the Nixon-Kissinger team, for whom Bush functioned as an international spokesman, and to whom no Kissinger policy was too odious to be enthusiastically proclaimed before the international community and world public opinion. Through this doggedly loyal service, Bush forged a link with Nixon that would be ephemeral but vital for his career, while it lasted, and a link with Kissinger that would be decisive in shaping Bush's own administration in 1988–89.

The way in which Bush set about organizing the anti-Iraq coalition of 1990–91 was decisively shaped by his United Nations experience. His initial approach to the Security Council, the types of resolutions that were put forward by the U.S., and the alternation of military escalation with consultations among the five permanent members of the Security Council—all this harkened back to the experience Bush acquired as Kissinger's envoy to the world body.

Toward the close of Bush's posting to the U.N., his father, Prescott Bush, died at the Sloan-Kettering Hospital in New York City. It was October 8, 1972. Prescott Bush had been diagnosed as suffering from lung cancer.

Notes for Chapter XI

1. In 1970, Bush's portfolio included 29 companies in which he had an interest of more than $4000. He had 10,000 shares of American General Insurance Co., 5,500 shares of American Standard, 200 shares of AT&T, 832 shares of CBS, and 581 shares of Industries Exchange Fund. He also held stock in the Kroger Company, Simplex Wire and Cable Co. (25,000 shares), IBM, and Allied Chemical. In addition, he had created a trust fund for his children.

2. James Reston, Jr., *The Lone Star: The Life of John Connally* (New York: Harper & Row, 1989), p. 380.

3. William Safire, *Before the Fall* (New York: Doubleday, 1977).

4. Walter Pincus and Bob Woodward, "Presidential Posts and Dashed Hopes," *Washington Post,* Aug. 9, 1988.

5. Reston, *op. cit.,* p. 382.

6. George Bush and Victor Gold, *Looking Forward* (New York: Doubleday, 1987), p. 110.

7. For the Nixon side of the Bush U.N. appointment, see William Safire, *op. cit.,* especially "The President Falls in Love," pp. 642 ff.

8. On Kissinger, see *Executive Intelligence Review,* March 3, 1989.

9. For text of Kissinger's speech, see *Executive Intelligence Review,* June 1, 1982.

10. Tom Mangold, *Cold Warrior* (New York: Simon and Schuster, 1991), p. 305.

11. See Tad Szulc, *The Illusion of Peace* (New York: Viking Press, 1978), p. 498.

12. Henry Kissinger, *White House Years* (Boston: Little, Brown, 1979), p. 715.

13. Szulc, *op. cit.,* p. 500, and *Washington Post,* Aug. 12, 1971.

14. *Washington Post,* Oct. 31, 1971.

15. See Seymour M. Hersh, *The Price of Power* (New York: Summit Books, 1983), pp. 444 ff.

16. Henry Kissinger, *op. cit.,* p. 897. The general outlines of these remarks were first published in Jack Anderson's syndicated column, and reprinted in Jack Anderson, *The Anderson Papers* (New York: Random House, 1973).

17. Kissinger, *op. cit.,* p. 896.

18. Elmo Zumwalt, *On Watch* (New York: Quadrangle/New York Times Book Co., 1976), p. 367.

19. Kissinger, *op. cit.,* p. 909.

20. Hersh, *op. cit.,* p. 457.

21. Kissinger, *op. cit.,* pp. 911–12.

22. See R.C. Gupta, *U.S. Policy Toward India and Pakistan* (Delhi: B.R. Publishing Corp., 1977), pp. 84 ff.

23. *Washington Post,* July 27, 1972.

24. *Washington Post,* Sept. 11, 1972.

Emblem of Skull and Bones, George Bush's blueblood secret society at Yale University.

NSIPS/George Canning

"The Tomb": Skull and Bones headquarters at Yale University in New Haven.

In 1988, the Washington Post *reported on charges that Prescott Bush had robbed the grave of Geronimo at Fort Sill, Oklahoma.*

George and Barbara Bush
with George's parents, Texas,
1948. Did they actually arrive
on this private Dresser
Company airplane, and not in
the red Studebaker of Bush
biographical legend?

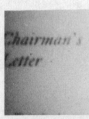

A letter from Zapata Offshore
Chairman George Bush in the
1963-4 annual report.

J. Hugh Liedtke,
Pennzoil chairman,
and his brother
William were
Bush's partners in
Zapata, Watergate
and China oil deals.

Carlos Wesley

Cuban exile community, with strong links to George Bush, was manipulated and used in Watergate and Iran-Contra.

Bottom right, Cuban exiles train for invasion. Top, under fire from Castro's troops at Bay of Pigs, as invasion becomes fiasco for the intelligence community.

Library of Congress/U.S. News and World Report Collection

5. Based on the above, it is my conclusion that I am not the Mr. George Bush of the Central Intelligence Agency referred to in the memorandum.

Assassination Archives and Research Center, Washington, D.C.

On November 23, 1963, the day after the murder of President John Kennedy, agents of the FBI spoke with "Mr. George Bush of the CIA" about the possible consequences of the assassination within the Cuban exile community. This November 29, 1963 memorandum (obtained at the Assassination Archives and Research Center, Washington, D.C.) of FBI Director J. Edgar Hoover records that discussion. When he was Vice President, George Bush denied any knowledge of the FBI briefing. In a sworn statement (shown here) one George William Bush, a "lowly researcher and analyst" for the CIA, who had been fingered by the CIA as the supposed respondent in the discussion, denied any knowledge of it. Had George Bush been caught again in the web of conspiracy and lies that has marked his career from the beginning?

Senator Ralph Yarborough (left), who beat Bush in Texas in 1964. His idea was to "put the jam on the lower shelf so the little man can get his hand in."

Yarborough, the "FDR Democrat" Bush could not defeat with racist jibes, corruption slanders, and Establishment money.

Congressman George Bush's population control leadership was lauded by the Population Crisis Committee—a group founded by Nazi banker Gen. William H. Draper, Jr.

United Nations/T. Chen

George Bush, ambassador to the U.N., welcomes Chinese Communist delegate Huang Hua to the Security Council in November 1971, after Kissinger China-card diplomacy had ousted Taiwan.

United Nations/T. Chen

Henry Kissinger, Bush's real boss at the United Nations.

XII
CHAIRMAN GEORGE
IN WATERGATE

In November 1972, Bush's "most influential patron," Richard Nixon,[1] won reelection to the White House for a second term in a landslide victory over the McGovern-Shriver Democratic ticket. Nixon's election victory had proceeded in spite of the arrest of five White House-linked burglars in the offices of the Democratic National Committee at the Watergate building in Washington early on June 17 of the same year. This was the beginning of the infamous Watergate scandal, which would overshadow and ultimately terminate Nixon's second term in 1974.

After the election, Bush received a telephone call informing him that Nixon wanted to talk to him at the Camp David retreat in the Catoctin Mountains of Maryland. Bush had been looking to Washington for the inevitable personnel changes that would be made in preparation for Nixon's second term. Bush tells us that he was aware of Nixon's plan to reorganize his cabinet around the idea of a "super cabinet" of top-level, inner cabinet ministers or "super secretaries" who would work closely with the White House while relegating the day-to-day functioning of their executive departments to sub-cabinet deputies. One of the big winners under this plan was scheduled to be George Shultz, the former Labor Secretary who was now supposed to become "Super" Secretary of the Treasury. Shultz was a Bechtel executive who went on to be Reagan's second Secretary of State after Al Haig. Bush and Shultz were future members of the Bohemian Club of San Francisco and of the Bohemian Grove summer gathering. Shultz was a Princeton graduate who was reputed to have a tiger, the school's symbol, tattooed on his rump.

Bush says he received a call from Nixon's top domestic aide, John Ehrlichman (along with Haldeman a partner in the "Chinese wall" around Nixon maintained by the White House palace guard). Ehrlichman told Bush that George Shultz wanted to see him before he went on to meet with Nixon at Camp David. As it turned out, Shultz wanted to offer Bush the post of Undersecretary of the Treasury, which would amount to *de facto* administrative control over the department while Shultz concentrated on his projected super secretary policy functions.

Bush says he thanked Shultz for his "flattering" offer, took it under consideration, and then pressed on to Camp David.[2]

At Camp David, Bush says that Nixon talked to him in the following terms: "George, I know that Shultz has talked to you about the Treasury job, and if that's what you'd like, that's fine with me. However, the job I really want you to do, the place I really need you, is over at the National Committee running things. This is an important time for the Republican Party, George. We have a chance to build a new coalition in the next four years, and you're the one who can do it."[3]

But this was not the job that George really wanted. He wanted to be promoted, but he wanted to continue in the personal retinue of Henry Kissinger. "At first Bush tried to persuade the President to give him, instead, the number-two job at the State Department, as deputy to Secretary Henry Kissinger. Foreign affairs was his top priority, he said. Nixon was cool to this idea, and Bush capitulated."[4]

According to Bush's own account, he asked Nixon for some time to ponder the offer of the RNC chairmanship. Among those whom Bush said he consulted on whether or not to accept was Rogers C.B. Morton, the former Congressman whom Nixon had made Secretary of Commerce. Morton suggested that if Bush wanted to accept, he insist that he continue as a member of the Nixon cabinet, where, it should be recalled, he had been sitting since he was named to the U.N. Pennsylvania Senator Hugh Scott, one of the Republican congressional leaders, also advised Bush to demand to continue on in the cabinet: "Insist on it," Bush recalls him saying. Bush also consulted Barbara. The story goes that Bar had demanded that George pledge that the one job he would never take was the RNC post. But now he wanted to take precisely that post, which appeared to be a political graveyard. George explained his wimpish obedience to Nixon: "Boy, you can't turn a President down."[5] Bush then told Ehrlichman that he would accept provided he could stay on in the cabinet. Nixon approved this condition, and the era of Chairman George had begun.

Of course, making the chairman of the Republican Party an ex-officio member of the President's cabinet seems to imply something resembling a one-party state. But George was not deterred by such difficulties.

Nixon's choice of Bush to head the RNC was announced on December 11, 1972. The outgoing RNC Chairman was Senator Bob Dole of Kansas, an asset of the grain cartel, but, in that period, not totally devoid of human qualities. According to press reports, Nixon palace guard heavies like Haldeman and Charles W. Colson, later a central Watergate figure, were not happy with Dole because he would not take orders from the White House.[6]

Bush's own account of how he got the RNC post ignores Dole, who was Bush's most serious rival for the 1988 Republican presidential nomination. According to Dole's version, he conferred with Nixon about the RNC post on November 28, and told the President that he would have to quit the RNC in 1973 in order to get ready to run for reelection in 1974. According to Dole, it was he who recommended Bush to Nixon. Dole even said that he had gone to New York to convince Bush to accept the post. Dole sought to remove any implication that he had been fired by Nixon, and contradicted "speculation that I went to the mountaintop to be pushed off," for "that was not the case." What was clear was that Nixon and his retainers had chosen a replacement for Dole, whom they expected to be more obedient to the commands of the White House palace guard.

Bush assumed his new post in January 1973, in the midst of the trial of the Watergate burglars. He sought at once to convey the image of a pragmatic technocrat on the lookout for Republican candidates who could win, rather than an ideologue. "There's kind of a narrow line between standing for nothing and imposing one's views," Bush told the press. He stressed that the RNC would have a lot of money to spend for recruiting candidates, and that he would personally control this money. "The White House is simply not going to control the budget," said Bush. "I believe in the importance of this job and I have confidence I can do it," he added. "I couldn't do it if I were some reluctant dragon being dragged away from a three-wine luncheon."[7]

Bush inaugurated his new post with a pledge that the Republican Party, from President Nixon on down, would do "everything we possibly can" to make sure that the GOP was not involved in political dirty tricks in the future. "I don't think it is good for politics in this country and I am sure I am reflecting the President's views on that as head of the party," intoned Bush in an appearance on "Issues and Answers."[8]

The Coup

By the beginning of the 1990s, it has become something of a commonplace to refer to the complex of events surrounding the fall of Nixon as a coup d'état.[9] It was, to be sure, a coup d'état, but one whose organizers and beneficiaries most commentators and historians are reluctant to name, much less to confront. Broadly speaking, Watergate was a coup d'état which was instrumental in laying the basis for the specific new type of authoritarian-totalitarian regime which now rules the United States. The purpose of the coup was to rearrange the dominant institutions of the U.S. government so as to enhance their ability to carry out policies agreeable to the increasingly urgent dictates of the Morgan-Rockefeller-Mellon-Harriman financier faction. The immediate beneficiaries of the coup have been that class of bureaucratic, technocratic administrators who have held the highest public offices, exercising power in many cases almost without interruption, since the days of the Watergate scandal. It is obvious that George Bush himself is one of the most prominent of such beneficiaries. As the Roman playwright Seneca warns us, "Cui prodest scelus, est fecit"—the one who derives advantage from the crime is the one most likely to have committed it.

The policies of the Wall Street investment banking interests named are those of usury and Malthusianism, stressing the decline of a productive industrial economy in favor of savage Third World looting and anti-population measures. The changes subsumed by Watergate included the abolition of government's function as a means to distribute the rewards and benefits of economic progress among the principal constituency groups, upon whose support the shifting political coalitions depended for their success. Henceforth, government would appear as the means by which the sacrifices and penalties of austerity and declining standards of living would be imposed on a passive and stupefied population. The constitutional office of the President was to be virtually destroyed, and the power of the usurious banking elites above and behind the presidency was to be radically enhanced.

The reason why the Watergate scandal escalated into the overthrow of Nixon has to do with the international monetary crisis of those years, and with Nixon's inability to manage the collapse of the Bretton Woods system and the U.S. dollar in a way satisfactory to the Anglo-American financial elite. One real-time observer of the events of these years, who emphasized the intimate relation between the international monetary upheavals on the one hand and the *peripeteia* of Nixon on the other, was Lyndon LaRouche. The following comments by LaRouche are excerpted from a July 1973 commentary on the conjuncture of a revaluation of the deutsche-mark with John Dean's testimony before Senator Sam Ervin's Watergate investigating committee:

> Last week's newest up-valuation of the West German D-Mark pushed the inflation-soaked Nixon Administration one very large step closer toward "Watergate" impeachment. Broad bi-partisan support and press enthusiasm for the televised Senate Select Committee airing of wide-ranging revelations coincides with surging contempt for the government's handling of international and domestic financial problems over the past six months.

LaRouche went on to point out why the same financiers and news media who had encouraged a coverup of the Watergate scandal during 1972 had decided during 1973 to use the break-in and coverup as a means of overthrowing Nixon.

> Then came the January [1973] Paris meeting of the International Monetary Fund. The world monetary system was glutted with over $60 billions of inconvertible reserves. The world economy was technically bankrupt. It was kept out of actual bankruptcy proceedings throughout 1972 solely by the commitment of the U.S.A. to agree to some January 1973 plan by which most of these $60 billions would begin to become convertible. The leading suggestion was that the excess dollars would be gradually sopped in exchange for IMF Special Drawing Rights (SDRs). With some such White House IMF action promised for January 1973, the financial world had kept itself more or less wired together by sheer political will throughout 1972.
>
> Then, into the delicate January Paris IMF sessions stepped Mr. Nixon's representatives. His delegates proceeded to break up the meeting with demands for trade and tariff concessions—a virtual declaration of trade war.
>
> Promptly, the financial markets registered their reaction to Mr. Nixon's bungling by plunging into crisis.
>
> To this, Mr. Nixon shortly responded with devaluation of the dollar, a temporary expedient giving a very brief breathing-space to get back to the work of establishing dollar convertibility. Nixon continued his bungling, suggesting that this devaluation made condi-

tions more favorable for negotiating trade and tariff concessions—more trade war.

The financiers of the world weighed Mr. Nixon's wisdom, and began selling the dollar at still-greater discounts. Through successive crises, Mr. Nixon continued to speak only of John Connally's Holy Remedies of trade and tariff concessions. Financiers thereupon rushed substantially out of all currencies into such hedges as world-wide commodity speculation on a scale unprecedented in modern history. Still, Mr. Nixon had nothing to propose on dollar convertibility—only trade wars. The U.S. domestic economy exploded into Latin American-style inflation.

General commodity speculation, reflecting a total loss of confidence in all currencies, seized upon basic agricultural commodities—among others. Feed prices soared, driving meat, poultry, and produce costs and prices toward the stratosphere.

It was during this period, as Nixon's credibility seemed so much less important than during late 1972, that a sudden rush of enthusiasm developed for the moral sensibilities of Chairman Sam Ervin's Senate Select Committee.[10]

As LaRouche points out, it was the leading Anglo-American financier factions which decided to dump Nixon, and availed themselves of the pre-existing Watergate affair in order to reach their goal. The financiers were able to implement their decision all the more easily thanks to the numerous operatives of the intelligence community who had been embedded within the Plumbers from the moment of their creation, in response to an explicit demand coming from George Bush's personal mentor, Henry Kissinger.

Watergate included the option of rapid steps in the direction of a dictatorship, not so much of the military as of the intelligence community and the law enforcement agencies, acting as executors of the will of the Wall Street circles indicated. The "Seven Days in May" overtone of Watergate, the more or less overt break with constitutional forms and rituals, was never excluded. We must recall that the backdrop for Watergate had been provided first of all by the collapse of the international monetary system, as made official by Nixon's austerity decrees imposing a wage and price freeze starting on the fateful day of August 15, 1971. What followed was an attempt to run the entire U.S. economy under the top-down *diktat* of the Pay Board and the Price Commission.

This economic state of emergency was then compounded by the artificial oil shortages orchestrated by the companies of the international oil cartel during late 1973 and 1974, all in the wake of Kissinger's October 1973 Middle East war and the Arab oil boycott.

Preponderant power during the last years of Nixon and during the Ford years was in any case exercised by Henry Kissinger, the *de facto* President, about whose pedigree and strategy something has been said above. The preserving of constitutional form and ritual as a hollow facade behind which to realize practices more and more dictatorial in their substance was a typical pragmatic adaptation made possible by the ability of the financiers to engineer the slow and gradual decline of the economy, avoiding upheavals of popular protest.

But in retrospect there can be no doubt that Watergate was a coup d'état, a creeping and muffled cold coup in the institutions which has extended its consequences over almost two decades. Among contemporary observers, the one who grasped this significance most lucidly in the midst of the events themselves was Lyndon LaRouche, who produced a wealth of journalistic and analytical material during 1973 and 1974. The roots of the administrative fascism of the Reagan and Bush years are to be found in the institutional tremors and changed power relations set off by the banal farce of the Watergate break-in.

In the view of the dominant school of pro-regime journalism, the essence of the Watergate scandal lies in the illegal espionage and surveillance activity of the White House covert operations team, the so-called Plumbers, who are alleged to have been caught during an attempt to burglarize the offices of the Democratic National Committee in the Watergate office building near the Potomac. The supposed goal of the break-in was to filch information and documents while planting bugs. According to the official legend of the *Washington Post* and Hollywood, Nixon and his retainers responded to the arrest of the burglars by compounding their original crime with obstruction of justice and all of the abuses of a coverup. Then the *Washington Post* journalists Bob Woodward and Carl Bernstein, dedicated partisans of the "truth," blew the story open with the help of Woodward's mysterious source, Deep Throat, setting into motion the investigation of the Senate committee under Sam Ervin, leading to impeachment proceedings by Rep. Peter Rodino's House Judiciary Committee, which ultimately forced Nixon to resign.

The received interpretation of the salient facts of the Watergate episode is a fantastic and grotesque distortion of historical truth. Even the kind of cursory examination of the facts in Watergate which we can permit ourselves within the context of a biography of Watergate figure George Bush will reveal that the actions which caused the fall of Nixon cannot be reduced to the simplistic account just summarized. There is, for example, the question of the infiltration of the White House staff and of the Plumbers themselves by members and assets of the intelligence community whose loyalty was not to Nixon, but to the Anglo-American financier elite. This includes the presence among the Plumbers of numerous assets of the Central Intelligence Agency, and specifically of the CIA bureaus traditionally linked to George Bush, such as the Office of Security-Security Research Staff and the Miami Station with its pool of Cuban operatives.

The Plumbers were created at the demand of Henry Kissinger, who told Nixon that something had to be done to stop leaks in the wake of the "Pentagon Papers" affair of 1971. But if the Plumbers were called into existence by Kissinger, they were funded through a mechanism set up by Kissinger-clone George Bush. A salient fact about the White House Special Investigations Unit (or Plumbers) of 1971–72 is that the money used to finance it was provided by George Bush's business partner and lifelong intimate friend, Bill Liedtke, the president of Pennzoil. Bill Liedtke was a regional finance chairman for the Nixon campaigns of 1968 and 1972, and he was one of the most successful, reportedly exceeding his quota by the largest margin among all his fellow regional chairmen. Liedtke says that he accepted this post as a personal favor to George Bush. In 1972, Bill Liedtke raised $700,000 in anonymous contributions, including what appears to have been a single contribution of $100,000 that was laundered through a bank account in Mexico. According to Harry Hurt, part of this money came from Bush's bosom crony Robert Mosbacher, his former Secretary of Commerce, then head of Bush's reelection campaign. According to one account, "two days before a new law was scheduled to begin making anonymous donations illegal, the $700,000 in cash, checks, and securities was loaded into a briefcase at Pennzoil headquarters and picked up by a company vice president, who boarded a Washington-bound Pennzoil jet and delivered the funds to the Committee to Re-Elect the President at ten o'clock that night."[11]

These Mexican checks were turned over first to Maurice Stans of the CREEP, who transferred them in turn to Watergate burglar G. Gordon Liddy. Liddy passed them on to Bernard Barker, one of the Miami Station Cubans arrested on the night of the final Watergate break-in. Barker was actually carrying some of the cash left over from these checks when he was apprehended. When Barker was arrested, his bank records were subpoenaed by the Dade County, Florida district attorney, Richard E. Gerstein, and were obtained by Gerstein's chief investigator, Martin Dardis. As Dardis told Carl

Bernstein of the *Washington Post*, about $100,000 in four cashier's checks had been issued in Mexico City by Manuel Ogarrio Daguerre, a prominent lawyer who handled Stans's money-laundering operation there.[12] Bill Liedtke eventually appeared before three grand juries investigating the different aspects of the Watergate affair, but neither he nor Pennzoil was ever brought to trial for the CREEP contributions. But it is a matter of more than passing interest that the money for the Plumbers came from one of Bush's intimates and, at the request of Bush, a member of the Nixon cabinet from February 1971 on. How much did Bush himself know about the activities of the Plumbers, and when did he know it?

Who Paid the Plumbers?

The U.S. House of Representatives Banking and Currency Committee, chaired by Texas Democrat Wright Patman, soon began a vigorous investigation of the money financing the break-in, large amounts of which were found as cash in the pockets of the burglars. Chairman Patman opened the following explosive leads:

Patman confirmed that the largest amount of the funds going into the Miami bank account of Watergate burglar Bernard Barker, a CIA operative since the Bay of Pigs invasion, was the $100,000 sent in by Texas CREEP chairman William Liedtke (longtime business partner of George Bush). The money was sent from Houston down to Mexico, where it was "laundered" to eliminate its accounting trail. It then came back to Barker's account as four checks totaling $89,000 and $11,000 in cash. A smaller amount, an anonymous $25,000 contribution, was sent in by Minnesota CREEP officer Kenneth Dahlberg in the form of a cashier's check.

Patman relentlessly pursued the true sources of this money, as the best route to the truth about who ran the break-in, and for what purpose. CREEP National Chairman Maurice Stans later described the situation just after the burglars were arrested, made dangerous by ". . . Congressman Wright Patman and several of his political hatchet men working on the staff of the House Banking and Currency Committee. Without specific authorization by his committee, Patman announced that he was going to investigate the Watergate matter, using as his entry the banking transactions of the Dahlberg and Mexican checks. In the guise of covering that ground, he obviously intended to roam widely, and he almost did, but his own committee, despite its Democratic majority, eventually stopped him."[13]

These are the facts that Patman had established—before "his own committee . . . stopped him."

The anonymous Minnesota $25,000 had in fact been provided to Dahlberg by Dwayne Andreas, chief executive of the Archer Daniels Midland grain trading company.

The Texas $100,000, sent by William Liedtke, in fact came from Robert H. Allen, a mysterious nuclear weapons materials executive. Allen was chairman of Gulf Resources and Chemical Corporation in Houston. His company controlled half the world's supply of lithium, an essential component of hydrogen bombs.

On April 3, 1972 (75 days before the Watergate arrests), $100,000 was transferred by telephone from a bank account of Gulf Resources and Chemical Corp. into a Mexico City account of an officially defunct subsidiary of Gulf Resources. Gulf Resources' Mexican lawyer, Manuel Ogarrio Daguerre, withdrew it and sent back to Houston the package of four checks and cash, which Liedtke forwarded for the CIA burglars.[14]

Robert H. Allen was Texas CREEP's chief financial officer, while Bush partner William Liedtke was overall chairman. But what did Allen represent?

In keeping with its strategic nuclear holdings, Allen's Gulf Resources was a kind of committee of the main components of the London-New York oligarchy. Formed in the late 1960s, Gulf Resources had taken over the New York-based Lithium Corporation of America. The president of this subsidiary was Gulf Resources Executive Vice President Harry D. Feltenstein, Jr. John Roger Menke, a director of both Gulf Resources and Lithium Corp., was also a consultant and director of the United Nuclear Corporation, and a director of the Hebrew Technical Institute. The ethnic background of the Lithium subsidiary is of interest due to Israel's known preoccupation with developing a nuclear weapons arsenal.

Another Gulf Resources and Lithium Corp. director was Minnesotan Samuel H. Rogers, who was also a director of Dwayne Andreas's Archer Daniels Midland Corp. Andreas was a large financial backer of the "Zionist lobby" through the Anti-Defamation League of B'nai B'rith.

Gulf Resources Chairman Robert H. Allen received the "Torch of Liberty" award of the Anti-Defamation League in 1982. Allen was a white Anglo-Saxon conservative. No credible reason for this award was supplied to the press, and the ADL stated their satisfaction that Mr. Allen's financing of the Watergate break-in was simply a mistake, now in the distant past.

From the beginning of Gulf Resources, there was always a representative on its board of New York's Bear Stearns firm, whose partner, Jerome Kohlberg, Jr., pioneered leveraged buyouts and merged with Bush's friend Henry Kravis.

The most prestigious board member of Allen's Gulf Resources was George A. Butler, otherwise the chairman of Houston's Post Oak Bank. Butler represented the ultra-secretive W.S. ("Auschwitz") Farish III, confidant of George Bush and U.S. host of Queen Elizabeth. Farish was the founder and controlling owner of Butler's Post Oak Bank, and was chairman of the bank's executive committee as of 1988.[15]

A decade after Watergate, it was revealed that the Hunt family had controlled about 15 percent of Gulf Resources shares. This Texas oil family hired George Bush in 1977 to be the executive committee chairman of their family enterprise, the First International Bank in Houston. In the 1980s, Ray Hunt secured a massive oil contract with the ruler of North Yemen under the sponsorship of then-Vice President Bush. Ray Hunt continues in the 1991–92 presidential campaign as George Bush's biggest Texas financial angel.

Here, in this one powerful Houston corporation, we see early indications of the alliance of George Bush with the "Zionist lobby"—an alliance which for political reasons the Bush camp wishes to keep covert.

These, then, are the Anglo-American moguls whose money paid for the burglary of the Watergate Hotel. It was their money that Richard Nixon was talking about on the famous "smoking gun" tape which lost him the presidency.

The Investigation is Derailed

On Oct. 3, 1972, the House Banking and Currency Committee voted 20–15 against Chairman Wright Patman's investigation. The vote prevented the issuance of 23 subpoenas for CREEP officials to come to Congress to testify.

The margin of protection to the moguls was provided by six Democratic members of the Committee who voted with the Republicans against Chairman Patman. As CREEP Chairman Maurice Stans put it, "There were . . . indirect approaches to Democratic [committee] members. An all-out campaign was conducted to see that the investigation was killed off, as it successfully was."[16]

Certain elements of this infamous "campaign" are known.

Banking Committee member Frank Brasco, a liberal Democratic Congressman from New York, voted to stop the probe. New York Governor Nelson Rockefeller had arranged a meeting between Brasco and U.S. Attorney General John Mitchell. Brasco had been a target of a Justice Department investigation for alleged fraud and bribery since 1970, and Mitchell successfully warned Brasco not to back Patman. Later, in 1974, Brasco was convicted of bribery.

Before Watergate, both John Mitchell and Henry Kissinger had FBI reports implicating California Congressman Richard Hanna in the receipt of illegal campaign contributions from the Korean Central Intelligence Agency. Hanna surprised Patman by voting against the investigation. Hanna was later convicted for his role in the Koreagate scandal in 1978.

The secretary of Congressman William Chappell complained in 1969 that the Florida Democrat had forced her to kick back some of her salary. The Justice Department, holding this information, had declined to prosecute. Chappell, a member of the Banking Committee, voted to stop Patman's investigation.

Kentucky Democratic Congressman William Curlin, Jr. revealed in 1973 that "certain members of the committee were reminded of various past political indiscretions, or of relatives who might suffer as a result of [a] pro-subpoena vote."

The Justice Department worked overtime to smear Patman, including an attempt to link him to "Communist agents" in Greece.[17]

The day before the committee vote, the Justice Department released a letter to Patman claiming that any congressional investigation would compromise the rights of the accused Watergate burglars before their trial.

House Republican leader Gerald Ford led the attack on Patman from within the Congress. Though he later stated his regrets for this vicious campaign, his eventual reward was the U.S. presidency.

Canceling the Patman probe meant that there would be no investigation of Watergate before the 1972 presidential election. The *Washington Post* virtually ended reference to the Watergate affair, and spoke of Nixon's opponent, George McGovern, as unqualified for the presidency.

The Republican Party was handed another four-year administration. Bush, Kissinger, Rockefeller and Ford were the gainers.

But then Richard Nixon became the focus of all Establishment attacks for Watergate, while the money trail that Patman had pursued was forgotten. Wright Patman was forced out of his committee chairmanship in 1974. On the day Nixon resigned the presidency,

Patman wrote to Peter Rodino, chairman of the House Judiciary Committee, asking him not to stop investigating Watergate. Though Patman died in 1976, his advice still holds good.

The CIA Plumbers

As the late FBI Director J. Edgar Hoover told the journalist Andrew Tully in the days before June 1972, "By God, he's [Nixon's] got some former CIA men working for him that I'd kick out of my office. Someday, that bunch will serve him up a fine mess."[18] The CIA men in question were among the Plumbers, a unit allegedly created in the first place to stanch the flow of leaks, including the Jack Anderson material about such episodes as the December 1971 brush with nuclear war discussed above (see Chapter 11). Leading Plumbers included retired high officials of the CIA. Plumber and Watergate burglar E. Howard Hunt had been a GS–15 CIA staff officer; he had played a role in the 1954 toppling of Guatemalan President Jacobo Arbenz Guzman, and later had been one of the planners in the Bay of Pigs invasion of 1961. After the failure of the Bay of Pigs, Hunt is thought to have been a part of the continuing CIA attempts to assassinate Castro, code-named Operation Mongoose, ongoing at the time of the Kennedy assassination. All of this puts him in the thick of the CIA Miami Station. One of Hunt's close personal friends was Howard Osborne, an official of the CIA Office of Security who was the immediate superior of James McCord. In the spring of 1971, Hunt went to Miami to recruit from among the Cubans the contingent of Watergate burglars, including Bernard Barker, Eugenio Martínez, and the rest. This was two months before the publication of the Pentagon Papers, leaked by Daniel Ellsberg, provided Kissinger with the pretext he needed to get Nixon to initiate what would shortly become the Plumbers.

Another leading Watergate burglar was James McCord, a former top official of the CIA Office of Security, the agency bureau which is supposed to maintain contacts with U.S. police agencies in order to facilitate its basic task of providing security for CIA installations and personnel. The Office of Security was thus heavily implicated in the CIA's illegal domestic operations, including "cointelpro" operations against political dissidents and groups, and was the vehicle for such mind-control experiments as Operations Bluebird, Artichoke, and MK-Ultra. The Office of Security also utilized male and female prostitutes and other sex operatives for purposes of compromising and blackmailing public figures, information gathering, and control. According to author Jim Hougan, the Office of

Security maintained a "fag file" of some 300,000 U.S. citizens, with heavy stress on homosexuals. The Office of Security also had responsibility for Soviet and other defectors. James McCord was at one time responsible for the physical security of all CIA premises in the U.S. McCord was also a close friend of CIA Counterintelligence Director James Jesus Angleton. McCord was anxious to cover the CIA's role; at one point he wrote to his superior, General Gaynor, urging him to "flood the newspapers with leaks or anonymous letters" to discredit those who wanted to establish the responsibility of "the company."[19] But according to one of McCord's own police contacts, Garey Bittenbender of the Washington, D.C. Police Intelligence Division, who recognized him after his arrest, McCord had averred to him that the Watergate break-ins had been "a CIA operation," an account which McCord heatedly denied later.[20]

The third leader of the Watergate burglars, G. Gordon Liddy, had worked for the FBI and the Treasury. Liddy's autobiography, *Will*, published in 1980, and various other statements show that Liddy's world outlook had a number of similarities with that of George Bush: He was, for example, obsessed with the maintenance and transmission of his "family gene pool."

Another key member of the Plumbers unit was John Paisley, who functioned as the official CIA liaison to the White House investigative unit. It was Paisley who assumed responsibility for the overall "leak analysis," that is to say, for defining the problem of unauthorized divulging of classified material which the Plumbers were supposed to combat. Paisley, along with Howard Osborne of the Office of Security, met with the Plumbers, led by Kissinger operative David Young, at CIA headquarters in Langley, Virginia on August 9, 1971. Paisley's important place on the Plumbers' roster is most revealing, since Paisley was later to become an important appointee of CIA Director George Bush. In the middle of 1976, Bush decided to authorize a group of experts, ostensibly from outside the CIA, to produce an analysis which would be compared with the CIA's own National Intelligence Estimates on Soviet capabilities and intentions. The panel of outside experts was given the designation of "Team B." Bush chose Paisley to be the CIA's "coordinator" of the three subdivisions of Team B. Paisley would later disappear while sailing on Chesapeake Bay in September of 1978.

In a White House memorandum by David Young summarizing the August 9, 1971 meeting between the Plumbers and the official CIA leaders, we find that Young "met with Howard Osborne and a Mr. Paisley to review what it was that we wanted CIA to do in connection with their files on leaks from January 1969 to the present." There then follows a 14-point list of leaks and their classification, including the frequency of leaks associated with certain journalists, the gravity of the leaks, and so forth. A data base was called for, and "it was decided that Mr. Paisley would get this done by next Monday, August 16, 1971." On areas where more clarification was needed, the memo noted, "the above questions should be reviewed with Paisley within the next two days."[21]

The lesser Watergate burglars came from the ranks of the CIA Miami Station Cubans: Bernard Barker, Eugenio Martínez, Felipe de Diego, Frank Sturgis, Virgilio González and Reinaldo Pico. Once they had started working for Hunt, Martínez asked the Miami Station chief, Jake Esterline, if he was familiar with the activities now being carried out under White House cover. Esterline in turn asked Langley for its opinion of Hunt's White House position. A reply was written by Cord Meyer, later openly profiled as a Bush admirer, to Deputy Director for Plans (that is to say, covert operations) Thomas Karamessines. The import of Meyer's directions to Esterline was that the latter should "not . . . concern himself with the travels of Hunt in Miami, that Hunt was on domestic White House business of an unknown nature and that the Chief of Station should 'cool it.' "[22]

Enter Lou Russell

One of the major sub-plots of Watergate, and one that will eventually lead us back to the documented public record of George Bush, is the relation of the various activities of the Plumbers to the wiretapping of a group of prostitutes who operated out of a brothel in the Columbia Plaza Apartments, located in the immediate vicinity of the Watergate buildings.[23] Among the customers of the prostitutes there appear to have been a U.S. Senator, an astronaut, a Saudi prince (the embassy of Saudi Arabia is nearby), U.S. and South Korean intelligence officials, and above all, numerous Democratic Party leaders whose presence can be partially explained by the propinquity of the Democratic National Committee offices in the Watergate. The Columbia Plaza Apartments brothel was under intense CIA surveillance by the Office of Security/Security Research Staff through one of their assets, an aging private detective out of the pages of Damon Runyon who went by the name of Louis James Russell. Russell was, according to Jim Hougan, especially interested in bugging a hotline phone that linked the DNC with the nearby brothel. During the Watergate break-ins, James McCord's recruit to the Plumbers, Alfred C. Baldwin, would appear to have been bugging the telephones of the Columbia Plaza brothel.

Lou Russell, in the period between June 20 and July 2, 1973, was working for a detective agency that was helping George Bush prepare for an upcoming press conference. In this sense, Russell was working for Bush.

Russell is relevant because he seems (although he denied it) to have been the fabled sixth man of the Watergate break-in, the burglar who got away. He may also have been the burglar who tipped off the police, if indeed anyone did. Russell was a harlequin who had been the servant of many masters. Lou Russell had once been the chief investigator for the House Un-American Activities Committee. He had worked for the FBI. He had been a stringer for Jack Anderson, the columnist. In September 1972, well after the scandal had become notorious, Russell seems to have joined with one Nick Beltrante in carrying out electronic countermeasures sweeps of the DNC headquarters, and during one of these he appears to have planted an electronic eavesdropping device in the phone of DNC worker Spencer Oliver which, when it was discovered, refocused public attention on the Watergate scandal at the end of the summer of 1972.

Russell was well acquainted with Carmine Bellino, the chief investigator on the staff of Sam Ervin's Senate Select Committee on Presidential Campaign Practices. Bellino was a Kennedy operative who had superintended the seamy side of the JFK White House, including such figures as Judith Exner, the President's alleged paramour. Later, Bellino would become the target of George Bush's most revealing public action during the Watergate period. Bellino's friend, William Birely, later provided Russell with an apartment in Silver Spring, Maryland (thus allowing him to leave his room in a rooming house on Q Street in the District), a new car, and sums of money.

Russell had been a heavy drinker, and his social circle was that of the prostitutes, whom he sometimes patronized and sometimes served as a bouncer and goon. His familiarity with the brothel milieu facilitated his service for the Office of Security, which was to oversee the bugging and other surveillance of Columbia Plaza and other locations.

Lou Russell was incontestably one of the most fascinating figures of Watergate. How remarkable, then, that the indefatigable ferrets Woodward and Bernstein devoted so little attention to him, deeming him worthy of mention in neither of their two books. Woodward and Bernstein met with Russell, but had ostensibly decided that there was "nothing to the story." Woodward claims to have seen nothing in Russell beyond the obvious "old drunk."[24]

The FBI had questioned Russell after the DNC break-ins, probing his whereabouts on June 16–17 with the suspicion that he had indeed been one of the burglars. But this questioning led to nothing. Instead, Russell was contacted by Carmine Bellino, and later by Bellino's broker Birely, who set Russell up in the new apartment (or safe house) already mentioned, where one of the Columbia Plaza prostitutes moved in with him.

By 1973, minority Republican staffers at the Ervin committee began to realize the importance of Russell to a revisionist account of the scandal that might exonerate Nixon to some extent by shifting the burden of guilt elsewhere. On May 9, 1973, the Ervin committee accordingly subpoenaed Russell's telephone, job and bank records. Two days later, Russell replied to the committee that he had no job records or diaries, had no bank account, made long-distance calls only to his daughter, and could do nothing for the committee.

On May 16–17, Deep Throat warned Woodward that "everybody's life is in danger." On May 18, while the staff of the Ervin committee were pondering their next move vis-a-vis Russell, Russell suffered a massive heart attack. This was the same day that James McCord, advised by Bud Fensterwald, his and Russell's lawyer, began his public testimony to the Ervin committee on the coverup. Russell was taken to Washington Adventist Hospital, where he recovered to some degree and convalesced until June 20. Russell was convinced that he had been the victim of an attempted assassination. He told his daughter after leaving the hospital that he believed that he had been poisoned, that someone had entered his apartment (the Bellino-Birely safe house in Silver Spring) and "switched pills on me."[25]

Leaving the hospital on June 20, Russell was still very weak and pale. But now, although he remained on the payroll of James McCord, he also accepted a retainer from his friend John Leon, who had been engaged by the Republicans to carry out a counterinvestigation of the Watergate affair. Leon was in contact with Jerris Leonard, a lawyer associated with Nixon, the GOP, the Republican National Committee, and with Chairman George Bush. Leonard was a former Assistant Attorney General for Civil Rights in the Nixon administration. Leonard had stepped down as head of the Law Enforcement Assistance Administration (LEAA) on March 17, 1973. In June 1973, Leonard was special counsel to George Bush personally, hired by Bush and not by the RNC. Leonard says today that his job consisted in helping to keep the Republican Party separate from Watergate, deflecting Watergate from the party "so it would not be a party thing."[26] As Hougan tells it,

Leon was convinced that Watergate was a set-up, that prostitution was at the heart of the affair, and that the Watergate arrests had taken place following a tip-off to the police; in other words, the June 17 burglary had been sabotaged from within, Leon believed, and he intended to prove it. . . . Integral to Leon's theory of the affair was Russell's relationship to the Ervin committee's chief investigator, Carmine Bellino, and the circumstances surrounding Russell's relocation to Silver Spring in the immediate aftermath of the Watergate arrests. In an investigative memorandum submitted to GOP lawyer Jerris Leonard, Leon described what he hoped to prove: that Russell, reporting to Bellino, had been a spy for the Democrats within the CRP, and that Russell had tipped off Bellino (and the police) to the June 17 break-in. The man who knew most about this was, of course, Leon's new employee, Lou Russell.[27]

Is it possible that Jerris Leonard communicated the contents of Leon's memorandum to the RNC and to its chairman George Bush during the days after he received it? It is possible. But for Russell, the game was over: On July 2, 1973, barely two weeks after his release from the hospital, Russell suffered a second heart attack, which killed him. He was buried with quite suspicious haste the following day. The potential witness with perhaps the largest number of personal ties to Watergate protagonists, and the witness who might have redirected the scandal, not just toward Bellino, but toward the prime movers behind and above McCord and Hunt and Paisley, had perished in a way that recalls the fate of so many knowledgeable Iran-Contra figures.

With Russell silenced forever, Leon appears to have turned his attention to targeting Bellino, perhaps with a view to forcing him to submit to depositioning or other questioning in which questions about his relationship to Russell might be asked. Leon, who had been convicted in 1964 of wiretapping in a case involving El Paso Natural Gas Co. and Tennessee Gas Co., had weapons in his own possession that could be used against Bellino. During the time that Russell was still in the hospital, on June 8, Leon had signed an affidavit for Jerris Leonard in which he stated that he had been hired by Democratic operative Bellino during the 1960 presidential campaign to "infiltrate the operations" of Albert B. "Ab" Hermann, a staff member of the Republican National Committee. Leon asserted in the affidavit that although he had not been able to infiltrate Hermann's office, he observed the office with field glasses and employed "an electronic device known as 'the big ear' aimed at Mr. Hermann's window." Leon recounted that he had been assisted by former CIA officer John Frank, Oliver W. Angelone, and former congressional investigator Ed Jones in the anti-Nixon 1960 operations.

Leon collected other sworn statements that all went in the same direction, portraying Bellino as a Democratic dirty tricks operative unleashed by the Kennedy faction against Nixon. Joseph Shimon, who had been an inspector for the Washington Police Department, told of how he had been approached by Kennedy operative Oliver W. Angelone, who alleged that he was working for Bellino, with a request to help Angelone gain access to the two top floors of the Wardman Park Hotel (now the Sheraton Park) just before they were occupied by Nixon on the eve of the Nixon-Kennedy television debate. Edward Murray Jones, then living in the Philippines, said in his affidavit that he had been assigned by Bellino to tail individuals at Washington National Airport and in downtown Washington.[28] According to Hougan,

> these sensational allegations were provided by Leon to Republican attorneys on July 10, 1973, exactly a week after Russell's funeral. Immediately, attorney Jerris Leonard conferred with RNC Chairman George Bush. It appeared to both men that a way had been found to place the Watergate affair in a new perspective, and, perhaps, to turn the tide. A statement was prepared and a press conference scheduled at which Leon was to be the star witness, or speaker. Before the press conference could be held, however, Leon suffered a heart attack on July 13, 1973, and died the same day.[29]

Two important witnesses, each of whom represented a threat to reopen the most basic questions of Watergate, dead in little more than a week! Bush is likely to have known of the import of Russell's testimony, and he is proven to have known of the content of Leon's. Jerris Leonard later told Hougan that the death of John Leon "came as a complete shock. It was . . . well, to be honest with you, it was frightening. It was only a week after Russell's death, or something like that, and it happened on the very eve of the press conference. We didn't know what was going on. We were scared."[30] Hougan comments: "With the principal witness against Bellino no longer available, and with Russell dead as well, Nixon's last hope of diverting attention from Watergate—slim from the beginning—was laid to rest forever."

Diversion and Damage Control

But George Bush went ahead with the press conference that had been announced, even if John Leon, the principal speaker, was now dead. According to Nixon, Bush had been "privately pleading for some action that would get us off the defensive" since back in the springtime.[31] On July 24, 1973, Bush made public the affidavits by Leon, Jones, and Shimon which charged that the Ervin committee chief investigator Carmine Bellino had recruited spies to help defeat Nixon back in 1960. "I cannot and do not vouch for the veracity of the statements contained in the affidavits," said Bush, "but I do believe that this matter is serious enough to concern the Senate Watergate committee, and particularly since its chief investigator is the subject of the charges contained in the affidavits. If these charges are true, a taint would most certainly be attached to some of the committee's work." Bush's statement to the press prediscounted Democratic charges that his revelations were part of a Nixon administration counteroffensive to deflect Watergate.

Bush specified that on the basis of the Shimon and Leon affidavits, he was "confident" that Ed Jones and Angelone "had bugged the Nixon space or tapped his phones prior to the television debate." He conceded that "there was corruption" in the ranks of the GOP. "But now I have presented some serious allegations that if true could well have affected the outcome of the 1960 presidential race. The Nixon-Kennedy election was a real cliff-hanger, and the debates bore heavily on the outcome of the people's decision." Bush rejected any charge that he was releasing the affidavits in a bid to "justify Watergate." He asserted that he was acting in the interest of "fair play."

Bush said that he had taken the affidavits to Sen. Sam Ervin, the Democratic chairman of the Senate Watergate committee, and to Sen. Howard Baker, that committee's ranking Republican, but that the committee had failed to act so far. "I haven't seen much action on it," Bush added. When the accuracy of the affidavits was challenged, Bush replied, "We've heard a lot more hearsay bandied about the [Watergate] committee than is presented here. I'd like to know how serious it is. I'd like to see it looked into," said Bush. He called on Sam Ervin and his committee to probe all the charges forthwith. Bush was "convinced that there is in fact substance to the allegations."

Bellino labeled Bush's charges "absolutely false." "I categorically and unequivocally deny that I have ever ordered, requested, directed, or participated in any electronic surveillance whatsoever in connection with any political campaign," said Bellino. "By attacking me on the basis of such false and malicious lies, Mr. Bush has attempted to distract me from carrying out what I consider one of the most important assignments of my life. I shall continue to exert all my efforts to ascertain the facts and the truth pertinent to this investigation."

Here Bush was operating on several levels of reality at once. The implications of the Russell-Leon interstices would be suspected only in retrospect. What appeared on the surface was a loyal Republican mounting a diversionary attack in succor of his embattled President. At deeper levels, the reality might be the reverse: the stiffing of Nixon in order to defend the forces behind the break-in and the scandal.

Back in April, as the Ervin committee was preparing to go into action against the White House, Bush had participated in the argument about whether the committee sessions should be televised or not. Bush discussed this issue with Senators Baker and Brock, both Republicans who wanted the hearings to be televised—in Baker's case, so that he could be on television himself as the ranking Republican on the panel. John Ehrlichman, to whom Bush reported in the White House, mindful of the obvious potential damage to the administration, wanted the hearings not televised, not even public, but in executive session with a sanitized transcript handed out later. So Bush, having no firm convictions of his own, but always looking for his own advantage, told Ehrlichman he sympathized with both sides of the argument, and was "sitting happily on the middle of the fence with a picket sticking up my you know what. I'll see you."[32] But Nixon's damage control interest had been sacrificed by Bush's vacillating advocacy, and the devastating testimony of figures like John Dean and James McCord would have its maximum impact.

Bush had talked in public about the Ervin committee during a visit to Seattle on June 29 in response to speculation that Nixon might be called to testify. Bush argued that the presidency would be diminished if Nixon were to appear. Bush was adamant that Nixon could not be subpoenaed and that he should not testify voluntarily. Shortly thereafter, Bush had demanded that the Ervin committee wrap up its proceedings to "end the speculation" about Nixon's role in the coverup. "Let's get all the facts out, let's get the whole thing over with, get all the people up there before the Watergate committee. I don't believe John Dean's testimony."[33]

Senator Sam Ervin placed Bush's intervention against Carmine Bellino in the context of other diversionary efforts launched by the RNC. Ervin, along with Democratic Senators Talmadge and Inouye, were targeted by a campaign inspired by Bush's RNC which alleged that they had tried to prevent a full probe of LBJ intimate Bobby Baker back in 1963. Later, speaking on the Senate floor on October 9, 1973, Ervin commented: "One can but admire the zeal exhibited by the Republican National Committee and its journalistic allies in their desperate effort to invent a red herring to drag across the trail which leads to the truth concerning Watergate."[34]

But Ervin saw Bush's Bellino material as a more serious assault. "Bush's charge distressed me very much for two reasons. First, I deemed it unjust to Bellino, who denied it and whom I had known for many years to be an honorable man and a faithful public servant; and, second, it was out of character with the high opinion I entertained of Bush. Copies of the affidavits had been privately submitted to me before the news conference, and I had expressed my opinion that there was not a scintilla of competent or credible evidence in them to sustain the charges against Bellino."[35]

Sam Dash, the chief counsel to the Ervin committee, had a darker and more detailed view of Bush's actions. Dash later recounted:

> In the midst of the pressure to complete a shortened witness list by the beginning of August, a nasty incident occurred that was clearly meant to sidetrack the committee and destroy or immobilize one of my most valuable staff assistants—Carmine Bellino, my chief investigator. On July 24, 1973, the day after the committee subpoena for the White House tapes was served on the President, the Republican national chairman, George Bush, called a press conference. . . . Three days later, as if carefully orchestrated, twenty-two Republican senators signed a letter to Senator Ervin, urging the Senate Watergate Committee to investigate Bush's charges and calling for Bellino's suspension pending the outcome of the investigation. Ervin was forced into a corner, and on August 3 he appointed a subcommittee consisting of Senators Talmadge, Inouye, and Gurney to investigate the charges. The White House knew that Carmine Bellino, a wizard at reconstructing the receipts and expenditures of funds despite laundering techniques and the destruction of records, was hot on the trail of Herbert Kalmbach and Bebe Rebozo. Bellino's diligent, meticulous work would ultimately disclose Kalmbach's funding scheme for the White House's dirty tricks campaign and unravel a substantial segment of Rebozo's secret cash transactions on behalf of Nixon.[36]

Dash writes that Bellino was devastated by Bush's attacks, "rendered emotionally unable to work because of the charges."

The mechanism targeted by Bellino is of course relevant to Bill Liedtke's funding of the CREEP described above. Perhaps Bush was in fact seeking to shut down Bellino solely to defend only himself and his confederates.

Members of Dash's staff soon realized that there had been another participant in the process of assembling the material that

Bush had presented. According to Dash, "the charges became even murkier when our staff discovered that the person who had put them together was a man named Jack Buckley. In their dirty tricks investigation of the 1972 presidential campaign, Terry Lenzner and his staff had identified Buckley as the Republican spy, known as Fat Jack, who had intercepted and photographed Muskie's mail between his campaign and Senate offices as part of Ruby I (a project code named in Liddy's Gemstone political espionage plan)." It would appear that Fat Jack Buckley was now working for George Bush. Ervin then found that Senators Gurney and Baker, both Republicans, might be willing to listen to additional charges made by Buckley against Bellino. Dash says he "smelled the ugly odor of blackmail on the part of somebody and I did not like it." Later, Senators Talmadge and Inouye filed a report completely exonerating Bellino, while Gurney conceded that there was no direct evidence against Bellino, but that there was some conflicting testimony that ought to be noted. Dash sums up that in late November 1973, "the matter ended with little fanfare and almost no newspaper comment. The reputation of a public official with many years' service as a dedicated and incorruptible investigator had been deeply wounded and tarnished, and Bellino would retire from federal service believing— rightly—that he had not been given the fullest opportunity he deserved to clear his good name."

Another Bush concern during the summer of 1973 was his desire to liquidate the CREEP, not out of moralistic motives, but because of his desire to seize the CREEP's $4 millon-plus cash surplus. During the middle of 1973, some of this money had already been used to pay the legal fees of Watergate conspirators, as in the case of Maurice Stans.[37]

During August, Bush went into an offensive of sanctimonious moralizing. Bush appears to have concluded that Nixon was doomed, and that it was imperative to distance himself and his operation from Nixon's impending downfall. On the NBC "Today" show, Bush objected to John D. Ehrlichman's defense before the Ervin committee of the campaign practice of probing the sex and drinking habits of political opponents. "Crawling around in the gutter to find some weakness of a man, I don't think we need that," said Bush. "I think opponent research is valid. I think if an opponent is thought to have done something horrendous or thought to be unfit to serve, research is valid. But the idea of just kind of digging up dirt with the purpose of blackmail or embarrassing somebody so he'd lose, I don't think that is a legitimate purpose," postured

Bush. By this time Ehrlichman, who had hired retired cops to dig up such dirt, had been thrown to the wolves.[38]

A couple of days later Bush delivered a speech to the American Bar Association on "The Role and Responsibility of the Political Candidate." His theme was that restoring public trust in the political system would require candidates who would set a higher moral tone for their campaigns.[39]

The next day Bush was at it again, announcing that he was reopening an investigation into alleged courses in political sabotage and dirty tricks taught by the GOP to college Republicans in weekend seminars during 1971 and 1972. Bush pledged to "get to the bottom" of charges that the College Republican National Committee, with 1,000 campus clubs and 100,000 members listed had provided instruction in dirty tricks.[40]

Bush had clearly distanced himself from the fate of the Nixon White House. By the time Spiro Agnew resigned as Vice President on October 10, 1973, Bush was in a position to praise Agnew for his "great personal courage" while endorsing the resignation as "in the best interest of the country."[41]

Later the same month came Nixon's "Saturday night massacre," the firing of Special Prosecutor Archibald Cox and the resignation of Attorney General Elliot Richardson and his deputy, William Ruckelshaus. To placate public opinion, Nixon agreed to obey a court order compelling him to hand over his White House tapes. Bush had said that Nixon was suffering from a "confidence crisis" about the tapes, but now commented that what Nixon had done "will have a soothing effect. Clearly it will help politically. . . . Hopefully, his move will cool the emotions and permit the President to deal with matters of enormous domestic and international concern."[42]

Later, in November, Bush bowed out of a possible candidacy in the 1974 Texas gubernatorial race. Speculation was that "the specter of Watergate" would have been used against him, but Bush preferred sanctimonious explanations. "Very candidly," he said, "being governor of Texas has enormous appeal to me, but our political system is under fire and I have an overriding sense of responsibility that compels me to remain in my present job."[43]

By the spring of 1974, the impending doom of the Nixon regime was the cue for Bush's characteristic reedy whining. In May of 1974, after a meeting of the Republican congressional leadership with Nixon, Bush told his friend Congressman Barber Conable that he was considering resigning from the RNC. Conable did not urge him to stay on. A few days later, John Rhodes, who had replaced Gerald Ford as House Minority Leader when Ford was tapped by Nixon for the vice-presidency, told a meeting of House Republicans that Bush was getting ready to resign, and if he did so, it would be impossible for the White House to "get anybody of stature to take his place."[44]

But even in the midst of the final collapse, Bush still made occasional ingratiating gestures to Nixon. Nixon pathetically recounts how Bush made him an encouraging offer in July 1974, about a month before the end: "There were other signs of the sort that political pros might be expected to appreciate: NC Chairman George Bush called the White House to say that he would like to have me appear on a fund-raising telethon."[45] This is what Bush was telling Nixon. But during this same period, Father John McLaughlin of the Nixon staff asked Bush for RNC lists of GOP diehards across the country for the purpose of generating support statements for Nixon. Bush refused to provide them.[46]

The Smoking Gun

On August 5, 1974, the White House released the transcript of the celebrated "smoking gun" taped conversation of June 23, 1972 in which Nixon discussed ways to frustrate the investigation of the Watergate break-ins. Chairman George was one of the leading Nixon administration figures consulting with Al Haig in the course of the morning. When Bush heard the news, he was very upset, undoubtedly concerned about all the very negative publicity that he himself was destined to receive in the blowback of Nixon's now imminent downfall. Then after a while he calmed down somewhat. One account describes Bush as "somewhat relieved" by the news that the *coup de grace* tape was going to be made public, "an act probably fatal," as Haig had said. "Finally there was some one thing the national chairman could see clearly. The ambiguities in the evidence had been tearing the party apart, Bush thought."[47] At this point Bush became the most outspoken and militant organizer of Nixon's resignation, a Cassius of the Imperial Presidency.

A little later, White House congressional liaison William Timmons wanted to make sure that everyone had been fully briefed about the transcripts going out, and he turned to Nixon's political counselor Dean Burch. "Dean, does Bush know about the transcript yet?" Timmons asked. Burch replied, "Yes." "Well, what did he do?" Timmons asked.

"He broke out in assholes and shit himself to death," was Burch's answer.[48]

But why, it may be asked, the dermal diarrhea? Why should Bush be so distraught over the release to the press of the transcript of the notorious White House meeting of June 23, 1972, whose exchanges between Nixon and Haldeman were to prove the *coup de grace* to the agony of the Nixon regime? As we have seen, there is plenty of evidence that the final fall of Nixon was just the denouement that Bush wanted. The answer is that Bush was upset about the fabulous "smoking gun" tape because his friend Mosbacher, his business partner Bill Liedtke, and he himself were referred to in the most sensitive passages. Yes, a generation of Americans has grown up recalling something about a "smoking gun" tape, but not many now recall that when Nixon referred to "the Texans," he meant George Bush.

The open secret of the much-cited but little-analyzed "smoking gun" tape is that it refers to Nixon's desire to mobilize the CIA to halt the FBI investigation of the Watergate burglars on the grounds that money can be traced from donors in Texas and elsewhere to the coffers of the CREEP and thence to the pockets of Bernard Barker and the other Cubans arrested. The money referred to, of course, is part of Bill Liedtke's $700,000 discussed above. A first crucial passage of the "smoking gun" tape goes as follows, with the first speaker being Haldeman:

> H: Now, on the investigation, you know the Democratic break-in thing, we're back in the problem area because the FBI is not under control, because [FBI chief] Gray doesn't exactly know how to control it and they have—their investigation is leading into some productive areas because they've been able to trace the money—not through the money itself—but through the bank sources—the banker. And, and it goes in some directions we don't want it to go. Ah, also there have been some things—like an informant came in off the street to the FBI in Miami who was a photographer or has a friend who was a photographer who developed some films through this guy Barker and the films had pictures of Democratic National Committee letterhead documents and things. So it's things like that that are filtering in. Mitchell came up with yesterday, and John Dean analyzed very carefully last night and concludes, concurs now with Mitchell's recommendation that the only way to solve this, and we're set up beautifully to do it, ah, in that and that—the only network that paid any attention to it last night was NBC—they did a massive story on the Cuban thing.
>
> P: [Nixon] That's right.
>
> H: That the way to handle this now is for us to have [CIA Deputy Director Vernon] Walters call Pat Gray and just say "Stay the hell out of this—this is ah, business here we don't want you to go any

further on it." That's not an unusual development, and ah, that would take care of it.

P: What about Pat Gray—you mean Pat Gray doesn't want to?

H: Pat does want to. He doesn't know how to, and he doesn't have, he doesn't have any basis for doing it. Given this, he will then have the basis. He'll call Mark Felt in, and the two of them—and Mark Felt wants to cooperate because he's ambitious—

P: Yeah.

H: He'll call him in and say, "We've got the signal from across the river to put the hold on this." And that will fit rather well because the FBI agents who are working the case, at this point, feel that's what it is.

P: This is CIA? They've traced the money? Who'd they trace it to?

H: Well they've traced it to a name, but they haven't gotten to the guy yet.

P: Would it be somebody here?

H: Ken Dahlberg.

P: Who the hell is Ken Dahlberg?

H: He gave $25,000 in Minnesota and, ah, the check went directly to this guy Barker.

P: It isn't from the committee though, from Stans?

H: Yeah. It is. It's directly traceable and there's some more through some Texas people that went to the Mexican bank which can also be traced to the Mexican bank—they'll get their names today. And (pause)

P: Well, I mean, there's no way—I'm just thinking if they don't cooperate, what do they say? That they were approached by the Cubans. That's what Dahlberg has to say, the Texans too, that they—

H: Well, if they will. But then we're relying on more and more people all the time. That's the problem, and they'll stop if we could take this other route.

P: All right.

H: And you seem to think the thing to do is get them to stop?

P: Right, fine.

Kenneth Dahlberg was a front man for Dwayne Andreas of Archer Daniels Midland. Nixon wanted to protect himself, of course, but there is no doubt that he is talking about Bill Liedtke, Pennzoil, Robert Mosbacher—his Bush-league Texas money-raising squad. With that comment, Nixon had dug his own grave with what was widely viewed as a *prima facie* case of obstruction of justice when this tape was released on August 5. But Nixon and Haldeman had a few other interesting things to say to each other that day, several of which evoke associations redolent of Bush.

Shortly after the excerpts provided above, Nixon himself sums up why the CIA ought to have its own interest in putting a lid on the Watergate affair:

> P: Of course, this Hunt, that will uncover a lot of things. You open that scab there's a hell of a lot of things and we just feel that it would be very detrimental to have this thing go any further. This involves these Cubans, Hunt, and a lot of hanky-panky that we have nothing to do with ourselves. Well, what the hell, did Mitchell know about this?
>
> H: I think so. I don't think he knew the details, but I think he knew.
>
> P: He didn't know how it was going to be handled through—with Dahlberg and the Texans and so forth? Well who was the asshole that did? Is it Liddy? Is that the fellow? He must be a little nuts!

Shortly after this, the conversation turned to Bus Mosbacher, Robert's elder brother, who was resigning as the Chief of Protocol. Nixon joked that while Mosbacher was escorting the visiting dignitaries, bachelor Henry Kissinger always ended up escorting Mosbacher's wife. But before too long Nixon was back to the CIA again:

> P: When you get in—when you get in (unintelligible) people, say, "Look the whole problem is that this will open the whole, the whole Bay of Pigs thing and the President just feels that ah, without going into the details—don't, don't lie to them to the extent to say there is no involvement, but just say this is a comedy of errors, without getting into it, the President believes that it is going to open the whole Bay of Pigs thing up again. And, ah, because these people are plugging for (unintelligible) and that they should call the FBI in and (unintelligible) don't go any further into this case, period! (inaudible) our cause.

It would also appear that Nixon's references to Howard Hunt and the Bay of Pigs are an oblique allusion to the Kennedy assassination, about which Nixon may have known more than he has ever told. Later the same day Haldeman reported back to Nixon about his meeting with Vernon Walters:

> H: Well, it was kind of interesting. Walters made the point and I didn't mention Hunt. I just said that the thing was leading into directions that were going to create potential problems because they were exploring leads that led back into areas that would be harmful to the CIA and harmful to the government (unintelligible) didn't have anything to do (unintelligible).

Later Haldeman returned to this same theme:

H: Gray called Helms and said I think we've run right into the middle of a CIA covert operation.

P: Gray said that?

H: Yeah. And (unintelligible) said nothing we've done at this point and ah (unintelligible) says well it sure looks to me like it is (unintelligible) and ah, that was the end of that conversation (unintelligible) the problem is it tracks back to the Bay of Pigs and it tracks back to some other of the leads run out to people who had no involvement in this, except by contracts and connection, but it gets to areas that are liable to be raised? The whole problem (unintelligible) Hunt. So at that point he kind of got the picture. He said, he said we'll be very happy to be helpful (unintelligible) handle anything you want. I would like to know the reason for being helpful, and I made it clear to him he wasn't going to get explicit (unintelligible) generality, and he said fine. And Walters (unintelligible), Walters is going to make a call to Gray. That's the way we put it and that's the way it was left.

P: How does that work though, how they've got to (unintelligible) somebody from the Miami bank.

H: (Unintelligible) The point John makes—the Bureau is going on this because they don't know what they are uncovering (unintelligible) continue to pursue it. They don't need to because they already have their case as far as the charges against these men (unintelligible). One thing Helms did raise. He said. Gray—he asked Gray why they thought they had run into a CIA thing and Gray said because of the amount of money involved, a lot of dough (unintelligible) and ah (unintelligible).

P: (Unintelligible).

H: Well, I think they will. If it runs (unintelligible) what the hell who knows (unintelligible) contributed CIA.

H: Ya, it's money CIA gets money (unintelligible) I mean their money moves in a lot of different ways, too.[49]

Nixon's train of associations takes him from the Pennzoil-Liedtke Mosbacher-Bush slush fund operation to Howard Hunt and the Bay of Pigs and "a lot of hanky-panky" and then back to Bus Mosbacher. Later on, Haldeman stresses that the FBI, discovering a large money-laundering operation between Pennzoil and Bill Liedtke in Houston, Mexico City, Maurice Stans and the CREEP in Washington, and some CIA Miami Station Cubans, simply concluded that this was all a CIA covert operation.

As Haldeman himself later summed it up:

If the Mexican bank connection was actually a CIA operation all along, unknown to Nixon; and Nixon was destroyed for asking the FBI to stop investigating the bank because it might uncover a CIA operation (which the Helms memo seems to indicate it actually was after all), the multiple layers of deception by the CIA are astounding.[50]

Later, on Nixon's last Monday, Bush joined White House Counsel J. Fred Buzhardt and Dean Burch on a visit to Congressman John Rhodes, and showed him the transcript of the smoking gun tape. "This means that there's just no chance in the world that he's not going to be impeached," said Rhodes. "In fact, there's no chance in the world that I won't vote to impeach him." Bush must have heaved a sigh of relief, since this is what he had wanted Rhodes to tell Nixon to get him to quit. "Rhodes later let it be known that he was offended that Bush had been briefed before he was," but of course, Bush was a top official of the Nixon White House.[51]

But Nixon still refused to quit, raising the prospect of a trial before the Senate that could be damaging to many besides Nixon. The next day, Tuesday, August 6, 1974, saw the last meeting of the Nixon cabinet, with Chairman George in attendance. This was the Cabinet meeting described as "unreal" by Bush later. Nixon's opening statement was: "I would like to discuss the most important issue confronting this nation, and confronting us internationally too—inflation." Nixon then argued adamantly for some minutes that he had examined the course of events over the recent past and that he had "not found an impeachable offense, and therefore resignation is not an acceptable course." Vice President Ford predicted that there would be certain impeachment by the House, but that the outcome in the Senate could not be predicted. Otherwise, said Ford, he was an interested party on the resignation issue and would make no further comment.

Nixon then wanted to talk about the budget again, and about an upcoming summit conference on the economy. Attorney General Saxbe interrupted him. "Mr. President, I don't think we ought to have a summit conference. We ought to make sure you have the ability to govern." Nixon quietly assured Saxbe that he had the ability to govern. Then Chairman George piped up, in support of Saxbe. The President's ability to govern was impaired, said George. The Republican Party was in a shambles, he went on, and the forthcoming congressional election threatened to be a disaster. Watergate had to be brought to an end expeditiously, Bush argued. From his vantage point at Nixon's right elbow, Kissinger could see that Bush was advancing toward the conclusion that Nixon had to resign. "It was cruel. And it was necessary," thought Kissinger. "More than enough had been said," was the Secretary of State's impression. Kissinger was seeking to avoid backing Nixon into a corner where he would become more stubborn and more resistant to the idea of resignation, making that dreaded Senate trial more likely. And this was the likely consequence of Bush's line of argument.

"Mr. President, can't we just wait a week or two and see what happens?" asked Saxbe. Bush started to support Saxbe again, but now Nixon was getting more angry. Nixon glared at Bush and Saxbe, the open advocates of his resignation. "No," he snapped. "This is too important to wait."

Now the senior cabinet officer decided he had to take the floor to avoid a total confrontation that would leave Nixon besieged but still holding the Oval Office. Kissinger's guttural accents were heard in the cabinet room: "We are not here to offer excuses for what we cannot do. We are here to do the nation's business. This is a very difficult time for our country. Our duty is to show confidence. It is essential that we show it is not safe for any country to take a run at us. For the sake of foreign policy we must act with assurance and total unity. If we can do that, we can vindicate the structure of peace." The main purpose of this pompous tirade had been to bring the meeting to a rapid end, and it worked. "There was a moment of embarrassed silence around the table," recalls Nixon, and after a few more remarks on the economy, the meeting broke up.

Kissinger stayed behind with Nixon to urge him to resign, which Nixon now said he felt compelled to do. Bush sought out Al Haig to ponder how Nixon might be forced out. "What are we going to do?" asked Bush. Haig told Bush to calm down, explaining: "We get him up to the mountaintop, then he comes down again, then we get him up again."[52] Kissinger walked back to his office in the West Wing and met Gen. Brent Scowcroft, the NSC Director. Kissinger told Scowcroft that "there was precious little support" for the President. Kissinger, no mean hypocrite in his own right, thought that Saxbe had been "weak-livered." Bush and Saxbe had both been petty and insensitive, Kissinger thought. He compared Bush and Saxbe and the rest to a seventeenth-century royal court with the courtiers scurrying about, concerned with themselves rather than with their country.

During this cabinet meeting, Bush was already carrying a letter to Nixon that would soon become the unkindest cut of all for Chairman George's wretched patron. This letter was delivered to Nixon on August 7. It read as follows:

Dear Mr. President,

It is my considered judgment that you should now resign. I expect in your lonely embattled position this would seem to you as an act of disloyalty from one you have supported and helped in so many ways. My own view is that I would now ill serve a President whose massive accomplishments I will always respect and whose family I love, if I did not now give you my judgment. Until this moment resignation has been no answer at all, but given the impact of the latest development, and it will be a lasting one, I now firmly feel resignation is best for the country, best for this President. I believe this view is held by most Republican leaders across the country. This letter is much more difficult because of the gratitude I will always have for you. If you do leave office history will properly record your achievements with a lasting respect.[53]

During Bush's confirmation hearings for the post of CIA Director in December 1976, when it became important to show how independent Bush had been, Senator Barry Goldwater volunteered that Bush had been "the first man to my knowledge to let the President know he should go." That presumably meant, the first among cabinet and White House officials.

The next day, August 8, 1974, Nixon delivered his resignation to Henry Kissinger. Kissinger could now look forward to exercising the powers of the presidency at least until January 1977, and perhaps well beyond.

Notes for Chapter XII

1. Fitzhugh Green, *George Bush: An Intimate Portrait* (New York: Hippocrene Books, 1989), p. 137.

2. George Bush and Victor Gold, *Looking Forward* (New York: Doubleday, 1987), pp. 120–21.

3. *Ibid.,* p. 121.

4. Green, *op. cit.,* p. 129.

5. Harry Hurt III, "George Bush, Plucky Lad," in *Texas Monthly,* June 1983.

6. *Washington Post,* Dec. 12, 1972.

7. *Washington Post,* Jan. 22, 1973.

8. *Washington Post,* Jan. 22, 1973.

9. See for example Len Cholodny and Robert Gettlin, *Silent Coup* (New York: St. Martin's Press, 1991).

10. Lyn Marcus, "Up-Valuation of German Mark Fuels Watergate Attack on Nixon," *New Solidarity,* July 9–13, 1973, pp. 10–11.

11. See Thomas Petzinger, *Oil and Honor* (New York: Putnam, 1987), pp. 64–65. See also Harry Hurt's article mentioned above. Wright Patman's House Banking Committee revealed part of the activities of Bill Liedtke and Mosbacher during the Watergate era.

12. Carl Bernstein and Bob Woodward, *All the President's Men* (New York: Simon and Schuster, 1974), present the checks received by Barker as one of the ways they breached the wall of secrecy around the CREEP, with the aid of their anonymous source "Bookkeeper." But neither in this book nor in *The Final Days* (New York: Simon and Schuster, 1976), do "Woodstein" get around to mentioning that the Mexico City money came from Bill Liedtke. This marked pattern of silence and reticence on matters pertaining to George Bush, certainly one of the most prominent of the President's men, is a characteristic of Watergate journalism in general.

For more information regarding William Liedtke's role in financing the CREEP, see Hearings

Before the Select Committee on Presidential Campaign Activities, 93rd Congress, including testimony by Hugh Sloan, June 6, 1973; and by Maurice Stans, June 12, 1973; see also the Final Report of the committee, issued in June 1974. Relevant press coverage from the period includes "Stans Scathes Report," by Woodward and Bernstein, *Washington Post*, Sept. 14, 1972; and "Liedtke Linked to FPC Choice," United Press International, June 26, 1973. Liedtke also influenced Nixon appointments in areas of interest to himself.

13. Maurice H. Stans, *The Terrors of Justice: The Untold Side of Watergate* (New York: Everest, 1978).

14. *New York Times,* Aug. 26, 1972 and Nov. 1, 1972.

15. Interview with a Post Oak Bank executive, Nov. 21, 1991. See also *Houston Post*, Dec. 27, 1988.

16. Stans, *op. cit.*

17. Stanley L. Kutler, *The Wars of Watergate: The Last Crisis of Richard Nixon* (New York: Knopf, distributed by Random House, 1990), pp. 229–33.

18. See Jim Hougan, *Secret Agenda* (New York: Random House, 1984), p. 92.

19. Ervin Committee Hearings, Book 9, pp. 3441–46; and Report of the Nedzi Committee of the House of Representatives, p. 201, cited by Hougan, *op. cit.,* p. 318.

20. Nezdi Committee Report, pp. 442–43, quoted in Hougan, *op. cit.,* p. 261.

21. Hougan, *op. cit.,* pp. 46–47.

22. Ervin Committee Final Report, pp. 1146–49, and Hougan, *op. cit.,* pp. 131–32.

23. The question of the Columbia Plaza Apartments is a central theme of Jim Hougan's *Secret Agenda, op. cit.* We have also relied on Hougan's version of the Russell-Leon-Bellino subplot described below. Hougan's book, although it studiously avoids drawing obvious conclusions about Bush, Kissinger, Rockefeller, and many others, is a convenient starting point for the necessary metacritique of Watergate. By contrast, the Cholodny-Gettlin *Silent Coup, op. cit.* represents a step backward, away from the truth of the matter on numerous points.

24. Hougan, *op. cit.,* pp. 324.

25. *Ibid.,* p. 370.

26. Interview of Jerris Leonard with Anton Chaitkin, Aug. 26, 1991.

27. Hougan, *op. cit.,* p. 374–75.

28. See Jules Witcover, "Political Spies Accuse Committee Investigator," *Washington Post,* July 25, 1973, and John Geddie, "Bush Alleges Bugs," *Dallas News,* July 25, 1973. See also Victor Lasky, *It Didn't Start with Watergate* (New York: Dial Press, 1977), pp. 41–55.

29. Hougan, *op. cit.,* p. 376. Notice that the day of Leon's death was also the day that White House staffer Butterfield told congressional investigators of the existence of Nixon's taping system.

30. Hougan, *op. cit.*

31. Richard Nixon, *RN: The Memoirs of Richard Nixon* (New York: Warner Books, 1979), p. 811.

32. Walter Pincus and Bob Woodward, "Presidential Posts and Dashed Hopes," *Washington Post,* Aug. 9, 1988.

33. *Washington Post,* July 12, 1973.

34. Sam J. Ervin, Jr., *The Whole Truth* (New York: Random House, 1980), p. 28.

35. *Ibid.,* p. 29.

36. Samuel Dash, *Chief Counsel* (New York: Random House, 1976), p. 192.

37. Evans and Novak, July 11, 1973.

38. *Washington Post,* Aug. 7, 1973.

39. *Washington Post,* Aug. 9, 1973.

40. *Washington Post,* Aug. 10, 1973.

41. *Washington Post,* Oct. 11, 1973.

42. *Washington Post,* Oct. 24, 1973.

43. *Washington Post,* Nov. 17, 1973.

44. Bernstein and Woodward, *The Final Days,* pp. 159, 176.

45. Nixon, *op. cit.,* p. 1042.

46. Green, *op cit.,* p. 135.

47. Bernstein and Woodward, *The Final Days,* p. 368.

48. *Ibid.,* p. 369.

49. For the "smoking gun" transcript of June 23, 1972, see *Washington Post,* Aug. 6, 1974.

50. H.R. Haldeman, *The Ends of Power* (New York: Times Books, 1978), p. 64.

51. Bernstein and Woodward, *The Final Days,* p. 374.

52. Available accounts of Nixon's last cabinet meeting are fragmentary, but see: *RN: The Memoirs of Richard Nixon,* p. 1066; *The Final Days,* pp. 386–89; Theodore H. White, *Breach of Faith: The Fall of Richard Nixon* (New York: Atheneum Publishers, 1975), p. 24; Henry

Kissinger, *Years of Upheaval* (Boston: Little, Brown, 1982), pp. 1202–3; J. Anthony Lukas, *Nightmare: The Underside of the Nixon Years* (New York: Viking Press, 1976), pp. 558–59. These have been collated for the account offered here.

53. The ostensible full text of this letter is found in Nicholas King, *George Bush: A Biography* (New York: Dodd, Mead & Company, 1980), p. 87. Vic Gold gives only seven lines of excerpts. Fitzhugh Green, in his post-November 1988 hagiography, liquidates the matter in fewer than five lines. In each case the calculating eye of the public relations man is observing the reader like the sucker in a medicine show. Apparently Bush's handlers concluded that there was less and less to gain from distancing their candidate from Nixon; perhaps their polls were showing that popular resentment against Nixon had somewhat declined.

XIII

BUSH IN BEIJING

As Nixon left the White House for his home in San Clemente, California, in the early afternoon of August 9, 1974, Chairman George was already plotting how to scale still further up the dizzy heights of state. Ford was now President, and the vice-presidency was vacant. According to the 25th Amendment, it was now up to Ford to designate a Vice President, who would then require a majority vote of both houses of Congress to be confirmed. Seeing a golden opportunity to seize an office that he had long regarded as the final stepping-stone to his ultimate goal of the White House, Bush immediately mobilized his extensive Brown Brothers Harriman/ Skull and Bones network, including as many Zionist lobby auxiliaries as he could muster. George had learned in 1968 that an organized effort commensurate with his own boundless lust for power would be required to succeed.

But because he was so redolent of Nixonian sleaze, Bush's maximum exertions for the vice-presidency were a failure. Ford announced his choice of Nelson Rockefeller on August 20, 1974. It was nevertheless astounding that Bush had come close. He was defeated for the moment, but he had established a claim on the office of the vice-presidency that he would not relinquish. Despite his hollow, arrogant ambition, and total incompetence for the office, he would automatically be considered for the vice-presidency in 1976 and then again in 1980. For George Bush was an aristocrat of senatorial rank, although denied the Senate, and his conduct betrayed the conviction that he was owed not just a place at the public trough, but the accolade of national political office.

Several minutes before President Ford appeared for the first time before the television cameras with Nelson Rockefeller, his Vice President-designate, he had placed a call to Bush to inform him that he had not been chosen, and to reassure him that he would be offered an important post as a consolation. Two days later, Bush met Ford at the White House. Bush claims that Ford told him that he could choose between a future as U.S. envoy to the Court of St. James in London, or presenting his credentials to the Elysée Palace in Paris. Bush would have us believe that he then told Ford that he wanted neither London nor Paris, but Beijing. Bush's accounts then portray Ford, never the quickest, as tamping his pipe, scratching his head, and asking, "Why Beijing?" Here Bush is lying once again. Ford was certainly no genius, but no one was better situated than he to know that it would have been utter folly to propose Bush for an ambassadorship that had to be approved by the Senate.

Why Beijing? The first consideration, and it was an imperative one, was that under no circumstances could Bush face Senate confirmation hearings for any executive branch appointment for at least one to two years. There would have been questions about the Townhouse slush fund, about his intervention on Carmine Bellino, perhaps about Leon and Russell, and about many other acutely embarrassing themes. All of the reasons which had led Ford to exclude Bush as Vice President, for which he would have needed the approval of both houses of Congress, were valid in ruling out any nomination that had to get past the Senate. After Watergate, Bush's name was just too smelly to send up to the Hill for any reason, despite all the power of the usual Brown Brothers Harriman/Skull and Bones network mobilization. It would take time to cauterize certain lesions and to cool off certain investigative tracks. Certain scandals had to be fixed. Perhaps in a year or two things might cool down, and the climate of opinion alter. But while the psychology of Watergate dominated the legislative branch, a high-profile job for Bush was out of the question.

As Bush himself slyly notes: "The United States didn't maintain formal diplomatic relations with the People's Republic at the time, so my appointment wouldn't need Senate confirmation." An asterisk sends us to the additional fact that "because I'd been ambassador to the United Nations I carried the title 'ambassador' to China." The person who would have to be convinced, Bush correctly noted, was Henry Kissinger, who monopolized all decisions on his prized China card.[1] But George was right about the confirmation. Official diplomatic relations between the U.S. and mainland China came only with the Carter China card of 1979. In 1974, what Bush was asking for was the U.S. Liaison Office (USLO), which did not have the official status of an embassy. The chief of that office was the President's personal representative in China, but it was a post that did not require Senate confirmation.

Bush's notorious crony Robert Mosbacher, certainly well versed enough to qualify as a connoisseur of sleaze, was uncharacteristically close to the heart of the matter when he opined that in late August 1974, Bush "wanted to get as far away from the stench [of Watergate] as possible."[2] Like Don Gregg in 1989, Bush wanted to get out of town and let things blow over for a while. His own story that Beijing would be a "challenge, a journey into the unknown" is pure tripe. More imaginative, but equally mendacious is the late Dean Burch's explanation that Bush had "a Marco Polo complex, thinking he could penetrate the mystery of the place." The truth is, that with Washington teeming with congressional committees, special prosecutors, grand juries, all in a furor of ostracism, Bush wanted to get as far away as he could, and Beijing was ideal.

Other attractions inherent in the Beijing posting are suggested by the fact that Bush's predecessor in Beijing was Harrimanite David K.E. Bruce, who had opened the liaison office in March 1973. Bruce had been in charge of the W.A. Harriman & Co. branch in Boston, while George's father was the firm's vice president back in the 1920s. Bruce had been chief of the London bureau of the Office of Strategic Services during World War II, which meant that he had been the boss of all European OSS operations, including Allen Dulles in Switzerland and all the rest. The presence in Beijing of Bruce, a true éminence grise of Anglo-American intelligence, points up the importance of the post, especially in the covert and intelligence domain.

Otherwise, serving in Beijing meant further close subordination to Henry Kissinger. Kissinger told Bush before he left that policy would be implemented directly by Kissinger himself, in contact with the Chinese liaison in Washington and the Chinese representative at the United Nations. In practice, Bush would be ordered about by such Kissinger clones as Richard Solomon of the NSC, Assistant Secretary of State Philip Habib, and Winston Lord, director of the State Department's Policy Planning Staff and the scion of an old Skull and Bones family. But then again, Bush was a leading Kissinger clone in his own right.

Finally, anyone who has observed Bush's stubborn, obsessive, morally insane support for Deng Xiaoping, Li Peng, and Yang Shankun during the aftermath of the Tiananmen massacre of June

1989, is driven toward the conclusion that Bush gravitated toward China because of an elective affinity, because of a profound attraction for the methods and outlook of Chinese leaders like Mao Zedong, Zhou Enlai, and Deng, for whom Bush has manifested a steadfast and unshakable devotion in the face of heinous crimes and significant political pressure to repudiate them. Bush wanted to go to China because he found Chinese Communists genuinely congenial.

When Bush was about to leave for China, his crony Dean Burch arranged for a 15-minute send-off meeting with Ford, but this was reduced to ten minutes by NSC Director Brent Scowcroft, at that time the most important Kissinger clone of them all.

Bush's staff in Beijing included Deputy Station Chief John Holdridge, Don Anderson, Herbert Horowitz, Bill Thomas and Bush's "executive assistant," Jennifer Fitzgerald, who has remained very close to Bush, and who has sometimes been rumored to be his mistress. Jennifer Fitzgerald in 1991 was the deputy chief of protocol in the White House; when German Chancellor Kohl visited Bush in the spring of 1991, he was greeted on the White House steps by Jennifer Fitzgerald.

Bush's closest contacts among Chinese officialdom included Vice Minister of Foreign Affairs Qiao Guanhua and his wife Zhang Hanzhi, also a top official of the foreign ministry. This is the same Qiao who is repeatedly mentioned in Kissinger's memoirs as one of his most important Red Chinese diplomatic interlocutors. This is the "Lord Qiao" enigmatically mentioned by Mao during Kissinger's meeting with Mao and Zhou Enlai on November 12, 1973. Qiao and Zhang later lost power because they sided with the left extremist Gang of Four after the death of Mao in 1976, Bush tells us. But in 1974–75, the power of the proto-Gang of Four faction was at its height, and it was toward this group that Bush quickly gravitated. In moving instinctively toward the hardline Mao faction, Bush was also doubtless aware of Mao's connections with the Yale in China Program around the time of World War I. The Skull and Bones network could turn up in unexpected places.

George and Barbara were careful to create the impression that they were rusticating away in Beijing. Barbara told Don Oberdorfer in early December: "Back in Washington or at the United Nations the telephone was ringing all the time. George would come home and say, excuse me, and pick up the phone. It's very different here. In the first five weeks I think he received two telephone calls, except for the ones from me. I try to call him once a day. I think he misses the phone as much as anything."

NSSM 200

When Bush had been in Beijing for about a month, Henry Kissinger arrived for one of his periodic visits to discuss current business with the Beijing leadership. Kissinger arrived with his usual army of retainers and Secret Service guards. During this visit, Bush went with Kissinger to see Vice-Premier Deng Xiaoping and Foreign Minister Qiao. This was one of three reported visits by Kissinger that would punctuate Bush's stay.

Bush's tenure in Beijing must be understood in the context of the Malthusian and frankly genocidal policies of the Kissinger White House. These are aptly summed up for reference in the recently declassified National Security Study Memorandum 200 (NSSM 200), "Implications of Worldwide Population Growth for U.S. Security and Overseas Interests," dated December 10, 1974.[3] NSSM 200, a joint effort by Kissinger and his deputy, Gen. Brent Scowcroft, provided a hit list of 13 developing countries for which the NSC posited a "special U.S. political and strategic interest" in population reduction or limitation. The list included India, Bangladesh, Pakistan, Nigeria, Mexico, Indonesia, Brazil, the Philippines, Thailand, Egypt, Turkey, Ethiopia and Colombia. Demographic growth in these and other Third World nations was to be halted, and if possible reversed, for the brutal reason that population growth represented increased strategic and military power for the countries in question.

Population growth, argues NSSM 200, will also increase pressure for the economic and industrial development of these countries, an eventuality which the study sees as a threat to the United States. In addition, bigger populations in the Third World are alleged to lead to higher prices and greater scarcity of strategic raw materials. As Kissinger summed up: "Development of a worldwide political and popular commitment to population stabilization is fundamental to any effective strategy. . . . The U.S. should encourage LDC leaders to take the lead in advancing family planning." When NSSM 200 goes on to ask, "would food be considered an instrument of national power?" it is clear to all that active measures of genocide are at the heart of the policy being propounded. A later Kissinger report praises the Chinese Communist leadership for their commitment to population control. During 1975, these Chinese Communists, Henry Kissinger, and George Bush were to team up to create a demonstration model of the NSSM 200 policy: the Pol Pot regime in Cambodia.

During the time that Bush was in Beijing, the fighting in Vietnam came to an end as the South Vietnamese Army collapsed in the face of a large-scale invasion from the north. The insane adventure of Vietnam had been organized by Bush's own Brown Brothers Harriman/Skull and Bones network. When John F. Kennedy had been elected President in 1960, he had turned to Brown Brothers Harriman partner Robert Lovett to provide him a list of likely choices for his cabinet. From this list were drawn Dean Rusk and Robert McNamara, the leading hawks in the cabinet. McGeorge Bundy and William Bundy, descendants of the Lowells of Boston, but closely related to the Stimson-Acheson circles, were mainstays of the party of escalation. Henry Cabot Lodge was the U.S. ambassador in Saigon when the State Department and the CIA insisted on assassinating President Ngo Dinh Diem, the leader of the country the U.S. was supposedly defending. And W. Averell Harriman himself, starting as assistant secretary for Southeast Asian affairs, worked his way up through the State Department with the same program of expanding the war, now that Harriman-Lovett policy had led to the inevitable debacle. But the post-war suffering of Southeast Asia was only beginning.

Target Cambodia

One of the gambits used by Kissinger to demonstrate to the Beijing Communist leaders the utility of rapprochement with the U.S. has to do with the unhappy nation of Cambodia. The pro-U.S. government of Cambodia was headed by Marshal Lon Nol, who had taken power in 1970, the year of the public and massive U.S. ground incursion into the country. By the spring of 1975, while the North Vietnamese advanced on Saigon, the Lon Nol government was fighting for its life against the armed insurrection of the Cambodian Communist Party or Khmer Rouge guerrillas, who were supported by mainland China. Kissinger was as anxious as usual to serve the interests of Beijing, and now even more so, because of the alleged need to increase the power of the Chinese and their assets, the Khmer Rouge, against the triumphant North Vietnamese. The most important consideration remained to ally with China, the second-strongest land power, against the U.S.S.R. Secondarily, it was important to maintain the balance of power in Southeast Asia as the U.S. policy collapsed. Kissinger's policy was therefore to jettison the Lon Nol government, and to replace it with the Khmer Rouge. George Bush, as Kissinger's liaison man in Beijing, was one of the instruments through which this policy was executed. Bush did his part, and the result is known to world history under the heading of the Pol Pot regime, which committed a genocide against its own population proportionally greater than any other in recent world history.

Until 1970, the government of Cambodia was led by Prince Norodom Sihanouk, a former king who had stepped down from the throne to become prime minister. Despite his many limitations, Sihanouk was then, and remains today, the most viable symbol of the national unity and hope for sovereignty of Cambodia. Under Sihanouk, Cambodia had maintained a measure of stability and had above all managed to avoid being completely engulfed by the swirling maelstrom of the wars in Laos and in Vietnam. But during 1969, Nixon and Kissinger had ordered a secret bombing campaign against North Vietnamese troop concentrations on Cambodian territory under the code name of "Menu." This bombing would have been a real and substantive ground for the impeachment of Nixon, and it did constitute the fourth proposed article of impeachment against Nixon submitted to the House Judiciary Committee on July 30, 1974. But after three articles of impeachment, having to do with the Watergate break-ins and subsequent coverup, were approved by the committee, the most important article, the one on genocide in Cambodia, was defeated by a vote of 26 to 12.

Cambodia was dragged into the Indo-China war by the U.S.-sponsored coup d'état in Phnom Penh in March 1970, which ousted Sihanouk in favor of Marshal Lon Nol of the Cambodian Army, whose regime was never able to achieve even a modicum of stability. Shortly thereafter, at the end of April 1970, Nixon and Kissinger launched a large-scale U.S. military invasion of Cambodia, citing the use of Cambodian territory by the North Vietnamese armed forces for their "Ho Chi Minh trail" supply line to sustain their forces deployed in South Vietnam. The "parrot's beak" area of Cambodia, which extended deep into South Vietnam, was occupied.

Prince Sihanouk, who described himself as a neutralist, established himself in Beijing after the seizure of power by Lon Nol. In May of 1970, he became the titular leader and head of state of a Cambodian government in exile, the Gouvernement Royal d'Union Nationale du Kampuchea, or GRUNK. The GRUNK was in essence a united front between Sihanouk and the Khmer Rouge, with the latter exercising most of the real power and commanding the armed forces and secret police. Sihanouk was merely a figurehead, and he knew it. He told Italian journalist Oriana Fallaci in 1973 that when "they [the Khmer Rouge] no longer need me, they will spit me out like a cherry pit."

During these years, the Khmer Rouge, which had launched a small guerrilla insurrection during 1968, was a negligible military factor in Cambodia, fielding only a very few thousand guerrilla fighters. One of its leaders was Saloth Sar, who had studied in Paris, and who had then sojourned at length in Red China at the height of the Red Guards' agitation. Saloth Sar was one of the most important leaders of the Khmer Rouge, and would later become infamous under his *nom de guerre,* Pol Pot. Decisive support for Pol Pot and for the later genocidal policies of the Khmer Rouge always came from Beijing, despite the attempts of misguided or lying commentators (like Henry Kissinger) to depict the Khmer Rouge as a creation of Hanoi.

But in the years after 1970, the Khmer Rouge, who were determined immediately to transform Cambodia into a Communist "utopia" beyond the dreams even of the wildest Maoist Red Guards, made rapid gains. The most important single ingredient in the rise of the Khmer Rouge was provided by Kissinger and Nixon, through their systematic campaign of terror-bombing against Cambodian territory during 1973. This was called Arclight, and began shortly after the January 1973 Paris Accords on Vietnam. With the pretext of halting a Khmer Rouge attack on Phnom Penh, U.S. forces carried out 79,959 officially confirmed sorties with B–52 and F–111 bombers against targets inside Cambodia, dropping 539,129 tons of explosives. Many of these bombs fell upon the most densely populated sections of Cambodia, including the countryside around Phnom Penh. The number of deaths caused by this genocidal campaign has been estimated at between 30,000 and 500,000.[4] Accounts of the devastating impact of this mass terror-bombing leave no doubt that it shattered most of what remained of Cambodian society and provided ideal preconditions for the further expansion of the Khmer Rouge insurgency, in much the same way that the catastrophe of World War I weakened European society so as to open the door for the mass irrationalist movements of fascism and Bolshevism.

During 1974, the Khmer Rouge consolidated their hold over parts of Cambodia. In these enclaves, they showed their characteristic methods of genocide, dispersing the inhabitants of the cities into the countryside, while executing teachers, civil servants, intellectuals— sometimes all those who could read and write. This policy was remarkably similar to the one being carried out by the U.S. under Theodore Shackley's Operation Phoenix in neighboring South Vietnam, and Kissinger and other officials began to see the potential of the Khmer Rouge for implementing the genocidal population reductions that had now been made the official doctrine of the U.S. regime.

Support for the Khmer Rouge was even more attractive to Kissinger and Nixon because it provided an opportunity for the geopolitical propitiation of the Maoist regime in China. Indeed, in the development of the China card between 1973 and 1975, during most of Bush's stay in Beijing, Cambodia loomed very large as the single most important bilateral issue between the U.S. and Red China. Already in November 1972, Kissinger told Bush's later prime contact, Qiao Guanhua, that the U.S. would have no real objection to a Sihanouk-Khmer Rouge government of the type that later emerged: "Whoever can best preserve it [Cambodia] as an independent neutral country, is consistent with our policy, and we believe with yours," said Kissinger.[5] Zhou Enlai told Kissinger in February 1973, that if North Vietnam were to extend its domination over Cambodia, this "would result in even greater problems."

When Bush's predecessor, David Bruce, arrived in Beijing to open the new U.S. Liaison Office in the spring of 1973, he sought contact with Zhou Enlai. On May 18, 1973, Zhou stressed that the only solution for Cambodia would be for North Vietnamese forces to leave that country entirely. A few days later, Kissinger told Chinese delegate Huang Hua in New York that U.S. and Red Chinese interests in Cambodia were compatible, since both sought to avoid "a bloc which could support the hegemonical objectives of outside powers," meaning North Vietnam and Hanoi's backers in Moscow. The genocidal terror-bombing of Cambodia was ordered by Kissinger during this period. Kissinger was apoplectic over the move by the U.S. Congress to prohibit further bombing of Cambodia after August 15, 1973, which he called "a totally unpredictable and senseless event."[6] Kissinger always pretends that the Khmer Rouge were a tool of Hanoi, and in his memoirs he spins out an absurd theory that the weakening of Zhou and the ascendancy of the Gang of Four was caused by Kissinger's own inability to keep bombing Cambodia. In reality, Beijing was backing its own allies, the Khmer Rouge, as is obvious from the account that Kissinger himself provides of his meeting with Bush's friend Qiao in October 1973.[7]

Starting in the second half of 1974, George Bush was heavily engaged on this Sino-Cambodian front, particularly in his contacts with his main negotiating partner, Qiao. Bush had the advantage that secret diplomacy carried on with the Red Chinese regime during those days was subject to very little public scrutiny. The summaries of Bush's dealings with the Red Chinese now await the liberation of the files of the Foreign Ministry in Beijing or of the State Department in Washington, whichever comes first. Bush's involvement on the Cambodian question has been established by later interviews with Prince Sihanouk's cabinet chief, Pung Peng Cheng, as well as with French and U.S. officials knowledgeable about Bush's activities in Beijing during that time. What we have here is admittedly the tip of the iceberg, the merest hints of the monstrous iniquity yet to be unearthed.[8]

The Khmer Rouge launched a dry-season offensive against Phnom Penh in early 1974, which fell short of its goal. They tried again the following year with a dry-season offensive launched on January 1, 1975. Soon supplies to Phnom Penh were cut off, both on the land and along the Mekong River. Units of Lon Nol's forces fought the battle of the Phnom Penh perimeter through March. On April 1, 1975, President Lon Nol resigned and fled the country under the pressure of the U.S. embassy, which wanted him out as quickly as possible as part of the program to appease Beijing.[9]

When Lon Nol had left the country, Kissinger became concerned that the open conquest of Phnom Penh by the Khmer Rouge Communist guerrillas would create public relations and political problems for the shaky Ford regime in the United States. Kissinger accordingly became interested in having Prince Sihanouk, the titular head of the insurgent coalition of which the Khmer Rouge was the leading part, travel from Beijing to Phnom Penh, so that the new government in Cambodia could be portrayed more as a neutralist-nationalist, and less as a frankly Communist, regime. This turns out to be the episode of the Cambodian tragedy in which George Bush's personal involvement is most readily demonstrated.

Prince Sihanouk had repeatedly sought direct contacts with Kissinger. At the end of March, 1975, he tried again to open a channel to Washington, this time with the help of the French embassy in Beijing. Sihanouk's cabinet chief, Pung Peng Cheng, requested a meeting with John Holdridge, Bush's deputy station chief. This meeting was held at the French embassy. Pung told Holdridge that Prince Sihanouk had a favor to ask of President Ford. According to Shawcross,

> "'in [Sihanouk's] old home in Phnom Penh were copies of the films of Cambodia he had made in the sixties when he had been a cinema enthusiast. They constituted a unique cultural record of a Cambodia that was gone forever: would the Americans please rescue them? Kissinger ordered Dean [the U.S. ambassador in Cambodia] to find the films and also instructed Bush to seek a meeting with Sihanouk. The Prince refused, and during the first ten days of April, as the noose around Phnom Penh tightened, he continued his public tirades [against the U.S. and its Cambodian puppets].[10]

On the same day, April 11, Ford announced that he would not request any further aid for Cambodia from the U.S. Congress, since any aid for Cambodia approved now would be "too late" anyway. Ford had originally been asking for $333 million to save the government of Cambodia. Several days later, Ford would reverse himself and renew his request for the aid, but by that time it was really too late.

On April 11, the U.S. embassy was preparing a dramatic evacuation, but the embassy was being kept open as part of Kissinger's effort to bring Prince Sihanouk back to Phnom Penh.

> It was now, on April 11, 1975, as Dean was telling government leaders he might soon be leaving, that Kissinger decided that Sihanouk should be brought back to Cambodia. In Peking, George Bush was ordered to seek another meeting; that afternoon John Holdridge met once more with Pung Peng Cheng at the French embassy. The American diplomat explained that Dr. Kissinger and President Ford were now convinced that only the Prince could end the crisis. Would he please ask the Chinese for an aircraft to fly him straight back to Phnom Penh? The United States would guarantee to remain there until he arrived. Dr. Kissinger wished to impose no conditions. . . . On April 12 at 5 A.M. Peking time Holdridge again met with Pung. He told him that the Phnom Penh perimeter was degenerating so fast that the Americans were pulling out at once. Sihanouk had already issued a statement rejecting and denouncing Kissinger's invitation.[11]

Sihanouk had a certain following among liberal members of the U.S. Senate, and his presence in Phnom Penh in the midst of the debacle of the old Lon Nol forces would doubtless have been reassuring for U.S. public opinion. But Sihanouk at this time had no ability to act independently of the Khmer Rouge leaders, who were hostile to him and who held the real power, including the inside track to the Red Chinese. Prince Sihanouk did return to Phnom Penh later in 1975, and his strained relations with Pol Pot and his colleagues soon became evident. Early in 1976, Sihanouk was placed under house arrest by the Khmer Rouge, who appear to have intended to execute him. Sihanouk remained under detention until the North Vietnamese drove Pol Pot and his forces out of Phnom Penh in 1978 and set up their own government there.

In following the Kissinger-Bush machinations to bring Prince Sihanouk back to Cambodia in mid-April 1975, one is also suspicious that an included option was to increase the likelihood that Sihanouk might be liquidated by the Khmer Rouge. When the Khmer Rouge entered Phnom Penh, they immediately carried out a massacre on a grand scale, slaying any members of the Lon Nol and Long

Boret cabinets they could get their hands on. There were mass executions of teachers and government officials, and all of the 2.5 million residents of Phnom Penh were driven into the countryside, including seriously ill hospital patients. Under these circumstances, it would have been relatively easy to assassinate Sihanouk amidst the general orgy of slaughter. Such an eventuality was explicitly referred to in a Kissinger NSC briefing paper circulated in March 1975, in which Sihanouk was quoted as follows in remarks made December 10, 1971: "If I go on as chief of state after victory, I run the risk of being pushed out the window by the Communists, like Masaryk, or that I might be imprisoned for revisionism or deviationism."

More than two million Cambodians out of an estimated total population of slightly more than seven million perished under the Khmer Rouge; according to some estimates, the genocide killed 32 percent of the total population.[12] The United States and Red China, acting together under the Kissinger "China card" policy, had liquidated one Cambodian government, destroyed the fabric of civil society in the country, ousted a pro-U.S. government, and installed a new regime they knew to be genocidal in its intentions. For Kissinger, it was the exemplification of the new U.S. strategic doctrine contained in NSSM 200. For George Bush, it was the fulfillment of his family's fanatically held belief in the need for genocide to prevent the allegedly "inferior" races of the earth, in this case those with yellow skins, from "out-breeding" the imperial Anglo-Saxon racial stock.

Meeting of the Monsters

Kissinger made four visits to Beijing during Bush's tenure there, three solo appearances and a final junket accompanied by Ford. On October 19, 1975, Kissinger arrived in Beijing to prepare for Ford's visit, set for December. There were talks between Kissinger and Deng Xiaoping, with Bush, Philip Habib, Winston Lord and Foreign Minister Qiao taking part. It was during this visit, Bush would have us believe, that he had his first face-to-face meeting with Mao Zedong, the leader of a Communist revolution which had claimed the lives of some 100 million Chinese since the end of the Second World War.

Mao, one of the greatest monsters of the twentieth century, was 81 years old at that time. He was in very bad health; when he opened his mouth to meet Kissinger, "only guttural noises emerged." Mao's study contained tables covered with tubes and medical apparatus, and a small oxygen tank. Mao was unable to speak coherently, but had to write Chinese characters and an occasional word in English on a note pad which he showed to his interpreters. Kissinger inquired as to Mao's health. Mao pointed to his head saying, "This part works well. I can eat and sleep." Then Mao tapped his legs: "These parts do not work well. They are not strong when I walk. I also have some trouble with my lungs. In a word, I am not well. I am a showcase for visitors," Mao summed up. The croaking, guttural voice continued: "I am going to heaven soon. I have already received an invitation from God."

If Mao was a basso profondo of guttural croaking, then Kissinger was at least a bass-baritone: "Don't accept it too soon," he replied. "I accept the orders of the Doctor," wrote Mao on his note pad. Mao at this point had slightly less than a year to live. Bush provided counterpoint to these lower registers with his own whining tenor.

Bush was much impressed by Mao's rustic background and repertoire of Chinese barnyard expressions. Referring to a certain problem in Sino-American relations, Mao dismissed it as no more important than a "fang go pi," no more important than a dog fart.

Mao went on, commenting about U.S. military superiority, and then saying: "God blesses you, not us. God does not like us because I am a militant warlord, also a Communist. No, he doesn't like me. He likes you three." Mao pointed to Kissinger, Bush and Winston Lord.

Toward the end of the encounter, this lugubrious monster singled out Bush for special attention. Mao turned to Winston Lord. "This ambassador," said Mao while gesturing toward Bush, "is in a plight. Why don't you come visit?" "I would be honored," Bush replied according to his own account, "but I'm afraid you're very busy." "Oh, I'm not busy," said Mao. "I don't look after internal affairs. I only read the international news. You should really come visit."

Bush claims[13] that he never accepted Chairman Mao's invitation to come around for private talks. Bush says that he was convinced by members of his own staff that Mao did not really mean to invite him, but was only being polite. Was Bush really so reticent, or is this another one of the falsifications with which his official biographies are studded? The world must await the opening of the Beijing and Foggy Bottom archives. In the meantime, we must take a moment to contemplate that gathering of October 1975 in Chairman Mao's private villa, secluded behind many courtyards and screens in the Chungnanhai enclave of Chinese rulers not far from the Great Hall of the People and Tiananmen, where less than a year later an initial round of pro-democracy demonstrations would be put down in blood in the wake of the funeral of Zhou Enlai.

Mao, Kissinger, and Bush: Has history ever seen a tête-à-tête of such mass murderers? Mao, identifying himself with Chin Shih Huang, the first Emperor of all of China and founder of the Chin dynasty, who had built the Great Wall, burned the books, and killed the Confucian scholars—this Mao had massacred ten percent of his own people, ravaged Korea, strangled Tibet. Kissinger's crimes were endless, from the Middle East to Vietnam, from the oil crisis of '73–'74, with the endless death in the Sahel, to India-Pakistan, Chile and many more. Kissinger, Mao and Bush had collaborated to install the Pol Pot Khmer Rouge regime in Cambodia, which was now approaching the zenith of its genocidal career. Compared to the other two, Bush may have appeared as an apprentice of genocide: He had done some filibustering in the Caribbean, had been part of the cheering section for the Indonesia massacres of 1965, and then he had become a part of the Kissinger apparatus, sharing in the responsibility for India-Pakistan, the Middle East, Cambodia. But as Bush advanced through his personal *cursus honorum,* his power and his genocidal dexterity were growing, foreshadowing such future triumphs as the devastation of El Chorillo in Panama in December 1989, and his later masterwork of savagery, the Gulf war of 1991. By the time of Bush's own administration, Anglo-American finance and the International Monetary Fund were averaging some 50 million needless deaths per year in the developing sector.

But Mao, Kissinger and Bush exchanged pleasantries that day in Mao's sitting room in Chungnanhai. If the shades of Hitler or Stalin had sought admission to that murderers' colloquium, they might have been denied entrance as pikers.

The Next Step

Bush was now obsessed with the idea that he had a right to become Vice President in 1976. As a member of the senatorial caste, he had a right to enter the Senate, and if the plebeians with their changeable humors barred the elective route, then the only answer was to be appointed to the second spot on the ticket and enter the Senate as its presiding officer. As Bush wrote in his campaign autobiography: "Having lost out to Rockefeller as Ford's vice-presidential choice in 1974, I might be considered by some as a leading contender for the number two spot in Kansas City. . . ."[14]

Accordingly, when Kissinger visited Bush in Beijing in October 1975, he pointedly inquired as to whether Bush intended to enter any of the Republican presidential primaries during the 1976 season. This was the principal question that Ford had directed Kissinger to ask of Bush.

Bush's exit from Beijing occurred within the context of Ford's celebrated "Halloween massacre" of early November 1975. This "massacre," reminiscent of Nixon's cabinet purge of 1973 ("the Saturday night massacre"), was a number of firings and transfers of high officials at the top of the executive branch, through which Ford sought to figure forth the political profile which he intended to carry into the primaries and, if he were successful in the winter and spring, into the Republican convention and, beyond that, into the fall campaign. So each of these changes had a purpose that was ultimately rooted in electioneering.

In the Halloween massacre, it was announced that Vice President Nelson Rockefeller would under no circumstances be a candidate to continue in that office. Nelson's negatives were simply too high, owing in part to a vigorous campaign directed against him by Lyndon LaRouche. James "Rodney the Robot" Schlesinger was summarily ousted as the Secretary of Defense; James Schlesinger's "Dr. Strangelove" overtones were judged not presentable during an election year. To replace Schlesinger, Ford's White House chief of staff, Donald Rumsfeld, was given the Pentagon. Henry Kissinger, who up to this moment had been running the administration from two posts, NSC Director and Secretary of State, had to give up his White House office and was obliged to direct the business of the government from Foggy Bottom. In consolation to him, the NSC job was assigned to his devoted clone and later business associate, retired Air Force Lt. Gen. Brent Scowcroft, a Mormon who would later play the role of exterminating demon during Bush's Gulf war adventure. At the Department of Commerce, the secretary's post was being vacated by Rogers Morton. Finally, William Colby, his public reputation thoroughly delapidated as a result of the revelations made during the Church Committee and Pike Committee investigations of the abuses and crimes of the CIA, especially within the U.S. domestic sphere, was canned as Director of Central Intelligence.

Could this elaborate reshuffle be made to yield a job for Bush? It was anything but guaranteed. The post of CIA Director was offered to Washington lawyer and influence-broker Edward Bennett Williams. But he turned it down.

Then there was the post at Commerce. This was one that Bush came very close to getting. In the Jack Marsh files at the Gerald Ford Library there is a draft marked "Suggested cable to George

Bush," but which is undated. The telegram begins: "Congratulations on your selection by the President as Secretary of Commerce." The job title is crossed out, and "Director of the Central Intelligence Agency" is penciled in.

So Bush almost went to Commerce, but then was proposed for Langley instead. Bush in his campaign autobiography suggests that the CIA appointment was a tactical defeat, the one new job that was more or less guaranteed to keep him off the GOP ticket in 1976. As CIA Director, if he got that far, he would have to spend "the next six months serving as point man for a controversial agency being investigated by two major congressional committees. The scars left by that experience would put me out of contention, leaving the spot open for others."[15] Bush suggests that "the Langley thing" was the handiwork of Donald Rumsfeld, who had a leading role in designing the reshuffle.

On All Saints' Day, November 1, 1975, Bush received a telegram from Kissinger informing him that "the President is planning to announce some major personnel shifts on Monday, November 3, at 7:30 P.M., Washington time. Among those shifts will be the transfer of Bill Colby from CIA. The President asks that you consent to his nominating you as the new Director of the Central Intelligence Agency."[16]

Bush promptly accepted.

Notes for Chapter XIII

1. George Bush and Victor Gold, *Looking Forward* (New York: Doubleday, 1987), p. 130.
2. Walter Pincus and Bob Woodward, "Presidential Posts and Dashed Hopes," *Washington Post*, Aug. 9, 1988.
3. See Hassan Ahmed and Joseph Brewda, "Kissinger, Scowcroft, Bush Plotted Third World Genocide," *Executive Intelligence Review*, May 3, 1991, pp. 26–30.
4. Russell R. Ross, ed., *Cambodia: A Country Study* (Washington: U.S. G.P.O., 1990), p. 46.
5. Henry Kissinger, *Years of Upheaval* (Boston: Little, Brown, 1982), p. 341. This second volume of Kissinger's memoirs, published when his close ally Bush had already become Vice President, has much less to say about George's activities, with only one reference to him in more than 1,200 pages. We see again that Bush prefers that most of his actual record remain covert.
6. *Ibid.*, p. 367.
7. *Ibid.*, p. 681.
8. See William Shawcross, *Sideshow: Kissinger, Nixon, and the Destruction of Cambodia* (New York: Simon and Schuster, 1987), pp. 360–61.
9. Lt. Gen. Sak Sutsakhan, the leader of the last Cambodian government before the advent of the Khmer Rouge, argues that the victory of the Communists was not a foregone conclusion, and that modest American aid, in the form of 20 aircraft and a few dozen obsolescent tanks waiting for delivery in Thailand, could have materially changed the military outcome. See Sutsakhan's *The Khmer Republic at War and the Final Collapse* (Washington: U.S. Army Center of Military History, 1980) pp. 163, 166.
10. Shawcross, *op. cit.*, p. 360.
11. *Ibid.;* p. 361.
12. Ross, *op. cit.*, p. 51.

13. See Bush and Gold, *op. cit.*, pp. 145–49 for Bush's account of his alleged first meeting with Mao.

14. Bush and Gold, *op. cit.*, p. 157.

15. *Ibid.*, pp. 157–58.

16. *Ibid.*, p. 153.

XIV

CIA DIRECTOR

In late 1975, as a result in particular of his role in Watergate, Bush's confirmation as CIA Director was not automatic. And though the debate at his confirmation was superficial, some Senators, including in particular the late Frank Church of Idaho, made some observations about the dangers inherent in the Bush nomination that have turned out in retrospect to be useful.

The political scene on the home front, from which Bush had been so anxious to be absent during 1975, was the so-called "Year of Intelligence," in that it had been a year of intense scrutiny of the illegal activities and abuses of the intelligence community, including CIA domestic and covert operations. On December 22, 1974, the *New York Times* published the first of a series of articles by Seymour M. Hersh, which relied on leaked reports of CIA activities assembled by Director James Rodney Schlesinger to expose alleged misdeeds by the agency.

It was widely recognized at the time that the Hersh articles were a self-exposure by the CIA that was designed to set the agenda for the Ford-appointed Rockefeller Commission, which was set up a few days later, on January 4. The Rockefeller Commission members included John T. Connor, C. Douglas Dillon, Erwin N. Griswold, Lane Kirkland, Lyman Lemnitzer, Ronald Reagan, and Edgar F. Shannon, Jr. The Rockefeller Commission was supposed to examine the malfeasance of the intelligence agencies and make recommendations about how they could be reorganized and reformed. In reality, the Rockefeller Commission proposals would reflect the transition of the structures of the 1970s toward the growing totalitarian tendencies of the 1980s.

While the Rockefeller Commission was a tightly controlled vehicle of the Eastern Anglophile Liberal Establishment, congressional investigating committees were impaneled during 1975 whose proceedings were somewhat less rigidly controlled. These included the Senate Intelligence Committee, known as the Church Committee, and the corresponding House committee, first chaired by Rep. Lucien Nedzi (who had previously chaired one of the principal Watergate-era probes), and then (after July) by Rep. Otis Pike. One example was the Pike Committee's issuance of a contempt of Congress citation against Henry Kissinger for his refusal to provide documentation of covert operations in November 1975. Another was Church's role in leading the opposition to the Bush nomination.

The Church Committee launched an investigation of the use of covert operations for the purpose of assassinating foreign leaders. By the nature of things, this probe was led to grapple with the problem of whether covert operations sanctioned to eliminate foreign leaders had been re-targeted against domestic political figures. The obvious case was the Kennedy assassination.

Frank Church—whom, we must keep in mind, was himself an ambitious politician—was especially diligent in attacking CIA covert operations, which Bush would be anxious to defend. The CIA's covert branch, Church thought, was a "self-serving apparatus." "It's a bureaucracy which feeds on itself, and those involved are constantly sitting around thinking up schemes for [foreign] intervention which will win them promotions and justify further additions to the staff. . . . It self-generates interventions that otherwise never would be thought of, let alone authorized."[1]

It will be seen that at the beginning of Bush's tenure at the CIA, the congressional committees were on the offensive against the intelligence agencies. By the time that Bush departed Langley, the tables were turned, and it was the Congress which was the focus of scandals, including Koreagate. Soon thereafter, the Congress would undergo the assault of Abscam.

The announcement of Bush's nomination occasioned a storm of criticism, whose themes included the inadvisability of choosing a Watergate figure for such a sensitive post so soon after that scandal had finally begun to subside. References were made to Bush's receipt of financial largesse from Nixon's Townhouse fund and related operations. There was also the question of whether the domestic CIA apparatus would get mixed up in Bush's expected campaign for the vice-presidency. These themes were developed in editorials during the month of November 1976, while Bush was kept in Beijing by the requirements of preparing the Ford-Mao meetings of early December. To some degree, Bush was just hanging there and slowly, slowly twisting in the wind. The slow-witted Ford soon realized that he had been inept in summarily firing William Colby, since Bush would have to remain in China for some weeks and then return to face confirmation hearings. Ford had to ask Colby to stay on in a caretaker capacity until Bush took office. The delay allowed opposition against Bush to crystallize to some degree, but his own network was also quick to spring to his defense.

Former CIA officer Tom Braden, writing in the *Fort Lauderdale News*, noted that the Bush appointment to the CIA looked bad, and looked bad at a time when public confidence in the CIA was so low that everything about the agency desperately needed to look good. Braden's column was entitled "George Bush, Bad Choice for CIA Job."

Rowland Evans and Robert Novak, writing in the *Washington Post*, commented that "the Bush nomination is regarded by some intelligence experts as another grave morale deflator. They reason that any identified politician, no matter how resolved to be politically pure, would aggravate the CIA's credibility gap. Instead of an identified politician like Bush . . . what is needed, they feel, is a respected non-politician, perhaps from business or the academic world."

The *Washington Post* came out against Bush in an editorial entitled "The Bush Appointment." Here the reasoning was that this position "should not be regarded as a political parking spot," and that public confidence in the CIA had to be restored after the recent revelations of wrongdoing.

After a long-winded argument, the conservative columnist George Will came to the conclusion that Ambassador Bush at the CIA would be "the wrong kind of guy at the wrong place at the worst possible time."

Senator Church viewed the Bush appointment in the context of a letter sent to him by Ford on October 31, 1975, demanding that the committee's report on U.S. assassination plots against foreign leaders be kept secret. In Church's opinion, these two developments were part of a pattern, and amounted to a new stonewalling defense by what Church had called "the rogue elephant." Church issued a press statement in response to Ford's letter attempting to impose a blackout on the assassination report. "I am astonished that President Ford wants to suppress the committee's report on assassination and keep it concealed from the American people," said Church. Then, on November 3, Church was approached by reporters outside of his Senate hearing room and asked by Daniel Schorr about the firing of Colby and his likely replacement by Bush. Church responded with a voice that was trembling with anger. "There is no question in my mind but that concealment is the new order of the day," he said. "Hiding evil is the trademark of a totalitarian government."[2] Schorr said that he had never seen Church so upset.

The following day, November 4, Church read Leslie Gelb's column in the *New York Times* suggesting that Colby had been fired, among other things, "for not doing a good job containing the congressional investigations." George Bush, Gelb thought, "would be able to go to Congress and ask for a grace period before pressing their investigations further." A *Washington Star* headline of this period summed up this argument: "CIA Needs Bush's PR Talent." Church talked with his staff that day about what he saw as an ominous pattern of events. He told reporters: "First came the very determined administration effort to prevent any revelations concerning NSA, their stonewalling of public hearings. Then came the president's letter. Now comes the firing of Colby, Mr. Schlesinger, and the general belief that Secretary Kissinger is behind these latest developments." For Church, "clearly a pattern has emerged now to try and disrupt this [Senate Intelligence Committee] investigation. As far as I'm concerned, it won't be disrupted," said Church grimly.

One of Church's former aides, speechwriter Loch K. Johnson, describes how he worked with Church to prepare a speech scheduled for delivery on November 11, 1975, in which Church would stake out a position opposing the Bush nomination:

> The nomination of George Bush to succeed Colby disturbed him and he wanted to wind up the speech by opposing the nomination. . . . He hoped to influence Senate opinion on the nomination on the eve of Armed Services Committee hearings to confirm Bush.
>
> I rapidly jotted down notes as Church discussed the lines he would like to take against the nomination. "Once they used to give former national party chairmen [as Bush had been under President Nixon] postmaster generalships—the most political and least sensitive job in government," he said. "Now they have given this former party chairman the most sensitive and least political agency." Church wanted me to stress how Bush "might compromise the independence of the CIA—the agency could be politicized."

Some days later, Church appeared on the CBS program "Face the Nation." He was asked by George Herman if his opposition to Bush would mean that anyone with political experience would be *a priori* unacceptable for such a post. Church replied: "I think that whoever is chosen should be one who has demonstrated a capacity for independence, who has shown that he can stand up to the many pressures." Church hinted that Bush had never stood up for principle at the cost of political office. Moreover, "a man whose background is as partisan as a past chairman of the Republican party does serious damage to the agency and its intended purposes."[3]

The Brown Brothers Harriman/Skull and Bones crowd counterattacked in favor of Bush, mobilizing some significant resources. One was none other than Leon Jaworski, the former Watergate special prosecutor. Jaworski's mission for the Bush network appears to have been to get the Townhouse and related Nixon slush fund issues off the table of the public debate and confirmation hearings. Jaworski, speaking at a convention of former FBI special agents meeting in Houston, defended Bush against charges that he had accepted illegal or improper payments from Nixon and CREEP operatives. "This was investigated by me when I served as Watergate special prosecutor. I found no involvement of George Bush and gave him full clearance. I hope that in the interest of fairness, the matter will not be bandied about unless something new has appeared on the horizon."[4]

Negative mail from both houses of Congress was also coming in to the White House. On November 12, Ford received a singular note from GOP Congressman James M. Collins of Dallas, Texas. Collins wrote to Ford: "I hope you will reconsider the appointment of George Bush to the CIA. At this time it seems to me that it would be a greater service for the country for George to continue his service in China. He is not the right man for the CIA," wrote Collins, who had been willing to support Bush for the vice-presidency back in 1974.[5]

There was also a letter to Ford from Democratic Congressman Lucien Nedzi of Michigan, who had been the chairman of one of the principal House Watergate investigating committees. Nedzi wrote as follows:

> The purpose of my letter is to express deep concern over the announced appointment of George Bush as the new Director of the Central Intelligence Agency. . . . [H]is proposed appointment would bring with it inevitable complications for the intelligence community. Mr. Bush is a man with a recent partisan political past and a probable near-term partisan political future. This is a burden neither the Agency, nor the legislative oversight committee, nor the Executive should have to bear as the CIA enters perhaps the most difficult period of its history.

The Director of the CIA must be unfettered by any doubts as to his politics. He must be free of the appearance, as well as the substance, that he is acting, or not acting, with partisan political considerations in mind. . . .

Accordingly, I respectfully urge that you reconsider your appointment of Mr. Bush to this most sensitive of positions.[6]

Senator William V. Roth of Delaware sent Bush a letter on November 20 which made a related point:

Dear George:

It is my deep conviction that the security of this nation depends upon an effective viable Central Intelligence Agency. This depends in part upon the intelligence agency being involved in no way in domestic politics, especially in the aftermath of Watergate. For that reason, I believe you have no choice but to withdraw your name unequivocally from consideration for the Vice Presidency, if you desire to become Director of the CIA. . . .

If Bush still wanted to pursue national office, wrote Roth, "then I believe the wise decision is for you to ask the President to withdraw your nomination for the CIA Directorship."[7] Roth sent a copy of the same letter to Ford.

Within just a couple of days of making Bush's nomination public, the Ford White House was aware that it had a significant public relations problem. To get reelected, Ford had to appear as a reformer, breaking decisively with the bad old days of Nixon and the Plumbers. But with the Bush nomination, Ford was putting a former party chairman and future candidate for national office at the head of the entire intelligence community.

Ford's staff began to marshal attempted rebuttals for the attacks on Bush. On November 5, Jim Connor of Ford's staff had some trite boiler-plate inserted into Ford's Briefing Book in case he were asked if the advent of Bush represented a move to obstruct the Church and Pike Committees. Ford was told to answer that he "has asked Director Colby to cooperate fully with the Committee" and "expects Ambassador Bush to do likewise once he becomes Director. As you are aware, the work of both the Church and Pike Committees is slated to wind up shortly."[8] In case he were asked about Bush politicizing the CIA, Ford was to answer: "I believe that Republicans and Democrats who know George Bush and have worked with him know that he does not let politics and partisanship interfere with the performance of public duty." That was a mouthful. "Nearly all of the men and women in this and preceding administrations have had partisan identities and have held partisan party posts. . . . George Bush is a part of that American tradition and he will demonstrate this when he assumes his new duties."

But when Ford, in an appearance on a Sunday talk show, was asked if he were ready to exclude Bush as a possible vice-presidential candidate, he refused to do so, answering, "I don't think people of talent ought to be excluded from any field of public service." At a press conference, Ford said, "I don't think he's eliminated from consideration by anybody, the delegates or the convention or myself.

Confirmation Hearings

Bush's confirmation hearings got under way on December 15, 1975. Even judged by Bush's standards of today, they constitute a landmark exercise in sanctimonious hypocrisy so astounding as to defy comprehension.

Bush's sponsor was GOP Senator Strom Thurmond of South Carolina, the ranking Republican on Senator John Stennis's Senate Armed Services Committee. Thurmond unloaded a mawkish panegyric in favor of Bush: "I think all of this shows an interest on your part in humanity, in civic development, love of your country, and willingness to serve your fellow man." Could the aide writing that, even if it were Lee Atwater, have kept a straight face?

Bush's opening statement was also in the main a tissue of banality and clichés. He indicated his support for the Rockefeller Commission report without having mastered its contents in detail. He pointed out that he had attended cabinet meetings from 1971 to 1974, without mentioning who the President was in those days. Everybody was waiting for this consummate pontificator to get to the issue of whether he was going to attempt the vice-presidency in 1976. Readers of Bush's propaganda biographies know that he never decides on his own to run for office, but always responds to the urging of his friends. Within those limits, his answer was that he was available for the second spot on the ticket. More remarkably, he indicated that he had a hereditary right to it—it was, as he said, his "birthright."

Would Bush accept a draft? "I cannot in all honesty tell you that I would not accept, and I do not think, gentlemen, that any American should be asked to say he would not accept, and to my knowledge, no one in the history of this Republic has been asked to renounce his political birthright as the price of confirmation for any office. And I can tell you that I will not seek any office while I hold the job of CIA Director. I will put politics wholly out of my sphere of activities." Even more, Bush argued, his willingness to serve at the CIA reflected his sense of noblesse oblige. Friends had asked him why he wanted to go to Langley at all, "with all the controversy swirling around the CIA, with its obvious barriers to political future?"

Magnanimously, Bush replied to his own rhetorical question: "My answer is simple. First, the work is desperately important to the survival of this country, and to the survival of freedom around the world. And second, old fashioned as it may seem to some, it is my duty to serve my country. And I did not seek this job but I want to do it and I will do my very best."[9]

Stennis responded with a joke that sounds eerie in retrospect: "If I thought that you were seeking the Vice Presidential nomination or Presidential nomination by way of the route of being Director of the CIA, I would question your judgment most severely." There was laughter in the committee room.

Senators Barry Goldwater and Stuart Symington made clear that they would give Bush a free ride not only out of deference to Ford, but also out of regard for the late Prescott Bush, with whom they had both started out in the Senate in 1952. Senator Thomas McIntyre was more demanding, and raised the issue of enemies list operations, a notorious abuse of the Nixon (and subsequent) administrations:

"What if you get a call from the President, next July or August, saying 'George, I would like to see you.' You go in the White House. He takes you over in the corner and says, 'Look, things are not going too well in my campaign. This Reagan is gaining on me all the time. Now, he is a movie star of some renown and has traveled with the fast set. He was a Hollywood star. I want you to get any dirt you can on this guy because I need it.' "

What would Bush do? "I do not think that is difficult, sir," intoned Bush. "I would simply say that it gets back to character and it gets back to integrity; and furthermore, I cannot conceive of the incumbent doing that sort of thing. But if I were put into that kind of position where you had a clear moral issue, I would simply say 'no,' because you see I think, and maybe—I have the advantages as everyone on this committee of 20–20 hindsight, that this agency must stay in the foreign intelligence business and must not harass American citizens, like in Operation Chaos, and that these kinds of things have no business in the foreign intelligence business." This was the same Bush whose 1980 campaign was heavily staffed by CIA veterans, some retired, some on active service and in flagrant violation of the Hatch Act. This is the Vice President who ran Iran-Contra out of his own private office, and so forth.

Gary Hart also had a few questions. How did Bush feel about assassinations? Bush "found them morally offensive and I am pleased the President has made that position very, very clear to the Intelligence Committee. . . ." How about "coups d'état in various countries around the world," Hart wanted to know.

"You mean in the covert field?" replied Bush. "Yes." "I would want to have full benefit of all the intelligence. I would want to have full benefit of how these matters were taking place but I cannot tell you, and I do not think I should, that there would never be any support for a coup d'état; in other words, I cannot tell you I cannot conceive of a situation where I would not support such action." In retrospect, this was a moment of refreshing candor.

Gary Hart knew where at least one of Bush's bodies was buried:

> Senator Hart: You raised the question of getting the CIA out of domestic areas totally. Let us hypothesize a situation where a President has stepped over the bounds. Let us say the FBI is investigating some people who are involved, and they go right to the White House. There is some possible CIA interest. The President calls you and says, I want you as Director of the CIA to call the Director of the FBI to tell him to call off this operation because it may jeopardize some CIA activities.
>
> Mr. Bush: Well, generally speaking, and I think you are hypothecating a case without spelling it out in enough detail to know if there is any real legitimate foreign intelligence aspect. . . .

There it was: the smoking gun tape again, the notorious Bush-Liedtke-Mosbacher-Pennzoil contribution to the CREEP again, the money that had been found in the pockets of Bernard Barker and the Plumbers after the Watergate break-in. But Hart did not mention it overtly, only in this oblique, Byzantine manner. Hart went on:

> I am hypothesizing a case that actually happened in June 1972. There might have been some tangential CIA interest in something in Mexico. Funds were laundered and so forth.
>
> Mr. Bush: Using a 50–50 hindsight on that case, I hope I would have said the CIA is not going to get involved in that if we are talking about the same one.
>
> Senator Hart: We are.
>
> Senator [Patrick] Leahy: Are there others?

Bush was on the edge of having his entire Watergate past come out in the wash, but the liberal Democrats were already far too devoted to the one-party state to grill Bush seriously. In a few seconds, responding to another question from Hart, Bush was off the hook, droning on about plausible deniability, of all things.

The next day, December 16, 1975, Church, appearing as a witness, delivered his philippic against Bush. After citing evidence of widespread public concern about the renewed intrusion of the CIA in domestic politics under Bush, Church reviewed the situation:

> So here we stand. Need we find or look to higher places than the Presidency and the nominee himself to confirm the fact that this door [of the Vice Presidency in 1976] is left open and that he remains under active consideration for the ticket in 1976? We stand in this position in the close wake of Watergate, and this committee has before it a candidate for Director of the CIA, a man of strong partisan political background and a beckoning political future.
>
> Under these circumstances I find the appointment astonishing. Now, as never before, the Director of the CIA must be completely above political suspicion. At the very least this committee, I believe, should insist that the nominee disavow any place on the 1976 Presidential ticket. . . .
>
> If Ambassador Bush wants to be Director of the CIA, he should seek that position. If he wants to be Vice President, then that ought to be his goal. It is wrong for him to want both positions, even in a Bicentennial year.

It was an argument that conceded far too much to Bush in the effort to be fair. Bush was incompetent for the post, and the argument should have ended there. Church's unwillingness to demand the unqualified rejection of such a nominee no matter what future goodies he was willing temporarily to renounce has cast long shadows over subsequent American history. But even so, Bush was in trouble.

Church was at his ironic best when he compared Bush to a recent chairman of the Democratic National Committee: ". . . [I]f a Democrat were President, Mr. Larry O'Brien ought not to be nominated to be Director of the CIA. Of all times to do it, this is the worst, right at a time when it is obvious that public confidence needs to be restored in the professional, impartial, and nonpolitical character of the agency. So, we have the worst of all possible worlds." Church tellingly underlined that "Bush's birthright does not include being Director of the CIA. It includes the right to run for public office, to be sure, but that is quite a different matter than confirming him now for this particular position."

Church said he would under no circumstance vote for Bush, but that if the latter renounced the '76 ticket, he would refrain from attempting to canvass other votes against Bush. It was an ambiguous position.

Bush came back to the witness chair in an unmistakably whining mood. He was offended above all by the comparison of his august self to the upstart Larry O'Brien: "I think there is some difference in the qualifications," said Bush in a hyperthyroid rage. "Larry O'Brien did not serve in the Congress of the United States for 4 years. Larry O'Brien did not serve, with no partisanship, at the United Nations for 2 years. Larry O'Brien did not serve as the Chief of the U.S. Liaison Office in the People's Republic of China." Not only Bush but his whole *cursus honorum* was insulted! "I will never apologize," said Bush a few seconds later, referring to his own record. Then Bush pulled out his "you must resign" letter to Nixon: "Now, I submit that for the record that that is demonstrable independence. I did not do it by calling the newspapers and saying, 'Look, I am having a press conference. Here is a sensational statement to make me, to separate me from a President in great agony.' "

Bush had been savaged in the hearings, and his nomination was now in grave danger of being rejected by the committee, and then by the full Senate. Later in the afternoon of November 16, a damage control party met at the White House to assess the situation for Ford.[10] According to Patrick O'Donnell of Ford's Congressional Relations Office, the most Bush could hope for was a bare majority of 9 out of 16 votes on the Stennis Committee.

Ford was inclined to give the Senators what they wanted, and exclude Bush *a priori* from the vice-presidential contest. When Ford called George over to the Oval Office on December 18, he already had the text of a letter to Stennis announcing that Bush was summarily ruled off the ticket if Ford were the candidate (which was anything but certain). Ford showed Bush the letter. We do not know what whining may have been heard in the White House that day from a senatorial patrician deprived (for the moment) of his birthright. Ford could not yield; it would have thrown his entire election campaign into acute embarrassment just as he was trying to get it off the ground. When George saw that Ford was obdurate, he proposed that the letter be amended to make it look as if the initiative to rule him out as a running mate had originated with Bush. The fateful letter read:

Dear Mr. Chairman:

As we both know, the nation must have a strong and effective foreign intelligence capability. Just over two weeks ago, on December 7 while in Pearl Harbor, I said that we must never drop our guard nor unilaterally dismantle our defenses. The Central Intelligence Agency is essential to maintaining our national security.

I nominated Ambassador George Bush to be CIA Director so we can now get on with appropriate decisions concerning the intelligence community. I need—and the nation needs—his leadership at CIA as we rebuild and strengthen the foreign intelligence community in a manner which earns the confidence of the American people.

Ambassador Bush and I agree that the Nation's immediate foreign intelligence needs must take precedence over other considerations and there should be continuity in his CIA leadership. Therefore, if Ambassador Bush is confirmed by the Senate as Director of Central Intelligence, I will not consider him as my Vice Presidential running mate in 1976.

He and I have discussed this in detail. In fact, he urged that I make this decision. This says something about the man and about his desire to do this job for the nation. . . .

On December 19, this letter was received by Stennis, who announced its contents to his committee. The committee promptly approved the Bush appointment by a vote of 12 to 4, with Gary Hart, Leahy, Culver and McIntyre voting against him. Bush's name could now be sent to the floor, where a recrudescence of anti-Bush sentiment was not likely, but could not be ruled out.

Bush was now engulfed by a profound rage. He had fought to get elected to the Senate twice, in 1964 and 1970, and failed both times. He had tried for the vice-presidency in 1968 and in 1972, had been passed over by Nixon in late 1973 in favor of Ford, again in 1974 in favor of Rockefeller, and was now out of the running in 1976. This was simply intolerable for a senatorial patrician, and that was indeed Bush's concept of his own "birthright."

Then, two days before Christmas, the CIA chief in Athens, Richard Welch, was gunned down in front of his home by masked assassins as he returned home with his wife from a Christmas party. A group calling itself the "November 19 Organization" later claimed credit for the killing.

Certain networks immediately began to use the Welch assassination as a bludgeon against the Church and Pike Committees. An example came from columnist Charles Bartlett, writing in the now-defunct *Washington Star*: "The assassination of the CIA Station

Chief, Richard Welch, in Athens is a direct consequence of the stagy hearings of the Church Committee. Spies traditionally function in a gray world of immunity from such crudities. But the Committee's prolonged focus on CIA activities in Greece left agents there exposed to random vengeance."[11] Staffers of the Church Committee pointed out that the Church Committee had never said a word about Greece or mentioned the name of Welch.

CIA Director Colby first blamed the death of Welch on *Counterspy* magazine, which had published the name of Welch some months before. The next day, Colby backed off, blaming a more general climate of hysteria regarding the CIA which had led to the assassination of Richard Welch. In his book, *Honorable Men*, published some years later, Colby continued to attribute the killing to the "sensational and hysterical way the CIA investigations had been handled and trumpeted around the world."

The Ford White House resolved to exploit this tragic incident to the limit. Liberals raised a hue and cry in response. Les Aspin later recalled that "the air transport plane carrying [Welch's] body circled Andrews Air Force Base for three-quarters of an hour in order to land live on the 'Today' Show." Ford waived restrictions in order to allow interment at Arlington Cemetery. The funeral on January 7 was described by the *Washington Post* as "a show of pomp usually reserved for the nation's most renowned military heroes." Anthony Lewis of the *New York Times* described the funeral as "a political device" with ceremonies "being manipulated in order to arouse a political backlash against legitimate criticism." Norman Kempster in the *Washington Star* found that "only a few hours after the CIA's Athens station chief was gunned down in front of his home, the agency began a subtle campaign intended to persuade Americans that his death was the indirect result of congressional investigations and the direct result of an article in an obscure magazine." Here, in the words of a *Washington Star* headline, was "one CIA effort that worked."

Between Christmas and New Year's in Kennebunkport, looking forward to the decisive floor vote on his confirmation, Bush was at work tending and mobilizing key parts of his network. One of these was a certain Leo Cherne.

Leo Cherne is not a household word, but he has been a powerful figure in the U.S. intelligence community over the period since World War II. Leo Cherne was to be one of Bush's most important allies when he was CIA Director and throughout Bush's subsequent career.

Cherne has been a part of B'nai B'rith all his life. He was (and still is) an ardent Zionist. He is typical to that extent of the so-called "neoconservatives" who have been prominent in government and policy circles under Reagan-Bush, and Bush. Cherne was the founder of the International Rescue Committee (IRC), a conduit for neo-Bukharinite operations between East and West in the Cold War, and also reputedly a CIA front organization.

Cherne was a close friend of William Casey, who was working in the Nixon administration as Undersecretary of State for Economic Affairs in mid-1973. That was when Cherne was named to the President's Foreign Intelligence Advisory Board (PFIAB) by Nixon. On March 15, 1976, Cherne became the chairman of this body, which specializes in conduiting the demands of financier and related interests into the intelligence community. Cherne, as we will see, would be, along with Bush, a leading beneficiary of Ford's spring 1976 intelligence reorganization.

Bush's correspondence with Cherne leaves no doubt that theirs was a very special relationship. Cherne represented for Bush a strengthening of his links to the Zionist-neoconservative milieu, with options for backchanneling into the Soviet bloc. Bush wrote to Cherne: "I read your testimony with keen interest and appreciation. I am really looking forward to meeting you and working with you in connection with your PFIAB chores. Have a wonderful 1976."

January 1976 was not auspicious for Bush. He had to wait until almost the end of the month for his confirmation vote, hanging there, slowly twisting in the wind. In the meantime, the Pike Committee report was approaching completion, after months of probing and haggling, and was sent to the Government Printing Office on January 23, despite continuing arguments from the White House and from the GOP that the committee could not reveal confidential and secret material provided by the executive branch. On Sunday, January 25, a copy of the report was leaked to Daniel Schorr of CBS News, and was exhibited on television that evening. The following morning, the *New York Times* published an extensive summary of the entire Pike Committee report.

Despite all this exposure, the House voted on January 29 that the Pike Committee report could not be released. A few days later it was published in full in the *Village Voice*, and CBS correspondent Daniel Schorr was held responsible for its appearance. The Pike Committee report attacked Henry Kissinger, "whose comments," it said, "are at variance with the facts." In the midst of his imperial regency over the United States, an unamused Kissinger responded that "we are facing a new version of McCarthyism." A few days later, Kissinger said of the Pike Committee: "I think they have used classified information in a reckless way, and the version of covert operations they have leaked to the press has the cumulative effect of being totally untrue and damaging to the nation."[12]

Thus, as Bush's confirmation vote approached, the Ford White House on the one hand, and the Pike and Church Committees on the other, were close to "open political warfare," as the *Washington Post* put it at the time. One explanation of the leaking of the Pike report was offered by Otis Pike himself on February 11: "A copy was sent to the CIA. It would be to their advantage to leak it for publication." By now, Ford was raving about mobilizing the FBI to find out how the report had been leaked.

On January 19, George Bush was present in the Executive Gallery of the House of Representatives, seated close to the unfortunate Betty Ford, for the President's State of the Union Address. This was a photo opportunity so that Ford's CIA candidate could get on television for a cameo appearance that might boost his standing on the eve of confirmation.

Confirmed, at Last

Senate floor debate was underway on January 26, and Senator McIntyre lashed out at the Bush nomination as "an insensitive affront to the American people."

In further debate on the day of the vote, January 27, Senator Joseph Biden joined other Democrats in assailing Bush as "the wrong appointment for the wrong job at the wrong time." Church appealed to the Senate to reject Bush, a man "too deeply embroiled in partisan politics and too intertwined with the political destiny of the President himself" to be able to lead the CIA. Goldwater, Tower, Percy, Howard Baker and Clifford Case all spoke up for Bush. Bush's floor leader was Strom Thurmond, who supported Bush by attacking the Church and Pike Committees.

Finally it came to a roll call and Bush passed by a vote of 64–27, with Lowell Weicker of Connecticut voting present. Church's staff felt they had failed lamentably, having gotten only liberal Democrats and the single Republican vote of Jesse Helms.[13]

It was the day after Bush's confirmation that the House Rules Committee voted 9 to 7 to block the publication of the Pike Committee report. The issue then went to the full House on January 29, which voted, 146 to 124, that the Pike Committee must submit its report to censorship by the White House and thus by the CIA. At almost the same time, Senator Howard Baker joined Tower and Goldwater in opposing the principal final recommendation of the

Church Committee, such as it was—the establishment of a permanent intelligence oversight committee.

Pike found that the attempt to censor his report had made "a complete travesty of the whole doctrine of separation of powers." In the view of a staffer of the Church Committee, "all within two days, the House Intelligence Committee had ground to a halt, and the Senate Intelligence Committee had split asunder over the centerpiece of its recommendations. The White House must have rejoiced; the Welch death and leaks from the Pike Committee report had produced, at last, a backlash against the congressional investigations."[14]

Riding the crest of that wave of backlash was George Bush. The constellation of events around his confirmation prefigures the wretched state of Congress today: a rubber stamp parliament in a totalitarian state, incapable of overriding even one of Bush's 22 vetoes.

On Friday, January 30, Ford and Bush were joined at the CIA auditorium for Bush's swearing-in ceremony before a large gathering of agency employees. Colby was also there: Some said he had been fired primarily because Kissinger thought that he was divulging too much to the congressional committees, but Kissinger later told Colby that the latter's stratagems had been correct.

Colby opened the ceremony with a few brief words: "Mr. President, and Mr. Bush, I have the great honor to present you to an organization of dedicated professionals. Despite the turmoil and tumult of the last year, they continue to produce the best intelligence in the world." This was met by a burst of applause.[15] Ford's line was: "We cannot improve this agency by destroying it." Bush promised to make "CIA an instrument of peace and an object of pride for all our people."

The CIA Team

Before proceeding, let us take a look at Bush's team of associates at the CIA, since we will find them in many of his later political campaigns and office staffs.

When Bush became Director of Central Intelligence (DCI), the incumbent principal deputy director was Gen. Vernon Walters, a former Army lieutenant general. This is the same Gen. Vernon Walters who was mentioned by Haldeman and Nixon in the notorious "smoking gun" tape already discussed, but who of course denied that he ever did any of the things that Haldeman and Ehrlichman said that he had promised to do. Walters had been at the CIA as

DCI since May 1972—a Nixon appointee who had been with Nixon when the then-Vice President's car was stoned in Caracas, Venezuela. Ever since then, Nixon had seen him as part of the old guard. Walters left to become a private consultant in July 1976.

To replace Walters, Bush picked Enno Henry Knoche, who had joined CIA in 1953 as an intelligence analyst specializing in Far Eastern political and military affairs. Knoche came from the Navy and knew Chinese. From 1962 to 1967 he had been the chief of the National Photographic Interpretation Center. In 1969, he had become deputy director of planning and budgeting, and chaired the internal CIA committee in charge of computerization. (This was reflected during the Bush tenure by heavy emphasis on satellites and SIGINT communications monitoring.) Next, Knoche was deputy director of the Office of Current Intelligence, which produces ongoing assessments of international events for the President and the NSC. After 1972, Knoche headed the Intelligence Directorate's Office of Strategic Research, charged with evaluating strategic threats to the U.S. In 1975, Knoche had been a special liaison between Colby and the Rockefeller Commission, as well as with the Church and Pike Committees. This was a very sensitive post, and Bush clearly looked to Knoche to help him deal with continuing challenges coming from the Congress. In the fall of 1975, Knoche had become number two on Colby's staff for the coordination and management of the intelligence community. According to some, Knoche was to function as Bush's "Indian guide" through the secrets of Langley; he knew "where the bodies were buried."

Knoche was highly critical of Colby's policy of handing over limited amounts of classified material to the Pike and Church Committees, while fighting to save the core of covert operations. Knoche told a group of friends during this period: "There is no counterintelligence any more." This implies a condemnation of the congressional committees with whom Knoche had served as liaison, and can also be read as a lament for the ousting of James Jesus Angleton, chief of the CIA's counterintelligence operations until 1975 and director of the mail-opening operation that had been exposed by various probers.[16]

Here was a deputy who could protect Bush's flank with his congressional tormentors, who would call Bush to the Hill more than 50 times during his approximately one year of CIA tenure. He would also appear to have had enough administrative experience to run things, shielding Bush from the defect that Governor William Scranton had pointed out years before—the lack of administrative ability.

Adm. Daniel J. Murphy was Bush's deputy director for the intelligence community, and later became Bush's chief of staff during his first term as Vice President. Much later, in November 1987, Murphy visited Panama in the company of South Korean businessman and intelligence operative Tongsun Park, and met with Gen. Manuel Antonio Noriega. Murphy was later obliged to testify to the Senate Foreign Relations Committee about his meeting with Noriega. Murphy claimed that he was only in Panama to "make a buck," but there are indications that he was carrying messages to Noriega from Bush. Tongsun Park, Murphy's ostensible business associate, will soon turn out to have been the central figure of the Koreagate scandal of 1976, a very important development on Bush's CIA watch.[17]

Other names on the Bush flow chart included holdover Edward Proctor, followed by Bush appointee Sayre Stevens in the slot of deputy director for intelligence; holdover Carl Duckett, followed by Bush appointee Leslie Dirks as deputy director for science and technology; John Blake, holdover as deputy director for administration; and holdover William Nelson, followed by Bush appointee William Wells, deputy director for operations.

William Wells as deputy director for operations was a very significant choice. He was a career covert operations specialist who had graduated from Yale a few years before Bush. Wells soon acquired his own deputy, recommended by him and approved by Bush: This was the infamous Theodore Shackley, whose title thus became associate deputy director for covert operations. Shackley later emerged as one of the central figures of the Iran-Contra scandal of the 1980s. He is reputedly one of the dominant personalities of a CIA old boys' network known as The Enterprise, which was at the heart of Iran-Contra and the other illegal covert operations of the Reagan-Bush years.

During the early 1960s, after the Bay of Pigs, Theodore Shackley had been the head of the CIA Miami Station during the years in which Operation Mongoose was at its peak. This was the E. Howard Hunt and Watergate Cubans crowd, circles familiar to Felix Rodriguez (Max Gomez), who in the 1980s ran Contra gun-running and drug-running out of Bush's vice-presidential office.

Later, Shackley was reportedly the chief of the CIA station in Vientiane, Laos, between July 1966 and December 1968. Some time after that, he moved on to become the CIA station chief in Saigon, where he directed the implementation of the Civilian Operations and Rural Development Support (CORDS) program, better known as Operation Phoenix, a genocidal crime against humanity which killed tens of thousands of Vietnamese civilians because they were suspected of working for the Vietcong, or sometimes simply because they were able to read and write. As for Shackley, there are also reports that he worked for a time in the late 1960s in Rome, during the period when the CIA's GLADIO capabilities were being used to launch a wave of terrorism in that country that went on for well over a decade. Such was the man whom Bush chose to appoint to a position of responsibility in the CIA. Later, Shackley will turn up as a "speechwriter" for Bush during the 1979–80 campaign.

Along with Shackley came his associate and former Miami Station second in command, Thomas Clines, a partner of Gen. Richard Secord and Albert Hakim during the Iran-Contra operation, convicted in September 1990 on four felony tax counts for not reporting his ill-gotten gains, and sentenced to 16 months in prison and a fine of $40,000.

Another career covert operations man, John Waller, became the inspector general, the officer who was supposed to keep track of illegal operations. For legal advice, Bush turned first to holdover General Counsel Mitchell Rogovin, who had in December 1975 theorized that intelligence activities belonged to the "inherent powers" of the presidency, and that no special congressional legislation was required to permit such things as covert operations to go on. Later, Bush appointed Anthony Lapham, Yale '58, as CIA general counsel. Lapham was the scion of an old San Francisco banking family, and his brother was Lewis Lapham, the editor of *Harper's* magazine. Lapham would take a leading role in the CIA coverup of the Letelier assassination case.[18]

Typical of the broad section of CIA officers who were delighted with their new boss from Brown Brothers Harriman/Skull and Bones was Cord Meyer, who had most recently been the station chief in London from 1973 on, a wild and woolly time in the tight little island, as we will see. Meyer, a covert action veteran and Watergate operative, writes at length in his autobiography about his enthusiasm for the Bush regime at CIA, which induced him to prolong his own career there.[19]

And what did other CIA officers, such as intelligence analysts, think of Bush? A common impression is that he was a superficial lightweight with no serious interest in intelligence. Deputy Director for Science and Technology Carl Duckett, who was ousted by Bush after three months, commented that he "never saw George Bush feel he had to understand the depth of something. . . . [He] is not a man tremendously dedicated to a cause or ideas. He's not fervent. He goes with the flow, looking for how it will play politically." According to

Maurice Ernst, the head of the CIA's Office of Economic Research from 1970 to 1980, "George Bush doesn't like to get into the middle of an intellectual debate . . . he liked to delegate it. I never really had a serious discussion with him on economics." Hans Heymann was Bush's national intelligence officer for economics, and he remembers having been impressed by Bush's Phi Beta Kappa Yale degree in economics. As Heymann later recalled Bush's response, "He looked at me in horror and said, 'I don't remember a thing. It was so long ago, so I'm going to have to rely on you.' "[20]

Intelligence Czar

During the first few weeks of Bush's tenure, the Ford administration was gripped by a "first strike" psychosis. This had nothing to do with the Soviet Union, but was rather Ford's desire to preempt any proposals for reform of the intelligence agencies coming out of the Pike or Church Committees with a pseudo-reform of his own, premised on his own in-house study, the Rockefeller report, which recommended an increase of secrecy for covert operations and classified information. Since about the time of the Bush nomination, an interagency task force armed with the Rockefeller Commission recommendations had been meeting under the chairmanship of Ford's counselor Jack O. Marsh. This was the Intelligence Coordinating Group, which included delegates of the intelligence agencies, plus NSC, OMB and others. This group worked up a series of final recommendations that were given to Ford to study on his Christmas vacation in Vail, Colorado. At this point, Ford was inclined to "go slow and work with Congress."

But on January 10, Marsh and the intelligence agency bosses met again with Ford, and the strategy began to shift toward preempting Congress. On January 30, Ford and Bush came back from their appearance at the CIA auditorium swearing-in session and met with other officials in the Cabinet Room. Attending besides Ford and Bush were Secretary of State Kissinger, Secretary of Defense Donald Rumsfeld, Attorney General Edward Levi, Jack Marsh, Philip Buchen, Brent Scowcroft, Mike Duval, and Peter Wallison, representing Vice President Rockefeller, who was out of town that day.[21] Here Ford presented his tentative conclusions for further discussion. The general line was to preempt the Congress, not to cooperate with it, to increase secrecy, and to increase authoritarian tendencies.

Ford scheduled a White House press conference for the evening of February 17. In his press conference, Ford scooped the Congress and touted his bureaucratic reshuffle of the intelligence agencies as the most sweeping reform and reorganization of the United States' intelligence agencies since the passage of the National Security Act of 1947. "I will not be a party to the dismantling of the CIA or other intelligence agencies," he intoned. He repeated that the intelligence community had to function under the direction of the National Security Council, as if that were something earth-shaking and new; from the perspective of Oliver North and Admiral Poindexter we can see in retrospect that it guaranteed nothing. A new NSC committee chaired by Bush was entrusted with the task of giving greater central coordination to the intelligence community as a whole. This committee was to consist of Bush, Kissinger clone William Hyland of the National Security Council staff, and Robert Ellsworth, the assistant secretary of defense for intelligence. This committee was jointly to formulate the budget of the intelligence community and allocate its resources to the various tasks.

The 40 Committee, which had overseen covert operations, was now to be called the Operations Advisory Group, with its membership reshuffled to include Scowcroft of NSC, Kissinger, Rumsfeld, Chairman of the Joint Chiefs of Staff George Brown, plus observers from the Attorney General and the Office of Management and Budget.

An innovation was the creation of the Intelligence Oversight Board (in addition to the President's Foreign Intelligence Advisory Board), which was chaired by Ambassador Robert D. Murphy, the old adversary of Charles de Gaulle during World War II. The IOB was supposed to be a watchdog to prevent new abuses from coming out of the intelligence community. Also on this board were Stephen Ailes, who had been Undersecretary of Defense for Kennedy and Secretary of the Army for LBJ. The third figure on this IOB was Leo Cherne, who was soon to be promoted to chairman of PFIAB as well. The increasingly complicit relationship of Cherne to Bush meant that all alleged oversight by the IOB was a mockery.

Ford also wanted a version of the Official Secrets Act: He called for "special legislation to guard critical intelligence secrets. This legislation would make it a crime for a government employee who has access to certain highly classified information to reveal that information improperly"—which would have made the Washington leak game rather more dicey than it is at present.

The Official Secrets Act would have to be passed by Congress, but most of the rest of what Ford announced was embodied in Executive Order 11905. Church thought that this was overreaching, since it amounted to changing some provisions of the National Security Act by presidential fiat. But this was now the new temper of the times.

As for the CIA, Executive Order 11905 authorized it "to conduct foreign counterintelligence activities . . . in the United States," which opened the door to many things. Apart from restrictions on physical searches and electronic bugging, it was still open season on Americans abroad. The FBI was promised the Levi guidelines, and other agencies would get charters written for them. In the interim, the power of the FBI to combat various "subversive" activities was reaffirmed. Political assassination was banned, but there were no limitations or regulations placed on covert operations, and there was nothing about measures to improve the intelligence and analytical product of the agencies.

In the view of the *New York Times*, the big winner was Bush: "From a management point of view, Mr. Ford tonight centralized more power in the hands of the Director of Central Intelligence than any had had since the creation of the CIA. The director has always been the nominal head of the intelligence community, but in fact has had little power over the other agencies, particularly the Department of Defense." Bush was now de facto intelligence czar.[22]

Poor Ford was unable to realize that his interest was to be seen as a reformer, not as someone who wanted to reimpose secrecy. When he was asked if his Official Secrets Act could not be used to deter whistle-blowers on future bureaucratic abuses, Ford responded that all federal employees would be made to sign a statement pledging that they would not divulge classified information, and that they could expect draconian punishment if they ever did so.

Congressman Pike said that Ford's reorganization was bent "largely on preserving all of the secrets in the executive branch and very little on guaranteeing a lack of any further abuses." Church commented that what Ford was really after was "to give the CIA a bigger shield and a longer sword with which to stab about."

An incident of those days reveals something of what was going on. Daniel Schorr of CBS, whose name had popped up on the Nixon enemies list during the Watergate hearings, had obtained a copy of the Pike Committee report and passed it on to the *Village Voice*. Schorr had attended Ford's press conference, and listened as Ford denounced the leaking of the Pike report. The next day, covering Capitol Hill, Schorr encountered Bush while the new CIA boss was on his way to testify before the Senate Foreign Relations Committee. A wirephoto of an angry Bush gesticulating at Schorr wound up on the front page of the *Washington Star* under the headline: "Another Confrontation." With that, Schorr's 20-year career with CBS was over, and he was soon to face a witch-hunt by the House Ethics Committee. Other reporters soon caught on that under the new Bush regime, political opponents would be slammed. Schorr later speculated about CIA links to CBS owner William Paley; there was no need to look any further than the fact that Prescott Bush had personally arranged the credit to give Paley ownership of CBS, and Prescott had been a director of CBS and its financial czar up through the 1950s, giving the Bushman network a firm presence there.

The Church Committee was still functioning, and was looking into journalists controlled by the CIA, whom some Senators wanted to expose by name. On the same day as Ford's press conference, Senators Walter Huddleston and Charles Mathias drove out to Langley to confront Bush and demand that he divulge the names of these CIA media assets. The CIA was "not at liberty to reveal the names," Bush told the two Senators. Instead, Bush offered documents that generally described the CIA's use of reporters and scholars over the years, but with no names. Senators Baker, Hart and Mondale then called Bush and urged that the names be made public. Bush refused.

Bush pointed to his statement, made on February 12 as the first public act of his CIA career, removing all "full-time or part-time news correspondents accredited by any U.S. news service, newspaper, periodicals, radio or TV network or station" from the CIA payroll. He also claimed that there were no clergymen or missionaries on the CIA payroll at all. As far as the journalists were concerned, in April the Senate Select Committee on Intelligence Activities announced that they had already caught Bush lying, and that at least 25 journalists and reporters were still on the CIA payroll, and the CIA was determined to keep them there. Bush had quibbled on the word "accredited." This limited the purge to accredited correspondents issued news credentials. But this excluded freelance reporters, editors, news executives, and foreign news organizations at all levels. When dealing with Bush, it pays to read the fine print.

The Bush-Kissinger-Ford counteroffensive against the congressional committees went forward. On March 5, the CIA leaked the story that the Pike Committee had lost more than 232 secret documents which had been turned over from the files of the executive branch. Pike said that this was another classic CIA provocation designed to discredit his committee, which had ceased its activity. Bush denied that he had engineered the leak.

In March, Bush had to take action in the wake of the leaking of a CIA report showing that Israel had between 10 and 20 nuclear bombs; the report was published by Arthur Kranish, the editor of *Science Trends* magazine. Church, who had Zionist lobby ties of his own and who was in the midst of a bid for the Democratic presidential nomination, demanded an investigation: "Can you imagine how a leak of that kind would have been treated if it had come out of the Congress of the United States!" In retrospect, the report may have been some timely window-dressing for Israeli prowess in a Ford regime in which Israel's military value as an ally was hotly contested; a little later, Gen. George Brown, the Chairman of the Joint Chiefs, was quoted to the effect that Israel and its armed forces had "got to be considered a burden" for the United States.

In May, FBI Director Clarence Kelley apologized to the American people for the abuses committed by his secret police. Kelley said that he was "truly sorry" for past abuses of power, all of which were neatly laid at the door of the deceased former director, J. Edgar Hoover. Bush, for his part, aggressively refused to apologize. Bush conceded that he felt "outrage" at the illegal CIA domestic operations of the Watergate era, but that "that's all I'm going to say about it . . . you can interpret it any way you want." Bush's line was that all abuses had already been halted under Colby by the latter's "administrative dictum," and that the issue now was the implementation of the Rockefeller Commission report, to which Bush once again pledged fealty. Bush had no comment on the Lockheed scandal, which had begun to destabilize the Japanese, German, Italian and Netherlands governments. The advance of the Italian Communists and the Panama Canal treaties were all "policy questions for the White House" in his view. Although China was being rocked by the "democracy wall" movement and the first Tiananmen-style massacre of 1976, Bush, ever loyal to his Chinese Communist cronies, found that all that did not add up to anything "dramatically different."

By September, Bush could boast in public that he had won the immediate engagement: His adversaries in the congressional investigating committees were defeated. "The CIA," Bush announced, "has weathered the storm. . . . The mood in Congress has changed. . . . No one is campaigning against strong intelligence. The adversary thing, how we can ferret out corruption, has given way to the more serious question how we can have better intelligence."

Such was the public profile of Bush's CIA tenure up until about the time of the November 1976 elections. If this had been the whole story, then we might accept the usual talk about Bush's period of uneventful rebuilding and morale boosting while he was at Langley.

We might share the conclusions of one author that "Bush was picked because he could be trusted to provide no surprises. Amiable and well-liked by old CIA hands, he sincerely believed in the agency and its mission."[23]

Bush's Real Agenda

Reality looked different. The administration Bush served had Ford as its titular head, but most of the real power, especially in foreign affairs, was in the hands of Kissinger. Bush was more than willing to play along with the Kissinger agenda.

The first priority was to put an end to such episodes as contempt citations for Henry Kissinger. Thanks to the presence of Don Gregg as CIA station chief in Seoul, South Korea, that was easy to arrange. This was the same Don Gregg of the CIA who would later serve as Bush's national security advisor during the second vice-presidential term, and who would manage decisive parts of the Iran-Contra operations from Bush's own office. Gregg knew of an agent of the Korean CIA, Tongsun Park, who had for a number of years been making large payments to members of Congress, above all to Democratic members of the House of Representatives, in order to secure their support for legislation that was of interest to Park Chung Hee, the South Korean leader. It was therefore a simple matter to blow the lid off this story, causing a wave of hysteria among the literally hundreds of members of Congress who had attended parties organized by Tongsun Park, who had become the Perle Mesta of the 1970s when it came to entertaining congressional bigwigs. Tongsun Park also had a stable of call girls available, and could provide other services. The U.S. ambassador to the Republic of Korea during this period was Richard Sneider.

The Koreagate headlines began to appear a few days after Bush had taken over at Langley. In February, there was a story by Maxine Cheshire of the *Washington Post* reporting that the Department of Justice was investigating Congressmen Bob Leggett and Joseph Addabbo for allegedly accepting bribes from the Korean government. Both men were linked to Suzi Park Thomson, who had been hosting parties of the Korean embassy. Later, it turned out that Speaker of the House Carl Albert had kept Suzi Park Thomson on his payroll for all of the six years that he had been Speaker. Congressmen Richard Hanna, Cornelius Gallagher, William Broomfield, Hugh Carey and Lester Wolf were all implicated. The names of Tip O'Neill, John Brademas and John McFall also came up. The *New York Times* estimated that as many as 115 Congressmen were involved.

In reality the number was much lower, but former Watergate Special Prosecutor Leon Jaworski was brought back from Houston to become special prosecutor for this case as well. This underlined the press line that "the Democrats' Watergate" had finally arrived. It was embarrassing to the Bush CIA when Tongsun Park's official agency file disappeared for several months, and finally turned up shorn of key information on the CIA officers who had been working most closely with Park. Eventually, Congressman Richard Hanna was convicted and sent to jail, while Congressman Otto Passman of Louisiana was acquitted, largely because he had had the presence of mind to secure a venue in his own state. A number of other congressmen quit, and it is thought that the principal reason for the decision by Democratic Speaker of the House Carl Albert to retire at the end of 1976 was the fact that he had been touched by the breath of this scandal, which would go into the chronicles as "Koreagate."[24]

With Koreagate, the Congress was terrorized and brought to heel. In this atmosphere, Bush moved to reach a secret foreign policy consensus with key congressional leaders of both parties of the one-party state. According to two senior government officials involved, limited covert operations in such places as Angola were continued under the pretext that they were necessary for phasing out the earlier, larger, and more expensive operations. Bush's secret deal was especially successful with the post-Church Senate Intelligence Committee. Because of the climate of restoration that prevailed, a number of Democrats on this committee concluded that they must break off their aggressive inquiries ("the adversary thing") and make peace with Bush, according to reports of remarks by two senior members of the committee staff. The result was an interregnum during which the Senate committee would neither set specific reporting requirements, nor attempt to pass any binding legislation to restrict CIA covert and related activity. In return, Bush would pretend to make a few disclosures to create a veneer of cooperation.[25] These 1976 deals set the stage for many of the foreign intelligence monstrosities of the Jimmy Carter era. Ever since, the pretense of congressional oversight over the intelligence community has been a mockery.

During Bush's first months in Langley, the CIA, under orders from Henry Kissinger, launched a campaign of destabilization of Jamaica for the purpose of preventing the reelection of Prime Minister Michael Manley. This included a large-scale campaign to foment violence during the election, and large amounts of illegal arms were shipped into the island. Some $10 million was spent on the attempt to overthrow Manley, and at least three assassination attempts took place with the connivance of the CIA.[26]

The Bush CIA also continued a program in Iran which went under the name of IBEX. This aimed at building and operating a $500 million electronic and photographic capability to cover the entire region, including parts of the Soviet Union. On August 28, 1976, three Americans working on the project were assassinated in Teheran. According to a *Washington Post* account by Bob Woodward, a month before these killings, the former CIA Director and then-U.S. ambassador to Iran, Richard Helms, sent Bush a note complaining about abuses connected with the project, and in particular demanding that Bush investigate corrupt practices which Helms suspected were involved with the project. Helms apparently wanted to be spared more embarrassment in case IBEX were to become the object of a new scandal.[27]

During Bush's time at the CIA, a series of governments around the world was destabilized by the Lockheed bribery scandal, the greatest multinational scandal of the 1970s. This scandal grew out of hearings before a Senate subcommittee chaired by Frank Church, although separate from the Intelligence Committee mentioned above. A number of Lockheed executives testified that they had systematically bribed officials of allied governments to secure contracts for the sale of their military aircraft. This system of unreported payments eventually implicated such figures as former Japanese Prime Minister Kakuei Tanaka, the leader of the most important faction in the Liberal Democratic Party; and Franz Josef Strauss, a former West German Defense Minister, Prime Minister of Bavaria, and the leader of the Christian Social Union, then a part of the opposition in the Bundestag in Bonn. Also implicated was a series of Italian Christian Democratic and Social Democratic political leaders, including then-Prime Minister Giulio Andreotti, President of the Italian Republic Giovanni Leone, and former defense ministers Mario Tanassi of the PSDI (Social Democratic party) and Luigi Gui of the DC (Christian Democratic party). In the Netherlands, Prince Bernhard, the consort of Queen Juliana, was implicated, and virtually no NATO country was spared.

The Lockheed scandal, coming as it did out of a milieu full of military intelligence connections, was coherent with a long-term Anglo-American design of destabilizing and weakening allied governments and the political forces that constituted those governments.

The Letelier Affair

One of the most spectacular scandals of Bush's tenure at the CIA was the assassination in Washington, D.C. of Orlando Letelier, the Chilean exile leader. Letelier had been a minister in the Allende government, which had been overthrown by Kissinger in 1973. Letelier, along with Ronnie Moffitt of the Washington Institute for Policy Studies, died on September 21, 1976 in the explosion of a car bomb on Sheridan Circle, in the heart of Washington's Embassy Row district along Massachusetts Avenue.

Relatively few cases of international terrorism have taken place on the territory of the United States, but this was certainly an exception. Bush's activities before and after this assassination amount to one of the most bizarre episodes in the annals of secret intelligence operations.

One of the assassins of Letelier was unquestionably one Michael Vernon Townley, a CIA agent who had worked for David Atlee Phillips in Chile. Phillips had become the director of the CIA's Western Hemisphere operations after the overthrow of Allende and the advent of the dictatorship of Augusto Pinochet Ugarte, and its Milton Friedman/Chicago School economic policies. In 1975, Phillips founded AFIO, the Association of Former Intelligence Officers, which has supported George Bush in every campaign he has ever waged since that time. Townley, as a "former" CIA agent, had gone to work for the DINA, the Chilean secret police, and had been assigned by the DINA as its liaison man with a group called CORU. CORU was the acronym for Command of United Revolutionary Organizations, a united front of four anti-Castro Cuban organizations based primarily in the neighborhood of Miami called Little Havana. With CORU, we are back in the milieu of Miami anti-Castro Cubans, whose political godfather George Bush had been since very early in the 1960s. CORU was at that time working together with the intelligence services of Chile's Pinochet, Paraguay's Alfredo Stroessner, and Nicaragua's Anastasio Somoza, for operations against common enemies, including Chilean left-wing emigrés and Castro assets. Soon after the foundation of CORU, bombs began to go off at the Cuban Mission to the United Nations in New York.

During this period, a Miami doctor named Orlando Bosch was arrested, allegedly because he had been planning to assassinate Henry Kissinger, and that ostensibly because of Kissinger's concessions to Castro. During the same period, the Chilean DINA was mounting its so-called Operation Condor, a plan to assassinate emigré opponents of the Pinochet dictatorship.[28]

It was under these circumstances that the U.S. ambassador to Chile, George Landau, sent a cable to the State Department with the singular request that two agents of the DINA be allowed to enter the United States with Paraguayan passports. One of these agents is likely to have been Townley. The cable also indicated that the two DINA agents also wanted to meet with Gen. Vernon Walters, the outgoing Deputy Director of Central Intelligence, and so the cable also went to Langley. Here the cable was read by Walters, and also passed into the hands of Director George Bush. Bush not only had this cable in his hands; Bush and Walters discussed the contents of the cable and what to do about it, including whether Walters ought to meet with the DINA agents. The cable also reached the desk of Henry Kissinger. One of Landau's questions appears to have been whether the mission of the DINA men had been approved in advance by Langley; his cable was accompanied by photocopies of the Paraguayan passports. (Later on, in 1980, Bush denied that he had ever seen this cable; he had not just been out of the loop, he claims; he had been in China.) The red Studebaker hacks, including Bush himself in his campaign autobiography, do not bother denying anything about the Letelier case; they simply omit it.[29]

On August 4, on the basis of the conversations between Bush and Vernon Walters, the CIA sent a reply from Walters to Landau, stating that the former "was unaware of the visit and that his Agency did not desire to have any contact with the Chileans." Ambassador Landau responded by revoking the visas that he had already granted and telling the Immigration and Naturalization Service to put the two DINA men on their watch list to be picked up if they tried to enter the United States. The two DINA men entered the United States anyway on August 22, with no apparent difficulty. The DINA men reached Washington, and it is clear that they were hardly traveling incognito: They appear to have asked a Chilean embassy official to call the CIA to repeat their request for a meeting.

According to other reports, the DINA men met with New York Senator James Buckley, the brother of conservative columnist William Buckley of Skull and Bones. It is also said that the DINA men met with Frank Terpil, a close associate of Ed Wilson, and no stranger to the operations of the Shackley-Clines Enterprise. According to one such version, "Townley met with Frank Terpil one week before the Letelier murder, on the same day that he met with Senator James Buckley and aides in New York City. The explosives sent to the United States on Chilean airlines were to replace explosives supplied by Edwin Wilson, according to a source close to the office of Assistant U.S. Attorney Lawrence Barcella."[30] The bomb that killed Letelier and Moffitt was of the same type that the FBI believed that Ed Wilson was selling, with the same timer mechanism.

Bush therefore had plenty of warning that a DINA operation was about to take place in Washington, and it was no secret that it would be wetwork. As authors John Dinges and Saul Landau point out, when the DINA hitmen arrived in Washington they "alerted the CIA by having a Chilean embassy employee call General Walters' office at the CIA's Langley headquarters. It is quite beyond belief that the CIA is so lax in its counterespionage functions that it would simply have ignored a clandestine operation by a foreign intelligence service in Washington, D.C., or anywhere in the United States. It is equally implausible that Bush, Walters, [Ambassador George] Landau and other officials were unaware of the chain of international assassinations that had been attributed to DINA."[31] One might say that Bush had been an accessory before the fact.

Bush's complicity deepens when we turn to the post-assassination coverup. The prosecutor in the Letelier-Moffitt murders was Assistant U.S. Attorney Eugene M. Propper. Nine days after the assassinations, Propper was trying without success to get some cooperation from the CIA, since it was obvious enough to anyone that the Chilean regime was the prime suspect in the killing of one of its most prominent political opponents. The CIA had been crudely stonewalling Propper. He had even been unable to secure the requisite security clearance to see documents in the case. Then Propper received a telephone call from Stanley Pottinger, assistant attorney general in charge of the Civil Rights Division of the Justice Department. Pottinger said that he had been in contact with members of the Institute for Policy Studies, who had argued that the Civil Rights Division ought to take over the Letelier case because of its clear political implications. Propper argued that he should keep control of the case since the Protection of Foreign Officials Act gave him jurisdiction. Pottinger agreed that Propper was right, and that he ought to keep the case. When Pottinger offered to be of help in any possible way, Propper asked if Pottinger could expedite cooperation with the CIA.

As Propper later recounted this conversation:

> Instant, warm confidence shot through the telephone line. The assistant attorney general replied that he happened to be a personal friend of the CIA Director himself, George Bush. Pottinger called him

"George." For him, the CIA Director was only a phone call away. Would Propper like an appointment? By that afternoon he [an FBI agent working on the case] and Pottinger were scheduled for lunch with Director Bush at CIA headquarters on Monday. A Justice Department limousine would pick them up at noon. Propper whistled to himself. This was known in Washington as access.[32]

At CIA headquarters, Pottinger introduced Propper to Director Bush, and Bush introduced the two lawyers to Tony Lapham, his general counsel. There was some polite conversation. Then,

> when finally called on to state his business, Propper said that the Letelier-Moffitt murders were more than likely political assassinations, and that the investigation would probably move outside the United States into the Agency's realm of foreign intelligence. Therefore, Propper wanted CIA cooperation in the form of reports from within Chile, reports on assassins, reports on foreign operatives entering the United States, and the like. He wanted anything he could get that might bear upon the murders.

If Bush had wanted to be candid, he could have informed Propper that he had been informed of the coming of the DINA team twice, once before they left South America and once when they had arrived in Washington. But Bush never volunteered this highly pertinent information. Instead, he went into a sophisticated stonewall routine:

> "Look," said Bush, "I'm appalled by the bombing. Obviously we can't allow people to come right here into the capital and kill foreign diplomats and American citizens like this. It would be a hideous precedent. So, as Director, I want to help you. As an American citizen, I want to help. But, as Director, I also know that the Agency can't help in a lot of situations like this. We've got some problems. Tony, tell him what they are."

Lapham launched into a consummate Aristotelian obfuscation, recounted in Branch and Propper's *Labrinth*. Lapham and Propper finally agreed that they could handle the matter best through an exchange of letters between the CIA Director and Attorney General Levi. George Bush summed up: "If you two come up with something that Tony thinks will protect us, we'll be all right." The date was October 4, 1976.

Contrary to that pledge, Bush and the CIA began actively to sabotage Propper's investigation in public as well as behind the scenes. By Saturday, the *Washington Post* was reporting many details of Propper's arrangement with the CIA. Even more interesting was the following item in the "Periscope" column of *Newsweek* magazine of October 11: "After studying FBI and other field investigations, the CIA has concluded that the Chilean secret police were not involved in the death of Orlando Letelier. . . . The agency reached its decision because the bomb was too crude to be the work of experts and because the murder, coming while Chile's rulers were wooing U.S. support, could only damage the Santiago regime."

On November 1, the *Washington Post* reported a leak from Bush personally: "CIA officials say . . . they believe that operatives of the present Chilean military junta did not take part in Letelier's killing. According to informed sources, CIA Director Bush expressed this view in a conversation last week with Secretary of State Kissinger, the sources said. What evidence the CIA has obtained to support this initial conclusion was not disclosed."

Most remarkably, Bush is reported to have flown to Miami on November 8 with the purpose or pretext of taking "a walking tour of little Havana." As author Donald Freed tells it, "Actually [Bush] met with the Miami FBI Special Agent in Charge Julius Matson and the chief of the anti-Castro terrorism squad. According to a source close to the meeting, Bush warned the FBI against allowing the investigation to go any further than the lowest level Cubans."[33]

In a meeting presided over by Pottinger, Propper was only able to get Lapham to agree that the Justice Department could ask the CIA to report any information on the Letelier murder that might relate to the security of the United States against foreign intervention. It was two years before any word of the July–August cables was divulged.

Ultimately, some low-level Cubans were convicted in a trial that saw Townley plea bargain and get off with a lighter sentence than the rest. Material about Townley under his various aliases strangely disappeared from the Immigration and Naturalization Service files, and records of the July–August cable traffic with Vernon Walters (and Bush) was expunged. No doubt there had been obstruction of justice; no doubt there had been a coverup.

Team A and Team B

Now what about the intelligence product of the CIA, in particular the National Intelligence Estimates that are the centerpiece of the CIA's work? Here Bush was to oversee a maneuver to markedly enhance the influence of the pro-Zionist wing of the intelligence community.

In June 1976, Bush accepted a proposal from Leo Cherne to carry out an experiment in "competitive analysis" in the area of National Intelligence Estimates of Soviet air defenses, Soviet missile accuracy, and overall Soviet strategic objectives. Bush and Cherne decided to conduct the competitive analysis by commissioning two separate groups, each of which would present and argue for its own conclusions. On the one, Team A would be the CIA's own National Intelligence Officers and their staffs. But there would also be a separate Team B, a group of ostensibly independent outside experts.

The group leader of Team B was Harvard history professor Richard Pipes, who was working in the British Museum in London when he was appointed by Bush and Cherne.

The liaison between Pipes's Team B and Team A, the official CIA, was provided by John Paisley, who had earlier served as the liaison between Langley and the McCord-Hunt-Liddy Plumbers. In this sense, Paisley served as the staff director of the Team A-Team B experiment. Pipes then began choosing the members of Team B. First, he selected from a list provided by the CIA two military men, Lt. Gen. John Vogt and Brig. Gen. Jasper Welch, Jr., both of the Air Force. Pipes then added seven additional members: Paul Nitze; Gen. Daniel Graham, the retiring head of the Defense Intelligence Agency; Professor William van Cleave of the University of Southern California; former U.S. Ambassador to Moscow Foy Kohler; Paul Wolfowitz of the Arms Control and Disarmament Agency; Thomas Wolfe of the RAND Corporation; and Seymour Weiss, a former top State Department official. Two other choices by Pipes were rejected by Bush.

Team B began meeting during late August of 1976. Paisley and Don Suda provided Team B with the same raw intelligence being used by National Intelligence Officer Howard Stoertz's Team A. Team B's basic conclusion was that the Soviet military preparations were not exclusively defensive, but rather represented the attempt to acquire a first-strike capability that would allow the U.S.S.R. to unleash and prevail in thermonuclear war. The U.S. would face a window of vulnerability during the 1980s. But it is clear from Pipes's own discussion of the debate,[34] that Team B was less interested in the Soviet Union and its capabilities than in seizing hegemony in the intelligence and think-tank community in preparation for seizing the key posts in the Republican administration that might follow Carter in 1980. Pipes was livid when, at the final Team A-Team B meeting, he was not allowed to sit at Bush's table for lunch.

The argument in Team B quarters was that since the Soviets were turning aggressive once again, the U.S. must do everything possible to strengthen the only staunch and reliable American ally in the Middle East or possibly anywhere in the world, Israel. This meant not just that Israel had to be financed without stint, but that Israel had to be brought into Central America, the Far East, and Africa. There was even a design for a new NATO, constructed around Israel, while junking the old NATO because it was absorbing vital U.S. resources needed by Israel.

By contrast, Team B supporters like Richard Perle, who served as Assistant Secretary of Defense under Reagan, were bitterly hostile to the Strategic Defense Initiative, which was plainly the only rational response to the Soviet buildup, which was very real indeed. The "window of vulnerability" argument had merit, but the policy conclusions favored by Team B had none, since their idea of responding to the Soviet threat was, once again, to subordinate everything to Israeli demands.

Team A and Team B were supposed to be secret, but leaks appeared in the *Boston Globe* in October. Pipes was surprised to find an even more detailed account of Team B and its grim estimate of Soviet intent in the *New York Times* shortly after Christmas, but Paisley told him that Bush and CIA official Richard Lehman had already been talking to the press, and urged Pipes to begin to offer some interviews of his own.[35]

Typically enough, Bush appeared on "Face the Nation" early in the new year, before the inauguration of the new President, Jimmy Carter, to say that he was "appalled" by the leaks of Team B's conclusions. Bush confessed that "outside expertise has enormous appeal to me." He refused to discuss the Team B conclusions themselves, but did say that he wanted to "gun down" speculation that the CIA had leaked a tough estimate of the Soviet Union's military buildup in order to stop Carter from cutting the defense budget. That speculation "just couldn't be further from the truth," said Bush, who was thus caught lying neither for the first nor last time in his existence.

Congress soon got into the act, and George Bush testified at a closed hearing of the Senate Foreign Relations Committee on January 18, 1977. It turned out that Team B and its "worst-case" scenario enjoyed strong support from Hubert Humphrey, Clifford Case, and Jacob Javits.

After the Team B conclusions had been bruited around the world, Pipes became a leading member of the Committee on the Present Danger, where his fellow Team B veteran, Paul Nitze, was already ensconced, along with Eugene V. Rostow, Dean Rusk, Lane Kirkland, Max Kampelman, Richard Allen, David Packard and Henry Fowler. About 30 members of the Committee on the Present Danger went on to become high officials of the Reagan administration.

Ronald Reagan himself embraced the "window of vulnerability" thesis, which worked as well for him as the bomber gap and missile gap arguments had worked in previous elections. When the Reagan administration was being assembled, Bush and James Baker had a lot to say about who got what appointments. Bush was the founder of Team B, and that is the fundamental reason why such pro-Zionist neoconservatives as Max Kampelman, Richard Perle, Steven Bryen, Noel Koch, Paul Wolfowitz and Dov Zakem showed up in the Reagan administration.

In a grim postlude to the Team B exercise, Bush's hand-picked staff director for the operation, John Paisley, the Soviet analyst (Paisley was the former deputy director of the CIA's Office of Strategic Research) and CIA liaison to the Plumbers, disappeared on September 24, 1978 while sailing on Chesapeake Bay in his sloop, the *Brillig*. Several days later, a body was found floating in the bay in an advanced state of decomposition, and with a gun shot wound behind the left ear. The corpse was weighted down by two sets of ponderous diving belts. The body was four inches shorter than Paisley's own height, and Paisley's wife later asserted that the body found was not that of her husband. Despite all this, the body was positively identified as Paisley's, the death summarily ruled a suicide, and the body quickly cremated at a funeral home approved by the Office of Security. Paisley had been involved along with Angleton in the debriefing and managing of Soviet defectors like Nosenko and Nikolai Artamonov ("Nick Shadrin"), and various aspects of this case show that the Bush-Cherne Team B had not really ceased its operations after 1976–77, but had continued to function. Some have attempted to identify Paisley as Deep Throat. Others have suggested that he was a KGB mole. Either story, if true, might lead to highly embarrassing consequences for George Bush.[36]

The question raised by these cases was almost universally dodged during the 1988 election campaign: "Do the American people really want to elect a former director of the CIA as their President?" as Tom Wicker posed it in the *New York Times* of April 29, 1988. "That's hardly been discussed so far; but it seems obvious that a CIA chief might well be privy to the kind of 'black' secrets that could later make him—as a public figure—subject to blackmail." Here is one area where we can be sure that we have only scratched the surface.

Parting Shots

As he managed the formidable world-wide capabilities of the CIA during 1976, Bush was laying the groundwork for his personal advancement to higher office and greater power in the 1980s. As we have seen, there was some intermittent speculation during the year that, in spite of what Ford had promised the Senate, Bush might show up as Ford's running mate after all. But, at the Republican convention, Ford chose Kansas Senator Bob Dole for Vice President. If Ford had won the election, Bush would certainly have attempted to secure a further promotion, perhaps to Secretary of State, Defense, or Treasury as a springboard for a new presidential bid of his own in 1980. But if Carter won the election, Bush would attempt to raise the banner of the non-political status of the CIA in order to convince Carter to let him stay at Langley during the period 1977–81 as a "non-partisan" administrator.

In the close 1976 election, Carter prevailed by vote fraud in New York, Ohio and other states, but Ford was convinced by William Nelson and Happy Rockefeller, as well as by his own distraught wife Betty, that he must concede in order to preserve the work of "healing" that he had accomplished since Watergate. Carter would therefore enter the White House.

Bush prepared to make his bid for continuity at the CIA. Shortly after the election, he was scheduled to journey to Plains to brief Carter with the help of his deputy Henry Knoche. The critical meeting with Carter went very badly indeed. Bush took Carter aside and argued that in 1960 and 1968, CIA directors were retained during presidential transitions, and that it would make Carter look good if he did the same. Carter signaled that he wasn't interested. Then Bush lamely stammered that if Carter wanted his own man in Langley, Bush would be willing to resign, which is of course standard procedure for all agency heads when a new President takes office. Carter said that that was indeed exactly what he wanted, and that he would have his own new DCI ready by January 21, 1977. Bush and Knoche then briefed Carter and his people for some six hours. Carter insiders told the press that Bush's briefing had been a "disaster." "Jimmy just wasn't impressed with Bush," said a key Carter staffer.[37]

Bush and Knoche then flew back to Washington, and on the plane Bush wrote a memo for Henry Kissinger describing his exchanges with Carter. At midnight, Bush drove to Kissinger's home and briefed him for an hour.

Bush left Langley with Carter's inauguration, leaving Knoche to serve a couple of months as acting DCI. In early February, Bush wrote again to Leo Cherne, with whom he was now on a first-name basis:

> . . . The past has been fantastic; but now I am determined to look to the future. I know it will be full of challenge. I hope it holds frequent contacts with Leo Cherne.
>
> I will follow with interest the President's decisions on PFIAB. Holler if I can ever be of help to you. I value our friendship.[38]

Carter abolished PFIAB and fired Cherne from the IOB. George Bush now turned to his family business of international banking.

Notes for Chapter XIV

1. Nathan Miller, *Spying for America* (New York: Paragon House, 1989), p. 399. Box 5.

2. See Loch K. Johnson, *A Season of Inquiry: The Senate Intelligence Investigation* (University Press of Kentucky, 1985), pp. 108–9.

3. *Ibid.,* pp. 115–16.

4. Gerald R. Ford Library, Philip Buchen Files, Box 24. Article is from *Houston Post,* Nov. 8, 1975.

5. Collins to Ford, Nov. 12, 1975, Ford Library, John O. Marsh Files, Box 1.

6. Nedzi to Ford, Dec. 12, 1975, Ford Library, John O. Marsh Files, Box 1.

7. Roth to Bush, Nov. 20, 1975, Ford Library, John O. Marsh Files, Box 1.

8. Ford Library, William T. Kendall Files, Box 7.

9. U.S. Senate, Committee on Armed Services, Nomination of George Bush to be Director of Central Intelligence, Dec. 15–16, 1975, p. 10.

10. Memo of Dec. 16, 1975 from O'Donnell to Marsh through Friedersdorf on the likely vote in the Stennis Senate Armed Services Committee. Ford Library, William T. Kendall Files, Box 7.

11. For an account of the exploitation of the Welch incident by the Ford administration, see Johnson, *op. cit.,* pp. 161–62.

12. For an account of the leaking of the Pike Committee Report and the situation in late Jan. and Feb. 1976, see Daniel Schorr, *Clearing the Air* (Boston: Houghton Mifflin, 1977) especially pp. 179–207, and Johnson, *op. cit.,* pp. 172–91.

13. Johnson, *op. cit.,* p. 180.

14. *Ibid.,* p. 182.

15. Thomas Powers, *The Man Who Kept the Secrets: Richard Helms and the CIA* (New York: Knopf, 1979), p. 12.

16. William Colby, *Honorable Men* (New York: Simon and Schuster, 1978), p. 452.

17. On Murphy and Noriega, see Frank McNeil, *War and Peace in Central America* (New York: Scribner, 1988), p. 278.

18. See John Prados, *Presidents' Secret Wars* (New York: William Morrow, 1986); Powers, *op. cit.;* and John Ranelagh, *The Agency: The Rise and Decline of the CIA* (New York: Simon and Schuster, 1987).

19. Cord Meyer, *Facing Reality: From World Federalism to the CIA* (Washington, D.C.: University Press of America, 1982), pp. 225–26.

20. *Washington Post,* Aug. 10, 1988.

21. Ford Library, Philip W. Buchen Files, Box 2.

22. For Ford's reorganization, see Johnson, *op. cit.,* pp. 194–97, and *New York Times,* Feb. 18, 1976.

23. Nathan Miller, *Spying For America: The Hidden History of U.S. Intelligence* (New York: Paragon House, 1989), pp. 402–3.

24. For Koreagate, see Robert B. Boettcher, *Gifts of Deceit* (New York: Holt Rinehart and Winston, 1980).

25. Scott Armstrong and Jeff Nason, "Company Man," *Mother Jones,* October 1988.

26. David Corn, "The Same Old Dirty Tricks," *The Nation,* Aug. 23, 1988.

27. *Ibid.*

28. Accounts of the Letelier affair include John Dinges and Saul Landau, *Assassination on Embassy Row* (New York: Pantheon Books, 1980); Donald Freed, *Death in Washington* (Westport, Connecticut: Lawrence Hill, 1980); and Armstrong and Nason, *op. cit.*

29. See Armstrong and Nason, *op. cit.*, p. 43.

30. Freed, *op. cit.*, p. 174.

31. Dinges and Landau, *op. cit.*, p. 384.

32. Taylor Branch and Eugene M. Propper, *Labyrinth* (New York: Viking Press, 1982), p. 72.

33. Freed, *op. cit.*, p. 174.

34. Richard Pipes, "Team B: The Reality Behind the Myth," *Commentary*, Oct. 1986.

35. *Ibid.*, p. 34. Pipes makes clear that it was Bush and Richard Lehman who both leaked to David Binder of the *New York Times*. Lehman also encouraged Pipes to leak. The version offered by William R. Corson, Susan B. Trento and Joseph J. Trento in *Widows* (New York: Crown, 1989), namely that Paisley did the leaking, may also be true, but will not exonerate Bush. The authors of *Widows* are in grave danger of being banished to the red Studebaker school of coverup in that they ignore Pipes's account and its included fingering of Bush as the lead leaker.

36. See Corson et al., *op. cit.*

37. Evans and Novak column, *Houston Post*, Dec. 1, 1976. For the pro-Bush account of these events, see Nicholas King, *George Bush: A Biography* (New York: Dodd, Mead & Company, 1980), pp. 109–10.

38. Ford Library, Leo Cherne Papers, Box 1.

XV
CAMPAIGN 1980

*Le mercennarie et ausiliarie sono inutili e pericolose; e, se uno tiene
lo stato suo fondato in sulle arme mercennarie, non sará mai fermo
né sicuro.* *
   —Machiavelli, *The Prince*

Shortly after leaving Langley, Bush asserted his birthright as an
international financier in the way he had indicated to his close friend
Leo Cherne; that is to say, by becoming a member of the board of
directors of a large bank. On February 22, 1977, Robert H. Stewart
III, the chairman of the holding company for First International
Bankshares of Dallas, announced that Bush would become the chairman of the executive committee of First International Bank of Houston, and would simultaneously become a director of First International Bankshares Ltd. of London, a merchant bank owned by First
International Bankshares, Inc. Bush also became a director of First
International Bankshares, Inc. ("Interfirst"), which was the Dallas-
based holding company for the entire international group.

Thus, less than two years before Margaret Thatcher came to
power, Bush acquired the status of investment banker in the City of
London, the home of the Eurodollar market and the home of British
imperial financial circles in which such figures as Lord Victor Rothschild, Tiny Rowland, the Sultan of Brunei, King Fahd of Saudi
Arabia, and the Emir of Kuwait were at home. An annual fee of

---

*Mercenaries and auxiliaries are useless and dangerous, and if anyone founds his
state on mercenary forces, that state will never be stable or secure.

$75,000 as a "consultant" also sweetened this pot. During the 1988 campaign, Bush gave the implacable stonewall to any questions about the services he performed for the First International Bankshares group or about any other aspects of his business activities during the pre-1980 interlude. Interfirst was then the largest bank in Texas and was reportedly running speculation all over South America, China and Europe.

Later, after the Reagan-Bush orgy of speculation and usury had ruined the Texas economy, the Texas commercial banks began to collapse into bankruptcy. Interfirst merged with RepublicBank during 1987 to form First RepublicBank, which became the biggest commercial bank in Texas. Bankruptcy overtook the new colossus just a few months later, but federal regulators delayed their inevitable intervention until after the Texas primary, in the spring of 1988, in order to avoid a potentially acute embarrassment for Bush. Once Bush had the presidential nomination locked up, the Federal Deposit Insurance Corporation, with the connivance of the IRS, awarded the assets of First RepublicBank to the North Carolina National Bank in exchange for no payment whatsoever on the part of NCNB (now NationsBank), which is reputedly a darling of the intelligence community.

During the heady days of Bush's directorship at Interfirst, the bank retained a law firm in which one Lawrence Gibbs was a partner. Two partners of Gibbs "joined three representatives of the energy department of Interfirst Bank on a trip to Peking, where they conducted a week-long seminar on financing the production of natural resources for the Oil and Gas Ministry of the People's Republic of China."[1] This visit was made in the context of trips to China by Bush for the purpose of setting up a lucrative oil concession for J. Hugh Liedtke of Pennzoil, Bush's old business partner.

Gibbs, a clear Bush asset, was made Commissioner of the Internal Revenue Service on August 4, 1986. Here, he engineered the sweetheart deal for NCNB by decreeing $1.6 billion in tax breaks for this bank. This is typical of the massive favors and graft for pro-Bush financier interests at the expense of the taxpayer which are the hallmark of the Bush machine. Lawrence Gibbs also approved IRS participation in the October 6, 1986 federal-state police raid against premises and persons associated with the political movement of Lyndon H. LaRouche in Leesburg, Virginia. This raid was a leading part of the Bush machine's long-term effort to eliminate centers of political opposition to Bush's 1988 presidential bid. And LaRouche had been a key adversary of Bush dating back to the 1979–80 New Hampshire primary campaign, as we will shortly document.

Bush also joined the board of Purolator Oil Company in Rahway, New Jersey, where his crony, Wall Street raider Nicholas Brady (later Bush's Secretary of the Treasury) was the chairman. Bush also joined the board of Eli Lilly & Co., a very large and very sinister pharmaceutical company. The third board Bush joined was that of Texas Gulf, Inc. Bush's total 1977 rakeoff from the four companies with which he was involved was $112,000, according to Bush's 1977 tax return.

During this time, Bush became a director of Baylor Medical College, a trustee of Trinity Medical College in San Antonio, and a trustee of Phillips Academy in Andover, Mass.

Bush also found time to line his pockets in a series of high-yield deals that begin to give us some flavor of what would later be described as the "financial excesses of the 1980s," in which Bush's circle was to play a decisive role.

A typical Bush venture of this period was Ponderosa Forest Apartments, a highly remunerative speculative play in real estate. Ponderosa bought up a 180-unit apartment complex near Houston that was in financial trouble, gentrified the interiors, and hiked the rents. Horace T. Ardinger, a Dallas real estate man who was among Bush's partners in this deal, described the transaction as "a good tax gimmick . . . and a typical Texas joint venture offering."

According to Bush's tax returns from 1977 through 1985, the Ponderosa partnership accrued to Bush a paper loss of $225,160, which allowed him to avoid payment of some $100,000 in federal taxes alone, plus a direct profit of over $14,000 and a capital gain of $217,278. This type of windfall represents precisely the form of real estate swindle that contributed to the Texas real estate and banking crisis of the mid-1980s. The deal illustrates one of the important ways in which the federal tax base has been eroded through real estate scams. We also see why it is no surprise that the one fiscal innovation which has earned Bush's sustained attention is the idea of a reduction in the capital gains tax to allow those who engage in swindles like these to pay an even smaller federal tax bite. It is also typical of the Bush style that Fred M. Zeder, the promoter of the Ponderosa deal, was made U.S. ambassador to the Marshall Islands in the South Pacific by the Bush administration after he had contributed over $30,000 to Bush's 1988 campaign.

But Bush's main preoccupation during these years was to assemble a political machine with which he could bludgeon his way to power. After his numerous frustrations of the past, Bush was resolved to organize a campaign that would go far beyond the innocuous exercise of appealing for citizens' votes. If such a machine were actually to succeed in seizing power in Washington, tendencies toward the creation of an authoritarian police state would inevitably increase.

The Spook Campaign Machine

One of the central figures of the Bush effort would be James Baker III, Bush's friend of ten years' standing. Baker's power base derived first of all from his family's Houston law firm, Baker & Botts, which was founded just after the end of the Civil War by defeated partizans of the Confederate cause. Judge Peter Gray and Walter Browne Botts established a law partnership in 1866, and this became Baker & Botts during the 1870s when Captain James A. Baker (the great-grandfather of Bush's Secretary of State) joined the firm.

Baker & Botts founder Peter Gray had been Assistant Treasurer of the Confederate States of America and financial supervisor of the CSA's "Trans-Mississippi Department." Gray, acting on orders of Confederate Secretary of State Robert Toombs, financed the subversive work of Confederate Gen. Albert Pike among the Indian tribes of the Southwest. The close of the war in 1865 had found Pike hiding in Canada, and Toombs in exile in England. Pike was excluded from the general U.S. amnesty for rebels because he was thought to have induced Indians to commit massacres and war crimes.

Pike and Toombs reestablished the "Southern Jurisdiction" of the Scottish Rite of Freemasonry, of which Pike had been the leader in the slave states before the Civil War. Pike's deputy, one Phillip C. Tucker, returned from Scottish Rite indoctrination in Great Britain to set up a Scottish Rite lodge in Houston in the spring of 1867. Tucker designated Walter Browne Botts and his relative Benjamin Botts as the leaders of this new Scottish Rite lodge.[2] The policy of the Scottish Rite was to regroup unreconstructed Confederates to secure the disenfranchisement of black citizens and to promote Anglophile domination of finance and business.

By the beginning of the twentieth century, there were two great powers dominating Texas: On the one hand, the railroad empire of E.H. Harriman, served by the law firm of Baker & Botts; and on the other, the British-trained political operative Colonel Edward M. House, the controller of President Woodrow Wilson. The close relation between Baker & Botts and the Harriman interests has remained in place down to the present. And since the time that Captain James A. Baker founded the Texas Commerce Bank, the Baker family has helped the London-New York axis run the Texas banking system.

In 1901, the discovery of large oil deposits in Texas offered great promise for the future economic development of the state, but also attracted the Anglo-American oil cartel. The Baker family law firm in Texas, like the Bush and Dulles families in New York, was aligned with the Harriman-Rockefeller cartel. Robert S. Lovett, a Baker & Botts partner from 1882 on, later became the chairman of Harriman's Union Pacific Railroad and chief counsel to E.H. Harriman.

The Bakers were prominent in supporting eugenics and utopian-feudalist social engineering. Captain James A. Baker, so the story goes, the grandfather of the current boss of Foggy Bottom, solved the murder of his client William Marsh Rice and took control of Rice's huge estate. Baker used the money to start Rice University and became the chairman of the school's board of trustees. Baker sought to create a center for diffusion of racist eugenics, and for this purpose brought in Julian Huxley of the infamous British oligarchical family to found the biology program at Rice starting in 1912.[3] Huxley was the vice president of the British Eugenics Society and actually helped to organize "race science" programs for the Nazi Interior Ministry, before becoming the founding director general of UNESCO in 1946–48. Bush was named adjunct professor at Rice after his CIA term ended.

James A. Baker III was born April 28, 1930, in the fourth generation of his family's wealth. Baker holdings have included Exxon, Mobil, Atlantic Richfield, Standard Oil of California, Standard Oil of Indiana, Kerr-McGee, Merck, and Freeport Minerals. Baker also held stock in some large New York banks during the time that he was negotiating the Latin American debt crisis in his capacity as Secretary of the Treasury.[4]

James Baker grew up in patrician surroundings. His social profile has been described as "Tex-prep." Like his father, James III attended the Hill School near Philadelphia, and then went on to Princeton, where he was a member of the Ivy Club, a traditional preserve of Eastern Anglophile Liberal Establishment oligarchs. Nancy Reagan was enchanted by Baker's sartorial elegance and smooth savoir faire. Nancy liked Baker far more than she ever did Bush, and this was a key advantage for Bush-Baker during the factional struggles of the Reagan years.

Baker & Botts maintains an "anti-nepotism" policy, so James III became a boss of Houston's Andrews, Kurth, Campbell & Jones law firm, a satellite of Baker & Botts. Baker's relation to Bush extends across both law firms: In 1977, Baker & Botts partner Blaine Kerr became president of Pennzoil, and in 1979, Baker & Botts partner B.J. Mackin became chairman of Zapata Corporation.

Baker & Botts have always represented Zapata, and are often listed as counsel for Schlumberger, the oil services firm. James Baker and his Andrews, Kurth partners were the Houston attorneys for First International Bank of Houston when George Bush was chairman of the bank's executive committee.

During the 1980 campaign, Baker became the chairman of the Reagan-Bush campaign committee, while fellow Texan Bob Strauss was chairman of the Carter-Mondale campaign. But Baker and Strauss were at the very same time business partners in Herman Brothers, one of America's largest beer distributors. Bush Democrat Strauss later went to Moscow as Bush's ambassador to the U.S.S.R., and later, to Russia.

Another leading Bush supporter was Ray Cline. During 1979, it was Ray Cline who had gone virtually public with a loose and informal, but highly effective, campaign network mainly composed of former intelligence officers. Cline had been the CIA station chief in Taiwan from 1958 to 1962. He had been deputy director of central intelligence from 1962 to 1966, and had then gone on to direct the intelligence-gathering operation at the State Department. Cline became a de facto White House official during the first Bush administration, and wrote the White House boiler plate entitled "National Security Strategy of the United States," under which the Gulf war was carried out.

Cline later said that his approach to Bush's 1979–80 primary campaign was to "organize something like one of my old CIA staffs." "I found there was a tremendous constituency for the CIA when everyone in Washington was still urinating all over it," commented Cline to the *Washington Post* of March 1, 1980. "It's panned out almost too good to be true. The country is waking up just in time for George's candidacy."

Heading up the Bush campaign muckraking "research" staff was Stephan Halper, Ray Cline's son-in-law and a former official of the Nixon White House.

A member of Halper's staff was a CIA veteran named Robert Gambino. Gambino had held the sensitive post of director of the CIA's Office of Security. It will be recalled that the Office of Security constitutes the interface between Langley and state and local police departments all across the United States, with whom it must cooperate to protect the security of CIA buildings and CIA personnel, as for example in cases in which these latter may run afoul of the law. The Office of Security is reputed to possess extensive files on the domestic activities of American citizens. David Aaron, Brzezinski's deputy at the Carter National Security Council, recalled that some high Carter officials were "upset" that Gambino had gone to work for the Bush camp. According to Aaron, "several [CIA] people took early retirement and went to work for Bush's so-called security staff. The thing that upset us, was that a guy who has been head of security for the CIA has been privy to a lot of dossiers, and the possibility of abuse was quite high, although we never heard of any occasion when Gambino called someone up and forced them to do something for the campaign."[5]

Other high-level spooks active in the Bush campaign included Lt. Gen. Sam V. Wilson and Lt. Gen. Harold A. Aaron, both former directors of the Defense Intelligence Agency. Another enthusiastic Bushman was retired Gen. Richard Stillwell, formerly the CIA's chief of covert operations for the Far East. The former deputy director for operations, Theodore Shackley, was also on board, reportedly as a speechwriter, but more likely for somewhat heavier work.

According to one estimate, at least 25 former intelligence officials worked directly for the Bush campaign. As Bill Peterson of the *Washington Post* wrote on March 1, 1980, "Simply put, no presidential campaign in recent memory—perhaps ever—has attracted as much support from the intelligence community as the campaign of former CIA Director George Bush."

Further intelligence veterans among the Bushmen included Daniel C. Arnold, the former CIA station chief in Bangkok, Thailand, who retired early to join the campaign during 1979. Harry Webster, a former clandestine agent, became a member of Bush's paid staff for the Florida primary. CIA veteran Bruce Rounds was Bush's "director of operations" during the key New Hampshire primary. Also on board with the Bushmen was Jon R. Thomas, a former clandestine operative who had been listed as a State Department official during a tour of duty in Spain, and who later worked on terrorism and drug-trafficking at the State Department. Andrew Falkiewicz, the former spokesman of the CIA in Langley, attended some of Bush's pre-campaign brainstorming sessions as a consultant on foreign policy matters.

One leading bastion of the Bushmen was predictably David Atlee Phillips's AFIO, the Association of Former Intelligence Officers. Jack Coakley was a former director and Bush's campaign coordinator for Virginia. He certified that at the AFIO annual meeting in the fall of 1979, he counted 190 "Bush for President" buttons among 240 delegates to the convention.[6]

James Baker was the obvious choice to be Bush's campaign manager. He had served Bush in this function in the failed Senate campaign of 1970. During the Ford years, Baker had advanced to become Deputy Secretary of Commerce. Baker had been the manager of Ford's failed 1976 campaign. Bringing Baker into the Bush campaign meant that he could bring with him many of the Ford political operatives and much of the Ford political apparatus and volunteers in a number of states. In 1978, Baker had attempted to get himself elected Attorney General of Texas, but had been defeated.

David Keene was political adviser. And, as always, no Bush campaign would be complete without Robert Mosbacher heading up the national finance operation. Mosbacher's experience, as we have seen, reached back to the Bill Liedtke conveyances to Maurice Stans of the CREEP in 1972. Teaming up with Mosbacher were Fred Bush in Houston and Jack Sloat in Washington.

With the help of Baker and Mosbacher, Bush began to set up political campaign committees that could be used to convoy quasi-legal "soft money" into his campaign coffers. This is the classic stratagem of setting up political action committees that are registered with the Federal Election Commission for the alleged purpose of channeling funds into the campaigns of deserving Republican (or Democratic) candidates. In reality, almost all of the money is used for the presidential candidate's own staff, office, mailings, travel and related expenses. Bush's principal vehicle for this type of funding was called the Fund for Limited Government. During the first six months of 1987, this group collected $99,000 and spent $46,000, of which only $2,500 went to other candidates. The rest was in effect spent to finance Bush's campaign preparations. Bush had a second PAC called the Congressional Leadership Committee, with Senator Howard Baker and Representative John Rhodes on the board, which did manage to dole out the princely sum of $500 to each of 21 GOP office-seekers.

The cash for the Fund for Limited Government came from 54 fat-cat contributors, half of them in Texas, including Pennzoil, Haggar Slacks, McCormick Oil and Gas, Houston Oil and Minerals, and Texas Instruments. Money also came in from Exxon, McDonnell-Douglas, and Clairol cosmetics.[7]

Despite the happy facade, Bush's campaign staff was plagued by turmoil and morale problems, leading to a high rate of turnover in key posts.

One who has stayed on all along has been Jennifer Fitzgerald, a British woman born in 1932 who had been with Bush at least since Beijing. Fitzgerald later worked in Bush's vice-presidential office, first as appointments secretary, and later as executive assistant. According to some Washington wags, she controlled access to Bush in the same way that Martin Bormann controlled access to Hitler. According to Harry Hurt, among former Bush staffers,

> "Fitzgerald gets vituperative reviews. She has been accused of bungling the 1980 presidential campaign by canceling Bush appearances at factory sites in favor of luncheon club speeches. Critics of her performance say she misrepresents staff scheduling requests and blocks access to her boss. . . . A number of the vice president's close friends worry that "the Jennifer problem"—or the appearance of one—may inhibit Bush's future political career. "There's just something about her that makes him feel good," says one trusted Bush confidant. "I don't think it's sexual. I don't know what it is. But if Bush ever runs for president again, I think he's going to have to make a change on that score."[8]

The Establishment's Candidate

Bush formally announced his presidential candidacy on May 1, 1979. One of Bush's themes was the idea of a "Union of the English-Speaking Peoples." Bush was asked later in his campaign by a reporter to elaborate on this. Bush stated at that time that "the British are the best friend America has in the world today. I believe we can benefit greatly from much close collaboration in the economic, military, and political spheres. Sure, I am an Anglophile. We should all be. Britain has never done anything bad to the United States."[9]

Jules Witcover and Jack Germond, two experienced observers of presidential campaigns, observed that Bush's was the first campaign in history to have peaked before it ever started.

Thanks to Mosbacher's operation, the Bush campaign would advance on a cushion of money—he spent $1.3 million for the Illinois primary alone. The biggest item would be media buys—above all television. This time Bush brought in Baltimore media expert Robert Goodman, who designed a series of television shorts that were described as "fast-moving, newsfilmlike portraits of an energetic, dynamic Bush creating excitement and moving through crowds, with an upbeat musical track behind him. Each of the advertisements used a slogan that attempted to capitalize on Bush's experience, while hitting Carter's wretched on-the-job performance and Ronald Reagan's inexperience on the national scene: 'George Bush,' the announcer intoned, 'a President we won't have to train.' "[10] One of these shorts showed Bush talking about inflation to a group of approving factory workers. In another, Bush climbed out of a private plane at a small airport, surrounded by supporters with straw hats and placards, and yelled "We're going all the way" to the accompaniment of applause and music Goodman hoped would sound "presidential." The inevitable footage of Bush getting fished out of the drink after the Chichi Jima shootdown was also aired.

In a rather slavish imitation of the Carter victory scenario, Bush also chose to imitate what had been called Carter's "fuzziness," or unwillingness to say anything of substance about issues. Bush was the unabashed demagogue, telling Diane Sawyer of CBS when he would finally talk about the issues: "[I]f they can show me how it will get me more votes someplace, I'll be glad to do it."

On November 3, 1979, Bush bested Sen. Howard Baker in a "beauty contest" straw poll taken at the Maine Republican convention in Portland. Bush won by a paper-thin margin of 20 votes out of 1,336 cast, and Maine was really his home state, but the Brown Brothers Harriman networks at the *New York Times* delivered a front-page lead story with a subhead that read, "Bush gaining stature as '80 contender."

Bush's biggest lift of the 1980 campaign came when he won a plurality in the January 21 Iowa caucuses, narrowly besting Reagan, who had not put any effort into the state. At this point, the Brown Brothers Harriman/Skull and Bones media operation went into high gear. That same night Walter Cronkite told viewers: "George Bush has apparently done what he hoped to do, coming out of the pack as the principal challenger to front-runner Ronald Reagan."

In the interval between January 21 and the New Hampshire primary of February 26, the Eastern Liberal Establishment labored mightily to put George Bush into power as President that same year. The press hype in favor of Bush was overwhelming. *Newsweek*'s cover featured a happy and smiling Bush talking with his supporters: "Bush Breaks Out of the Pack," went the headline. Smaller pictures showed a scowling Senator Howard Baker and a decidedly untelegenic Reagan grimacing before a microphone.

Time, which had been founded by Henry Luce of Skull and Bones, showed a huge, grinning Bush and a smaller, very cross Reagan, headlined: "BUSH SOARS." The leading polls, always doctored by the intelligence agencies and other interests, showed a Bush boom: Lou Harris found that whereas Reagan had led Bush into Iowa by 32–6 nationwide, Bush had pulled even with Reagan at 27–27 within 24 hours after the Iowa result had become known.

Robert Healy of the *Boston Globe* stuck his neck out even further for the neo-Harrimanite cause with a forecast that "even though he is still called leading candidate in some places, Reagan does not look like he'll be on the Presidential stage much longer."[11]

NBC's Tom Brokaw started calling Reagan the "former front-runner." Tom Pettit of the same network was more direct: "I would like to suggest that Ronald Reagan is politically dead." Once again the choice of pictures made Bush look good, Reagan bad.

The Eastern Liberal Establishment had left no doubt who its darling was: Bush, and not Reagan. In their arrogance, the Olympians had once again committed the error of confusing their collective patrician whim with real processes ongoing in the real world. The New Hampshire primary was to prove a devastating setback for Bush, in spite of all the hype the Bushman networks were able to crank out. How did it happen?

New Hampshire: The LaRouche Factor

George Bush was, of course, a lifelong member of the Skull and Bones secret society of Yale University, through which he advanced toward the freemasonic upper reaches of the Anglo-American Establishment, toward those exalted circles of London, New York and Washington, in which the transatlantic destiny of the self-styled Anglo-Saxon master race is elaborated. The entrees provided by Skull and Bones membership would always be, for Bush, the most vital ones. But, in addition to such exalted feudal brotherhoods as Skull and Bones, the Anglo-American Establishment also maintains a series of broader-based elite organizations whose function is to manifest the hegemonic Anglo-American policy line to the broader layers of the Establishment, including bureaucrats, businessmen, bankers, journalists, professors and other such assorted retainers and stewards of power.

George Bush had thus found it politic over the years to become a member of the New York Council on Foreign Relations. By 1979, Bush was a member of the board of the CFR, where he sat next to his old patron Henry Kissinger. The president of the CFR during this period was Kissinger clone Winston Lord of the traditional Skull and Bones family.

George was also a member of the Bohemian Club of San Francisco, which had been founded by Ambrose Bierce after the Civil War to cater to the Stanfords, Huntingtons, Crockers, Hopkinses and the other nouveau-riche tycoons that had emerged from the gold rush. The Bohemian Club made a summer outing every year to its camp at Bohemian Grove, a secluded, 2,700-acre stand of majestic redwoods about 75 miles from San Francisco. A sign over the gate advises: "Spiders Weave Not Here." Up to 1,600 members, with the occasional foreign guest like German Chancellor Helmut Schmidt, gather in midsummer for freemasonic ceremonies featuring the ritual interment of "dull care," cavort in women's pantyhose in female impersonator theatricals, or better yet, frolic in the nude near the banks of the Russian River. Herbert Hoover was a devoted regular; Eisenhower and Allen Dulles made Cold War speeches there; Nixon and Reagan discussed prospects for the 1968 election; Stephen Bechtel was always big; and Henry Kissinger loved to pontificate, all at the Grove.

Then there was the Trilateral Commission, founded by David Rockefeller in 1973–74. One branch from North America, one branch from Europe, one branch from Japan, with the resulting organism a kind of policy forum aiming at an international consensus among financier factions, under overall Anglo-American domination. The Trilateral Commission emerged at the same time that the Rockefeller-Kissinger interests perpetrated the first oil hoax. Some of its first studies were devoted to the mechanics of imposing authoritarian-totalitarian forms of government in the U.S., Europe and Japan to manage the austerity and economic decay that would be the results of Trilateral policies. The Carter administration was very overtly a Trilateral administration. Popular hatred of Carter and his crew made the Trilterals an attractive target; their existence had been publicized by *New Solidarity*, the newspaper associated with Lyndon LaRouche, during 1974 in the context of a highly effective anti-Rockefeller campaign. Reagan promised that he would change all that, but his government was also dominated by the Trilateraloids.

Bush was also a member of the Alibi Club, a society of Washington insiders who gather periodically to assert the primacy of oligarchism over such partisan or other divisions that have been concocted to divert the masses. Bush had also joined another Washington association, the Alfalfa Club (of which his father had been president in 1963), with much the same ethos and a slightly different cast of characters.

As we saw briefly during Bush's Senate campaign, the combination of bankruptcy and arrogance which was the hallmark of Eastern Liberal Establishment rule over the United States generated resentments which could make membership in such organizations a distinct political liability. That the issue exploded in New Hampshire during the 1979–80 campaign in such a way as to wreck the Bush campaign was largely the merit of Lyndon LaRouche, who had launched an outsider bid in the Democratic primary.

LaRouche conducted a vigorous campaign in New Hampshire during late 1979, focusing on the need to put forward an economic policy to undo the devastation being wrought by the 22 percent prime rate being charged by many banks as a result of the high-interest, usurious policies of Paul Volcker, whom Carter had made the head of the Federal Reserve. But in addition to contesting Carter, Ted Kennedy and Jerry Brown on the Democratic side, LaRouche's campaign also noticed George Bush, whom LaRouche correctly identified as a liberal Republican in the Theodore Roosevelt-House of Morgan "Bull Moose" tradition of 1912. LaRouche also noticed that a majority of the wealthy "blue blood" families who dominated New Hampshire political life were Bush backers. These were the families who could—and often did—organize ballot-box fraud on a vast scale.

During late 1979, the LaRouche campaign began to call attention to Bush as a threat against which other candidates, Republicans and Democrats, ought to unite. LaRouche attacked Bush as the spokesman for "the folks who live on the hill," for petty oligarchs and blue bloods who think that it is up to them to dictate political decisions to the average citizen. These broadsides were the first to raise the issue of Bush's membership in David Rockefeller's Trilateral Commission and in the New York Council on Foreign Relations. Soon Bush's membership in the Trilateral Commission became for many voters a symbol of Bush's plutocratic and arrogant claim on high public office as some kind of a "birthright," quite independent of the judgment of the voters.

While on the hustings in New Hampshire, especially in the Connecticut River Valley in the western part of the state, LaRouche observed the high correlation between preppy, liberal Republican, blue-blooded support for Bush and mental pathology. As LaRouche wrote, "In the course of campaigning in New Hampshire during 1979 and 1980, I have encountered minds, especially in western New Hampshire, who represent, in a decayed sort of way, exactly the treasonous outlook our patriotic forefathers combatted more than a century or more ago. Naturally, since I am an American Whig by family ancestry stretching back into the early 19th century, born a New Hampshire Whig, and a Whig Democrat by profession today, the blue-blooded kooks of certain 'respected' Connecticut River Valley families get my dander up."[12]

LaRouche's principal charge was that George Bush was a "cult-ridden kook, and more besides." He cited Bush's membership in "the secret society which largely controls George Bush's personal destiny, the Russell Trust Association, otherwise known as 'Skull and Bones'. . . . Understanding the importance of the Russell Trust Association in Bush's adult life will help the ordinary citizen to understand why one must place a question mark on Bush's political candidacy today. Is George Bush a 'Manchurian candidate'?"

After noting that the wealth of many of the Skull and Bones families was derived from the British East India Company's trade in black slaves and in opium, LaRouche went on to discuss "How Yale Turned 'Gay' ":

> Today, visiting Yale, one sees male students walking hand in hand, lovers, blatantly, on the streets. One does not permit one's boy children to visit certain of the residences on or around that campus. There have been too many incidents to be overlooked. One is reminded of the naked wrestling in the mud which initiates to the Yale Skull and Bones Society practice. One thinks of 'Skull and Boneser' William F. Buckley's advocacy of the dangerous, mind-wrecking substance, marijuana, and of Buckley's recent, publicly expressed sympathies for sodomy between male public school teachers and students.
> . . .
> As the anglophile commitments [of the blue-blooded families] deepened and decayed, the families reflected this in part by a growth of the incidence of "homosexuality" for which British public schools and universities are rightly notorious. Skull and Bones is a concentrated expression of that moral and intellectual degeneration.

LaRouche pointed out that the symbol of Skull and Bones is the skull and crossbones of the pirate Jolly Roger with "322" placed under the crossbones. The 322 is thought to refer to 322 B.C., the year of the death of the Athenian orator Demosthenes, whom LaRouche identified as a traitor to Athens and an agent provocateur in the service of King Philip of Macedonia. The Skull and Bones ceremony of induction and initiation is modeled on the death and resurrection fetish of the cult of Osiris in ancient Egypt. LaRouche described the so-called "Persian model" of oligarchical rule sought by Skull and Bones:

> The "oligarchical" or "Persian" model was what might be called today a "neo-Malthusian" sort of "One World" scheme. Science and technological progress were to be essentially crushed and most of the world turned back into labor-intensive, "appropriate" technologies. By driving civilization back toward barbarism in that way, the spon-

sors of the "oligarchical model" proposed to ensure the perpetuation of a kind of "one world" rule by what we would term today a "feudal landlord" class. To aid in bringing about that *"One World Order,"* the sponsors of the project utilized a variety of religious cults. Some of these cults were designed for the most illiterate strata of the population, and, at the other extreme, other cults were designed for the indoctrination and control of the ruling elite themselves. The cult-organization under the Roman Empire is an excellent example of what was intended.

LaRouche went on:

Skull and Bones is no mere fraternity, no special alumni association with added mumbo-jumbo. It is a very serious, very dedicated cult-conspiracy against the U.S. Constitution. Like the Cambridge Apostles, the initiate to the Skull and Bones is a dedicated agent of British secret intelligence for life. The fifteen Yale recruits added each year function as a powerful secret intelligence association for life, penetrating into our nation's intelligence services as well as related high levels of national policy-making.

Representatives of the cult who have functioned in that way include Averell Harriman, Henry Luce, Henry Stimson, Justice Potter Stewart, McGeorge Bundy, Rev. William Sloane Coffin (who recruited William F. Buckley), William Bundy, J. Richardson Dilworth, and George Bush . . . and many more notables. The list of related Yalies in the history of the CIA accounts for many of the CIA's failures and ultimate destruction by the Kennedy machine, including the reason Yalie James Jesus Angleton failed to uncover H. "Kim" Philby's passing of CIA secrets to Moscow.

Now, the ordinary citizen should begin to realize how George Bush became a kook-cultist, and also how so incompetent a figure as Bush was appointed for a while Director of Central Intelligence for the CIA. . . .

On the record, the ordinary citizen who knew something of Bush's policies and sympathies would class him as a "Peking sympathizer," hence a Communist sympathizer.

Focusing on Bush's links with the Maoist regime, LaRouche stressed the recent genocide in Cambodia:

The genocide of three out of seven million Cambodians by the Peking puppet regime of Pol Pot (1975–78) was done under the direction of battalions of Peking bureaucrats controlling every detail of the genocide—the worst genocide of the present century to date. This genocide, which was aimed especially against all merely literate Cambodians as well as professional strata, had the purpose of sending all of Southeast Asia back into a "dark age." That "dark age" policy is the policy of the present Peking regime. That is the regime which Kissinger, Bush and Brzezinski admire so much as an "ally". . . .

The leading circles of London have no difficulty in recognizing what "Peking Communism" is. It is their philosophy, their policy in a Chinese mandarin culture form. To the extent that Yalies of the Skull and Bones sort are brought into the same culture as their superiors in London, such Yalies, like Bush, also have deep affection for "Peking Communism."

Like Bush, who supports neo-Malthusian doctrines and zero-growth and anti-nuclear policies, the Peking rulers are dedicated to a "one world" order in which the population is halved over the next twenty years (i.e. genocide far greater than Hitler's), and most of the survivors are driven into barbarism and cultism under the rule of parasitical blue blood families of the sort represented in the membership of the Skull and Bones.

In that sense, Bush is to be viewed without quibble as a "Manchurian candidate." From the vantage point of the U.S. Constitution and American System of technological progress and capital formation, Bush is in effect an agent of the same evil philosophies and policies as the rulers of Peking.

That, dear friends, is not mere opinion; that is hard fact.[13]

This leaflet represented the most accurate and devastating personal and political indictment Bush had ever received in his career. It was clear that LaRouche had Bush's number. The linking of Bush with the Cambodian genocide is all the more surprising, since most of the evidence on Bush's role was at that time not in the public domain. Other aspects of LaRouche's comments are prophetic: Bush's "deep affection" for Chinese Communism was to become an international scandal when Bush maintained his solidarity with Deng Xiaoping after the Tiananmen massacre of 1989. Outstanding is LaRouche's reference to the "One World Order" which the world began to wonder about as the "New World Order" in the late summer of 1990, during the buildup for Bush's Gulf war; LaRouche had identified the policy content of the term way back in 1980.

Bush's handlers were stunned, then enraged. No one had ever dared to stand up to George Bush and Skull and Bones like this before. The Bush entourage wanted revenge. A vote fraud to deprive LaRouche of virtually all the votes cast in the Democratic primary, and transfer as many of them as possible to the Bush column, would be the first installment. Bush is vindictive, and he would not forget this attack by LaRouche. Later Gary Howard and Ron Tucker, two agents provocateur from Midland, Texas, were dispatched to try to infiltrate pro-LaRouche political circles. From 1986 on, Bush would emerge as a principal sponsor of a judicial vendetta by the Department of Justice that would see LaRouche and several of his supporters twice indicted, and finally convicted, on a series of trumped-up charges. One week after George Bush's inauguration as President, his most capable and determined opponent, Lyndon LaRouche, would be thrown into federal prison, where he remains to this day.

But in the New Hampshire of 1979–80, LaRouche's attacks on Bush brought into precise focus many aspects of Bush's personality that voters found profoundly distasteful. LaRouche's attack sent out a shock wave, which, as it advanced, detonated one turbulent assault on Bush after the other. The spell was broken; Bush was vulnerable.

One who was caught up in the turbulence was William Loeb, the opinionated curmudgeon of Pride's Crossing, Massachusetts who was the publisher of the Manchester *Union Leader*, the most important newspaper in the state. Loeb had supported Reagan in 1976 and was for him again in 1980. Loeb might have dispersed his fire against all of Reagan's Republican rivals, including Howard Baker, Robert Dole, Phil Crane, John Anderson, John Connally and Bush. It was the LaRouche campaign which demonstrated to Loeb long before the Iowa caucuses that Bush was the main rival to Reagan, and therefore the principal target. As a result, Loeb would launch a barrage of slashing attacks on Bush. The other GOP contenders would be virtually ignored by Loeb.

Loeb had assailed Ford as "Gerry the Jerk" in 1976; his attacks on Sen. Edmund Muskie reduced the latter to tears during the 1972 primary. Loeb began to play up the theme of Bush as a liberal, as a candidate controlled by the "internationalist" (or Kissinger) wing of the GOP and the Wall Street bankers, always soft on communism and always ready to undermine liberty through Big Government here at home. A February editorial by Loeb reacted to Bush's Iowa success with these warnings of vote fraud:

> The Bush operation in Iowa had all the smell of a CIA covert operation. . . . Strange aspects of the Iowa operation [included] a long, slow count and then the computers broke down at a very convenient point, with Bush having a six per cent bulge over Reagan. . . . Will the elite nominate their man, or will we nominate Reagan?[14]

For Loeb, the most damning evidence was Bush's membership in the Trilateral Commission, the creature of David Rockefeller and the international bankers. Carter and his administration had been packed with Trilateral members; there were indications that the

Establishment choice of Carter to be the next U.S. President had been made at a meeting of the Trilateral Commission in Kyodo, Japan, where Carter had been introduced by Gianni Agnelli of Italy's FIAT Motor Company.

Loeb simplified all that: "George Bush is a Liberal" was the title of his editorial published the day before the primary. Loeb flayed Bush as a "spoiled little rich kid who has been wet-nursed to succeed and now, packaged by David Rockefeller's Trilateral Commission, thinks he is entitled to the White House as his latest toy."

Shortly before the election Loeb ran a cartoon entitled "Silk Stocking Republicans," which showed Bush at a cocktail party with a cigarette and glass in hand. Bush and the other participants, all male, were wearing women's pantyhose. This was the message that Loeb had apparently gotten from Bush's body language.

Paid political ads began to appear in the *Union Leader* sponsored by groups from all over the country, some helped along by John Sears of the Reagan campaign. One showed a drawing of Bush juxtaposed with a Mr. Peanut logo: "The same people who gave you Jimmy Carter want now to give you George Bush," read the headline. The text described a "coalition of liberals, multinational corporate executives, big-city bankers, and hungry power brokers" led by David Rockefeller, whose "purpose is to control the American government, regardless of which political party—Democrat or Republican—wins the presidency this coming November!. . . The Trojan horse for this scheme is Connecticut-Yankee-turned-Texas oilman George Bush—the out-of-nowhere Republican who openly admits he is using the same 'game-plan' developed for Jimmy Carter in the 1976 presidential nomination campaign." The ad went on to mention the Council on Foreign Relations and the "Rockefeller money" that was the lifeblood of Bush's effort.

While campaigning, Bush was asked once again about the money he received from Nixon's 1970 Townhouse slush fund. Bush's stock reply was that his friend Leon Jaworski had cleared him: "The answer came back, clean, clean, clean," said Bush.

By now the Reagan camp had caught on that something important was happening, something which could benefit Reagan enormously. First Reagan's crony Edwin Meese piped up an oblique reference to the Trilateral membership of some candidates, including Bush: "[A]ll these people come out of an international economic industrial organization with a pattern of thinking on world affairs" that led to a "softening on defense." That played well, and Reagan decided he would pick up the theme. On February 7, 1980, Reagan observed in a speech that 19 key members of the Carter administration, including Carter, were members of the Trilateral Commission. According to Reagan, this influence had indeed led to a "softening on defense" because of the Trilateraloids' belief that business "should transcend, perhaps, the national defense."[15] Voters whose fathers remembered the complaint of a beaten Bonesman, Robert Taft, in 1952—that every GOP presidential candidate since 1936 had been chosen by Chase Bank and the Rockefellers—found this touched a responsive chord.

Bush realized that he was faced with an ugly problem. He summarily resigned from both the Trilateral Commission and from the New York Council on Foreign Relations. But his situation in New Hampshire was desperate. His cover had been largely blown.

Now the real polls, the ones that are generally not published, showed Bush collapsing, and even media that would normally have been rabidly pro-Bush were obliged to distance themselves from him in order to defend their own "credibility," meaning their future ability to ply the citizens with lies and disorientation. Part of Reagan's support reflected a desire by voters to stick it to the media.

Bush was now running scared, sufficiently so as to entertain the prospect of a debate among candidates.

Epiphany of a Scoundrel

John Sears of the Reagan campaign signaled to the *Nashua Telegraph*, a paper published in southern New Hampshire, that Reagan would accept a one-on-one debate with Bush. James Baker was gulled: He welcomed the idea because the debate format would establish Bush as the main alternative to Reagan. "We thought it was the best thing since sliced bread," said Baker. Bob Dole complained to the Federal Elections Commission about being excluded, and the Reagan camp suggested that the debate be paid for out of campaign funds, half by Reagan and half by Bush. Bush refused to pay, but Reagan pronounced himself willing to defray the entire cost. Thus it came to pass that a bilateral Bush-Reagan debate was scheduled for February 23 at a gymnasium in Nashua.

For many, this evening would provide the epiphany of George Bush, a moment when his personal essence was made manifest.

Bush propaganda has always tried to portray the *Nashua Telegraph* debate as some kind of ambush planned by Reagan's diabolical campaign manager, John Sears. Established facts include that the *Nashua Telegraph* owner, blue blood J. Herman Pouliot, and *Telegraph* editor John Breen, were both close personal friends of former Governor Hugh Gregg, who was Bush's campaign director in the state. Bush had met with Breen before the debate. Perhaps it was Bush who was trying to set some kind of a trap for Reagan.

On the night of February 23, the gymnasium was packed with more than 2,400 people. Bush's crony Rep. Barber Conable (or "Barbarian Cannibal," later Bush's man at the World Bank) was there with a group of Congressmen for Bush. Then the excluded GOP candidates, John Anderson, Howard Baker, Bob Dole and Phil Crane, all arrived and asked to meet with Reagan and Bush to discuss opening the debate up to them as well. (Connally, also a candidate, was in South Carolina.) Reagan agreed to meet with them and went backstage into a small office with the other candidates. He expressed a general willingness to let them join in. But Bush refused to talk to the other candidates, and sat on the stage waiting impatiently for the debate to begin. John Sears told Bush's press secretary, Peter Teeley, that Sears wanted to talk to Bush about the debate format. "It doesn't work that way," hissed the liberal Teeley, who sent James Baker to talk with Sears. Sears said it was time to have an open debate. Baker passed the buck to the *Nashua Telegraph*.

From the room behind the stage where the candidates were meeting, the Reagan people sent U.S. Senator Gordon Humphrey out to urge Bush to come and confer with the rest of them. "If you don't come now," said Humphrey to Bush, "you're doing a disservice to party unity." Bush whined in reply: "Don't tell me about unifying the Republican Party! I've done more for this party than you'll ever do! I've worked too hard for this and they're not going to take it away from me!" In the back room, there was a proposal that Reagan, Baker, Dole, Anderson and Crane should go on stage together and announce that Reagan would refuse to debate unless the others were included.

"Everyone seemed quite irritated with Bush, whom they viewed as acting like a spoiled child," wrote an aide to Anderson later.[16] Bush refused to even acknowledge the presence of Dole, who had helped him get started as GOP chairman; of Anderson and Crane, former House colleagues; and of Howard Baker, who had helped him get confirmed at the CIA. George kept telling anybody who came close that he was sticking with the original rules.

The audience was cheering for the four excluded candidates, demanding that they be allowed to speak. Publisher Pouliot addressed the crowd: "This is getting to sound more like a boxing match. In the rear are four other candidates who have not been invited by the *Nashua Telegraph*," said Pouliot. He was roundly booed. "Get them chairs," cried a woman, and she was applauded.

Bush kept staring straight ahead into space, and the hostility of the crowd was focusing more and more on him.

Reagan started to speak, motivating why the debate should be opened up. Editor Breen, a rubbery-looking hack with a bald pate and glasses, piped up: "Turn Mr. Reagan's microphone off." There was pandemonium. "You Hitler!" screamed a man in the front row right at Breen.

Reagan replied: "I'm paying for this microphone, Mr. Green." The crowd broke out in wild cheers. Bush still stared straight ahead in his temper tantrum. Reagan spoke on to ask that the others be included, saying that exclusion was unfair. But he was unsure of himself, looking to Nancy Reagan for a sign as to what he should do. At the end Reagan said he would prefer an open debate, but that he would accept the bilateral format if that were the only way.

With that the other candidates left the podium in a towering rage. "There'll be another day, George," growled Bob Dole.

Reagan and Bush then debated, and those who were still paying attention agreed that Bush was the loser. A staff member later told Bush, "The good news is that nobody paid any attention to the debate. The bad news is you lost that, too."

Film footage of Reagan grabbing the microphone while Bush stewed in his temper tantrum was all over local and network television for the next 48 hours. It was the epiphany of a scoundrel.

Now the Bush damage control apparatus went into that mode it finds so congenial: lying. A radio commercial was prepared under orders from James Baker for New Hampshire stations: Here an announcer, not Bush, intoned that "at no time did George Bush object to a full candidate forum. This accusation by the other candidates is without foundation whatsoever."

Walter Cronkite heard a whining voice from Houston, Texas as he interviewed Bush on his new program: "I wanted to do what I agreed to do," said the whine. "I wanted to debate with Ronald Reagan."

The New Hampshire primary was a debacle for Bush. Reagan won 50 percent of the votes to George's 23 percent, with 13 percent for Baker and 10 percent for Anderson.[17]

Bush played out the string through the primaries, but he won only four states (Massachusetts, Connecticut, Pennsylvania and Michigan) plus Puerto Rico. Reagan took 29. Even in Pennsylvania, where the Bushmen outspent Reagan by a colossal margin, Reagan managed to garner more delegates even though Bush got more votes.

Bush was able to keep going after New Hampshire because Mosbacher's machinations had given him a post-New Hampshire war chest of $3 million. The Reagan camp had spent two-thirds of their legal total expenditure of $18 million before the primaries had begun. This had proven effective, but it meant that in more than a dozen primaries, Reagan could afford no television purchases at all. This allowed Bush to move in and smother Reagan under a cascade of greenbacks in a few states, even though Reagan was on his way to the nomination. That was the story in Pennsylvania and Michigan. The important thing for Bush now was to outlast the other candidates and to build his credentials for the vice-presidency, since that was what he was now running for.

Bush officially capitulated on May 26, 1980, and declared that he would support Reagan all the way to November. Reagan, campaigning that day at the San Bernardino County Fairgrounds, commended Bush's campaign and thanked him for his support.

Seeking his 'Birthright'

All the money and organization had not sufficed. After some expensive primary failures, Bush now turned his entire attention to the quest for his "birthright," the vice-presidency. This would be his fifth attempt to attain that office, and once again, despite the power of Bush's network, success was uncertain.

Inside the Reagan camp, one of Bush's greatest assets would be William Casey, who had been closely associated with the late Prescott Bush. Casey was to be Reagan's campaign manager for the final phase of the 1980 elections. In 1962, Prescott and Casey had cofounded a think tank called the National Strategy Information Center in New York City, a forum where Wall Street lawyers like Casey could join hands with politicians from Prescott's wing of the Republican Party, financiers, and the intelligence community. The National Strategy Information Center provided material for a news agency called Forum World Features, a CIA proprietary that operated in London, and which was in liaison with the British Information Research Department, a Cold War propaganda unit set up by Christopher Mayhew of British intelligence with the approval of Prime Minister Clement Attlee.[18]

This Prescott Bush-William Casey think tank promoted the creation of endowed chairs in strategic analysis, national intelligence and the like on a number of campuses. The Georgetown Center for Strategic and International Studies, later the home of Kissinger, Michael Ledeen and a whole stable of ideologues of the Anglo-American empire, was in part a result of the work of Casey and Prescott.

Casey was also a close associate of George Bush. During 1976, Ford appointed Casey to PFIAB, where Casey was an enthusiastic supporter of the Team B operation along with Bush and Cherne. George Bush and Casey would play decisive roles in the secret government operations of the Reagan years.

As the Republican convention gathered in Detroit in July 1980, the problem was to convince Reagan of the inevitability of tapping Bush as his running mate. But Reagan did not want Bush. He had conceived an antipathy, even a hostility, for George. What Reagan had experienced personally from Bush during the *Nashua Telegraph* debate, had left a lasting and highly derogatory impression.

According to one account of this phase, "ever since the episode in Nashua in February, Reagan had come to hold the preppy Yankee transplant in, as the late Senator Robert Kerr of Oklahoma used to say, minimum high regard. 'Reagan is a very gracious contestant,' one of his inner circle said, 'and he generally views his opponents with a good deal of respect. The thing he couldn't understand was Bush's conduct at the *Nashua Telegraph* debate. It imprinted with Reagan that Bush was a wimp. He remembered that night clearly when we had our vice-presidential discussions. He couldn't understand how a man could have sat there so passively. He felt it showed a lack of courage." And now that it was time to think about a running mate, the prospective presidential nominee gave a sympathetic ear to those who objected to Bush for reasons that ran, one of the group said later, from his behavior at Nashua to 'anti-Trilateralism.' " According to this account, conservatives seeking to stop Bush at the convention were citing their suspicions about a " 'conspiracy' backed by Rockefeller to gain control of the American government."[19]

Drew Lewis was a leading Bushman submarine in the Reagan camp, telling the candidate that Bush could help him in electoral college megastates like Pennsylvania and Michigan where Ted Kennedy had demonstrated that Carter was vulnerable during the primaries. Lewis badgered Reagan with the prospect that if he waited too long, he would have to accept a politically neutral running mate in the way that Ford took Dole in 1976, which might end up costing him the election. According to Lewis, Reagan needed to broaden his base, and Bush was the most palatable and practical vehicle for doing so.

Much to his credit, Reagan resisted; "[H]e told several staff members and advisers that he still harbored 'doubts' about Bush, based on Nashua. 'If he can't stand up to that kind of pressure,' Reagan told one intimate, 'how could he stand up to the pressure of being president?' To another, he said: 'I want to be very frank with you. I have strong reservations about George Bush. I'm concerned about turning the country over to him.' "

As the convention came closer, Reagan continued to be hounded by Bushmen from inside and outside his own campaign. A few days before the convention, it began to dawn on Reagan that one alternative to the unpalatable Bush might be former President Gerald Ford, assuming the latter could be convinced to make the run. Two days before Reagan left for Detroit, according to one of his strategists, Reagan "came to the conclusion that it would be Bush, but he wasn't all that happy about it."[20] But this was not yet the last word.

Casey, Meese and Michael Deaver sounded out Ford, who was reluctant but did not issue a categorical rejection. Stuart Spencer, Ford's 1976 campaign manager, reported to Reagan on his contacts with Ford. "Ron," Spencer said, "Ford ain't gonna do it, and you're gonna pick Bush." But judging from Reagan's reaction, Spencer recalled later, "There was no way he was going to pick Bush," and the reason was simple: Reagan just didn't like the guy. "It was chemistry," Spencer said.[21]

Reagan now had to be ground down by an assortment of Eastern Liberal Establishment perception-mongers and political heavies. Much of the well-known process of negotiation between Reagan and Ford for the "Dream Ticket" of 1980 was simply a charade to disorient and demoralize Reagan while eating up the clock, until the point was reached when Reagan would have no choice but to make the classic phone call to Bush. It is obvious that Reagan offered the vice-presidency to Ford, and that the latter refused to accept it outright, but engaged in a process of negotiations ostensibly in order to establish the conditions under which he might, eventually, accept.[22] Casey called in Henry Kissinger and asked him to intercede with Ford. What then developed was a marathon of haggling in which Ford was represented by Kissinger, Alan Greenspan, Jack Marsh and Bob Barrett. Reagan was represented by Casey, Meese and perception-monger Richard Wirthlin. Dick Cheney, Ford's former chief of staff, who is now Bush's pro-genocide Secretary of Defense, also got into the act.

This complex strategy of intrigue culminated in Ford's notorious interview with Walter Cronkite, in which the CBS anchor man asked Ford if "It's got to be something like a co-presidency?" "That's something Governor Reagan really ought to consider," replied Ford, which was not what a serious vice-presidential candidate might say, but did correspond rather well to what "Gerry the Jerk" would say if he wanted to embarrass Reagan and help Bush.

The best indication that Ford had been working all along as an agent of Bush was provided by Ford himself to Germond and Witcover: "Ford, incidentally, told us after the election that one of his prime objectives at the convention had been 'to subtly help George Bush get the [vice-presidential] nomination.' "[23]

Drew Lewis helped Reagan make the call that he found so distasteful. Reagan came on the line: "Hello, George, this is Ron Reagan. I'd like to go over to the convention and announce that you're my choice for vice president . . . if that's all right with you."

"I'd be honored, Governor."

Reagan now proceeded to the convention floor, where he would announce his choice of Bush. Knowing that this decision would alienate many of Reagan's ideological backers, the Reagan campaign leaked the news that Bush had been chosen to the media, so that it would quickly spread to the convention floor. They were seeking to cushion the blow, to avoid mass expressions of disgust when Bush's name was announced. Even as it was, there was much groaning and booing among the Reagan faithful.

In retrospect, the success of Bush's machinations at the 1980 convention can be seen to have had a very sinister precedent at the GOP convention held in Philadelphia just 80 years earlier. At that convention, William McKinley, one of the last of the Lincoln Republicans, was nominated for a second term.

The New York bankers, especially the House of Morgan, wanted Theodore Roosevelt for Vice President, but McKinley and his chief political ally, Senator Marc Hanna, were adamant that they wanted no part of the infantile and megalomaniac New York governor. At one point Hanna exclaimed to a group of southern delegates, "Don't any of you realize that there's only one life between this madman and the White House!" Eventually McKinley's hand was forced by a group of New York delegates who were motivated primarily by their desire to get the unpopular and erratic Roosevelt out of the state at any cost. They told Hanna that unless Roosevelt were on the ticket, McKinley might lose the vital New York electoral votes. McKinley and Hanna capitulated, and Theodore Roosevelt joined the ticket.[24]

Within one year, President McKinley was assassinated at Buffalo, and Theodore Roosevelt assumed power in the name of the fanatical and imbecilic Anglo-Saxon imperial strategy of world domination which helped to precipitate the First World War.

As the Detroit convention came to a close, the Reagan and Bush campaign staffs were merged, with James Baker assuming a prominent position in the Casey-run Reagan campaign. The Ray Cline, Halper and Gambino operations were all continued. From this point on, Reagan's entourage would be heavily infiltrated by Bushmen.

The October Surprise

The Reagan-Bush campaign, now chock full of Bush's Brown Brothers Harriman/Skull and Bones assets, announced a campaign of espionage. This campaign told reporters that it was going to spy on the Carter regime.

Back in April, Carter had taken to live television at 7:00 A.M. one morning to announce some ephemeral progress in his efforts to secure the release of State Department officials and others from the U.S. embassy in Teheran, who were being held as hostages by the Khomeini forces in Iran. This announcement was timed to coincide with Democratic primaries in Kansas and Wisconsin, in which Carter was able to overwhelm challenges from Teddy Kennedy and Jerry Brown. A memo from Richard Wirthlin to Casey and Reagan initiated a discussion of how the Carter gang might exploit the advantages of incumbency in order to influence the outcome of the election, perhaps by attempting to stampede the public by some dramatic event at the last minute, such as the freeing of the hostages in Teheran. On April 24, a military task force failed to free the hostages. Casey began to institute countermeasures even before the Detroit GOP convention.

During the convention, at a July 14 press conference, Casey told reporters of his concern that Carter might spring an "October Surprise" in foreign or domestic policy on the eve of the November elections. He announced that he had set up what he called an "incumbency watch" to monitor Carter's activities and decisions. Casey explained that an "intelligence operation" directed against the Carter White House was functioning "already in germinal form." Ed Meese, who was with Casey at this press conference, added that the October Surprise "could be anything from a summit conference on energy" or development in Latin America, or perhaps the imposition of "wage and price controls" on the domestic economy.

"We've talked about the October surprise and what the October surprise will be," said Casey. "I think it's immoral and improper."[25]

The previous evening, in a television appearance, Reagan had suggested that "the Soviet Union is going to throw a few bones to Mr. Carter during this coming campaign to help him continue as president."

Although Casey and Meese had defined a broad range of possibilities for the October Surprise, the most prominent of these was certainly the liberation of the American hostages in Iran. A poll showed that if the hostages were to be released during the period between October 18 and October 25, Carter could receive a ten percent increase in popular vote on election day.

The "incumbency watch" set up by Casey would go beyond surveillance and become a dirty tricks operation against Carter.

What followed was in essence a pitched battle between two fascist gangs, the Carter White House and the Bush-Casey forces. Out of this 1980 gang warfare, the post-1981 United States regime would emerge.

Carter and Brzezinski had deliberately toppled the Shah of Iran, and deliberately installed Khomeini in power. This was an integral part of Brzezinski's "arc of crisis" geopolitical lunacy, another made-in-London artifact which called for the U.S. to support the rise of Khomeini, and his personal brand of fanaticism, a militant heresy within Islam. U.S. arms deliveries were made to Iran during the time of the Shah; during the short-lived Shahpour Bakhtiar government at the end of the Shah's reign; and continuously after the advent of Khomeini. There are indications that the Carter regime might even have connived with Khomeini to get the hostages taken in the first place; the existence of the hostages would allow Carter to continue arms deliveries and other vital forms of support for Khomeini under the pretext that he was doing it not out of love for Khomeini, but in order to free the hostages. It was, in short, the same charade that was later acted out under Reagan.

Subsequently, President Carter and senior members of his administration have suggested that the Reagan/Bush campaign cut a deal with the Khomeini regime to block the liberation of the hostages before the November 1980 election. By early 1992, the charges and countercharges reached such a fever pitch that a preliminary congressional investigation of the affair had been initiated.

In March 1992, *Executive Intelligence Review* issued a Special Report titled, "Treason in Washington: New Evidence on the 'October Surprise,' "[26] which presented extensive new evidence from internal FBI and CIA documents, released under the Freedom of Information Act, that suggests that the then-Republican vice-presidential candidate played a personal role in keeping the hostages in Khomeini's hands until after Election Day 1980; and that Casey, a personal friend of Bush's father and Reagan's CIA Director, coordinated the operation.

The central link suggesting Bush's role in the scandal was Cyrus

Hashemi, an Iranian arms dealer and agent of the Iranian SAVAK secret police, whom Casey seems to have recruited as a liaison to the mullahs.

On December 7, 1979, less than two months after the hostages were seized, Carter's Assistant Secretary of State, Harold Saunders, was contacted by an intermediary for Cyrus Hashemi. The Iranian arms merchant proposed a deal to free the hostages, and submitted a memorandum calling for the following: removal of the ailing expatriate Shah from U.S. territory; an apology by the United States to the people of Iran for past U.S. interference; the creation of a United Nations Commission; the unfreezing of the Iranian financial assets seized by Carter; and arms and spare parts deliveries by the United States to Iran. All of this was summed up in a memorandum submitted to Secretary of State Cyrus Vance following meetings with Hashemi and his attorney.[27]

The notable aspect of this encounter is the identity of the American lawyer who was both the business partner and the intermediary for the Iranian gun-runner: John Stanley Pottinger. The account of the 1976 Letelier case provided above (see Chapter 14) has established that Pottinger was a close friend of George Bush. Pottinger, it will be recalled, had served as Assistant Attorney General for Civil Rights in the Nixon and Ford administrations between 1973 and 1977, after having directed the U.S. Office of Civil Rights in the Justice Department between 1970 and 1973. Pottinger had also stayed on into the early Carter administration, serving as special assistant to the Attorney General from February to April 1977. Pottinger had then joined the law firm of Tracy, Malin and Pottinger of Washington, London and Paris. After the 1980 election, Pottinger was being considered for a high-level post in the Reagan/Bush administration.

This same Pottinger was now the representative for gun-runner Cyrus Hashemi. Given Pottinger's proven relation to Bush, we may wonder to what extent was Bush informed of Hashemi's proposal, and of the responses of the Carter administration. Bush may have known, for example, that during the Christmas season of 1979, one Captain Siavash Setoudeh, an Iranian naval officer and the former Iranian military attaché before the breaking of diplomatic relations between the United States and Iran, was arranging arms deliveries to Khomeini out of a premises of the U.S. Office of Naval Research in Arlington, Virginia. If Bush had been in contact with Pottinger, he might have known something about the Carter offers of arms deliveries.

Relevant evidence that might help us to determine what Bush

knew and when he knew it is still being withheld by the Bush regime. The FBI bugged Cyrus Hashemi's phones and office from August 1980 to February 1981, and many of the conversations that were recorded were between Hashemi and Bush's friend Pottinger. Ten years later, in November 1991, the FBI released heavily redacted summaries of some of the conversations, but most of the summaries and transcripts are still classified. Are they being withheld to protect Pottinger, and to prevent disclosure of information which would show the involvement of Bush and others in his administration?

EIR's Special Report thoroughly documented how Pottinger was protected from indictment by the Reagan-Bush Justice Department. For years, prosecution of Hashemi and Pottinger, for illegally conspiring to ship weapons to the Khomeini regime, was blocked by the administration on "national security" grounds. Declassified FBI documents show that an indictment of Pottinger had been drawn up, but that the indictment was killed at the last minute in 1984 when the FBI "lost" crucial taped evidence. The FBI conducted an extensive internal investigation of the missing "Pottinger tapes" but the results have never been disclosed.

Other information on the intentions of the Khomeini regime and secret dealings may have reached Bush from his old friend and associate Mitchell Rogovin, the former CIA general counsel. During 1976, Rogovin had accompanied Bush on many trips to the capital to testify before congressional committees; the two were known to be close. Rogovin was credited with having saved the CIA after it came under major congressional and media attack in the mid 1970s. In the spring of 1980, Rogovin told the Carter administration that he had been approached by Iranian-American arms dealer Houshang Lavi with an offer to start negotiations for the release of the hostages. Lavi claimed to be an emissary of Iranian President Abol Hassan Bani-Sadr; Rogovin at this time was working as the lawyer for the John Anderson GOP presidential campaign.

Bush's family friend Casey had also been in direct contact with Iranian representatives. Jamshid Hashemi, the brother of Cyrus Hashemi (who died under suspicious circumstances during 1986), has told Gary Sick, a former official of Carter's National Security Council, that he met with William Casey at the Mayflower Hotel in Washington, D.C. in March of 1980 to discuss the hostages. According to Jamshid Hashemi, "Casey quickly made clear that he wanted to prevent Jimmy Carter from gaining any political advantage from the hostage crisis. The Hashemis agreed to cooperate with Casey without the knowledge of the Carter Administration."[28]

Casey's "intelligence operation" included the spying on the opposing candidate that has been routine in U.S. political campaigns for decades, but went far beyond it. As journalists like Witcover and Germond knew during the course of the campaign, and as the 1984 Albosta committee "Debategate" investigation showed, Casey set up at least two "October Surprise" espionage groups.

The first of these watched the Carter White House, the Washington bureaucracy, and diplomatic and intelligence posts overseas. This group was headed by Reagan's principal foreign policy adviser and later NSC Chairman, Richard Allen. Allen was assisted by Fred Ikle and John Lehman, who later got top jobs in the Pentagon, and by Admiral Thomas Moorer. This group also included Robert McFarlane. Allen was in touch with some 120 foreign policy and national security experts sympathetic to the Reagan campaign. Casey helped Allen to interface with the Bush campaign network of retired and active duty assets in the intelligence community. This network reached into the Carter NSC, where Bush crony Don Gregg worked as the CIA liaison man, and into Carter's top-secret White House situation room.

Another October Surprise monitoring group was headed by Adm. Robert Garrick, who was assisted by Stephan Halper, Ray Cline's son-in-law. The task of this group was the physical surveillance of U.S. military bases by on-the-ground observers, often retired and sometimes active duty military officers. Lookouts were posted to watch Tinker Air Force Base in Oklahoma, Andrews Air Force Base near Washington, McGuire Air Force Base in New Jersey (where weapons already bought and paid for by the Shah were stockpiled), and Norton and March Air Force bases in California.

Garrick, Casey, Meese, Wirthlin and other campaign officials met each morning in Falls Church, Virginia, just outside of Washington, to review intelligence gathered. Bush was certainly informed of these meetings. Did he also attend them?

This group soon became operational. It was clear that Khomeini was keeping the hostages to sell them to the highest bidder. Bush and Casey were not reticent about putting their own offer on the table.

Shortly after the GOP convention, Casey appears to have traveled to Europe for a meeting in Madrid in late July with Mehdi Karrubi, a leading Khomeini supporter, now the Speaker of the Iranian Parliament. Jamshid Hashemi said that he and his late brother Cyrus were present at this meeting and at another one in Madrid during August, which they say Casey also attended. The present government of Iran has declined to confirm or deny this contact, saying that "the Islamic Government of Iran sees no benefit to involve itself in the matter."

Casey's whereabouts in the last days of July 1980 are officially unknown. Part of the coverup on the story has been to create uncertainty and confusion on Casey's travels at the time. What is known is that as soon as Casey surfaced again in Washington on July 30, he reported back to vice-presidential candidate George Bush in a dinner meeting held at the Alibi Club. It is certain from the evidence that there were negotiations with the mullahs by the Reagan-Bush camp, and that Bush was heavily involved at every stage.

In early September, Bush's brother, Prescott Bush, Jr., became involved with a letter to James Baker in which he described his contacts with a certain Herbert Cohen, a consultant to the Carter administration on Middle East matters. Cohen had promised to abort any possible Carter moves to "politicize" the hostage issue by openly denouncing any machinations that Carter might attempt. Prescott offered Baker a meeting with Cohen. Were it not for the power of the Brown Brothers Harriman/Skull and Bones networks to control the media, George's brother Prescott Bush might have become something like the Billy Carter of the 1980s.

Sometime in fall 1980, there was a meeting at the L'Enfant Plaza Hotel in Washington among Richard Allen, Bud McFarlane, Laurence Silberman of the Reagan-Bush campaign, and a mysterious Iranian representative, thought to be an emissary of Hashemi Rafsanjani, currently Iranian President and an asset of U.S. intelligence who was then becoming one of the most powerful mullahs in Khomeini's entourage. The Iranian representative offered a deal whereby "he could get the hostages released directly to our campaign before the election," Silberman recalls. [Silberman went on to become a judge in the District of Columbia Appeals Court and led the vote in overturning Oliver North's conviction.] Allen has claimed that he cut this meeting short after 20 minutes. Allen, McFarlane and Silberman all failed to report this approach to the White House, the State Department or other authorities.

On September 22, Iraq invaded Iran, starting a war that would last until the middle of 1988 and which would claim more than a million lives. The U.S. intelligence estimate had been that Khomeini and the mullahs were in danger of losing power by the end of 1980 because of their incompetence, corruption and benighted stupidity. U.S. and other Western intelligence agencies, especially the French, thereupon encouraged Iraq to attack Iran, offering the prospect of an easy victory. The "easy victory" analysis was incorporated into a "secret" CIA report which was delivered to the Saudi Arabian government with the suggestion that it be leaked to Iraq. The real

U.S. estimate was that a war with Iraq would strengthen Khomeini against reformers who looked to President Bani-Sadr, and that the war emergency would assist in the imposition of a "new dark ages" regime in Iran. An added benefit was that Iran and Iraq as warring states would be forced vastly to increase their oil production, forcing down the oil price on the world market and thus providing the bankrupt U.S. dollar with an important subsidy in terms of the dollar's ability to command basic commodities in the real world. Bani-Sadr spoke in this connection of "an oil crisis in reverse" as a result of the Iran-Iraq war.

President Bani-Sadr, who was later deposed in a coup d'état by Khomeini, Rafsanjani and Beheshti, has recalled that during this period, Khomeini decided to bet on Reagan-Bush. "So what if Reagan wins," said Khomeini. "Nothing will really change since he and Carter are both enemies of Islam."[29]

This was the time of the Reagan-Carter presidential debates, and Casey's operation had also yielded booty in this regard. Bush ally and then-Congressman David Stockman boasted in Indiana in late October that he had used a "pilfered copy" of Carter's personal briefing book to coach Reagan prior to the debates.

Many sources agree that a conclusive series of meetings between the Reagan-Bush and Khomeini forces took place in the weeks and months prior to Election Day 1980. In late 1991, as the campaign season heated up, close to a score of articles appeared in the U.S. press responding to Gary Sick's *October Surprise* book, which gave credibility to the charge that the Reagan-Bush campaign had indeed made a dirty deal with the mullahs to prevent the release of the hostages. Even Carter, who said that he had heard such rumors back in 1980, now agreed that a congressional investigation would be helpful in settling the matter. President Bush and an entire gaggle of political operatives and neoconservative journalists denounced Sick's book and the accusation as the fantasies of "conspiracy theorists."

Sick and other journalists who published articles about the affair were severely criticized for retailing the stories of an assortment of intelligence informants, gun-runners, money launderers, pilots and other flotsam and jetsam from the seamy side of international espionage and intrigue by pro-Bush journalists and congressional leaders opposed to probing the accusations. Immediately after the Iran-Contra scandal made headlines in early 1987, numerous sources surfaced and began to contact journalists with purported eyewitness accounts of meetings between Reagan/Bush campaign representatives and Khomeini intermediaries. Several of the sources said they had seen Bush and Casey at meetings in Europe with Khomeini's emissaries. Others offered bits and pieces of information complementing the eyewitness reports.

One source, Richard Brenneke, a self-admitted money launderer and pilot for the CIA, was indicted for perjury by a U.S. Attorney in Colorado for saying he had been told by another alleged CIA pilot, Heinrich Rupp, that he had seen Bush in Paris in October 1980. Brenneke said that he had personally seen Casey and Donald Gregg in Paris at the same time. But a jury acquitted Brenneke. Later, Frank Snepp, a former CIA officer turned investigative reporter, did an exposé published in the *Village Voice*, allegedly proving that Brenneke could not have been in Paris in October 1980 because he had obtained credit card receipts showing that Brenneke was in Oregon at the time he had told others he had been in Paris. The original source on Bush's secret trip to Paris was Oscar LeWinter, a German-based professional snitch, who seems to have done some work for both the Israeli Mossad and the CIA. LeWinter later admitted that he had been paid, allegedly by the CIA, to spread false information about Bush and Casey's secret trips to Europe for meetings with messengers from the mullahs.

Does that mean there is no smoking gun linking Bush to the "coincidence" that the hostages were only released on Inauguration Day 1981, within minutes of Reagan taking his presidential oath? No. What is clear, is that some intelligence apparatus deployed an elaborate disinformation campaign which created a false trail which could be discredited. The intelligence community operation of "damage-control" is premised on revealing some of the truth, mixed with half-truths and blatantly false facts, which allows the bigger story to be undermined. It is possible that Bush was not in Paris in October 1980 to meet with an Iranian delegation to seal the deal. Bush has heatedly denied that he was in Paris at this time, and has said that he personally did not negotiate with Khomeini envoys. But he has generally avoided a blanket denial that the campaign, of which he was a principal, engaged in surreptitious dealings with the Khomeini mullahs.

There is another intriguing possibility: During the same time frame that LeWinter and Brenneke (Oct. 18–19, 1980) say Bush was in Paris, Iranian Prime Minister Ali Rajai was in New York. An adversary of then-President Bani-Sadr and puppet of Khomeini, Prime Minister Ali Rajai was in New York preparing to depart for Algiers after consultations at the United Nations. Rajai had refused all contact with Carter, Muskie and other U.S. officials, but he may have been more interested in meeting Bush or one of his representatives. What is now well documented is, that throughout 1980, many Reagan/Bush campaign officials were tripping over themselves to meet with anyone purporting to be an Iranian. If a deal were to be authenticated, there is no question that Khomeini and crew would have sought a handshake from someone who could not later deny the agreement.

Between October 21 and October 23, Israel dispatched a planeload of much-needed F–4 Phantom jet spare parts to Iran in violation of the U.S. arms boycott. Who in Washington had sanctioned these shipments? In Teheran, the U.S. hostages were reportedly dispersed into a multitude of locations on October 22. Also on October 22, Prime Minister Rajai, back from New York and Algiers, announced that Iran wanted neither American spare parts nor American arms.

The Iranian approach to the ongoing contacts with the Carter administration now began to favor evasive delaying tactics. There were multiple indications that Khomeini had decided that Reagan-Bush was a better bet than Carter, and that Reagan-Bush had made the more generous offer.

Barbara Honegger, then an official of the Reagan-Bush campaign, recalls that "on October 24th or 25th, an assistant to Stephan Halper's 'October Surprise' intelligence operation echoed William Casey's newfound confidence, boasting to the author in the operations center where [Reagan-Bush Iran-watcher Michel] Smith worked that the campaign no longer needed to worry about an 'October Surprise' because Dick [Allen] cut a deal."[30]

On October 27, Bush campaigned in Pittsburgh, where he addressed a gathering of labor leaders. His theme that day was the Iranian attempt to "manipulate" the outcome of the U.S. election through the exertion of "last-minute leverage" involving the hostages. "It's no secret that the Iranians do not want to see Ronald Reagan elected President," Bush lied. "They want to play a hand in the election—with our 52 hostages as the 52 cards in their negotiating deck." It was a "cool, cynical, unconscionable ploy" by the Khomeini regime. Bush asserted that it was "fair to ask how come right now there's talk of releasing them [the hostages] after nearly a year." His implication was that Carter was the one with the dirty deal. Bush concluded that he wanted the hostages "out as soon as possible. . . . We want them home and we'll worry about who to blame later."[31]

During the first week of December, *Executive Intelligence Review* reported that Henry Kissinger "held a series of meetings during the week of November 12 in Paris with representatives of Ayatollah

Beheshti, leader of the fundamentalist clergy in Iran. . . . Top-level intelligence sources in Reagan's inner circle confirmed Kissinger's unreported talks with the Iranian mullahs, but stressed that the Kissinger initiative was totally unauthorized by the president-elect." According to *EIR*, "it appears that the pattern of cooperation between the Khomeini people and circles nominally in Reagan's camp began approximately six to eight weeks ago, at the height of President Carter's efforts to secure an arms-for-hostages deal with Teheran. Carter's failure to secure the deal, which a number of observers believe cost him the November 4 election, apparently resulted from an intervention in Teheran by pro-Reagan British circles and the Kissinger faction."[32] These revelations from *EIR* are the first mention in the public record of the scandal which has come over the years to be known as the October Surprise.

The hostages were not released before the November election, which Reagan won convincingly. Khomeini kept the hostages imprisoned until January 20, the day of the Reagan-Bush inauguration, and let the hostage plane take off just as Reagan and Bush were taking their oaths of office.

Whether George Bush was personally present in Paris, or at other meetings with Iranian representatives where the hostage and arms questions were on the agenda, has yet to be conclusively proven. Here a thorough and intrusive congressional investigation of the Carter and Reagan machinations in this regard is long overdue. Such a probe might also shed light on the origins of the Iran-Iraq war, which set the stage for the more recent Gulf crisis. But, quite apart from questions regarding George Bush's presence at this or that meeting, there can be no doubt that both the Carter regime and the Reagan-Bush campaign were actively involved in dealings with the Khomeini regime concerning the hostages and concerning the timing of their possible release. In the case of the Reagan-Bush Iran connection, there is reason to believe that federal crimes in violation of the Logan Act and other applicable laws may have taken place.

George Bush had now grasped the interim prize that had eluded him since 1968: After more than a dozen years of effort, he had now become the Vice President of the United States.

Notes for Chapter XV

1. For Bush's business dealings of 1977–79, see Bob Woodward and Walter Pincus, "Doing Well With Help From Family, Friends," *Washington Post*, Aug. 11, 1988.

2. Albert Pike to Robert Toombs, May 20, 1861 in *The War of the Rebellion: A Compilation of the Official Records of the Union and Confederate Armies* (Washington: U.S. Government Printing Office, 1881), Series I, Vol. III, pp. 580–81. See also James David Carter, *History of the Supreme Council, 330 (Mother Council of the World), Ancient and Accepted Scottish Rite of*

Freemasonry Southern Jurisdiction, U.S.A., 1861–1891 (Washington: The Supreme Council, 330, 1967), pp. 5–24, and James David Carter, Ed., *The First Century of Scottish Rite Masonry in Texas: 1867–1967* (Texas Scottish Rite Bodies, 1967), pp. 32–33, 42.

3. Fredericka Meiners, *A History of Rice University: The Institute Years, 1907–1963* (Houston: Rice University, 1982).

4. Ronald Brownstein and Nina Easton, *Reagan's Ruling Class* (New York: Pantheon Books, 1983), p. 650.

5. Joe Conason, "Company Man," *Village Voice,* Oct. 1988.

6. Bob Callahan, "Agents for Bush," *Covert Action Information Bulletin,* No. 33 (Winter 1990), pp. 5 ff.

7. Harris Worcester, "Travels with Bush and Connally," *Texas Observer,* Sept. 22, 1978.

8. Harry Hurt III, "George Bush, Plucky Lad," *Texas Monthly,* June 1983, p. 206.

9. L. Wolfe, "King George VII Campaigns in New Hampshire," *New Solidarity,* Jan. 8, 1980.

10. Jeff Greenfield, *The Real Campaign* (New York: Summit Books, 1982), pp. 36–37.

11. See Jeff Greenfield, *op. cit.,* pp. 40–41.

12. See Lyndon LaRouche, "Is Republican George Bush a 'Manchurian Candidate'?" issued by Citizens for LaRouche, Manchester, New Hampshire, Jan. 12, 1980.

13. Quoted in Greenfield, *op. cit.,* p. 44.

14. Manchester *Union Leader,* Feb. 24, 1980.

15. Sidney Blumenthal, *The Rise of the Counter-Establishment* (New York: Perennial Library, 1988), pp. 82–83.

16. Mark Bisnow, *Diary of a Dark Horse: The 1980 Anderson Presidential Campaign* (Carbondale: Southern Illinois University Press, 1983), p. 136.

17. For the *Nashua Telegraph* debate, see: Jeff Greenfield, *op. cit.,* pp. 44 ff.; Mark Bisnow, *op. cit.,* pp. 134 ff.; Jules Witcover and Jack Germond, *Blue Smoke and Mirrors* (New York: Viking, 1981), pp. 116 ff.

18. David Leigh, *The Wilson Plot: The Intelligence Services and the Discrediting of a Prime Minister* (London: Heinemann, 1988), *passim.*

19. Germond and Witcover, *op. cit.,* p. 169.

20. *Ibid.,* p. 170.

21. *Ibid.,* p. 171.

22. The best testimony on this is Reagan's own response to a question from Witcover and Germond. Asked if "it was true that he was trying to get President Ford to run with him," Reagan promptly responded, "Oh, sure. That would be the best." See Germond and Witcover, *op. cit.,* p. 178.

23. Germond and Witcover, *op. cit.,* p. 188.

24. See Henry Pringle, *Theodore Roosevelt, A Biography* (New York: Harcourt Brace, 1931), p. 223.

25. *Washington Star,* July 15, 1980.

26. *EIR Special Report:* "Treason in Washington: New Evidence on the October Surprise," (Washington: March 1992).

27. See *EIR Special Report:* "Project Democracy: The 'Parallel Government' Behind the Iran-Contra Affair" (Washington, 1987), pp. 88–101.

28. Gary Sick, "The Election Story of the Decade," *New York Times,* April 15, 1991.

29. Abol Hassan Bani-Sadr, *My Turn to Speak* (New York: Brassey's, U.S., 1991), p. 33.

30. Barbara Honegger, *October Surprise* (New York: Tudor Publishing Co., 1989) p. 58.

31. *Washington Post,* Oct. 28, 1980.

32. *Executive Intelligence Review,* Dec. 2, 1980.

XVI

THE ATTEMPTED COUP D'ETAT OF MARCH 30, 1981

"Bizarre happenstance, a weird coincidence"
—Bush spokeswoman Shirley M. Green, March 31, 1981

Cui prodest scelus, est fecit*
—Seneca, first century A.D.

For Bush, the vice-presidency was not an end in itself, but merely another stage in the ascent toward the pinnacle of the federal bureaucracy, the White House. With the help of his Brown Brothers Harriman/Skull and Bones network, Bush had now reached the point where but a single human life stood between him and the presidency.

Ronald Reagan was 70 years old when he took office, the oldest man ever to be inaugurated as President. His mind wandered; long fits of slumber crept over his cognitive faculties. On some days, he may have kept bankers' hours with his papers and briefing books and meetings in the Oval Office, but he needed a long nap most afternoons and became distraught if he could not have one. His custom was to delegate all administrative decisions to the cabinet members, to the executive departments and agencies. Policy questions were delegated to the White House staff, who prepared the options and then guided Reagan's decisions among the pre-defined options. This was the staff that composed not just Reagan's speeches, but the script of his entire life: Normally, every word that Reagan spoke in meetings and conferences, every line down to and

*The one who benefits from the crime is the one who committed it.

including "Good morning, Senator," every word was typed on three-by-five file cards from which Reagan would read.

But sometimes Reagan was capable of lucidity, and even of inspired greatness, in the way a thunderstorm can momentarily illuminate a darkling countryside; these moments often involved direct personal impressions or feelings. Reagan's instinctive contempt for Bush after the *Nashua Telegraph* debate was one of his better moments. Reagan's greatest moment of conceptual clarity came in his television speech of March 23, 1983 on the Strategic Defense Initiative, a concept that had been drummed into the Washington bureaucracy through the indefatigable efforts of Lyndon LaRouche and a few others. The idea of defending against nuclear missiles, of not accepting Mutually Assured Destruction, and of using such a program as a science driver for rapid technological renewal was something Reagan permanently grasped and held onto, even under intense pressure in Hofdie House in Reykjavik in October 1986 during the summit with Gorbachov.

In addition, during the early years of Reagan's first term, there were enough Reaganite loyalists in the administration, typified by William Clark, to cause much trouble for the Bushmen. But as the years went by, the few men like Clark whom Reagan had brought with him from California would be ground up by endless bureaucratic warfare, and their replacements, like McFarlane at the NSC, would come more and more from the ranks of the Kissingerians. Unfortunately, Reagan never developed a plan to make the SDI an irreversible political and budgetary reality, and this critical shortcoming grew out of Reagan's failed economic policies, which never substantially departed from Carter's.

But apart from rare moments like the SDI, Reagan tended to drift. Don Regan called it "the guesswork presidency"; for Al Haig, frustrated in his own lust for power, it was government by an all-powerful staff. Who were the staff? At first, it was thought that Reagan would take most of his advice from his old friend Edwin Meese, his close associate from California days, loyal and devoted to Reagan, and sporting his Adam Smith tie. But it was soon evident that the White House was really run by a troika: Meese, Michael Deaver, and James Baker III, Bush's man.

Deaver gravitated by instinct toward Baker; Deaver tells us in his memoirs that he was a supporter of Bush for Vice President at the Detroit convention. This meant that James Baker-Michael Deaver became the dominant force over Ron and over Nancy; George Bush, in other words, already had an edge in the bureaucratic infighting.

Thus it was that White House Press Secretary James Brady could say in early March 1981: "Bush is functioning much like a co-president. George is involved in all the national security stuff because of his special background as CIA Director. All the budget working groups he was there, the economic working groups, the Cabinet meetings. He is included in almost all the meetings."[1]

During the first months of the Reagan administration, Bush found himself locked in a power struggle with Gen. Alexander Haig, whom Reagan had appointed to be Secretary of State. Haig was a real threat to the Bushmen. Haig was first of all a Kissinger clone with credentials to rival Bush's own; Haig had worked on Henry's staff during the Nixon years; he had been the White House chief of staff who had eased Nixon out the door with no trial, but with an imminent pardon. Haig's gifts of intrigue were considerable. And Haig was just as devoted to the Zionist neoconservatives as Bush was, with powerful ties in the direction of the Anti-Defamation League. It was, altogether, a challenge not to be taken lightly. Haig thought that he had been a rival to Bush for the vice-presidency at the Detroit convention, and perhaps he had been.

Inexorably, the Brown Brothers Harriman/Skull and Bones networks went into action against Haig. The idea was to paint him as a power-hungry megalomaniac bent on dominating the administration of the weak figurehead Reagan. This would then be supplemented by a vicious campaign of leaking by James Baker and Michael Deaver, designed to play Reagan against Haig and vice-versa, until the rival to Bush could be eliminated.

The wrecking operation against Haig started during his confirmation hearings, during which he had to answer more questions about Watergate than Bush had faced in 1975, when the facts were much more recent. Senator Paul Tsongas was wired in: Tsongas, motivating his negative vote against Haig's confirmation, told the nominee: "You are going to dominate this administration, if I may say so. You are by far the strongest personality that's going to be in there."[2]

Three weeks into the new administration, Haig concluded that "someone in the White House staff was attempting to communicate with me through the press," by a process of constant leakage, including leakage of the contents of secret diplomatic papers. Haig protested to Meese, NSC chief Richard Allen, James Baker and Bush. Shortly thereafter, Haig noted that "Baker's messengers sent rumors of my imminent departure or dismissal murmuring through the press. . . . Soon, a 'senior presidential aide' was quoted in a syndicated column as saying, 'We will get this man [Haig] under control.' "[3] It took more than a year for Baker and Bush to drive

Haig out of the administration. Ultimately, it was Haig's role in the Malvinas crisis in April 1982, where he played a filthy inside game for the British, which weakened Haig to the point that he could be finished off. Shortly before his ouster, Haig got a report of a White House meeting during which Baker was reported to have said, "Haig is going to go, and quickly, and we are going to make it happen."[4]

Haig's principal bureaucratic ploy during the first weeks of the Reagan administration was his submission to Reagan, on the day of his inauguration, of a draft executive order to organize the National Security Council and interagency task forces, including the crisis staffs, according to Haig's wishes. Haig refers to this document as National Security Decision Directive 1 (NSDD 1), and laments that it was never signed in its original form, and that no comparable directive for structuring the NSC interagency groups was signed for over a year. Ultimately a document called NSDD 1 would be signed, establishing a Special Situation Group (SSG) crisis management staff chaired by Bush. Haig's draft would have made the Secretary of State the chairman of the SSG crisis staff in conformity with Haig's demand to be recognized as Reagan's "vicar of foreign policy." This was unacceptable to Bush, who made sure, with the help of James Baker and probably also Deaver, that Haig's draft of NSDD 1 would never be signed.

Haig writes about this bureaucratic struggle as the battle for the IG's (Interagency Groups) and SIG's (Special or Senior Interagency Groups), generally populated by undersecretaries, assistant secretaries, and deputy assistant secretaries within the NSC framework. As Haig points out, these Kissingerian structures are the locus of much real power, especially under a weak President like Reagan. Haig notes that

> in organizational terms, the key to the system is the substructure of SIG's and IG's in which the fundamentals of policy (domestic and foreign) are decided. On instructions from the President, the IG's (as I will call the whole lot, for the sake of convenience), can summon up all the human and informational resources of the federal government, study specific issues, and develop policy options and recommendations. . . . IG chairmanships are parceled out to State and other departments and agencies according to their interests and their influence. As Kissinger, that canny veteran of marches and countermarches in the faculty of Harvard University, recognized, he who controls the key IG's controls the flow of options to the President and, therefore, to a degree, controls policy.[5]

The struggle between Haig and Bush culminated toward the end of Reagan's first 100 days in office. Haig was chafing because the

White House staff, meaning James Baker, was denying him access to the President. Haig's NSDD 1 had still not been signed. Then, on Sunday, March 22, Haig's attention was called to an elaborate leak to reporter Martin Schram that had appeared that day in the *Washington Post* under the headline "White House Revamps Top Policy Roles; Bush to Head Crisis Management." Haig's attention was drawn to the following paragraphs:

> Partly in an effort to bring harmony to the Reagan high command, it has been decided that Vice President George Bush will be placed in charge of a new structure for national security crisis management, according to senior presidential assistants. This assignment will amount to an unprecedented role for a vice president in modern times. In the Carter administration, the crisis management structure was chaired by Zbigniew Brzezinski, the national security adviser. . . .
>
> Bush's stature, by virtue of job title and experience, was cited as the reason that he was chosen to chair meetings in the Situation Room in time of crisis. Principal officials involved in crisis management will be the secretaries of state and defense, the Central Intelligence Agency director, the national security adviser, Meese, and Baker, officials said, adding that the structure has not been fully devised nor the presidential directive written.
>
> Reagan officials emphasized that Bush, a former director of the CIA and former United Nations ambassador, would be able to preserve White House control over crisis management without irritating Haig, who they stressed was probably the most experienced and able of all other officials who could serve in that function.
>
> "The reason for this [choice of Bush] is that the secretary of state might wish he were chairing the crisis management structure," said one Reagan official, "but it is pretty hard to argue with the vice president being in charge."[6]

Haig says that he called Ed Meese at the White House to check the truth of this report, and that Meese replied that there was no truth to it. Haig went to see Reagan at the White House. Reagan was concerned about the leak, and reassured Haig: "I want you to know that the story in the *Post* is a fabrication. It means that George would sit in for me in the NSC in my absence, and that's all it means. It doesn't affect your authority in any way." Haig also says that he received a further call from Reagan assuring him that his authority was not to be diminished in the slightest.

But later the same afternoon, White House Press Secretary James Brady read the following statement to the press: "I am confirming today the President's decision to have the Vice President chair the

Administration's 'crisis management' team, as a part of the National
Security Council system. . . . President Reagan's choice of the Vice
President was guided in large measure by the fact that management
of crises has traditionally—and appropriately—been done in the
White House."[7]

Haig says he then drew up his letter of resignation, but hesitated
to sign it. He called Bush to complain: "The American people can't
be served by this. It's an impossible situation for you and me to be
in. Of course, you chair the NSC in the President's absence. We
didn't need to say it. This is all mischief. Why the hell did they do
this without discussing it with me?" Haig went on: "I have been
dealt with duplicitously, George. The President has been used. I
need a public reaffirmation of my role or I can't stay here."

Can it be that Haig was so naive that he did not realize that Bush
was his ruthless rival and the source of many of his problems? Haig
undoubtedly knew, but chose not to say so in memoirs written after
he had been defeated. For Haig also knew that Bush was vindictive.
Haig does note that he was convinced that Meese was not part of
the cabal out to get him. Haig had further conversations with Reagan
during these days, which often seemed to have cleared up the confusion, but which in retrospect were never conclusive. In the meantime,
George Bush had seized control of the Special Situation Group,
which would take control of the executive branch in time of crisis
or national emergency. It was a superb starting point for a coup
d'état.

In the midst of the Bush-James Baker cabal's relentless drive
to seize control over the Reagan administration, John Warnock
Hinckley, Jr. carried out his attempt to assassinate President Reagan
on the afternoon of March 30, 1981. George Bush was visiting
Texas that day. Bush was flying from Fort Worth to Austin in his
Air Force Two Boeing 707. In Fort Worth, Bush had unveiled a
plaque at the Hyatt Regency Hotel, the old Hotel Texas, designating
it as a national historic site. This was the hotel, coincidentally, in
which John F. Kennedy had spent the last night of his life, before
going on to Dallas the next day, November 22, 1963.

In Austin, Bush was scheduled to deliver an address to a joint
session of the Texas state legislature. It was Al Haig who called Bush
and told him that the President had been shot, while forwarding
the details of Reagan's condition, insofar as they were known, by
scrambler as a classified message. Haig was in touch with James
Baker III, who was close to Reagan at George Washington University
hospital. Bush's man in the White House situation room was Adm.
Dan Murphy, who was standing right next to Haig. Bush agreed

with Haig's estimate that he ought to return to Washington at once. But first his plane needed to be refueled, so it landed at Carswell Air Force Base near Austin.

Bush says that his flight from Carswell to Andrews Air Force Base near Washington took about two and one-half hours, and that he arrived at Andrews at about 6:40 P.M. Bush says he was told by Ed Meese that the operation to remove the bullet that had struck Reagan was a success, and that the President was likely to survive.

Back at the White House, the principal cabinet officers had assembled in the Situation Room and had been running a crisis management committee during the afternoon. Haig says he was at first adamant that a conspiracy, if discovered, should be ruthlessly exposed: "It was essential that we get the facts and publish them quickly. Rumor must not be allowed to breed on this tragedy. Remembering the aftermath of the Kennedy assassination, I said to Woody Goldberg, 'No matter what the truth is about this shooting, the American people must know it.' "[8] But the truth has never been established.

Defense Secretary Caspar Weinberger's memoir of that afternoon reminds us of two highly relevant facts. The first is that a "NORAD [North American Air Defense Command] exercise with a simulated incoming missile attack had been planned for the next day." Weinberger agreed with Gen. David Jones, the Chairman of the Joint Chiefs of Staff, that this exercise should be canceled.[9]

Weinberger also recalls that the group in the Situation Room was informed by James Baker that "there had been a FEMA [Federal Emergency Management Agency] exercise scheduled for the next day on presidential succession, with the general title 'Nine Lives.' By an immediate consensus, it was agreed that exercise should also be canceled."[10]

As Weinberger further recalls, "at almost exactly 7:00, the Vice President came to the Situation Room and very calmly assumed the chair at the head of the table."[11] Bush asked Weinberger for a report on the status of U.S. forces, which Weinberger furnished.

Another eyewitness of these transactions was Don Regan, whom the Tower Commission later made the fall-guy for Bush's Iran-Contra escapades. Regan records that "the Vice President arrived with Ed Meese, who had met him when he landed to fill him in on the details. George asked for a condition report: 1) on the President; 2) on the other wounded; 3) on the assailant; 4) on the international scene. . . . After the reports were given and it was determined that there were no international complications and no domestic conspiracy, it was decided that the U.S. government would carry on business as usual. The Vice President would go on TV from the White House to reassure the nation and to demonstrate that he was in charge."[12]

As Weinberger recounts the same moments: "[Attorney General William French Smith] then reported that all FBI reports concurred with the information I had received; that the shooting was a completely isolated incident and that the assassin, John Hinckley, with a previous record in Nashville, seemed to be a 'Bremmer' type, a reference to the attempted assassin of George Wallace."[13]

Those who were not watching carefully here may have missed the fact that just a few minutes after George Bush had walked into the room, he had presided over the sweeping under the rug of the decisive question regarding Hinckley and his actions: Was Hinckley a part of a conspiracy, domestic or international? Not more than five hours after the attempt to kill Reagan, on the basis of the most fragmentary early reports, before Hinckley had been properly questioned, and before a full investigation had been carried out, a group of cabinet officers chaired by George Bush had ruled out *a priori* any conspiracy. Haig, whose memoirs talk most about the possibility of a conspiracy, does not seem to have objected to this incredible decision.

From that moment on, "no conspiracy" became the official doctrine of the U.S. regime, for the moment a Bush regime, and the most massive efforts were undertaken to stifle any suggestion to the contrary. The iron curtain came down on the truth about Hinckley.

The Conspiracy

Curiously enough, press accounts emerging over the next few days provided a *prima facie* case that there had been a conspiracy around the Hinckley attentat, and that the conspiracy had included members of Bush's immediate family. Most of the overt facts were not disputed, but were actually confirmed by Bush and his son Neil.

On Tuesday, March 31, the *Houston Post* published a copyrighted story under the headline: "Bush's Son Was to Dine with Suspect's Brother," by Arthur Wiese and Margaret Downing. The lead paragraph read as follows: "Scott Hinckley, the brother of John Hinckley, Jr., who is charged with shooting President Reagan and three others, was to have been a dinner guest Tuesday night at the home of Neil Bush, son of Vice President George Bush, the *Houston Post* has learned."

According to the article, Neil Bush had admitted on Monday, March 30 that he was personally acquainted with Scott Hinckley, having met with him on one occasion in the recent past. Neil Bush also stated that he knew the Hinckley family, and referred to large monetary contributions made by the Hinckleys to the Bush 1980 presidential campaign. Neil Bush and Scott Hinckley both lived in Denver at this time. Scott Hinckley was the vice president of Vanderbilt Energy Corporation, and Neil Bush was employed as a landman for Standard Oil of Indiana. John W. Hinckley, Jr., the would-be assassin, lived on and off with his family in Evergreen, Colorado, not far from Denver.

Neil Bush was reached for comment on Monday, March 30, and was asked if, in addition to Scott Hinckley, he also knew John W. Hinckley, Jr., the would-be killer. "I have no idea," said Neil Bush. "I don't recognize any pictures of him. I just wish I could see a better picture of him."

Sharon Bush, Neil's wife, was also asked about her acquaintance with the Hinckley family. "I don't even know the brother," she replied, suggesting that Scott Hinckley was coming to dinner as the date of a woman whom Sharon did know. "From what I know and have heard, they [the Hinckleys] are a very nice family . . . and have given a lot of money to the Bush campaign. I understand he [John W. Hinckley, Jr.] was just the renegade brother in the family. They must feel awful."

It also proved necessary for Bush's office to deny that the Vice President was familiar with the "Hinckley-Bush connection." Bush's press secretary, the British-born Peter Teeley, said when asked to comment: "I don't know a damn thing about it. I was talking to someone earlier tonight, and I couldn't even remember his [Hinckley's] name. All I know is what you're telling me." Teeley denied that Bush had revealed that he knew Hinckley or the Hinckley family when he first heard the assassin's name; the Vice President "made no mention of it whatsoever." Bush, repeated Teeley, "certainly didn't indicate anything like that."

Chase Untermeyer of Bush's staff, who had been with him throughout the day of the assassination attempt, put in that, in his recollection, Bush had not been told the assailant's name through the time that Bush reached the Naval Observatory in Washington on his way to the White House.

On April 1, 1981, the *Rocky Mountain News* of Denver carried an account of a press conference given the previous day in Denver by Neil Bush. During most of the day on March 31, Neil Bush had refused to answer phone calls from the media, referring them to the vice-presidential press office in Washington. But then he appeared in front of the Amoco Building at East 17th Avenue and Broadway in Denver, saying that he was willing to meet the media once, but then wanted to "leave it at that." As it turned out, his wishes were to be scrupulously respected, at least until the Silverado Savings and Loan scandal got out of hand some years later.

The *Rocky Mountain News* article signed by Charles Roos carried Neil Bush's confirmation that if the assassination attempt had not happened on March 30, Scott Hinckley would have been present at a dinner party at Neil Bush's home the night of March 31. According to Neil, Scott Hinckley had come to the home of Neil and Sharon Bush on January 23, 1981 to be present along with about 30 other guests at a surprise birthday party for Neil, who had turned 26 one day earlier. Scott Hinckley had come "through a close friend who brought him," according to this version, and this same close female friend was scheduled to come to dinner along with Scott Hinckley on that last night of March, 1981.

"My wife set up a surprise party for me, and it truly was a surprise, and it was an honor for me at that time to meet Scott Hinckley," said Neil Bush to reporters. "He is a good and decent man. I have no regrets whatsoever in saying Scott Hinckley can be considered a friend of mine. To have had one meeting doesn't make the best of friends, but I have no regrets in saying I do know him."

Neil Bush told the reporters that he had never met John W. Hinckley, Jr., the gunman, nor his father, John W. Hinckley, Sr., president and chairman of the board of Vanderbilt Energy Corporation of Denver. But Neil Bush also added that he would be interested in meeting the elder Hinckley: "I would like [to meet him]. I'm trying to learn the oil business, and he's in the oil business. I probably could learn something from Mr. Hinckley."

Neil Bush then announced that he wanted to "set straight" certain inaccuracies that had appeared the previous day in the *Houston Post* about the relations between the Bush and Hinckley families. The first was his own wife Sharon's reference to the large contributions from the Hinckleys to the Bush campaign. Neil asserted that the 1980 Bush campaign records showed no money whatever coming in from any of the Hinckleys. All that could be found, he argued, was a contribution to that "great Republican," John Connally.

The other issue the *Houston Post* had raised regarded the 1978 period, when George W. Bush of Midland, Texas, Neil's oldest brother, had run for Congress in Texas's 19th Congressional District. At that time Neil Bush had worked for George W. Bush as his campaign manager, and in this connection Neil had lived in Lubbock, Texas during most of the year. This raised the question of whether Neil might have been in touch with gunman John W. Hinckley, Jr. during that year of 1978, since gunman Hinckley had lived in Lubbock from 1974 through 1980, when he was an intermittent student at Texas Tech University there. Neil Bush ruled out any contact between the Bush family and gunman John W. Hinckley, Jr. in Lubbock during that time.

The previous day, elder son George W. Bush had been far less categorical about never having met gunman Hinckley. He had stated to the press: "It's certainly conceivable that I met him or might have been introduced to him. . . . I don't recognize his face from the brief, kind of distorted thing they had on TV, and the name doesn't ring any bells. I know he wasn't on our staff. I could check our volunteer rolls." But now Neil was adamant: There had been no contact.

Neil Bush's confirmation of his relations with Scott Hinckley was matched by a parallel confirmation from the Executive Office of the Vice President. This appeared in the *Houston Post*, April 1, 1981 under the headline, "Vice President Confirms his Son was to have Hosted Hinckley Brother," by *Post* Washington Bureau Chief Arthur Wiese. Here the second-string press secretary, Shirley M. Green, was doing the talking. "I've spoken to Neil," she said, "and he says they never saw [Scott] Hinckley again [after the birthday party]. They kept saying 'we've got to get together,' but they never made any plans until tonight." Contradicting Neil Bush's remarks, Ms. Green asserted that Neil Bush knew Scott Hinckley "only slightly."

Shirley Green described the Tuesday night dinner appointment as "a bizarre happenstance, a weird occurrence."

Later in the day, Bush spokesman Peter Teeley surfaced to deny any campaign donations from the Hinckley clan to the Bush campaign. When asked why Sharon Bush and Neil Bush had made reference to large political contributions from the Hinckleys to the Bush campaign, Teeley responded, "I don't have the vaguest idea." "We've gone through our files," said Teeley, "and we have absolutely no information that he [John W. Hinckley, Sr.] or anybody in the family were contributors, supporters, anything."

A summary of this material was made generally available through the Associated Press, which published a short note on March 31.

It is not known how many newspapers chose to print the AP dispatch; it would appear that the *Washington Post*, for one, did not do so. The electronic media also do not appear to have devoted much attention to this story. Once the cabinet had decided that there had been no conspiracy, all such facts were irrelevant anyway. There is no record of Neil Bush, George W. Bush, or Vice President George H.W. Bush ever having been questioned by the FBI in regard to the contacts described. They never appeared before a grand jury or a congressional investigating committee. Which is another way of saying that by March 1981, the United States government had degenerated into total lawlessness, with special exemptions for the now-ruling Bush family. Government by law had dissolved.

The media were not interested in the dinner date of Neil Bush and Scott Hinckley, but they were very interested indeed in the soap opera of what had gone on in the Situation Room in the White House during the afternoon of March 30. Since the media had been looking for ways to go after Haig for weeks, they simply continued this line into their coverage of the White House scene that afternoon. Haig had appeared before the television cameras to say:

> Constitutionally, gentlemen, you have the President, the Vice President, and the Secretary of State, in that order, and should the President decide that he wants to transfer the helm he will do so. He has not done that. As of now, I am in control here, in the White House, pending the return of the Vice President and in close touch with him. If something came up, I would check with him, of course.

The "I'm in control here" story on Haig was made into the leitmotif for his sacking, which was still a year in the future. Reagan's own ghostwritten biography published the year after he left office gives a good idea what James Baker and Michael Deaver fed the confused and wounded President about what had gone on during his absence:

> On the day I was shot, George Bush was out of town and Haig immediately came to the White House and claimed he was in charge of the country. Even after the vice-president was back in Washington, I was told he maintained that he, not George, should be in charge. I didn't know about this when it was going on. But I heard later that the rest of the cabinet was furious. They said he acted as if he thought he had the right to sit in the Oval Office and believed it was his constitutional right to take over—a position without any legal basis.[14]

This fantastic account finds no support in the Regan or Weinberger memoirs, but is a fair sample of the Bushman line.

Manchurian Candidate?

What also interested the media very much was the story of John W. Hinckley, Jr.'s obsession with the actress Jodie Foster, who had played the role of a teenage prostitute in the 1976 movie "Taxi Driver." The prostitute is befriended by a taxi driver, Travis Bickle, who threatens to kill a Senator who is running for President in order to win the love of the girl. Young John Hinckley had imitated the habits and mannerisms of Travis Bickle.

When John Hinckley, Jr. had left his hotel room in Washington, D.C. on his way to shoot Reagan, he had left behind a letter to Jodie Foster:

> Dear Jodie,
>   There is a definite possibility that I will be killed in my attempt to get Reagan. It is for this reason that I am writing you this letter now. As you well know by now, I love you very much. The past seven months I have left you dozens of poems, letters, and messages in the faint hope you would develop an interest in me. . . . Jodie, I'm asking you to please look into your heart and at least give me the chance with this historical deed to gain your respect and love.
>   I love you forever.
>   [signed] John Hinckley[15]

In 1980, Jodie Foster was enrolled at Yale University in New Haven, Connecticut, as an undergraduate. Hinckley spent three weeks in September 1980 in a New Haven hotel, according to the *New York Daily News*. In early October, he spent several days in New Haven, this time at the Colony Inn motel. Two bartenders in a bar near the Yale campus recalled Hinckley as having bragged about his relationship with Jodie Foster. Hinckley had been arrested by airport authorities in Nashville, Tennessee on October 9, 1980 for carrying three guns, and was quickly released. Reagan had been in Nashville on October 7, and Carter arrived there on October 9. The firearms charge on the same day that the President was coming to town should have landed Hinckley on the Secret Service watch list of potential presidential assassins, but the FBI apparently neglected to transmit the information to the Secret Service.

In February 1981, Hinckley was again near the Yale campus. During this time, Hinckley claimed that he was in contact with Jodie Foster by mail and telephone. Jodie Foster had indeed received a series of letters and notes from Hinckley, which she had passed on to her college dean. The dean allegedly gave the letters to the New Haven police, who supposedly gave them to the FBI. Nevertheless, nothing was done to restrain Hinckley, who had a record of psychiatric treatment. Hinckley had been buying guns in various locations across the United States. Was Hinckley a Manchurian candidate, brainwashed to carry out his role as an assassin? Was a network operating through the various law enforcement agencies responsible for the failure to restrain Hinckley or to put him under special surveillance?

The FBI soon officially rubber-stamped the order promulgated by the cabinet that no conspiracy be found: "There was no conspiracy and Hinckley acted alone," said the bureau. Hinckley's parents' memoir refers to some notes penciled by Hinckley which were found during a search of his cell and which "could sound bad." These notes "described an imaginary conspiracy—either with the political left or the political right . . . to assassinate the President." Hinckley's lawyers, from Edward Bennett Williams's law firm, said that the notes were too absurd to be taken seriously, and they have been suppressed.[16]

In July 1985, the FBI was compelled to release some details of its investigation of Hinckley under the Freedom of Information Act. No explanation was offered of how it was determined that Hinckley had acted alone, and the names of all witnesses were censored. According to a wire service account, "The file made no mention of papers seized from Hinckley's prison cell at Butner, North Carolina, which reportedly made reference to a conspiracy. Those writings were ruled inadmissible by the trial judge and never made public."[17]

The FBI has refused to release 22 pages of documents concerning Hinckley's "associates and organizations," 22 pages about his personal finances, and 37 pages about his personality and character. The Williams and Connally defense team argued that Hinckley was insane, controlled by his obsession with Jodie Foster. The jury accepted this version, and in July 1982, Hinckley was found not guilty by reason of insanity. He was remanded to St. Elizabeth's mental hospital where he remains to this day with no fixed term to serve; his mental condition is periodically reviewed by his doctors.

The other aspect of the case that would have merited more careful scrutiny was the relation of John W. Hinckley, Sr., the gunman's father, to the U.S. intelligence community. The line in the press right after the assassination attempt was that "the father of John Hinckley is a devout Christian who did work in Africa." Some papers also included the fact that John W. Hinckley, Sr. had also worked with World Vision, beginning in 1976. World Vision describes itself as the largest "international Christian relief and development agency" active in the Third World. It is officially a joint activity of the Episcopal and Presbyterian churches.

"Jack" Hinckley, as the gunman's father was frequently called, during the 1970s became a close associate of Robert Ainsworth, the director of U.S. Ministries for World Vision, Inc. Jack Hinckley's profile was that of a born-again Christian. Jack Hinckley and Ainsworth traveled together to the Sahel region of Africa, Zimbabwe, and South Africa. Even before joining World Vision, Jack Hinckley had carried on "relief work" in Guatemala. "Jack and I became very close," Ainsworth said. "Jack was a successful businessman. On occasion he would ask us to pray for his son. It's not that Jack felt that John would do something bad, just that John had no direction, John had not found himself."

World Vision is one of the notorious non-governmental organizations that function as a de facto arm of U.S. intelligence under current arrangements. Robert Ainsworth's pedigree is impressive: He was a foreign area analyst for the U.S. State Department; an adviser in Vietnam during the war there; and chaired an international committee involved in the negotiation of the Chemical and Bacteriological Warfare Treaty of 1973.

The largest contributor to World Vision is the U.S. State Department Agency for International Development (AID), whose program is frankly genocide. Pax Christi, the Catholic human rights organization, has accused world vision of functioning as a "Trojan horse for U.S. foreign policy."[18] The entire milieu is thus redolent of the U.S. intelligence agencies.

Reagan went into a long convalescence, first in the hospital and then at his ranch in California. Even when Reagan was pronounced fully recovered, he was even more detached than before, even more absent, even more dependent on his long afternoon nap.

Nancy Reagan, crazed by fear and unable to comprehend the forces that had been at work behind the assassination attempt, vastly increased her reliance on the astrological advice of her resident clairvoyant, Joan Quigley. Through this channel, the Occult Bureau of British Intelligence and its co-thinkers at Langley acquired an awesome capability of manipulation over the Reagan presidency, which could often be mobilized in favor of Bush. This was all the more true since Nancy Reagan's obsession was always her image, what the press was saying about her and how she looked in the media. Nancy appealed to her astrologer to secure her a better press image. Since the controlled press could be calibrated from day to day by the Bush networks, Nancy Reagan found herself in the grip of a many-leveled inside-outside operation whose true nature she was too shallow to suspect.

Bush Takes Over

Bush took up the duties of the presidency, all the while elaborately denying, in his self-deprecating way, that he had in fact taken control. During the time that Reagan was convalescing, the President was even less interested than usual in detailed briefings about government operations. Bush's visits to the chief executive were thus reduced to the merest courtesy calls, after which Bush was free to do what he wanted.

Bush's key man was James Baker III, White House chief of staff and the leading court favorite of Nancy Reagan. During this period Deaver was a wholly controlled appendage of Baker, and would remain one for as long as he was useful to the designs of the Bushmen. Among Baker, Deaver, and the astrologer, Nancy Reagan could also be manipulated into substantial subservience to Bush's designs.

And Baker and Deaver were not the only Bushmen in the White House. There were also Bush campaign veterans David Gergen and Jay Moorhead. In the cabinet, one Bush loyalist was Secretary of Commerce Malcolm Baldridge, who was flanked by his assistant secretary, Fred Bush (apparently not a member of the George Bush family). The Bushmen were strong in the sub-cabinet: Here were Assistant Secretary of State for East Asian and Pacific Affairs John Holdridge, who had served Bush on his Beijing mission staff and during the 1975 Pol Pot caper in Beijing; and Assistant Secretary of State for Congressional Affairs Richard Fairbanks; with these two in Foggy Bottom, Haig's days were numbered. At the Pentagon was Henry E. Catto, the Assistant Secretary of Defense for Public Affairs; Catto would later be rewarded by Bush with an appointment as U.S. ambassador to the Court of St. James in London, the post that foreign service officers spend their lives striving to attain. Bush was also strong among the agencies: His pal William H. Draper III, son of the Nazi banker, was the chairman and president of the Export-Import Bank. Loret Miller Ruppe, Bush's campaign chairman in Michigan, was director of the Peace Corps.

At the Treasury, Bush's cousin, John Walker, would be assistant secretary for enforcement. When the BCCI scandal exploded in the media during 1991, William von Raab, the former director of the U.S. Customs, complained loudly that, during Reagan's second term, his efforts to "go after" BCCI had been frustrated by reticence at the Treasury Department. By this time, James Baker III was Secretary of the Treasury, and Bush's kissing cousin, John Walker, was an official who would have had the primary responsibility for the intensity of such investigations.

At the Pentagon, Caspar Weinberger's deputy assistant secretary for East Asia, Richard Armitage, was no stranger to the circles of Shackley and Clines.

Bush's staff numbered slightly less than 60 during the early spring of 1981. He often operated out of a small office in the West Wing of the White House where he liked to spend time because it was "in the traffic pattern," but his staff was principally located in the Old Executive Office Building. Here Bush sat at a mammoth mahogany desk which had been used in 1903 by his lifetime ego ideal, the archetypal liberal Republican extravagant, Theodore Roosevelt. Bush also kept an office at the Senate.

Some of the leading Bush operatives included:

• Bush's chief of staff was Adm. Daniel J. Murphy, who had represented Bush in the Situation Room until the Vice President had returned from Texas. Murphy had served Melvin Laird and Elliot Richardson when they commanded the Pentagon under Nixon; he had commanded the Sixth Fleet in the Mediterranean during the 1973 Middle East war. Murphy habitually accompanied Bush to attend Reagan's national security briefing each morning in the Oval Office.

• Bush's executive assistant and special assignments man was Charles G. "Chase" Untermeyer, who had graduated from Harvard, worked as a newspaper reporter and served between 1977 and 1980 as a GOP member of the Texas House of Representatives for the silk-stocking Republican 83rd district in Houston, where James Baker, John Connally and Leon Jaworski own homes.

• Bush's general counsel was C. Boyden Gray, a Harvard-educated lawyer who had worked as a partner for the Washington power broker law firm of Wilmer, Cutler, and Pickering, where he specialized in antitrust litigation and representing businessmen's groups like the Business Roundtable and the American Mining Congress. Gray's family were plutocrats from North Carolina who had sponsored the forced sterilization programs described in Chapter 3. Gray's father, Gordon Gray, had served as chief of the National Security Council during the Eisenhower administration, and had directly overseen the very extensive covert operations of the later Eisenhower years.[19]

During and after Reagan's recovery, Bush put together a machine capable of steering many of the decisions of the Reagan administration. Bush had a standing invitation to sit in on all cabinet meetings and other executive activities, and James Baker was always there to make sure he knew what was going on. Bush was a part of every session of the National Security Council. Bush also possessed guaranteed access to Reagan, in case he ever needed that: Each Thursday Reagan and Bush would have lunch alone together in the Oval Office.

Each Tuesday, Bush attended the weekly meeting of GOP committee chairmen presided over by Senate Majority Leader Howard

Baker at the Senate. Then Bush would stay on the Hill for the weekly luncheon of the Republican Policy Committee hosted by Senator John Tower of Texas.

Prescott's old friend William Casey was beginning to work his deviltry at Langley, and kept in close touch with Bush. Reports of personality conflicts between Bush and Casey are the most transparent disinformation.

Problems might have come from the oversight functions of the Congress, but the Congress was now in the process of being destroyed as a constitutional force. Senator Harrison Williams of New Jersey was now on trial on charges resulting from the FBI's illegal "Abscam" entrapment operations. Williams's forced resignation from the Senate, after a number of Congressmen had been convicted on the same manufactured charges, would complete the subordination of Congress to police state controls.

Problems might have come from the Director of the National Security Council, but here the job had been downgraded: Richard Allen reported not to Reagan, but to Meese. Allen would in any case soon be ousted from office because he had accepted some watches from Japanese visitors. Allen would be followed in quick succession by William Clark, Bud McFarlane, John Poindexter, Frank Carlucci and Colin Powell—a new NSC Director a bit less than once a year. For Bush, the dangerous one had been Clark; the rest were quite prepared to go with the Kissinger line. In any case, this merry-go-round at the NSC meant that no serious challenge could emerge against Bush from this quarter. Al Haig was also finished off in this period.

The Attempt on the Pope

Forty-four days after the attempted assassination of Reagan, there followed the attempt to assassinate Pope John Paul II during a general audience in St. Peter's Square in Rome. During those 44 days, Bush had been running the U.S. government. It was as if a new and malignant evil had erupted onto the world stage, and was asserting its presence with an unprecedented violence and terror. Bush was certainly involved in the attempt to cover up the true authors of the attentat of St. Peter's Square. An accessory before the fact in the attempt to slay the pontiff appears to have been Bush's old cohort Frank Terpil, who had been one of the instructors who had trained Mehmet Ali Agca, who fired on the Pope.

After a lengthy investigation, the Italian investigative magistrate, Ilario Martella, in December 1982 issued seven arrest warrants in the case, five against Turks and two against Bulgarians. Ultimate responsibility for the attempt on the Pope's life belonged to Yuri Andropov of the Soviet KGB. On March 1, 1990, Viktor Ivanovich Sheymov, a KGB officer who had defected to the West, revealed at a press conference in Washington, D.C. that as early as 1979, shortly after Karol Woityla became Pope, the KGB had been instructed through an order signed by Yuri Andropov to gather all possible information on how to get "physically close to the Pope."[20]

According to one study of these events, during the second week of August 1980, when the agitation of the Polish trade union Solidarnosc was at its height, the Pope had dispatched a special emissary to Moscow with a personal letter for Soviet President Leonid Brezhnev. The Pope's message warned the Soviet dictator that if the Red Army were to invade Poland, as then seemed imminent, the Pope would fly to Warsaw and lead the resistance. It is very likely that shortly after this the Soviets gave the order to eliminate Pope John Paul II.[21]

With the Vatican supporting Judge Martella in his campaign to expose the true background of Ali Agca's assault, it appeared that the Bulgarian connection, and with it the Andropov-KGB connection, might soon be exposed. But in the meantime, Brezhnev had died, and had been succeeded by the sick and elderly Konstantin Chernenko. Bush was already in the "you die, we fly" business, representing Reagan at all important state funerals, and carrying on the summit diplomacy that belongs to such occasions. Bush attended Brezhnev's funeral in November 1982, and conferred at length with Yuri Andropov. Chernenko was a transitional figure, and the Anglo-American elites were looking to KGB boss Andropov as a desirable successor with whom a new series of condominium deals at the expense of peoples and nations all over the planet might be consummated. For the sake of the condominium, it was imperative that the hit against the Pope not be pinned on Moscow. There was also the scandal that would result if it turned out that U.S. assets had also been involved within the framework of derivative assassination networks.

During the first days of 1983, Bush lodged an urgent request with Monsignor Pio Laghi, the apostolic pro-nuncio in Washington, in which Bush asked for an immediate private audience with the Pope. By February 8, Bush was in Rome. According to reliable reports, during the private audience Bush "suggested that John Paul should not pursue quite so energetically his own interest in the plot."[22]

Bush's personal intervention had the effect of supplementing and accelerating a U.S. intelligence operation that was already in motion to sabotage and discredit Judge Martella and his investigation. On

May 13, 1983, the second anniversary of the attempt on the Pope's life, Vassily Dimitrov, the first secretary of the Bulgarian embassy in Rome, expressed his gratitude: "Thanks to the CIA, I feel as if I were born again!"[23]

Bush consistently expressed skepticism on Bulgarian support for Agca. On December 20, 1982, responding to the Martella indictments, Bush told the *Christian Science Monitor*: "Maybe I speak defensively as a former head of the CIA, but leave out the operational side of the KGB—the naughty things they allegedly do: Here's a man, Andropov, who has had access to a tremendous amount of intelligence over the years. In my judgment, he would be less apt to misread the intentions of the U.S.A. That offers potential. And the other side of that is that he's tough, and he appears to have solidified his leadership position."

According to one study, the German foreign intelligence service (the Bundesnachrichtendienst) believed at this time that "a common link between the CIA and the Bulgarians" existed.[24]

Martella was convinced that Agca had been sent into action by Sergei Antonov, a Bulgarian working in Rome. According to author Gordon Thomas, Martella was aware that the White House, and Bush specifically, were determined to sabotage the exposure of this connection. Martella brought Agca and Antonov together, and Agca identified Antonov in a line-up. Agca also described the interior of Antonov's apartment in Rome. "Later, Martella told his staff that the CIA or anyone else can spread as much disinformation as they like; he is satisfied that Agca is telling the truth about knowing Antonov."[25]

Later, U.S. intelligence networks would redouble these sabotage efforts with some success. Agca was made to appear a lunatic, and two key Bulgarian witnesses changed their testimony. A campaign of leaks was also mounted. In a bizarre but significant episode, even New York Senator Al D'Amato got into the act. D'Amato alleged that he had heard about the Pope's letter warning Brezhnev about invading Poland while he was visiting the Vatican during early 1981. As the *New York Times* reported on February 9, 1983, "D'Amato says he informed the CIA about the letter and identified his source in the Vatican when he returned to the U.S. from a 1981 trip to Rome." Later, D'Amato was told that the Rome CIA station had never heard anything from Langley about his report of the Pope's letter. "I gave them important information and they clearly never followed it up," complained D'Amato to reporters.

In February 1983, D'Amato visited Rome once again on a fact-finding mission in connection with the Agca plot. He asked the

U.S. embassy in Rome to set up appointments for him with Italian political leaders and law enforcement officials, but his visit was sabotaged by U.S. Ambassador Maxwell Raab. The day before D'Amato was scheduled to leave Washington, he found that he had no meetings set up in Rome. Then an Italian-speaking member of the staff of the Senate Intelligence Committee, who was familiar with the Agca investigation and who was scheduled to accompany D'Amato to Rome, informed the Senator that he would not make the trip. D'Amato told the press that this last-minute cancellation was due to pressure from the CIA.

Much to D'Amato's irritation, it turned out that George Bush personally had been responsible for a rather thorough sabotage of his trip. D'Amato showed the Rome press "a telegram from the American Ambassador in Rome urging him to postpone the visit because the embassy was preoccupied with an overlapping appearance by Vice President Bush," as the *New York Times* reported. This was Bush's mission to warn the Pope not to pursue the Bulgarian connection. D'Amato said he was shocked that no one on the CIA staff in Rome had been assigned to track the Agca investigation.

The CIA station chief in Rome during the early 1980s was William Mulligan, a close associate of former CIA Deputy Assistant Director for Operations Theodore Shackley. Shackley, as we have seen, was a part of the Bush for President campaign of 1980.

Mehmet Ali Agca received training in the use of explosives, firearms and other subjects from the "former" CIA agent Frank Terpil. Terpil was known to Agca as "Major Frank," and the training appears to have taken place in Syria and in Libya.

Agca's identification of Terpil had been very precise and detailed on Major Frank and on the training program. Terpil himself granted a television interview, which was incorporated into a telecast on his activities and entitled "The Most Dangerous Man in the World," broadcast in January 1982, during which Terpil described in some detail how he had trained Agca. Shortly after this, Terpil left his apartment in Beirut, accompanied by three unidentified men, and disappeared. Terpil and Ed Wilson had gone to Libya and begun a program of terrorist training at about the time that George Bush became the CIA Director. Wilson was indicted for supplying explosives to Libya, for conspiring to assassinate one of Qaddafi's opponents in Egypt, and for recruiting former U.S. pilots and Green Berets to work for Qaddafi. Wilson was later lured back to the U.S. and jailed. Frank Terpil presumably continues to operate, if he is still alive. Was Terpil actually a triple agent?

What further relation might George Bush have had to the attempt to take the life of the Pope? Only a thorough and unhindered investigation will ever reveal the truth.

Notes for Chapter XVI

1. Clay F. Richards, "George Bush: 'co-president' in the Reagan administration," United Press International, March 10, 1981.
2. Alexander Haig, *Caveat* (New York: MacMillan, 1984), p. 54.
3. *Ibid.*, p. 115.
4. *Ibid.*, p. 302.
5. *Ibid.*, p. 60.
6. *Washington Post*, March 22, 1981.
7. Haig, *op. cit.*, pp. 144–45.
8. Haig, *op. cit.*, p. 151.
9. Caspar Weinberger, *Fighting for Peace* (New York: Warner Books, 1990), p. 91.
10. *Ibid.*, p. 93.
11. *Ibid.*, p. 94.
12. Donald T. Regan, *For the Record* (New York: Harcourt, Brace, Jovanovich, 1988), p. 168.
13. Weinberger, *op. cit.*, p. 95.
14. Ronald Reagan, *An American Life* (New York: Simon and Schuster, 1990), p. 271.
15. Jack and JoAnn Hinckley, *Breaking Points* (Grand Rapids: Chosen Books, 1985), p. 169.
16. *Ibid.*, p. 215.
17. Judy Hasson, United Press International, July 31, 1985.
18. *EIR Special Report:* "American Leviathan: Administrative Fascism under the Bush Regime" (Wiesbaden, Germany: Executive Intelligence Review Nachrichtenagentur, April 1990).
19. For Bush's staff see "George Bush—Keeping His Profile Low So He Can Keep His Influence High," *National Journal*, June 20, 1981, pp. 1096 ff.; and Arthur Wiese, "The Bush Team," *Houston Post*, April 1, 1981.
20. *Washington Post*, March 2, 1990.
21. See Gordon Thomas, *Pontiff* (New York: Doubleday, 1983).
22. Gordon Thomas, *Averting Armageddon* (New York: Doubleday, 1984), p. 74.
23. "American Leviathan," *op. cit.*
24. *Ibid.*, p. 268.
25. *Ibid.*, p. 75.

Congressman and Mrs. George Bush, newly arrived in Washington, 1966.

Washington Star photo, © Washington Post, courtesy Washington D.C. Public Library

Bernie Boston/Washington Star photo, © Washington Post, courtesy Washington D.C. Public Library

Freshman Congressman George Bush (left) tours civil rights protest encampment Resurrection City, May 22, 1968. Rev. James Bevel, second from right, appears skeptical.

Joseph Silverman/Washington Star photo, © Washington Post, courtesy Washington D.C. Public Library

Congressman George Bush visits President Nixon at the White House Jan. 12, 1970, to discuss Bush's political future.

Washington Star photo, © Washington Post, courtesy Washington D.C. Public Library

CIA covert operations manager E. Howard Hunt at Senate Watergate hearings.

Washington Star photo, © Washington Post, courtesy Washington D.C. Public Library

Congressman Wright Patman, whose investigation of the Watergate break-in was squelched before it could expose George Bush's Texas circle.

Joseph Silverman/Washington Star photo, © Washington Post, courtesy Washington D.C. Public Library

Watergate burglar James McCord shows Senate Watergate Committee how Democrats' phones were bugged. McCord blamed Nixon, though Bush's Texas partners had paid for the break-in.

Washington Star photo, © Washington Post, courtesy Washington D.C. Public Library

George and Barbara at Bush's installation as CIA Director, Jan. 30, 1976; Outgoing CIA Director William Colby (left), Deputy Director Vernon Walters (right), the CIA man named on Nixon's Watergate tapes.

Washington Star photo, © Washington Post, courtesy Washington D.C. Public Library

Supreme Court Justice Potter Stewart swears in fellow Skull and Bones member Bush as CIA Director. President Gerald Ford (right) had saved Bush by helping to squash the Patman investigation.

Washington Star photo, © Washington Post, courtesy Washington D.C. Public Library

With the Watergate scandal still smoldering, Bush prepares for confirmation hearings for his nomination as CIA Director, Dec. 15, 1975.

Ray Lustig/Washington Star photo, © Washington Post, courtesy Washington D.C. Public Library

Vice President Bush and Secretary of State Alexander Haig, April 3, 1981, four days after attempted murder of President Reagan. Bush and his allies soon purged Haig.

Washington Star photo, © Washington Post, courtesy Washington D.C. Public Library

Sen. John Tower sponsored Bush for CIA Director. Later, Tower whitewashed Bush in Iran-Contra, and Bush appointed Tower defense secretary.

Hinckley advocated violence, neo-Nazis say

Officials say gun arrests discretionary

Bush, Hinckley sons had appointment

Vice president confirms his son was to have hosted Hinckley brother

City Council prays for Reagan, other injured men

The Bush team
Tightly knit, highly touted but little-known

The Houston Post *Good morning!*

Reagan wounded

Press aide clinging to life; 2 law officers also injured

Bush's son to dine with suspect's brother
Post exclusive

Bush's son was to dine tonight with shooting suspect's brother

Kennedy gets federal guards

Hinckley bought 2 pistols in Dallas shop

Above: Bush family contacts with
Hinckley's family, then in the news, have
since disappeared from public view.

Left: Vice President Bush meets the press
following the attempt on Reagan's life.

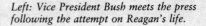

EIRNS/Stuart Lewis

Sen. Howard Baker and Vice President Bush, rivals to Reagan in the New Hampshire presidential primary election, February 1980, at a National Rifle Association candidates forum.

Reagan's opponent Bush became Reagan's running mate through maneuvers of Gerald Ford and Henry Kissinger.

XVII
IRAN-CONTRA

What pleases the prince has the force of law.
—Roman law
"As long as the police carries out the will of the leadership, it is acting legally."
—Gestapo officer Werner Best[1]

We cannot provide here a complete overview of the Iran-Contra affair. We shall attempt, rather, to give an account of George Bush's decisive, central role in those events, which occurred during his vice-presidency and spilled over into his presidency.

The principal elements of scandal in Iran-Contra may be reduced to the following points:

1) the secret arming of the Khomeini regime in Iran by the U.S. government, during an official U.S.-decreed arms embargo against Iran, while the U.S. publicly denounced the recipients of its secret deliveries as terrorists and kidnappers—a policy initiated under the Jimmy Carter presidency and accelerated by the Reagan-Bush administration;

2) the Reagan-Bush administration's secret arming of its "Contras" for war against the Sandinista regime in Nicaragua, while such aid was explicitly prohibited under U.S. law;

3) the use of communist and terrorist enemies—often *armed directly by the Anglo-Americans*—to justify a police state and co-vert, oligarchical rule at home;

4) paying for and protecting the gun-running projects with drug-smuggling, embezzlement, theft by diversion from authorized U.S.

programs, and the "silencing" of both opponents and knowledge-able participants in the schemes; and

5) the continual, routine perjury and deception of the public by government officials pretending to have no knowledge of these activities; and the routine acquiescence in that deception by Congressmen too frightened to oppose it.

When the scandal broke, in late 1986 and early 1987, George Bush maintained that he knew nothing about these illegal activities; that other government officials involved in them had kept him in the dark; that he had attended no important meetings where these subjects were under discussion.

Since that time, many once-classified documents have come to light, which suggest that Bush organized and supervised many, or most, of the criminal aspects of the Iran-Contra adventures.

The most significant events relevant to George Bush's role are presented here in the format of a chronology.

At the end of the chronology, parts of the testimony of George Bush's loyal assistant Donald Gregg will be provided, to allow for a comparison of the documented events with the Bush camp's account of things.

Over the time period covered, the reader will observe the emergence of new structures in the U.S. government:

• The "Special Situation Group," together with its subordinate "Standing Crisis Pre-Planning Group" (May 14, 1982).

• The "Crisis Management Center" (February 1983).

• The "Terrorist Incident Working Group" (April 3, 1984).

• The "Task Force on Combatting Terrorism" (or simply Terrorism Task Force) (July 1985).

• The "Operations Sub-Group" (January 20, 1986).

These were among the *official*, secret structures of the U.S. government created from 1982 through 1986. Other structures, whose existence has not yet come to light, may also have been created—or may have persisted from an earlier time. Nothing of this is to be found in the United States Constitution.

All of these structures revolved around the secret command role of the then-Vice President, George Bush.

The propaganda given out to justify these changes in government has stressed the need for secrecy to carry out necessary *covert acts* against enemies of the nation (or of its leaders). Certainly, a military command will act secretly in war, and will protect secrets of its vulnerable capabilities.

But the Bush apparatus, within and behind the government, was formed to carry out *covert policies:* to make war when the constitutional government had decided not to make war; to support enemies of the nation (terrorists and drug-runners) who are the friends or agents of the secret government.

In the period of the chronology, there are a number of meetings of public officials—secret meetings. Who really made the policies, which were then well or poorly executed by the covert action structure? By looking at the scant information that has come to light on these meetings, we may reach some conclusions about who advocated certain policy choices; but we have not then learned much about the actual origin of the policies that were being carried out. This is the rule of an oligarchy whose members are unknown to the public, an oligarchy which is bound by no known laws.

January 20, 1981:
Ronald Reagan was inaugurated as U.S. President.

March 25, 1981:
Vice President George Bush was named the leader of the United States "crisis management" staff, "as a part of the National Security Council system."

March 30, 1981:
The new President was shot in an attempted assassination. He survived his wounds, so Vice President Bush did not succeed to the presidency.

May 14, 1982:
Bush's position as chief of all covert action and *de facto* head of U.S. intelligence—in a sense, the acting President—was formalized in a secret memorandum.

The memo explained that "National Security Decision Directive 3, Crisis Management, establishes the Special Situation Group (SSG), chaired by the Vice President. The SSG is charged . . . with formulating plans in anticipation of crises."

It is most astonishing that, in all of the reports, articles and books about the Iran-Contra covert actions, the existence of Bush's SSG has received no significant attention. Yet its importance in the management of those covert actions is obvious and unmistakable, as soon as an investigative light is thrown upon it.

The memo in question also announced the birth of another organization, the Standing Crisis Pre-Planning Group (CPPG), which was to work as an intelligence-gathering agency for Bush and his

SSG. This new subordinate group, consisting of representatives of Vice President Bush, National Security Council (NSC) staff members, the CIA, the military and the State Department, was to "meet periodically in the White House Situation Room. . . ." They were to identify areas of potential crisis and "[p]resent . . . plans and policy options to the SSG" under Chairman Bush. And they were to provide to Bush and his assistants, "as crises develop, alternative plans," "action/options" and "coordinated implementation plans" to resolve the "crises."

Finally, the subordinate group was to give to Chairman Bush and his assistants "recommended security, cover, and media plans that will enhance the likelihood of successful execution." It was announced that the CPPG would meet for the first time on May 20, 1982, and that agencies were to "provide the name of their CPPG representative to Oliver North, NSC staff. . . ."

The memo was signed **"for the President"** by Reagan's national security adviser, William P. Clark. It was declassified during the congressional Iran-Contra hearings.[2]

Gregg, Rodriguez and North Join the Bush Team

August 1982:

Vice President Bush hired Donald P. Gregg as his principal adviser on national security affairs. Gregg now officially retired from the Central Intelligence Agency.

Donald Gregg brought along into the Vice President's office his old relationship with mid-level CIA assassinations manager **Felix I. Rodriguez.** Gregg had been Rodriguez's boss in Vietnam.

Donald Gregg worked under Bush in Washington from 1976— when Bush was CIA Director—through the later 1970s, when the Bush clique was at war with President Carter and his CIA Director, Stansfield Turner. Gregg was detailed to work at the National Security Council between 1979 and 1982. From 1976 right up through that NSC assignment, CIA officer Gregg saw CIA agent Rodriguez regularly. Both men were intensely loyal to Bush.[3]

Their continuing collaboration was crucial to Vice President Bush's organization of covert action. Rodriguez was now to operate out of the Vice President's office.

December 21, 1982:

The first "Boland Amendment" became law: "None of the funds provided in this Act [the Defense Appropriations Bill] may be used by the Central Intelligence Agency or the Department of Defense to furnish military equipment, military training or advice, or other support for military activities, to any group or individual . . . for the purpose of overthrowing the government of Nicaragua."

"Boland I," as it was called, remained in effect until Oct. 3, 1984, when it was superseded by a stronger prohibition known as "Boland II."[4]

February 1983:

Fawn Hall joined Oliver North as his assistant. Ms. Hall reported that she worked with North on the development of a secret "Crisis Management Center."

Lt. Colonel North, an employee of the National Security Council, is seen here managing a new structure within the Bush-directed SSG/CPPG arrangements of 1981–82.[5]

March 3, 1983:

In the spring of 1983, the National Security Council established an office of "Public Diplomacy" to propagandize in favor of and run cover for the Iran-Contra operations, and to coordinate published attacks on opponents of the program.

Former CIA Director of Propaganda Walter Raymond was put in charge of the effort. The unit was to work with domestic and international news media, as well as private foundations. The Bush family-affiliated Smith Richardson Foundation was part of a National Security Council "private donors' steering committee" charged with coordinating this propaganda effort.

A March 3, 1983 memorandum from Walter Raymond to then-NSC Director William Clark, provided details of the program:

"As you will remember you and I briefly mentioned to the President when we briefed him on the N[ational] S[ecurity] D[ecision] D[irective] on public diplomacy that we would like to get together with some potential donors at a later date. . . .

"To accomplish these objectives Charlie [United States Information Agency Director Charles Z. Wick] has had two lengthy meetings with a group of people representing the private sector. This group had included principally program directors rather than funders. The group was largely pulled together by Frank Barnett, Dan McMichael (Dick [Richard Mellon] Scaife's man), Mike Joyce (Olin Foundation), Les Lenkowsky (Smith Richardson Foundation) plus Leonard Sussman and Leo Cherne of Freedom House. A number of others including Roy Godson have also participated." [Everything above in parentheses is in the original].[6]

Elsewhere, Raymond described Cherne and Godson as the coordinators of this group. Frank Barnett was the director of the Bush family's National Strategy Information Center, for which Godson was the Washington, D.C. director. Barnett had been the project director of the Smith Richardson Foundation prior to being assigned to that post.

The Smith Richardson Foundation has sunk millions of dollars into the Iran-Contra projects. Some Smith Richardson grantees, receiving money since the establishment of the National Security Council's "private steering committee" (according to the foundation's annual reports) include the following:

• **Dennis King,** to write the book *Lyndon LaRouche and the New American Fascism*, used as the basis for arguments against LaRouche and his associates by federal and state prosecutors around the country. (See the LaRouche section at the end of this chapter.)

• **Freedom House.** This was formed by Leo Cherne, business partner of CIA Director William Casey. Cherne oversaw Walter Raymond's "private donor's committee."

• **National Strategy Information Center,** founded in 1962 by Casey, Cherne and the Bush family (see Chapter 4).

Thus, when an item appeared in a daily newspaper, supporting the Contras, or attacking their opponents—calling them "extremists," etc.—it is likely to have been planted by the U.S. government, by the George Bush-NSC "private donors' " apparatus.

March 17, 1983:

Professional assassinations manager Felix I. Rodriguez met with Bush aide Donald P. Gregg, officially and secretly, at the White House. Gregg then recommended to National Security Council adviser Robert "Bud" McFarlane a plan for El Salvador-based military attacks on a target area of Central American nations including Nicaragua.

Gregg's March 17, 1983 memo to McFarlane said: "The attached plan, written in March of last year, grew out of two experiences:

"—Anti-Vietcong operations run under my direction in III Corps Vietnam from 1970–1972. These operations [see below], based on . . . a small elite force . . . produced very favorable results.

"—Rudy Enders, who is now in charge of what is left of the paramilitary capability of the CIA, went to El Salvador in 1981 to do a survey and develop plans for effective anti-guerrilla operations. He came back and endorsed the attached plan. (I should add that Enders and Felix Rodriguez, who wrote the attached plan, both worked for me in Vietnam and carried out the actual operations outlined above.)

"This plan encountered opposition and skepticism from the U.S. military. . . .

"I believe the plan can work based on my experience in Vietnam. . . ."[7]

Three years later, Bush agent Rodriguez would be publicly exposed as the supervisor of the covert Central American network illegally supplying arms to the Contras; that exposure of Rodriguez would begin the explosive public phase of the "Iran-Contra scandal."

Rodriguez's uncle had been Cuba's public works minister under Fulgencio Batista, and his family fled Castro's 1959 revolution. Felix Rodriguez joined the CIA, and was posted to the CIA's notorious Miami Station in the early 1960s. The Ted Shackley-E. Howard Hunt organization there, assisted by Meyer Lansky's and Santos Trafficante's mafiosi, trained Rodriguez and other Cubans in the arts of murder and sabotage. Rodriguez and his fellow CIA trainees took part in numerous terror raids against Castro's Cuba.

Felix Rodriguez recounted his early adventures in gun-running under false pretexts in a ghost-written book, *Shadow Warrior*:

> [J]ust around the time President Kennedy was assassinated, I left for Central America.
> I spent almost two years in Nicaragua, running the communications network for [our enterprise]. . . . [O]ur arms cache was in Costa Rica. The funding for the project came from the CIA, but the money's origin was hidden through the use of a cover corporation, a company called Maritima BAM, which was [Manuel] Artim's initials spelled backwards. Periodically, deposits of hundreds of thousands of dollars would be made in Maritima BAM's accounts, and disbursed by Cuban corporation officers. The U.S. government had the deniability it wanted; we got the money we needed. . . .
> In fact, what we did in Nicaragua twenty-five years ago has some pretty close parallels to the Contra operation today.[8]

Rodriguez followed his CIA boss Ted Shackley to Southeast Asia in 1970. Shackley and Donald Gregg put Rodriguez into the huge assassination and dope business which Shackley and his colleagues ran during the Indochina war; this bunch became the heart of the "Enterprise" that went into action 15 to 20 years later in Iran-Contra.

Shackley funded opium-growing Meo tribesmen in murder, and used the dope proceeds in turn to fund his hit squads. He formed the Military Assistance Group-Special Operations Group (MAG-SOG) political murder unit; Gen. John K. Singlaub was a commander of MAG-SOG; Oliver North and Richard Secord were officers of the unit. By 1971, the Shackley group had killed about 100,000 civilians in Southeast Asia as part of the CIA's Operation Phoenix.

After Vietnam, Felix Rodriguez went back to Latin American CIA operations, while other parts of the Shackley organization went on to drug-selling and gun-running in the Middle East.

By 1983, both the Mideast Shackley group and the self-styled "Shadow Warrior," Felix Rodriguez, were attached to the shadow commander-in-chief, George Bush.

May 25, 1983:

Secretary of State George Shultz wrote a memorandum for President Reagan, trying to stop George Bush from running Central American operations for the U.S. government. Shultz included a draft National Security Decision Directive for the President to sign, and an organizational chart ("Proposed Structure") showing Shultz's proposal for the line of authority—from the President and his NSC, through Secretary of State Shultz and his assistant secretary, down to an interagency group.

The last line of the Shultz memo says bluntly what role is reserved for the Bush-supervised CPPG: "The Crisis Pre-Planning Group is relieved of its assignments in this area."

Back came a memorandum for The Honorable George P. Shultz, on a White House letterhead but bearing no signature, saying no to Shultz: "The institutional arrangements established in NSDD–2 are, I believe, appropriate to fulfill [our national security requirements in Central America]. . . ." With the put-down is a chart headlined **"NSDD–2 Structure for Central America."** At the top is the President; just below is a complex of Bush's SSG and CPPG as managers of the NSC; then below that is the Secretary of State, and below him various agencies and interagency groups.[9]

July 12, 1983:

Kenneth De Graffenreid, new manager of the Intelligence Directorate of the National Security Council, sent a secret memo to George Bush's aide, Admiral Daniel Murphy:

". . . Bud McFarlane has asked that I meet with you today, if possible, to review procedures for obtaining the Vice President's comments and concurrence on all N[ational] S[ecurity] C[ouncil] P[lanning] G[roup] covert action and MONs."[10]

The Bush Regency in Action

October 20, 1983:

The U.S. invasion of the Caribbean island-nation of Grenada was decided upon in a secret meeting of the metagovernment—the National Security State—under the leadership of George Bush. National Security Council operative Constantine Menges, a stalwart participant in these events, described the action for posterity:

> My job that afternoon was to write the background memorandum that would be used by the vice president, who in his role as "crisis manager" would chair this first NSC meeting on the [Grenada] issue. . . .
>
> [F]ortunately I had help from Oliver North, who in his nearly three years with NSC had become expert in the memo formats and formal procedures. After the morning CPPG meeting, North had begun to get interested in Grenada. . . .
>
> Shortly before 6:00 P.M., the participants began to arrive: Vice President Bush, [Secretary of Defense Caspar] Weinberger, [Attorney General Edwin] Meese, J[oint] C[hiefs of] S[taff] Chairman General Vessey, acting CIA Director McMahon, [State Dept. officer Lawrence] Eagleburger, . . . North and myself. We all went to the Situation Room in the White House.
>
> President Reagan was travelling, as were [CIA Director] Bill Casey and Jeane Kirkpatrick. . . .
>
> Vice President Bush sat in the president's chair.

Menges continued: ". . . A factual update was the first order of business. Then the discussion moved to the availability of military forces and how long it would take to ready them. The objective, right from the beginning, was to plan a rescue [of American students detained on Grenada] that would guarantee quick success, but with a minimum of casualties. . . ."

"The first suggested presidential decision was to prepare for possible military action by shifting navy ships, which were taking a marine unit to rotate forces in Lebanon, plus other naval units, toward Grenada.

"Secrecy was imperative. . . . As part of this plan, there would be no change in the schedule of the top man. President Reagan . . . would travel to Augusta, Georgia, for a golf weekend. Secretary of State Shultz would go too. . . ."

Work now proceeded on detailed action plans, under the guidance of the Vice President's Special Situation Group.

"Late Friday afternoon [Oct. 21] . . . the CPPG . . . [met] in room

208. . . . Now the tone of our discussions had shifted from whether we would act to how this could be accomplished. . . .

"[The] most secure means [were to] be used to order U.S. ships to change course . . . toward Grenada. Nevertheless, ABC news had learned about this and was broadcasting it."

Thus, the course of action decided upon without the President was "leaked" to the news media, and became a *fait-accompli.* Menges's memo continues:

It pleased me to see that now our government was working as a team. . . . That evening Ollie North and I worked together . . . writing the background and decision memoranda. Early in the evening [NSC officer Admiral John] Poindexter reviewed our first draft and made a few minor revisions. Then the Grenada memoranda were sent to the President, Shultz and McFarlane at the golf course in Georgia. . . .

Shortly before 9:00 A.M. [Oct. 22], members of the foreign policy cabinet [sic!] began arriving at the White House—all out of sight of reporters. The participants included Weinberger, Vessey, and Fred Ikle from Defense; Eagleburger and Motley from State; McMahon and an operations officer from CIA; and Poindexter, North and myself from NSC. Vice President Bush chaired the Washington group.

All participants were escorted to room 208, which many had never seen before. The vice president sat at one end of the long table and Poindexter at the other, with speaker phones positioned so that everyone could hear President Reagan, Shultz, and McFarlane.

The meeting began with an overview and an update. . . . There were animated discussions. . . . The conclusion was that by early Tuesday, October 25, the United States and allied forces would be in a position to initiate military action. . . .

The only legal authority on Grenada was the governor general, Sir Paul N. Scoon, . . . a Grenadan citizen appointed by the British crown. . . . Ingeniously, he had smuggled out a request for external help in restoring law and order. . . .

The detailed hour-by-hour plan was circulated to everyone at the meeting. There was also a short discussion of the War Powers Resolution, which requires the president to get approval of Congress if he intends to deploy U.S. troops in combat for more than sixty days. There was little question that U.S. combat forces would be out before that time. . . .

The president had participated and asked questions over the speaker phone; he made his decision. The U.S. would answer the call from our Caribbean neighbors. We would assure the safety of our citizens.[11]

Clearly, there was no perceived need to follow the U.S. Constitution and leave the question of whether to make war up to the Congress. After all, President Reagan had concurred, from the golf course, with Acting President Bush's decision in the matter. And the British nominee in the target country had requested Mr. Bush's help!

November 3, 1983:
Bush aide Donald Gregg met with Felix Rodriguez to discuss "the general situation in Central America."[12]

December 1983:
Oliver North accompanied Vice President Bush to El Salvador as his assistant. Bush met with Salvadoran army commanders. North helped Bush prepare a speech, in which he publicly called upon them to end their support for the use of "death squads." North later testified that Bush's speech "was one of the bravest things I've seen for anybody [sic]."[13]

Attack from Jupiter

January 1 through March 1984:
The *Wall Street Journal* of March 6, 1985 gave a de-romanticized version of certain aquatic adventures in Central America:

> Armed speedboats and a helicopter launched from a Central Intelligence Agency "mother ship" attacked Nicaragua's Pacific port, Puerto Sandino on a moonless New Year's night in 1984.
>
> A week later the speedboats returned to mine the oil terminal. Over the next three months, they laid more than 30 mines in Puerto Sandino and also in the harbors at Corinto and El Bluff. In air and sea raids on coastal positions, Americans flew—and fired from—an armed helicopter that accompanied the U.S.-financed Latino force, while a CIA plane provided sophisticated reconaissance guidance for the nighttime attacks.
>
> The operation, outlined in a classified CIA document, marked the peak of U.S. involvement in the four-year guerrilla war in Nicaragua. More than any single event, it solidified congressional opposition to the covert war, and in the year since then, no new money has been approved beyond the last CIA checks drawn early [in the] summer [of 1984]. . . .
>
> CIA paramilitary officers were upset by the ineffectiveness of the Contras. . . . As the insurgency force grew . . . during 1983 . . . the CIA began to use the guerrilla army as a cover for its own small "Latino" force. . . .

[The] most celebrated attack, by armed speedboats, came Oct. 11, 1983, against oil facilities at Corinto. Three days later, an underwater pipeline at Puerto Sandino was sabotaged by Latino [sic] frogmen. The message wasn't lost on Exxon Corp.'s Esso unit [formerly Standard Oil of New Jersey], and the international giant informed the Sandinista government that it would no longer provide tankers for transporting oil to Nicaragua.

The CIA's success in scaring off a major shipper fit well into its mining strategy. . . .

The mother ship used in the mining operation is described by sources as a private chartered vessel with a configuration similar to an oil-field service and towing ship with a long, flat stern section where helicopters could land. . . .

The reader may have already surmised that Vice President Bush (with his background in "oilfield service") sat in his Washington office and planned these brilliant schemes. But such a guess is probably incorrect—it is off by about 800 miles.

On Jupiter Island, Florida, where the Bush family has had a seasonal residence for the past several decades (see Chapter 4) is the headquarters of Continental Shelf Associates, Inc. (CSA).[14]

This company describes itself as "an environmental consulting firm specializing in applied marine science and technology . . . founded in 1970. . . . The main office . . . is located in Jupiter, Florida, approximately 75 miles north of Miami." CSA has "Offshore and Onshore divisions." It lists among its clients Exxon Company, U.S.A.; Military Sealift Command; Pennzoil Company; U.S. Department of Defense/Army Corps of Engineers; and other oil companies and government agencies.

CSA's main advertised concern is with underwater engineering, often involving oil or nuclear facilities. It has many "classified" projects. It employs the world's most sophisticated subsurface vehicles and monitoring equipment.

The founder and chief executive of CSA is Robert "Stretch" Stevens. A former lieutenant commander in naval special operations, Stevens has been a close associate of CIA officer **Theodore Shackley**, and of Bush agent **Felix Rodriguez** since the early 1960s, when Stevens served as a boat captain in the invasion of Cuba at the Bay of Pigs, and through the Vietnam War.

During the period 1982–85, CSA was contracted by the U.S. intelligence community, including the CIA, to carry out coastal and on-the-ground reconnaissance and logistical support work in the eastern Mediterranean in support of the U.S. Marine deployment into Lebanon; and coastal mapping and reconnaissance of the Caribbean island of Grenada prior to the October 1983 U.S. military action.

Beginning in approximately the autumn of 1983, CSA was employed to design and execute a program for the mining of several Nicaraguan harbors. After the U.S. Senate restricted such activities to non-U.S. personnel only, CSA trained "Latin American nationals" at a facility located on El Bravo Island off the eastern coast of Nicaragua.

Acta Non Verba (Deeds Not Words) is a "subsidiary" of CSA, incorporated in 1986 and located at the identical Jupiter address.

Rudy Enders, the head of the CIA's paramilitary section—and deployed by George Bush aide Donald Gregg—is a minority owner of Acta Non Verba (ANV).

ANV's own tough-talking promotional literature says that it concentrates on "counter-terrorist activities in the maritime environment."

A very high-level retired CIA officer, whose private interview was used in preparation for this book, described this "Fish Farm" in the following more realistic terms:

"Assassination operations and training company controlled by Ted Shackley, under the cover of a private corporation with a regular board of directors, stockholders, etc., located in Florida. They covertly bring in Haitian and Southeast Asian boat people as recruits, as well as Koreans, Cubans, and Americans. They hire out assassinations and intelligence services to governments, corporations, and individuals, and also use them for covering or implementing 'Fish Farm' projects/activities."

The upshot of the attack from Jupiter—the mining of Nicaragua's harbors—was that the Congress got angry enough to pass the "Boland II" amendment, re-tightening the laws against this public-private warfare (see entry for Oct. 3, 1984).

April 3, 1984:
Another subcommittee of the Bush terrorism apparatus was formed, as President Reagan signed National Security Decision Directive 138. The new "Terrorist Incident Working Group" reported to Bush's Special Situation Group. The TIWG geared up government agencies to support militant counterterrorism assaults, on the Israeli model.[15]

"How Can Anyone Object?"

June 25, 1984:

The National Security Planning Group, including Reagan, Bush and other top officials, met secretly in the White House situation room at 2:00 P.M. They discussed whether to risk seeking "third-country aid" to the Contras, to get around the congressional ban enacted Dec. 21, 1982.

George Bush spoke in favor, according to minutes of the meeting.

Bush said, "How can anyone object to the U.S. encouraging third parties to provide help to the anti-Sandinistas under the [intelligence] finding. The only problem that might come up is if the United States were to promise to give these third parties something in return so that *some people might interpret* this as some kind of an exchange" [emphasis added].

Warning that this would be illegal, Secretary of State Shultz said: "I would like to get money for the contras also, but another lawyer [then-Treasury Secretary] Jim Baker said if we go out and try to get money from third countries, it is an impeachable offense."

CIA Director Casey reminded Shultz that "Jim Baker changed his mind [and now supported the circumvention]. . . ."

NSC adviser Robert McFarlane cautioned, "I propose that there be no authority for anyone to seek third party support for the anti-Sandinistas until we have the information we need, and I certainly hope none of this discussion will be made public in any way."

President Ronald Reagan then closed the meeting with a warning against anyone leaking the fact they were considering how to circumvent the law: "If such a story gets out, we'll all be hanging by our thumbs in front of the White House until we find out who did it." In March of the following year, Bush personally arranged the transfer of funds to the Contras by the Honduran government, assuring them they would receive compensating U.S. aid.

The minutes of this meeting, originally marked "secret," were released five years later, at Oliver North's trial in the spring of 1989.[16]

October 3, 1984:

Congress enacted a new version of the earlier attempt to outlaw the U.S. secret war in Central America. This "Boland II" amendment was designed to prevent any conceivable form of deceit by the covert action apparatus:

"During fiscal year 1985, no funds available to the Central Intelligence Agency, the Department of Defense, or any other agency or entity of the United States involved in intelligence activities may be obligated or expended for the purpose or which would have the effect of supporting, directly or indirectly, military or paramilitary operations in Nicaragua by any nation, group, organization, movement, or individual."

This law was effective from October 3, 1984, to December 5, 1985, when it was superceded by various aid-limitation laws which, taken together, were referred to as "Boland III."[17]

November 1, 1984:

Felix Rodriguez's partner, Gerard Latchinian, was arrested by the Federal Bureau of Investigation. Latchinian was then tried and convicted of smuggling $10.3 million in cocaine into the United States. The dope was to finance the murder and overthrow of the President of Honduras, Roberto Suazo Cordova. Latchinian was sentenced to a 30-year prison term.

On Nov. 10, 1983, a year before the arrest, Felix Rodriguez had filed the annual registration with Florida's secretary of state on behalf of Latchinian's and Rodriguez's joint enterprise, "Giro Aviation Corp."[18]

December 21, 1984:

Felix Rodriguez met in the office of the Vice President with Bush adviser Donald Gregg. Immediately after this meeting, Rodriguez met with Oliver North, supposedly for the first time in his life. But Bush's adviser strenuously denied to investigators that he "introduced" his CIA employee to North.[19]

January 18, 1985 (Friday):

Felix Rodriguez met with Ramon Milian Rodriguez (not known to be a relative of Felix), accountant and money launderer, who had moved $1.5 billion for the Medellín cocaine cartel. Milian testified before a Senate investigation of the Contras' drug-smuggling, that more than a year earlier he had granted Felix's request and given $10 million from the cocaine cartel to Felix for the Contras.

Milian Rodriguez was interviewed in his prison cell in Butner, North Carolina, by investigative journalist Martha Honey. He said Felix Rodriguez had offered that "in exchange for money for the Contra cause he would use his influence in high places to get the [Cocaine] cartel U.S. 'good will'. . . . Frankly, one of the selling points was that he could talk directly to Bush. The issue of good will wasn't something that was going to go through 27 bureaucratic hands. It was something that was directly between him and Bush."

Ramon Milian Rodriguez was a Republican contributor, who had partied by invitation at the 1981 Reagan-Bush inauguration ceremonies. He had been arrested aboard a Panama-bound private jet by federal agents in May 1983, while carrying over $5 million in cash. According to Felix Rodriguez, Milian was seeking a way out of the narcotics charges when he met with Felix on January 18, 1985.

This meeting remained secret until two years later, when Felix Rodriguez had become notorious in the Iran-Contra scandal. The *Miami Herald* broke the story on June 30, 1987. Felix Rodriguez at first denied ever meeting with Ramon Milian Rodriguez. But then a new story was worked out with various agencies. Felix "remembered" the Jan. 18, 1985 meeting, claimed he had "said nothing" during it, and "remembered" that he had filed documents with the FBI and CIA telling them about the meeting just afterwards.[20]

January 22, 1985 (Tuesday):

George Bush met with Felix Rodriguez in the Executive Office Building. The agenda may have included the results of the meeting five days before with Medellín cocaine cartel representative Milian Rodriguez.

Felix's ghost writer doesn't tell us what was said, only that Felix was "able to show [Bush] some of the photos from my album. The honor of being with the Vice President . . . was overwhelming. Mr. Bush was easy to talk to, and he was interested in my stories."[21]

Late January, 1985:

George Bush's office officially organized contacts through the State Department for Felix Rodriguez to operate in Central America from a base in El Salvador, in a false "private" capacity.

The U.S. ambassador to El Salvador, Thomas Pickering, then cabled to Gen. Paul F. Gorman, commander of the U.S. Army Southern Command: "Rodriguez has high-level contacts at the White House, DOS [State Dept] and DOD [Defense Department], some of whom are strongly supporting his use in El Salvador.

"It would be in our best interests that Mr. Rodriguez confer with you personally prior to coming to El Salvador. I have some obvious concerns about this arrangement. . . ."

Felix Rodriguez flew to Panama to speak to General Gorman. They discussed his covert aid to the Contras "since the early eighties."[22]

Rodriguez, by George Bush's story the private, volunteer helper of the Contras, flew from Panama to El Salvador on General Gorman's personal C–12 airplane. General Gorman also sent a confidential cable to Ambassador Pickering and Col. James Steele, U.S. military liaison man with the Contra resupply operation in El Salvador:

"I have just met here with Felix Rodriguez, [deleted, probably "CIA"] pensioner from Miami. Born in Cuba, a veteran of guerrilla operations [several lines deleted]. . . .

"He is operating as a private citizen, but his acquaintanceship with the V[ice] P[resident] is real enough, going back to the latter's days as D[irector of] C[entral] I[ntelligence].

"Rodriguez' primary commitment to the region is in [deleted] where he wants to assist the FDN [Contras military forces]. I told him that the FDN deserved his priority. . . . He will want to fly with the E[l] S[alvador] A[ir] F[orce] to establish his credibility, but that . . . seems to me both unnecessary and unwise. . . ."[23]

February 7, 1985:

The Crisis Pre-Planning Group (CPPG), subordinate to Chairman Bush of the Special Situation Group (SSG), met to discuss means to circumvent the Boland amendment's ban on aid to the Contras. They agreed on a "Presidential letter" to be sent to President Suazo of Honduras, "to provide several enticements to Honduras in exchange for its continued support of the Nicaraguan Resistance. These enticements included expedited delivery of military supplies ordered by Honduras, a phased release of withheld economic assistance (ESF) funds, and other support."

The preceding was the admission of the United States government in the 1989 Oliver North trial—number 51 in a series of "stipulations" that was given to the court to avoid having to release classified documents.

February 12, 1985:

The government admissions in the North trial continued:

"52: . . . North proposed that McFarlane send a memo [to top officials on] the recommendation of the CPPG [the Bush-supervised body, often chaired by Bush adviser Don Gregg]. . . . The memo stated that this part of the message [to the Honduran president] should not be contained in a written document but should be delivered verbally by a discreet emissary." [This was to be George Bush himself—see March 16, 1985.]

Honduras would be given increased aid, to be diverted to the Contras, so as to deceive Congress and the American population.[24]

February 15, 1985 (Friday):

After Rodriguez had arrived in El Salvador and had begun setting up the central resupply depot for the Contras—at Ilopango Airbase—Ambassador Thomas Pickering sent an "Eyes Only" cable to the State Department on his conversation with Rodriguez. Pickering's cable bore the postscript, "Please brief Don Gregg in the V.P.'s office for me."[25]

February 19, 1985 (Tuesday):
Felix Rodriguez met with Bush's staff in the vice-presidential offices in the Executive Office Building, briefing them on the progress of his mission.

Over the next two years, Rodriguez met frequently with Bush staff members in Washington and in Central America, often jointly with CIA and other officials, and conferred with Bush's staff by telephone countless times.[26]

March 15–16, 1985 (Friday and Saturday):
George Bush and Felix Rodriguez were in Central America on their common project.

On Friday, Rodriguez supervised delivery in Honduras of military supplies for the FDN Contras whose main base was there in Honduras.

On Saturday, George Bush met with Honduran President Roberto Suazo Cordova. Bush told Suazo that the Reagan-Bush administration was expediting delivery of more than $110 million in economic and military aid to Suazo's government. This was the "quid pro quo": a bribe for Suazo's support for the U.S. mercenary force, and a transfer through Honduras of the Contra military supplies, which had been directly prohibited by the Congress.

Government as Counterterror

June 14, 1985:
"Shiite Muslim terrorists" hijacked an Athens-to-Rome airliner. One American was killed, 39 Americans were held hostage and released June 30.

July 1985:
Vice President George Bush was designated by President Reagan to lead the **Task Force on Combatting Terrorism** (or Terrorism Task Force).

Bush's task force was a means to sharply concentrate the powers of government into the hands of the Bush clique, for such policies as the Iran-Contra armaments schemes.

The Terrorism Task Force had the following cast of characters:

GEORGE BUSH, U.S. Vice President:	CHAIRMAN
Admiral James L. Holloway III:	Executive assistant to Chairman Bush
Craig Coy:	Bush's deputy assistant under Holloway
Vice Admiral John Poindexter:	Senior NSC representative to Chairman Bush
Marine Corps Lt. Col. Oliver North:	Day-to-day NSC representative to George Bush
Amiram Nir:	Counterterror adviser to Israeli Premier Shimon Peres
Lt. Col. Robert Earl:	Staff member
Terry Arnold:	Principal consultant
Charles E. Allen, CIA officer:	Senior Review Group
Robert Oakley, Director, State Dept. Counter Terrorism Office:	Senior Review Group
Noel Koch, Deputy to Asst. Secretary of Defense Richard Armitage:	Senior Review Group
Lt. Gen. John Moellering, Joint Chiefs of Staff:	Senior Review Group
Oliver "Buck" Revell, FBI executive:	Senior Review Group

This was the first known official contact of the Israeli Nir with the U.S. government in the Iran-Contra affair. In the future, Nir would serve as the main Israeli agent in the covert arms-for-hostages negotiations with Iran, alongside such other well-known U.S. participants as Oliver North and Robert McFarlane.

The Terrorism Task Force organization, as we shall see, was a permanent affair.[27]

August 8, 1985:

George Bush met with the National Security Planning Group in the residence section of the White House. Spurring on their deliberations on the terrorism problem, a car bomb had blown up that day at a U.S. air base in Germany, with 22 American casualties.

The officials discussed shipment of U.S.-made arms to Iran through Israel—to replenish Israeli stocks of TOW missiles and to permit Israel to sell arms to Iran.

According to testimony by Robert McFarlane, the transfer was supported by George Bush, Casey and Donald Regan, and opposed by Shultz and Weinberger.[28]

August 18, 1985:

Luis Posada Carriles escaped from prison in Venezuela, where he was being held for the terrorist murder of 73 persons. Using forged documents falsely identifying him as a Venezuelan named "Ramon Medina," Posada flew to Central America. Within a few weeks, Felix Rodriguez assigned him to supervise the Bush office's Contra resupply operations being run from the El Salvador air base. Posada personally ran the safe-houses used for the CIA flight crews.

Rodriguez explained the arrangement in his book: "Because of my relationship with [El Salvador Air Force] Gen. Bustillo, I was able to pave the way for [the operations attributed to Oliver] North to use the facilities at Ilopango [El Salvador air force base]. . . . I found someone to manage the Salvadorian-based resupply operation on a day-to-day basis. They knew that person as Ramon Medina. I knew him by his real name: Luis Posada Carriles. . . . I first [sic!] met Posada in 1963 at Fort Benning, Georgia, where we went through basic training together . . . as U.S. Army second lieutenants. . . ."

Rodriguez neglects to explain that agent Posada Carilles was originally recruited and trained by the same CIA murder operation, "JM/WAVE" in Miami, as was Rodriguez himself.

Felix continues: "In the sixties, he reportedly went to work for DISIP, the Venezuelan intelligence service, and rose to considerable power within its ranks. It was rumored that he held one of the top half-dozen jobs in the organization. . . .

"After the midair bombing of a Cubana airliner on October 6, 1976, in which seventy-three people were killed, Posada was charged with planning the attack and was thrown in prison. . . . Posada was confined in prison for more than nine years. . . ."[29]

September 10, 1985:

George Bush's national security adviser, Donald Gregg, met at 4:30 P.M. with Oliver North and Col. James Steele, the U.S. military official in El Salvador who oversaw flights of cargo going to the Contras from various points in Central America. They discussed information given to one or more of them by arms dealer Mario DelAmico, supplier to the Contras. According to the entry in Oliver North's notebook, they discussed particularities of the supply flights, and the operations of FDN commander Enrique Bermudez.

Elsewhere in the diary pages for that day, Colonel North noted that DelAmico had procured a certain 1,000 munitions items for the Contras.[30]

November 1985 (ca. American Thanksgiving Day):

George Bush sent Oliver North a note, with thanks for "your dedication and tireless work with the hostage thing and with Central America."[31]

December 1985:

Congress passed new laws limiting U.S. aid to the Contras. The CIA, the Defense Department, and "any other agency or entity of the United States involved in intelligence activities" were prohibited from providing *armaments* to the Contras. The CIA was permitted to provide communications equipment and training. "Humanitarian" aid was allowed.

These laws, known together as "Boland III," were in effect from December 4, 1985 to October 17, 1986.

December 18, 1985:

CIA official Charles E. Allen, a member of George Bush's Terrorism Task Force, wrote an update on the arms-for-hostages dealings with Iran. Allen's memo was a debriefing of an unnamed member of the group of U.S. government officials participating in the arms negotiations with the Iranians. The unnamed U.S. official (from the context, probably NSC terrorism consultant Michael Ledeen) is referred to in Allen's memo as "Subject".

Allen wrote: "[Speaker of the Iranian Parliament Hashemi] Rafsanjani . . . believes Vice President George Bush is orchestrating the U.S. initiative with Iran. In fact, according to Subject, Rafsanjani believes that Bush is the most powerful man in the U.S. because in addition to being Vice President, he was once Director of CIA."[32]

December 1985–January 1986:

George Bush completed his official study of terrorism in December 1985. John Poindexter now directed Oliver North to go back to work with Amiram Nir.

Amiram Nir came to Washington and met with Oliver North. He told U.S. officials that the Iranians had promised to free all hostages in exchange for more arms. Reportedly after this Nir visit, in an atmosphere of constant terrorism and rumors of terrorism, President Reagan was persuaded of the necessity of revving up the arms shipments to Iran.[33]

December 27, 1985:

Terrorists bombed Rome and Vienna airports, killing 20 people, including five Americans. The Crisis Pre-Planning Group (CPPG), supervised by Bush's office and reporting to Bush, blamed Libyans for the attack and began planning for a military strike on Libya. Yet an unpublished CIA analysis and the Israelis both acknowledged that the Abu Nidal group (in effect, the Israeli Mossad agency) carried out the attacks.[34]

Bush's CPPG later organized the U.S. bombing of Libya, which occurred in mid-April 1986.

December 31, 1985 (Tuesday):

Iranian arms dealer Cyrus Hashemi told Paris-based CIA agent Bernard Veillot that Vice President Bush was backing arms sales to Iran, and that official U.S. approval for private sales to Iran, amounting to $2 billion, was "going to be signed by Mr. Bush and [U.S. Marine Corps commandant] Gen. [Paul X.] Kelley on Friday."[35]

Loudly and publicly exposed in the midst of Iran arms deals, Veillot was indicted by the U.S. Then the charges were quietly dropped, and Veillot went underground. A few months later Hashemi died suddenly of "leukemia."[36]

January 2, 1986 (Thursday):

Israeli counterterrorism chief Amiram Nir met with North and Poindexter in Washington. The Bush report on terrorism had now been issued within the government but was not yet published. Bush's report was urging that a counterterrorism coordinator be named for the entire U.S. government—and Oliver North was the one man intended for that slot.

At this meeting, Nir proposed specifically that prisoners held by Israeli-controlled Lebanese, and 3,000 American TOW missiles, be exchanged for U.S. hostages held by Iran. Other discussions between Nir and Bush's nominee involved the supposedly new idea that the Iranians be overcharged for the weapons shipped to them, and the surplus funds be diverted to the Contras.[37]

January 6, 1986 (Monday):

President Reagan met with George Bush, Donald Regan, McFarlane and Poindexter. The President was handed a draft "Presidential Finding" that called for shipping arms to Iran through Israel. The President signed this document, drafted following the discussions with Amiram Nir.

The draft consciously violated the National Security Act which had established the Central Intelligence Agency, requiring notification of Congress. But Bush joined in urging President Reagan to sign this "finding":

"I hereby find that the following operation in a foreign country ... is important to the national security of the United States, and due to its extreme sensitivity and security risks, I determine it is essential to *limit prior notice, and direct the Director of Central Intelligence to refrain from reporting this finding to the Congress as provided in Section 501 of the National Security Act of 1947, as amended, until I otherwise direct*" [emphasis added].

"... The USG[overnment] will act to facilitate efforts by third parties and third countries to establish contacts with *moderate elements* within and outside the Government of Iran by providing these elements with arms, equipment and related materiel in order to enhance the credibility of these elements. ..."

Of course, Bush, Casey and their Israeli allies had never sought to bolster "moderate elements" in Iran, but overthrew them at every opportunity—beginning with President Abol Hassan Bani-Sadr.[38]

January 7, 1986:

President Reagan and Vice President Bush met at the White House with several other administration officials. There was an argument over new proposals by Amiram Nir and Iranian arms dealer Manucher Ghorbanifar to swap arms for hostages.

Secretary of State George Shultz later told the Tower Commission that George Bush supported the arms-for-hostages deal at this meeting, as did President Reagan, Casey, Meese, Regan and Poindexter. Shultz reported that he himself and Secretary of Defense Caspar Weinberger both opposed further arms shipments.[39]

January 9, 1986:

Lt. Col. Oliver North complained, in his notebook, that "Felix [Rodriguez]" has been "talking too much about the V[ice] P[resident] connection."[40]

January 15, 1986:

CIA and Mossad employee Richard Brenneke wrote a letter to Vice President Bush giving full details, alerting Bush about his own work on behalf of the CIA in illegal—but U.S. government-sanctioned—sales of arms to Iran.[41]

Mid–January, 1986:

George Bush and Oliver North worked together on the illegal Iran-Contra plan.

Later, at North's trial, the Bush administration—portraying Colonel North as the master strategist in the case!—stipulated that North "prepared talking points for a meeting between Admiral Poindexter, Vice-President Bush, and [the new] Honduran President [José Simón] Azcona. North recommended that Admiral Poindexter and Vice-President Bush tell President Azcona of the need for Honduras to work with the U.S. government on increasing regional involvement with and support for the Resistance. Poindexter and Bush were also to raise the subject of better U.S. government support for the states bordering Nicaragua."

That is, Honduras, which of course "borders on Nicaragua," was to get more U.S. aid and was to pass some of it through to the Contras.

In preparation for the January 1986 Bush-Azcona meeting, the U.S. State Department sent to Bush adviser Donald Gregg a memorandum, which "alerted Gregg that Azcona would insist on receiving clear economic and social benefits from its [Honduras's] cooperation with the United States."[42]

Two months after the January Bush-Azcona meeting, President Reagan asked Congress for $20 million in emergency aid to Honduras, needed to repel a cross-border raid by Nicaraguan forces against Contra camps. Congress voted the "emergency" expenditure.

January 17, 1986:

George Bush met with President Reagan, John Poindexter, Donald Regan, and NSC staff member Donald Fortier to review the final version of the January 7 arms-to-Iran draft document.

With the encouragement of Bush, and the absence of opponents to the scheme, President Reagan signed the authorization to arm the Khomeini regime with missiles, and keep the facts of this scheme from congressional oversight committees.

This was the reality of the Bush "counterstrategy" to terrorism, for whose implementation his Terrorism Task Force was just then creating the covert mechanism.

The official story about this meeting—given in the Tower Commission Report—is as follows:

"[T]he proposal to shift to direct U.S. arms sales to Iran . . . was considered by the president at a meeting on January 17 which only the Vice President, Mr. Regan, Mr. Fortier, and VADM Poindexter attended. Thereafter, the only senior-level review the Iran initiative received was during one or another of the President's daily national security briefings. These were routinely attended only by the President, the Vice President, Mr. Regan, and VADM Poindexter. There was no subsequent collective consideration of the Iran initiative by the NSC principals before it became public 11 months later. . . .

"Because of the obsession with secrecy, interagency consideration of the initiative was limited to the cabinet level. With the exception of the NSC staff and, after January 17, 1986, a handful of CIA officials, the rest of the executive departments and agencies were largely excluded.

"The National Security Act also requires notification of Congress of covert intelligence activities. If not done in advance, notification must be 'in timely fashion.' The Presidential Finding of January 17 directed that congressional notification be withheld, and this decision appears to have never been reconsidered."[43]

January 18, 1986:
Defense Secretary Caspar Weinberger was directed to prepare the transfer of 4,000 TOW anti-tank missiles to the CIA, which was to ship them to Khomeini's Iran. Bypassing normal channels for covert shipments, he elected to have his senior military assistant, Lt. Gen. Colin L. Powell, handle the arrangements for the arms transfer.[44]

January 19–21, 1986:
George Bush's deputy national security aide, Col. Samuel Watson, worked with Felix Rodriguez in El Salvador, and met with Col. James Steele, the U.S. military liaison officer with the covert Contra resupply organization in El Salvador.[45]

Bush Sets Up North as Counterterrorism Boss—and "Fall Guy"

January 20, 1986:
Following the recommendations of an as yet unofficial report of the George Bush Terrorism Task Force, President Reagan signed National Security Decision Directive (NSDD) 207.

The unofficial Bush report, the official Bush report released in February, and the Bush-organized NSDD 207, together put forward Oliver North as "Mr. Iran-Contra." North became the nominal, up-front coordinator of the administration's counterterrorism program, hiding as best he could Bush's hand in these matters. He was given a secret office and staff (the Office to Combat Terrorism), separate from regular NSC staff members.

George Bush now reassigned his Terrorism Task Force employees, Craig Coy and Robert Earl, to do the daily work of the North secret office. The Bush men spent the next year working on Iran arms sales: Earl devoted one-quarter to one-half of his time on Iran and Contra support operations; Coy "knew everything" about Project Democracy. North traveled much of the time. Earl and Coy were at this time officially attached to the Crisis Management Center, which North worked on in 1983.[46]

FBI Assistant Director Revell, often George Bush's "hit man" against Bush's domestic opponents, partially disclosed this shell game in a letter to Sen. David Boren (D-Ok.), explaining the FBI's contacts with North:

> At the time [April 1986], North was the NSC official charged by the President with the coordination of our national counterterrorist program. He was responsible for working closely with designated lead agencies and was responsible for participating in all interagency groups, maintaining the national programming documents, assisting in the coordination of research and development in relation to counterterrorism, facilitating the development of response options and overseeing the implementation of the Vice President's Terrorism Task Force recommendations.
>
> This description of Col. North's position is set forth in the public report of the Vice President's Task Force on Combatting Terrorism, February 1986. There is an even more detailed and comprehensive description of Col. North's position in the classified National Security Decision Directive #207 issued by the President on January 20, 1986.[47]

The Bush Terrorism Task Force, having completed its official work, had simply made itself into a renamed, permanent, covert agency. Its new name was **Operations Sub-Group** (OSG).

In this transformation, CIA Contra-handler Duane Clarridge had been added to the Task Force to form the "OSG," which included North, Poindexter, Charles Allen, Robert Oakley, Noel Koch, General Moellering and "Buck" Revell.

According to the Oliver North diaries, even before this final phase of the Bush-North apparatus there were at least 14 meetings between North and the Bush Task Force's senior members Holloway, Oakley and Allen, its principal consultant Terry Arnold, and its staff men Robert Earl and Craig Coy. The North diaries from July 1985 through January 1986, show one meeting with President Reagan, and four meetings with Vice President Bush: either the two alone, North with Bush and Amiram Nir, or North with Bush and Donald Gregg.

The Bush counterterrorism apparatus had its own communications channels, and a global antiterrorist computer network called Flashboard outside of all constitutional government arrangements. Those opposed to the arming of terrorists, including cabinet members, had no access to these communications.[48]

This apparatus had responsibility for Iran arms sales; the private funding of the Contras, from contributions, theft, dope-running; the "public diplomacy" of Project Democracy to back these efforts; and counterintelligence against other government agencies and against domestic opponents of the policy.[49]

January 28, 1986:

George Bush met with Oliver North and FDN Contra Political Director Adolfo Calero in the Old Executive Office Building.[50] North and Calero would work together to protect George Bush when the Contra supply effort blew apart in October 1986.

January 31, 1986:

Iranian arms dealer Cyrus Hashemi was told by a French arms agent that "[a]n assistant of the vice president's going to be in Germany . . . and the indication is very clear that the transaction can go forward" referring to George Bush's supposed approval of the private arms sale to Iran.[51]

February 6, 1986:

Responding to the January 15 letter from Richard Brenneke, Bush aide Lt. Col. E. Douglas Menarczik wrote to Brenneke: "The U.S. government will not permit or participate in the provision of war materiel to Iran and will prosecute any such efforts by U.S. citizens to the fullest extent of the law."[52]

February 7, 1986:

Samuel M. Evans, a representative of Saudi and Israeli arms dealers, told Cyrus Hashemi that "[t]he green light now finally has been given [for the private sale of arms to Iran], that Bush is in favor, Shultz against, but nevertheless they are willing to proceed."[53]

February 25, 1986:

Richard Brenneke wrote again to Bush's office, to Lt. Col. Menarczik, documenting a secret project for U.S. arms sales to Iran going on since 1984.

Brenneke later said publicly that early in 1986, he called Menarczik to warn that he had learned that the U.S. planned to buy weapons for the Contras with money from Iran arms sales. Menarczik reportedly said, "We will look into it." Menarczik claimed not to have "any specific recollection of telephone conversations with" Brenneke.[54]

Late February, 1986:

Vice President George Bush issued the public report of his Terrorism Task Force. In his introduction to the report, Bush asserted: "Our Task Force was briefed by more than 25 government agencies . . . traveled to embassies and military commands throughout the world. . . . Our conclusion: . . . We firmly oppose terrorism in all forms and wherever it takes place. . . . We will make no concessions to terrorists."[55]

March 1986:

According to a sworn statement of pilot Michael Tolliver, Felix Rodriguez had met him in July 1985. Now Rodriguez instructed Tolliver to go to Miami International Airport. Tolliver picked up a DC–6 aircraft and a crew, and flew the plane to a Contra base in Honduras. There Tolliver watched the unloading of 14 tons of military supplies, and the loading of 12 and 2/3 tons of marijuana. Following his instructions from Rodriguez, Tolliver flew the dope to Homestead Air Force Base in Florida. The next day Rodriguez paid Tolliver $75,000.[56]

Tolliver says that another of the flights he performed for Rodriguez carried cocaine on the return trip to the U.S.A. He made a series of arms deliveries from Miami into the air base at Agucate, Honduras. He was paid in cash by Rodriguez and his old Miami CIA colleague, Rafael "Chi Chi" Quintero.

In another circuit of flights, Tolliver and his crew flew between Miami and El Salvador's Ilopango air base. Tolliver said that Rodriguez and Quintero "instructed me where to go and who to see." While making these flights, he "could go by any route available without any interference from any agency. We didn't need a stamp of approval from Customs or anybody. . . ."[57]

With reference to the covert arms shipments out of Miami, George Bush's son Jeb said: "Sure, there's a pretty good chance that arms were shipped, but does that break any law? I'm not sure it's illegal. The Neutrality Act is a completely untested notion, established in the 1800s."[58]

Smuggling Missiles and Reporting to the Boss

Trafficking in lethal weapons without government authorization is always a tricky business for covert operators. But when the operatives are smuggling weapons in a particular traffic which the U.S. Congress has expressly prohibited, a good deal of criminal expertise and certain crucial contacts are required for success.

And when the smugglers report to the Vice President, who wishes his role to remain concealed, the whole thing can become very sticky—or even ludicrous to the point of low comedy.

March 26, 1986:

Oliver North sent a message to Robert McFarlane about his efforts to procure missiles for the Contras, and to circumvent many U.S. laws, as well as the customs services and police forces of several nations. The most important component of such transactions, aside from the purchase money, was a falsified document showing the supposed recipient of the arms, the *end-user certificate* (EUC).

In the message he wrote, North said that "we have" an EUC; that is, a false document has been acquired for this arms sale: "[W]e are trying to find a way to get 10 BLOWPIPE launchers and 20 missiles from [a South American country] . . . thru the Short Bros. Rep. . . . Short Bros., the mfgr. of the BLOWPIPE, is willing to arrange the deal, conduct the training and even send U.K. 'tech. reps' . . . if we can close the arrangement. Dick Secord has already paid 10% down on the delivery and we have a [country deleted] EUC which is acceptable to [that South American country]."[59]

Now, since this particular illegal sale somehow came to light in the Iran-Contra scandal, another participant in this one deal decided not to bother hiding his own part in it. Thus, we are able to see how Colonel North got his false certificate.

April 20, 1986:

Felix Rodriguez met in San Salvador with Oliver North and Enrique Bermudez, the Contras' military commander. Rodriguez informs us of the following in his own, ghost-written book:

"Shortly before that April 20 meeting, Rafael Quintero had asked me to impose upon my good relations with the Salvadoran military to obtain 'end-user' certificates made out to Lake Resources, which he told me was a Chilean company. . . ."[60]

The plan was to acquire false end-user certificates from his contacts in the Salvadoran armed forces for Blowpipe ground-to-air missiles supposedly being shipped into El Salvador. The missiles would then be illegally diverted to the Contras in Honduras and Nicaragua.

Rodriguez continues, with self-puffery: "The Salvadorans complied with my request, and in turn I supplied the certificates, handing them over personally to Richard Secord at that April 20 meeting."[61]

While arranging the forgery for the munitions sale, Rodriguez was in touch with the George Bush staff back in his home office. On April 16, four days before the Rodriguez-North missile meeting, Bush national security adviser Donald Gregg asked his staff to put a meeting with Rodriguez on George Bush's calendar.

Gregg said the purpose of the White House meeting would be "to brief the Vice President on the war in El Salvador and resupply of the Contras." The meeting was arranged for 11:30 A.M. on May 1.[62]

Due its explicitly stated purpose—clandestine weapons trafficking in an undeclared war against the rigid congressional prohibition—the planned meeting was to become one of the most notorious of the Iran-Contra scandal.

April 30, 1986 (Wednesday):
Felix Rodriguez met in Washington with Bush aide Col. Sam Watson.

The following reminder message was sent to George Bush:

Briefing Memorandum for the Vice President
Event: Meeting with Felix Rodriguez
Date: Thursday, May 1, 1986
Time: 11:30–11:45 a.m.—West Wing
From: Don Gregg

I. PURPOSE
Felix Rodriguez, a counterinsurgency expert who is visiting from El Salvador, will provide a briefing on the status of the war in El Salvador and resupply of the Contras.

III. [sic] PARTICIPANTS
The Vice President   Felix Rodriguez
Craig Fuller
Don Gregg
Sam Watson

IV. MEDIA COVERAGE
Staff photographer. [i.e. internal-use photographs, no media coverage][63]

May 1, 1986:
Vice President Bush and his staff met in the White House with Felix Rodriguez, Oliver North, financier Nicholas Brady, and the new U.S. ambassador to El Salvador, Edwin Corr.

At this meeting it was decided that "private citizen" Felix Rodriguez would continue his work in Central America.[64]

May 16, 1986:
George Bush met with President Reagan, and with cabinet members and other officials in the full National Security Planning Group. They discussed the urgent need to raise more money for the Contras to continue the anti-Sandinista war.

The participants decided to seek support for the Contras from nations ("third countries") which were not directly involved in the Central American conflict.

As a result of this initiative, George Bush's former business partners, the Sultan of Brunei, donated $10 million to the Contras. But after being deposited in secret Swiss bank accounts, the money was "lost."[65]

May 20, 1986:
George Bush met with Felix Rodriguez and El Salvador Air Force commander Gen. Juan Rafael Bustillo at a large reception in Miami on Cuban independence day.[66]

May 29, 1986:
George Bush, President Reagan, Donald Regan and John Poindexter met to hear from McFarlane and North on their latest arms-for-hostages negotiations with Iranian officials and Amiram Nir in Teheran, Iran. The two reported their arrangement with the Khomeini regime to establish a secure covert communications network between the two "enemy" governments.[67]

July 10, 1986:
Eugene Hasenfus, whose successful parachute landing would explode the Iran-Contra scandal into world headlines three months later, flew from Miami to El Salvador. He had just been hired to work for "Southern Air Transport," a CIA front company for which Hasenfus worked previously in the Indochina War.

Within a few days he was introduced to "Max Gomez"—the pseudonym of Felix Rodriguez—as "one of the Cuban coordinators of the company." Rodriguez ("Gomez") took him to the Ilopango air base security office where he and others hired with him were given identity cards.

He now began work as a cargo handler on flights carrying military supplies to Contra soldiers inside Nicaragua.[68]

July 29, 1986:

George Bush met in Jerusalem with Terrorism Task Force member Amiram Nir, the manager of Israel's participation in the arms-for hostages schemes. Bush did not want this meeting known about. The Vice President told his chief of staff, Craig Fuller, to send his notes of the meeting only to Oliver North—not to President Reagan, or to anyone else.

Craig Fuller's memorandum said, in part:

> 1. SUMMARY. Mr. Nir indicated that he had briefed Prime Minister Peres and had been asked to brief the V[ice] P[resident] by his White House contacts. He described the details of the efforts from last year through the current period to gain the release of the U.S. hostages. He reviewed what had been learned which was essentially that the radical group was the group that could deliver. He reviewed the issues to be considered—namely that there needed to be ad [sic] decision as to whether the items requested would be delivered in separate shipments or whether we would continue to press for the release of the hostages prior to delivering the items in an amount agreed to previously.
>
> 2. The VP's 25 minute meeting was arranged after Mr. Nir called Craig Fuller and requested the meeting and after it was discussed with the VP by Fuller and North. . . .
>
> 14. Nir described some of the lessons learned: 'We are dealing with the most radical elements. . . . They can deliver . . . that's for sure. . . . [W]e've learned they can deliver and the moderates can't.
> [69]
> . . .

July 30, 1986:

The day after his Jerusalem summit with Amiram Nir, Vice President Bush conferred with Oliver North. This meeting with North was never acknowledged by Bush until the North diaries were released in May 1990.

Early September, 1986:

Retired Army Maj. Gen. John K. Singlaub sent a memo to Oliver

North on the Contra resupply effort under Felix Rodriguez. Singlaub warned North that Rodriguez was boasting about having "daily contact" with George Bush's office. According to Singlaub, this could "damage President Reagan and the Republican Party."[70]

The Scandal Breaks—On George Bush

October 5, 1986:

A C–123k cargo aircraft left El Salvador's Ilopango air base at 9:30 A.M., carrying "10,000 pounds of small arms and ammunition, consisting mainly of AK rifles and AK ammunition, hand grenades, jungle boots." It was scheduled to make air drops to Contra soldiers in Nicaragua.[71]

The flight had been organized by elements of the CIA, the Defense Department, and the National Security Council, coordinated by the Office of Vice President George Bush.

At that time, such arms resupply was prohibited under U.S. law— prohibited by legislation which had been written to prevent precisely that type of flight.

The aircraft headed south along the Pacific coast of Nicaragua, turned east over Costa Rica, then headed up north into Nicaraguan air space. As it descended toward the point at which it was to drop the cargo, the plane was hit in the right engine and wing by a ground-to-air missile. The wing burst into flames and broke up. Cargo handler Eugene Hasenfus jumped out the left cargo door and opened his parachute. The other three crew members died in the crash.[72]

Meanwhile, Felix Rodriguez made a single telephone call—to the office of Vice President George Bush. He told Bush aide Samuel Watson that the C–123k aircraft was missing and was possibly down.

October 6, 1986:

Eugene Hasenfus, armed only with a pistol, took refuge in a small hut on a jungle hilltop inside Nicaragua. He was soon surrounded by Sandinista soldiers and gave himself up.[73]

Felix Rodriguez called George Bush's aide Sam Watson again. Watson now notified the White House Situation Room and the National Security Council staff about the missing aircraft.

Oliver North was immediately dispatched to El Salvador to prevent publicity over the event, and to arrange death benefits for the crew.[74]

After the shoot-down, several elaborate attempts were made by government agencies to provide false explanations for the origin of the aircraft.

A later press account, appearing on May 15, 1989, after Bush was safely installed as President, exposed one such attempted coverup:

> Official: Contras Lied to Protect VP Bush
> By Alfonso Chardy, Knight-Ridder Newspapers
> WASHINGTON—Nicaraguan rebels falsely assumed responsibility for an arms-laden plane downed over Nicaragua in 1986 in an effort to shield then-Vice President George Bush from the controversy that soon blossomed into the Iran-Contra scandal, a senior Contra official said in early May 1989.
> According to the Contra official, who requested anonymity but has direct knowledge of the events, a Contra spokesman, Bosco Matamoros [official FDN representative in Washington, D.C.], was ordered by [FDN Political Director] Adolfo Calero to claim ownership of the downed aircraft, even though the plane belonged to Oliver North's secret Contra supply network. . . .
> Calero called (Matamoros) and said, "Take responsibility for the Hasenfus plane because we need to take the heat off the vice president," the Contra source said. . . .
> The senior Contra official said that shortly after Calero talked to Matamoros, Matamoros called a reporter for the *New York Times* and "leaked" the bogus claim of responsibility. The *Times* ran a story about the claim on its front page.[75]

October 7, 1986:
Rep. Henry B. Gonzalez (D-Tx.) called for a congressional investigation of the Nicaraguan air crash, and the crash of a Southern Air Transport plane in Texas, to see if they were part of a covert CIA operation to overthrow the Nicaraguan government.

October 9, 1986:
At a news conference in Nicaragua, captured U.S. crew member Eugene Hasenfus exposed Felix Rodriguez, alias "Max Gomez," as the head of an international supply system for the Contras. The explosive, public phase of the Iran-Contra scandal had begun.

October 11, 1986:
The *Washington Post* ran two headlines side-by-side: "Captured American Flyer to be Tried in Nicaragua" and "Bush is Linked to Head of Contra Aid Network."
The *Post* reported:

Max Gomez, a Cuban American veteran of the CIA's ill-fated Bay of Pigs operation, has told associates that he reported to Vice President Bush about his activities as head of the secret air supply operation that lost a cargo plane to Nicaraguan missile fire. . . .

Gomez has said that he met with Bush twice and has been operating in Nicaragua with the Vice President's knowledge and approval, the sources said. . . .

Asked about these matters, a spokesman for Bush, Marlin Fitzwater, said: "Neither the vice president nor anyone on his staff is directing or coordinating an operation in Central America."

. . . The *San Francisco Examiner*, which earlier this week linked [Bush adviser Donald] Gregg to Gomez, reported that Gomez maintains daily contact with Bush's office. . . .

[M]embers of Congress said yesterday they wanted to investigate the administration's conduct further. And . . . several said that their focus had shifted from the CIA to the White House. . . .

[T]he Sunday crash will be among events covered by a [Senate] Foreign Relations Committee probe into allegations that the contras may have been involved in drug-running and abuse of U.S. aid funds, [Senator Richard G.] Lugar said. . . .

The Customs Service said yesterday it is investigating whether the downed plane may have carried guns out of Miami, which would violate federal restrictions on arms exports and other laws, including the Neutrality Act, which bars U.S. citizens from working to overthrow governments not at war with the United States. . . .

Hasenfus told reporters in Nicaragua the plane had flown out of Miami.[76]

George Bush's career was now on the line. News media throughout the world broke the story of the Hasenfus capture, and of the crewman's fingering of Bush and his underlings Rodriguez and Posada Carriles.

Bush was now besieged by inquiries from around the world, as to how and why he was directing the gun-running into Latin America.

Speaking in Charleston, South Carolina, George Bush described Max Gomez/Rodriguez as "a patriot." The Vice President denied that he himself was directing the illegal operations to supply the Contras: *"To say I'm running the operation . . . it's absolutely untrue."*

Bush said of Rodriguez: "I know what he was doing in El Salvador, and I strongly support it, as does the president of El Salvador, Mr. Napoleon Duarte, and as does the chief of the armed forces in El Salvador, because this man, an expert in counterinsurgency, was down there helping them put down a communist-led revolution [i.e. in El Salvador, not Nicaragua]."[77]

Two days later, Gen. Adolfo Blandón, armed forces chief of staff in El Salvador, denied Bush's contention that Felix Rodriguez worked for his country's military forces: "This intrigues me. It would have to be authorized [by our] joint chiefs of staff [and] the government." He said such authorization had not been given.[78]

October 12, 1986:

Eugene Hasenfus, the U.S. airman downed in Nicaragua, gave and signed an affidavit in which it was stated: "About Max Gomez [Felix Rodriguez], Hasenfus says that he was the head Cuban coordinator for the company and that he works for the CIA and that he is a very close friend of the Vice-President of the United States, George Bush. . . . Max Gomez, after receiving his orders was the one who had to . . . [say] where the air drops would be taking place.

"About Ramon Medina [escaped airplane bomber Luis Posada Carriles], Hasenfus says that he was also a CIA agent and that he did the 'small work' because *Max Gomez* was the 'senior man.' He says that *Ramon* took care of the rent of the houses, the maids, the food, transportation and drivers, and also, coordination of the fuel for the aircraft, etc." [emphasis in the original].[79]

His cover being blown, and knowing he was still wanted in Venezuela for blowing up an airliner and killing 73 persons, Posada Carriles now "vanished" and went underground.[80]

October 19, 1986:

Eugene Hasenfus, interviewed in Nicaragua by Mike Wallace on the CBS television program "60 Minutes," said that Vice President Bush was well aware of the covert arms supply operation. He felt the Reagan-Bush administration was "backing this 100 percent."

Wallace asked Hasenfus why he thought that Gomez/Rodriguez and the other managers of the covert arms resupply "had the blessing of Vice President Bush." Hasenfus replied, "They had his knowledge that he was working [on it] and what was happening, and whoever controlled this whole organization—which I do not know—Mr. Gomez, Mr. Bush, I believe a lot of these other people. They know how this is being run. I do not."[81]

Iran-Contra Characters Fall In and Out

November 3, 1986:

The Lebanese newspaper *Al-Shiraa* revealed that the U.S. government was secretly dealing arms to the Khomeini regime. This was three weeks after the Eugene Hasenfus exposé of George Bush made world headlines. Yet the Bush administration and its retainers have since decided that the Iran-Contra affair "began" with the *Al-Shiraa* story!

November 22, 1986:
President Reagan sent a message, *through Vice President George Bush,* to Secretary of State George Shultz, along the lines of "Support me or get off my team."[82]

December 18, 1986:
CIA Director William Casey, a close ally of George Bush who knew everything from the inside, was operated on for a "brain tumor" and lost the power of speech.

That same day, associates of Vice President George Bush said that Bush believed White House Chief of Staff Donald Regan should resign, but claim Bush had not yet broached the issue with the President. Donald Regan said that he had no intention of quitting.[83]

February 2, 1987:
CIA Director William Casey resigned. He soon died, literally without ever talking.

February 9, 1987:
Former National Security Director Robert McFarlane, a principal figure in the Reagan-Bush administration's covert operations, attempted suicide by taking an overdose of drugs. McFarlane survived.

February 26, 1987 (Thursday):
The President's Special Review Board, commonly known as the Tower Commission, issued its report. The commission heavily blamed White House Chief of Staff Donald Regan for the "chaos that descended upon the White House" in the Iran-Contra affair.

The Commission hardly mentioned Vice President George Bush except to praise him for his "vigorous reaffirmation of U.S. opposition to terrorism in all forms"!

The afternoon the Tower Commission report came out, George Bush summoned Donald Regan to his office. Bush said the President wanted to know what his plans were about resigning. Donald Regan blasted the President: "What's the matter—isn't he man enough to ask me that question?" Bush expressed sympathy. Donald Regan said he would leave in four days.[84]

February 27, 1987 (Friday):

Cable News Network televised a leaked report that Donald Regan had already been replaced as White House chief of staff. After submitting a one-sentence letter of resignation, Donald Regan said, "There's been a deliberate leak, and it's been done to humiliate me."[85]

George Bush, when President, rewarded the commission's chairman, Texas Senator John Tower, by appointing him U.S. Secretary of Defense. Tower was asked by a reporter at the National Press Club, whether his nomination was a "payoff" for the "clean bill of health" he gave Bush. Tower responded that "the commission was made up of three people, Brent Scowcroft and [Senator] Ed Muskie in addition to myself, that would be sort of impugning the integrity of Brent Scowcroft and Ed Muskie. . . . We found nothing to implicate the Vice President. . . . I wonder what kind of payoff they're going to get?"[86]

President Bush appointed Brent Scowcroft his chief national security adviser.

But the Senate refused to confirm Tower. Tower then wrote a book and began to talk about the injustice done to him. He died April 5, 1991 in a plane crash.

March 8, 1987:

In light of the Iran-Contra scandal, President Reagan called on George Bush to reconvene his Terrorism Task Force to evaluate the current program!

June 2, 1987:

Bush summarized his findings in a press release: "[O]ur current policy as articulated in the Task Force report is sound, effective, and fully in accord with our democratic principles, and national ideals of freedom."[87]

November 13, 1987:

The designated congressional committees filed their joint report on the Iran-Contra affair. Wyoming Representative Richard Cheney, the senior Republican member of the House Select Committee to Investigate Covert Arms Transactions with Iran, helped steer the joint committees to an impotent result. George Bush was totally exonerated, and was hardly mentioned.

George Bush, when President, rewarded Dick Cheney by appointing him U.S. Secretary of Defense, after the Senate refused to confirm John Tower.

The Mortification of the U.S. Congress

January 20, 1989:
George Bush was inaugurated President of the United States.

May 12, 1989:
President Bush's nomination of Donald Gregg to be U.S. ambassador to Korea was considered in hearings by the Senate Foreign Relations Committee.

Gregg was now famous in Washington as Bush's day-to-day controller of the criminal gun-running into Central America. Before the Gregg hearings began, both Republican and Democratic Senators on the committee tried to get President Bush to withdraw the Gregg nomination. This was to save them the embarrassment of confirming Gregg, knowing they were too intimidated to stop him.

What follows are excerpts from the typed transcript of the Gregg hearings. The transcript has never been reproduced, it has not been printed, and it will not be published by the Senate Foreign Relations Committee, which is evidently embarrassed by its contents.[88]

Gregg: [As] his national security adviser [for] six and a half years . . . I worked closely with the Vice President keeping him informed as best I could on matters of foreign policy, defense, and intelligence. . . . Travelling with the Vice President as I did . . . [in] a great variety of missions to more than 65 countries. . . .

[After Vietnam] I did not see [Felix Rodriguez] until the early eighties where he would drop into Washington sporadically . . . we remained friends. . . . So, some of those contacts would have been [1979–1982] when I was at the White House at the NSC.

Sen. Sarbanes: And Felix would come to see you there?

Gregg: No, at my home. . . . [Then] he brought me in '83 the plan which I have already discussed with Senator Cranston. . . . [At that point] I was working for the Vice President . . . [which I began in] August 1982.

Sen. Sarbanes: In December of 1984 he came to see you with the idea of going to El Salvador. You . . . cleared it with the Vice President?

Gregg: . . . I just said, "My friend Felix, who was a remarkable former agency employee . . . wants to go down and help with El Salvador. And I am going to introduce him to [State Department personnel] and see if he can sell himself to those men," and the Vice President said fine.

Gregg: Felix went down there about the first of March [1985].

Before he went . . . I introduced him to the Vice President . . . and the Vice President was struck by his character and wished him well in El Salvador.

Sen. Sarbanes: So before he went down, you undertook to introduce him to the Vice President. . . . Why did you do that?

Gregg: Well, the Vice President had always spoken very highly and enthusiastically of his career [!], or his one-year as DCI [Director of Central Intelligence]. I had gone out with him to the agency just after I joined him in '82 and I saw the tremendous response he got there and he got quite choked up about it and as we drove back in the car he said, you know, that is the best job I have ever had before I became Vice President.

So here it was, as I said probably the most extraordinary CIA comrade I had known, who was going down to help in a country that I knew that the Vice President was interested in. . . .

The Vice President was interested in the progress of the Contras.

There were two occasions on which he asked me, how are they doing and I, on one occasion went to a CIA officer who was knowledgeable and got a run-down on how they were doing from that and sent it to the Vice President and he sent it back with no comment.

On another occasion, he asked me again, how are they doing, and I went—I drew a memo up, I think on the basis of a conversation with North. Again, he returned that with no comment. So he was interested in the Contras as an instrument of putting pressure on the Sandinistas.

But what I said we had never discussed was the intricacies, or who was supplying what to whom. . . .

Sen. Simon: Let me read another section from Senator Cranston's statement. I believe the record suggests the following happened: After Boland II was signed in October 1984 [outlawing all U.S. aid to the Contras], you and certain others in the White House were encouraged to secure military aid for the Contras through unorthodox channels.

Your career training in establishing secrecy and deniability for covert operations, your decades-old friendship for Felix Rodriguez, apparently led you to believe you could serve the national interest by sponsoring a freelance covert operation out of the Vice President's office.

What is your response to that statement?

Gregg: Well, I think it is a rather full-blown conspiracy theory. That was not what I was doing. . . . I was involved in helping the Vice President's task force on antiterrorist measures write their report. But normally I had no operational responsibilities. . . .

Sen. Simon: When did you first find out the law was being violated?

Gregg: By the law, do you mean the Boland amendment?

Sen. Simon: That is correct.

Gregg: I guess my knowledge of that sort of came at me piecemeal after Hasenfus had been shot down [Oct. 5, 1986] and there were various revelations that came out. . . .

Sen. Simon: So what you are telling us, you found out about the law being violated the same time the rest of us found out the law was being violated?

Gregg: Yes, sir. . . .

Sen. Cranston: From February 1985 to August 1986, you have acknowledged that you spoke to Rodriguez many, many times on the telephone. Let me quote from your sworn deposition to the Iran-Contra Committee: "Felix called me quite often and frequently it was what I would call sort of combat catharsis. He used to do the same thing in Vietnam. He would come back from an operation in which some people had been lost and he would tell me about it."

Now, is it still your testimony that Rodriguez never mentioned his deep involvement in Contra supply activities during any of these phone conversations?

Gregg: That is my testimony.

Sen. Cranston: Is it still your testimony that prior to Aug. 8th, 1986, Rodriguez never mentioned the status of his Contra resupply efforts during his numerous face-to-face meetings with you in Washington?

Gregg: Never.

Sen. Cranston: Is it still your testimony that Rodriguez did not mention the status of his Contra resupply efforts in the very meetings that were convened according to two memos bearing your name, for Rodriguez to "brief the Vice President on the status of the war in El Salvador and efforts to resupply the Contras"?

Gregg: There was no intention to discuss resupply of the Contras and everyone at that meeting, including former Senator Nick Brady have testified that it was not discussed.

Sen. Cranston: As you know, it is difficult to reconcile those statements about what happened in the meeting with the statement and memos from you that the agenda was . . . two things, one of them being efforts to resupply the Contras. . . .

Gregg: Those memos first surfaced to my attention in December of 1986, when we undertook our first document search of the Vice President's office. They hit me rather hard because by that time I had put the pieces together of what had been going on and I realized the implications of that agenda item.

I did not shred the documents. I did not hide it. . . . [T]his is the worst thing I have found and here it is, and I cannot really explain it. . . . I have a speculative explanation which I would like to put forward if you would be interested.

Sen. Cranston: Fine.

Gregg: Again, turning to Felix [Rodriguez]'s book . . . Felix makes the following quote. . . . [By the way the book] is going to be published in October of this year. The text has been cleared by CIA and it is now with the publishers. I was given an advance copy. . . . This is the quote, sir: ". . . I had no qualms about calling [Sam Watson] or Don [Gregg] when I thought they could help run interference with the Pentagon to speed up deliveries of spare chopper parts." That means helicopters.

"I must have made many such calls during the spring of 1986. Without operating Hughes 500 helicopters it was impossible to carry out my strategy against the [El Salvadoran] insurgents. . . ." [There are] then documented steps that Colonel Watson had taken with the Pentagon to try to get spare parts expedited for El Salvador. . . .

So my construction is this, sir. I recall that in the meeting with the Vice President the question of spare parts for the helicopters in El Salvador was discussed and so that I think *what the agenda item on the two memos is, is a garbled reference to something like resupply of the copters, instead of resupply of the Contras* [emphasis added].

[At this point there was laughter and whistling in the hearing room. Afterwards, Gregg told reporters, "I don't know how it went over, but it was the best I could do."]

Sen. Sarbanes: How did the scheduling proposal of April 16, 1986 and the briefing memorandum of April 30th take place?

Gregg: They were prepared by my assistant, Mrs. Byrne, acting on advice from Colonel Watson. She signed my initials, but those are not my initials. I did not see the documents until December 1986, when I called them to the attention of the House Intelligence Committee. . . . And if, you know, if you do not—if my speculation does not hold up, I have to refer you to a memorandum that I turned over to the Iran-Contra Committee on the 14th of May 1987, which—

Sen. Sarbanes: I am looking at that memorandum now.

Gregg: Okay. That has been my explanation up until now.

Sen. Sarbanes: But you are now providing a different explanation?

Gregg: It is the only one—I have been thinking about these documents for over two years, and it is the only thing that I can come up with that would come close to explaining that agenda item—given the fact that there was no intention of discussing resupply to the Contras. That resupply of the Contras was not discussed, according to the testimony of everyone who was in the meeting. . . ."

Sen. Kerry: Douglas Minarczik is who?

Gregg: He was one of my assistants in my office responsible for Mid-East and African affairs. . . .

Sen. Kerry: And he was working for you in 1985 and 1986, that period?

Gregg: Yes.

Sen. Kerry: Now, when I began first investigating allegations of the *gun-running* that was taking place out of Miami, one of the very first references that my staff, frankly, frequently heard, and I think you and I have talked about this, that *Miami was buzzing with the notion that the Vice President's office was somehow involved in monitoring that, at least* [emphasis added].

Now, Jesus Garcia was a Miami corrections official who got into trouble and wound up going to jail on weapons offenses. Through that connection, we came across telephone records. And those telephone records demonstrate calls from Garcia's house to Contra camps in Honduras, to John Hull in Costa Rica, and Douglas Minarczik in, not necessarily in your office, but directly to the White House.

However, there is incontrovertible evidence that he had in his possession the name of Mr. Minarczik, a piece of paper in our possession, in Garcia's home in connection with monitoring those paramilitary operations, in August of 1985.

Now, how do you account for the fact that Minarczik's—that the people involved with the Contra supply operations out of Miami . . . had Minarczik's name and telephone number, and that there is a record of calls to the White House at that time?

Gregg: I cannot account for it. Could it have anything to do with our old friend Mr. Brenicke [sic]? Because Brenicke did have Minarczik's phone number. . . .

Sen. Kerry: . . . No. Totally separate.

Gregg: This is all new. I do not have an explanation, sir. . . .

Sen. Kerry: Do you recall the downing of a Cuban airliner in [1976] in which 72 people lost their lives as a result; do you remember that?

Gregg: Yes.

Sen. Kerry: A terrorist bomb. And a Cuban-American named

Luis Posada [Carriles] was arrested in Venezuela in connection with that. He then escaped in 1985 with assistance from Felix Rodriguez—I do not know if this is going to be in the [Rodriguez] book or not—

Gregg: It is.

Sen. Kerry: Okay, and he brought him to Central America to help the Contras under pseudonym of Ramon Medina, correct?

Gregg: Now, I know that; yes.

Sen. Kerry: . . . [Is] it appropriate for a Felix Rodriguez to help a man indicted in a terrorist bombing to escape from prison, and then appropriate for him to take him to become involved in supply operations, which we are supporting?

Gregg: I cannot justify that, sir. And I am not certain what role Felix played in getting him out. . . . I thought that Orlando Boche [sic], or someone of that nature, had been responsible for that.

Sen. Kerry: When did you first learn that [i.e. about Posada's hiring for Contra resupply], Don?

Gregg: When I learned who the various aliases were, which was some time in November/December [1986], after the whole thing came out.

COMMITTEE SESSION JUNE 15, 1989

Sen. Cranston: Before proceeding in this matter, I would like to state clearly for the record what the central purpose of this investigation is about and in my view what it is not about.

It is not about who is for or against the Contras. . . .

Similarly, this investigation is not about building up or tearing down our new President [Bush]. We have tried throughout this proceeding to avoid partisan attacks. Indeed, *Republicans and Democrats alike* have sought Mr. Gregg's withdrawal as one way to avoid casting aspersions on the [Bush] White House. . . . [emphasis added].

Mr. Gregg remains steadfast in his loyalty to his boss, then-Vice President Bush, and to his long-time friend, Felix Rodriguez. Mr. Gregg has served his country in the foreign policy field for more than three decades.

By all accounts he is a loyal American. . . .

As Mr. Gregg himself conceded last month, there are substantial reasons for senators to suspect his version of events and to raise questions about his judgement.

It does not take a suspicious or partisan mind to look at the documentary evidence, the back channel cables, the "eyes only" memos, and then to conclude that Mr. Gregg has not been straight with us. Indeed, I am informed that more than one Republican senator who has looked at the accumulated weight of the evidence against Mr. Gregg, has remained unconvinced and has sought Mr. Gregg's withdrawal.

Mr. Gregg, this committee has a fundamental dilemma. If we are to promote a man we believe to have misled us under oath, we would make a mockery of this institution. We would invite contempt for our enquiries. We would encourage frustration of our constitutional obligations.

. . . [It] has been established that when you are confronted with written evidence undermining your story, you point the finger of blame elsewhere. At our last hearing you said Gorman's cables were wrong, North's notebooks were wrong, Steele's memory was wrong, North's sworn testimony [that Gregg introduced Rodriguez to him] was wrong, you concocted a theory that your aide, Watson, and your secretary erred by writing "Contras" instead of "helicopters" on those infamous briefing memos for the Vice President.

In sum, you have told a tale of an elaborate plan in which your professional colleagues and long-time friends conspired to keep you ignorant of crucial facts through days of meetings, monthly phone calls and nearly two years' worth of cables and memos.

Incredibly, when senators confront you with the documentary evidence which undermines your story, you accuse us of concocting conspiracy theories and you do so with a straight face.

. . . I think it is clear by now that many important questions may never be answered satisfactorily, especially because we have been stonewalled by the administration.

The National Security Agency has rejected our legitimate enquiries out of hand. The Central Intelligence Agency provided a response with access restrictions so severe . . . as to be laughable.

The Department of Defense has given an unsatisfactory response two days late. The State Department's response was utterly unresponsive. They answered our letter after their self-imposed deadline and failed to produce specific documents we requested and which we know exist.

This Committee has been stonewalled by Oliver North, too. He has not complied with the Committee subpoena for his unredacted notebooks. The redacted notebooks contain repeated January 1985 references to Felix Rodriguez which suggests North's involvement in Rodriguez' briefings of the Vice President.

No member of the Senate can escape the conclusion that these administration actions are contemptuous of this Committee. *I find this highly regrettable, with potential long-term ramifications, but I recognize the will of the majority to come to a committee vote soon, up or down, and to move on to other pressing business* [emphasis added]. . . .

Sen. McConnell: . . . During the period of the Boland Amendment, were you ever asked to inform the Vice President's office or lend his name to private, nonprofit efforts to support the Contras?

Gregg: Yes. I recall one instance, in particular, where there was a request—I guess it was probably from one aspect of the Spitz Channell organization, which had a variety of things going on in and around Nicaragua.

We got, on December 2nd, 1985, a letter to the Vice President, asking him to get involved in something called the Friends of the Americas, which was aid to the Meskito Indians . . . in Nicaragua that had been badly mistreated by the Sandinistas. . . . And so I have a document here which shows how we dealt with it. I sent it to Boyden Gray, the counsel of the Vice President and said, "Boyden, this looks okay as a charity issue, but there is the question of precedent. Please give me a legal opinion. Thanks." . . . Boyden Gray wrote back to me and said, "No, should not do. Raises questions about indirect circumvention of congressional funding limits or restriction, vis-a-vis Nicaragua."

That is the only time I recall that we had a specific request like that, and this is how we dealt with it.

[In fact, George Bush had a much more interesting relationship to the affairs of Carl R. "Spitz" Channell than Mr. Gregg discusses here. Channell worked with Bush's covert action apparatus, moving his wealthy contacts toward what he termed "the total embrace of the Vice President."]

Sen. Pell [Chairman of the Committee]: . . . First, you say that you offered to resign twice, I think.

Knowing that you are a very loyal servant of what you view as the national interest, and knowing the embarrassment that this nomination has caused the administration, I was wondering why you did not ask your name to be withdrawn . . . to pull your name back. . . . [w]hich has been recommended by many of us as being a way to resolve this problem.

Gregg: Well, I haven't because I think I'm fully qualified to be Ambassador to South Korea. And so does the Vice President [sic].

So I am here because he has asked me to serve. . . .

Sen. Cranston: . . . Senators will recall that on Oct. 5th of '86 a plane bearing military supplies to the Contras was shot down over Nicaragua. The sole survivor, Eugene Hasenfus, spoke publicly of the role of Felix Rodriguez, alias Max Gomez, in aiding military resupply and noted Gomez's ties to the Vice President's office.

Could you please describe your understanding of why it was that the first call to official Washington regarding the shootdown was from Felix Rodriguez to your aid[e] in Washington?

Gregg: . . . [It] was because on the 25th of June of that year he had come to Washington to confront North about what he regarded as corruption in the supply process of the Contras. . . . [H]e broke with North on the 25th of June and has not been on speaking terms with the man since then. . . . [H]e tried to get me—he could not—he reached Colonel Watson. . . .

Sen. Cranston: As you recall, the Vice President was besieged at that time with inquiries regarding Rodriguez's ties to the Vice President's office. What did you tell [Bush press spokesman] Marlin Fitzwater regarding that relationship?

Gregg: . . . The thrust of the press inquiries was always that from the outset I had had in mind that Rodriguez should play some role in the Contra support operation, and my comments to Marlin . . . were that that had not been in my mind. . . .

Sen. Cranston: Let me quote again from the *New York Times*, George Bush quoted October 13, '86. Bush said, "To the best of my knowledge, this man, Felix Rodriguez, is not working for the United States government."

Now Mr. Gregg, you knew that Rodriguez was aiding the Contras and receiving material assistance in the form of cars, housing, communications equipment and transportation from the U.S. government. Did you inform Bush of those facts so that he could make calculated misleading statements in ignorance of his staff's activities?

Gregg: . . . At that point I had no idea that Felix—you said—you mentioned communications equipment. I had no idea he had been given by North one of those encryption devices. I think I was aware that Colonel Steele had given him access to a car, and I knew he was living in a BOQ at the air base. He was not being paid any salary. His main source of income was, as it is now, his retirement pension from CIA.

Sen. Cranston: . . . You told the Iran-Contra committee that you and Bush never discussed the Contras, had no expertise on the issue, no responsibility for it, and the details of Watergate-sized scandal involving NSC staff and the [Edwin] Wilson gang was not Vice Presidential.

Your testimony on that point I think is demonstrably false. There are at least six memos from Don Gregg to George Bush regarding detailed Contra issues. . . .

Sen Cranston: Am I correct in this, that you have confirmed . . . that senior U.S. military, diplomatic . . . and intelligence personnel, really looked with great doubt upon Rodriguez's mission and that they tolerated it only because Rodriguez used his contacts with the Vice President and his staff as part of the way to bolster his mission.

Gregg: . . . I was not aware of the diplomatic; I was aware of the military and intelligence, yes, sir.

The committee voted in favor of confirmation. Cranston voted no. But three Democrats—Charles Robb, Terry Sanford and Chairman Claiborne Pell—joined the Republicans.

Sanford confirmed Cranston's viewpoint, saying that he was allowing the nomination to go through because he was afraid "the path would lead to Bush," the new President. Sanford said, shamefacedly, *"If Gregg was lying, he was lying to protect the President, which is different from lying to protect himself."*[89]

In George Bush's government, the one-party state, the knives soon came out, and the prizes appeared.

The Senate Ethics Committee, including the shamefaced Terry Sanford, began in November 1989, its attack on the "Keating Five." These were U.S. Senators, among them Senator Alan Cranston, charged with savings and loan corruption. The attack soon narrowed down to one target only—the Iran-Contrary Senator Cranston.

On Aug. 2, 1991, Senator Terry Sanford, having forgotten his shame, took over as the new chairman of the Senate Ethics Committee.

Bush, LaRouche and Iran-Contra

George Bush and his friends have repeatedly told political pundits that America is "tired" and "bored" of hearing about the Iran-Contra affair.

Bush has taken a dim view of those who were not tired or bored, but fought him.

Oct. 6, 1986 was a fateful day in Washington. The secret government apparatus learned that the Hasenfus plane had been shot down the day before, and went scurrying about to protect its exposed parts. At the same time, it sent about 400 heavily armed FBI agents, other federal, state and local policemen storming into the Leesburg,

Virginia, publishing offices associated with the American dissident political leader Lyndon LaRouche, Jr.

LaRouche and his political movement had certified their danger to the Bush program. Six months before the raid, LaRouche associates Mark Fairchild and Janice Hart had gained the Democratic nominations for Illinois lieutenant governor and secretary of state; they won the primary elections after denouncing the government-mafia joint coordination of the narcotics trade. With this notoriety, LaRouche was certain to act in an even more unpredictable and dangerous fashion as a presidential candidate in 1988. LaRouche allies were at work throughout Latin America, promoting resistance to the Anglo-Americans. The LaRouche-founded *Executive Intelligence Review* had exposed U.S. government covert support for Khomeini's Iranians, beginning in 1980.

More directly, the LaRouchites were fighting the Bush apparatus for its money. Connecticut widow Barbara Newington, who had given Spitz Channell's National Endowment for the Preservation of Liberty $1,735,578 out of its total 1985 income of $3,360,990,[90] was also contributing substantial sums to LaRouche-related publishing efforts . . . which were exposing the Contras and their dope-pushing. Fundraiser Michael Billington argued with Mrs. Newington, warning her not to give money to the Bush-North-Spitz Channell gang.

Back on August 19, 1982, and on November 25, 1982, George Bush's old boss, Henry A. Kissinger, had written to FBI Director William Webster, asking for FBI action against "the LaRouche group." In promoting covert action against LaRouche, Kissinger also got help from James Jesus Angleton, who had retired as chief of counterintelligence for the CIA. After Yalie Angleton got going in this anti-dissident work, he mused "Fancy that, now I've become Kissinger's Rebbe."[91]

One week before the raid, an FBI secret memorandum described the LaRouche political movement as "subversive," and claimed that its "policy positions . . . dovetail nicely with Soviet propaganda and disinformation objectives."[92]

Three months after Spitz Channell's fraud confession, Vice President Bush denounced LaRouche at an Iowa campaign rally: "I don't like the things LaRouche does. . . . He's bilked people out of lots of money, and misrepresented what causes money was going to. LaRouche is in a lot of trouble, and deserves to be in a lot of trouble."[93]

LaRouche and several associates eventually went on trial in Boston, on a variety of "fraud" charges—neither "subversion" nor defunding the Contras was in the indictments. Bush was now running hard for the presidency.

Suddenly, in the midst of the primary elections, the LaRouche trial took a threatening turn. On March 10, 1988, Federal Judge Robert E. Keeton ordered a search of the indexes to Vice President George Bush's confidential files to determine whether his spies had infiltrated LaRouche-affiliated organizations.

Iran-Contra Special Prosecutor Lawrence Walsh had acquired, and turned over to the LaRouche defense, in response to an FOIA request, a secret memorandum found in Oliver North's safe. It was a message from Gen. Richard Secord to North, written May 5, 1986—four days after North had met with George Bush and Felix Rodriguez to confirm that Rodriguez would continue running guns to the Contras using Spitz Channell's payments to Richard Secord. The memo, released in the Boston courtroom, said, "Lewis has met with FBI and other agency reps and is apparently meeting again today. Our Man here claims Lewis has collected info against LaRouche."[94]

The government conceded that "our man here" in the memo was Bush Terrorism Task Force member Oliver "Buck" Revell, the assistant director of the FBI. "Lewis"—"soldier of fortune" Fred Lewis—together with Bush operatives Gary Howard and Ron Tucker, had met later in May 1986, with C. Boyden Gray, counsel to Vice President Bush.[95]

Howard and Tucker, deputy sheriffs from Bush-family-controlled Midland, Texas, were couriers and bagmen for money transfers between the National Security Council and private "counterterror" companies. They were also professional sting artists. Howard and Tucker had sold 100 battle tanks to a British arms dealer for shipment to Iran, and had taken his $1.6 million. Then they turned him in to British authorities and claimed a huge reward. A British jury, outraged at Howard and Tucker, threw out the criminal case in late 1983.

The LaRouche defense contended, with the North memo and other declassified documents, that the Bush apparatus had sent spies and provocateurs into the LaRouche political movement in an attempt to wreck it.

Judge Keeton demanded that the Justice Department tell him why information they withheld from the defense was now appearing in court in declassified documents.

The government was not forthcoming, and in May 1988, the

judge declared a mistrial. The jury told the newspapers they would have voted for acquittal.

But Bush could not afford to quit. LaRouche and his associates were simply indicted again, on new charges. This time they were brought to trial before a judge who could be counted on.

Judge Albert V. Bryan, Jr. was the organizer, lawyer and banker of the world's largest private weapons dealer, Interarms of Alexandria, Virginia. As the new LaRouche trial began, the CIA-front firm that the judge had founded controlled 90 percent of the world's official private weapons traffic. Judge Bryan had personally arranged the financing of more than a million weapons traded by Interarms between the CIA, Britain and Latin America.

Agency for International Development trucks carried small arms, rifles, machine guns and ammunition from Interarms in Alexandria for flights to Cuba—first for Castro's revolutionary forces. Then, Judge Bryan's company, Interarms, provided guns for the anti-Castro initiatives of the CIA Miami Station, for Rodriguez, Shackley, Posada Carriles, Howard Hunt, Frank Sturgis, et al. When George Bush was CIA Director, Albert V. Bryan's company was the leading private supplier of weapons to the CIA.[96]

In the LaRouche trial, Judge Bryan prohibited virtually all defense initiatives. The jury foreman, Buster Horton, had top secret clearance for government work with Oliver North and Oliver "Buck" Revell. LaRouche and his associates were declared guilty.

On January 27, 1989—one week after George Bush became President—Judge Albert V. Bryan sentenced the 66-year dissident leader LaRouche to 15 years in prison. Michael Billington, who had tried to wreck the illicit funding for the Contras, was jailed for three years with LaRouche; he was later railroaded into a Virginia court and sentenced to another 77 years in prison for "fundraising fraud."

Notes for Chapter XVII

1. William L. Shirer, *The Rise and Fall of the Third Reich: A History of Nazi Germany* (New York: Simon and Schuster, 1960), p. 271.

2. Memo, May 14, 1982, two pp. bearing the nos. 29464 and 29465. See also "NSDD–2 Structure for Central America," bearing the no. 29446, a chart showing the SSG and its CPPG as a guidance agency for the National Security Council.

Photostats of these documents are reproduced in the *EIR Special Report:* "Irangate, the Secret Government and the LaRouche Case," (Wiesbaden, Germany: Executive Intelligence Review Nachrichtenagentur, June 1989), p. 19.

3. Testimony of Donald P. Gregg, pp. 72–73 in Stenographic Transcript of Hearings Before the U.S. Senate Committee on Foreign Relations, Nomination Hearing for Donald Phinney Gregg to be Ambassador to the Republic of Korea. Washington, D.C., May 12, 1989 (hereinafter identified as "Gregg Hearings"). This transcript is available for reading at the office of the U.S. Senate Foreign Relations Committee, in the Capitol, Washington, D.C.

See also Felix Rodriguez and John Weisman, *Shadow Warrior* (New York: Simon and Schuster, 1989), pp. 213–14. The book was ghost written—and spook-approved—by the CIA and Donald Gregg before publication.

4. *Report of the Congressional Committees Investigating the Iran Contra Affair* (hereinafter identified as the "Iran-Contra Report"), published jointly by the U.S. House of Representatives Select Committee to Investigate Covert Arms Transactions with Iran, and the U.S. Senate Select Committee on Secret Military Assistance to Iran and the Nicaraguan Opposition, Nov. 17, 1987, Washington, D.C., pp. 395–97. Note that different sections of the Congressional Iran-Contra Report were published on different dates.

5. *CovertAction*, No. 33, Winter 1990, p. 12; drawn from Public Testimony of Fawn Hall, Iran-Contra Report, June 8, 1987, p. 15.

6. Memoranda and meetings of March 1983, in the "National Security Archive" Iran-Contra Collection on microfiche at the Library of Congress, Manuscript Reading Room (hereinafter identified as "Iran-Contra Collection").

7. Don Gregg Memorandum for Bud McFarlane, March 17, 1983, stamped SECRET, since declassified. Document no. 77 in the Iran-Contra Collection; on the memo is a handwritten note from "Bud" [McFarlane] to "Ollie" [North].

See also Gregg Hearings, pp. 54–55.

8. Rodriguez and Weisman, *op. cit.*, p. 119.

9. Shultz Memorandum, May 25, 1983 and White House reply, both stamped SECRET/ SENSITIVE. Documents beginning no. 00107 in the Iran-Contra Collection.

10. De Graffenreid Memorandum for Admiral Murphy, July 12, 1983, since declassified, bearing the no. 43673. Document no. 00137 in the Iran-Contra Collection.

11. Constantine C. Menges, *Inside the National Security Council* (New York, Simon and Schuster, 1988), pp. 70–78.

12. Chronology supplied by the Office of the Vice President, cited in *The Progressive*, May 18, 1987, London, England, p. 20.

13. Rodriguez and Weisman, *op. cit.*, p. 221.; *CovertAction*, No. 33, Winter 1990, p. 13, citing Testimony of Oliver North; *Iran-Contra Report* (June 8, 1987), pp. 643, 732–33.

14. This section is based on 1) literature supplied by CSA, Inc. and its subsidiary ANV, and 2) an exhaustive examination of CSA/ANV in Jupiter and other locations, including interviews with personnel employed by the company, and with military and CIA personnel who have worked with the company.

15. Scott Armstrong, Executive Editor for The National Security Archive, *The Chronology: The Documented Day-by-Day Account of the Secret Military Assistance to Iran and the Contras* (New York: Warner Books, 1987), p. 55.

Jonathan Marshall, Peter Dale Scott and Jane Hunter, *The Iran-Contra Connection: Secret Teams and Covert Operations in the Reagan Era* (Boston: South End Press, 1987), pp. 219–20.

16. National Security Planning Group Meeting Minutes, June 25, 1984, pp. 1 and 14, photostats reproduced in *EIR Special Report:* "American Leviathan: Administrative Fascism under the Bush Regime" (Wiesbaden, Germany: Executive Intelligence Review Nachrichtenagentur, April 1990), p. 159.

17. This is an excerpt from Section 8066 of Public Law 98–473, the Continuing Appropriations Act for Fiscal Year 1985; Iran-Contra Report, Nov. 13, 1987, p. 398l.

18. Armstrong, *op. cit.*, Nov. 1, 1984 entry, p. 70, citing *Miami Herald* 11/2/84 and 11/3/ 84, *Wall Street Journal* 11/2/84, *Washington Post* 8/15/85, *New York Times* 12/23/87.

Armstrong, *op. cit.*, Nov. 10, 1983 entry, p. 42, citing corporate records of the Florida secretary of state 7/14/86, *Miami Herald* 11/2/84, *New York Times* 11/3/84.

19. Rodriguez and Weisman, *op. cit.*, pp. 220–21; *EIR Special Report:* "American Leviathan," pp. 157–58.

20. Report of the Subcommittee on Terrorism, Narcotics and International Operations of the Committee on Foreign Relations, United States Senate, December 1988, pp. 61–62.

21. Rodriguez and Weisman, *op. cit.*, pp. 221–22.

22. *Ibid.*, pp. 224–25.

23. General Gorman "eyes only" cable to Pickering and Steele, Feb. 14, 1985. Partially declassified and released on July 30, 1987 by the National Security Council, bearing no. D 23179. Document no. 00833 in the Iran-Contra Collection.

See also Rodriguez and Weisman, *op. cit.*, pp. 225–26.

24. U.S. government stipulations in the trial of Oliver North, reproduced in *EIR Special Report:* "Irangate. . .," pp. 20, 22.

25. Gregg Hearings, p. 99.

26. Rodriguez and Weisman, *op. cit.*, p. 227.

Gregg Hearings, *New York Times*, Dec. 13, 1986.

27. *CovertAction*, No. 33, Winter 1990, pp. 13–14.

On Amiram Nir, see Armstrong, *op. cit.*, pp. 225–26, citing *Wall Street Journal* 12/22/86, *New York Times* 1/12/87.

On Poindexter and North, see Menges, *op. cit.*, p. 264.

28. Armstrong, *op. cit.*, pp. 140–41, citing Senate Select Committee on Intelligence, "Report on Preliminary Inquiry," Jan. 29, 1987.

29. Rodriguez and Weisman, *op. cit.*, pp. 239–41.

30. Oliver North's diary, since edited and partially declassified, entries for "10 Sep 85." Document no. 01527 in the Iran-Contra Collection.

31. *Washington Post*, June 10, 1990.

32. Charles E. Allen "Memorandum for the Record," December 18, 1985. Partially declassified/released (i.e. some parts are still deleted) by the National Security Council on January 26, 1988. Document no. 02014 in the Iran-Contra Collection.

33. Armstrong, *op. cit.*, pp. 226–27, citing *Wall Street Journal* 12/22/86, *New York Times* 12/25/86 and 1/12/87.

34. Armstrong, *op. cit.*, p. 231, citing *Washington Post* 2/20/87, *New York Times* 2/22/87.

35. *Ibid.*, p. 232, citing *Miami Herald* 11/30/86.

36. Interview with Herman Moll in *EIR Special Report:* "Irangate. . .," pp. 81–83.

37. Armstrong, *op. cit.*, p. 235, citing *Washington Post* 12/16/86, 12/27/86, 1/10/87 and 1/12/87; *Ibid.*, p. 238, citing Tower Commission Report; Menges, *op. cit.*, p. 271.

38. Armstrong, *op. cit.*, pp. 240–41, citing *Washington Post* 1/10/87 and 1/15/87; Sen. John Tower, Chairman, *The Tower Commission Report: The Full Text of the President's Special Review Board* (New York: Bantam Books, 1987), p. 217.

39. *Ibid.*, pp. 37, 225.

40. North notebook entry Jan. 9, 1986, Exhibits attached to Gregg Deposition in Tony Avirgan and Martha Honey v. John Hull, Rene Corbo, Felipe Vidal et al., 29 April 1988.

41. Armstrong, *op. cit.*, p. 258, citing the Brenneke letter, which was made available to the National Security Archive.

42. U.S. government stipulations at the North trial, in *EIR Special Report:* "Irangate. . .," p. 22.

43. *Tower Commission Report*, pp. 67–68, 78.

44. Armstrong, *op. cit.*, p. 266, citing *Washington Post* 1/10/87 and 1/15/87.

45. Chronology supplied by Office of Vice President Bush; Armstrong, *op. cit.*, p. 266, citing *Washington Post* 12/16/86.

46. Deposition of Robert Earl, *Iran-Contra Report,* May 2, 1987, Vol. 9, pp. 22–23; Deposition of Craig Coy, *Iran-Contra Report,* March 17, 1987, Vol. 7, pp. 24–25: cited in *CovertAction,* No. 33, Winter 1990, p. 13.

47. Oliver Revell to Sen. David Boren, chairman of Senate Select Committee on Intelligence, April 17, 1987; *Washington Post* Feb. 17, 20 and 22, 1987; *Wall Street Journal* Feb. 20, 1987: cited in *CovertAction,* No. 33, Winter 1990, p. 13.

48. *Newsweek,* Oct. 21, 1985, p. 26; Earl Exhibit, nos. 3–8, attached to Earl Deposition, *op. cit.*: cited in *CovertAction* No. 33, Winter 1990, p. 15.

49. Earl Deposition, *op. cit.*, May 30, 1987, pp. 33–37; May 15, 1987, pp. 117–21 (Channell and Miller); May 15, 1987, pp. 131, 119 (private contributors).

50. Donald Gregg Briefing Memorandum for the Vice President, Jan. 27, 1986; released by the National Security Council March 22, 1988. Document no. 02254 in Iran-Contra Collection.

51. Armstrong, *op. cit.*, p. 275, citing *Miami Herald* 11/30/86.

52. *Ibid.*, p. 280, citing the Menarczik letter to Brenneke which was made available to the National Security Archive.

53. *Ibid.*, citing *Miami Herald* 11/30/86.

54. *New York Times,* Nov. 30, 1986, Dec. 4, 1986. See Gregg testimony: Brenneke had M's number.

55. Quoted in Menges, *op. cit.*, p. 275.

56. Deposition of Michael Tolliver in Avirgan and Honey, *op. cit.*

57. Allan Nairn, "The Bush Connection," in *The Progressive* (London: May 18, 1987), pp. 21–22.

58. Nairn, *op. cit.*, pp. 19, 21–23.

59. *Tower Commission Report*, p. 465

60. Rodriguez and Weisman, *op. cit.*, pp. 244–45.

61. *Ibid.*

62. "Schedule Proposal," Office of the Vice President, April 16, 1986, exhibit attached to Gregg Deposition in Avirgan and Honey, *op. cit.*

63. Office of the Vice President Memorandum, April 30, 1986, released Aug. 28, 1987 by the National Security Council. Document no. 02738 in the Iran-Contra Collection.

64. Rodriguez and Weisman, *op. cit.*, pp. 245–46.

See also Gregg confirmation hearings, excerpted *infra,* and numerous other sources.

65. Armstrong, *op. cit.*, pp. 368–69, citing Senate Select Intelligence Committee Report, Jan. 29, 1987.

66. *Ibid.*, p. 373, citing *Washington Post* 12/16/86.

67. *Ibid.*, p. 388–89, citing McFarlane testimony to the Tower Commission.

68. Affidavit of Eugene Harry Hasenfus, October 12, 1986, pp. 2–3. Document no. 03575 in the Iran-Contra Collection.

69. *Tower Commission Report*, pp. 385–88.

70. *Washington Post*, Feb. 26, 1987.

71. Hasenfus Affidavit, pp. 6–7.

72. *Ibid.*

73. Hasenfus Affidavit, p. 7.

74. Armstrong, *op. cit.*, p. 508, citing the chronology provided by George Bush's office, *Washington Post* 12/16/86; *New York Times* 12/16/86, 12/17/86 and 12/25/86; *Wall Street Journal* 12/19/86 and 12/24/86.

75. *Laredo [Texas] Morning Times,* May 15, 1989, p. 1.

76. *Washington Post*, Oct. 11, 1986.

77. *Washington Post*, Oct. 12, 1986, Oct. 14, 1986.

78. *Washington Post*, Oct. 14, 1986.

79. Hasenfus Affidavit, p. 3.

80. Rodriguez and Weisman, *op. cit.*, p. 241.

81. *Washington Post*, Nov. 20, 1986.

82. *Washington Post*, Feb. 12, 1987.

83. *Washington Post*, Dec. 18, 1986, *Wall Street Journal*, Dec. 19, 1986.

84. Donald T. Regan, *For the Record: From Wall Street to Washington* (New York: Harcourt Brace Jovanovitch, 1988), pp. 368–73.

85. *Ibid.*

86. *New York Times*, March 2, 1989.

87. *CovertAction*, No. 33, Winter 1990, p. 15.

88. Stenographic Transcript of Hearings Before the U.S. Senate Committee on Foreign Relations, Nomination Hearing for Donald Phinney Gregg to be Ambassador to the Republic of Korea. Washington, D.C., May 12 and June 15, 1989. Some misspellings in the transcript have been corrected here.

89. Mary McCrory, "The Truth According to Gregg," *Washington Post,* June 22, 1989.

90. NEPL contributions 1985 printout, cited in Armstrong, *op. cit.*, p. 226.

91. Kissinger letters, declassified in 1984, photostats in *EIR Special Report:* "Irangate. . .," pp. 52, 55.

Angleton quote in Tom Mangold, *Cold Warrior* (New York: Simon and Schuster, 1991), p. 352. Mangold defines "rebbe" as "not a rabbi, but trusted counselor and family friend."

See also Burton Hersh, "In the Hall of Mirrors: The Cold War's Distorted Images," in *The Nation,* June 23, 1991. Hersh says: "I knew Angleton in the last five years of his life [he died May 11, 1987]. Angleton was amusing himself just then with a vendetta against Lyndon LaRouche."

92. Director FBI to D[efense] I[ntelligence] A[gency], Sept. 30, 1986, classified SECRET.

93. Bush at Shelton, Iowa, July 31, 1987, quoted in *EIR Special Report:* "Irangate. . .," p. 65.

94. Secord to North 5/5/86 memorandum marked SECRET, declassified Feb. 26, 1988 by Special Prosecutor Lawrence Walsh, photostat in *EIR Special Report:* "Irangate. . .," p. 31.

95. *Washington Post,* March 27, 1989.

96. Corporate records of the First National Bank of Alexandria and the First Citizens Bank of Alexandria, 1940s to 1960s, in *Polk's Bankers Directory.*

Clarence J. Robinson, *Reminiscences* (Fairfax, Va.: George Mason University, 1983). Robinson was the owner of the massive weapons warehouse, "Robinson's Terminal Warehouse," for which Albert V. Bryan was the registered agent.

Over 100 interviews with family, friends and associates of Judge Bryan in banking, freemasonry, armaments, Episcopal Church and other fields.

XVIII

THE LEVERAGED BUYOUT MOB

During the entire decade of the 1980s, the policies of the Reagan-Bush and Bush administrations encouraged one of the greatest paroxysms of speculation and usury that the world has ever seen. Starting especially in the summer of 1982, a malignant and cancerous mass of speculative paper spread through all the vital organs of the banking, credit and financial system. Capital had long since ceased to be used for the creation of new productive plant and equipment, new productive manufacturing jobs, investment in transportation, power systems and education; health services and other infrastructure declined well below the break-even level. Wall Street investors came more and more to resemble vampires who ranged over a ghoulish landscape in search of living prey whose blood they could suck to perpetuate their own lively form of death.

Industrial employment was out, the service sector was in. The post-industrial society meant that the production of tangible, physical wealth, of hard commodities, within U.S. borders was being terminated. The future would belong to parasitical legions of lawyers, financial services experts, accountants, and clerical support personnel, but the growth in the balance of payments deficit signaled that the game could not go on forever.

On the surface, wild speculation was the order of the day: There was the stock market boom, which underwent a crash in 1987, but then, thanks to Nicholas Brady's drugged futures and index options markets, kept rising until the Dow had passed 3,000, although by that time no one could remember why it was still called an industrial average. The stock market provided the right atmosphere for a much broader speculative boom, the one in commercial and residential real estate, which kept going until almost the end of the decade, but which then began to crash with a vengeance. When real estate began to implode, as in Texas at the middle of the 1980s or the Northeast after 1988, savings banks and commercial banks by the scores became insolvent. Thus, by the third year of the Bush administration, a different bankrupt savings and loan was being seized by federal regulators on every business day, and Congressman John Dingell of Michigan had to announce that Citibank, still the largest bank in the United States, was indeed "technically" bankrupt. Depositors in Hong Kong started a run on the Citibank branch there; their U.S. counterparts were slower to react, perhaps because deluded by the pathetic faith that the Federal Deposit Insurance Corporation could still cover their deposits.

Even more fundamental than speculation was the absolute primacy of debt. During the Reagan and Bush years, unprecedented federal deficits pushed the public debt of the United States into the ionosphere, with the total almost quadrupling during a little more than ten years, to approach the fantastic total of $3.25 thousand billion (or trillion). In 1989, it was estimated that total debt claims in the U.S. economy had attained almost $25 trillion and their total has increased exponentially ever since. The debt of state and local governments, corporate debt, consumer debt—all expanded into the wild blue yonder. In the meantime, the Great Lakes industrial region became the rust bowl, the Sun Belt oil and computer booms collapsed, the great cities of the East were rotten to the core with slums, and farmers went bankrupt more rapidly than at any other time in the memory of man.

Living standards had been in a gradual but constant decline since the days of Nixon, and it began to dawn on more and more families who considered themselves members of the middle class that they could no longer afford their own home, nor hope to send their children to college, all because of the prohibitive costs. The Bureau of the Census made sure in 1990 not to count the number of those who had become homeless during the 1980s, since the real figure would be an acute political embarrassment to George Bush: Were there five million, or six, as many as the total population of Sweden, or of Belgium?

New jobs were created, but most of them were dead-ends for losers, at or below the minimum wage, and presupposed illiteracy on the part of the applicant: Hamburger sales and pizza home delivery were the growth areas, although a smart kid might still aspire to become a croupier. Behind it all lurked the pervasive narcotics trade, with hundreds of billions of dollars a year in heroin, crack, marijuana.

For the vast majority of the U.S. population (to say nothing of the brutal immiseration in the developing countries) it was an epoch of austerity, sacrifice and decline, of the entropy of a society in which most people have no purpose and feel themselves becoming redundant. But for a paper-thin stratum of plutocrats and parasites, the 1980s was a time of unlimited opportunity. These were the practitioners of the disastrous financial swindles that marked the decade, the protagonists of the hostile takeovers, mergers and acquisitions, leveraged buyouts, greenmail and stock plays that occupied the admiration of Wall Street. These were corporate raiders like J. Hugh Liedtke, Blaine Kerr, T. Boone Pickens and Frank Lorenzo; Wall Street financiers like Henry Kravis and Nicholas Brady. And these men, surely not by coincidence, belonged to the intimate circle of personal friends and close political supporters of George Herbert Walker Bush.

If the orgy of usury and speculation during the 1980s could be compared to a glittering and exclusive dinner party, and Liedtke, Kerr, Pickens, Lorenzo, Kravis and Brady were the invited guests, then surely George Bush was the host who presided. By late 1991, the long-deferred bill for these Lucullian entertainments was about to arrive. The exhausted working people and destitute unemployed must present the bill to, among others, the founder of the feast, the whining and greedy spoiled child of the Anglo-American oligarchy, George Bush, the man whose idea of privation would be a life without servants, and whose concept of a domestic agenda would be a plan to hire two maids and a butler.

The Pennzoil Wars: A Case Study

One of the landmark corporate battles of the first Reagan administration was the battle over control of Getty Oil, a battle fought between Texaco—at that time the third largest oil company in the United States and the fourth largest industrial corporation—and J. Hugh Liedtke's Pennzoil. George Bush's old partner and constant crony, J. Hugh Liedtke, was obsessed with his dream of building Pennzoil into a major oil company, one that could become the seventh of the traditional Seven Sisters after Chevron and Gulf merged. But the sands of biological time were running out on "Chairman Mao" Liedtke, as the abrasive Pennzoil boss was known in the years after he became the first U.S. oilman to drill in China, thanks to Bush. The only way that Chairman Mao Liedtke could realize his lifelong dream would be by acquiring a large oil company and using its reserves to build Pennzoil up to world-class status.

Liedtke was the chairman of the Pennzoil board, and the Pennzoil president was now Blaine Kerr, a former lawyer from Baker & Botts in Houston. Blaine Kerr was also an old friend of George Bush. Back in 1970, when George was running against Lloyd Bentsen, Kerr had advised Bush on a proposed business deal involving a loan request from Victor A. Flaherty, who needed money to buy Fidelity Printing Company. Blaine Kerr was a hard bargainer: He recommended that Bush make the loan, but that he also demand some stock in Fidelity Printing as part of the deal. Three years later, when Fidelity Printing was sold, Bush cashed in his stock for $99,600 in profit, a gain of 1,900 percent on his original investment. That was the kind of return that George Bush liked, the kind that honest activities can so rarely produce.[1]

Chairman Mao Liedtke and his sidekick Blaine Kerr constantly scanned their radar screens for an oil company to acquire. They studied Superior Oil, which was in play, but Superior Oil did too much of its business in Canada, where there had been no equivalent of George Bush's Task Force on Regulatory Relief, and where the oil companies were thus still subject to some restraints. Chairman Mao ruled that one out. Then there was Gulf Oil, where T. Boone Pickens was attempting a takeover, but Liedtke reluctantly decided that Gulf was beyond his means. Then, Chairman Mao began to hear reports of conflicts on the board of Getty Oil. Getty Oil, with 20,000 employees, was a $12 billion corporation, about six times larger than Pennzoil. But Chairman Mao had already managed to gobble up United Gas when that company was about six times larger than his own Pennzoil. Getty Oil had about a billion barrels of oil in the ground. Now Chairman Mao was very interested.

Chairman Mao Liedtke gathered his team to attempt to seize control of Getty Oil: James Glanville of Lazard Freres was his investment banker, Arthur Liman of Paul, Weiss, Rifkind, Wharton & Garrison was his chief negotiator. Liedtke also had the services of the megafirm Baker & Botts of Houston.

In early 1984, Gordon Getty and his Sarah Getty Trust, plus the Getty Museum represented by the New York mergers and acquisitions lawyer Marty Lipton, combined to oblige the board of Getty Oil to give preliminary acceptance to a tender offer for Getty Oil stock at a price of about $112.50 per share. Arthur Liman thought he had a deal that would enable Chairman Mao to seize control of Getty Oil and its billion barrel reserves, but no contract or any other document was ever signed, and key provisions of the transaction remained to be negotiated.

When the news of these negotiations began to leak out, major oil companies who also wanted Getty and its reserves began to move in: Chevron showed signs of making a move, but it was Texaco, represented by Bruce Wasserstein of First Boston and the notorious Skadden, Arps, Slate, Meagher & Flom law firm, that got the attention of the Getty Museum and Gordon Getty with a bid (of $125 a share) that was sweeter than the tight-fisted Chairman Mao Liedtke had been willing to put forward. Gordon Getty and the Getty Museum accordingly signed a contract with Texaco. This was nominally the largest acquisition in human history up to that time, and the check received by Gordon Getty was for $4,071,051,264, the second largest check ever written in the history of the United States, second only to one that had been used to roll over a part of the post-World War II national debt.

But Chairman Mao Liedtke thought he had been cheated. "They've made off with a million dollars of my oil!" he bellowed. "We're going to sue everybody in sight!"

But Chairman Mao Liedtke's attempts to stop the deal in court were fruitless; he then concentrated his attention on a civil suit for damages on a claim that Texaco had been guilty of "tortious interference" with Pennzoil's alleged oral contract with Getty Oil. The charge was that Texaco had known that there already had been a contract, and had set out deliberately to breach it. After extensive forum shopping, Chairman Mao concluded that Houston, Texas was the right venue for a suit of this type. Liedtke and Pennzoil demanded $7 billion in actual damages and $7 billion in punitive damages for a total of at least $14 billion, a sum bigger than the entire public debt of the United States on December 7, 1941. Liedtke hired Houston lawyer Joe "King of Torts" Jamail, and backed up Jamail with Baker & Botts.

Interestingly, the judge who presided over the trial until the final phase, when the die had already been cast, was none other than Anthony J.P. "Tough Tony" Farris. Back in February 1963, the newly elected Republican county chairman for Harris County, George H.W. Bush, had named Tough Tony Farris as his first assistant county chairman.[2] This was when Bush was in the midst of preparations for his failed 1964 Senate bid. Farris had tried to get elected to Congress on the GOP ticket, but failed. During the Nixon administration, Farris became the United States Attorney in Houston. Given what we know of the relations between Nixon and

George Bush (to say nothing of the relations between Nixon and Prescott Bush), we must conclude that a patronage appointment of this type could hardly have been made without George Bush's involvement. Tough Tony Farris was decidedly an asset of the Bush networks.

Now Tough Tony Farris was a state district judge, whose remaining ambition in life was an appointment to the federal bench. Farris did not recuse himself because his patron, George Bush, was a former business partner and constant crony of J. Hugh Liedtke. Farris rather began issuing a string of rulings favorable to Pennzoil: He ruled that Pennzoil had a right to quick discovery from Texaco. Farris was an old friend of Pennzoil's lead trial lawyer, Joe Jamail, and Jamail had just given Tough Tony Farris a $10,000 contribution for his next election campaign. Jamail, in fact, was a member of Tough Tony's campaign committee. Texaco attempted to recuse Farris, but they failed. Farris claimed that he would have recused himself if Texaco's lawyers had come to him privately, but that their public attempt to get him pitched out of the case made him decide to fight to stay on. Just at that point the district courts of Harris County changed their rules in such a way as to allow Bush's man Tough Tony Farris, who had presided over the pretrial hearings, to actually try the case.

And try the case he did, for 15 weeks, during which the deck was stacked for Pennzoil's ultimate victory. With a few weeks left in the trial, Farris was diagnosed as suffering from terminal cancer, and he was forced to request a replacement district judge. The last-minute substitute was Judge Solomon Casseb, who finished up the case along the lines already clearly established by Farris. In late November 1985, the jury awarded Pennzoil damages of $10.53 billion, a figure that exceeded the total Gross National Product of 116 countries around the world. Casseb not only upheld this monstrous result, but increased it to a total of $11,120,976,110.83.

Before the trial, back in January 1985, Chairman Mao Liedtke had met with John K. McKinley, the chairman of Texaco, at the Hay-Adams Hotel across Lafayette Park from the White House in Washington, D.C. Liedtke told McKinley that he thought what Texaco had done was highly illegal, but McKinley responded that his lawyers had assured him that his legal position was "very sound." McKinley offered suggestions for an out-of-court settlement, but these were rejected by Chairman Mao, who made his own counter-offer: He wanted three-sevenths of Getty Oil, and was now willing to hike his price to $125 a share. According to one account of this meeting, Liedtke seemed to go out of his way to mention his friendship with George Bush, according to Bill Weitzel of Texaco. "Mr. Liedtke was quite outspoken with regard to the influence that he felt he had—and would and could expect in Washington—in connection with antitrust matters and legislative matters," McKinley would say in deposition. "The idea was that Pennzoil was not without political influence that could adversely affect the efforts of Texaco in completing its merger."[3]

Liedtke denied all this: "The political-influence thing isn't true. I don't have any and McKinley knows it!" Did Liedtke keep a straight face?

In any case, the Reagan-Bush regime made no secret of its support for Pennzoil. In the spring of 1987, after prolonged litigation, the U.S. Supreme Court required Texaco to post a bond of $11 billion. On April 13, 1987, the press announced that Texaco had filed for Chapter 11 bankruptcy protection. The Justice Department created two committees to represent the interests of Texaco's unsecured creditors, and Pennzoil was made the chairman of one of these committees. Texaco operations were subjected to severe disruptions.

During the closing weeks of 1987, Texaco was haggling with Chairman Mao about the sum of money that the bankrupt firm would pay to Pennzoil. At this point, Bushman Lawrence Gibbs was the Commissioner of the Internal Revenue Service, one of the principal targeting agencies of the growing police state. He slammed bankrupt and wounded Texaco with a demand for $6.5 billion in back taxes. This move was in the works behind the scenes during the Texaco-Pennzoil talks, and it certainly made clear to Texaco which side the government was on. The implication was that Texaco had better settle with Chairman Mao in a hurry, or face the prospect of being broken up by the various Wall Street sharks—Holmes à Court, T. Boone Pickens, Kohlberg, Kravis, Roberts and Carl Icahn—who had begun to circle the wounded company. In case Texaco had not gotten the message, the Department of Energy also launched an attack on Texaco, alleging that the bankrupt firm had overcharged its customers by $1.25 billion during the time before 1981 when oil price controls had been in effect.

Chairman Mao Liedtke finally got his pound of flesh: He would eventually receive $3 billion from Texaco. Texaco in late 1987 announced an asset write-down of $4.9 billion as a result of staggering losses, and began to sell assets to try to avoid liquidation. Texaco's Canadian and German operations were sold off, as were 600 oil properties in various locations. Later Texaco also sold off a

50 percent interest in its refining and marketing system to Saudi Arabia. A number of Texaco refineries were simply shut down. A total of $7 billion in assets were sold off during 1988–89 alone.

The entire affair represented a monstrous miscarriage of justice, a declaration that the entire U.S. legal system was bankrupt. At the heart of the matter was the pervasive influence of the Bush networks, which gave Liedtke the support he needed to fight all the way to the final settlement. The real losers in this affair were the Texaco and Getty workers whose jobs were destroyed, and the families of those workers, as well as Texaco's customers. Estimates of the numbers of these victims are hard to come by, but the count must reach into the tens of thousands.

KKR

But even the enormities of Chairman Mao Liedtke were destined to be eclipsed in the political and regulatory climate of savage greed created with the help of the Reagan-Bush administration and George Bush's Task Force on Regulatory Relief. Even Liedtke's colossal grasping was about to be out-topped by a small Wall Street firm, which, primarily during the second Reagan-Bush term, assembled a financial empire greater than that of J.P. Morgan at the height of Jupiter's power. This firm was Kohlberg, Kravis, Roberts (KKR) which had been founded in 1976 by a partner and some former employees of the Bear Stearns brokerage of lower Manhattan, and which by late 1990 had bought a total of 36 companies using some $58 billion lent to KKR by insurance companies, commercial banks, state pension funds, and junk bond king Michael Milken. The dominant personality of KKR was Henry Kravis, the man who inspired actor Michael Douglas (Kravis's former prep school classmate at the Loomis School) when Douglas played the role of corporate raider Gordon Gekko in Oliver Stone's movie *Wall Street*. Henry Kravis was in particular the motor force behind the KKR leveraged buyout of RJR Nabisco, which, with a price tag of almost $25 billion, was the largest transaction in recorded history up to that time.

Henry Kravis's epic achievements in speculation and usury perhaps had something to do with the fact that he was a close family friend of George Bush. As we have seen, when Prescott Bush was arranging a job for young George Herbert Walker Bush in 1948, he contacted Ray Kravis of Tulsa, Oklahoma, whose business included helping Brown Brothers Harriman to evaluate the oil reserves of companies (see Chapter 8). Ray Kravis over the years had kept in close touch with Senator Prescott Bush and George Bush, and young Henry Kravis, his son, had been introduced to George and had hob-nobbed with him at various Republican Party fundraising events. Henry Kravis by the early 1980s was a member of the Republican Party's elite Inner Circle.

Bush and Henry Kravis became even more closely associated during the time that Bush, ever mindful of campaign financing, was preparing his bid for the presidency. Among political contributors, Henry Kravis was a very high roller. In 1987–88, Kravis gave over $80,000 to various Senators, Congressmen, Republican political action committees, and the Republican National Committee. During 1988, Kravis gave $100,000 to the GOP Team 100, which meant a "soft money" contribution to the Bush campaign. Kravis's partner George Roberts also anted up $100,000 for the Republican Team 100. In 1989, the first year in which it was owned by KKR, RJR Nabisco also gave $100,000 to Team 100. During that year, Kravis and Roberts gave $25,000 each to the GOP. Kravis was also a leading financier of Zionist causes. During the 1988 primary season, Kravis was the co-chair of a lavish Bush fundraiser at the Vista Hotel in lower Manhattan at which Henry's fellow Wall Street dealmakers and financier fat cats coughed up a total of $550,000 for Bush. Part of Kravis's symbolic recompense was the prestigious title of co-chairman of Bush's Inaugural Dinner in January 1989. One year later, in January 1990, Kravis was the National Chairman of Bush's Inaugural Anniversary Dinner.[4]

According to Kravis, Bush "writes me handwritten notes all the time and he calls me and stuff, and we talk." The talk concerned what the U.S. government should do in areas of immediate interest to Kravis: "We talked on corporate debt—this was going back a few years—and what that meant to the private sector," said Kravis.

Henry Kravis certainly knows all about debt. The 1980s wit-nessed the triumph of debt over equity, with a tenfold increase in total corporate debt during the decade, while production, productive capacity, and employment stagnated and declined. One of the princi-pal ways in which this debt was loaded onto a shrinking productive base was through the technique of the hostile, junk bond-assisted leveraged buyout, of which Henry Kravis and his firm were the leading practitioners.

Small-scale leveraged buyouts were pioneered by KKR during the late 1970s. In its final form, the technique looked something like this: Corporate raiders looked around for companies that might be worth more than their current stock price if they were broken up and sold off. Using money borrowed from a number of sources, the raider would make a tender offer, or otherwise secure a majority of the shares. Often all outstanding shares in the company would be bought up, taking the company private, with ownership residing in a small group of financiers. The company would end up saddled with an immense amount of new debt, often in the form of high-yield, high-risk subordinated debt certificates called junk bonds. The risk on these was high, since, if the company were to go bankrupt and be auctioned off, the holders of the junk bonds would be the last to get any compensation.

Often, the first move of the raider after seizing control of the company and forcing out its existing management, would be to sell off the parts of the firm that produced the least cash flow, since enhanced cash flow was imperative to start paying the new debt. Proceeds from these sales could also be used to pay down some of the initial debt, but this process inevitably meant jobs destroyed and production diminished. These raiding operations were justified by a fascistoid-populist demagogy that accused the existing management of incompetence, indolence and greed. The LBO pirates professed to have the interests of the shareholders at heart, and made much of the fact that their operations increased the value of the stock and, in the case of tender offers, gave the stockholders a better price than they would have gotten otherwise. The litany of the corporate raider was built around his commitment to "maximize shareholder value"; workers, bondholders, the public, the firms themselves were all expendable in the short run. Ivan Boesky and others further embroidered this with a direct apology for greed as a motor force of progress in human affairs.

An important enticement to transform stocks and equity into bonded and other debt was provided by the insanity of the U.S. tax code, which taxed profits distributed to shareholders, but not the debt paid on junk bonds. The ascendancy of the leveraged buyout, therefore, was accompanied by the demolition of the U.S. corporate tax base, contributing in no small way to the growth of federal deficits.

Ultimately, the big profits were expected when the companies acquired, after having been downsized to "lean and mean" dimensions, had their stock sold back to the public. KKR reserved itself 20 percent of the profits on these final transactions. In the meantime Kravis and his associates collected investment banking fees, retainer fees, directors' fees, management fees, monitoring fees, and a plethora of other charges for their services.

The leverage was accomplished by the smaller amount of equity left outstanding in comparison with the vastly increased debt. This meant that if, after deducting the debt service, profits went up, the return to the investors could become very high. Naturally, if losses began to appear, reverse leverage would come into play, producing astronomical amounts of red ink. Most fundamental was that companies were being loaded with debt during the years of what the Reagan-Bush regime insisted on calling a boom. It was evident to any sober observer that as the depression asserted its existence, many of the companies that had succumbed to leveraged buyouts and related usury would very rapidly become insolvent.

This is why the "recession" (in reality the deterioration of the pre-existing depression) that George Bush was forced to acknowledge during late 1991 was so ominous in its implications. The leveraged buyouts of the 1980s were now doomed to collapse. The handwriting on the wall was clear by September–October of 1989, the first year of George Bush's presidency, when the $250 billion market for junk bonds collapsed just in advance of the mini-crash of the New York Stock Exchange.

All in all, during the years between 1982 and 1988, more than 10,000 merger and acquisition deals were completed within the borders of the United States, for a total capitalization of $1 trillion. There were, in addition, 3,500 international mergers and acquisitions for another $500 billion.[5] The enforcement of antitrust laws atrophied into nothing: As one observer said of the late 1980s, "such concentrations had not been allowed since the early days of antitrust at the beginning of the century."

George Bush's friend Henry Kravis raised money for his leveraged buyouts from a number of sources. Money came first of all from insurance companies such as the Metropolitan Life Insurance Company of New York, which cultivated a close relation with KKR over a number of years. Met was joined by Prudential, Aetna, and Northwestern Mutual. Then there were banks like Manufacturers Hanover Trust and Bankers Trust. All these institutions were attracted by astronomical rates of return on KKR investments, estimated at 32.2 percent in 1980, 41.8 percent in 1982, 28 percent in 1984, and 29.6 percent in 1986. By 1987, the KKR prospectus boasted that they had carried out the first large LBO of a publicly held company, the first billion-dollar LBO, the first large LBO of a public company via tender offer, and the largest LBO in history until then, Beatrice Foods.

Then came the state pension funds, which were also anxious to share in these very large returns. The first to begin investing with KKR was Oregon, which shoveled money to KKR like there was no tomorrow. Other states that joined in were Washington, Utah,

Minnesota, Michigan, New York, Wisconsin, Illinois, Iowa, Massachusetts and Montana. Some of these funds are so heavily committed to KKR that if any of the highly-leveraged deals should go sour in the current "recession," pensions for many retired state workers in those states would soon cease to exist. In that eventuality, which for many working people has already occurred, the victims should remember George Bush, the political godfather of Henry Kravis and KKR.

KKR had one other very important source of capital for its deals: This was the now-defunct Wall Street investment firm of Drexel Burnham Lambert and its California-based junk bond king, Michael Milken. Drexel and Milken were the most important single customers KKR had. (Drexel had its own Harriman link: It had merged with Harriman Ripley & Co. of New York in 1966.) During the period of close working alliance between KKR and Drexel, Milken's junk-bond operation raised an estimated $20 billion of funds for KKR. Junk bonds were those high-risk, high-yield, junior debt securities that Milken floated. He started off with junk bonds issued by fly-by-night insurance companies owned by financiers seeking to emerge from the penumbra of Meyer Lansky. These included Carl Lindner and his Great American; Saul Steinberg and his Reliance Insurance Co., Meshulam Riklis and his Rapid American group; Lawrence Tisch and CNA; Nelson Peltz; Victor Posner; Carl Icahn; Thomas Spiegel and his Columbia Savings and Loan; and Fred Carr, a financial gunslinger of the 1960s, and his First Executive Corp. insurance firm. Later, the circle of Milken's customers would expand to include commercial banks, savings and loans, mutual funds, upscale insurance companies and others who could not resist the high yields. These robber barons of modern usury were dubbed "Milken's monsters" by one of their number, Meshulam Riklis.

All of these personages pranced at Milken's annual meetings in Beverly Hills, which were followed by evenings of sumptuous entertainment. These became known as "the predators' ball," and attracted such people as T. Boone Pickens, Icahn, Irwin Jacobs, Sir James Goldsmith, Oscar Wyatt, Saul Steinberg, Ivan Boesky, Carl Lindner, the Canadian Belzberg family, Ron Perelman and so forth.

First Executive Corp. was the first great bankruptcy among the insurance companies in early 1991, giving the depression of the 1990s a dimension that the economic-financial conflagration of the 1930s had not possessed. First Executive Life succumbed to losses on its junk bond portfolio, and it will be the first of many insurance companies to find bankruptcy via this route. Shortly thereafter,

Mutual Benefit Life Insurance Company of New Jersey was seized by state regulators. Mutual Benefit was the victim of combined real estate and junk bond losses, and more retirement plans were threatened with annihilation. Those whose pensions are lost must recall the junk bond united front that reached from Milken to Kravis to Bush.

Milken's silent partner was Ivan Boesky, the arbitrager who went beyond mere program trading to become a silent partner to advance Milken's stockjobbing: Sometimes Milken would have Boesky begin to acquire the stock of a certain company so as to signal to the market that it was in play, setting off a stampede of buyers when this suited Milken's strategy.

The Beatrice Foods LBO illustrates how necessary Milken's role was to the overall strategy of Bush backer Kravis. With a price tag of $8.2 billion, Beatrice was the biggest LBO up to the time it was completed in January–February 1986. As part of this deal, Kravis gave Milken warrants for five million shares of stock in the new Beatrice corporation. These warrants could be used in the future to buy Beatrice shares at a small fraction of the market price. One result of this would be a dilution of the equity of the other investors. Milken kept the warrants for his own account, rather than offer them to his junk bond buyers, in order to get a better price for the Beatrice junk bonds. Later in the same year, KKR bought out Safeway grocery stores for $4.1 billion, of which a large part came from Milken.

After 1986, Henry Kravis and George Roberts were gripped by financial megalomania. Between 1987 and 1989, they acquired eight additional companies with an aggregate price tag of $43.9 billion. These new victims included Owens-Illinois Glass, Duracell, Stop and Shop food markets, and, in the landmark transaction of the 1980s, RJR Nabisco. RJR Nabisco was the product of a number of earlier mergers: National Biscuit Company had merged with Standard Brands to form Nabisco Brands, and this in turn merged with R.J. Reynolds Tobacco to create RJR Nabisco. It is important to recall that R.J. Reynolds was the concern traditionally controlled by the family of Bush's personal White House lawyer, C. Boyden "Boy" Gray.

Control of RJR Nabisco was sought by opposing gangs: A first group included RJR Nabisco chairman Ross Johnson, Peter Cohen of Shearson Lehman Hutton and the notorious John Gutfreund of Salomon Brothers. KKR was a second contender, and a third offer for RJR came from First Boston. The Johnson offer and the KKR were about the same, but a cover story in the Henry Luce-Skull and

Bones *Time* magazine in early December 1988 targeted Johnson as the greedy party. The attraction of RJR Nabisco, one of the 20 largest U.S. corporations, was an immense cash flow supplied especially by its cigarette sales, where profit margins were enormous. The crucial phases of the fight corresponded with the presidential election of 1988: Bush won the White House, and Kravis won RJR with a bid of about $109 per share compared to a stock price of about $55 per share before the company was put into play, giving the pre-buyout shareholders a capital gain of more than $13.3 billion. How much of that went to Boy Gray of the Bush White House?

The RJR Nabisco swindle generated senior bank debt of about $15 billion. Then came $5 billion of subordinated debt, with the largest offering of junk bonds ever made. Then came an echelon of even more junior debt with payment-in-kind securities: junk bonds that paid interest not in cash, but in other junk bonds. But even with all the wizardry of KKR, there could have been no deal without Milken and his junk bonds. The banks could not muster the cash required to complete the financing; KKR required bridge loans. Merrill Lynch and Drexel were in the running to provide an extra $5 billion of bridge financing. Drexel got Milken's monsters and many others to buy short-term junk notes with an interest rate that would increase the longer the owner refrained from cashing in the note. Drexel's "increasing rate notes" easily brought in the entire $5 billion required.

In November of 1986, Ivan Boesky pled guilty to one felony count of manipulating securities, and his testimony led to the indictment of Milken in March 1989, some months after the RJR Nabisco deal had been sewn up. In order to protect more important financial players, Milken was allowed to plead guilty in April 1990 to five counts of insider trading, for which he agreed to pay a fine of $600 million. On February 13, 1990, Drexel Burnham Lambert had declared itself bankrupt and gone into liquidation, much to the distress of junk bond holders everywhere, who saw the firm as a junk bond buyer of last resort.

By this time, many of the great LBOs had begun to collapse. Robert Campeau's retail sales empire of Allied and Federated Stores blew up in the fall of 1989, bringing down almost $10 billion of LBO debt. Revco, Fruehauf, Southland (Seven-Eleven stores), Resorts International, and many other LBOs went into Chapter 11 proceedings. As for KKR's deals, they also began to implode: SCI-TV, a spin-off of Storer Broadcasting, announced that it could not service its $1.3 billion of debt, and forced the holders of $500 million in junk bonds to settle for new stocks and bonds worth between 20 and 70 cents on the dollar. Hillsborough Holdings, a subsidiary of Jim Walker, went bankrupt, and Seamans Furniture put through a forced restructuring of its debt.

It was clear at the time of the RJR Nabisco LBO that the totality of the company's large cash flow would be necessary to maintain payments of $25 billion of debt. That will take a lot of animal crackers and Winstons. If RJR Nabisco had been a foreign country, it would have ranked among the top 15 debtor nations, coming in between Peru and the Philippines. Within a short time after the LBO, RJR Nabisco proved unable to maintain payments. KKR was forced to inject several billion dollars of new equity, take out new bank loans, and dun its clients for an extra $1.7 billion. RJR Nabisco by the early autumn of 1991 was a time bomb ticking away near the center of a ruined U.S. economy. If citizens are bright enough to follow the line that leads back from Milken to Kravis to Bush, RJR and similar horror stories could politically demolish George Bush.

In September 1987, very late in the day, Senator William Proxmire submitted a bill which aimed at restricting takeovers. Two weeks later, Rep. Dan Rostenkowski of Illinois offered a bill to limit the tax deductibility of the interest on takeover debt. The LBO gang in Wall Street was horrified, even though it was clear that the Reagan-Bush team would oppose such legislation using every trick in the book. Later, LBO ideologues blamed the Congress for causing the crash of October 1987.

Bush's 'Free Enterprise'

During the 1988 campaign, Bush presented his views on hostile takeovers, using the forum provided by his old friend T. Boone Pickens' *U.S.A. Advocate*, a monthly newsletter published by the United Shareholders Association, which Pickens runs. In the October 1988 issue of this publication, Bush made clear that he was not worried about leveraged buyouts. Rather, what concerned Bush was the need to prevent corporations from adopting defenses to deter such attempted hostile takeovers. Bush also railed against "golden parachutes," which provide lucrative settlements for top executives who are ousted as the result of a takeover.[6]

Bush was clearly hostile to any federal restrictions on hostile takeovers. If anything, he was closer to those who demanded that the federal government stop the states from passing laws that interfere with LBO activity. For that notorious corporate raider and disciple of Chairman Mao Liedtke, T. Boone Pickens, the message was clear: "I know that Vice President Bush is a free enterpriser."[7]

The expectations of Pickens and his ilk were not disappointed by the Bush cabinet that took office in January 1989. The new Secretary of the Treasury, Bush crony Nicholas Brady, was not only a supporter of leveraged buyouts; he had been one of the leading practitioners of the mergers and acquisitions game during his days in Wall Street as partner of the Harriman-allied investment bank of Dillon Read.

The family of Nicholas Brady has been allied for most of this century with the Bush-Walker clan. During his Wall Street career at Dillon Read, Brady, like Bush, cultivated the self-image of the patrician banker, becoming a member of the New York Jockey Club and racing his own thoroughbred horses at the New York tracks once presided over by George Herbert Walker and Prescott Bush. Brady, like Bush, is a member of the Bohemian Club of San Francisco and attends the Bohemian Grove every summer. Inside the Bohemian Grove oligarchic pantheon, Brady enjoys the special distinction of presiding over the prestigious Mandalay Camp (or cabin complex), the one to which Henry Kissinger habitually retires, and sometimes frequented by Gerald Ford.

Nick Brady got the job he presently occupies by heading up a study of the October 1987 stock market crash, the results of which Brady announced on a cold Friday afternoon in January 1988, just after the New York stock market had taken another 150-point dive.

The study of the October 1988 "market break" was produced by a group of Wall Street and Treasury insiders billed as the "Presidential Task Force on Market Mechanisms." At the center of the report's attention was the relation between the New York Stock Exchange, American Stock Exchange, and NASDAC over-the-counter stock trading, on the one hand, and the future, options, and index trading carried on at the Chicago Board of Trade, Chicago Board Options Exchange, and Chicago Mercantile Exchange. The Brady group examined the impact of program trading, index arbitrage and portfolio insurance strategies on the behavior of the markets that led to the crash. The Brady report recommended the centralization of all market oversight in a single federal agency, the unification of clearing systems, consistent margins, and the installation of circuit breaker mechanisms. That, at least, was the public content of the report.

The real purpose of the Brady report was to create a series of drugged and manipulated markets. The Brady group realized that if the Chicago futures price of a stock or stock index could be artificially inflated, this would be of great assistance in propping up the value of the underlying stock in New York.

The Brady group focused on the Major Market Index of 20 stock futures traded on the Chicago Board of Trade, which roughly corresponded to the principal stocks of the Dow Jones Industrial Average. As long as the MMI was trading at a higher price than the DJIA, the program traders and index arbitrageurs would tend to sell the MMI and buy the underlying stock in New York in order to lock in their parasitical profits. The great advantage of this system was first of all that some tens of millions of dollars in Chicago, where turnover was less intense than in New York, could generate hundreds of millions of dollars of demand in New York. In addition, the margin requirements for borrowing money to buy futures in Chicago were much less stringent than the requirements for margin-buying of stocks in New York. Liquidity for this operation could be drawn from banks and other institutions loyal to the Bush-Baker-Brady power cartel, with full backup and assistance from the district banks of the Federal Reserve.

The Brady "drugged market" mechanisms, with the refinements they have acquired since 1988, are a key factor behind the Dow Jones Industrial's seeming defiance of the law of gravity in attaining a new all-time high, well above the 3,000 mark during 1991.

Brady's exercise was nothing new: During the collapse of the Earl of Oxford's South Sea bubble in 1720, the South Sea Company attempted to support the astronomically inflated price of its shares by becoming a buyer of its own stock, until its cash and credit reserves were exhausted. Such maneuvers can indeed delay the onset of the final collapse for some period of time, but they guarantee that when the panic, crash and bankruptcy finally become overwhelming, the aggregate damage to society will be far greater than if the crash had been allowed to occur according to its own spontaneous dynamic. For this reason, a large part of the fearful price that is being exacted from the American people as the depression unfolds in its full fury is a result of the Bush-Brady measures to postpone the inevitable reckoning beyond the 1988 election.

In 1988, Bush boasted of his achievements in the field of deregulation. One important case study of the impact of Bush's Task Force on Regulatory Relief is the meatpacking industry. In February 1981, when Reagan gave Bush "line" authority for deregulation, he promulgated Executive Order 12291, which established the principle that federal regulations "be based upon adequate evidence that their potential benefits to society are greater than their potential costs to society." In practice, that meant that Bush threw health and safety standards out the window in order to ingratiate himself with gouging entrepreneurs. In March 1981, Bush wrote to businessmen and invited them to enumerate the ten areas they wanted to see deregulated, with specific recommendations on what they wanted done. By the end of the year Bush's office issued a self-congratulatory report boasting of a "significant reduction in the cost of federal regulation."

In the meatpacking industry, this translated into production line speedup as jobs were eliminated, with a cavalier attitude toward safety precautions. At the same time the Occupational Safety and Health Administration sharply reduced inspections, often arriving only after disabling or lethal accidents had already occurred. In 1980, there were 280 OSHA inspections in meatpacking plants, but in 1988 there were only 176. This is in an industry in which the rate of personal injury is 173 persons per working day, three times the average of all remaining U.S. industry.[8]

Bush used his Task Force on Regulatory Relief as a way to curry favor with various business groups whose support he wanted for his future plans to assume the presidency in his own right. According to one study made midway through the Reagan years, Bush converted his own office "into a convenient back door for corporate lobbyists" and "a hidden court of last resort for special interest groups that have lost their arguments in Congress, in the federal courts, or in the regulatory process. . . . Case by case, the vice president's office got involved in some mean and petty issues that directly affect people's health and lives, from the dumping of toxic pollutants to government warnings concerning potentially harmful drugs."[9]

There were also reports of serious abuses by Bush, especially in the area of conflicts of interest. In one case, Bush intervened in March 1981 in favor of Eli Lilly & Co., of which he had been a director in 1977–79. Bush had owned $145,000 of stock in Eli Lilly until January 1981, after which it was placed in a blind trust, meaning that Bush ostensibly had no way of knowing whether his trust still owned shares in the firm or not. The Treasury Department had wanted to make the terms of a tax break for U.S. pharmaceutical firms operating in Puerto Rico more stringent, but Vice President Bush had contacted the Treasury to urge that "technical" changes be made in the planned restriction of the tax break. By April 14, Bush was feeling some heat, and he wrote a second letter to Treasury Secretary Don Regan asking that his first request be withdrawn, because Bush was now "uncomfortable about the appearance of my active personal involvement in the details of a tax matter directly affecting a company with which I once had a close association."[10]

Bush's continuing interest in Eli Lilly is underlined by the fact that the Pulliam family of Indiana, the family clan of Bush's 1988 running mate, Dan Quayle, owned a large portion of the Eli Lilly shares. Bush's choice of Quayle was but a reaffirmation of a pre-existing financial and political alliance with the Pulliam interests, which also include a newspaper chain.

Ripping Up the Airline Industry

Bush's ideal of labor-management practices and corporate leadership in general appears to have been embodied by Frank Lorenzo, the most celebrated and hated *banquerotteur* of U.S. air transport. Before his downfall in early 1990, Lorenzo combined Texas Air, Continental Airlines, New York Air, People Express and Eastern Airlines into one holding, and then presided over its bankruptcy. Now Eastern has been liquidated, and the other components are likely to follow suit. Along the way to this debacle, Lorenzo won the sympathy of the Reagan-Bush crowd through his union-busting tactics: He had thrown Continental Airlines into bankruptcy court and used the bankruptcy statutes to break all union contracts, and to break the unions themselves. Continental pilots had been stripped of seniority, benefits and bargaining rights, and had been subjected to a massive pay cut under threat of being turned out into the street. In 1985, the average yearly wage of a pilot was $87,000 at TWA, but less than $30,000 at Continental. The hourly cost of a flight crew for a DC–10 at American Airlines was $703, while at Continental it was only $194. It is an interesting commentary on such wage-gouging that Lorenzo nevertheless managed to bankrupt Continental by the end of the decade.

George Bush has been on record as a dedicated union-buster going back to 1963–64, and he has always been very friendly with Lorenzo. When Bush became President, this went beyond the personal sphere and became a revolving door between the Texas Air group and the Bush administration. During 1989, the Airline Pilots Association issued a list of some 30 cases in which Texas Air officials had transferred to jobs in the Bush regime and vice versa. By the end of 1989, Bush's top congressional lobbyist was Frederick D. McClure, who had been a vice president and chief lobbyist for Texas Air. McClure had traded jobs with Rebecca Range, who had worked as a public liaison for Reagan until she moved over to the post of lead congressional lobbyist for Texas Air. John Robson, Bush's Deputy Secretary of the Treasury, was a former member of the Continental Airlines board of directors. Elliott Seiden, a top antitrust lawyer for the Justice Department, switched to being an attorney for Texas Air.

When questioned by columnist Jack Anderson, McClure and Robson claimed that they recused themselves from any matters involving Texas Air. But McClure signed a letter to Congress announcing Bush's opposition to any government investigation of the circumstances surrounding the Eastern Airlines strike in early 1989. This was a move in support of Lorenzo. Bush himself has always stonewalled in favor of Lorenzo. During the early months of that same Eastern Airlines strike, in which pilots, flight attendants and machinists all walked out to block Lorenzo's plan to asset strip the airline and bust the unions, the Congress attempted to set up a panel to investigate the dispute, but Bush was adamant in favor of Lorenzo and vetoed any government probes.[11]

Lorenzo's activities were decisive in the wrecking of U.S. airline transportation during the Reagan-Bush era. When Carl Icahn was in the process of taking over TWA, he was able to argue that the need to compete in many of the same markets in which Lorenzo's airlines were active made it mandatory that the TWA workforce accept similar sacrifices and wage cuts. The cost-cutting criteria pioneered with such ruthless aggressivity by Lorenzo have had the long-term effect of reducing safety margins and increasing the risk the traveling public must confront in any decision to board an airliner operating under U.S. jurisdiction. Eastern, Midway and Pan Am have disappeared, and Continental has been joined in bankruptcy by America West and TWA. Northwest, having been taken through the wringer of an LBO by Albert Cecchi, is now busy extorting subsidies from the state of Minnesota and other sources as a way to stay afloat.

It is widely believed that when the dust settles, only Delta, American and perhaps United will remain among the large nationwide carriers. At that point, hundreds of localities will be served by only one airline, and that airline will proceed to raise its fares without any fear of price competition or any other form of competition. With that, air travel will float beyond the reach of much of the American middle class, and the final fruits of airline deregulation will be manifest. In the meantime, it must be feared that the erosion of safety margins will exact a growing toll of human lives in airline accidents. If such tragedies occur, the bereaved relatives will perhaps recall George Bush's friend Frank Lorenzo.

And how, the reader may ask, was George Bush doing financially while surrounded by so many billions in junk bonds? Bush had always pontificated that he had led the fight for full public disclosure of personal financial interests by elected officials. He never tired of repeating that "in 1967, as a freshman member of the House of Representatives, I led the fight for full financial disclosure." But after he was elected to the vice-presidency, Bush stopped disclosing his investments in detail. He stated his net worth, which had risen to $2.1 million by the time of the 1984 election, representing an increase of some $300,000 over the previous five years. Bush justified his refusal to disclose his investments in detail by saying that he didn't know himself just what securities he held, since his portfolio was now in the blind trust mentioned above. The blind trust was administered by W.S. Farish & Co. of Houston, owned by Bush's best friend William Stamps Farish III of Beeville, Texas, the grandson and heir of the Standard Oil executive who had backed Heinrich Himmler and the Waffen SS.[12]

Notes for Chapter XVIII

1. Walter Pincus and Bob Woodward, "Doing Well with Help from Family, Friends," *Washington Post*, Aug. 11, 1988.

2. *Houston Chronicle*, Feb. 21, 1963. See clippings available in Texas Historical Society, Houston.

3. Thomas Petzinger, *Oil and Honor* (New York: Putnam, 1987), pp. 244–45.

4. For the relation between George Bush and Henry Kravis, see Sarah Bartlett, *The Money Machine: How KKR Manufactured Power & Profits* (New York: 1991), pp. 258–59 and 267–70.

5. Roy C. Smith, *The Money Wars* (New York: Dutton, 1990), p. 106.

6. *Washington Post*, Sept. 29, 1988.

7. *Ibid.*

8. Judy Mann, "Bush's Top Achievement," *Washington Post*, Nov. 2, 1988.

9. William Greider, *Rolling Stone*, April 12, 1984.

10. "Bush Denies Influencing Drug Firm Tax Proposal," *Washington Post*, May 20, 1981.

11. Jack Anderson and Dale Van Atta, "The Bush-Lorenzo Connections," *Washington Post*, Dec. 21, 1989.

12. James Ridgway, "The Tax Records of Reagan and Bush," *Texas Observer*, Sept. 28, 1984.

XIX

THE PHONY WAR ON DRUGS

An indispensable component of the mythical media profile which George Bush has built up over the years to buttress his electoral aspirations has been his role as an antidrug fighter. His first formally scheduled prime time presidential television address to the nation, in September 1989, was devoted to announcing his plans for measures to combat the illegal narcotics that continued to inundate the streets of the United States. During his 1988 election campaign, Bush had pointed with astounding complacency to his record as President Reagan's designated pointman in the administration's war on drugs.

In his acceptance speech to the Republican National Convention in 1988, Bush stated: "I want a drug-free America. Tonight, I challenge the young people of our country to shut down the drug dealers around the world. . . . My administration will be telling the dealers, 'Whatever we have to do, we'll do, but your day is over. You're history.' "

Indeed, Bush has an impressive resumé of bureaucratic titles to back up his claim to be America's top antidrug fighter. On January 28, 1982, Reagan created the South Florida Task Force under Bush's high-profile leadership, to coordinate the efforts of the various federal agencies to stem the tide of narcotics into Bush's old family bailiwick. On March 23, 1983, Bush was placed in charge of the National Narcotics Border Interdiction System, which was supposed to staunch the drug flow over all U.S. borders. In August 1986, U.S. officials presented to their Mexican counterparts a scheme called Operation Alliance, a new border enforcement initiative that was allegedly to do for the U.S.-Mexican border area what the South Florida Task Force had allegedly already done for the southeastern states. George Bush was appointed chief of Operation Alliance, which involved 20 federal agencies, 500 additional federal officers, and a budget of $266 million.

The drug plague is an area in which the national interest requires results. Illegal narcotics are one of the most important causes of the dissolution of American society at the present time. To interdict the drug flows and to prosecute the drug money launderers at the top of the banking community would have represented a real public service. But Bush had no intention of seriously pursuing such goals. For him, the war on drugs was, and is, a cruel hoax, a cynical exercise in demagogic self-promotion, designed in large part to camouflage activities by himself and his networks that promoted drug trafficking. A further shocking episode that has come to light in this regard involves Bush's 14-year friendship with a member of Meyer Lansky's Miami circles who sold Bush his prized trophy, the Cigarette boat *Fidelity*.

Bush's war on drugs was a rhetorical and public relations success for a time. On February 16, 1982, in a speech on his own turf in Miami, Florida, Bush promised to use sophisticated military aircraft to track the airplanes used by smugglers. Several days later, Bush ordered the U.S. Navy to send in its E2C surveillance aircraft for this purpose. If these were not available in sufficient numbers, said Bush, he was determined to bring in the larger and more sophisticated AWACS early warning aircraft to do the job. But Bush's skills as an interagency expediter left something to be desired: By May, two of the four E2C aircraft that originally had been in Florida were transferred out of the state. By June, airborne surveillance time was running a mere 40 hours per month, not the 360 hours promised by Bush, prompting Rep. Glenn English (D-Ok.) to call hearings on this topic. By October 1982, the General Accounting Office issued an opinion in which it found "it is doubtful whether the [South Florida] task force can have any substantial long-term impact on drug availability." But the headlines were grabbed by Bush, who stated in 1984 that the efforts of his task force had eliminated the marijuana trade in south Florida. That was an absurd claim, but it sounded very good. When Francis Mullen, Jr., the administrator of the Drug Enforcement Administration (DEA), criticized Bush for making this wildly inaccurate statement, he was soon ousted from his post at the DEA.

In 1988, Democratic Congressman Glenn English concluded that Bush's "war on drugs" had been fought with "little more than lip service and press releases." English wrote: "There has been very little substance behind the rhetoric, and some of the major interdiction problems have yet to be resolved. The President assigned . . . Bush to coordinate and direct federal antidrug-abuse programs among the various law enforcement agencies. However, eight years later it is apparent that the task has not been accomplished."[1] No observer still stationed in reality could dispute this very pessimistic assessment.

But the whole truth is much uglier. We have indicated how the Iran-Contra drug-running and gun-running operations run out of Bush's own office played their role in increasing the cocaine and marijuana brought into this country. We have reviewed Bush's relations with his close supporters in the Wall Street LBO gang, much of whose liquidity is derived from narcotics payments which the banking system is eager to recycle and launder. We recall Bush's 1990 meeting with Syrian President Hafez al Assad, who is personally one of the most prolific drug pushers on the planet, and whom Bush embraced as an ally during the Gulf war.

But there is an even more flagrant aspect of Bush's conduct which can be said to demolish once and for all the myth of the "war on drugs" and replace it with a reality so sinister that it goes beyond the imagination of most citizens.

Those who follow Bush's frenetic sports activities on television are doubtless familiar with Bush's speedboat, in which he is accustomed to cavort in the waters off his estate at Walker's Point in Kennebunkport, Maine.[2] The craft in question is the *Fidelity,* a powerboat capable of operating on the high seas. *Fidelity* is a class of boat marketed under the brand name of "Cigarette," a high-priced speedboat dubbed "the Ferrari of the high seas." This detail should awaken our interest, since Bush's profile as an Anglo-Saxon aristocrat would normally include a genteel predilection for sailing, rather than a preference for a vulgar hotrod like *Fidelity,* which evokes the ethos of rum-runners and smugglers.

The Cigarette boat *Fidelity* was purchased by George Bush from a certain Don Aronow. Bush reportedly met Aronow at a boat show in 1974, and decided to buy one of the Cigarette boats Aronow manufactured. Aronow was one of the most celebrated and successful powerboat racers of the 1960s, and had then turned his hand to designing and building these boats. But, according to at least one published account, there is compelling evidence to conclude that Aronow was a drug smuggler and suspected drug money launderer, linked to the Genovese family of New York and New Jersey within the more general framework of the Meyer Lansky organized crime syndicate. Aronow's role in marijuana smuggling was reportedly confirmed by Bill Norris, head of the Major Narcotics Unit at the Miami U.S. Attorney's office, and thus the top federal drug prosecution official in south Florida.[3]

Aronow numbered among his friends and acquaintances not just Bush, but many international public figures and celebrities, many of whom had purchased the boats he built. In May of 1986, Aronow received a letter from Nicolas Iliopoulos, the royal boat captain to King Hussein of Jordan, expressing on behalf of the King the latter's satisfaction with a powerboat purchased from Aronow, and conveying the compliments of King Juan Carlos of Spain and President Hosni Mubarak of Egypt, who had recently been the Jordanian sovereign's guests on board. Aronow sent a copy of this letter to Bush, from whom he received a reply dated June 6, 1986, in which Bush thanked him "with warm regards" for forwarding the royal note and added: "I can repeat that my old Cigarette, the 'Fidelity' is running well too. I've had her out a couple of weekends and the engines have been humming. I hope our paths cross soon, my friend."[4]

Aronow was reportedly a close friend of George Bush. Over the years, Bush had apparently consulted with Aronow concerning the servicing and upkeep of his Cigarette boat. During 1983, Bush began to seek out Aronow's company for fishing trips. The original engines on Bush's Cigarette boat needed replacement, and this was the ostensible occasion for renewing contact with Aronow. Aronow told Bush of a new model of boat that he had designed, supposedly a high-performance catamaran. Bush planned to come to Florida during the New Year's holiday for a short vacation during which he would go bonefishing with his crony Nick Brady. During this time he would also arrange to deliver an antidrug pep-talk.

On January 4, 1984, George Bush rendezvoused with Don Aronow at Islamorada in the Florida Keys. Earlier in the day, Bush had delivered one of his "war on drugs" speeches at the Omni International Hotel in Miami. Bush and Brady then proceeded by motorcade to Islamorada, where Aronow was waiting with his catamaran. Accompanied by a flotilla of Secret Service and Customs agents in Cigarette boats that had been seized from drug smugglers, Bush, Brady, Aronow and one of the latter's retainers proceeded aboard the catamaran through moderate swells to Miami, with White House photographers eternalizing the photo opportunity at every moment. Bush, who had donned designer racing goggles for the occasion, was allowed to take the wheel of the catamaran and seemed very thrilled and very happy. Nick Brady, sporting his own wraparound shades, found the seas too rough for his taste.

After the trip was over, Bush personally typed the following letter to Don Aronow on his vice-presidential stationery, which he sent accompanied by some photographs of Bush, Aronow, Brady and the others on board the catamaran:

> January 14, 1984
> Dear Don,
>   . . . Again Don this day was one of the greatest of my life. I love boats, always have. But ever since knowing you that private side of my life has become ever more exciting and fulfilling. Incidentally, I didn't get to tell you but my reliable 28 footer Cigarette that is still doing just fine . . . no trouble at all and the new last year engines.
>   All the best to you and all your exciting ventures. May all your boats bee [sic] number one and may the hosres [sic] be not far behind.

At the end of this message, before his signature, Bush wrote in by hand, "My typing stinks."[5]

As a result of this outing, Bush is said to have used his influence to see to it that Aronow received a lucrative contract to build the "Blue Thunder" catamarans at $150,000 apiece for the U.S. Customs Service. This contract was announced with great fanfare in Miami on February 4, 1985, and was celebrated a week later in a public ceremony in which Florida Senator Paula Hawkins and U.S. Customs Commissioner William von Raab mugged for photographers together with Aronow. The government purchase was hyped as the first time that Customs would receive boats especially designed and built to intercept drug-runners on the high seas, a big step forward in the war on drugs.

This was the same George Bush who in March 1988 had stated: "I will never bargain with drug dealers on U.S. or foreign soil."

As one local resident recalled of that time, "everyone in Miami knew that if you needed a favor from Bush, you spoke to Aronow."[6] It was proverbial among Florida pols and powerbrokers that Aronow had the Vice President's ear.

The Customs Service soon found that the Blue Thunder catamarans were highly unseaworthy and highly unsuitable for the task of chasing down other speedboats, including, above all, Aronow's earlier model Cigarette boats, which were now produced by a company not controlled by Aronow. Blue Thunder was a relatively slow class, capable of a top speed of only 56 miles per hour, despite the presence of twin 440-horsepower marine engines. The design of the catamaran hulls lacked any hydrodynamic advantages, and the boats were too heavy to attain sufficient lift. The stern drives were too weak for the powerful engines, leading to the problem of "grenading": When the drive shafts severed, which was often, the engines began to rev far beyond their red line, leading to the explosion or disintegration of the engines and the shrapnel-like scattering of red-hot steel fragments through the boat. This meant that the boats had to be kept well below their maximum speed. Most Blue Thunders spent more time undergoing repairs than chasing drug-runners in the coastal waters of Florida. Blue Thunder was in boating parlance "wet," a complete lemon, useful only for photo opportunities and publicity shots.

Documents found by Thomas Burdick in the Dade County land records office show that U.S.A. Racing, the company operated by Aronow which built the Blue Thunder catamarans for the Customs Service, was not owned by Aronow, but rather by a one Jack J. Kramer in his capacity as president of Super Chief South Corporation. Jack Kramer had married a niece of Meyer Lansky. Jack Kramer's son, Ben Kramer, was thus the great-nephew and one of the putative heirs of the top boss of the U.S. crime syndicate, Meyer Lansky. Ben Kramer was also a notorious organized crime figure in his own right. On March 28, 1990 Jack Kramer and Ben Kramer were found guilty of 23 and 28 counts (respectively) of federal money laundering charges. In the previous year, Ben Kramer had also been sentenced to life imprisonment without parole for having imported half a million pounds of marijuana. Bush had thus given a prime contract in waging the war on drugs to one of the leading drug-smuggling and money-laundering crime families in the U.S.

Don Aronow was murdered by Mafia-style professional killers on February 3, 1987. During the last days of his life, Aronow is reported to have made numerous personal telephone calls to Bush. Aronow had been aware that his life was in danger, and he had left a list of instructions to tell his wife what to do if anything should happen to him. The first point on the list was "#1. CALL GEORGE BUSH."[7] Lillian Aronow did call Bush, who reportedly responded by placing a personal call to the Metro-Dade Police Department homicide division to express his concern and to request an expeditious handling of the case. Bush did not attend Aronow's funeral, but a month later he sent a letter to Aronow's son Gavin in which he called the late Don Aronow "a hero."

When Lillian Aronow suspected that her telephone was being tapped, she called Bush, who urged her to be calm and promised to order an investigation of the matter. Shortly after that, the suspicious noises in Mrs. Aronow's telephone ceased. When Lillian Aronow received reports that her husband might have been murdered by rogue CIA operatives or other wayward federal agents, and that she herself and her children were still in danger, she shared her fears in a telephone call to Bush. Bush reportedly later called Mrs. Aronow and, as she recalled, "He said to me, 'Lillian, you're fine.' He said that 'ex-CIA people are really off.' That's the truth."[8]

In the summer of 1987, Bush snubbed Mrs. Aronow by pointedly avoiding her at a Miami dinner party. But during this same period, Bush frequently went fishing with former Aronow employee Willie Meyers. According to Thomas Burdick's sources, Willie Meyers was also a friend of Secretary of State George Shultz, and often expressed concern about damaging publicity for Bush and Shultz that might derive from the Aronow case.

According to Thomas Burdick, Meyers says that Bush talked to him about how the Vice President's staff was monitoring the Aronow story. Bush lamented that he did not have grounds to get federal agencies involved. "I just wish," said Bush to Meyers, "that there was some federal aspect to the murder. If the killers crossed state lines. Then I could get the FBI involved."[9] The form of the argument is reminiscent of the views expressed by Bush and Tony Lapham during the Orlando Letelier case.

In May or June of 1987, several months after Aronow had been killed, Mike Brittain, who owned a company called Aluminum Marine Products, located on "Thunderboat Alley" in the northern part of Miami (the same street where Aronow had worked), was approached by two FBI special agents, Joseph Usher and John Donovan, both of the Miami FBI field office. They were accompanied by a third FBI man, whom they presented as a member of George Bush's staff at the National Drug Task Force in Washington, D.C. The third agent, reportedly named William Temple, had, according to the other two, come to Miami on a special mission ordered by the Vice President of the United States.

As Brittain told his story to Burdick, Special Agent Temple "didn't ask about the murder or anything like that. All he wanted to know about was the merger."[10] The merger in question was the assumption of control over Aronow's company, U.S.A. Racing, by the Kramers' Super Chief South, which meant that a key contract in the Bush "war on drugs" had been awarded to a company controlled by persons who would later be convicted for marijuana smuggling and money laundering. Many of the FBI questions focused on this connection between Aronow and Kramer. Later, after

Bush's victory in the 1988 presidential election, the FBI again questioned Brittain, and again the central issue was the Aronow-Kramer connection, plus additional questions of whether Brittain had divulged any of his knowledge of these matters to other persons. A possible conclusion was that a damage control operation in favor of Bush was in progress.

Tommy Teagle, an ex-convict interviewed by Burdick, said he feared that George Bush would have him killed because information in his possession would implicate Jeb Bush in cocaine smuggling. Teagle's story was that Aronow and Jeb Bush had been partners in cocaine trafficking and were $2.5 million in debt to their Colombian suppliers. Dr. Robert Magoon, a friend of Aronow, is quoted in the same location as having heard a similar report. But Teagle rapidly changed his story.[11] Ultimately, an imprisoned convict was indicted for the murder of Aronow.

But the circumstances of the murder remain highly suspect. Starting in 1985, and with special intensity during 1987–88, more than two dozen persons involved in various aspects of the Iran-Contra gun-running and drug-running operation met their deaths. At the same time, other persons knowledgeable about Iran-Contra, but one or more steps removed from eyewitness knowledge of these operations, have been subjected to campaigns of discrediting and slander, often associated with indictments on a variety of charges, charges which often stemmed from the Iran-Contra operations themselves. Above and beyond the details of each particular case, the overall pattern of these deaths strongly suggests that they are coherent with a damage control operation by the networks involved, that has concentrated on liquidating those individuals whose testimony might prove to be most damning to the leading personalities of these networks. The death of Don Aronow occurred within the time frame of this general process of amputation and cauterization of the Iran-Contra and related networks. Many aspects of Aronow's life suggest that his assassination may have been a product of the same "damage control" logic.

Notes for Chapter XIX

1. For Bush's "war on drugs," see Jack Anderson and Dale Van Atta, "How Bush Commanded the War on Drugs," *Washington Post,* June 20, 1988; Lawrence Lifschultz, "Bush, Drugs and Pakistan: Inside the Kingdom of Heroin," *The Nation,* Nov. 14, 1988; "Drug Czars We Have Known," *The Nation,* Feb. 27, 1989; and Robert A. Pastor and Jorge Castaneda, *Limits to Friendship: The United States and Mexico* (New York: Knopf, dist. by Random House), p. 271.

2. See the cover of *Newsweek,* Oct. 19, 1987, "Fighting the 'Wimp Factor,' " which portrays Bush at the controls of *Fidelity.* A similar photo appears facing p. 223 in George Bush and Victor Gold, *Looking Forward* (New York: Doubleday, 1987).

3. See Thomas Burdick and Charlene Mitchell, *Blue Thunder* (New York: Simon and Schuster, 1990), p. 229. The following account of the relations between Bush and Aronow relies upon this remarkable study.

4. *Ibid.*, p. 182.
5. *Ibid.*, p. 18.
6. *Ibid.*, p. 34.
7. *Ibid.*, p. 71.
8. *Ibid.*, p. 95.
9. *Ibid.*, p. 103.
10. *Ibid.*, pp. 326–27.
11. *Ibid.*, pp. 351, 357.

XX

OMAHA

On the morning of June 29, 1989, pandemonium erupted in the corridors of power in the nation's capital. "Homosexual Prostitution Probe Ensnares Official of Bush, Reagan," screamed the front-page headline of the *Washington Times* with the kicker "Call Boys Took Midnight Tour of White House."

The *Times* reported, "A homosexual prostitution ring is under investigation by federal and District authorities and includes among its clients key officials of the Reagan and Bush administrations, military officers, congressional aides and U.S. and foreign business-men with close ties to Washington's political elite."

The exposé centered on the role of one Craig Spence, a Republican powerbroker known for his lavish "power cocktail" parties. Spence was well connected. He celebrated Independence Day 1988 by conducting a midnight tour of the White House in the company of two teenage male prostitutes among others in his party.

Rumors circulated that a list existed of some 200 Washington prominents who had used the call boy service. The Number Two in charge of personnel affairs at the White House, who was responsible for filling all the top civil service posts in the federal bureaucracy, and Secretary of Labor Elizabeth Dole's chief of staff, were two individuals publicly identified as patrons of the call boy ring.

Two of the ring's call boys were allegedly KGB operatives, according to a retired general from the Defense Intelligence Agency interviewed by the press. But the evidence seemed to point to a CIA sexual blackmail operation, instead. Spence's entire mansion was covered with hidden microphones, two-way mirrors and video cameras, ever ready to capture the indiscretions of Washington's high, mighty and perverse. The political criteria for proper sexual comportment had long been established in Washington: Any kinkiness goes, so long as you don't get caught. The popular proverb was that the only way a politician could hurt his career was if he were "caught with a dead woman or a live boy" in his bed.

Months after the scandal had died down, and a few weeks before he allegedly committed suicide, Spence was asked who had given him the "key" to the White House. The *Washington Times* reported that "Mr. Spence hinted the tours were arranged by 'top level' persons, including Donald Gregg, national security advisor to Vice President Bush"[1] and later U.S. ambassador to South Korea.

We have already had occasion to examine Don Gregg's role in Iran-Contra, and have observed his curious performance when testifying under oath before congressional committees. Gregg indignantly denied any connection to Spence, yet it is public record that Spence had sponsored a dinner in Gregg's honor in the spring of 1989 at Washington's posh Four Seasons Hotel in Georgetown.

George Bush was less than pleased with the media coverage of the prostitution charges and kept abreast of the scandal as it mushroomed. The *Washington Times* reported in an article titled "White House Mute on Call Boy Scandal," that "White House sources confirmed that President Bush has followed the story of the late night visit and Mr. Spence's links to a homosexual prostitution ring under investigation by federal authorities since they were disclosed June 29 in the *Washington Times*. But top officials will not discuss the story's substance, reportedly even among themselves.

"Press officers have rebuffed repeated requests to obtain Mr. Bush's reaction and decline to discuss investigations or fall out from the disclosures."[2] By midsummer, the scandal had been buried. The President had managed to avoid giving a single press conference where he would surely have been asked to comment.

As the call boy ring affair dominated the cocktail gossip circuit in Washington, another scandal, halfway across the country in the state of Nebraska, peaked. Again this scandal knocked on George Bush's door.

A black Republican who had been a leader in organizing minority support for Bush's 1988 presidential campaign and who proudly displayed a photo of himself and Bush, arm in arm, in his Omaha home, was at the center of a sex and money scandal that continues to rock the Cornhusker state.

The scandal originated with the collapse of the minority-oriented Franklin Community Credit Union in Omaha, directed by Lawrence

E. King, Jr., a nationally influential black Republican who sang the national anthem at both the 1984 and 1988 Republican conventions. King became the subject of the Nebraska Senate's investigation conducted by the specially created "Franklin Committee" to probe charges of embezzlement. In November 1988, King's offices were raided by the FBI and $40 million was discovered missing. Within weeks, the Nebraska Senate, which initially opened the inquiry to find out where the money had gone, instead found itself questioning young adults and teenagers who said that they had been child prostitutes. Social workers and state child-care administrators accused King of running a child prostitution ring. The charges grew with the former police chief of Omaha, the publisher of the state's largest daily newspaper, and several other political associates of King, finding themselves accused of patronizing the child prostitution ring.

King is now serving a 15-year federal prison sentence for defrauding the Omaha-based credit union. But the magazines *Avvenimenti* of Italy and *Pronto* of Spain, among others, have charged that King's crimes were more serious: that he ran a national child prostitution ring that serviced the political and business elite of both Republican and Democratic parties. Child victims of King's operations charged him with participation in at least one satanic ritual murder of a child several years ago. The *Washington Post*, *New York Times*, *Village Voice* and *National Law Journal* covered the full range of accusations after the story broke in November of 1988. King's money machinations were also linked to the Iran-Contra affair, and some say that King provided the CIA with information garnered from his alleged activities as a "pimp" for the high and mighty.

Pronto, the Barcelona-based, largest circulation weekly in Spain with 4.5 million readers, reported that the Lawrence E. King child prostitution scandal "appears to directly implicate politicos of the state of Nebraska and Washington, D.C. who are very close to the White House and George Bush himself."

The weekly stated that Roy Stephens, a private investigator who has worked on the case and heads the Missing Youth Foundation, "says there is reason to believe that the CIA is directly implicated," and that the "FBI refuses to help in the investigation and has sabotaged any efforts" to get to the bottom of the story. Stephens says that "Paul Bonnacci directly accused President Bush of being implicated" in the affair when he testified before the Franklin Committee.[3] Bonnacci, who had been one of the child prostitutes, is identified by leading child-abuse experts as a well-informed, credible witness.

Lawrence King was no stranger to President Bush. And Lawrence King was no stranger to Craig Spence. Several of the Omaha child prostitutes testified that they had traveled to Washington, D.C. with King in private planes to attend political events which were followed by sex parties. King and Spence had much in common. Not only were they both Republican Party activists but they had gone into business together procuring prostitutes for Washington's elite.

Bush's name had repeatedly surfaced in the Nebraska scandal. But his name was first put into print in July 1989, a little less than a month after the Washington call boy affair had first made headlines. Omaha's leading daily newspaper reported, "One child, who has been under psychiatric care, is said to believe she saw George Bush at one of King's parties."[4]

A full three years after the scandal had first made headlines, Bush's name again appeared in print. *Gentleman's Quarterly (GQ)* carried a lengthy article, viewed by many political observers in Nebraska as an attempt to refute the charges which would not die, despite the termination of all official inquiries. The GQ piece disputed the allegations as a conspiracy theory that went out of control and resonated because of some mystical sociological phenomena allegedly unique to Nebraskan rural folk who will believe anything and burn "with the mistrust of city life that once inflamed the prairie with populist passion." Numerous polls over the last few years have recorded over 90 percent saying they believe there has been a "cover up" of the truth.

GQ reported that yes, there was theft, corruption and homosexuality in this story, "but no children were ever involved in this case." In fact, "the only child even mentioned was a 9-year-old boy, whom the least reliable of Caradori's witnesses claimed to have seen in the company of George Bush at one of Larry King's Washington parties."

Gary Caradori was a retired state police investigator who had been hired by the Nebraska Senate to investigate the case, and who had died mysteriously during the course of his investigations.[5]

Sound crazy? Not to Steve Bowman, an Omaha businessman who is compiling a book about the Franklin money and sex scandal. "We do have some credible witnesses who say that 'Yes, George Bush does have a problem.'. . . Child abuse has become one of the epidemics of the 1990s," Bowman told GQ. Allegedly, one of Bowman's sources is a retired psychiatrist who worked for the CIA. He added that cocaine trafficking and political corruption were the other principal themes of his book.[6]

It didn't sound crazy to Peter Sawyer either. An Australian conservative activist who publishes a controversial newsletter, *Inside News*, with a circulation of 200,000, Sawyer dedicated his November 1991 issue entirely to the Nebraska scandal, focusing on President Bush's links to the affair. In a section captioned, "The Original Allegations: Bush First Named in 1985," Sawyer writes,

> Stories about child sex and pornography first became public knowledge in 1989, following the collapse of the Franklin Credit Union. That is not when the allegations started, however. Indeed, given the political flavor of the subsequent investigations, it would be easy to dismiss claims that George Bush had been involved. He was by then a very public figure. . . .
>
> If the first allegations about a massive child exploitation ring, centered around Larry King and leading all the way to the White House, had been made in 1989, and had all come from the same source, some shenanigans and mischievous collusion could be suspected. However, the allegations arising out of the Franklin Credit Union collapse were not the first.
>
> Way back in 1985, a young girl, Eulice (Lisa) Washington, was the center of an investigation by Andrea L. Carener, of the Nebraska Department of Social Services. The investigation was instigated because Lisa and her sister Tracey continually ran away from their foster parents, Jarrett and Barbara Webb. Initially reluctant to disclose information for fear of being further punished, the two girls eventually recounted a remarkable story, later backed up by other children who had been fostered out to the Webb's [sic].
>
> These debriefings were conducted by Mrs. Julie Walters, another welfare officer, who worked for Boys Town at the time, and who had been called in because of the constant reference by the Webb children and others, to that institution.
>
> Lisa, supported by her sister, detailed a massive child sex, homosexual, and pornography industry, run in Nebraska by Larry King. She described how she was regularly taken to Washington by plane, with other youths, to attend parties hosted by King and involving many prominent people, including businessmen and politicians. Lisa specifically named George Bush as being in attendance on at least two separate occasions.

"Remember, this was in 1985," emphasized the Australian newsletter.

The newsletter reproduces several documents on Lisa's case, including a Nebraska State Police report, a State of Nebraska Foster Care Review Board letter to the Attorney General, an investigative report prepared for the Franklin Committee of the Nebraska Senate, and a portion of the handwritten debriefing by Mrs. Julie Walters.

Peter Sawyer says that he obtained the documents from sympathetic Australian law enforcement officers who had helped Australian Channel Ten produce an exposé of a national child prostitution ring Down Under. The Australian cops seem to have been in communication with American law enforcement officers who apparently agreed that there had been a coverup on the Nebraska scandal. Subsequent investigations by the authors established that all four documents were authentic.

Mrs. Julie Walters, now a housewife in the Midwest, confirmed that in 1986 she had interviewed the alleged child prostitute, Lisa, who told her about Mr. Bush. Lisa and her sister Tracey were temporarily living at the time in the home of Kathleen Sorenson, another foster parent. Mrs. Walters explained that at first she was very surprised. But Lisa, who came from a very underprivileged background with no knowledge of political affairs, gave minute details of her attendance at political meetings around the country. From Julie Walters' 50-page handwritten report:

3/25/86. Met with Kathleen [Sorenson] and Lisa for about 2 hours in Blair [Neb.] questioning Lisa for more details about sexual abuse. . . . Lisa admitted to being used as a prostitute by Larry King when she was on trips with his family. She started going on trips when she was in 10th grade. Besides herself and Larry there was also Mrs. King, their son, Prince, and 2–3 other couples. They traveled in Larry's private plane, Lisa said that at these trip parties, which Larry hosted, she sat naked "looking pretty and innocent" and guests could engage in any sexual activity they wanted (but penetration was not allowed) with her. . . . Lisa said she first met V.P. George Bush at the Republican Convention (that Larry King sang the national anthem at) and saw him again at a Washington, D.C. party that Larry hosted. At that party, Lisa saw no women ("make-up was perfect—you had to check their legs to make sure they weren't a woman").

The polygraph test which Lisa took only centered around sexual abuse committed by Jarrett Webb. At that time, she had said only general things about Larry's trips (i.e. where they went, etc.). She only began talking about her involvement in prostitution during those trips on 3/25/86. . . .

Lisa also accompanied Mr. and Mrs. King and Prince on trips to Chicago, N.Y. and Washington, D.C. beginning when she was 15 years old. She missed twenty-two days of school almost totally due to these trips. Lisa was taken along on the pretense of being Prince's babysitter. Last year she met V.P. George Bush and saw him again at one of the parties Larry gave while on a Washington, D.C. trip. At some of the parties there are just men (as was the case at the party George Bush attended)—older men and younger men in their early

twenties. Lisa said she has seen sodomy committed at those parties.
. . .

At these parties, Lisa said every guest had a bodyguard and she saw some of the men wearing guns. All guests had to produce a card which was run through a machine to verify who the guest was, in fact, who they said they were. And then each guest was frisked down before entering the party.[7]

The details of the accusations against Mr. Bush are known to be in the hands of the FBI. A Franklin Committee report stated:

Apparently she [Lisa] was contacted on December 19 [1988] and voluntarily came to the FBI offices on December 30, 1988. She was interviewed by Brady, Tucker and Phillips.

She indicates that in September or October 1984, when [Lisa] Washington was fourteen or fifteen years of age, she went on a trip to Chicago with Larry King and fifteen to twenty boys from Omaha. She flew to Chicago on a private plane.

The plane was large and had rows of two seats apiece on either side of the interior middle aisle.

She indicates that King got the boys from Boys Town and the boys worked for him. She stated that Rod Evans and two other boys with the last name of Evans were on the plane. Could not recall the names of the other boys.

The boys who flew to Chicago with Washington and King were between the ages of fifteen and eighteen. Most of the boys were black but some were white. She was shown a color photograph of a boy and identified that boy as being one of the boys on the plane. She could not recall his name.

She indicates that she was coerced to going on the trip by Barbara Webb.

She indicates that she attended a party in Chicago with King and the male youths. She indicated George Bush was present.

She indicates that she set [sic] at a table at the party while wearing nothing but a negligee. She stated that George Bush saw her on the table. She stated she saw George Bush pay King money, and that Bush left the party with a nineteen year old black boy named Brent.

Lisa said the party George Bush attended was in Chicago in September or October 1984. According to the *Chicago Tribune* of October 31, 1984, Bush was in Illinois campaigning for congressional candidates at the end of October.

Lisa added more details on the Chicago trip, and told why she was sure it was George Bush she had seen. According to a May 8, 1989 report by investigator Jerry Lowe, "Eulice [Lisa] indicated that she recognized George Bush as coming to the party and that Bush had two large white males with him. Eulice indicated Bush came to the party approximately 45 minutes after it started and that he was greeted by Larry King. Eulice indicated that she knew George Bush due to the fact that he had been in political campaigns and also she had observed a picture of Bush with Larry King at Larry King's house in Omaha."

There is no question that Lisa and Tracey Webb were abused in the way they claimed. But, in keeping with the alleged pattern of coverup, a Washington County, Nebraska judge in December 1990 dismissed all charges against their abusers, Jarrett and Barbara Webb. The judge ignored presented testimony of the 1986 report by Boys Town official Julie Walters. The report stated: "Lisa was given four polygraph tests administered by a state trooper at the State Patrol office on Center Street in Omaha. The state trooper, after Lisa's testing was completed, told [another foster parent] he tried to 'break Lisa down,' but he was convinced she was telling the truth."[8]

Furthermore, numbers of foster care officials and youth workers debriefed the sisters. All of them fully believed not only their general story of abuse, but specifically their account of Bush's involvement. The March 1986 report on Bush was incorporated into the Foster Care Review Board's official report presented to the Senate Franklin Committee and to law enforcement. As Kathleen Sorenson wrote in a report dated May 1, 1989, "This was long before he [Bush] was president. It seems like there were more exciting people to 'lie' about if that's what they were doing."[9]

The rumors about Mr. Bush were given new life when Dr. Ronald Roskens, the head of the Agency for International Development (AID), found himself the object of controversy. *Executive Intelligence Review* reported in the fall of 1991 that Dr. Roskens

> is the subject of a scandal in which he is being charged with violating federal laws and ethics codes, according to the Oct. 6 *Washington Post*. A report prepared by AID Inspector General Herbert Beckington, dated April 5 and leaked to the *Post,* charges Roskens with accepting thousands of dollars in payments from "different organizations in compensation of his and his wife's travel expenses" while Roskens was on official government travel. He also took money for a private trip from a company "from which Roskens had agreed to divest himself as a condition of his presidential appointment."

The inspector general concluded that the money accepted by

Roskens was a clear conflict of interest and violated federal law against earning non-government income. But on Sept. 4, after reviewing the charges, the Department of Justice . . . informed Beckington that it had decided not to prosecute—giving no explanation for its decision. The White House is reviewing the case.

Congressional investigators are already looking into the allegations. Should they scratch below the surface, they will find that this is not the first time Roskens has been touched by scandal. Although President Bush promised that he would not tolerate even the appearance of impropriety in his administration, Congress should not be surprised if the White House threatens to start "breaking legs" in Roskens's defense.

It is not just that Roskens is a personal friend of the President—although he is. . . . [A]n unimpeded investigation into Roskens could expose the link between Bush's little publicized birth control mania—much of which is carried out through the State Department's AID in the Third World—and the sexual depravity rampant in U.S. political and intelligence elites. Any such scandal could shatter the illusions of Bush's conservative base, many of whom still accept the President's claims to being "pro-life," "anti-drug," and an American patriot. It should also make anyone who thinks of the propaganda about Bush being the "education President," deeply queasy.

Roskens left his home state of Nebraska for the nation's capital in early 1990 enmired in controversy. He had been fired suddenly as president of the University of Nebraska, in a secret meeting of the state Board of Regents in July 1989. No public explanation was given for his removal. Yet, within weeks, the White House offered Roskens the high-profile job in Washington. The administration knew about the controversy in Nebraska, but Roskens passed an FBI background check, and was confirmed to head AID.

The FBI appears to have overlooked a Feb. 19, 1990 investigative report by the late Gary Caradori [see footnote 5 below], an investigator for the "Franklin Committee" of the Nebraska Senate. He wrote, "I was informed that Roskins [sic] was terminated by the state because of sexual activities reported to the Regents and verified by them. Mr. Roskins [sic] was reported to have had young men at his residence for sexual encounters. As part of the separation from the state, he had to move out of the state-owned house because of the liability to the state if some of his sexual behavior was 'illegal.' "[10]

There has been no independent confirmation of the accusation. As of late December 1991, a congressional committee was looking into the charges.

Notes for Chapter XX

1. *Washington Times*, Aug. 9, 1989.
2. *Washington Times*, July 7, 1989.

3. *Pronto* (Barcelona, Spain), Aug. 3, 1991 and Aug. 10, 1991.

4. *Omaha World-Herald,* July 23, 1989.

5. On July 11, 1990, during the course of his investigations, Gary Caradori, 41, died in the crash of his small plane, together with his 8-year-old son, after a mid-air explosion whose cause has not yet been discovered. A skilled and cautious pilot, Caradori told friends repeatedly in the weeks before his death that he feared his plane would be sabotaged.

6. *Gentleman's Quarterly,* December 1991.

7. Report, written on March 25, 1986 by Julie Walters and authenticated by her in an interview in 1990.

8. Report, early 1989, compiled by Jerry Lowe, the first investigator for the Franklin Committee of the Nebraska State Senate.

9. A book recently published on the Nebraska affair by a former Republican state senator and decorated Vietnam veteran, John W. DeCamp, *The Franklin Cover-Up: Child Abuse, Satanism and Murder in Nebraska* (Lincoln, Nebraska: AWT, Inc., 1992) tells the whole story.

10. *Executive Intelligence Review,* Oct. 18, 1991.

XXI

BUSH TAKES
THE PRESIDENCY

*Oderint dum metuant**
—Accius, *Atreus* (c. 125 B.C.), attributed by Suetonius to Caligula

George Bush's quest for the summit of American political power was so sustained and so unrelenting that it is impossible to assign the beginning of his campaign for President to any specific date. It is more accurate to report that his entire tenure as Vice President was consumed by the renovation and expansion of his personal and family network for the purpose of seizing the presidency at some point in the future. During this phase, Bush was far more concerned with organizational and machine-building matters than with ideology or public relations. For most of the 1980s, it was convenient for Bush to cultivate the public profile of a faithful and even obsequious deputy to Reagan, while using the office of the Vice President to build a national and international overt/covert power cartel.

Bush had no regional constituency in any of the half-dozen places he tried to call home; his favorite son appeal was diluted all over the map. He had no base among labor, blacks or in the cities, like the Kennedy apparat. Blue-blooded financiers gravitated instinctively to Bush; his lifeline to the post-Meyer Lansky mob was robust indeed; and these were important factors, although not enough by themselves to win an election. Bush's networks could always tilt the media in his favor, but the Reagan experience had provided a painful

*Let them hate me, provided that they fear me.

479

lesson of how inadequate this could be against a clever populist rival. Otherwise, Bush's base was in the government, where eight years of patient work had packed the executive branch, the Congress and its staffs, and the judiciary with Bushmen.

Nor was it only that Bush lacked a loyal base of support. He also had very high negatives, meaning that there were a lot of people who disliked him intensely. Such animosity was especially strong among the ideological Reaganite conservatives, whom Bush had been purging from the Reagan administration from early on.

There would prove to be very little that Bush could do to lower his negative response rate, so the only answer would be to raise the negatives of all rival candidates on both sides of the partisan divide. This brutal imperative for the Bush machine has contributed significantly to the last half decade's increase in derogation and vilification in American life. Bush's discrediting campaigns would be subsumed within the "anything goes" approach advocated by the late Lee Atwater, the organizer of Reagan's 1984 campaign, who had signed on with Bush well in advance of 1988.

The *Washington Post* went after Bush as "the Cliff Barnes of American politics," a reference to a character in the TV soap opera "Dallas," whom the *Post* found "blustering, opportunistic, craven, and hopelessly ineffective all at once." Others, foreshadowing the thyroid revelations of 1991, talked about Bush's "hyperkinesis." Even the unsavory George Will commented that "the optimistic statement 'George Bush is not as silly as he frequently seems' now seems comparable to Mark Twain's statement that Wagner's music is better than it sounds."[1]

More than anything, Bush wanted an early endorsement from Reagan in order to suppress or at least undercut challenges to his presumptive front-runner status from GOP rivals in the primaries; it was already clear that Senator Bob Dole might be the most formidable of these. Bush feared Dole's challenge, and desperately wanted to be anointed as Reagan's heir-apparent as soon as possible before 1988. But Reagan had apparently not gotten over the antipathy to Bush he had conceived during the *Nashua Telegraph* debate of 1980. According to a high-level Reagan administration source speaking in the summer of 1986, "more than once the president [told Bush], 'Obviously, I'm going to stay neutral until after the convention, and then I'm going to work for whichever candidate comes out on top.' "[2] Despite Bush's "slavish devotion," Reagan wanted to keep the door open to his good friend, Senator Paul Laxalt of Nevada, whom Reagan apparently thought was getting ready to run for President. One can imagine Bush's rage and chagrin.

Reagan stubbornly refused to come out for Bush until the endorsement could no longer help him in the Republican primaries. Reagan chose to wait until Super Tuesday was over and the rest of the Republican field had been mathematically eliminated. Reagan actually waited until Bob Dole, the last of Bush's rivals, had dropped out. Then Reagan ignored the demands of Bush's media handlers and perception-mongers and gave his endorsement in the evening, too late for the main network news programs. The scene was a partisan event, a very large GOP congressional fundraising dinner. Reagan waited to the end of the speech, explained that he was now breaking his silence on the presidential contest, and in a perfunctory way said he would support Bush. "I'm going to work as hard as I can to make Vice President George Bush the next president of the United States," said old Ron. There were no accolades for Bush's real or imagined achievements, no stirring kudos. Seasoned observers found Reagan's statement "halfhearted . . . almost grudging."[3]

The Wimp Factor

Reagan's endless reticence meant that Bush had to work especially hard to pander to the right wing, to those people whom he despised but nevertheless needed to use. Here Bush stooped to boundless public degradation. In December 1985, Bush went to Canossa by accepting an invitation to a dinner in Manchester, New Hampshire held in honor of the late William Loeb, the former publisher of the Manchester *Union Leader*. We have already documented (Chapter 15) that old man Loeb hated Bush and worked doggedly for his defeat in 1980. Still, Bush was the "soul of humility," and he was willing to do anything to be able to take power in his own name. Bush gave a speech full of what the *Washington Post* chose to call "self-deprecating humor," but what others might have seen as groveling. Bush regaled 500 Republicans and rightists with a fairy tale about having tried in 1980 to woo Loeb by offering rewards of colored watchbands, LaCoste shirts and Topsider shoes to anyone who could win over Bill Loeb. The items named were preppy paraphernalia which Loeb and many others found repugnant.

Some of the assembled right-wingers repeated the line from the Doonesbury comic strip according to which Bush "had placed his manhood in a blind trust." Loeb's widow, Nackey Scripps Loeb, was noncommittal. "We have decided on a candidate for 1988— whoever best fights for the Reagan agenda," she announced. "Whether that person is here tonight remains to be seen," she added.[4]

Lawfully, Bush had earned only the contempt of these New Hampshire conservatives. In October 1987, when the New Hampshire primary season was again at hand, Mrs. Loeb rewarded Bush for his groveling with a blistering attack that featured reprints of Bill Loeb's 1980 barbs: "a preppy wimp, part of the self-appointed elite," and so forth. Mrs. Loeb wrote, "George Bush has been Bush for 63 years. He has been Ronald Reagan's errand boy for just the last seven. Without Ronald Reagan he will surely revert to the original George Bush." Mrs. Loeb repeated her late husband's 1980 advice: "Republicans should flee the presidential candidacy of George Bush as if it were the black plague itself."[5]

All of this culminated in the devastating *Newsweek* cover story of October 19, 1987, "Fighting the 'Wimp Factor.' " The article was more analytical than hostile, but did describe the "crippling handicap" of being seen as a "wimp." Bush had been a "vassal to Kissinger" at the United Nations and in Beijing, the article found, and now even Bush's second-term chief of staff said of Bush, "He's emasculated by the office of vice president." To avoid appearing as a television wimp, Bush had "tried for the past 10 years to master the medium, studying it as if it were a foreign language. He has consulted voice and television coaches. He tried changing his glasses and even wearing contact lenses. . . . Bush's tight, twangy voice is a common problem. Under stress, experts explain, the vocal cords tighten and the voice is higher than normal and lacks power." According to *Newsweek*, 51 percent of Americans found that "wimp" was a "serious problem" for Bush.

The *Newsweek* "wimp" cover soon had Bush chewing the carpet at the Naval Observatory. Bush's knuckle-dragging son, George W. Bush, called the story "a cheap shot" and added menacingly: ". . . I'd like to take the guy who wrote that headline out on that boat," i.e., the Aronow-built *Fidelity* in which Bush was depicted on the *Newsweek* cover—which sounded very much like a threat. George W. Bush also called *Newsweek* Washington bureau chief Evan Thomas to inform him that the Bush campaign had officially cut off all contact with *Newsweek* and its reporters. The decision to put *Newsweek* out of business was made by candidate Bush personally, and aborted a plan by *Newsweek* to publish a book on the 1988 campaign. The press got the message: Portray Bush in a favorable light or face vindictive and discriminatory countermeasures.

Big Bucks for Bush

Bush campaigns have always advanced on a cushion of money, and the 1988 effort was to push this characteristic to unheard-of extremes. In keeping with a tradition that had stretched over almost three decades, the Bush campaign finance chairman was Robert Mosbacher, whose Mosbacher Energy Corporation is one of the largest privately held independent oil companies in Texas. Mosbacher's net personal worth is estimated at $200 million. During the 1988 campaign, Mosbacher raised $60 million for the Bush campaign and $25 million for the Republican National Committee. It was Mosbacher who formed the Team 100 elite corps of 250 fat cats, among whom we have seen Henry Kravis. The trick was that many of these $100,000 contributors were promised ambassadorial posts and other prestigious appointments, a phenomenon that would reach scandalous proportions during 1989.

Bush's big money campaigning was especially dependent upon Texas oilmen, whose largesse he required to stoke his political machine. Bush was running a political action committee called the Fund for America's Future, which raised $3.9 million in off-year 1985, a hefty sum. Of that take, about a fifth was raised from 505 Texas donors, with Texans giving more than the residents of any other state. $135,095 of Bush's money harvest came from persons who could be clearly identified as oil industry figures, and the rakeoff here was probably much greater. When the price of a barrel of oil fell during this period from $39 to $12, Bush had a big problem. His donors began to squawk.

The collapse of the oil price posed a real problem that should have been answered by introducing an oil tariff with a trigger price of $25 per barrel, so that the domestic price of oil would never fall below that figure, as was proposed at the time by Lyndon LaRouche and a few spokesmen for the oil patch. That would have been the equivalent of setting up a parity price for oil, and would have given domestic producers solid certainties for long-term development and planning. But the Reagan administration in general was still wedded to the President's irrational fetishism of "the magic of the marketplace," and would violently oppose anything smacking of dirigism or re-regulation.

Bush was not interested in a parity price for oil. He rather took advantage of a scheduled trip to the Middle East in the spring of 1986, during which he was supposed to be discussing regional security matters, to talk up the price of oil with his long-time crony King Fahd of Saudi Arabia. Bush expressed his concern about "the free fall" of oil prices and talked with Fahd about "how [the Saudis] feel there can be some stability to a market that certainly can't be very happy to them." He denied that he had come to Saudi Arabia on a "price-fixing mission," but invoked national security. Bush lectured Saudi Oil Minister Zaki Yamani about the saturation of the world oil market. The implication was clear: The Saudis were supposed to cut back their production.[6] It was a few weeks later that the U.S. bombed Libya.

Bush sanctimoniously claimed that his remarks had nothing to do with the quest for political advantage. His performance may have played well in the oil patch, but reviews elsewhere were not laudatory. A Dole spokesman gloated that "given Bush's background, the last thing he needs to be doing is carrying water for the oil industry and the international banks. . . . It was as if his whole resumé was talking."

The Primary Campaign

James Baker was the titular head of the Bush campaign, but the person responsible for the overall concepts and specific tactics of the Bush campaign was Lee Atwater, a political protégé of Senator Strom Thurmond of South Carolina. Thurmond had been a Democrat, then a Dixiecrat in 1948, then a Democrat again, and finally a Republican. The exigencies of getting elected in South Carolina on the GOP ticket had taught Thurmond to reach deeply into that demagogue's bag of tricks called the wedge issues. Under Thurmond's tutelage, Atwater had become well versed in the essentials of the Southern Strategy, the key to that emergent Republican majority in presidential elections which Kevin Phillips had written about in 1968. Atwater had also imbibed political doctrine from the first practitioner of the Southern Strategy, the dark-jowled Richard M. Nixon himself.

In January 1983, for example, Lee Atwater, at that time deputy director of the White House office of political affairs (and a creature of the Bush-Baker connection), met with Nixon for three and a half hours in Columbia, South Carolina. Nixon held forth on three points: the decisive political importance of the Sun Belt, the numerical relations within the Electoral College, and the vast benefits of having no primary competition when seeking reelection.

In 1988 as well, Nixon was brought in to be the *spiritus rector* of the Bush campaign. During March of 1988, when it was clear that Bush was going to win the nomination, Nixon "slipped into town" to join George Bush, Bar and Lee Atwater for dinner at the Naval Observatory. This time it was Bush who received a one-hour lecture from Nixon on the need to cater to the Republican right wing, the imperative of a tough line on crime in the streets and the Soviets (again to propitiate the rightists), to construct an independent identity only after the convention, and to urge Reagan to campaign actively. And of course, where Nixon shows up, Kissinger cannot be far away.[7]

1988 saw another large-scale mobilization of the intelligence community in support of Bush's presidential ambitions. The late Miles Copeland, a high-level former CIA official who operated out of London during the 1980s, contributed a piece frankly titled "Old Spooks for Bush" to the March 18, 1988 issue of *National Review*. (Since the magazine's editor, William Buckley, was a notorious Skull and Bones cultist, the allusion to "spooks" assumed the character of an insider pun.)

Bush and Atwater feared all their competition. They feared former Governor Pierre DuPont of Delaware because of his appeal to liberal and blue-blooded Republicans who might otherwise automatically gravitate to Bush. They feared New York Congressman Jack Kemp because of his appeal to the GOP right wing and to blue-collar Reagan Democrats, and because of what they viewed as his disturbing habit of talking about the Strategic Defense Initiative and similar issues. They feared that Senator Bob Dole of Kansas, with his "root canal economics" and right-wing populism, and his solid backing from the international grain cartel, might appear more credible to the Wall Street bankers than Bush as an enforcer of austerity and sacrifices.

But at the same time, they knew that Bush had more money to spend and incomparably more state by state organization than any of his GOP rivals, to say nothing of the fabled Brown Brothers Harriman media edge. Bush also ruled the Republican National Committee with Stalin-like ferocity, denying these assets to all of his rivals. This allowed Bush to wheel toward the right in 1986–87 to placate some of his critics there, and then move back toward the center by the time of the primaries. Indeed, Bush's many layers of money and political *apparatchiki* made it possible for him to absorb even stunning defeats like the outcome of the Iowa caucuses without folding. Victory, thought Bush, would belong to the big battalions.

But all the money and the organization could not mask the fact that Bush was fundamentally a weak candidate. This began to become obvious to Atwater and his team of perception-mongers as the Iowa caucuses began to shape up. These were the caucuses that Bush had so niftily won in 1980. By 1988, Bush's Iowa effort had become complicated by reality, in the form of a farm crisis that was driving thousands of farmers into bankruptcy every week. Farm voters were now enraged against the avuncular thespian Ronald Reagan and were looking for a way to send a message to the pointy-headed set in Washington, D.C. Governor Terry Branstad of Iowa complained as early as February 1986: "I don't think his advisors are even keeping [Bush] informed on the extent of the farm crisis. We've got a crisis in agriculture and no one is in charge." Bush's Iowa campaign was dripping with lucre, but this now brought forth resentment among the grim and grey-faced rural voters.

In mid-October 1987, five of the six declared Republican candidates attended a traditional Iowa GOP rally in Ames, just north of Des Moines, on the campus of Iowa State University. Televangelist Pat Robertson surprised all the others by mobilizing 1,300 enthusiastic supporters for the Saturday event. The culmination of this rally was a presidential straw poll, which Robertson won with 1,293 votes to 958 for Dole. Bush trailed badly with 864. This was the occasion for Bush's incredible explanation of what had happened: "A lot of people that support me, they were off at the air show, they were at their daughters' coming out parties, or teeing up at the golf course for that all-important last round."[8] Many Iowans, including Republicans, had to ask what a debutante cotillion was, and began to meditate on the fact that they were not socially acceptable. But most concluded that George Bush was the imperial candidate from another planet, bereft of the foggiest notion of their lives and their everyday problems.

During the buildup to the Iowa caucuses, Bush continued to dodge questions on Iran-Contra. The famous "tension city" encounter with Dan Rather took place during this time. Lee Atwater considered that performance Bush's defining event for the campaign, a display which made him look like John Wayne, Clint Eastwood and Gary Cooper, especially in the South, where people like a pol who "can kick somebody's ass" and where that would make a big difference on Super Tuesday.

But Bush's handlers were nevertheless shocked when Dole won the Iowa caucuses with 37 percent of the vote, followed by Pat Robertson with 25 percent. Bush managed only a poor show, with 19 percent, a massive collapse in comparison with 1980, when he had been far less known to the public.

Bush had known that defeat was looming in Iowa, and he had scuttled out of the state and gone to New Hampshire before the results were known. Bush was nevertheless stunned by his ignominious third-place finish, and he consulted with Nick Brady, Lee Atwater, chief of staff Craig Fuller and pollster Bob Teeter. Atwater had boasted that he had built a "fire wall" in the southern Super Tuesday states that would prevent any rival from seizing the nomination out of Bush's grasp, but the Bush image-mongers were well aware that a loss in New Hampshire might well prove a fatal blow to their entire effort, the advantages of money, networks and organization notwithstanding.

Atwater accordingly ordered a huge media buy of 1,800 gross rating points, enough to ensure that the theoretical New Hampshire television viewer would be exposed to a Bush attack ad 18 times over the final three days before the election. The ad singled out Bob Dole, judged by the Bushmen as their most daunting New Hampshire challenger, and savaged him for "straddling" the question of whether or not new taxes ought to be imposed. The ad proclaimed that Bush "won't raise taxes," period. Bush was glorified as opposing an oil import tax, and for having supported Reagan's INF treaty on nuclear forces in Europe from the very beginning. It was during this desperate week in New Hampshire that Bush became indissolubly wedded to his lying and demagogic "no new taxes" pledge, which he repudiated with considerable fanfare during the spring of 1990.

When Bush had arrived in Manchester the night of the disastrous Iowa result, New Hampshire Governor John Sununu, his principal supporter in the state, had promised a nine-point victory for Bush in his state. Oddly enough, that turned out to be exactly right. The final result was 38 percent for Bush, 29 percent for Dole, 13 percent for Kemp, 10 percent for DuPont, and 9 percent for Robertson. Was Sununu a clairvoyant? Perhaps he was, but those familiar with the inner workings of the New Hampshire quadrennials are aware of a very formidable ballot-box stuffing potential assembled there by the blue-blooded political establishment. Lyndon LaRouche pointed to pervasive vote fraud in the 1988 New Hampshire primaries, and Pat Robertson, as we shall see, also raised this possibility. The Sununu machine delivered exactly as promised, securing the governor the post of White House chief of staff. (Sununu soon became so self-importantly inebriated with the trappings of the imperial presidency, as reflected in his travel habits, that it was suggested that the state motto appearing on New Hampshire license plates be changed from "Live Free or Die" to "Fly Free or Die.") In any case, for Bush, the heartfelt "Thank You, New Hampshire" he intoned after his surprising victory signaled that his machine had weathered its worst crisis.

In the South Carolina primary, the Bushmen were concerned about a possible threat from television evangelist Pat Robertson, who had mounted his major effort in the Palmetto state. Robertson was widely known through his appearances on his Christian Broadcasting Network. Shortly before the South Carolina vote, a scandal became public which involved another television evangelist, Jimmy Swaggart, a close friend of Robertson and an active supporter of Robertson's presidential campaign. Swaggart admitted to consorting with a prostitute, and this caused a severe crisis in his ministry. Jim Bakker of the PTL television ministry had already been tainted by a sex scandal.

Pat Robertson accused the Bush campaign of orchestrating the Swaggart revelations at a time that would be especially advantageous to their man. Talking to reporters, Robertson pointed to "the evidence that two weeks before the primary . . . it suddenly comes to light." Robertson added that the Bush campaign was prone to "sleazy" tricks, and suggested that his own last-place finish in New Hampshire was "quite possibly" the result of "dirty tricks" by the Bush campaign. Bush responded by dismissing Robertson's charges as "crazy" and "absurd." Robertson had been linking Bush to the "international banking community" in his South Carolina campaigning.[9]

True to his Southern Strategy, Atwater had "front-loaded" Bush's effort in the southern states with money, political operatives and television, straining the legal limit of what could be spent during the primary season as a whole. A few days before Super Tuesday came the South Carolina primary. Here Bush appeared before a group of two dozen evangelical fundamentalist ministers and declared with a straight face: "Jesus Christ is my personal savior." The state's governor, Caroll Campbell, was a former customer of Lee Atwater. Strom Thurmond was for Dole, but his endorsement proved to be valueless. Here Bush got all the state's 37 delegates by scoring 48 percent of the vote to 21 percent for Dole, 19 percent for Robertson and 11 percent for Kemp.

Then, in the March 8 Super Tuesday polling, Bush scored an across-the-board triumph, winning in Florida, Texas, Alabama, Arkansas, Georgia, Kentucky, Louisiana, Mississippi, North Carolina, Oklahoma, Tennessee, Virginia, Missouri and Maryland, plus Massachusetts and Rhode Island outside of the region. It was better than one of Napoleon Bonaparte's plebiscites. With this, Bush took 600 of 803 delegates at stake that day. Four and a half million Republicans had voted, the best turnout ever in southern GOP primaries. Most of the votes were votes for Reagan in the part of the country that felt least disillusioned by the Great Communicator, but they were all scored as votes for Bush. When Bush beat Dole by a three-to-two margin in Illinois, supposedly a part of Dole's base, it was all over. Bush prepared for the convention and the choice of a Vice President.

The Wedge Issues Campaign

The Bush campaign of 1988 had no issues, but only demagogic themes. These were basically all on the table by June, well before the Republican convention. The first was the pledge of no new taxes, later embroidered with the Clint Eastwood tough-guy overtones of "Read My Lips—No New Taxes." The other themes reflected Atwater's studies of how to drive up the negatives of Bush's Democratic opponent, who would be Massachusetts Governor Michael Dukakis. Very early on, Bush began to harp on Dukakis's veto of a bill requiring teachers to lead their class each day in the pledge of allegiance. Speaking in Orange County, California on June 7, Bush said: "I'll never understand, when it came to his desk, why he vetoed a bill that called for the pledge of allegiance to be said in the schools of Massachusetts. I'll never understand it. We are one nation under God. Our kids should say the pledge of allegiance."[10]

This theme lent itself very well to a highly cathexized visual portrayal, with flags and bunting. Atwater was assisted in these matters by Roger Ailes, a television professional who had been the executive producer of the Mike Douglas Show by the time he was 27 years old. That was in 1967, when he was hired by Richard Nixon and Leonard Garment. Ailes had been one of the most cynical designers of the selling of the President in 1968, and he had remained in the political media game ever since. Between them, Atwater and Ailes would produce the modern American television equivalent of a 1930s Nuremburg party rally.

At about this time, the Bush network we have seen in operation at the *Reader's Digest* since the 1964 campaign conveniently printed an article about a certain Willie Horton, a black convicted murderer who was released from a Massachusetts jail on a furlough, and then absconded to Maryland, where he raped a white woman and stabbed her fiancé. The Massachusetts furlough program had been started by Republican Governor Frank Sargent, but this meant nothing. Bush was to use Willie Horton in the same way that Hitler and the Nazis exploited the grisly crimes of one Harmann, a serial killer in Germany of the early 1930s, in their calls for law and order. In Illinois in mid-June, Bush began to talk about how Dukakis let "murderers out on vacation to terrorize innocent people." "Democrats can't find it in their hearts to get tough on criminals," Bush ranted.

As packaged by Bush's handlers, it was thoroughly racist without being nominally so, like Nixon's "crime in the streets" shorthand for racist backlash during the 1968 campaign. Later, Bush would embroider this theme with his demand for the death penalty, his own Final Solution to the problem of criminals like Willie Horton. These themes fit very well into the standard Bush campaign event, which was very often Bush appearing before a local police department to receive their endorsement. Bush's ability to organize these events in places like Boston, to the great embarrassment of Dukakis, doubtless reflected strong support from the CIA Office of Security, which was the bureau that kept in contact with police departments all over the country and, inevitably, infiltrated them.

All of Bush's themes corresponded to wedge issues, the divisive Pavlovian ploys the southern Republicans had become expert in during their decades of battering and dismantling the classic Franklin D. Roosevelt coalition of labor, the cities, blacks, farmers and intellectuals. They were designed to propitiate the vilest prejudices of a majority, while offending a minority, and studiously avoiding any real politics or economics that might be detrimental to the imperatives of Wall Street or the Washington bureaucracy.

To crown this demagogy, George H.W. Bush of Skull and Bones portrayed Dukakis as an elitist insider: "Governor Dukakis, his foreign-policy views born in Harvard Yard's boutique, would cut the muscle of our defense." Bush's frequent litany of "liberal Massachusetts governor" was shameless in its main purpose of suggesting that Bush himself was *not* a liberal.

When Bush arrived in New Orleans for the Republican National Convention, he was accompanied by Baker, Teeter, Fuller, Atwater, Ailes and James Baker's Girl Friday, Margaret Tutwiler. Up to this point, Bush's staff had expected him to generate a little suspense around the convention by withholding the name of his vice-presidential choice until the morning of the last day of the convention, when Bush could share his momentous secret with the Texas caucus and then tell it to the world.

Bush's vetting of Vice Presidents was carried out between Bush and Robert Kimmitt, the Washington lawyer and Baker crony who later joined Baker's ruling clique at the State Department, before being put up for ambassador to Germany when Vernon Walters quit in the spring of 1991. United Germany can now boast a U.S. ambassador whose greatest achievement was to guide Bush toward the choice of J. Danforth Quayle. Bush and Kimmitt reviewed the obvious choices: Kemp was out because he lectured Bush on the SDI and was too concerned about issues. Dole was out because he kept sniping at Bush with his patented sardonic zingers. Elizabeth Dole was a choice to be deemed imprudent. John Danforth, Pete Domenici, Al Simpson and some others were eliminated. Many were the possible choices who had to be ruled out not because of lack of stature, but because they might seem to have more stature than Bush himself.

Quayle had shown up on lists prepared by Fuller and Ailes. Ed Rollins, attuned to the Reagan Democrats, could not believe that Quayle was being seriously considered. But now, at Belle Chase Naval Air Station north of New Orleans, Bush told his staff that he had chosen Dan Quayle. Not only was it Quayle, but Bush's thyroid was now in overdrive: He wanted to announce his selection within hours. Quayle was contacted by telephone and instructed to meet Bush at the dock in New Orleans when the paddle-wheel steamer *Natchez* brought Bush down the Mississippi to that city's Spanish Plaza.

Why J. Danforth Quayle?

Quayle turned up at the dock in a state of inebriated euphoria, grabbing Bush's arm, prancing and capering around Bush. As soon as the dossiers on Quayle came out, a few questions were posed. Had his Senate office been a staging point for Contra resupply efforts? One of the Iran-Contra figures, Rob Owen, had indeed worked for Quayle, but Quayle denied everything. Had Quayle, now a hawk, been in Vietnam? Tom Brokaw asked Quayle if he had gotten help in joining the National Guard as a way of ducking the draft. Quayle stammered that it had been 20 years earlier, but maybe "phone calls were made." Then Dan Rather asked Quayle what his worst fear was. "Paula Parkinson," was the reply. This was the woman lobbyist and *Playboy* nude model who had been present with Quayle at a wild weekend at a Florida country club back in 1980.

The Bush image-mongers hurriedly convened damage control sessions, and Quayle was given two professional handlers, Stuart Spencer and Joe Canzeri. Spencer was an experienced GOP operative who had done public relations and consulting work worth $350,000 for General Noriega of Panama during the mid-1980s.[11] After a couple of Bush-Quayle joint appearances before groups of war veterans to attempt to dissipate Quayle's National Guard issue, Quayle was then shunted into the secondary media markets under the iron control of his new handlers.

Although Bush's impulsive proclamation of his choice of Quayle does indeed raise the question of the hyperthyroid snap decision, the choice of Quayle was not impulsive, but rather perfectly coherent with Bush's profile and pedigree. Bush told James Baker that Quayle had been "my first and only choice."[12] Bush's selection of political appointees is very often the product of Bush-Walker family alliances over more than a generation—as in the case of Baker, Brady, Boy Gray and Henry Kravis—or at least of a long and often lucrative business collaboration, as in the case of Mosbacher. The choice of Quayle lies somewhere in between, and was strengthened by a deep ideological affinity in the area of racism.

J. Danforth Quayle's grandfather was Eugene C. Pulliam, who built an important press empire starting with his purchase of the Atchison (Kansas) *Champion* in 1912. The bulk of these papers were in Indiana, the home state of the Pulliam clan, and in Arizona. "Gene" Pulliam had died in 1975, but his newspaper chain was worth an estimated $1.4 billion by the time Dan Quayle became a household word. Pulliam was a self-proclaimed ideologue: "If I wanted to make money, I'd go into the bond business. I've never been interested in the money I make but the influence we have."[13]

Old Gene was a firm opponent of racial integration. When Martin Luther King, Jr. was assassinated in 1968, Gene Pulliam sent a note to the editors of his papers in Indianapolis, Indiana ordering them not to give the King tragedy "much exposure" because he considered the civil rights leader a "rabble rouser." He instructed that the news of King's death be summarized in as few words as possible and relegated to the bottom of the front page.

The Bush-Quayle alliance thus reposed first of all on a shared premise of racism.

Quayle is known to the vast majority of the American public as a virtual cretin. Quayle is the first representative of the post-war Baby Boom to advance to national elective office. Unfortunately, he seems to exhibit some of the mental impairment that is known to overtake long-term, habitual marijuana users.

Quayle was admitted by the University of Indiana Law School in violation of that school's usual policy of rejecting all applicants with an academic average of less than 2.6. He wanted to be a lawyer because he had heard that "lawyers make lots of money and do little," as he told his fraternity brothers at De Pauw. As it turned out, the dean of admissions at the University of Indiana Law School was one G. Kent Frandsen, who was a Republican city judge in Lebanon, Indiana, a town where the Pulliam family controls the local newspaper. He had always been endorsed by the Pulliam interests. Two years later, Frandsen would officiate at the marriage of J. Danforth Quayle to Marilyn Tucker. Still later, Frandsen would serve as Quayle's campaign manager in Boone County during the 1986 Senate race. It was thus no surprise that Frandsen was willing to admit Dan Quayle to law school as part of a program for disadvantaged students, primarily those from the black community.

After all this, it may appear as a miracle that Dan Quayle was ever able to obtain a law degree. J. Danforth's receipt of that degree appears to have been mightily facilitated by the plutocratic Quayle family, who made large donations to the law school each year during Dan's time as a law student.

What were Quayle's pastimes during his law school years? According to one account, they included recreational drugs. During the summer of 1988, a Mr. Brett Kimberlin told Dennis Bernstein and a radio audience of WBAI in New York that he had first met J. Danforth during this period at a fraternity party at which marijuana was indeed being consumed. "He found out that I had marijuana available at the time," said Kimberlin. "It was good quality, and he asked if I had any for sale. . . . I thought it was kind of strange. He looked kind of straight. I thought he might be a narc [DEA agent] at first. But we talked and I felt a little more comfortable, and finally I gave him my phone number and said, 'Hey, well, give me a call.' He called me a couple weeks later, and said, 'Hey, this is DQ. Can we get together?' and I said 'Yes, meet me at the Burger Chef restaurant.' We struck up a relationship that lasted for 18 months. I sold him small quantities of marijuana for his personal use about once a month during that period. He was a good customer. He was a friend of mine. We had a pretty good relationship. He always paid cash. . . . When him and Marilyn got married in 1972, I gave him a wedding present of some Afghanistan hashish and some Acapulco gold."[14]

Kimberlin repeated these charges in a pre-election interview on NBC News on November 4, 1988. Kimberlin was a federal prisoner serving time in Tennessee after conviction on charges of drug smuggling and explosives. Later that same day, Kimberlin was scheduled to address a news conference by telephone conference call. But before Kimberlin could speak to the press, he was placed in solitary confinement, and was moved in and out of solitary confinement until well after the November 8 presidential election. A second attempted press conference by telephone hookup on the eve of the election did not take place, because Kimberlin was still being held incommunicado. On August 6, 1991, U.S. District Judge Harold H. Greene ruled that the allegations made by Kimberlin against U.S. Bureau of Prisons Director J. Michael Quinlan were "tangible and detailed" enough to justify a trial. Kimberlin had accused Quinlan of ordering solitary confinement for him when it became clear that his ability to further inform the media about Quayle's drug use would damage the Bush-Quayle effort. The trial is still pending as of our publication date.

In March 1977, Congressman Dan Quayle contributed an article to the Fort Wayne, Indiana *News-Sentinel* in which he recommended that Congress take a "serious" look at marijuana decriminalization. In April 1978, Quayle repeated this proposal, specifying he supported decriminalization for first-time users.[15]

The Last Lap

The final stages of the campaign were played out amid great public indifference. Some interest was generated in the final weeks by a matter of prurient, rather than policy interest: Rumors were flying of a Bush sex scandal. This talk, fed by the old Jennifer Fitzgerald story, had surfaced during 1987 in the wake of the successful covert operation against Gary Hart. The gossip became intense enough that George W. Bush asked his father if he had been guilty of philandering. The young Bush reported back to the press that "the answer to the Big A [adultery] question is N-O." Lee Atwater accused David Keene of the Dole campaign of helping to circulate the rumor, and Keene, speaking on a television talk show, responded that Atwater was "a liar." Shortly thereafter, a "sex summit" was convened between the Bush and Dole camps for the purpose of maintaining correct GOP decorum even amidst the acrimony of the campaign.[16]

Evans and Novak opined that "Atwater and the rest of the Bush high command, convinced that the rumors would soon be published, reacted in a way that spelled panic to friend and foe alike." On June 17, 1987, Michael Sneed of the *Chicago Sun-Times* had written that "several major newspapers are sifting . . . reported dalliances of Mr. Boring."[17] But during that summer of 1987, the Brown Brothers Harriman/Skull and Bones networks were powerful enough to suppress the story and spare Bush any embarrassment.

During the weeks before the election, the *LA Weekly,* an alternative paper in Los Angeles, devoted an entire issue to "the dark side of George Bush." British newspapers like the tabloid *London Evening Standard* repeated some details, but U.S. news organizations were monolithic in refusing to report anything; the Bush networks were in total command. Then rumors began to fly that the *Washington Post* was preparing to publish an account of Bush's sex peccadillos. On Wednesday, October 19, the New York Stock Exchange was swept by reports that stories damaging to Bush were about to appear, and this was cited as a contributing factor in a 43-

point drop in the Dow Jones Industrial Average. The *Wall Street Journal* and *USA Today* gingerly picked up the story, albeit in very vague terms. The *Wall Street Journal* wrote that the *Washington Post* was preparing a story that "Bush had carried on an extramarital affair," with a "report that he [Bush] has had a mistress for several years." One of the allegations was that Bush had had an extramarital affair during the mid-1970s with a woman who was no longer in his entourage.

After an Associated Press wire sent out on Thursday, October 20 had offered another summary of the rumor, Bush's press aide Sheila Tate dismissed the entire story as "warmed over garbage."[18] But in the end, the *Washington Post* published no story, and the entire issue was stifled by the brutal power of the Bush media networks.

In the end, the greatest trump card of Bush's 1988 campaign was Bush's opponent Michael Dukakis. There is every reason to believe that Dukakis was chosen by Bush Democrat power brokers and the Eastern Establishment bankers primarily because he was so manifestly unwilling and unable seriously to oppose Bush. Many are the indications that the Massachusetts governor had been selected to take a dive. The gravest suspicions are in order as to whether there ever was a Dukakis campaign at all. Well before Dukakis received the nomination, supporters of Lyndon LaRouche in the National Democratic Policy Committee called attention to the indications of personal and mental instability in Dukakis's personal history, but the Democratic Convention in Atlanta chose to ignore these highly relevant issues.

As the NDPC leaflet pointed out, "There is strong evidence that Michael Dukakis suffers from a deep-seated mental instability that could paralyze him, and decapitate our government, in the event of a severe economic or strategic crisis. This is a tendency for psychological breakdown in a situation of adversity and perceived personal rejection."[19] The best proof of the validity of this assessment is the pitiful election campaign that Dukakis then conducted. The NDPC leaflet had warned that the GOP would exploit this obvious issue, and Reagan soon made his celebrated quip, "I'm not going to pick on an invalid," focusing intense public attention on Dukakis's refusal to release his medical records.

The colored maps used by the television networks on the night of November 8 presented a Bush victory which, although less convincing than Reagan's two landslides, nevertheless seemed impressive. A closer examination of the actual vote totals reveals a much different lesson: Even in competition with the bumbling and craven Dukakis campaign, Bush remained a pitifully weak candidate who, despite overwhelming advantages of incumbency, money, organization, years of enemies-list operations, a free ride from the controlled media, and a pathetic opponent, just managed to eke out a hairs-breadth margin.

Bush had won 53 percent of the popular vote, but if just 535,000 voters in 11 states (or 600,000 voters in nine states) had switched to Dukakis, the latter would have been the winner. The GOP had ruled the terrain west of the Mississippi for many moons, but Bush had managed to lose three Pacific states: Oregon, Washington and Hawaii. Bush won megastates like Illinois and Pennsylvania by paper-thin margins of 51 percent, and the all-important California vote, which went to Bush by just 52 percent, had been too close for George's comfort. Missouri had also been a 52 percent close call for George. In the farm states, the devastation wrought by eight years of GOP free enterprise caused both Iowa and Wisconsin to join Minnesota in the Democratic column. Chronically depressed West Virginia was having none of George. In the oil patch, the Democrats posted percentage gains even though Bush carried these states: In Texas, Oklahoma and Louisiana the Democratic presidential vote was up between 7 and 11 percent compared to the Mondale disaster of 1984. In the Midwest, Dukakis managed to carry four dozen counties that had not gone for a Democratic presidential contender since 1964. All in all, half of Bush's electoral votes came from states in which he got less than 55.5 percent of the two-party vote, showing that there was no runaway Bush landslide.

The voter turnout hit a new postwar low, with just 49.1 percent of eligible voters showing up at the polls, significantly worse than the Harry Truman-Thomas Dewey matchup of 1948, when just 51 percent had deemed it worthwhile to vote. This means that Bush expected to govern the country with the votes of just 26.8 percent of the eligible voters in his pocket. Bush had won a number of southern states by lop-sided margins of about 20 percent, but this was correlated in many cases with very low overall voter turnout, which dipped below 40 percent in Georgia and South Carolina. A big plus factor for George was the very low black voter turnout in the South, where a significant black vote had helped the Democrats retake control of the Senate in 1986. With Dukakis capturing 90 percent of the black vote, a bigger black turnout would have created some serious problems for George. Bush knows that victory in 1992 will depend on keeping the black turnout low, and this is part of the rationale behind his "wedge issue" nomination of the black rightist Clarence Thomas to the Supreme Court, which successfully split national black organizations in such a way that Bush hopes he will be able to ignore them in 1992.

More generally, it would appear that Bush would be very happy to keep across-the-board voter turnout at such depressed levels, since a larger vote could only threaten his results. Dukakis was able to attract only about half of the Reagan Democrats back to their traditional party, despite the preppy, blue-blooded aura of the Bush campaign, which these voters would normally have found highly offensive. The Bush cause is therefore well served by public scandals and media campaigns that tend to elicit widespread disgust with politics and government, since these increase the probability that citizens will stay home on election day, leaving George to dominate the field. It is no surprise that precisely such scandals, from congressional pay raises and the Keating five to the Thomas nomination hearings have proliferated during the years of the Bush regime.

Among those Republicans who had succeeded in winning the White House in two-way races (excluding years like 1948 or 1968, when the totals were impacted by Henry Wallace and Strom Thurmond's Dixiecrats, or by George Wallace), Bush's result was the weakest since fellow Skull and Bones alumnus William Howard Taft in 1908.[20] These patterns might also indicate that the dominant role of the electoral votes of the former Confederate States of America within the Electoral College under the post-1968 Southern Strategy of the national Republican Party may be subjected to erosion in 1992, especially under the impact of the Bush economic depression.

It is also to be hoped that 1988 will prove in retrospect to have represented the high-water mark of hired-gun media and campaign consultants in presidential elections. Atwater at one time boasted that his staff contained at least 28 media experts and political operatives who had worked in at least three previous presidential elections, many of whom were also winning efforts for the GOP. These men were drawn from New York's Madison Avenue and from Washington's Connecticut Avenue "Power Alley," where many of the best-connected political consulting firms have their offices. It is clear that men like Atwater, Ailes, Spencer, Deaver and others have performed a function in the consolidation of a modern American leviathan state that is exactly analogous to the vital services rendered to the Third Reich by Propaganda Minister Dr. Josef Goebbels between 1933 and 1945.

Some months later, Atwater was found to be suffering from a malignant brain cancer. It is rumored around Washington that

Atwater in his final days became a convert to Roman Catholicism and expressed repentance for many of the deeds he performed during his political career. It appears certain that he personally apologized to some of the candidates whom he had vilified during the course of various political campaigns. When Atwater died in April 1991 at the age of 40, it was widely rumored in Washington that he had expressed the deepest remorse for having contributed to the creation of the Bush administration.

Notes for Chapter XXI

1. George Will column, Jan. 30, 1986, in George Will, *The Morning After* (New York: Free Press London, Collier-MacMillan, 1986), p. 254.

2. Jack Anderson and Dale Van Atta, "Bush Waits and Hopes for Reagan Nod," *Washington Post,* Aug. 18, 1986.

3. Jack W. Germond and Jules Witcover, *Whose Broad Stripes and Bright Stars: The Trivial Pursuit of the Presidency, 1988* (New York: Warner Books, 1989), p. 156.

4. "Bush Proves Successful in Ticklish Appearance," *Washington Post,* Dec. 12, 1985.

5. "New Hampshire Chill," *Washington Post,* Oct. 11, 1987.

6. *Washington Post,* April 7, 1986.

7. For Bush in the 1988 campaign, see *Whose Broad Stripes and Bright Stars.*

8. *Washington Post,* Oct. 16, 1987.

9. "Robertson Links Bush to Swaggart Scandal," *Washington Post,* Feb. 24, 1988.

10. Germond and Witcover *op. cit.,* p. 161.

11. Frank McNeil, *War and Peace in Central America* (New York: Scribner's, 1988), p. 277.

12. Germond and Witcover *op. cit.,* p. 385.

13. Eleanor Randolph, "Ghost of Dan Quayle's Grandfather Laid to Rest," *Dallas Times-Herald,* Aug. 23, 1988.

14. Joel Bleifuss, "In Short," *In These Times,* Nov. 16–22, 1988, p. 5, cited by Arthur Frederick Ide, *Bush-Quayle: The Reagan Legacy* (Irving, Texas: Scholars Books, 1989), pp. 55–56.

15. *Ibid.*

16. *Washington Post,* July 1, 1987.

17. *Washington Post,* June 26, 1987.

18. Eleanor Randolph, "Bush Rumor Created Dilemma for Media," *Washington Post,* Oct. 22, 1988.

19. See "Is Dukakis the New Senator Eagleton?" in "Dukakis's Mental Health: An Objective Assessment," *Executive Intelligence Review Reprint,* Aug. 15, 1988, p. 8.

20. See Kevin Phillips, *The Politics of Rich and Poor* (New York: Random House, 1990), p. 215; *Facts on File,* Nov. 11, 1988; and Paul R. Abramson, John H. Aldrich and David W. Rohde, *Change and Continuity in the 1988 Elections* (Washington: Congressional Quarterly, 1991).

XXII

THE END OF HISTORY

"If the Emperor Tiberius—George Bush—is elected, this country will become a fascist state in the first year he is in office, I guarantee it."
  —Lyndon H. LaRouche, Jr., April 15, 1988
  campaign speech in Buffalo, N.Y.

George Bush's inaugural address of January 21, 1989, was on the whole an eminently colorless and forgettable oration. The speech was for the most part a rehash of the tired demagogy of Bush's election campaign, with the ritual references to "a thousand points of light" and the hollow pledge that when it came to the drug inundation which Bush had supposedly been fighting for most of the decade, "This scourge will stop." Bush talked of "stewardship" being passed on from one generation to another. There was almost nothing about the state of the U.S. economy. Bush was preoccupied with the "divisiveness" left over from the Vietnam era, and this he pledged to end in favor of a return to bipartisan consensus between the President and the Congress, since "the statute of limitations has been reached. This is a fact: The final lesson of Vietnam is that no great nation can long afford to be sundered by a memory." There is good reason to believe that Bush was already contemplating the new round of foreign military adventures which were not long in coming.

The characteristic note of Bush's remarks came at the outset, in the passages in which he celebrated the triumph of the American variant of the bureaucratic-authoritarian police state, based on usury, which chooses to characterize itself as "freedom":

> We know what works: Freedom works. We know what's right: Freedom is right. We know how to secure a more just and prosperous life for man on Earth—through free markets, free speech, free elections, and the exercise of free will unhampered by the state.
>
> For the first time in this century, for the first time perhaps in all history, man does not have to invent a system by which to live. We don't have to talk late into the night about which form of government is better. We don't have to wrest justice from the kings. We only have to summon it from within ourselves. We must act on what we know.[1]

After the inauguration ceremonies at the Capitol were completed, George and Barbara Bush descended Pennsylvania Avenue toward the White House in a triumphant progress, getting out of their limousine every block or two to walk among the crowds and savor the ovations. George Bush, imperial administrator and bureaucrat, had now reached the apex of his career, the last station of the *cursus honorum:* the chief magistracy. Bush now assumed leadership of a Washington bureaucracy that was increasingly focused on itself and its own aspirations, convinced of its own omnipotence and infallibility, of its own manifest destiny to dominate the world. It was a heady moment, full of the stuff of megalomaniac delusion.

Imperial Washington was now aware of the increasing symptoms of collapse in the Soviet Empire. The feared adversary of four decades of cold war was collapsing. Germany and Japan were formidable economic powers, but they were led by a generation of politicians who had been well schooled in the necessity of following Anglo-Saxon orders. France had abandoned her traditional Gaullist policy of independence and sovereignty, and had returned to the *suivisme* of the old Fourth Republic under Bush's freemasonic brother François Mitterrand. Opposition to Washington's imperial designs might still come from leading states of the developing sector, from India, Brazil, Iraq and Malaysia, but the imperial administrators, puffed up with their xenophobic contempt for the former colonials, were confident that these states could be easily defeated, and that the Third World would meekly succumb to the installation of Anglo-American puppet regimes in the way that the Philippines and so many Latin American countries had during the 1980s.

Bush could also survey the home front with self-congratulatory complacency. He had won a congressional election in his designer district in Houston, but in 1964 and 1970 majorities at the polls had proven mockingly elusive. Now, for just the second time in his life, he had solved the problem of winning a contested election, and this time it had been the big one. Bush had at one stroke fulfilled his greatest ambition and solved his most persistent problem, that of getting himself elected to public office. He had dealt successfully with the thorny issue of governance in the domestic sphere, foiling the jinx that had dogged all sitting Vice Presidents seeking to move up past a live retired President, after Martin Van Buren's success in 1836.

Bush assembled a team of his fellow Malthusian bureaucrats and administrators from among those officials who had staffed Republican administrations going back to 1969, the year that Nixon chose Kissinger for the National Security Council. Persons like Brent Scowcroft, James Baker, Carla Hills, and Bush himself had, with few exceptions, been in or around the federal government and especially the executive branch for most of two decades, with only the brief hiatus of Jimmy Carter to let them fill their pockets in private sector influence-peddling. Bush's cabinet and staff were convinced they boasted the most powerful battery of resumés, the consummate experience, the most impeccable credentials, of any management team in the history of the world.

All the great issues of policy had been solved under Nixon, Ford and Reagan; the geopolitical situation was being brought under control; all that remained was to consolidate and perfect the total administration of the world according to the policies and procedures already established, while delivering mass consensus through the same methods that had just proven unbeatable in the presidential campaign. The Bush team was convinced of its own inherent superiority to the Mandarin Chinese, the Roman and Byzantine, the Ottoman, the Austrian, the Prussian, the Soviet, and to all other bureaucratic-authoritarian regimes that had ever existed on the planet. Only the British East India Company was even in the same league, thought the theorists of usury on the Bush team.

Pride goeth ever before a fall.

The imperial functionaries of the Bush team had chosen to ignore certain gross facts, most importantly the demonstrable bankruptcy and insolvency of their own leading institutions of finance, credit and government. Their ability to command production and otherwise to act upon the material world was in sharp decline. How long would the American population remain in its state of stupefied passivity in the face of deteriorating standards of living that were now falling more rapidly than at any time in the last 20 years? And now, the speculative orgy of the 1980s would have to be paid for. Even their advantage over the crumbling Soviet empire was ultimately only a marginal, relative and temporary one, due primarily to a faster rate of collapse on the Soviet side; but the day of reckoning for the Anglo-Americans was coming, too.

This was the triumphalism that pervaded the opening weeks of the Bush administration. Bush gave more press conferences during the transition period than Reagan had given during most of his second term; he reveled in the accoutrements of his new office, and gave the White House press corps all the photo opportunities and interviews they wanted, to butter them up and get them in his pocket.

These fatuous delusions of grandeur were duly projected upon the plane of the philosophy of history by an official of the Bush administration, Francis Fukuyama, the deputy director of the State Department Policy Planning Staff, the old haunt of Harrimanites like Paul Nitze and George Kennan. In the winter of 1989, during Bush's first hundred days in office, Fukuyama delivered a lecture to the Olin Foundation which was later published in *The National Interest* quarterly under the title of "The End of History?"[2] Imperial administrator Fukuyama had studied under the reactionary elitist Allan Bloom, and was conversant with the French neo-Enlightenment semiotic (or semi-idiotic) school of Derrida, Foucault and Roland Barthes, whose "zero degree of writing" Fukuyama may have been striving to attain. Above all, Fukuyama was a follower of Hegel in the interpretation of the French postwar neo-Hegelian Alexandre Kojeve.

Fukuyama qualifies as the official ideologue of the Bush regime. His starting point is the "unabashed victory of economic and social liberalism," meaning by that the economic and political system reaching its maturity under Bush—what the State Department usually calls "democracy."

> The triumph of the West, of the Western idea, is evident first of all in the total exhaustion of viable systematic alternatives to Western liberalism. . . . The triumph of the Western political idea is complete. Its rivals have been routed. . . . Political theory, at least the part concerned with defining the good polity, is finished. The Western idea of governance has prevailed. . . . What we may be witnessing is not just the end of the Cold War, or the passing of a particular period of postwar history, but the end of history as such: that is, the end point of mankind's ideological evolution and the universalization of Western liberal democracy as the final form of human government.

According to Fukuyama, communism as an alternative system had been thoroughly discredited in the U.S.S.R., China, and the other communist countries. Since there are no other visible models contending for the right to shape the future, he concludes that the modern American state is the "final, rational form of society and state."

There are of course large areas of the world where governments and forms of society prevail which diverge radically from Fukuyama's Western model, but he answers this objection by explaining that backward, still historic parts of the world exist and will continue to exist for some time. It is just that they will never be able to present their forms of society as a credible model or alternative to "liberalism." Since Fukuyama presumably knew something of what was in the Bush administration pipeline, he carefully kept the door open for new wars and military conflicts, especially among historical states, or between historical and post-historical powers. Both Panama and Iraq would, according to Fukuyama's typology, fall into the latter category.

Thus, in the view of the early Bush administration, the planet would come to be dominated more and more by the "universal homogenous state," a mixture of "liberal democracy in the political sphere combined with easy access to VCRs and stereos in the economic." The arid banality of that definition is matched by Fukuyama's dazzling tribute to "the spectacular abundance of advanced liberal economies and the infinitely diverse consumer culture." Fukuyama, it turns out, is a resident of the privileged enclave for imperial functionaries that is northeast Virginia, and so has little understanding of the scope of U.S. domestic poverty and immiseration: For Fukuyama, writing at a moment when American class divisions were more pronounced than at any time in human memory, "the egalitarianism of modern America represents the essential achievement of the classless society envisaged by Marx." As a purveyor of official doctrine for the Bush regime, Fukuyama is bound to ignore 20 years of increasing poverty and declining standards of living for all Americans which have caused an even greater retrogression for the minority population.

It is not far from the End of History to Bush's later slogans of the New World Order and the imperial Pax Universalis. It is ironic but lawful that Bush should have chosen a neo-Hegelian as apologist for his regime. Hegel was the arch-obscurantist, philosophical dictator, and saboteur of the natural sciences; he was the ideologue of Metternich's Holy Alliance system of police states in the post-1815 oligarchic restoration in Europe imposed by the Congress of Vienna. When we mention Metternich, we have at once brought Bush's old patron Kissinger into play, since Metternich is well known as his ego ideal. Hegel deified the bureaucratic-authoritarian state machinery of which he was a part as the final embodiment of rationality in human affairs, beyond which it was impossible to go. Hegel told intellectuals to be reconciled with the world they found around them, and pronounced philosophy incapable of producing ideas for the reform of the world.

The Bush regime thus took shape as a bureaucratic-authoritarian stewardship of the financial interests of Wall Street and the City of London. Many saw in the Bush team the patrician financiers of the Nelson Rockefeller administration that never was. The groups in society which were to be served were so narrowly restricted that the Bush administration often looked like a government that had totally separated itself from the underlying society and had constituted itself to govern in the interests of the bureaucracy itself. Since Bush was irrevocably committed to carrying forward the policies that had been consolidated and institutionalized during the previous eight years, the regime became more and more rigid and inflexible. Active opposition, or even the dislocations occasioned by administration policies were therefore dealt with by the repressive means of the police state. The Bush regime could not govern, but it could indict, and the Discrediting Committee was always ready to vilify. Some observers spoke of a new form of Bonapartism *sui generis,* but the most accurate description for the Bush combination was the "administrative fascism" coined by political prisoner Lyndon LaRouche, who was thrown in jail just seven days after the Bush inauguration.

The Bush Cabinet

Bush's cabinet reflected several sets of optimizing criteria:

The best way to attain a top cabinet post was to belong to a family that had been allied with the Bush-Walker clan over a period of at least half a century, and to have served as a functionary or fundraiser for the Bush campaign. This applied to Secretary of State James Baker III, Treasury Secretary Nicholas Brady, Commerce Secretary Robert Mosbacher, and Bush's White House counsel and top political adviser, C. Boyden Gray.

A second royal road to high office was to have been an officer of Kissinger Associates, the international consulting firm set up by Bush's lifelong patron, Henry Kissinger. In this category we find

Gen. Brent Scowcroft, the former chief of the Kiss. Ass. Washington office, and Lawrence Eagleburger, the dissipated wreck who was named to the number two post in the State Department, undersecretary of state. Eagleburger had been the president of Kissinger Associates. The ambassadorial (or proconsul) list was also rife with Kissingerian pedigrees: a prominent one was John Negroponte, Bush's ambassador to Mexico.

Overlapping with this last group were the veterans of the 1974– 77 Ford administration. National Security Council Director Brent Scowcroft, for example, was simply returning to the job that he had held under Ford as Kissinger's alter ego inside the White House. Dick Cheney, who eventually became Secretary of Defense, had been Ford's White House chief of staff. Cheney had been executive assistant to the director of Nixon's Office of Economic Opportunity way back in 1969. In 1971, he had joined Nixon's White House staff as Don Rumsfeld's deputy. From 1971 to 1973, Cheney was at the Cost of Living Council, working as an enforcer for the infamous Phase II wage freeze in Nixon's "Economic Stabilization Program." The charming Carla Hills, who became Bush's trade representative, had been Ford's Secretary of Housing and Urban Development. William Seidman and James Baker (and Federal Reserve Board Chairman Alan Greenspan, a Reagan holdover who was the chairman of Ford's Council of Economic Advisers) had also been in the picture under Gerry Ford.

Bush also extended largesse to those who had assisted him in the election campaign just concluded. At the top of this list was Governor John Sununu of New Hampshire, who would have qualified as the modern Nostradamus for his exact prediction of Bush's 9 percent margin of victory over Dole in the New Hampshire primary—unless he had helped to arrange it with vote fraud.

Another way to carry off a top plum in the Bush regime was to have participated in the coverup of the Iran-Contra scandal. The leading role in that coverup had been assumed by Reagan's own blue ribbon commission of notables, the Tower Commission, which carried out the White House's own in-house review of what had allegedly gone wrong, and had scapegoated Don Regan for a series of misdeeds that actually belonged at the doorstep of George Bush. The members of that board were former GOP Senator John Tower of Texas, Gen. Brent Scowcroft, and former Sen. Edmund Muskie, who had been Secretary of State for Carter after the resignation of Cyrus Vance. Scowcroft, who shows up under many headings, was ensconced at the NSC. Bush's original candidate for Secretary of Defense was John Tower, who had been the point man of the

1986–87 coverup of Iran-Contra during the months before the congressional investigating committees formally got into the act. Tower's nomination was rejected by the Senate after he was accused of being drunken and promiscuous by Paul Weyrich, a Buckleyite activist, and others. Some observers thought that the Tower nomination had been deliberately torpedoed by Bush's own discrediting committee so as to avoid the presence of a top cabinet officer with the ability to blackmail Bush. Perhaps Tower had overplayed his hand. In any case, Dick Cheney, a Wyoming Congressman with strong intelligence community connections, was speedily nominated and confirmed after Tower had been shot down, prompting speculation that Cheney was the one Bush had really wanted all the time.

Another Iran-Contra veteran in line to get a reward was Bush's former national security adviser, Don Gregg, who had served Bush since at least the time of the 1976 Koreagate scandal. Gregg, as we have seen, was more than willing to commit the most maladroit and blatant perjury in order to save his boss from the wolves (see Chapter 17). Later, when William Webster retired as Director of the CIA, there were persistent rumors that the hyperthyroid Bush had originally demanded that Don Gregg be nominated to take his place. According to these reports, it required all the energy of Bush's handlers to convince the President that Gregg was too dirty to pass confirmation; Bush relented, but then announced to his dismayed and exhausted staff that his second and non-negotiable choice for Langley was Robert Gates, the former CIA Deputy Director who had been working as Scowcroft's number two at the National Security Council. The problem was that Gates, who had already dropped out of an earlier confirmation battle for the CIA Director's post, was about as thoroughly compromised as Don Gregg. But at that point, Bush could not be budged a second time, so the name of Gates was sent to the Senate, bringing the entire Iran-Contra complex into full public view once again. As it turned out, the Bush Democrats in the Senate proved more than willing to approve Gates.

Still on the Iran-Contra list was Gen. Colin Powell, whom Bush appointed as Chairman of the Joint Chiefs of Staff. After Vice Admiral John Poindexter and Lt. Col. Oliver North had departed from the Old Executive Office Building in November 1986, Reagan had appointed Frank Carlucci to lead the NSC. Carlucci had brought along General Powell, who had been commanding an army corps in Germany. With Colin Powell as his deputy, Carlucci cleaned up the Augean stables of the OEOB-NSC complex in such a way as to minimize damage to Bush. Powell was otherwise a protégé of the very Anglophile Caspar Weinberger, and of Carlucci, a man with strong links to Project Democracy and to the Sears, Roebuck interests.

The State Department, too, had its Iran-Contra coverup brigade. First came Thomas R. Pickering, chosen by Bush to take over his old post as U.S. ambassador to the United Nations, a job with cabinet rank. When Pickering was U.S. ambassador to El Salvador during the 1984–85 period, he helped arrange shipment of more than $1 million of military equipment to the Contras, all during a time when this was forbidden by U.S. law, according to his own testimony before the congressional Iran-Contra investigating committees. Pickering did not report any of his doings to the State Department, but instead kept in close touch with Bushmen Don Gregg, Felix Rodriguez and Oliver North. Pickering, when he was ambassador to Israel in 1985–86, was also in on Israeli third-country arms shipments to Iran, that were supposed to secure the release of certain hostages held in nearby Lebanon.[3] This vulgar, gun-running filibusterer is now the arrogant spokesman for Bush's New World Order among the five permanent members of the United Nations Security Council, where he dispenses imperial threats and platitudes.

Still on the Iran-Contra coverup honors list we find Reginald Bartholomew, Bush's choice as undersecretary of state for security affairs, science and technology. Bartholomew was U.S. ambassador in Beirut in September–November 1985, when an Israeli shipment of 508 U.S.-made TOW antitank missiles was followed by the release of Rev. Benjamin Weir, an American hostage held by the pro-Iranian Islamic Jihad. According to the testimony of then Secretary of State George Shultz to the Tower Commission, Bartholomew was working closely with Oliver North on a scheme to use Delta Force commandos to free any hostages not spontaneously released by Islamic Jihad. According to Shultz, Bartholomew told him on September 4, 1985 that "North was handling an operation that would lead to the release of all seven hostages."[4] Needless to say, the actual transactions involved not force but massive support to the terrorists with payments of cash and weapons.

Other choice appointments went to long-time members of the Bush network. These included Manuel Lujan, who was tapped for the Department of the Interior, and former Rep. Ed Derwinski, who was given the Veterans Administration, shortly to be upgraded to a cabinet post. A prominent figure of Bush's first year in office was William Reilly, tapped to be administrator of the Environmental Protection Agency, the green police of the regime. Reilly had been closely associated with the oligarchical financier Russell Train at the U.S. branch of Prince Philip's World Wildlife Fund and the Conservation Foundation.

So many top cabinet posts were thus assigned on the basis of direct personal services rendered to George Bush that the collegial principle of any oligarchic system would appear to have been neglected. There were relatively few key posts left over for distribution to political-financial factions who might reasonably expect to be brought on board by being given a seat at the cabinet table. Richard Thornburgh, a creature of the Mellon interests who had been given his job under Reagan, was allowed to stay on, but this led to a constant guerrilla war between Thornburgh and James Baker with the obvious issue being the 1996 succession to Bush. Clayton Yeutter went to the Department of Agriculture because that was what the international grain cartel wanted. The choice of Jack Kemp, a 1988 presidential candidate with a loyal conservative-populist base, for Housing and Urban Development, appeared inspired more by Bush's desire to prevent a challenge from emerging on his right in the GOP primaries of 1992 than by the need to cater to an identifiable financier faction. The tapping of Reagan's Secretary of Education, William Bennett, a leading right-wing ideologue and possible presidential prospect, to be Drug Czar, is a further example of the same thinking. The selection of Elizabeth Hanford Dole to be Secretary of Labor was dictated by similar intra-GOP considerations, namely the need to placate the angry Republican Minority Leader, Sen. Bob Dole of Kansas, a darling of Dwayne Andreas of Archer Daniels Midland and the rest of the grain cartel.

Later reshuffling of the Bush cabinet has conformed to the needs of getting an intrinsically weak candidate reelected, especially by accentuating the Southern Strategy: When Lauro Cavazo left the Department of Education, he was replaced by former Tennessee Governor Lamar Alexander. When Bennett had to be replaced as Drug Czar, the nod went to another Republican former southern governor, Bob Martinez of Florida. All of this was to build the southern base for 1992. When Thornburgh quit as Attorney General to run for the Senate in Pennsylvania in the vain hope of positioning himself for 1996, Bush tapped Thornburgh's former number two at Justice, William P. Barr, who had been a CIA officer when Bush was CIA Director in 1976, for this key police-state post.

But all in all, this cabinet was very much an immediate reflection of the personal network and interests of George Bush, even more than it represented the principal financier factions who control the United States. We see here once more the very strong sense of national government as personal property for private exploitation which was evident in Bush's oil price ploy of 1986, and which also characterized his choreography of the Gulf crisis of 1990–91—as we shall see. This approach to cabinet appointments could give rise to a surprising weakness on the part of the Bush regime, should the principal financier factions become disaffected in the wake of the banking and currency panic toward which Bush's policies are steering the country.

Bush's shameless exploitation of political appointments and plum jobs for blatant personal advantage became a national scandal when he began to assign certain ambassadorial posts. It became clear that the job of representing the United States abroad had been virtually sold at auction, with the most flagrant disregard for qualifications and ability, in return for cash contributions to the Bush campaign and the coffers of the Republican Party. These appointments were carried out with Bush's approval by a transition team of GOP pollster Bob Teeter, Bush's campaign aide Craig Fuller, who had lost out on his bid to be White House chief of staff, campaign press secretary Sheila Tate, and long-time Bush staffer Chase Untermeyer. Calvin Howard Wilkins, Jr., who had given over $178,000 to the GOP over a number of years, including $92,000 to the Kansas Republican National State Election Committee on September 6, 1988, became the new ambassador to the Netherlands. Penne Percy Korth was Bush's selection for ambassador to Mauritius; Ms. Korth was a crack GOP fundraiser. Della M. Newman, tapped for New Zealand, had been Bush's campaign chairman in Washington state. Joy Silverman, Bush's choice for Barbados, had contributed $180,000. Joseph B. Gilderhorn, destined for Switzerland, had coughed up $200,000. Fred Bush, allegedly not a relative but certainly a former aide and leading fundraiser, was the new President's original pick for Luxembourg. Joseph Zappala, who gave $100,000, was put up for the Madrid embassy. Melvin Sembler, another member of Team 100, was tapped for Australia. Fred Zeder, a Bush crony who had already been the ambassador to Micronesia, was nominated for the Overseas Private Investment Corporation.[5]

The Dismal Hundred Days

Bush's first hundred days in office fulfilled Fukuyama's prophecy that the End of History would be "a very sad time." If "post-history" meant that very little was accomplished, Bush filled the bill. Three weeks after his inauguration, Bush addressed a joint session of the Congress on certain changes that he had proposed in Reagan's last budget. The litany was hollow and predictable: Bush wanted to be the Education President, but was willing to spend less than a billion dollars of new money in order to do it. He froze the U.S. military budget, and announced a review of the previous policy toward the Soviet Union. This last point meant that Bush wanted to wait to see how fast the Soviets would in fact collapse before he would even discuss trade normalization, which had been the perspective held out to Moscow by Reagan and others. Bush said he wanted to join with Drug Czar William Bennett in "leading the charge" in the war on drugs.

Bush also wanted to be the Environmental President. This was a far more serious aspiration. Shortly after the election, Bush had attended the gala centennial awards dinner of the very oligarchical National Geographic Society, for many years a personal fiefdom of the feudal-minded Grosvenor family. Bush promised the audience that night that there was "one issue my administration is going to address, and I'm talking about the environment." Bush confided that he had been coordinating his plans with British Prime Minister Margaret Thatcher, and that he had agreed with her on the necessity for "international cooperation" on green issues. "We will support you," intoned Gilbert Grosvenor, a fellow Yale alumnus, ". . . Planet Earth is at risk."[6]

In order to be the Environmental President, Bush was willing to propose a disastrous Clean Air Act that would drain the economy of hundreds of billions of dollars over time in the name of fighting acid rain. Bush's first hundred days coincided with the notable phenomenon of the "greening" of Margaret Thatcher, who had previously denounced environmentalists as "the enemy within," and fellow travelers of the British Labour Party and the loonie left. Thatcher's resident ideologue, Nicholas Ridley, had referred to the green movement in Britain as "pseudo-Marxists." But in the early months of 1989, allegedly under the guidance of Sir Crispin Tickell, the British ambassador to the United Nations, Thatcher embraced the orthodoxy that the erosion of the ozone layer, the greenhouse effect and acid rain—every one of them a pseudo-scientific hoax— were indeed at the top of the list of the urgent problems of the human species. Thatcher's acceptance of the green orthodoxy permitted the swift establishment of a total environmentalist-Malthusian consensus in the European Community, the Group of 7 and other key international forums.

Characteristically, Bush followed Thatcher's lead, as he would on so many other issues. During the first hundred days, Bush called for the elimination of all chlorofluorocarbons (CFCs) by the end of the century, thus accepting the position assumed by the European

Community as a result of Mrs. Thatcher's turning green. Bush told the National Academy of Sciences that new "scientific advancements" had permitted the identification of a serious threat to the ozone layer; Bush stressed the need to "reduce CFCs that deplete our precious upper atmospheric resources." A treaty had been signed in Montreal in 1987 that called for cutting the production of CFCs by one half within a ten-year period. "But recent studies indicate that this 50 percent reduction may not be enough," Bush now opined. Senator Albert Gore, Jr. of Tennessee was calling for complete elimination of CFCs within five years. Here a pattern emerged that was to be repeated frequently during the Bush years: Bush would make sweeping concessions to the environmentalist Luddites, but would then be denounced by them for measures that were insufficiently radical. This would be the case when Bush's Clean Air Bill was going through the Congress during the summer of 1990.

(It should also be noted that the Du Pont interests, a leading light of the Eastern Establishment, stand to make a fortune through the sale of CFC substitutes on which they hold the patents, such as HFC–134a. Three newly built Du Pont plants are already producing CFC substitutes.)

After Bush's appearance before the Congress with his revised budget, the new regime exploited the honeymoon to seal a sweetheart contract with the rubber-stamp congressional Democrats, who under no circumstances could be confused with an opposition. The *de facto* one-party state was alive and well, personified by milquetoast Senator George Mitchell of Maine, the Democrats' Majority Leader. The collusion between Bush and the Democratic leadership involved new sleight of hand in order to meet the deficit-reduction targets stipulated by the Gramm-Rudman-Hollings law. This involved mobilizing more than $100 billion from surpluses in the Social Security, highway and other special trust funds which had not previously been counted. The Democrats also went along with a $28 billion package of asset sales, financing tricks and unspecified new revenues. They also bought Bush's rosy economic forecast of higher economic growth and lower interest rates. Senate Majority Leader Mitchell, accepting his pathetic rubber-stamp role, commented only that "much sterner measures will be required in the future." Since the Democrats were incapable of proposing an economic recovery program in order to deal with the depression, they were condemned to give Bush what he wanted. This particular swindle would come back to haunt all concerned, but not before the spectacular budget debacle of October 1990.

In the spring of 1990, according to an estimate by Sid Taylor of the National Taxpayers Union, the total potential liabilities of the federal government exceeded $14 trillion. At that point, the official national debt totaled $2.8 trillion, but this estimate excluded the commitments of the Federal Savings and Loan Insurance Corporation, the Federal Deposit Insurance Corporation, the Pension Benefit Guarantee Corporation, and other agencies.

Bush's inability to pull his regime together for a serious round of domestic austerity was not appreciated by the crowd at the Bank for International Settlements in Geneva. Evelyn Rothschild's London *Economist* summed up the international banking view of George's temporizing on this score with its headline, "Bush Bumbles."

A few weeks into the new administration, it was the collapse of the FSLIC, studiously ignored by the waning Reagan administration, that reached critical mass. On February 6, 1989, Bush announced measures that his image-mongers billed as the most sweeping and significant piece of financial legislation since the creation of the Federal Reserve Board on the eve of World War I. This was the savings and loan bailout, a new orgy in the monetization of debt and a giant step toward the consolidation of a neo-fascist corporate state.

At the heart of Bush's policy was his refusal to acknowledge the existence of an economic crisis of colossal proportions, which had among its symptoms the gathering collapse of the real estate market after the stock market crash of October 1987. The sequence of a stock market panic, followed by a real estate and banking crisis, closely followed the sequence of the Great Depression of the 1930s. But Bush violently rejected the existence of such a crisis, and was grimly determined to push on with more of the same. This meant that the federal government would simply take control of the savings banks, the majority of which were bankrupt or imminently bankrupt. The depositors might get their money, but the result would be the debasement of the currency and a deepening depression all around. In the process, the U.S. government would become one of the main owners of real estate, buildings and the worthless junk bonds that had been spewed out by Bush's friend Henry Kravis and his partner Michael Milken during the heady days of the boom.

The federal government would create a new world of bonded debt to pay for the savings banks that would be seized. When Bush announced his bailout that February, he stated that $40 billion had already been poured into the S&L sinkhole, and that he proposed to issue an additional $50 billion in new bonds through a financing corporation, a subsidiary of the new Resolution Trust Corporation. By August 1989, when Bush's legislation had been passed, the estimated cost of the S&L bailout had increased to $164 billion over a period of ten years, with $20 billion of that scheduled to be spent by the end of September 1989.

Within a few months, Bush was forced to increase his estimates once again. "It's a whale of a mess, and we'll see where we go," Bush told a group of newspaper editorial writers at the White House in mid-December. "We've had this one refinancing. I am told that that might not be enough." By this time, academic experts were suggesting that the bailout might exceed the administration's $164 billion by as much as $100 billion more. Every new estimate was swiftly overtaken by the ghastly spectacle of a real estate market in free fall, with no bottom in sight. The growing public awareness of this situation, compounded by the ongoing bankruptcy of the commercial banking system as well, would lead in July 1990 to a very ugly public relations crisis for the Bush regime around the role of the President's son (and Scott Hinckley's old friend) Neil Bush, in the insolvency of the Silverado Savings and Loan of Denver, Colorado. One of the obvious reasons for Bush's enthusiastic choice of war in the Persian Gulf was the need to get Neil Bush off the front page. But even the Gulf war bought no respite in the collapse of the real estate markets and the chain-reaction bankruptcies of the savings banks: By the summer of 1991, federal regulators were seizing S&Ls at the rate of just under one every business day, and the estimates of the total price tag of the bailout had ballooned to over $500 billion, with every certainty that this figure would also be surpassed.[7]

The carnage among the S&Ls did not prevent Bush from seeking an increase in the U.S. contribution to the International Monetary Fund, the main agency of a world austerity that claims upwards of 50 million human lives each year as the needless victims of its Malthusian conditionalities. The members of the IMF had been debating an increase in the funds each member must pay into the IMF (which has been bankrupt for years as a matter of reality), with Managing Director Michel Camdessus proposing a 100 percent increase, and Britain and Saudi Arabia arguing for a much smaller 25 percent hike. Bush attempted to mediate and resolve the dispute with a proposal for a 35 percent increase, equal to an $8 billion additional payment by the U.S. This sum was equal to more than three times the yearly expenditure for the highly successful Women, Infants and Children (WIC) program of the U.S. Department of Agriculture, savagely cut during Bush's first year, which attempted to provide a high-protein and balanced food supplement to mothers and their offspring.[8]

As the depression deepened, Bush had only one idea: to reduce the capital gains tax rate from 28 percent to 15 percent. This was a proposal for a direct public subsidy to the vulture legions of Kravis, Liedtke, Pickens, Milken, Brady, Mosbacher and the rest of Bush's apostles of greed. The Bushmen estimated that a capital gains tax reduction in this magnitude would cost the Treasury some $25 billion in lost receipts over six years, a crass underestimate. These funds, argued the Bushmen, would then be invested in high-tech plant and equipment, creating new jobs and new production. In reality, the funds would have flowed into bigger and better leveraged buyouts, which were still being attempted after the crash of the junk bond market with the failure of the United Airlines buyout in October 1989. But Bush had no serious interest in, or even awareness of, commodity production. His policies had now brought the country to the brink of a financial panic in which 75 percent of the current prices of all stocks, bonds, debentures, mortgages and other financial paper would be wiped out.

If there was a constant note in Bush's first year in office, it was a callously flaunted contempt for the misery of the American people. During the spring of 1989, the Congress passed a bill that would have raised the minimum wage in interstate commerce from $3.55 per hour to $4.55 per hour by a series of increments over three years. This legislation would even have permitted a subminimum wage that could be paid to certain newly hired workers over a 60-day training period. Bush vetoed this measure because the $4.55 minimum wage was 30 cents an hour higher than he wanted, and because he demanded a subminimum wage for all new employees for the first six months on the job, regardless of their previous experience or training. On June 14, 1989, the House of Representatives failed to override this veto, by a margin of 37 votes. (Later, Bush signed legislation to raise the minimum wage to $4.25 per hour over two years, with a subminimum training wage applicable only to teenagers and only during the first 90 days of the teenagers' employment, with the possibility of a second 90-day training wage stint if they moved on to a different employer.)[9]

This was the same George Bush who had proposed $164 billion for bankrupt S&Ls, and $8 billion for the International Monetary Fund, all without batting an eye.

This is also the George Bush who, customarily during holiday periods, joins his millionaire crony William Stamps ("Auschwitz") Farish III at his Lazy F Ranch near Beeville, Texas, for the two men's traditional holiday quail hunt. This is the same William Stamps Farish III whose grandfather, the president of Standard Oil of New

Jersey, had financed Heinrich Himmler (see Chapter 3). William Stamps Farish III's investment bank in Houston, W.S. Farish & Co., had at one time managed the blind trust into which Bush had placed his personal investment portfolio. Farish was rich enough to vaunt five addresses: Beeville, Texas; Lane's End Farm in the Versailles, Kentucky bluegrass; Florida, and two others. Farish's hobby for the past several decades has been the creation of his own top-flight farm for the raising of thoroughbred horses, the 3,000-acre Lazy F Ranch, with its ten horse barns and four sumptuous residences. Over the years, Farish has saddled winners in the 1972 Preakness and the 1987 Belmont Stakes, and bred 80 stakes winners over the past decade. Farish, who is married to Sarah Sharp, the daughter of a Du Pont heiress, had worked with Bush as an aide during the 1964 Senate campaign.

Farish III is rich enough to extend his largesse even to Queen Elizabeth II of the United Kingdom, probably the richest individual in the world. The queen regularly visits Farish's horse farm, traveling by Royal Air Force jetliner to the Blue Grass Airport in Lexington, Kentucky, accompanied by mares which Her Majesty wishes to breed with Farish's million-dollar prize stallions. Farish magnanimously waives the usual stud fees for the queen, resulting in an estimated savings to Her Majesty of some $800,000.

Farish III has been described as the Bush regime's counterpart to Bebe Rebozo, Richard Nixon's sleazy crony. According to Bush, when he is watching movies, hunting and playing tennis with his old friend Farish, "we talk about issues. He's very up on things, but it's a comfortable thing, not probing beyond what I want to say." With a cabal of friends and advisers like William Stamps Farish III and Henry Kravis, we begin to comprehend the wellsprings of Bush's policies of parasitical looting of infrastructure and the work force.[10]

Smear, Scandal and Sanctions

For George Bush, the exercise of power has always been inseparable from the use of smear, scandal, and the final sanctions of police-state methods against political rivals and other branches of government. A classic example was the Koreagate scandal of 1976, unleashed with the help of Bush's long-time retainer, Don Gregg. It will be recalled that Koreagate included the toppling of Democratic Speaker of the House Carl Albert of Oklahoma, who quietly retired from the House at the end of 1976. That was in the year when Bush had returned from Beijing to Langley. Was it merely coincidence that, in the first year of Bush's tenure in the White House, not just the Democratic Speaker of the House, but also the House Majority Whip, were driven from office?

The campaign against Speaker of the House Jim Wright was spearheaded by Georgia Republican Congressman Newt Gingrich, a typical "wedge issue" ideologue of the GOP's Southern Strategy. Gingrich's campaign against Wright could never have succeeded without systematic support from the news media, who regularly trumpeted his charges and lent him a wholly undeserved importance. Gingrich's pretext was a story about the financing of a small book in which Wright had collected some of his old speeches, which Gingrich claimed had been sold to lobbyists in such a way as to constitute an unreported gift in violation of the House rules. One of Gingrich's first steps when he launched the assault on Wright during 1988 was to send letters to Bush and to Assistant Attorney General William Weld, whose family investment bank, White Weld, had purchased Uncle Herbie Walker's G.H. Walker & Co. brokerage when Bush's favorite uncle was ready to retire. Newt Gingrich wrote: "May I suggest, the next time the news media asks about corruption in the White House, you ask them about corruption in the Speaker's office?" A similar letter went out from the "Conservative Campaign Fund" to all GOP House candidates with the message: "We write to encourage you to make . . . House Speaker Jim Wright a major issue in your campaign."[11] Bush placed himself in the vanguard of this campaign.

When Bush, in the midst of his presidential campaign, was asked by reporters about the investigation of Reagan Attorney General Edwin Meese (no friend of Bush) concerning his dealings with the Wedtech Corporation, he replied: "You talk about Ed Meese. How about talking about what Common Cause raised against the Speaker the other day? Are they going to go for an independent counsel so the nation will have this full investigation? Why don't people call out for that? I will right now. I think they ought to."[12] Reagan followed Bush's lead in calling for Wright to be investigated.

In January–February 1989, the House took under consideration a pay increase for members. Both Reagan and Bush had endorsed such a pay increase, but Lee Atwater, now installed at the Republican National Committee, launched a series of mailings and public statements to make the pay increase into a new wedge issue. It was a brilliant success, with the help of a few old Prescott Bush strings pulled on key talk show hosts across the country. Bush accomplished the coup of thoroughly destabilizing the Congress at the outset of his tenure. Jim Wright was hounded out of office and into retirement a few months later, followed by Tony Coelho, the Democratic Whip.

What remained was the meek Tom Foley, a pliable rubber stamp, and Richard Gephardt, who briefly got in trouble with Bush during 1989, but who found his way to a deal with Bush that allowed him to rubber-stamp Bush's "fast track" formula for the free trade zone with Mexico, which effectively killed any hope of resistance to that measure. The fall of Jim Wright was a decisive step in the domestication of the Congress by the Bush regime.

Bush was also able to rely on an extensive swamp of "Bush Democrats" who would support his proposals under virtually all circumstances. The basis of this phenomenon was the obvious fact that the national leadership of the Democratic Party had long been a gang of Harrimanites. The Brown Brothers Harriman grip on the Democratic Party had been represented by W. Averell Harriman until his death, and after that was carried on by his widow, Pamela Churchill Harriman, the former wife of Sir Winston Churchill's alcoholic son, Randolph. The very extensive Meyer Lansky/Anti-Defamation League networks among the Democrats were oriented toward cooperation with Bush, sometimes directly, and sometimes through the orchestration of gang vs. countergang charades for the manipulation of public opinion. A special source of Bush strength among southern Democrats is the cooperation between Skull and Bones and southern jurisdiction freemasons in the tradition of the infamous Albert Pike. These southern jurisdiction freemasonic networks have been most obviously decisive in the Senate, where a group of southern Democratic Senators has routinely joined with Bush to block overrides of Bush's many vetoes, or to provide a pro-Bush majority on key votes like the Gulf war resolution.

Bush's style in the Oval Office was described during this period as "extremely secretive." Many members of Bush's staff felt that the President had his own long-term plans, but refused to discuss them with his own top White House personnel. During Bush's first year, the White House was described as "a tomb," without the usual dense barrage of leaks, counter-leaks, trial balloons and signals which government insiders customarily employ to influence public debate on policy matters. Bush is said to employ a "need to know" approach even with his closest White House collaborators, keeping each one of them in the dark about what the others are doing. Aides have complained of their inability to keep up with Bush's phone calls when he goes into his famous "speed-dialing mode," in which he can contact dozens of politicians, bankers or world leaders within a couple of hours. Unauthorized passages of information from one office to another inside the White House constitute leaks in Bush's opinion, and he has been at pains to suppress them. When information was given to the press about a planned meeting with Gorbachov, Bush threatened his top-level advisers: "If we cannot maintain proper secrecy with this group, we will cut the circle down."

Bush routinely humiliates and mortifies his subordinates. This recalls his style in dealing with the numerous hapless servants and domestics who populated his patrician youth; it may also have been reinforced by the characteristic style of Henry Kissinger. If advisers or staff dare to manifest disagreement, the typical Bush retort is a whining "If you're so damned smart, why are you doing what you're doing and I'm the president of the United States?"[13]

In one sense, Bush's style reflects his desire to seem "absolute and autocratic" in the tradition of the Romanov czars and other Byzantine rulers. He refuses to be advised or dissuaded on many issues, relying on his enraged, hyperthyroid intuitions. More profoundly, Bush's "absolute and autocratic" act is a cover for the fact that many of his initiatives, ideas and policies came from outside of the U.S. government, since they originated in the rarefied ether of those international finance circles where names like Harriman, Kravis and Gammell are the coin of the realm. Indeed, many of Bush's policies come from outside of the United States altogether, deriving from the oligarchical financial circles of the City of London. The classic case is the Gulf crisis of 1990–91. When the documents on the Bush administration are finally thrown open to the public, it is a safe bet that some top British financiers and Foreign Office types will be found to have combined remarkable access and power with a non-existent public profile.

The Tiananmen Disgrace

One of the defining moments in the first year of the Bush presidency was his reaction to the Tiananmen massacre of June 4, 1989. No one can forget the magnificent movement of the anti-totalitarian Chinese students, who used the occasion of the funeral of Hu Yaobang in the spring of 1989 to launch a movement of protest and reform against the monstrous dictatorship of Deng Xiaoping, Yang Shankun, and Prime Minister Li Peng. As the portrait of the old butcher Mao Zedong looked down from the former imperial palace, the students erected a statue of liberty and filled the square with the Ode to Joy from Beethoven's Ninth Symphony. By the end of May, it was clear that the Deng regime was attempting to pull itself together to attempt a convulsive massacre of its political opposition. At this point, it is likely that a pointed and unequivocal public warning from the United States government might have avoided the looming bloody crackdown against the students. Even a warning through secret diplomatic channels might have sufficed. Bush undertook neither, and he must bear responsibility for this blatant omission.

The nonviolent protest of the students was then crushed by the martial law troops of the hated and discredited Communist regime. Untold thousands of students were killed outright, and thousands more died in the merciless death hunt against political dissidents which followed. Mankind was horrified. For Bush, however, the main considerations were that Deng Xiaoping was part of his own personal network, with whom Bush had maintained close contact since at least 1975. Bush's devotion to the immoral British doctrine of "geopolitics" further dictated that, unless and until the U.S.S.R. had totally collapsed as a military power, the U.S. alliance with China as the second strongest land power must be maintained at all costs. Additionally, Bush was acutely sensitive to the views on China policy held by his mentor, Henry Kissinger, whose paw-prints were still to be found all over U.S. relations with Deng. In the wake of Tiananmen, Kissinger (who had lucrative consulting contracts with the Beijing regime) was exceptionally vocal in condemning any proposed U.S. countermeasures against Deng. These were the decisive factors in Bush's reactions to Tiananmen.

In the pre-1911 imperial court of China, the etiquette of the Forbidden City required that a person approaching the throne of the "Son of Heaven" must prostrate himself before that living deity, touching both hands and the forehead to the floor three times. This is the celebrated "kow-tow." And it was "kow-tow" which sprang to the lips and pens of commentators all over the world as they observed Bush's elaborate propitiation of the Deng regime. Even cynics were astounded that Bush could be so deferential to a regime that was obviously so hated by its own population that it had to be considered as being on its last legs; the best estimate was that when octogenarian Deng finally died, the Communist regime would pass from the scene with him.

In a press conference held on June 9, in the immediate wake of the massacre, Bush astounded even the meretricious White House press corps by his mild and obsequious tone toward Deng and his cohorts. Bush limited his retaliation to a momentary cutoff of some military sales. That would be all: "I'm one who lived in China; I understand the importance of the relationship with the Chinese people and with the government. It is in the interest of the United

States to have good relations. . . ."[14] Would Bush consider further measures, such as the minor step of temporarily recalling the U.S. ambassador, Bush's CIA crony and fellow patrician James Lilly?

> Well, some have suggested, for example, to show our forcefulness, that I bring the American ambassador back. I disagree with that 180 degrees, and we've seen in the last few days a very good reason to have him there. . . .
>
> What I do want to do is take whatever steps are most likely to demonstrate the concern that America feels. And I think I've done that. I'll be looking for other ways to do it if we possibly can.

This was the wimp with a vengeance, groveling and scraping like Neville Chamberlain before the dictators, but there was more to come. As part of his meek and pathetic response, Bush had pledged to terminate all "high-level exchanges" with the Deng crowd. With this public promise, Bush had cynically lied to the American people. Shortly before Bush's invasion of Panama in December, it became known that Bush had dispatched the two most prominent Kissinger clones in his retinue, NSC Chairman Brent Scowcroft and Undersecretary of State Lawrence Eagleburger, on a secret mission to Beijing over the July 4th weekend, less than a month after the massacre in Tiananmen. Bush regarded this mission as so sensitive that he reportedly kept it a secret even from White House Chief of Staff Sununu, who only learned of the trip when two of his aides stumbled across the paper trail of the planning. The story about Scowcroft and Eagleburger, both veterans of Kissinger Associates, spending the glorious Fourth toasting the butchers of Beijing was itself leaked in the wake of a high-profile public mission to China involving the same Kissingerian duo that started December 7, 1989. Bush's cover story for the second trip was that he wanted to get a briefing to Deng on the results of the Bush-Gorbachov Malta summit, which had just concluded. The second trip was supposed to lead to the quick release of Chinese physicist and dissident Fang Lizhi, who had taken refuge in the U.S. embassy in Beijing during the massacre; this did not occur until some time later.

During a press conference primarily devoted to the ongoing Panama invasion, Bush provided an unambiguous signal that the inspiration for his China policy, and indeed for his entire foreign policy, was Kissinger:

> There's a lot of going on that, in the conduct of the foreign policy or a debate within the U.S. government, has to be sorted out without

the spotlight of the news. There has to be that way. The whole opening to China would never have happened . . . if Kissinger hadn't undertaken that mission. It would have fallen apart. So you have to use your own judgment.[15]

The news of Bush's secret diplomacy in favor of Deng caused a widespread wave of sincere and healthy public disgust with Bush, but this was shortly overwhelmed by the jingoist hysteria that accompanied Bush's invasion of Panama.

Bush's handling of the issue of the immigration status of the Chinese students who had enrolled at U.S. universities also illuminated Bush's character in the wake of Tiananmen. In Bush's pronouncements in the immediate wake of the massacre, he absurdly asserted that there were no Chinese students who wanted political asylum here, but also promised that the visas of these (non-existent) students would be extended so that they would not be forced to return to political persecution and possible death in mainland China. It later turned out that Bush had neglected to promulgate the executive orders that would have been necessary. In response to Bush's prevarication about the lives and well-being of the Chinese students, the Congress subsequently passed legislation that would have waived the requirement that holders of J-visas, the type commonly obtained by Chinese students, be required to return to their home country for two years before being able to apply for permanent residence in the U.S. Bush, in an act of loathsome cynicism, vetoed this bill. The House voted to override by a majority of 390 to 25, but Bush Democrats in the Senate allowed Bush's veto to be sustained by a vote of 62 to 37. Bush, squirming under the broad public obloquy brought on by his despicable behavior, finally issued regulations that would temporarily waive the requirement of returning home for most of the students.

Bush came back from his summer in Kennebunkport with a series of "policy initiatives" that turned out to be no more than demagogic photo opportunities. In early September, Bush made his first scheduled evening television address to the nation on the subject of his alleged war on drugs. The highlight of this speech was the moment when Bush produced a bag of crack which had been sold in a transaction in Lafayette Park, directly across the street from the White House. The transaction had been staged with the help of the Drug Enforcement Administration. This was George Bush, the friend of Felix Rodriguez, Hafez al Assad, Hashemi Rafsanjani and Don Aronow. The funds and the targets set for Bush's program were minimal. A real war on drugs remained a vital necessity, but it was clear that there would be none under the Bush administration.

Later the same month, on September 27–28, Bush met with the governors of all 50 states in Charlottesville, Virginia for what was billed as an "education summit." This was truly a glorified photo opportunity, since all discussions were kept rigorously off the record, and everything was carefully choreographed by White House image-mongers.

Ironically, the best perspective on Bush's "education summit" eyewash came from within his own regime. Obviously piqued at the bad reviews his previous performance as Reagan's Secretary of Education was getting, Bush Drug Czar William Bennett told reporters that the proceedings in Charlottesville were "standard Democratic and Republican pap—and something that rhymes with pap. Much of the discussion proceeded in a total absence of knowledge about what takes place in schools."

By the autumn of 1989, Bush was facing a crisis of confidence in his regime. His domination of Congress on all substantive matters was complete; at the same time, he had nothing to propose except vast public subsidies to bankrupt financial and speculative interests. Except for exertions to shovel hundreds of billions of dollars into Wall Street, the entire government appeared as paralyzed and adrift. This was soon accentuated by colossal upheavals in China, Eastern Europe and the U.S.S.R. On Friday, October 13, timed approximately with the second anniversary of the great stock market crash of 1987, there was a fall in the Dow Jones Industrial Average of 190.58 points during the last hour of trading. This was triggered by the failure of a labor-management group to procure sufficient financing to carry out the leveraged buyout of United Airlines. The stage for this failure had been set during the preceding weeks by the crisis of the highly leveraged retail empire or Robert Campeau, which made many junk bonds wholly illiquid for a time. The autumn was full of symptoms of a deflationary contraction of overall production and employment. For a time, Bush appeared to be approaching that delicate moment in which a President is faced with the loss of his mandate to rule.

Criticism Mounts

October 1989 was full of anxiety and apprehension about the economic future, and worry about where Bush was leading the country. Included in the many mood pieces was an evident desire of the Eastern Liberal Establishment circles to spur Bush on to more decisive and aggressive action in imposing austerity at home, and in increasing the rate of primitive accumulation in favor of the dollar abroad.

A typical sample of these October lucubrations was a widely read essay by Kevin Phillips (the traditional Republican theoretician of ethnic splitting and the Southern Strategy), entitled "George Bush and Congress—Brain-Dead Politics of '89." Phillips faulted Bush for his apparent decision "to imitate the low-key, centrist operating mode of President Dwight D. Eisenhower. But imitating Ike in the 1990s makes as little sense as trying to imitate Queen Victoria in the 1930s."[16]

Phillips catalogued the absurd complacency of the Bushmen, with Brady saying of the U.S. economy that "it couldn't get much better than it is." Phillips's basic thesis was that Bush and his ostensible opposition had joined hands simply to ignore the existence of the leading problems threatening U.S. national life, while hiding behind an "irrelevant consensus" forged 10 to 20 years in the past, and reminiscent overall of the pre-1860 tacit understanding of Democrats and Whigs to sweep sectionalism and slavery under the rug. One result of this conspiracy of the incumbents to ignore the real world was the "unhappy duality that the United States and Russia are *both* weakening empires in haphazard retreat from their post-1945 bipolar dominance."

Kevin Phillips's conclusion was that while reality might begin to force a change in the "political agenda" by 1990, it was more likely that a shift would occur in 1992 when an aroused electorate, smarting from decades of decline in standards of living and economic aspirations, might "hand out surprising political rewards. . . . Honesty's day is coming," summed up Phillips, with the clear implication that George Bush would not be a beneficiary of the new day.

Similar themes were developed in the Bonesmen's own *Time* magazine toward the end of the month, in coverage entitled "Is Government Dead?" which featured a cover picture of George Washington shedding a big tear and a blurb warning that "unwilling to lead, politicians are letting America slip into paralysis."[17] *Time* discovered that Bush and the Congress were "conspiring to hide" $96 billion of a $206 billion deficit through various stratagems, while the bill for the S&L bailout had levitated upwards to $300 billion. *Time* held up to ridicule the "paltry $115 million" Bush had offered as economic aid to Poland during his visit there during the summer. Grave responsibility for the growing malaise was assigned by *Time* to Bush: "Leadership is generally left to the President. Yet George Bush seems to have as much trouble as ever with the 'vision thing.' Handcuffed by his simplistic 'read my lips' campaign rhetoric against a tax increase as well as by his cautious personality, Bush too often appears self-satisfied and reactive."

Bush, Baker and Brady were thus confronted with some clear signals of an ugly mood of discontent on the part of key Establishment financier circles inside their own traditional base. These groups were demanding more austerity, more primitive accumulation against the U.S. population than George had been able to deliver. A further ingredient in the dangerous dissatisfaction on Wall Street and environs was that Bush had botched and bungled a U.S.-sponsored coup d'état against the Panamanian government loyal to Gen. Manuel Antonio Noriega. Noriega's survival and continued defiance of Washington seemed to certify, in the eyes of the ruling financiers, that Bush was indeed a wimp incapable of conducting their international or domestic business. By November 1989, the ten-month-old Bush regime was drifting toward the Niagara of serious trouble. It was under these circumstances that the Bush networks responded with their invasion of Panama.

Noriega and the Thornburgh Doctrine

George Bush's involvement with Panama goes back to operations conducted in Central America and the Caribbean by Senator Prescott Bush's Jupiter Island Harrimanite cabal. For the Bush clan, the cathexis of Panama is very deep, since it is bound up with the exploits of Theodore Roosevelt, the founder of the twentieth-century U.S. imperialism, which the Bush family is determined to defend to the farthest corners of the planet. It was Theodore Roosevelt who had used the U.S.S. *Nashville* and other U.S. naval forces to prevent the Colombian military from repressing the U.S.-fomented revolt of Panamanian soldiers in November 1903, thus setting the stage for the creation of an independent Panama and for the signing of the Hay-Bunau-Varilla Treaty, which created a Panama Canal Zone under U.S. control. Roosevelt's "cowboy diplomacy" had been excoriated in the U.S. press of those days as "piracy."

Theodore Roosevelt had in December 1904 expounded his so-called "Roosevelt Corollary" to the Monroe Doctrine, in reality a complete repudiation and perversion of the anti-colonial essence of John Quincy Adams's original warning to the British and other imperialists. The self-righteous Teddy Roosevelt had stated, "Chronic wrongdoing . . . may in America, as elsewhere, ultimately require intervention by some civilized nation, and in the Western Hemisphere the adherence of the United States to the Monroe Doctrine may force the United States, however reluctantly, in flagrant cases of such wrongdoing or impotence, to the exercise of an international police power."[18]

The old imperialist idea of Theodore Roosevelt was quickly revived by the Bush administration during 1989. Through a series of actions by Attorney General Richard Thornburgh, the U.S. Supreme Court, and CIA Director William Webster, the Bush regime arrogated to itself a sweeping carte blanche for extraterritorial interference in the internal affairs of sovereign states, all in open defiance of the norms of international law. These illegal innovations can be summarized under the heading of the "Thornburgh Doctrine." The Federal Bureau of Investigation arrogated to itself the "right" to search premises outside of U.S. territory and to arrest and kidnap foreign citizens outside of U.S. jurisdiction, all without the concurrence of the judicial process of the other countries whose territory was thus subject to violation. U.S. armed forces were endowed with the "right" to take police measures against civilians. The CIA demanded that an Executive Order prohibiting the participation of U.S. government officials and military personnel in the assassination of foreign political leaders, which had been issued by President Ford in October 1976, be rescinded. There is every indication that this presidential ban on assassinations of foreign officials and politicians, which had been promulgated in response to the Church and Pike Committees' investigations of CIA abuses, has indeed been abrogated. To round out this lawless package, an opinion of the U.S. Supreme Court issued on February 28, 1990 permitted U.S. officials abroad to arrest (or kidnap) and search foreign citizens without regard to the laws or policy of the foreign nation subject to this interference. Through these actions, the Bush regime effectively staked its claim to universal extraterritorial jurisdiction, the classic posture of an empire seeking to assert universal police power. The Bush regime aspired to the status of a world power *legibus solutus,* a superpower exempted from all legal restrictions.[19]

Back in January 1972, at the extraordinary session of the United Nations Security Council in Addis Ababa, the Panamanian delegate, Aquilino Boyd, had delivered a scathing condemnation of the American "occupation" of the Canal Zone, which most Panamanians found increasingly intolerable. At that time, Ambassador Bush had wormed his way out of a tough situation by pleading that Boyd was out of order, since Panama had not been placed on the agenda for the meeting. Boyd was relentless in pressing for a special session of the Security Council in Panama City at which he could bring up the issue of sovereignty over the Canal Zone and the canal. Later, in

March 1973, Bush's successor at the U.N. post, John Scali, was forced to resort to a veto in order to kill a resolution calling for "full respect for Panama's effective sovereignty over all its territory." This veto had been a big political embarrassment, since it was cast in the face of vociferous condemnation from the visitors' gallery, which was full of Panamanian patriots. To make matters worse, the U.S. had been totally isolated, with 13 countries supporting the resolution and one abstention.[20]

The hostility of the U.S. government against General Noriega was occasioned first of all by Noriega's refusal to be subservient to the U.S. policy of waging war against the Sandinista regime. This was explained by Noriega in an interview with CBS journalist Mike Wallace on February 4, 1988, in which General Noriega described the U.S. campaign against him as a "political conspiracy of the Department of Justice." General Noriega described a visit to Panama on December 17, 1985 by Admiral John Poindexter, then the chief of the U.S. National Security Council, who demanded that General Noriega join in acts of war against Nicaragua, and then threatened Panama with economic warfare and political destabilization when Noriega refused to go along with Poindexter's plans:

> Noriega: Poindexter said he came in the name of President Reagan. He said that Panama and Mexico were acting against U.S. policy in Central America because we were saying that the Nicaragua conflict must be settled peacefully. And that wasn't good enough for the plans of the Reagan administration. The single thing that will protect us from being economically and politically attacked by the United States is that we allow the Contras to be trained in Panama for the fight against Nicaragua.
>
> Wallace: He told you that you would be economically attacked if you didn't do that?
>
> Noriega: It was stated, Panama must expect economic consequences. Your interest was that we should aid the Contras, and we said "no" to that.

Poindexter outlined plans for a U.S. invasion of Nicaragua that would require the fig leaf of participation of troops from other countries in the region.

Noriega: "Yes, they wanted to attack Nicaragua and the only reason it hadn't already happened was that Panama was in the way, and all they wanted was that Panama would open the way and make it possible for them to continue their plans."

According to Noriega's adviser, Panamanian Defense Forces

Captain Cortiso, "[the U.S.] wanted that Panamanian forces attack first. Then we would receive support from U.S. troops."[21]

It was in this same December 1985 period that Bush and Don Gregg met with Ambassador Briggs to discuss Noriega's refusal to follow dictation from Washington. According to Gregg in his deposition in the Christic Institute lawsuit, "I think we [i.e., Bush and Gregg] came away from the meeting with Ambassador Briggs with the sense that Noriega was a growing problem, politically, militarily, and possibly in the drug area." When pressed to comment about Noriega's alleged relations to drug trafficking, Gregg could only add: "It would have been part of the general picture of Noriega as a political problem, corruption, and a general policy problem. . . . I don't recall any specific discussion of Noriega's involvement in drugs," Gregg testified.[22]

In this case it is quite possible that Don Gregg is for once providing accurate testimony: The U.S. government decision to begin interference in Panama's internal affairs for the overthrow of Noriega had nothing to do with questions of drug trafficking. It was predicated on Noriega's rejection of Poindexter's ultimatum demanding support for the Nicaraguan Contras, themselves a notorious gang of drug-pushers enjoying the full support of Bush and the U.S. government. Colonel Samuel J. Watson III, deputy national security adviser to Bush during those years, invoked executive privilege during the course of his Christic Institute deposition on the advice of his lawyer, in order to avoid answering questions about Bush's 1985 meeting with Everett Briggs.[23]

In addition to the question of Contra aid, another rationale for official U.S. rage against Noriega had emerged during 1985. Panamanian President Nicky Barletta, a darling of the State Department and a former vice president of the genocidal World Bank, attempted to impose a package of conditionalities and economic adjustment measures dictated by the International Monetary Fund. This was a package of brutal austerity, and riots soon erupted in protest against Barletta. Noriega refused to comply with Barletta's request to use the Panamanian military forces to put down these anti-austerity riots, and the IMF austerity package was thus compromised. Barletta was shortly forced out as President.

During 1986–87, Noriega cooperated with U.S. law enforcement officials in a number of highly effective antidrug operations. This successful joint effort was documented by letters of commendation sent to Noriega by John C. Lawn, at that time head of the U.S. Drug Enforcement Administration. On February 13, 1987, Lawn wrote to Noriega: "Your longstanding support of the Drug Enforcement

Administration is greatly appreciated. International police cooperation and vigorous pursuit of drug traffickers are our common goal."
Later in the same year, Lawn wrote to Noriega to commend the
latter's contributions to Operation Pisces, a joint U.S.-Panamanian
effort against drug-smuggling and drug money laundering. Panamanian participation was facilitated by a tough new law, called Law
23, which contained tough new provisions against drug money
laundering. Lawn's letter to Noriega of May 27, 1987 includes the
following:

> As you know, the recently concluded Operation Pisces was enor-
> mously successful: many millions of dollars and many thousands
> of pounds of drugs have been taken from the drug traffickers and
> international money launderers. . . .
> Again, the DEA and officials of Panama have together dealt an
> effective blow against drug dealers and international money launder-
> ers. Your personal commitment to Operation Pisces and the compe-
> tent, professional, and tireless efforts of other officials in the Republic
> of Panama were essential to the final positive outcome of this investi-
> gation. Drugs dealers throughout the world now know that the profits
> of their illegal operations are not welcome in Panama. The operation
> of May 6 led to the freezing of millions of dollars in the bank accounts
> of drug dealers. Simultaneously, bank papers were confiscated that
> gave officials important insights into the drug trade and the laun-
> dering operations of the drug trade. The DEA has always valued
> close cooperation, and we are prepared to proceed together against
> international drug dealers whenever the opportunity presents itself.[24]

By a striking coincidence, it was in June 1987, just one month
after this glowing tribute had been written, that the U.S. government
declared war against Panama, initiating a campaign to destabilize
Noriega on the pretexts of lack of democracy and corruption. On
June 30, 1987, the U.S. State Department demanded the ouster of
General Noriega. Elliott Abrams, the assistant secretary of state for
Latin American affairs, later indicted for perjury in 1991 for his role
in the Iran-Contra scandal and coverup, to which he pled guilty,
made the announcement. Abrams took note of a resolution passed
on June 23 by the Senate Foreign Relations Committee demanding
the creation of a "democratic government" in Panama, and officially
concurred, thus making the toppling of Noriega the official U.S.
policy. Abrams also demanded that the Panamanian military be
freed of "political corruption."

These were precisely the destabilization measures which Poindexter had threatened 18 months earlier. The actual timing of the U.S.

demand for the ouster of Noriega appears to have been dictated by resentment in the U.S. financial community over Noriega's apparent violation of certain taboos in his measures against drug money laundering. As the *New York Times* commented on August 10, 1987: "The political crisis follows closely what bankers here saw as a serious breach of bank secrecy regulations. Earlier this year, as part of an American campaign against the laundering of drug money, the Panamanian government froze a few suspect accounts here in a manner that bankers and lawyers regarded as arbitrary." These were precisely the actions lauded by the DEA's John Lawn. Had Noriega shut down operations sanctioned by the U.S. intelligence community, or confiscated assets of the New York banks?

On August 12, 1987, Noriega responded to the opposition campaigns fomented by the U.S. inside Panama by declaring that the aim of Washington and its Panamanian minions was "to smash Panama as a free and independent nation. It is a repetition of what Teddy Roosevelt did when he militarily attacked following the separation of Panama from Colombia."

On August 13, 1987, the *Los Angeles Times* reported that U.S. Assistant Attorney General Stephen Trott, who had headed up the Department of Justice "Get Noriega" Task Force for more than a year, had sent out orders to "pull together everything that we have on him [Noriega] in order to see if he is prosecutable." This classic enemies-list operation was clearly aimed at fabricating drug charges against Noriega, since that was the political spin which the U.S. regime wished to impart to its attack on Panama. In February 1988, Noriega was indicted on U.S. drug charges, despite a lack of evidence and an even more compelling lack of jurisdiction. This indictment was quickly followed by economic sanctions, an embargo on trade and other economic warfare measures that were invoked by Washington on March 2, 1988. All of these measures were timed to coincide with the "Super Tuesday" presidential preference primaries in the southern states, where Bush was able to benefit from the racist appeal of the assault on Noriega, who is of mestizo background and has a swarthy complexion.

During the spring of 1988, the Reagan administration conducted a negotiation with Noriega with the declared aim of convincing him to relinquish power in exchange for having the drug charges against him dropped. In May, Michael G. Kozak, the deputy assistant secretary of state for Inter-American affairs, had been sent to Panama to meet with Noriega. Bush had come under attack from other presidential candidates, especially Dukakis, for being soft on Noriega and seeking a plea bargain with the Panamanian leader. Bush first took the floor during the course of an administration policy-making meeting to advocate an end of the bargaining with Noriega. According to press reports, this proposal was "hotly contested." Then, in a speech in Los Angeles, Bush made one of his exceedingly rare departures from the Reagan line, by announcing with a straight face that a Bush administration would not "bargain with drug dealers" at home or abroad.[25]

Bush's interest in Noriega continued after he had assumed the presidency. On April 6, 1989, Bush formally declared that the government of Panama represented an "unusual and extraordinary threat" to U.S. national security and foreign policy. He invoked the National Emergencies Act and the International Emergency Act to declare a state of "national emergency" in this country to meet the menace allegedly posed by the nationalists of little Panama. The May 1, 1989 issue of *U.S. News and World Report* revealed that Bush had authorized the expenditure of $10 million in CIA funds for operations against the Panamanian government. These funds were obviously to be employed to influence the Panamanian elections, which were scheduled for early May. The money was delivered to Panama by CIA bagman Carlos Eleta Almaran, who had just been arrested in Georgia on charges of drug trafficking. On May 2, with one eye on those elections, Bush attempted to refurbish his wimp image with a blustering tirade delivered to the David Rockefeller-controlled Council of the Americas in which he stated: "Let me say one thing clearly. The U.S.A. will not accept the results of fraudulent elections that serve to keep the supreme commander of the Panamanian armed forces in power." This made clear that Bush intended to declare the elections undemocratic if the pro-Noriega candidates were not defeated.

The CIA's $10 million and other monies were used to finance an extensive covert operation which aimed at stealing the elections on May 7. The U.S.-supported Civic Democratic Alliance, whose candidate was Guillermo Endara, purchased votes, bribed the election officials, and finally physically absconded with the official vote tallies. Because of the massive pattern of fraud and irregularities, the Panamanian government annulled the election. Somewhere along the line, the usual U.S.-staged "people power" upsurge had failed to materialize. The inability of Bush to force through a victory by the anti-Noriega opposition was a first moment of humiliation for the would-be Rough Rider.

This was the occasion for a new outburst of hypocritical breast-beating from Bush, whose vote fraud operation had not worked so well in Panama as it had in New Hampshire. Speaking at the commencement ceremonies of Mississippi State University in Starkville, Mississippi, Bush issued a formal call to the citizens and soldiers of Panama to overthrow Noriega, asserting that "they ought to do everything they can to get Mr. Noriega out of there." Asked whether this was a call for a military coup against Noriega, Bush replied: "I would love to see them get him out of there. Not just the PDF—the will of the people of Panama." Bush elaborated that his was a call for "a revolution. . ."

Bush seemed also to invite the assassination of Noriega by blurting out, "No, I would add no words of caution" on how to do any of this. He slyly kept an escape hatch open in case a coup leader called on the U.S. for support, as in fact later happened: "If the PDF asks for support to get rid of Noriega, they wouldn't need support from the United States in order to get rid of Noriega. He's one man, and they have a well-trained force."

During this period, Admiral William Crowe, the chairman of the U.S. Joint Chiefs of Staff, attempted to convince the U.S. commander in Panama, Gen. Frederick F. Woerner, to accept a brigade-sized reinforcement of 3,000 troops in addition to the 12,000 men already stationed in Panama. Woerner declined the additional men, which the Pentagon had intended to dispatch with great fanfare in an attempt to intimidate Noriega and his triumphant supporters.

Operation Blue Spoon

At this point, the Pentagon activated preparations for Operation Blue Spoon, which included a contingency plan to kidnap Noriega with the help of a Delta Force unit. There were discussions about whether an attempt could be made to abduct Noriega with any likelihood of success; it was concluded that Noriega was very wily and exceedingly difficult to track. It was in the course of these deliberations that Defense Secretary Cheney is reported to have told Crowe, "You know, the President has got a long history of vindictive political actions. Cross Bush and you pay," he said, supplying the names of a few victims and adding: "Bush remembers and you have to be careful."[26] Thus intimidated by Bush, the military commanders concurred in Bush's announcement of a brigade-sized reinforcement for Woerner, plus the secret dispatch of Delta Forces and Navy Seals. On July 17, Bush approved a plan to "assert U.S. treaty rights" by undertaking demonstrative military provocations in violation of the treaty. Woerner was soon replaced by Gen. Maxwell Reid "Mad Max" Thurman, who would bring no qualms to his assignment of aggression. Thurman took over at the Southern Command on September 30.

In the wake of this tirade, the U.S. forces in Panama began a systematic campaign of military provocations. In July, the U.S. forces began practicing how to seize control of important Panamanian military installations and civilian objectives, all in flagrant violation of the Panama Canal Treaty. On July 1, for example, the town of Gamboa was seized and held for 24 hours by U.S. troops, tanks and helicopters. The mayor of the town and 30 other persons were illegally detained during this "maneuver." In Chilibre, the U.S. forces occupied the key water purification plant serving Panama City and Colon. On August 15, Bush escalated the rhetoric still further by proclaiming that he had the obligation "to kidnap Noriega." Then, during the first days of October, there came an abortive U.S.-sponsored coup attempt, followed by the public humiliation of George Bush, who had failed to measure up to the standards of efficacy set by Theodore Roosevelt.

The provocations continued all the way up to the December 20 invasion.

In his speech delivered at 7:20 A.M. on December 21, 1989 announcing the U.S. invasion, Bush said:

> Many attempts have been made to resolve this crisis through diplomacy and negotiations. All were rejected by the dictator of Panama, Gen. Manuel Noriega, an indicted drug trafficker.
>
> Last Friday, Noriega declared his military dictatorship to be in a state of war with the United States and publicly threatened the lives of Americans in Panama. The very next day forces under his command shot and killed an unarmed American serviceman, wounded another, arrested and brutally beat a third American serviceman and then brutally interrogated his wife, threatening her with sexual abuse. That was enough.[27]

On December 22, Bush was asked what had made him decide to launch the attack now. He replied: "I think what changed my mind was the events that I cited in briefing the American people on this yesterday: the death of the Marine, the brutalizing, really obscene torture of the Navy lieutenant, and the threat of sexual abuse and the terror inflicted on that Navy lieutenant's wife. . . ."[28]

Later in the same press conference, Bush obsessively returned to the same topic, this time answering a question about the Soviet reaction to the U.S. move:

> And I also need to let him [Gorbachov] know—look, if an American Marine is killed, if they kill an American Marine—that's real bad. And if they threaten and brutalize the wife of an American

citizen, sexually threatening the lieutenant's wife while kicking him in the groin over and over again, then, Mr. Gorbachov, please understand, this president is going to do something about it."

Blacks and mestizos make up the vast majority of the population of Panama. The principal enemy image was constructed around the figure of Noriega, who was ridiculed as "the pineapple" in the U.S. media loyal to Bush. Noriega was not, however, the only target: Francisco Rodriguez, the pro-Noriega President of Panama, is, like Noriega, a mestizo, while the Minister of Government and Justice, the Minister of the Treasury, and the Minister of Labor are all black. Noriega's Foreign Minister is of Chinese background, as is the head of the small Air Force. A number of Noriega's leading PDF colleagues are black. By contrast, Guillermo Endara, the new U.S. puppet President who was now administered his oath of office by U.S. military officers on a U.S. military base, is white, and lily-white is his retinue, including First Vice President Ricardo Arias Calderon and Second Vice President Guillermo "Billy" Ford. There would be only one non-white in the new Endara cabinet, a black woman who is Minister of Education. The rest of the U.S. assets belonged to the lily-white oligarchy of Panama, the *rabiblancos* or "cottontails," who had ruled the country with supreme incompetence and maximum corruption until the advent of the nationalist revolution of Gen. Omar Torrijos, Noriega's patron, in 1968. Endara's base was among the "BMW revolutionaries" who had attended anti-Noriega rallies only in the comfort of their air-conditioned limousines. These were Bush's kind of people. One of Bush's *soldatesca* in Panama, Gen. Marc Cisneros, boasted that the Panamanians "need to have a little infusion of Anglo values."

Bush Orders Holocaust

The U.S. military operations, which got under way just after midnight on Tuesday, December 19, were conducted with unusual ferocity. Mad Max Thurman sent in the new Stealth and A–7 fighter-bombers, and AC–13 gunships. The neighborhood around Noriega's Comandancia, called El Chorillo, was bombarded with a vengeance and virtually razed, as was the working-class district of San Miguelito, and large parts of the city of Colon.

U.S. commanders had been instructed that Bush wished to avoid U.S. casualties at all costs, and that any hostile fire was to be answered by overwhelming U.S. firepower, without regard to the number of civilian casualties that this might produce among the

Panamanians. Many of the Panamanian civilian dead were secretly buried in unmarked mass graves during the dead of night by the U.S. forces; many other bodies were consumed in the holocaust of fires that leveled El Chorillo. The Institute of Seismology counted 417 bomb bursts in Panama City alone during the first 14 hours of the U.S. invasion. For many days there were no U.S. estimates of the civilian dead (or "collateral damage"), and eventually the Bush regime set the death toll for Panamanian noncombatants at slightly over 200. In reality, as *Executive Intelligence Review* and former U.S. Attorney General Ramsey Clark pointed out, there had been approximately 5,000 innocent civilian victims, including large numbers of women and children.

U.S. forces rounded up 10,000 suspected political opponents of "democracy" and incarcerated them in concentration camps, calling many of them prisoners of war. Many political prisoners were held for months after the invasion without being charged with any specific offense, a clear violation of the norms of *habeas corpus*. The combined economic devastation caused by 30 months of U.S. sanctions and economic warfare, plus the results of bombardments, firefights and torchings, had taken an estimated $7 billion out of the Panamanian economy, in which severe poverty was the lot of most of the population, apart from the *rabiblanco* bankers who were the main support for Bush's intervention. The bombing left 15,000 homeless. The Endara government purged several thousand government officials and civil servants under the pretext that they had been tainted by their association with Noriega.

Perhaps not by accident, the new U.S. puppet regime could only be described as a congeries of drug-pushers and drug money launderers. The most succinct summary was provided by the *International Herald Tribune* on February 7, 1990, which reported: "The nation's new President Guillermo Endara has for years been a director of one of the Panamanian banks used by Colombia's drug traffickers. Guillermo Ford, the Second Vice President and chairman of the banking commission, is a part owner of the Dadeland Bank of Florida, which was named in a court case two years ago as a central financial institution for one of the biggest Medellín money launderers, Gonzalo Mora. Rogelio Cruz, the new Attorney General, has been a director of the First Interamericas Bank, owned by Rodriguez Orejuela, one of the bosses of the Cali Cartel gang in Colombia."

The portly Guillermo Endara was also the business partner and corporate attorney of Carlos Eleta Almaran, the CIA bagman already mentioned. Eleta Almaran, the owner of the Panamanian branch of Philip Morris Tobacco, was arraigned in Bibb County,

Georgia in April 1989 by DEA officials, who accused him of conspiracy to import 600 kilos of cocaine per month into the U.S., and to set up dummy corporations to launder the estimated $300 million in profits this project was expected to produce. Eleta was first freed on $8 million bail; after the "successful" U.S. invasion of Panama, all charges against him were ordered dropped by Bush and Thornburgh.

As for Endara's First Vice President, Ricardo Arias Calderon, his brother, Jaime Arias Calderon, was president of the First Interamericas Bank when that bank was controlled by the Cali Cartel. Jaime Arias Calderon was also the co-owner of the Banco Continental, which laundered $40 million in drug money, part of which was used to finance the activities of the anti-Noriega opposition. Thus, all of Bush's most important newly installed puppets were implicated in drug-dealing.

The invasion presented some very difficult moments for Bush. From the beginning of the operation late on December 19, until Christmas Eve, the imposing U.S. martial apparatus had proven incapable of locating and capturing Noriega. The U.S. Southern Command was terrorized when a few Noriega loyalists launched a surprise attack on U.S. headquarters with mortars, scattering the media personnel who had been grinding out their propaganda.

There was great fear throughout the U.S. command that Noriega had successfully implemented a plan for the PDF to melt away to arms caches and secret bases in the Panamanian jungle for a prolonged guerrilla warfare effort. As it turned out, Noriega had failed to give the order to disperse.

Then, on the evening of December 24, it was reported that Noriega, armed with an Uzi machine gun, had made his way unchallenged and undetected to the Papal Nunciature in Panama City where he had asked for and obtained political asylum. There are no reports of how far George Bush gnawed into the White House Bigelows upon hearing that news, but it is clear that there was important damage to the deep pile in the Oval Office.

The standoff that then developed encapsulated the hereditary war of the Bush family with the Holy See and the Roman Catholic Church. For eight days, U.S. troops surrounded the Nunciature, which they proceeded to bombard with deafening decibels of explicitly satanic heavy metal and other hard rock music, which according to some reports had been personally chosen by Mad Max Thurman in order to "unnerve Noriega and the Nuncio," Monsignor LaBoa. Noriega was reputed to be an opera lover.

At the same time, Bush ordered the State Department to carry out real acts of thuggery in making threatening representations to the Holy See. It became clear that Roman Catholic priests, nuns, monks and prelates would soon be in danger in many countries of Ibero-America. Nevertheless, the Vatican declined to expel Noriega from the Nunciature in accordance with U.S. demands. Bush's forces in Panama had shown they were ready to play fast and loose with diplomatic immunity. A number of foreign embassies were broken into by U.S. troops while they were frantically searching for Noriega, and the Cuban and Nicaraguan embassies were ringed with tanks and troops in a ham-handed gesture of intimidation. It is clear that in this context, Bush contemplated the storming of the Nunciature by U.S. forces.

In Panama City, the Endara-Ford-Arias Calderon forces mobilized their BMW base and hired hundreds of those who had nothing to eat for militant demonstrations outside of the Nunciature. These were liberally seeded with U.S. special forces and other commandos in civilian clothes. As the demonstrations grew more menacing, and the U.S. troops and tanks made no move to restrain them, it was clear that the U.S. forces were preparing to stage a violent but "spontaneous" assault by the masses on the Nunciature that would include the assassination of Noriega and the small group of his co-workers who had accompanied him into that building. At about this time, Monsignor LaBoa warned Noriega, "you could be lynched like Mussolini." Noriega appears to have concluded that remaining in the Nunciature meant certain death for himself and his subordinates at the hands of the U.S. commandos operating under the cover of the mob. LaBoa and the other religious on the staff of the Nunciature would also be in grave danger. On January 3, 1990, after thanking LaBoa and giving him a letter to the Pope, Noriega, dressed in his general's uniform, left the Nunciature and surrendered to General Cisneros.

A Crime and a Failure

In Bush's speech of December 21 he had offered the following justification for his act of war, Operation Just Cause: "The goals of the United States have been to safeguard the lives of Americans, to defend democracy in Panama, to combat drug trafficking, and to protect the integrity of the Panama Canal Treaty."

If these were the goals, then Bush's invasion of Panama must be counted not only a crime, but also a failure.

On April 5, 1991, newspapers all over Ibero-America carried details of a new report by the U.S. Drug Enforcement Administration confirming that the U.S.-installed puppet President of Panama, Guillermo Endara, had been an officer of at least six companies which had been demonstrably implicated in laundering drug money. These were the Banco General, the Banco de Colombia, the Union Bank of Switzerland, the Banco Aleman, the Primer Banco de Ahorros, Sudameris, Banaico and the Banco del Istmo. The money laundered came from a drug-smuggling ring headed up by Augusto Falcon and Salvador Magluta of Colombia, who are reported to have smuggled an average of one ton of cocaine per month into Florida during the decade 1977–87, including many of the years during which Bush's much-touted South Florida Task Force and related operations were in operation.

With the puppet President so heavily implicated in the activity of the international drug mafia, it can be no surprise that the plague of illegal drugs has markedly worsened in the wake of Bush's invasion. According to the London *Independent* of March 5, 1991, "statistics now indicate that since General Noriega's departure, cocaine trafficking has, in fact, prospered" in the country. On March 1, the State Department had conceded that the turnover of drug money laundered in Panama had at least regained the levels attained before the 1989 invasion. According to the *Los Angeles Times* of April 28, 1991, current levels of drug trafficking in Panama "in some cases exceed" what existed before the December 20 invasion, and U.S. officials "say the trend is sharply upward and includes serious movements by the Colombian cartels into areas largely ignored under Noriega." This was all real drug activity, and not the cornmeal tamales wrapped in banana leaves that Bush's mind war experts found in one of Noriega's residences and labeled as "cocaine" during the invasion.

Bush's invasion of Panama has done nothing to fight the scourge of illegal narcotics. Rather, the fact that so many of Bush's hand-picked puppets can be shown to be top figures in the drug mafia suggests that drug trafficking through Panama toward the United States has increased after the ouster of Noriega. If drug shipments to the United States have increased, this exposes Bush's pledge to "safeguard the lives of Americans" as a lie.

As far as the promise of democracy is concerned, it must be stressed that Panama has remained under direct U.S. military dictatorship and virtual martial law until this writing in the late autumn of 1991, two years after Bush's adventure was launched. The congressional and local elections that were conducted during early 1991 were thoroughly orchestrated by the U.S. occupation forces. Army intelligence units interrogated potential voters, and medical battalions handed out vaccines and medicines to urban and rural populations to encourage them to vote. Every important official in the Panamanian government from Endara on down has U.S. military "liaison officers" assigned on a permanent basis. These officers are from the Defense Department's Civic Action-Country Area Team (or CA-CAT), a counterinsurgency apparatus that parallels the "civic action" teams unleashed during the Vietnam War. CA-CAT officers supervise all government ministries and even supervise police precincts in Panama City. The Panamanian Defense Forces have been dissolved, and the CA-CAT officers are busily creating a new constabulary, the Fuerza Publica.

Radio stations and newspapers which spoke out against the U.S. invasion or criticized the puppet regime were jailed or intimidated, as in the case of the publisher Escolastico Calvo, who was held in concentration camps and jails for some months after the invasion without an arrest warrant and without specific charges.

Trade union rights are non-existent: After a demonstration by 100,000 persons in December 1990 had protested growing unemployment and Endara's plans to "privatize" the state sector by selling it off for a song to the *rabiblanco* bankers, all of the labor leaders who had organized the march were fired from their jobs, and arrest warrants were issued against 100 union officials by the government.

In the wake of Bush's invasion, the economy of Panama has not been rebuilt, but has rather collapsed further into misery. The Bush administration has set as the first imperative for the puppet regime the maintenance of debt service on Panama's $6 billion in international debt. Debt service payments take precedence over spending on public works, public health and all other categories. Bush had promised Panama $2 billion for post-invasion reconstruction, but he later reduced this to $1 billion. What was finally forthcoming was just $460 million, most of which was simply transferred to the Wall Street banks in order to defray the debt service owed by Panama. The figure of $460 million scarcely exceeds the $400 million in Panamanian holdings that were supposedly frozen by the United States during the period of economic warfare against Noriega, but which were then given to the New York banks, also for debt service payments.

As far as the "integrity" of the Panama Canal Treaty signed by Torrijos and Carter, and ratified by the U.S. Senate, is concerned, on February 7, 1989, Rep. Philip Crane (R-Il.) introduced a House Joint Resolution, with 26 co-sponsors, to express "the sense of the Congress that the President or the Congress should abrogate the

Panama Canal Treaties of 1977 and the Neutrality Treaty." Then on March 21, 1991, Senator Larry Craig (R-Id.), together with Rep. Philip Crane on the House side, introduced a concurrent resolution, calling on George Bush to renegotiate the Canal Treaties "to permit the United States Armed Forces to remain in Panama beyond Dec. 31, 1999, and to permit the U.S. to act independently to continue to protect the Panama Canal"—i.e., for the U.S. to keep a military presence in Panama indefinitely. These resolutions are still pending before the Congress.

Thus, on every point enumerated by Bush as basic to his policy—the lives of Americans, Panamanian democracy, antidrug operations, and the integrity of the treaty—Bush has obtained a fiasco. Bush's invasion of Panama will stand as a chapter of shame and infamy in the recent history of the United States.

Bush's performance during the Panama crisis was especially ominous because of the President's clearly emerging mental imbalance. Several outbursts during the Noriega press conferences resembled genuine public fits. These gross phenomena did not receive the attention they would have merited from journalists, television commentators and pundits, who rather preferred studiously to ignore them. One public figure who called attention to Bush's psychopathology was political prisoner Lyndon LaRouche, who made the following courageous observations from a jail cell in a federal prison in Minnesota after viewing several of Bush's press briefings during the last days of December:

George is a very shallow-minded person, very impulsive. He's a person of rage-driven obsession, and impulses flowing from rage-driven obsessions. Very shallow-minded. He's sort of a jock of one kind or another, in his mentality. He talks like it, he acts like it, his body language is that of it. He can't present a concept. The man is incapable of carrying a concept in his head. He's a poor little fellow who's so rage-driven that very little intellectual activity can occur in his head; that's his conceptual style. He's a man characterized by sudden fits of jock-style rage, of obsessions which flow from seizure by that rage, and of impulses which flow from those obsessions.

If you were a psychiatrist and you had such a fellow on your couch, what's your prognosis of the way he's going to react to this situation? He'll react only when he becomes sly. And he becomes sly in the face of great pressure. He'll duck, he'll be sneaky, when he faces something he knows he can't cope with. And he'll duck and hope to come back to hit another day.

But now he's in a manic fit. He's the President. He said so at his press conference. "I'm the President. I'm Queen of the May." So you've got a rage-driven man, with rage-driven obsession with impulses flowing from that, in a man who thinks he's the Queen of the May. In other words, in Aeschylean language, *a law unto himself.* What's your prognosis?[29]

It was during these waning days of 1989 that Bush's mental disintegration became unmistakable, foreshadowing the greater furors yet to come.

Notes for Chapter XXII

1. *Washington Post,* Jan. 21, 1991.
2. For Fukuyama's "End of History," see *The National Interest,* Summer 1989, and Henry Allen, "The End. Or Is It?" *Washington Post,* Sept. 27, 1989.
3. *Washington Post,* Dec. 8, 1988.
4. *Washington Post,* April 17, 1989.
5. See Jack Anderson and Dale Van Atta, "Another Test of Loyalty and Standards," *Washington Post,* April 26, 1989; "Overseas Spoils for GOP Loyalists," *Washington Post,* Sept. 22, 1989; and Ann Devroy, "Bush Ambassadorial Nomination in Limbo," *Washington Post,* Sept. 12, 1989.
6. "Bush's Earthly Pursuits," *Washington Post,* Nov. 18, 1988.
7. See the transcript of Bush's statement and news conference, *Washington Post,* Feb. 7, 1989; "With Signs and Ceremony, S&L Bailout Begins," *Washington Post,* Aug. 10, 1989; and "Bush: S&Ls May Need More Help," *Washington Post,* Dec. 12, 1989.
8. "Bush Backs Increase in IMF Funds," *Washington Post,* Nov. 23, 1989.
9. See House Democratic Study Group, Special Report No. 101–45, "Legislation Vetoed by the President," p. 83.
10. *Washington Post,* April 29, 1990, p. F1.
11. John M. Barry, *The Ambition and the Power* (New York: Viking Press, 1989) pp. 621–22.
12. *Ibid.*
13. "Bush: The Secret Presidency," *Newsweek,* Jan. 1, 1990.
14. Transcript of President Bush's press conference, *Washington Post,* June 9, 1989.
15. Transcript of President Bush's press conference, *Washington Post,* Dec. 22, 1989.
16. Kevin Phillips, "George Bush and Congress—Brain-Dead Politics of '89," *Washington Post,* Oct. 1, 1989.
17. *Time,* Oct. 23, 1989.
18. *Congressional Record,* 58th Congress, 3rd session, p. 19.
19. See "Police State and Global Gendarme: The United States under the Thornburgh Doctrine," *American Leviathan: Administrative Fascism under the Bush Regime,* (Wiesbaden: EIR News Service, 1990), pp. 61–102.
20. Kenneth J. Jones, *The Enemy Within,* (Cali, Colombia: Carvajal, 1990), p. 22.
21. "Panama: Atrocities of the 'Big Stick,' " in *American Leviathan,* pp. 39–40.
22. For Gregg's testimony on Bush-Noriega relations, see "Testimony on Bush Meeting With Panama Ambassador," *New York Times,* May 21, 1988.
23. "Bush Aide Invokes Executive Privilege," *Washington Post,* May 20, 1988.
24. *American Leviathan,* pp. 41–42.
25. "Bush Presses to Cut Off Talks with Noriega," *Washington Post,* May 20, 1988.
26. Bob Woodward, *The Commanders* (New York: Simon and Schuster, 1991), p. 89.
27. Text of President Bush's Address, *Washington Post,* Dec. 21, 1989.
28. Text of President Bush's press conference, *Washington Post,* Dec. 22, 1989.
29. *What Does Candidate LaRouche Think of Bush's Mental Health?* (Washington: Democrats for Economic Recovery-LaRouche in 92, 1991), p. 7.

Willard Velz/Washington Star photo, © Washington Post, courtesy Washington D.C. Public Library

Frank Lorenzo, a pioneer in Bush's Wall Street buyout mob, looted U.S. airlines after breaking their labor force.

Bush associates hammered Texaco in favor of Liedtke's Pennzoil, with a railroaded court verdict and a billion dollar IRS tax demand.

White House photo

Vice President Bush, in designer racing goggles, rides in the Blue Thunder *catamaran of Don Aronow (extreme right), reputed drug trafficker, who was later mysteriously murdered.*

Oliver North: George Bush's key operative in the Iran-Contra gun-running and drug-running enterprise.

Robert Gates: He covered up Iran-Contra, and Bush nominated him CIA Director.

Donald Gregg before the Senate Foreign Relations Committee May 11, 1989. Gregg ran the Contra guns-for-drugs operations as Bush's national security advisor.

Stanley Pottinger as a top Justice Department official with instant access to CIA Director George Bush. Later Pottinger helped run Jimmy Carter's weapons trafficking with Khomeini.

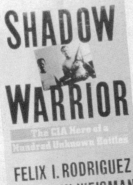

Autobiography of Felix Rodriguez, manager of Contra resupply in Central America.

Ex-Franklin Investigators:
'Sen. Schmit Told of Pressure to Halt Probe'

Lowe: Schmit Told of Pressure

Omaha World-Herald
Grand Jury Says Abuse Stories Were a 'Carefully Crafted Hoax'

Many Rumors Are Debunked In Report; Three Are Indicted

Schmit Rejects Report, Defends His Committee

COLUMBUS TELEGRAM
Franklin Credit puzzle may include incidents of homicide, Satanism

A pedophile ring allegedly reaching into the highest levels of government operated out of Omaha, Nebraska during the 1980s. Unconfirmed reports have implicated George Bush.

THE FRANKLIN COVER-UP

Child Abuse, Satanism, and Murder in Nebraska

by John W. DeCamp

Legislator John de Camp's 1992 book blew the lid off crimes against humanity in Nebraska.

Carlos Wesley

U.S. troops in Panama prior to Bush's 1989 invasion, which killed an estimated 5,000 defenseless civilians.

General Noriega: The Bush administration produced reams of propaganda, but no hard evidence, to back up its accusation of drug trafficking.

Carlos Martinez

The new Endara government, installed after Bush ousted Noriega, has turned Panama over to the rabiblanco bankers and the drug-runners.

Carlos Wesley

EIRNS/Stuart Lewis

*Bush at the White House
with an old family friend
and business associate:
The Amir Jabir al-Ahmad
al-Jabir al-Sabah, the
slave-holding Emir
of Kuwait.*

*George's son Neil Mallon
Bush testifies in the
Silverado scandal, May 23,
1990. Neil's troubles
helped propel George into
the Gulf War adventure.*

EIRNS/Stuart Lewis

U.S. Army

Operation Desert Shield/Desert Storm troops land in Saudi Arabia.

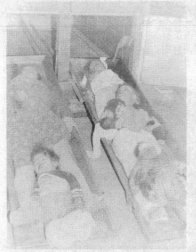

The infrastructure bombing and economic sanctions have killed countless thousands of Iraqis.

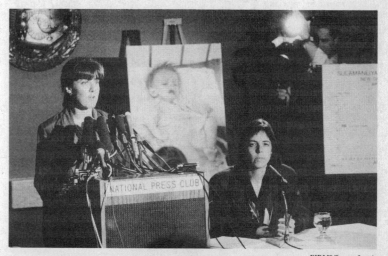

EIRNS/Stuart Lewis

Dr. Megan Passey of the Harvard Study Team discloses their report in May 1991, on the public health holocaust resulting from the bombing and sanctions.

British Prime Minister Margaret Thatcher with Bush in Washington August 6, 1990. Thatcher had virtually ordered Bush to commit the United States to war with Iraq.

EIRNS/Stuart Lewis

Queen Elizabeth II visits U.S. May 14, 1991. Anglophile George Bush raised eyebrows by referring to the United Kingdom as "the mother country."

EIRNS/Stuart Lewis

With Mikhail Gorbachov at the White House May 31, 1990. Bush did everything in his power to shore up the discredited and crumbling Kremlin regime.

EIRNS/Stuart Lewis

XXIII

THE NEW WORLD ORDER

*Roma caput mundi regit orbis frena rotundi.**
—Inscription on the imperial crown of Diocletian

During late 1989 and 1990, George Bush traversed a decisive watershed in his political career and in his own personal mental life. During this period, the tensions converging on Bush's personal psychological structures were greatly magnified, not just by the Panama adventure and the Gulf war, but also by the crisis of the Anglo-American financial interests, by the threat posed to Anglo-American plans by German reunification, by the thorny problems of preparing his own reelection, and by the foundering of his condominium partners in the Kremlin. As a result of this surfeit of tensions, Bush's personality entered into a process of disintegration. The whining accents of the wimp, so familiar to Bush-watchers of years past, were now increasingly supplanted by the hiss of frenetic spleen.

The successor personality which emerged from this upheaval differed in several important respects from the George Bush who had sought and occupied the vice-presidency. The George Bush who emerged in late 1990 after the dust had settled was far less restrained than the man who had languished in Reagan's shadow. The hyperthyroid "presidential" persona of Bush was equipped with little self-control, and rather featured a series of compulsive, quasi-psychotic episodes exhibited in the public glare of the television lights. These were typically rage-induced outbursts of verbal abuse and threats

*Rome, the chief of the world, holds the reins of this round orb.

made in the context of international crises, first against Noriega and later against Iraqi President Saddam Hussein.

Some might argue that the public rage fits that became increasingly frequent during 1989–90 were calculated and scripted performances, calibrated and staged according to the methods of mind war for the express purpose of intimidating foreign adversaries and, not least of all, the American population itself. Bush's apprenticeship with Kissinger would have taught him the techniques we have seen Kissinger employ in his secret communications with Moscow during the Indo-Pakistani war of 1970: Kissinger makes clear that an integral part of his crisis management style is the studied attempt to convince his adversary that the latter is dealing with a madman who will shun no expedient, however irrational, in order to prevail. But with the Bush of 1990 we are far beyond such calculating histrionics. There were still traces of method in George Bush's madness, but the central factor was now the madness itself.

The thesis of this chapter is, that while it is clear that the Gulf war was a deliberate and calculated provocation by the Anglo-American oligarchical and financier elite, the mental instability and psychological disintegration of George Bush was an indispensable ingredient in implementing the actions which the oligarchs and bankers desired. Without a George Bush who was increasingly *non compos mentis,* the imperialist grand design for the destruction of the leading Arab state and the intimidation of the Third World might have remained on the shelf. Especially since the Bay of Pigs and the Vietnam debacle, American Presidents have seen excellent reasons to mistrust their advisers when the latter came bearing plans for military adventures overseas. The destruction of the once powerful Lyndon B. Johnson, in particular, has stood as an eloquent warning to his successors that a President who wants to have a political future must be very reticent before he attempts to write a new page in the martial exploits of imperialism. Eisenhower's repudiation of the Anglo-French Suez invasion of 1956 can serve to remind us that even a relatively weak U.S. President may find reasons not to leap into the vanguard of the latest hare-brained scheme to come out of the London clubs. The difficulty of orchestrating a "splendid little war" is all the more evident when the various bureaucratic, military and financier factions of the U.S. Establishment are not at all convinced that the project is a winner or even worthwhile, as the pro-sanctions, wait-and-see stance of many Democratic members of the House and Senate indicates. The subjectivity of George Bush is therefore a vital link in the chain of any explanation of why the war happened, and that subjectivity centers on an increasingly desperate, aggravated, infantile id, tormented by the fires of a raging thyroid storm.

The process of mental and moral degeneration, the loss of previous self-control observable in Bush during this period, is not merely an individual matter. The geek act in the White House was typical of the collective mental and political behavior of the faction to which Bush belongs by birth and pedigree, the Anglo-American financiers. During 1989 and 1990, outbursts of megalomania, racism and manic flight-forward were common enough, not just in Washington, but in Wall Street, Whitehall and the City of London as well. These moods provided the psychic raw material for the strategic construct which Bush would proclaim during the late summer of 1990 as "The New World Order."

By the autumn of 1989, it was evident that the Soviet Empire, the Cold War antagonist and then the uneasy partner of the Anglo-Americans over more than four decades, was falling apart. During the middle 1980s, the Anglo-Americans and their counterparts in the Kremlin had arrived at the conclusion that, since they could no longer dominate the planet through their rivalry, they must now attempt to dominate it through their collusion. The new detente of Reagan's second term, in which Bush had played a decisive role, was a worldwide condominium of the Soviets and Anglo-Saxons, the two increasingly feeble and gutted empires which now leaned on each other like two drunks, each one propping the other up. That had been the condominium, incarnated in the figure of Gorbachov.

Both empires were collapsing at an exceedingly rapid pace, but during the second half of the 1980s, the rate of Soviet decay outstripped that of the Anglo-Americans. That took some doing, since between 1985 and 1990, the global edifice of Anglo-American speculation and usury had been shaken by the panic of 1987, and by the deflationary contraction of 1989, both symptoms of a lethal disorder. But the Anglo-Americans, unlike the Soviets, were insulated within their North Atlantic metropolis by the possession of a global, as distinct from a merely continental, base of economic rapine, so the economic and political manifestations of the Soviet collapse were more spectacular.

The day of reckoning for the Anglo-Americans was not far off, but in the meantime the breathtaking collapse of the Soviets opened up megalomaniacal vistas to the custodians of the imperial idea in London drawing rooms and English country houses. The practitioners of the Great Game of geopolitics were now enticed by the perspective of the Single Empire, a worldwide Imperium that would be a purely Anglo-Saxon show, with the Russians and Chinese forced to knuckle under. Like the contemporaries of the Duke of Wellington in 1815, the imbecilic Anglo-American think-tankers and financiers contemplated the chimera of a new century of world domination, not unlike the British world supremacy that had extended from the Congress of Vienna until the First World War. The old Skull and Bones slogan of Henry Luce's "American Century" of 1945, which had been robbed of its splendid lustre by the Russians and the Cold War, could now ride again.

True, there were still some obstacles. The Great Russian rout meant that German reunification could not be avoided, which brought with it the danger of a *Wirtschaftswunder* reaching from the Atlantic to the Urals. That, and the continued economic dynamism of the Japanese-oriented sphere in the Far East, would be combatted by economic conflicts and trade wars that would take advantage of the Anglo-American control of raw materials and, above all, oil, with the Anglo-American lease on the Persian Gulf to be vigorously reaffirmed. Even so, the end of the partition of Germany was a real trauma for the Anglo-Saxons, and would elicit a wave of true hysteria on the part of Mrs. Thatcher, Nicholas Ridley and the rest of their circle, and a parallel public episode of consternation and chagrin on the part of Bush. The Anglo-Americans were moved to sweeping countermeasures. A little further down the line, a war in the Balkans could bring chaos to the German economic hinterland. From the standpoint of British and Kissingerian geopolitics, the countermeasures were necessary to restore the balance of power, which now risked shifting in favor of the new Germany. German ascendancy would mean that London would occupy the place to which Thatcher's economics had entitled that wretched nation—a niche of impotence, impoverishment, isolation and irrelevance. But the British were determined to be important, and war was a way to attain that goal.

There were also governments in the developing sector whose obedience to the Anglo-Saxon supermen was in doubt. The 250 million Arabs, who were in turn the vanguard of a billion Moslems, would always be intractable. The out-of-area deployments doctrine of the Atlantic Alliance would now be the framework for the ritual immolation of the leading Arab state, which happened to be Iraq. Later, there would be time to crush and dismember India, Malaysia, Brazil, Indonesia, Libya, and some others.

Then there was the inherent demographic weakness of the Anglo-Saxons, especially the falling birth rate, now exacerbated by Hollywood, television and heavy metal. How could such a small master race prevail against the black, brown, yellow, Mediterranean and

Slavic masses? The answer to that could only be genocide on a colossal scale, with economic breakdown, famine, epidemics and pestilence completing the job that war had begun. If the birth rate of Nigeria seemed destined to catapult that country into second place among the world demographic powers, the AIDS epidemic in central Africa was the remedy. General Death was the main ally of the Anglo-Saxons.

Despite these problems, Bush and his co-thinkers were confident that they could subjugate the planet for a full century. But they had to hurry. Unless the Soviets, Chinese, Germans, Japanese and Third World powers could be rapidly dealt with, the Anglo-Americans might be overtaken by their own accelerating economic collapse, and they might soon find themselves too weak to extend their yoke over the world. The military machine that attacked Iraq was in the process of shrinking by more than 25 percent because of growing American economic weakness, so it was important to act fast.

The Anglo-American system depended on squeezing enough wealth out of the world economy to feed the insatiable demands of the debt and capital structures in London and New York. During the 1980s, those capital structures had swelled like malignant tumors, while the depleted world economy was bled white. Now, crazed after their October 1987 and October 1989 brushes with bottomless financial and currency panic, the masters of usury in London and New York demanded that the rate of primitive accumulation be stepped up all over the world. The old Soviet sphere would pass from the frying pan of the Comecon to the fires of the IMF. By the spring of 1991, Bush would issue his calls for a free trade zone from the North Pole to Tierra del Fuego, and then for worldwide free trade. Bush's handling of the General Agreement on Tariffs and Trade and the North American Free Trade Agreement soon convinced the Europe '92 crowd in Brussels that the Anglo-Americans were hell-bent on global trade war.

These were the impulses and perspectives which impinged on Bush from what he later called "the Mother Country," and which were vigorously imparted to him in his frequent consultations with British Prime Minister Margaret Thatcher, who now loomed very large in the configuration of Bush's personal network.

Malta-Yalta

The November 1989 historic collapse of the East German Communist regime, and subsequent fall of the Berlin Wall, served as a detonator of one of Bush's most severe episodes thus far of public emotional disturbance. The entire Cold War condominium relationship, now centered on Margaret Thatcher's "Gorby Doll," seemed to be collapsing into the dustbin of history.

When the wall came down, Bush could not avoid a group of reporters in the Oval Office, where he sat in a swivel chair in the company of James Baker. Bush told the reporters that he was "elated" by the news, but his mood was at once funereal and testy. If he was so elated, why was he so unhappy? Why the long face? "I'm just not an emotional kind of guy." The main chord was one of caution. "It's way too early" to speculate about German reunification, although Bush was forced to concede, through clenched teeth, that the Berlin Wall "will have very little relevance" from now on.[1]

After an enraged and tongue-tied monologue with the reporters, Bush privately asked his staff: "How about if I give them one of these?" Then he jumped in the air, waved his hands and yelled "Whoooopppeee!" at the top of his lungs.[2] Bush's spin doctors went into action, explaining that the President had been "restrained" because of his desire to avoid gloating or otherwise offending Gorbachov and the Kremlin.

Bush's gagged emotional clutch attracted a great deal of attention in the press and media. "Why did the leader of the western world look as though he had lost his last friend the day they brought him the news of the fall of the Berlin Wall?" asked Mary McGrory. "George Bush's stricken expression and lame words about an event that had the rest of mankind quickly singing hosannas were an awful letdown at a high moment in history."[3]

In reality, Bush's suppressed rage was another real epiphany of his character. Bush's family tradition was to support totalitarian rule in Germany, starting with Daddy Prescott's role in the Hitler project, and continuing with Averell Harriman's machinations of 1945, which helped to solidify a Communist dictatorship for 40 years in the Eastern zone after the Nazis had fallen. But Bush's reaction was also illustrative of the Anglo-American perception that the resurgence of German industrialism in central Europe was a deadly threat.

Over in London, Thatcher's brain-truster Nicholas Ridley was forced to quit the cabinet after he foamed at the mouth in observations about German unity, which he equated with a Nazi resurgence seeking to enslave Britain within the coils of the EEC. The Anglo-Saxon oligarchs were truly dismayed, and it is in this hysteria that we must seek the roots of the Gulf crisis and the war against Iraq.

But in the meantime, the collapse of the old Pankow regime

in East Berlin meant that Bush had urgent issues to discuss with Gorbachov. The two agreed to meet on ships in Malta during the first week of December.

Bush talked about his summit plans in a special televised address before Thanksgiving 1989. He tried to claim credit for the terminal crisis of communism, citing his own inaugural address: "The day of the dictator is over." But mainly he sought to reassure Gorbachov: ". . . [W]e will give him our assurance that America welcomes this reform not as an adversary seeking advantage but as a people offering support. . . . I will assure him that there is no greater advocate of *perestroika* than the president of the United States." Bush also had to protect his flank from criticism from Europeans and domestic critics like Lyndon LaRouche, who had warned that the Malta meeting contained the threat of an attempted new Yalta of the superpowers at the expense of Europe. "We are not meeting to determine the future of Europe," Bush promised.[4]

At the Malta-Yalta table, Bush and Gorbachov haggled over the "architecture" of the new Europe. Gorbachov wanted NATO to be dissolved as the Warsaw Pact ceased to exist, but this was something Bush and the British refused to grant. Bush explained that Germany was best bound within NATO in order to avoid the potential for independent initiatives that neither Moscow nor Washington wanted. A free hand for each empire within its respective sphere was reaffirmed, as suggested by the symmetry of Bush's assault on Panama during the Romanian crisis that liquidated Ceausescu, but left a neo-Communist government of old Comintern types like Ion Iliescu and Petre Roman in power. Bush would also support the Kremlin against both Armenia and Azerbaijan when hostilities and massacres broke out between these regions during the following month.

Bush's reciprocal services to Gorbachov included a monstrous diplomatic first: Just as the Communist regime in East Germany was in its death agony, Bush dispatched James Baker to Potsdam to meet with the East German "reform Communist" leader, Hans Modrow. No U.S. Secretary of State had ever set foot in the D.D.R. during its entire history after 1949, but now, in the last days of the Pankow Communist regime, Baker would go there. His visit was an insult to those East Germans who had marched for freedom, always having to reckon with the danger that Erich Honecker's tanks would open fire. Baker's visit was designed to delay, sabotage and stall German reunification in whatever ways were still possible, while shoring up the Communist regime. Baker gave it his best shot, but his sleazy deal-making skills were of no use in the face of an aroused populace. Nevertheless, after Tiananmen and Postdam, Bush was rapidly emerging as one of the few world leaders who could be counted on to support world communism.

During the early months of 1990, certain forces in Moscow, Bonn and other capitals gravitated toward a new Rapallo arrangement in a positive key: There was the potential that the inmates of the prison-house of nations might attain freedom and self-determination, while German capital investments in infrastructure and economic modern-ization could guarantee that the emerging states would be economi-cally viable, a process from which the entire world could benefit.

A rational policy for the United States under these circumstances would have entailed a large-scale commitment to taking part in rebuilding the infrastructure of the former Soviet sphere in transpor-tation, communications, energy, education and health services, com-bined with capital investments in industrial modernization. Such investment might also have served as a means to restart the depressed U.S. economy. The precondition for economic cooperation would have been a recognition by the Soviet authorities that the aspirations of their subject nationalities for self-determination had to be hon-ored, including through the independence of the former Soviet re-publics in the Baltic, the Transcaucasus, central Asia, Ukraine and elsewhere. As long as the Soviet military potential remained formida-ble, adequate military preparedness in the West was also indispens-able, and should have featured a significant commitment to the "new physical principles" anti-missile defenses that had inspired the original Strategic Defense Initiative of 1983. Obviously, none of these measures would have been possible without a decisive break with the economic policy of the Reagan-Bush years, in favor of an economic recovery program focused on fostering high-technology growth in capital-intensive industrial employment producing tangi-ble, physical commodities. The single U.S. political figure who had proposed such a program for war-avoidance and stability was Lyn-don LaRouche, who had put forward such a package during a press conference in West Berlin in October 1988, in the context of a prophetic forecast that German reunification was very much on the agenda for the immediate future.

Bush was responsible for the jailing of LaRouche, and his policy in these matters was diametrically opposite to this approach. Bush never made a serious proposal for the economic reconstruction of the areas included within the old U.S.S.R., and was niggardly even in loans to let the Russians buy agricultural commodities. In November 1990, Gorbachov addressed a desperate plea to world governments to alleviate the U.S.S.R. food shortage, and sent Foreign Minister

Shevardnadze to Washington in the following month, in hopes of obtaining a significant infusion of outright cash grants for food purchases from U.S. stocks. After photo opportunities with James Baker in Texas and with Bush at the White House, all Shevardnadze had to take back to Moscow was a paltry $1 billion and change. Within a week of Shevardnadze's return, he resigned his post under fire from critics, referring to sinister plans for a coup against Gorbachov. The coup, of course, came the following August. It should have been obvious that Bush's policy was maximizing the probability of ugly surprises further down the road.

Bush did not demand self-determination for the subject nationalities, but sided with the Kremlin against the republics again and again, ignoring the January 1991 bloodbath in Lithuania, or winning himself the title of "Chicken Kiev" during a July 1991 trip to Ukraine in which he told that republic's Supreme Soviet to avoid the pitfalls of "suicidal" nationalism. Even though the Soviet missile park was largely intact, Bush was compelled by his budget penury to take down significant areas of U.S. military capacities. And finally, his stubborn refusal to throw the bankrupt policies of the Reagan-Bush years overboard guaranteed further U.S. economic collapse.

The Broccoli Connection

But Bush was mindful neither of war avoidance nor economic recovery. In the months after Panama, he basked in the afterglow of a dramatic increase in his popularity, as reflected by the public opinion polls. A full-scale state visit by Gorbachov was scheduled for late May. Rumblings were being heard in the Middle East. But, in early April, Bush's mind was focused on other matters. It was now that he made his famous remarks on the subject of broccoli. The issue surfaced when the White House decreed that henceforth, by order of the President himself, broccoli would no longer be served to Bush. Reporters determined to use the next available photo opportunity to ask what this was all about.

Bush's infantile anti-broccoli outburst came in the context of a White House state dinner held in honor of visiting Polish Prime Minister Tadeusz Mazowiecki. Although Bush was obsessed with broccoli, he did make some attempt to relate his new obsession to the social context in which he found himself: "Just as Poland had a rebellion against totalitarianism, I am rebelling against broccoli, and I refuse to give ground. I do not like broccoli, and I haven't liked it since I was a little kid and my mother made me eat it. And I'm president of the United States, and I'm not going to eat any more broccoli."

Out in California, where broccoli is big business as a cash crop, producers were aroused sufficiently to dispatch ten tons of broccoli, equivalent to about 80,000 servings, to the White House. Bush was still adamant: "Barbara loves broccoli. She's tried to make me eat it. She eats it all the time herself. So she can go out and meet the caravan."[5]

These statements were an illumination in themselves, since the internal evidence pointed conclusively to a choleric infantile tantrum being experienced by the President. But what could have occasioned an outburst on broccoli, of all things? Slightly more than a year later, when it became known that Bush was suffering from Basedow's disease, some observers recalled the broccoli outburst. It turns out that broccoli, along with cabbage and some other vegetables, belongs to a category of foods called goitrogens. Some schools of medicine recommend frequent servings of broccoli and other goitrogens in order to help cool off an overactive thyroid.[7] There was much speculation that Bush's hyperthyroid syndrome had been diagnosed by March–April, or perhaps earlier, and that broccoli had been appearing more often on the White House menu as part of a therapy to return Bush's thyroid and metabolism to more normal functioning. Was the celebrated broccoli outburst a case of an irascible President, in the grip of psychopathological symptoms his physicians were attempting to treat, rebelling against his doctors' orders?

At their spring summit, Bush and Gorbachov continued to disagree about whether united Germany would be a member of NATO. Much time was spent on strategic arms, the Vienna conventional arms reduction talks, and the other aspects of the emerging European architecture, where their mutual counterrevolutionary commitments went very deep. Both stressed that they had taken their Malta consultations as their point of departure. Bush's hostility to the cause of Lithuania and the other Baltic republics, now subject to crippling economic blockade by Moscow, was writ large. The central exchanges of this summit were doubtless those which occurred in the bucolic isolation of Camp David among a small shirtsleeve group that comprehended Bush, Gorbachov, Shevardnadze, James Baker and Brent Scowcroft. Bush was unusually closed-mouthed, but the very loquacious Gorbachov volunteered that they had come to talk about the "planet and its flash-points" and the "regional issues." There was the distinct impression that these talks were sweeping and futurological in their scope.[8]

Did Bush and Gorbachov use their Camp David afternoon to coordinate their respective roles in the Gulf crisis, which the Anglo-

Americans were now about to provoke? It is very likely that they did.[9]

"Dead from the Neck Up"

Bush's political stock was declining during the summer of 1990. One indication was provided by the astoundingly frank remarks of Justice Thurgood Marshall of the U.S. Supreme Court in an interview with Sam Donaldson on the ABC News television program "Prime Time Live." Justice Marshall, the sole black justice on the Supreme Court, was asked for his reaction to Bush's nomination of the "stealth candidate," David Souter, to fill the place of the retiring Justice William Brennan, a friend of Marshall. Souter was a man who appeared to have no documentable opinions on any subject, although he had a sinister look. "I just don't understand what he's doing. I just don't understand it. I mean this last appointment is . . . the epitome of what he's been doing," said Marshall of Bush. Marshall didn't have "the slightest idea" of Bush's motives in the Souter nomination. Would Marshall comment on Bush's civil rights record? asked correspondent Sam Donaldson. "Let me put it this way. It's said that if you can't say something good about a dead person, don't say it. Well, I consider him dead." Who was dead? asked Donaldson. "Bush!" was Marshall's reply. "He's dead from the neck up."

Thurgood Marshall added that he regarded Bush's chief of staff, John Sununu of New Hampshire, the state Souter was from, as the one "calling the shots." "If he came up for election," said Marshall of Bush, "I'd vote against him. No question about it. I don't think he's ever stopped" running for reelection since he took office. Marshall and Donaldson had the following exchange about Souter:

> Donaldson: Do you know Judge David Souter?
> Marshall: No, never heard of him.
> Donaldson: He may be the man to replace Brennan.
> Marshall: I still never heard of him. When his name came down I listened to television. And the first thing, I called my wife. Have I ever heard of this man? She said, "No, I haven't either." So I promptly called Brennan, because it's his circuit [the First Circuit in Boston]. And his wife answered the phone, and I told her. She said: "He's never heard of him either."

Thurgood Marshall and Brennan had often been at odds with the Bush administration's promotion of the death penalty. In this connection, Marshall commented: "My argument is that if you make a mistake in a trial and it's corrected later on—you find out it was an error—you correct it. But if you kill a man, what do you say? 'Oops?' 'I'm sorry?' 'Wait a minute?' That's the trouble with death. Death is so lasting."

On this occasion, Marshall renewed his pledge that he would never resign, but would die in office: "I said before, and I repeat that, I'm serving out my life term. I have a deal with my wife that when I begin to show signs of senility, she'll tell me. And she will."[10] Yet, less than one year later, Thurgood Marshall announced his retirement from the bench, giving Bush the chance to split the organizations of black America with the Clarence Thomas appointment. Those who saw Marshall's farewell press conference would have to agree that he still possessed one of the most lucid and trenchant minds anywhere in the government. Had Bush's vindictiveness expressed itself once again through its inevitable instruments of secret blackmail and threats?

During June and July, domestic economic issues edged their way back to center stage of U.S. politics. As always, that was bad news for Bush.

'Read My Lips—I Lied'

Bush's biggest problem during 1990 was the collision between his favorite bit of campaign demagogy, his "read my lips, no new taxes" mantra of 1988, and the looming national bankruptcy of the United States. Bush had sent his budget to the Hill on January 29 where the Democrats, despite the afterglow of Panama, had promptly pronounced it Dead on Arrival. During March and April, there were rounds of haggling between the Congress and Bush's budget pointman, Richard Darman of OMB. Then, on the sunny spring Sunday afternoon of May 6, Bush used the occasion of a White House lecture on his ego ideal, Theodore Roosevelt, to hold a discreet meeting with Democratic congressional leaders for the purpose of quietly deep-sixing the no new taxes litany. Bush was extremely surreptitious in the jettisoning of his favorite throwaway line, but the word leaked out in Monday's newspapers that the White House, in the person of hatchet-man Sununu, was willing to go to a budget summit with "no preconditions." Responding to questions on Monday, Bush's publicity man, Marlin Fitzwater, explained that Bush wanted budget negotiations "unfettered with conclusions about positions taken in the past." That sounded like new taxes.

Bush had been compelled to act by a rising chorus of panicked screaming from the City of London and Wall Street, who had been demanding a serious austerity campaign ever since Bush had arrived at the White House. After the failure of the $13 billion Bank of New England in January, Wall Street corporatist financier Felix Rohatyn had commented: "I have never been so uneasy about the outlook in 40 years. Everywhere you look, you see red lights blinking. I see something beyond recession, but short of depression."[11] At the point that Bush became a tax apostate, estimates were that the budget deficit for fiscal 1990 would top $200 billion and after that disappear into the wild blue yonder. The IMF-BIS bankers wanted Bush to extract more of that wealth from the blood and bones of the American people, and George would now go through the motions of compliance.

The political blowback was severe. Ed Rollins, the co-chairman of the National Republican Congressional Committee, was a Reagan Democrat who had decided to stick with the GOP, and he had developed a plan, which turned out to be a chimera, about how the Republicans could gain some ground in the Congress. As a professional political operative, Rollins was acutely sensitive to the fact that Bush's betrayal of his "no new taxes pledge" would remove the one thing that George and his party supposedly stood for. "The biggest difference between Republicans and Democrats in the public perception is that Republicans don't want to raise taxes," complained Rollins. "Obviously, this makes that go right out the door. Politically, I think it's a disaster."[12] With that, Rollins was locked in a feud with Bush that would play out all the way to the end of the year.

But Democrats were also unhappy, since "no preconditions" was an evasive euphemism, and they wanted Bush to take the full opprobrium of calling for "new taxes." The White House remained duplicitous and evasive. In mid-May, *pourparlers* were held in the White House on a comprehensive deficit-reduction agreement. The Democrats demanded that Bush go on national television to motivate drastic, merciless austerity all along the line, with tax increases to be combined with the gouging of domestic and social programs. Bush demurred. All during June, the haggling about who would take the public rap went forward. On June 26, during a White House breakfast meeting with Bush, Sununu, Darman and congressional leaders, Speaker of the House Thomas Foley threatened to walk out of the talks unless Bush went public with a call for tax hikes. For a moment, the dollar, the Treasury bill market, and the entire insane house of cards of Anglo-American finance hung suspended by a thread. If the talks blew up, a worldwide financial panic might ensue, and the voters would hold George responsible for the consequences. Bush's Byzantine response was to issue a low-profile White House press statement. "It is clear to me that both the size of the deficit problem and the need for a package that can be enacted require all of the following: entitlement and mandatory program reform; tax revenue increases; growth incentives; discretionary spending reductions; orderly reductions in defense expenditures; and budget process reform."

"Tax revenue increases" was the big one. June 26 is remembered by the GOP right wing as a Day of Infamy; Bush cannot forget it either, since it was on that day that his poll ratings began to fall, and kept falling until late November, when war hysteria bailed him out. Many congressional Republicans, who for years had had no other talking point than taxes, were on a collision course with the nominal head of their party; a back-benchers' revolt was in full swing. Fitzwater and a few others still argued that "tax revenue increases" did not mean "new taxes," but this sophistry was received with scorn.

Nixon's spokesman Ron Nessen had been more candid when he once announced, "All previous statements are inoperative." When Fitzwater was asked if he would agree that Bush had now formally broken his no tax pledge, Fitzwater replied: "No. Are you crazy?" On July 11, congressional Democrats blocked Bush's favorite economic panacea, the reduction of the capital gains tax rate, by demanding that any such cut be combined with an overall increase of income tax rates on the wealthy. This yielded a deadlock which lasted until the last days of September.

Bush hid out in the White House for a few days, but then he had to face the press. There would be only one topic: his tax pledge. The first question—"I'd like to ask you about your reversal on 'no new taxes' "—occasioned evasive verbiage. Other questions were all on the same point. Bush attempted to pull himself together:

> I'll say I take a look at a new situation. I see an enormous deficit. I see a savings and loan problem out there that has to be resolved. And like Abraham Lincoln said, "I'll think anew." I'm not—but I'm not violating or getting away from my fundamental conviction on taxes or anything of that nature. Not in the least. But what I have said is on the table, and let's see where we go. . . .
>
> And look, I knew I'd catch some flak on this decision. . . . But I've got to do what I think is right, and then I'll ask the people for support. But more important than posturing now, or even negotiating, is the result. . . .

It was a landmark of impudence and dissembling. One of Bush's main objectives as he zig-zagged through the press conference was to avoid any television sound bites that would show him endorsing new taxes. So all his formulations were as diffuse as possible.

A questioner cited a tabloid headline: "Read My Lips: I Lied." Bush had been prepped by an historical review of how other Presidents had allegedly changed their minds or lied, which had convinced Bush that he, although a liar, was actually in the same class with Lincoln. "I've been more relaxed about it than I thought I'd be," quipped Bush. "I feel comfortable about that because I've gone back and done a little research and seen these firestorms come and go, people who feel just as strongly on one side or another of an issue as I do and haven't gotten their way exactly." Bush's basic idea was that he could get away with it, in the way that Reagan had gotten away with the 1982 recession. But for many voters, and even for many Republican loyalists, this had been yet another epiphany of a scoundrel. Many were convinced that Bush believed in absolutely nothing except hanging on to power.

Neil Bush

It was also in the early summer of 1990 that it gradually dawned on many taxpayers that, according to the terms of the savings and loan bailout championed by Bush during the first weeks of his regime, they would be left holding the bag to the tune of *at least* $500 billion. Their future was now weighted with the crushing burden of a *de facto* second mortgage, in addition to the astronomical national debt that Reagan and Bush had rolled up. This unhappy consciousness was compounded by the personal carnage of the continuing economic contraction, which had been accelerated by the shocks of September–October 1989. An ugly mood was abroad, with angry people seeking a point of cathexis.

They found it in Neil Bush, the President's marplot cadet son, the one we saw explaining his March 31, 1981 dinner engagement with Scott Hinckley (see Chapter 16). Neil Bush was a member of the board of directors of Silverado Savings and Loan of Denver, Colorado, which went bankrupt and had to be seized by federal regulators during 1988. Preliminary estimates of the costs to the taxpayers were on the order of $1.6 billion, but this was sure to go higher. The picture was complicated by the fact that Neil Bush had received a $100,000 personal loan (never repaid, and formally forgiven) and a $1.25 million line of credit from two local land speculators, Kenneth Good and William Walters, both also prominent money-bags for the Republican Party. In return for the favors he had received, Neil Bush certainly did nothing to prevent Silverado from lending $35 million to Good for a real estate speculation that soon went into default. Walters received $200 million in loans from Silverado, which were never called in. This was a *prima facie* case of violation of conflict of interest regulations. But instead of keeping quiet, Neil Bush showed that the family tradition of self-righteous posturing even when caught with both hands in the cookie jar was well represented by him: He launched an aggressive campaign of proclaiming his own innocence; it was all political, thought Neil, and all because people wanted to get at his august father through him.

Neil was looking forward to public hearings organized by the Federal Deposit Insurance Corporation to probe his malfeasance; there was talk of a criminal indictment, but this eventually dwindled into a $200 million civil suit brought against Neil and ten other former Silverado officials for "gross negligence" in their running of the affairs of the bank.

Bush's immediate reaction to the dense clouds gathering over Neil's head was to step up a scandal he saw as a counterweight: This was the "Keating Five" or "Lincoln Brigade" affair, which hit Senate Democrats Alan Cranston, Don Riegle, John Glenn and Dennis DeConcini, plus Republican John McCain. Some S&L loans showed "excesses," Bush was now ready to concede, and some were "foolish and ill-advised." But, he quickly stipulated: "I don't want to argue in favor of re-regulating the industry." And Bush was also on the defensive because, while he mandated $500 billion for the S&Ls, he wanted to veto a measure providing for unpaid parental leave for working mothers, despite a campaign promise that "we need to assure that women don't have to worry about getting their jobs back after having a child or caring for a child during serious illness."

But there was no doubt that Neil Bush had been acting as an influence peddler. Documents released by the Office of Thrift Supervision, which detailed the conflict of interest charges against Neil, conveyed a very low view of the dyslexic young man's business acumen: The regulators described him as "unqualified and untrained" to be a director of a financial institution. In the words of the OTS, "certainly he had no experience in managing a large corporation, especially a financial institution with almost $2 billion in assets."

As the end of July approached, Neil Bush was becoming a severe public relations problem for his father George. To make matters worse, economist Dan Brumbaugh, who enjoyed a certain notoriety as the Cassandra of the S&L debacle, appeared on television to confirm what the insiders already knew, that not just the S&Ls, but the entire commercial banking system of the United States, from the Wall Street giants down through the other money center banks, was all bankrupt. Economic reality, Bush's old nemesis, was once again threatening his ambition to rule. Then, in the last days of July, the White House received information that a national news magazine, probably *Newsweek*, was planning a cover story on Neil Bush.[13]

Such were the events in the political and personal life of George Bush that provided the backdrop for Bush's precipitous and choleric decision to go to war with Iraq. This is not to say that the decision to go to war was caused by these unpleasant developments; the causes of the Gulf war are much more complicated than that. But it is equally clear that Bush's bellicose enthusiasm for the first war that came along was notably facilitated by the complex of problems which he would thus sweep off the front page.

Preparing the War

There is much evidence that the Bush regime was committed to a new, large-scale war in the Middle East from the very day of its inauguration. The following analysis was filed on Palm Sunday, March 19, 1989 by one of the authors of the present study, and was published in *Executive Intelligence Review* under the title "Is Bush courting a Middle East war and a new oil crisis?":

Is the Bush administration preparing a military attack on Iran, Libya, Syria, or other Middle East nations in a flight forward intended to cut off or destroy a significant part of the world's oil supply and drastically raise the dollar price of crude on the world markets? A worldwide pattern of events monitored on Palm Sunday by *Executive Intelligence Review* suggests that such a move may be in the works. If the script does indeed call for a Middle East conflict and a new oil shock, it can be safely assumed that Henry Kissinger, the schemer behind the 1973 Yom Kippur war, is in the thick of things, through National Security Adviser Brent Scowcroft and the State Department's number-two man Lawrence Eagleburger. . . .

Why should the Bush administration now be a candidate to launch an attack on Libya and Iran, with large-scale hostilities likely in the Gulf? The basic answer is, as part of a manic flight-forward fit of "American Century" megalomania designed to distract attention from the fiasco of the new President's first 60 days in office.[14]

Despite the numerous shortcomings in this account, including the failure to identify Iraq as the target, it did capture the essential truth that Bush was planning a Gulf war. By August 1988 at the latest, when Iraq had emerged as the decisive victor in the eight-year-long Iran-Iraq war, British geopolitical thinkers had identified Iraq as the leading Arab state, and the leading threat to the Israeli-dominated balance of power in the Middle East. This estimate was seconded by those Zionist observers for whom the definition of minimal security is the capability of Israel to defeat the combined coalition of all Arab states. By August of 1988, leading circles in both Britain and Israel were contemplating ways of preventing Iraq from rebuilding its postwar economy, and were exploring options for a new war to liquidate the undeniable economic achievements of the Baath Party. Bush would have been a part of these deliberations starting at a very early phase.

A more precise outline of the coming war was issued in early March 1990, by Bush's political prisoner, Lyndon LaRouche. From his prison cell, LaRouche warned on March 10, 1990:

> It is apparent that during the next 60 days, more or less, the world is being plunged into the greatest pre-war crisis of the twentieth century. . . .
> Israel is preparing for war. The state of Israel is now marshalled in preparation for war, which, from one standpoint, might be described as Israel's attempted "final solution" to the Arab problem. This means a war, presumably against Iraq and other states, and the destruction of Jordan.[15]

During June and July, this warning was seconded by King Hussein of Jordan, Yassir Arafat of the PLO, Prince Hassan of Jordan and Saddam Hussein himself.

The Bush regime's contributions to the orchestration of the Gulf crisis of 1990–91 were many and indispensable. First there was a campaign of tough talking by Bush and Baker, designed to goad the new Likud-centered coalition of Shamir (in many respects the most belligerent and confrontational regime Israel had ever known) into postures of increased bellicosity. Bush personally referred to Israel as one of the countries in the Middle East that held hostages. In early March 1990, Bush said that the U.S. government position was to oppose Israeli settlements not only on the West Bank of the Jordan and the Gaza Strip, but also in East Jerusalem. A few days before that, James Baker had suggested that U.S. support for a $400 million loan guarantee program for settling Soviet Jews in Israel

would be forthcoming only if Israel stopped setting up new settlements in the occupied territories. Bush's mention of East Jerusalem
had toughened that line.[16] Baker had added some tough talk of his
own when he had told a congressional committee that if and when
the Israeli government wanted peace, they had only to call the White
House switchboard, whose number he proceeded to give. But on
June 20, Bush suspended the U.S. dialogue with the PLO, which he
had caused to be started during December 1988. The pretext was a
staged terror incident at an Israeli beach.

July 1990 was full of the hyperkinetic travel and diplomacy which
has become George's trademark. Over the July Fourth weekend,
Bush went to Kennebunkport to prepare for the London NATO
summit and the successive Houston summit of the seven leading
industrial nations.

The secret agenda at this summit was dominated by the NATO
out-of-area deployments, transforming the alliance into the white
man's vengeful knout against the Third World. According to a
senior NATO consultant, the Lancaster House summit focused on
"increasing tension and rearmament in a number of countries, in
North Africa, the Middle East including Palestine, and Asia through,
increasingly, to Southeast Asia. There are new dangers from new
directions. We are shifting from an exclusive focus on the east-west
conflict, to a situation of risk coming eventually or potentially from
all directions." The talk in London in that July was about a possible
new Middle East war, which "would tend to escalate horizontally
and vertically. A real conflict in the Levant would extend from the
Turkish border to the Suez canal. It would involve the neighbors of
the main combatants. The whole thing would be in a state of flux,
because the great powers couldn't afford just to sit there." In order
to avoid public relations problems for the continental European
governments, who still had qualms about their domestic public
opinion, these debates were not featured in the final communiqué,
which complacently proclaimed the end of the Cold War and invited
Gorbachov to come and visit NATO headquarters to make a
speech.[17]

After hobnobbing with Thatcher, Queen Elizabeth II and other
members of the royal family, Bush flew to Houston to assume the
role of host of the Group of 7 yearly economic summit. At this
summit, the Anglo-Saxon master race, as represented by Bush and
Thatcher, found itself in a highly embarrassing position. Everyone
knew that the worst economic plague outside of the Communist
bloc was the English-speaking economic depression, which held not
just the United States, the United Kingdom and Canada, but also

Australia, New Zealand and other former imperial outposts in its grip. The continental Europeans were interested in organizing emergency aid and investment packages for the emerging countries of eastern Europe and the Soviet republics, but this the Anglo-Saxons adamantly opposed. Rather, Bush and Thatcher were on a full trade-war line against the European Community and Japan when it came to the General Agreement on Tariffs and Trade and other matters of international economics.

In the following week, the Anglo-Saxon supermen were once again plunged into gloom when Gorbachov and Kohl, meeting on July 16 in the south Russian town of Mineralny Vody near Stavropol, announced the Soviet acquiescence to the membership of united Germany in NATO. This was an issue that Bush and Thatcher had hoped would cause a much longer delay and much greater acrimony, but now there were no more barriers to the successful completion of the "two plus four" talks on the future of Germany, which meant that German reunification before the end of the year was unavoidable.

On the same day that Kohl and Gorbachov were meeting, satellite photographs monitored in the Pentagon showed that Iraq's crack Hammurabi division, the elite corps of the Republican Guard, was moving south toward the border of Kuwait. By July 17, Pentagon analysts would be contemplating new satellite photos showing the entire division, with 300 tanks and over 10,000 men, in place along the Iraq-Kuwait border. A second division, the Medina Luminous, was beginning to arrive along the border, and a third division was marching south.[18]

The disputes between Iraq and Kuwait were well known, and the Anglo-Americans had done everything possible to exacerbate them. Iraq had defended Kuwait, Saudi Arabia and the other Gulf Cooperation Council countries against the fanatic legions of Khomeini during the Iran-Iraq war. Iraq had emerged from the conflict victorious, but burdened by $65 billion in foreign debt. Iraq demanded debt relief from the rich Gulf Arabs, who had not lifted a finger for their own defense. As for Kuwait, it had been a British puppet state since 1899. Both Kuwait and the United Arab Emirates were acknowledged to be exceeding their OPEC production quotas by some 500,000 barrels per day. This was part of a strategy to keep the price of oil artificially low; the low price was a boon to the dollar and the U.S. banking system, and it also prevented Iraq from acquiring the necessary funds for its postwar demobilization and reconstruction. Kuwait was also known to be stealing oil by over-pumping the Rumaila oil field, which lay along the Iraq-Kuwait border. The border through the Rumaila oil field was thus a bone of contention between Iraq and Kuwait, as was the ownership of Bubiyan and Warba islands, which controlled the access to Umm Qasr, Iraq's chief port and naval base as long as the Shatt-el-Arab was disputed with Iran. It later became known that the Emir of Kuwait was preparing further measures of economic warfare against Iraq, including the printing of masses of counterfeit Iraqi currency notes, which he was preparing to dump on the market in order to produce a crisis of hyperinflation in Iraq. Many of these themes were developed by Saddam Hussein in a July 17 address in which he accused the Emir of Kuwait of participation in a U.S.-Zionist conspiracy to keep the price of oil depressed.

The Emir of Kuwait, Jabir al-Sabah, was a widely hated figure among Arabs and Moslems. He is a sybaritic degenerate, fabulously wealthy, a complete parasite and nepotist, the keeper of a harem, and the owner of slaves, especially black slaves, for domestic use in his palace. The Sabah family ran Kuwait as the private plantation of their clan, and Sabah officials were notoriously cruel and stupid. Iraq, by contrast, was a modern secular state with high rates of economic growth, and possessed one of the highest standards of living and literacy rates in the Arab world. The status of women was one of the most advanced in the region, and religious freedom was extended to all churches.

Anglo-American strategy was thus to use economic warfare measures, including embargoes on key technologies, to back Saddam Hussein into a corner. When the position of Iraq was judged sufficiently desperate, secret feelers from the Anglo-Americans offered Saddam Hussein encouragement to attack Kuwait, with secret guarantees that there would be no Anglo-American reaction. Reliable reports from the Middle East indicate that Saddam Hussein was told before he took Kuwait that London and Washington would not go to war against him. Saddam Hussein was given further assurances through December and January 1991 that the military potential being assembled in his front yard would not be used against him, but would only permanently occupy Saudi Arabia. It is obvious that, in order to be believable on the part of the Iraqi leadership, these assurances had to come from persons known to exercise great power and influence in London and Washington—persons, let us say, in the same league with Henry Kissinger. One prime suspect who would fill the bill is Tiny Rowland, a property custodian of the British royal family and administrator of British post-colonial and neo-colonial interests in Africa and elsewhere. Tiny Rowland had been in Iraq in July, shortly before the Iraqi military made its move.

It is important to note that every aspect of the public conduct of the Bush regime until after the Iraqi invasion of Kuwait had become a fait accompli was perfectly coherent with the assurances Saddam Hussein was receiving, namely that there would be no U.S. military retaliation against Iraq for taking Kuwait.

The British geopoliticians so much admired by Bush are past masters of the intrigue of the *invitatio ad offerendum,* the suckering of another power into war. *Invitatio ad offerendum* means in effect "let's you and him fight." Saddam Hussein's attack on Iran in 1980 had been encouraged by U.S. and British assurances that the Teheran government was collapsing and incapable of resistance.

As we have seen, the Pentagon knew of Iraqi troops massing on the border with Kuwait as early as July 16–17. If Kuwait had been so vital to the security of the United States and the West, then it is clear that at any time between July 17 and August 1—and that is to say during a period of almost two weeks—Bush could have issued a warning to Iraq to stay out of Kuwait, backing it up with some bloodcurdling threats and serious, high-profile military demonstrations. Instead, Bush maintained a studied public silence on the situation and allowed his ambassador to convey a message to Saddam Hussein that was wholly misleading, but wholly coherent with the hypothesis of a British plan to sucker Saddam into war.

On July 24, press releases from the White House, the State Department and the Pentagon were balanced between support for the "moderate" Kuwaitis and Saudis on the one hand, and encouragement for an Arab-mediated peaceful settlement. Margaret Tutwiler at the State Department stressed that the United States had no commitment to defend Kuwait:

> We do not have any defense treaties with Kuwait and there are no special defense or security commitments to Kuwait. We also remain strongly committed to supporting the individual and collective self-defense of our friends in the Gulf, with whom we have deep and long-standing ties.

On July 25, U.S. Ambassador April Glaspie met with Saddam Hussein, and conveyed a highly misleading message about the U.S. view of the crisis. Glaspie assured Saddam Hussein that she was acting on direct instructions from Bush, and then delivered her celebrated line: "We have no opinion on the Arab-Arab conflict, like your border disagreement with Kuwait." There is every indication that these were indeed the instructions that had been given directly by the chief agent provocateur in the White House, Bush. "I have direct instructions from the president to seek better relations with Iraq," Glaspie told Saddam. According to the Iraqi transcript of this meeting, Glaspie stressed that this had always been the U.S. position: "I was in the American embassy in Kuwait during the late 1960s. The instruction we had during this period was that we should express no opinion on this issue and the issue is not associated with America."[19] Saddam Hussein illustrated Iraq's economic grievances and need of economic assistance for postwar reconstruction, points for which Ms. Glaspie expressed full U.S. official comprehension. Shortly after this, April Glaspie left Kuwait to take her summer vacation, another signal of elaborate U.S. government disinterest in the Kuwait-Iraq crisis.

According to the *Washington Post* of July 26, Saddam Hussein used the meeting with Glaspie to send Bush a message that " 'nothing will happen' on the military front while this weekend's mediation efforts are taking place." The mediation referred to an effort by Egyptian President Hosni Mubarak and the Saudi government to organize direct talks between Iraq and Kuwait, which were tentatively set for the weekend of July 28–29 in Jeddah. Over that weekend, Bush still had absolutely nothing to say about the Gulf crisis.

According to the *Washington Post* of July 30, the Saudi government announced on July 29 that the Iraqi-Kuwaiti talks, which had been postponed, would take place in Jeddah starting Tuesday, July 31. The Kuwaiti delegation abruptly walked out of these talks, a grandstanding gesture obviously calculated to incense the Iraqi leadership. On the morning of July 31, the *Washington Post* reported that the Iraqi troop buildup had now reached 100,000 men between Basra and the Kuwaiti border.

Bush would have known all about the additional Iraqi troops at least 36 hours earlier, through satellite photos and embassy reports. But still Bush remained silent as a tomb. Bush had plenty of opportunity that day to say something about the Gulf; he met with the GOP congressional leadership for more than an hour on the morning of July 31 and, according to participants, told them he was "annoyed" at the pace of the budget talks, which remained stalemated. At this time the White House was receiving intelligence reports that made an Iraqi invasion seem more likely, and some officials were quoted in the *New York Times* of the next day as having "expressed growing concern that hostilities could break out. . . ." But Bush said nothing, did nothing.

Enter the Iron Lady

On Thursday, August 2, Bush was scheduled to fly to Aspen for a meeting with Margaret Thatcher, whom Bush held in awe. Thatcher had now been in power for over 11 years, and had assured her place in the pantheon of Anglo-Saxon worthies. This desiccated mummy of British imperialism had been invited to Aspen, Colorado, to hold forth on the future of the West, and Bush was scheduled to confer with her there. At 5:00 A.M., Bush was awakened by Scowcroft, who had brought him the executive orders freezing all Iraqi and Kuwaiti assets in the U.S. At 8:00 A.M., the National Security Council gathered in the Cabinet Room. At the opening of this session there was a photo opportunity to let Bush put out the preliminary line on Iraq and Kuwait. Bush told the reporters:

"We're not discussing intervention."

Q: "You're not contemplating any intervention or sending troops?"

Bush: "I'm not contemplating such action, and I, again, would not discuss it if I were."

According to published accounts, during the meeting that followed, the one prospect that got a rise out of Bush was the alleged Iraqi threat to Saudi Arabia. This, as we will see, was one of the main arguments used by Thatcher later in the day to goad Bush to irreversible commitment to massive troop deployment and to war. This meeting ended without any firm decisions for further measures beyond the freezing of assets already decided. During Bush's flight to Aspen, Bush got on the telephone with several Middle East leaders, who, he said, had urged him to forestall U.S. intervention and allow ample time for an "Arab solution."

Bush's meetings with Thatcher in Aspen on Thursday, August 2, and on Monday, August 6 at the White House, are of the most decisive importance in understanding the way in which the Anglo-Americans connived to unleash the Gulf war. Before meeting with Thatcher, Bush was clearly in an agitated and disturbed mental state, but had no bedrock commitment to act in the Gulf crisis. After the sessions with Thatcher, Bush was rapidly transformed into a raving, monomaniacal warmonger and hawk. The transition was accompanied by a marked accentuation of Bush's overall psychological impairment, with a much increased tendency toward rage episodes.

The impact of Bush's Aspen meeting with Thatcher was thus to brainwash Bush toward a greater psychological disintegration, and toward a greater pliability and suggestibility in regard to London's imperial plans. One can speculate that the "Iron Lady" was armed with a Tavistock Institute psychological profile of Bush, possibly centering on young George's feelings of inadequacy when he was denied the love of his cold, demanding Anglo-Saxon sportswoman mother. Perhaps Thatcher's underlying psychological gameplan in this (and previous) encounters with Bush was to place herself along the line of emotional cathexis associated in Bush's psyche with the internalized image of his mother, Dorothy Bush, especially in her demanding and domineering capacity as the grey eminence of the Ranking Committee. George had to do something to save the embattled English-speaking peoples, Thatcher might have hinted. Otherwise, he would be letting down the side in precisely the way which he had always feared would lose him his mother's love. But to do something for the Anglo-Saxons in their hour of need, George would have to be selfless and staunch and not think of himself, just as Mother Dorothy had always demanded: He would have to risk his entire political career by deploying U.S. forces in overwhelming strength to the Gulf.

On a more explicit level, Thatcher also possessed an array of potent arguments. Back in 1982, she might have recalled, she had fallen in the polls and was being written off for a second term as a result of her dismal economic performance. But then the Argentineans seized the Malvinas, and she, Thatcher, acting in defiance of her entire cabinet and of much of British public opinion, had sent the fleet into the desperate gamble of the Malvinas war. The British had reconquered the islands, and the resultant wave of jingoism and racist chauvinism had permitted Thatcher to consolidate her regime until the present day. Thatcher knew about the "no new taxes" controversy and the Neil Bush affair, but all of that would be quickly suppressed and forgotten once the regiments began to march off to the Saudi front. For Bush, this would have been a compelling package.

As far as Saddam Hussein was concerned, Thatcher's argument is known to have been built around the ominous warning, "He won't stop!" Her message was that MI-6 and the rest of the fabled British intelligence apparatus had concluded that Saddam Hussein's goal would be an immediate military invasion and occupation of the immense Kingdom of Saudi Arabia, with its sensitive Moslem holy places, its trackless deserts and its warlike Bedouins. Since Thatcher was familiar with Bush's racist contempt for Arabs and other dark-skinned peoples, which she emphatically shared, she would also have laid great stress on the figure of Saddam Hussein and the threat he posed to Anglo-Saxon interests. The Tavistock profile would have included how threatened Bush felt in his psycho-sexual impotence by tough customers like Saddam, whom nobody had ever referred to as little Lord Fauntleroy.

At this moment in the Gulf crisis, the only competent political-military estimate of Iraqi intentions was that Saddam Hussein had no intent of going beyond Kuwait, a territory to which Baghdad had a longstanding claim, arguing that the British Empire had illegally established its secret protectorate over the southern part of the Ottoman Empire's province of Basra in 1899. This estimate, that Iraq had no desire to become embroiled with Saudi Arabia, was repeated during the first week of the crisis by such qualified experts as former U.S. Ambassador to Saudi Arabia James Aikens, and by the prominent French military leader Gen. Jeannou Lacaze. Even Gen. Norman Schwarzkopf thought it highly unlikely that Saddam would move against Saudi Arabia.

In her public remarks in Aspen, Thatcher began the new phase in the racist demonization of Saddam Hussein by calling his actions "intolerable," in a way that Syrian and Israeli occupations of other countries' lands seemingly were not. She asserted that "a collective and effective will of the nations belonging to the U.N." would be necessary to deal with the crisis. Thatcher's traveling entourage from the Foreign Office had come equipped with a strategy to press for mandatory economic sanctions and possible mandatory military action against Iraq under the provisions of Chapter VII of the United Nations Charter. Soon Bush's entourage had also picked up this new line.

Bush now changed his tune markedly. He suddenly and publicly reacquired his military options. When asked about his response, he stated: "We're not ruling any options in but we're not ruling any options out."

Bush also revealed that he had told the Arab leaders with whom he had been in contact during the morning that the Gulf crisis "had gone beyond simply a regional dispute because of the naked aggression that violates the United Nations charter." These formula-tions were I.D. format Thatcher-speak. Bush condemned Saddam for "his intolerable behavior," again parroting Thatcher's line. Bush was now "very much concerned" about the safety of other small Gulf states. Bush also referred to the hostage question, saying that threats to American citizens would "affect the United States in a very dramatic way because I view a fundamental responsibility of my presidency [as being] to protect American citizens." Bush added that he had talked with Thatcher about British proposals to press for "collective efforts" by members of the United Nations against

Iraq. The Iraqi invasion was a "totally unjustified act," Bush went on. It was now imperative that the "international community act together to ensure that Iraqi forces leave Kuwait immediately. Bush revealed that he and his advisers were now examining the "next steps" to end the crisis.

There is every reason to believe that Bush's decision to launch U.S. military intervention and war was taken in Aspen, under the hypnotic influence of Thatcher. Any residual hesitancy displayed in secret councils was merely dissembling to prevent his staffs from opposing that decision. Making a strategic decision of such colossal implications on the basis of a psycho-manipulative pep talk from Thatcher suggests that Bush's hyperthyroid condition was already operating; the hyperthyroid patient notoriously tends to resolve complicated and far-reaching alternatives with quick, snap decisions. Several published accounts have sought to argue that the decision for large-scale intervention did not come until Saturday at Camp David, but these accounts belong to the "red Studebaker" school of coverup. The truth is that Bush went to war as the racist tail on the British imperial kite, cheered on by the Kissinger cabal that permeated and dominated his administration. As the London *Daily Telegraph* gloated, Mrs. Thatcher had "stiffened [Bush's] resolve."

Bush had been scheduled to stay overnight in Aspen, but he now departed immediately for Washington. Later, the White House said that Bush had been on the phone with Saudi King Fahd, who had agreed that the Iraqi invasion was "absolutely unacceptable."[20] On the return trip and through the evening, the Kissingerian operative Scowcroft continued to press for military intervention, playing down the difficulties which other advisers had been citing. Given Kissinger's longstanding relationship with London and the Foreign Office, it was no surprise that Scowcroft was fully on the London line.

The next morning was Friday, August 3, and Bush called another NSC meeting at the White House. The Establishment media like the *New York Times* were full of accounts of how Iraq was allegedly massing troops along the southern border of Kuwait, about to pounce on Saudi Arabia. Scowcroft, with Bush's approval, bludgeoned the doubters into a discussion of war options. Bush ordered the CIA to prepare a plan to overthrow or assassinate Saddam Hussein, and told Dick Cheney, Colin Powell and General Schwarzkopf to prepare military options for the next day. Bush was opening the door to war slowly, so as to keep all of his civilian and military advisers on board. Later on Friday, Prince Bandar, the Saudi Arabian ambassador to Washington, met with Bush. According to one version, Bush pledged his word of honor to Bandar that he would "see this through with you." Bandar was widely reputed to be working for the CIA and other Western intelligence agencies.

When the time came in the afternoon to walk to his helicopter on the White House south lawn for the short flight to the Camp David retreat in the Catoctin Mountains of Maryland, Bush stopped at the microphones that were set up there, a procedure that became a habit during the Gulf crisis. At this point, Bush was psyching himself up toward the fit that he would act out on his Sunday afternoon return. But there was already no doubt that Bush's bellicosity was rising by the hour. With Kuwait under occupation, he said, "the status quo is unacceptable and further expansion" by Iraq "would be even more unacceptable." This formulation already pointed to an advance into Kuwait. He also stressed Saudi Arabia: "If they ask for specific help—it depends obviously on what it is— I would be inclined to help in any way we possibly can."[21]

War Psychosis

Over the weekend, Bush conducted several NSC meetings, during which Dick Cheney was sent to Saudi Arabia. A Sunday press conference was held for the purpose of "spleen-venting," as Maureen Dowd of the *New York Times* observed. This was the beginning of the war psychosis, with George Bush the leading psychotic.[22]

Later on Sunday, Bush went into the White House for yet another meeting of the NSC. At this meeting, it was already a foregone conclusion that there would be a large U.S. military deployment, although that had never been formally deliberated by the NSC. It had been a solo decision by Bush. There was now only the formality of Saudi assent.

Monday at the White House was dominated by the presence of Margaret Thatcher at her staunchest. Thatcher's theme was now that the enforcement of the economic sanctions voted by the U.N. would require a naval blockade in which the Anglo-Saxon combined fleets would play the leading role. Thatcher's first priority was that the sanctions had to be made to work. But if Washington and London were to conclude that a naval blockade were necessary for that end, she went on, "you would have to consider such a move."

Bush immediately took Thatcher's cue: "We need to discuss full and total implementation of these sanctions, ruling out nothing at all. These sanctions must be enforced.

The breast-beating about the enforcement of the sanctions signaled that the Anglo-Americans were going on a diplomatic offensive against countries like Germany, Japan and many in the Third World who might have assumed a neutral or pacifist position in the crisis. Baker had been traveling in Siberia with Shevardnadze when Iraq had entered Kuwait, and Soviet condemnation of Iraq had been immediate. Many countries, especially in the Third World, now found that with the Soviets closing ranks with the Anglo-Americans, the margin of maneuver they had enjoyed during the Cold War was now totally gone. Countries like Jordan, Sudan and Yemen, and the PLO and others who expressed understanding for Iraqi motives went to the top of the Anglo-American hit list. Bush assumed the role of top cop himself, with gusto: according to Fitzwater, the "speed-dialing mode" had produced 20 calls to 12 different world leaders over slightly more than three days.

When Cheney arrived in Saudi Arabia, the essence of his mission was to convey to King Fahd and his retinue that the first elements of the 82nd Airborne Division would be landing within an hour or two, and that the Saudi monarchy would be well advised to welcome them. In effect, Cheney was there to tell the Saudis that they were an occupied country, and that the United States would assume physical possession of most of the Arabian peninsula, with all of its fabulous oil wealth. Did King Fahd think of protesting the arrogance of Cheney's ultimatum? If he did, he had only to think of the fate of his predecessor, King Faisal, who had been murdered by the CIA in 1975. By the time King Fahd acquiesced, the first U.S. units were already on the ground. Bahrain, the United Arab Emirates, Qatar, Oman, all the members of the Gulf Cooperation Council would soon be subject to the same process of military occupation.

The U.S. expeditionary force in Saudi Arabia became widely known in Washington on Tuesday, August 7, as White House officials hastened to share the news with journalists. Bush personally wanted to stay out of the spotlight. At a cabinet meeting, Bush told his advisers that his regime had warned the Saudi government that the threat posed by the Iraqi military to Saudi Arabia was also a threat to the national security of the United States. According to Fitzwater, Saddam Hussein met with the U.S. chargé d'affaires in Baghdad, Joseph Wilson, to tell him that "he had no intention of leaving Kuwait and every intention of staying and claiming it as his own."

On Wednesday morning, Bush delivered a televised address to the American people from the Oval Office. He told the public that his troop deployments were "to take up defensive positions in Saudi Arabia." These U.S. forces would "work together with those of Saudi Arabia and other nations to preserve the integrity of Saudi

Arabia and to deter further Iraqi aggression." He inaugurated the Anglo-American Big Lie that the Iraqi actions had been "without provocation," which readers of daily newspapers knew not to be true. He also minted the story that Iraq possessed "the fourth largest military in the world," a wild exaggeration that was repeated many times. The "new Hitler" theme was already prominent: "Appeasement does not work," Bush asserted. "As was the case in the 1930s, we see in Saddam Hussein an aggressive dictator threatening his neighbors. . . . His promises mean nothing." Bush summed up the goals of his policy as follows:

> First, we seek the immediate, unconditional and complete withdrawal of all Iraqi forces from Kuwait. Second, Kuwait's legitimate government must be restored to replace the puppet regime. And third, my administration, as has been the case with every president from President [Franklin] Roosevelt to President Reagan, is committed to the security and stability of the Persian Gulf. And fourth, I am determined to protect the lives of American citizens abroad.[23]

None of this appeared to include offensive military action. Bush attempted to reinforce that false impression in his news conference later the same afternoon. It was during this appearance that the extent of Bush's mental disintegration and psychic dissociation became most evident. But first, Bush wanted to stress his "defensive" cover story: "Well, as you know, from what I said, they're there in a defensive mode right now, and therefore that is not the mission, to drive the Iraqis out of Kuwait. We have economic sanctions that I hope will be effective to that end."

The purpose, he stressed, was the "defense of the Saudis." "We're not in a war," Bush added. After several exchanges, he was asked what had tipped his hand in deciding to send troops and aircraft into Saudi Arabia. Bush lied: "There was no one single thing that I can think of. But when King Fahd requested such support we were prompt to respond. . . . If there was one it would perhaps be the Saudis moving south when they said they were withdrawing. . . ."

The press corps stirred uneasily and one or two voices could be heard prompting Bush: "The Iraqis . . . the Iraqis." There was acute embarrassment on the faces of Sununu and Fitzwater; this was the classic gaffe of Cold War Presidents who confused North Korea and South Korea, or East Germany and West Germany. Bush's forte was supposedly international affairs; he had traveled to both Saudi Arabia and Kuwait as a government official and before that as a businessman. So this gaffe pointed to a disorder of the synapses.

Bush realized what he had done and tried to recover: "I mean the Iraqis, thank you very much. It's been a long night. The Iraqis moving down to the Kuwait-Saudi border, when indeed they have given their word that they were withdrawing. That heightened our concern."

A little later there was another sensitive question, touching on the mission of the troops and the possible future occupation of Saudi Arabia, postwar bases, and the like: "Could you share with us the precise military objective of this mission? Will the American troops remain there only until Saddam Hussein removes his troops from the Saudi border?" Bush, obviously in deep water, answered: "I can't answer that because we have to—we have a major objective with those troops, which is the defense of the Soviet Union, so I think it beyond a defense of Saudi Arabia. So I think it's beyond the—I think it's beyond just the question of tanks along the border. . . ."

The defense of the Soviet Union! But Bush pressed on: "I'm not preparing for a long ground war in the Persian Gulf. . . . My military objective is to see Saudi Arabia defended."

The final portion of the press conference was devoted to the very important theme of the U.N. sanctions railroaded through the Security Council by the Anglo-Americans with the help of their willing French, Soviet and Chinese partners. The sanctions were in themselves an act of genocide against Iraq and the other populations impacted in the region. The sanctions, maintained after the war had ceased with the pretext that Saddam Hussein was still in power, have proven more lasting than the war itself, and they may yet prove more lethal. The congressional debate in January was fought almost exclusively between the stranglers of the Democratic Party, who wanted to "give the sanctions more time to work," and the bombers of the Bush administration and the Republican Party, who wanted to initiate an air war. Both positions constituted high crimes against humanity.

Bush's final response shows that he was fully aware that the economic sanctions designed by the State Department and the Foreign Office would mean genocide against Iraqi children, since they contained an unprecedented prohibition of food imports:

> Well, I don't know what they owe us for food, but I know that this embargo, to be successful, has got to encompass everything. And if there are—you know, if there's a humanitarian concern, pockets of starving children, or something of this nature, why, I would take a look. But other than that this embargo is going to be all-encom-

passing, and it will include food, and I don't know what Iraq owes us now for food. Generally speaking, in normal times, we have felt that food might be separated out from—you know, grain, wheat, might be separated out from other economic sanctions. But this one is all-encompassing and the language is pretty clear in the United Nations resolutions.[24]

As a final gesture, Bush acknowledged to the journalists that he had "slipped up a couple times here," and thanked them for having corrected him, so that his slips and gaffes would not stand as a part of the permanent record. Bush had now done his work; he had set into motion the military machine that would first strangle, and then bomb, Iraq. Within two days, Bush was on his way to Walker's Point in Kennebunkport, where his handlers hoped that the dervish would pull himself together.

During August, Bush pursued a hyperactive round of sports activities in Kennebunkport, while cartoonists compared the Middle East to the sand traps that Bush so often landed in during his frenetic daily round of golf.

The New World Order

It was during these August days that Scowcroft coined the slogan of Bush's Gulf war. On August 23, Scowcroft told reporters, "We believe we are creating the beginning of a new world order out of the collapse of U.S.-Soviet antagonisms."[25]

Bush was now conducting a systematic "mind war" campaign to coerce the American people into accepting the war he had already chosen. On August 20, Bush introduced a new rhetorical note, now calling the American citizens detained in Iraq "hostages." Under international law, the imminent threat of acts of war against a country entitles that country to intern enemy aliens as a matter of self-defense; this had been the rule in earlier wars. Henceforth, Bush would attempt to turn the hostage issue on and off according to his propaganda needs, until Iraq freed all the Americans in early December.

On August 27, Bush opined that "Saddam Hussein has been so resistant to complying with international law that I don't yet see fruitful negotiations."[26] Statements like these were made to cloak the fact that Bush was adamantly refusing to negotiate with Iraq, and preventing other nations from doing so. Bush's diplomatic posture was in effect an ultimatum to Iraq to get out of Kuwait, with the Iraqi departure to come before any discussions. Bush called this a refusal to reward aggression; it was in fact a refusal to negotiate in good faith, and made clear that Bush wanted war. His problem was that the U.S. military buildup was taking longer than expected, with ship convoys forced to turn back in the Atlantic because freighters broke down and were left dead in the water.

Bush returned to Washington at the end of August to address members of Congress. In the public part of this meeting, Bush reiterated that his goal was to "persuade Iraq to withdraw." There followed an executive session behind closed doors. The next day Bush recorded a broadcast to the U.S. forces in the Gulf, which was beamed to Saudi Arabia by the Armed Forces Radio. "Soldiers of peace will always be more than a match for a tyrant bent on aggression," Bush told the troops.

During early September, it became evident that the U.S. and Soviet approaches to the Gulf crisis were beginning to show some signs of divergence. Up to this point, Foreign Minister Shevardnadze had backed every step made by Bush and Baker, but the U.S. Gulf intervention was not popular among Red Army commanders and among Soviet Moslems, who were disturbed by the infidel occupation of the holy places. On September 9, Bush met with Gorbachov in Helsinki, Finland in order to discuss this and other matters of interest to a condominium in which the Anglo-Saxons were now more than ever the senior partners. Gorbachov spoke up for "a political solution" to the conflict, but his government willingly took part in every vote of the U.N. Security Council which opened the way to the Gulf war.

A few days later, on September 15, Bush received precious support from his masonic brother François Mitterrand, who exploited a trifling incident involving French diplomatic premises in Kuwait— the sort of thing that Bush had done repeatedly in Panama—massively to escalate the French troop presence and rhetoric in the Gulf.

To while away the weeks of the buildup, Bush busied himself with extortion. This was directed especially against Germany and Japan, two countries that were targets of the Gulf war, and whom Bush now called upon to pay for it. The constitutions of these countries prevented them from sending military contingents, and intervention would have been unpopular with domestic public opinion in any case. Japan was assessed $4 billion in tribute, and Germany a similar sum. By the end of the crisis, Bush and Baker had organized a $55 billion shakedown at the expense of a series of countries. These combined to produce the first balance of payments surplus for the United States in recent memory during the first quarter of 1991, obtaining breathing space for the dollar.

But even prediscounting this extorted tribute, the fiscal crisis of the U.S. Treasury was becoming overwhelming. On September 11, Bush was to address the Congress on the need for austerity measures to reduce the deficit for the coming fiscal year. But Bush did not wish to appear before the Congress as a simple bankrupt; he wanted to strut before them as a warrior. The resulting speech was a curious hybrid, first addressing the Gulf crisis, and only then turning to the dolorous balance sheets of the regime. It was in this speech that Bush repeated the Scowcroft slogan that will accompany his regime into the dust bin of history: The New World Order. After gloatingly quoting Gorbachov's condemnation of "Iraq's aggression," Bush came to the relevant passage:

> Clearly, no longer can a dictator count on East-West confrontation to stymie concerted United Nations action against aggression. A new partnership of nations has begun, and we stand today at a unique and extraordinary moment. The crisis in the Persian Gulf, as grave as it is, also offers a rare opportunity to move toward an historic period of cooperation. Out of these troubled times, our fifth objective—a new world order—can emerge: a new era—freer from the threat of terror, stronger in the pursuit of justice and more secure in the quest for peace. An era in which the nations of the world, east and west, north and south, can prosper and live in harmony.[27]

Of all the statements that might be adduced to illustrate the dissociation of the mind of George Bush from reality, this is surely the most telling. What Bush means by the New World Order is clearly the Single Empire, the new century of undisputed world dominion of the Anglo-Saxon powers. It is a world of neo-imperialism and neo-colonialism, in which a human species exhausted by two world wars, by fascism and communism, and by the cultural paradigm degeneration of the Western world during the last quarter-century, is called upon to accept the pacification of the planet. The terminology of a "new order" had been recently used, most notably, in the Rome-Berlin-Tokyo Axis. The "new world order" was revealed as the oldest: the slogan of every conqueror bent on world domination. The only thing notable about Bush's slogan was its monumental hypocrisy: Racist genocide against non-white peoples and the replanting of colonial flags (camouflaged as new mandates or "trusteeship territories") were allegedly no longer brutal crimes against humanity, but steps toward universal harmony. In any case, the New World Order could never become the permanent basis for planetary civilization, since the Malthusian, anti-industrial economics of its bearers could only guarantee the early doom of populations foolish or cowardly enough to submit to it.

Reality Hits

During August and September, Bush's Gulf offensive had allowed him to dominate the headlines and news broadcasts with bellicose posturing and saber-rattling in the crisis which he had assiduously helped to create. Now, during October, the awesome economic depression produced by the bipartisan economic policies of the Eastern Liberal Establishment over a quarter-century reasserted its presence with all the explosive force of reality long denied.

All during August and September, the haggling had continued between Bush and the congressional leadership about how optimally to inflict more drastic austerity on the American people. The haggling had recessed in August, but had resumed in great secrecy on September 7, with the elite group of participants sequestered from the world at Andrews Air Force Base near Washington. The haggling proceeded slowly, and key budget deadlines built into the Gramm-Rudman calendar began to slip by: September 10, September 15 and September 25 were missed. It was now apparent that the final deadline posed for the beginning of the fiscal year on October 1 could not be met; there was a danger of a Gramm-Rudman "train wreck" or automatic, across-the-board sequester of budget spending authority.

On September 30, Bush and the elite congressional summiteers appeared in a Rose Garden ceremony to announce a five-year, $500 billion deficit-reduction package, allegedly featuring $40 billion in deficit reduction during the first year, to be submitted to Congress for rubber-stamping. This plan contained higher taxes on gasoline, cigarettes, liquor, luxury items, plus savage cuts in defense, Medicare for the elderly, and farm payments. It was unsweetened by Bush's favorite nostrum for fat cats, a cut in the capital gains tax. Tax deductions were limited for the most wealthy.

Bush called the package "balanced" and "fair." "Now comes the hard part," said Senator George Mitchell, referring to the irritating formality of congressional passage. Believing the assurances of Mitchell and Foley, Dole and Bob Michel, that the resulting deal could be passed, Bush signed a continuing resolution to keep the government going from October 1 until October 5, while also avoiding the Gramm-Rudman guillotine.

Republicans were incensed that Bush had given away the "crown jewels" of their party just in order to get a deal. Right-wing Republicans lamented that the package was a "road-map to recession" and a "cave-in to the liberal Democrats." "I wouldn't vote for it if it cured cancer," said Congressman James A. Traficant, Jr. of Ohio.

Democrats were angered by the new excise tax, which was regressive, and by income tax rate increases for lower income groups.

When the plan came up for a vote in the House on the fateful day of October 5, with the stopgap legislation about to run out, many Democrats deferred voting until they could see that a clear majority of the Republicans were voting against their own President's plan. Then the Democrats also cast negative votes. The deficit package was soundly defeated, 254–179. Bush was humiliated: only 71 Republicans stuck with their President, joined by 108 Democrats. 105 GOPers had revolted, and joined with 149 Democrats to sink the accord Bush had pleaded for on television. Even Rep. Newt Gingrich of Georgia, who as House GOP Minority Whip should have superintended efforts to dragoon votes for Bush, had jumped ship on October 1, encouraging other GOP defections.

The Congress then quickly passed and sent to Bush a further continuing resolution to keep the government going; it was now the Friday before the Columbus Day weekend. Bush had threatened to veto any such legislation, and he now made good on his threat, intoning that "the hour of reckoning is at hand." The federal government thereupon began to shut down, except for Desert Shield and some other operations the bureaucracy considered essential. Tourists in Washington noticed that the toilets maintained by the National Park Service were shutting down. Bush, wanting to set a good example, decided that Sunday that he would drive back from Camp David by car: He got a rude taste of how the other half lives, ending up stalled in a typical traffic jam on the interstate.

After a week of great political hemorrhaging, Bush relented and signed a short-term continuing resolution.

By the weekend of October 13–14, there were at least three draft tax bills in circulation. Even hard-core Bushmen were unable to tell the legislators what the President wanted, and what he would veto. The most degraded and revealing moment came when Bush was out jogging, and reporters asked him about his position on taxes. "Read my hips!" shouted Bush, pointing toward his posterior with both hands. It was not clear who had scripted that one, but the message was clear: The American people were invited to kiss Bush's ass.

The haggling went on into the third week of October, and then into the fourth. Would it last to Halloween, to permit a macabre night of the living dead at the Capitol? Newt Gingrich told David Brinkley on "This Week" of October 21 that most House Republicans were prepared to vote against any plan to increase taxes, totally disregarding the wishes of Bush. At this point the Democrats wanted to place a one percent surtax on all income over $41 million, while the GOP favored reducing the deductions for the rich. In yet another flip-flop, Bush had conceded on October 20 that he would accept an increase in the top income tax rate from 28 percent to 31 percent. By October 24, a deal was finally reached which could be passed, and the next day Bush attempted to put the best possible face on things by assembling the bruised and bleeding Republican congressional leadership, including the renegade Gingrich, for another Rose Garden ceremony.

The final budget plan set the top income tax rate at 31 percent, and increased taxes on gasoline, cigarettes and airline tickets, and increased Medicare payroll taxes and premiums, while cutting Medicare benefit payouts and government payments to farmers. Another part of the package replaced the Gramm-Rudman-Hollings once-a-year sequester threat with a "triple, rolling sequester" with rigid spending caps for each of the three categories of defense, foreign aid and discretionary domestic spending, and no transfers permitted among these. The entire apparatus will require super-majorities of 60 votes to change in the future.

Naturally, this package was of no use whatever in deficit reduction, given the existence of an accelerating economic depression. In Bush's famous New World Order speech on September 11, he had frightened the Congress with the prospect of a deficit of $232 billion. In October of 1991, it was announced that the deficit for the fiscal year ending September 31, 1991, the one that was supposed to show improvement, had come in at $268.7 billion, the worst in all history. Predictions for the deficit in the year beginning on October 1, 1991 were in excess of $350 billion, guaranteeing that the 1991 record would not stand long. Bush's travail of October 1990 had done nothing to improve the picture.

Bush's predicament was that the Reaganomics of the 1980s (which had in fact been in force since the period after the Kennedy assassination) had produced more than a depression: It had engendered the national bankruptcy of the United States. That bankruptcy was now lawfully dismembering the Reagan coalition, the coalition which Bush had still been able to ride to power in 1988. Since Bush refused to replace the suicidal, post-industrial economic policies of the last quarter-century, he was obliged to attempt to smother irrepressible political conflicts with police-state methods, and with war hysteria.

Typhoid Mary

On the campaign trail, Bush was finally receiving treatment commensurate with his merits. October 23 was a day he will never forget. George had gotten up before dawn to make a day of it on the hustings, only to find that he was being shunned as the new Typhoid Mary of American politics.

The first stop was an early-morning fundraiser in Burlington, Vermont, designed to benefit Rep. Peter Smith, a freshman Congressman. Smith was supposed to give Bush a rousing introduction and then bask in the warmth of Bush's support. But instead, Smith astounded Bush and his handlers by launching into a tortured monologue on all the points of disagreement that divided him from Bush. Smith told of how he had been loyal to Bush on October 5, and of how his constituents had then rebelled, with the result that he caught political hell for his pro-Bush vote. Smith demanded that Bush now raise taxes on the wealthy. Smith also mentioned the civil rights bill: "My specific disagreements with this administration are a matter of record," Smith stressed. Poor Smith: His pro-Bush vote on October 5 had doomed him to defeat in his close race with Bernie Sanders, the socialist former mayor of Burlington.

Bush stewed, raged and squirmed. He looked around to see if anyone would come to his aid. Sitting next to Bush was GOP Senator James M. Jeffords, who had voted in favor of the civil rights bill Bush had vetoed. He had made an emotional speech in the Senate lambasting Bush for trying to punch giant "loopholes" in the civil rights of citizens. Jeffords sat staring straight ahead, doing a fair imitation of Bush at the *Nashua Telegraph* debate. When Bush got up, he was dissociated and tongue-tied. He stumbled through his speech, improvising a few lines in which he praised the independent-mindedness of Vermonters like Smith, but whined that he wished it would not come at his expense. Bush then asserted that "we have a sluggish economy out there nationally. That's one of the reasons why I favor this deficit so much."[28]

The crowd was puzzled. The mental disintegration of George Bush went on apace.

Bush's second stop of the day was in Manchester, New Hampshire. Here he was greeted by his old friend, the Manchester *Union Leader*, with a front page cartoon of the granite-faced man in the mountain saying "Read His Lips, Mr. President. Go Home and Take Your Taxes with You." Here there was no attack on Bush's economics; the candidate he was supposed to be helping, Rep. Robert C. Smith, had obviously concluded that any film footage showing him in the same picture with Bush would pose the threat of disaster, so he had simply stayed in Washington. The Congressman's wife was there to tell the audience that her husband had stayed in Washington for House votes he could not miss; an apoplectic Bush ferociously chewed on an apple before he rose for perfunctory remarks.

Bush's third stop was in Waterbury, Connecticut, where the beneficiary of his presence was Gary Franks, a black Republican whom Bush needed as a fig leaf for his veto of the civil rights bill. Franks solved the Typhoid Mary problem by barring the news media from the campaign event, so no sound bites associating him with Bush could be used against him by his opponent. Later there was a brief photo opportunity with Bush and Franks together.

Surely Bush had cut a ridiculous figure. But how many Iraqis would die in January, February and beyond to assuage Bush's humiliations of this day?

Bush's last pre-election campaign trip would eliminate stops in Oregon, Nebraska, Illinois and North Carolina, where Republicans teetered on the edge of defeat. Bush was trying to cut his losses, and he was not alone. During the months before the election, Bush had spent hours sweating under television lights to tape endorsement commercials for over 80 GOP candidates. One Congressman, Rep. Alfred A. McCandless of California, used pieces of Bush's tape in a commercial designed to highlight his differences with Bush. Many of the other tapes were never used; many of those endorsed pleaded as an excuse that their fundraising had been ruined by Bush's tax policy, so they never had the money to put them on the air.

Bush went back to his staple offering: hysterical, rage-driven warmongering, with an extra dividend for some audiences coming through the clear racist overtones. Once Congress had adjourned, one observer noted, "Bush was able to switch to his favorite script, 'Desperately Seeking Saddam.' "[29] Bush grimaced and pouted against the "butcher of Baghdad." Saddam was now "Hitler revisited." Later, there were estimates that Bush's exclusive concentration on the war theme had saved one to two Senate seats, and perhaps half a dozen in the House.

But Bush came dangerously close to overdoing it. In the last days of October, he had begun a demagogic effort to whip up hysteria about the U.S. citizens interned by Iraq. "I have had it" with the Iraqi handling of the internees, was now Bush's favorite line. When Bush wrapped himself in the flag, he expected the Democrats to kow-tow, but now there was some opposition. Bush met with some 15 congressional leaders active in foreign policy, and began raving about the "horrible, barbarous" conditions of the hostages. Sharp questions were immediately posed by Democrats, many of them facing reelection in a few days. According to one Congressman, "They were asking, in not so many words, Is this trumped up? If it isn't, how come we just have started hearing about it in the middle of this political mess the president is in? It seems to be coming out of nowhere." Dante Fascell said the Democrats had told Bush, "If there is additional provocation [by Iraq], it better be real and able to stand up to press scrutiny." Too bad the Democrats had not applied that standard to the whole trumped-up Gulf crisis.[30]

The result of the November 6 election was a deep disappointment to Republicans; Bush's party lost one Senate seat, nine House seats, and one governorship. Not all of these gains went to Democrats, since disgruntled voters gave two governorships and one House seat to independents outside of the two-party system. Most dramatic was the anti-incumbent mood against Governors, where economic crisis and tax revolt had been on the agenda all year: The governing party, whether Republican or Democrat, was ousted in 14 of the 36 state houses that were contested. For Bush there were very special disappointments: He had campaigned very hard for Clayton Williams in Texas and for Governor Bob Martinez in Florida, but Bush's coattails proved non-existent to negative; Democrats won both governorships. The loss of Texas and Florida was a very ominous threat for Bush's 1992 reelection campaign, since these were the two indispensable keystones of the Southern Strategy. Now, that GOP lock on the Electoral College might be drawing to a close.

Toward Aggressive War

But well before the dust had settled from the election debacle, Bush had resumed his march toward a holocaust in the Middle East. On the day after the election, Baker, speaking in Moscow, launched Bush's all-out press for a U.N. Security Council resolution legitimizing the use of armed force against Iraq over the Kuwait question. Bush had to push his war through both the U.S. Congress and the U.N. permanent five; his estimate was that the world powers would be easier to dragoon, and that the assent of the Security Council could then be used to bludgeon the Congress into acquiescence.

It is important to note that in shifting his policy toward aggressive war, Bush was once again dancing to the tune being piped in from London. On Wednesday, November 7, the racist crone Thatcher, now on her way out as Prime Minister, issued her most warmongering statement so far on the Gulf crisis: "Either [Saddam Hussein] gets out of Kuwait soon or we and our allies will remove him by force and he will go down to defeat with all the consequences. He has been warned."[31]

Yet again, the United States was to be drawn into a useless and genocidal war as the tail on the British imperial kite.

And so, flaunting his vicious contempt for the democratic process, on Thursday, November 8, just two days after the election, Bush made what any serious, intelligent person must have recognized as a declaration of preemptive war in the Gulf:

> After consultation with King Fahd and our other allies I have today directed the Secretary of Defense to increase the size of U.S. forces committed to Desert Shield to ensure that the coalition has an adequate offensive military option should that be necessary to achieve our common goals. Towards this end we will continue to discuss the possibility of both additional allied force contributions and appropriate United Nations actions. Iraq's brutality, aggression, and violations of international law cannot be allowed to succeed.[32]

For those who had ever believed Bush's verbal declarations, here was an entirely new policy, advanced without the slightest motivation. Bush argued that the current U.S. troop strength of 230,000 was enough to defend Saudi Arabia, but that was no longer good enough. Bush's only argument was that gradual strangulation by sanctions might take too long. Reporters pointed out that Thatcher had threatened to use military force the day before. Did Bush want war? "I would love to see a peaceful resolution to this question, and that's what I want." Some of the more lucid minds had now figured out that Bush was indeed a pathological liar.

For the rest of the month of November, a modest wave of anti-war sentiment was observed in the United States. On Sunday, November 11, Sen. Sam Nunn questioned Bush's rush to war. But Nunn did not call for a denial of funds to wage war on the model of the Hatfield-McGovern amendment, which had finally tied Nixon's hands in Vietnam. Nunn was a leader of the strangler group, urging reliance on the sanctions. James Reston wrote in the *New York Times* that "Bush's comparison of Hussein to Hitler, a madman with superior military forces in the center of industrial Europe, is ridiculous. . . . Saying 'my President, right or wrong,' in such circumstances, is a little like saying, 'my driver, drunk or sober,' and not many passengers like to go that far."[33] The following day, under a headline reading "Tide against war grows at home, abroad," the *Washington Times* carried a warning from New York Senator Daniel Patrick Moynihan: "If George Bush wants his presidency to die in the Arabian desert, he's going at it very steadily and as if it were a plan. He will wreck our military, he will wreck his administration, and he'll spoil the chance to get a collective security system working. It breaks the heart." Sen. Kerrey of Nebraska declared himself "not convinced this administration will do everything in its power to avoid war. And if ever there was an avoidable war, it is this one."

On the following day, Gorbachov's special envoy to the Middle East, Yevgeny Primakov, called for a delay in the resolution on the use of force against Iraq to allow Saddam Hussein a "face-saving" way out. One week later, in the context of the Paris Conference on Security and Cooperation in Europe, Gorbachov directed his desperate appeal to the world for food shipments to the U.S.S.R. Even if the Kremlin had wished to resist Bush's war drive, its weakness was evident. The Soviet Union, like China, would soon vote for the resolution that would justify Bush's January attack.

James Baker, groping for reasons for the coming war, thought he had found one: "If you want to sum it up in one word, it's jobs. Because an economic recession, worldwide, caused by the control of one nation, one dictator, of the West's economic lifeline will result in the loss of jobs on the part of American citizens."[34] Many citizens were offended by Baker's patronizing condescension, which was coordinated with Bush's remarks of the same day in which he admitted that the country was in a "downturn," and hinted that the depth of any recession would depend on whether or not the Gulf crisis turned into a prolonged standoff. If recession were to come, said Bush, "it will not be deep and we will come out of it relatively soon—six months at most."[35] Commenting on what really concerned him, Bush commented, "holding public opinion forever is very difficult to do."

In the House of Representatives, a group of 45 House Democrats went to federal court in a vain attempt to stop Bush from initiating hostilities, and Rep. Henry Gonzalez of Texas, the honorable maverick, offered a bill of impeachment against Bush.

On November 16, Bush left on a multi-country blitz of Europe and the Middle East which was intended to shore up the anti-Iraq coalition until the buildup could be completed and the war unleashed. In Prague, Bush was lionized by large crowds; President Vaclav Havel gave Bush a testimonial of support about the lessons of Munich 1938 and appeasement that Bush would wave around all through the war. It was unfortunate that freedom from communist tyranny for some politicians seemed to mean the freedom to lick Bush's boots. In Speyer, Germany, Bush had another apoplectic moment when Catholic Bishop Anton Schlembach wished Bush success "but without war and bloodshed." Germans were not happy about Bush's extortion of their country when they needed money to rebuild the newly freed federal states in the east; Germany was now reunified. Bush had a strained meeting with Kohl, and, at the CSCE finale in Paris, a cordial one with Mitterrand, with whom his rapport was excellent.

On Thanksgiving Day, Bush and Bar were with the troops in Saudi Arabia. Many soldiers told reporters that they were not happy to be there, and were not in favor of war. One trooper asked Bush, "Why not make a deal with Saddam Hussein, Mr. President?"

Flying westward the next day, Bush stopped in Geneva for a meeting with Hafez al Assad of Syria, a true villain and butcher, who had, during the month of October, taken advantage of his deal with Bush to finish off Gen. Michel Aoun's independent Lebanese state. Bush's meeting with Assad lasted for three hours. Assad had provided 7,500 Syrian troops for the coalition attack force in Saudi Arabia, which he promised to increase to 20,000. "Mr. Assad is lined up with us with a commitment to force," said Bush. "They are on the front line, or will be, standing up to this aggression."

It was during this period that Lyndon LaRouche, from his jail cell in Minnesota, called attention to Bush's increasingly psychotic behavior. On November 24, LaRouche commented:

> I have been obliged today to use nothing other than the term "psycho-sexual impotence" to describe the characteristic features exhibited by a visibly paranoid President George Herbert "Hoover" Walker Bush in the context of his reactions simultaneously to knowledge of the certainty of the ongoing economic depression, and the mess in the Persian Gulf, in which he, guided largely by certain Israeli influences and Margaret Thatcher, has enmired himself, the nation, and a good deal of the world.
>
> There is no question that President George Bush is suffering a more acute form of implicitly schizophrenic paranoia than he showed during the height of the moments of uncertainty during the Panama atrocity by forces under his direction.
>
> The President, in short, is CRACKING: HE IS GOING NUTS.
>
> The proper term to be used, to understand this particular problem of the President as President, is "psycho-sexual impotence" as I have used the term, in connection with, for example, the "Beyond Psychoanalysis" series. . . .
>
> Bush . . . is a killer; he is a heartless, amoral, immoral bureaucrat, who's capable of any dirty thing in the book, for the sake of expediency; he probably has a sense of ethics, which means ethics in the sense of *Nichomachean Ethics*, which means a complete lack of morality. . . .
>
> And George simply reacts like a Nietzschean fascist, to say that he will impose by brute force and by exercise of the will, his arbitrary values, his belief structure, upon an uncooperative Creator and Creation.

That is the case in which the psycho-sexual impotent goes over to the practice of RAPE—because the woman, or women, refuse to be responsive to his advances, and therefore he says, "I'll make you responsive; I'll rape you." That's George Bush. Therefore, one must use the concept of psycho-sexual impotence in the case of Bush in order to understand him, and to understand the crisis which besets the presidency at this time. You have a man who is intellectually distinguished by the banality of his mediocrity, who is faced with a situation in which there is no room for mediocrity, in any part of the world, with respect to any important domestic or international policy matter. But, you have a mediocrity who, at the same time, is a megalomaniac mediocrity who refuses to accept anything which might suggest the slightest tinge of mediocrity in his mediocrity. And he's gone over to a Nietzschean kind of triumph of the arbitrary will, which he conceives of, as did Hitler, as a new world order, at the behest of the impulse of this poor mediocrity himself.[36]

On November 30, the U.N. Security Council, now reduced to a discredited tool of the Anglo-Americans, voted for a resolution authorizing the use of force against Iraq. This piece of infamy was labeled Resolution 648, and passed with twelve assenting votes against the no votes of Cuba and Yemen, with the People's Republic of China abstaining. (International jurists later pointed out that according to the text of the U.N. Charter, which requires the positive votes of all five permanent members to approve substantive resolutions, the resolution had not passed, and that in acting on it the U.N. had entered a phase of anarchy and lawlessness.) Iraq was given 47 days to leave Kuwait, and this ultimatum was to expire on January 15. Bush clearly hoped that this resolution could be used to silence his congressional critics.

Anti-war sentiment now crystallized around the hearings being held by Sam Nunn's Senate Armed Services Committee. Two former chairmen of the Joint Chiefs of Staff, Adm. William J. Crowe and Gen. David C. Jones, urged a policy of continued reliance on the sanctions. They were soon joined by former Secretary of Defense James R. Schlesinger, Gen. William Odom, and other figures of past regimes. Bush's principal support came from the croaking voice of Henry Kissinger, who was for war as soon as practicable. Bush wanted the Congress to pass a resolution giving him a blank check to wage war, but he hesitated to set off a debate that might go on all the way to January 15 and beyond, and in which he risked being beaten.

Now, on Friday, November 30, Bush executed the cynical tactic that would ultimately paralyze his craven domestic opposition and clear the way to war: He made a fake offer of negotiations with Iraq:

> However, to go the extra mile for peace, I will issue an invitation to Foreign Minister Tariq Aziz to come to Washington at a mutually convenient time during the latter part of the week of December 10th to meet with me. And I'll invite ambassadors of several of our coalition partners in the gulf to join me in that meeting.
>
> In addition, I am asking Secretary Jim Baker to go to Baghdad to see Saddam Hussein, and I will suggest to Iraq's president that he receive the secretary of state at a mutually convenient time between December 15 and January 15 of next year.[37]

It was all a fiendish lie, even down to the offer of times and venues for the talks. When Iraq responded with proposals for the schedule of meetings, Bush welshed and reneged. Iraq released the U.S. internees, but Bush still wanted war. "We've got to continue to keep the pressure on," was his reaction. Then came a full month of useless haggling, which was exactly what Bush wanted. As his text had pointed out, he was not interested in real negotiation anyway; the U.N. resolutions had already resolved everything. The real purpose of this gambit was to suppress the domestic opposition, since negotiations were allegedly now ongoing.

The most important opposition to a January 15 war, according to the deadline railroaded through the U.N. by Bush, came from the U.S. Army, the service least enthralled by the idea of a needless war. During a visit by Powell and Cheney to Saudi Arabia, Lt. Gen. Calvin A.H. Waller, the second-in-command of U.S. forces in the Gulf, remarked that there was a "distinct possibility that every unit will not be fully combat-ready until some time after February 1," or perhaps as late as mid-February." "If the owner asks me if I'm ready to go, I'd tell him, 'No, I'm not ready to do the job,' " Waller told the press. It was understood that Waller was acting as spokesman for a broad stratum of senior officers. The Bush White House was once again infuriated. "This is not the message we were trying to send now," said one top Bushman.[38] Waller and the other active duty officers would henceforth remain silent.

Bush's buildup went on inexorably through the Christmas holidays. In the first week of the new year, Bush offered a meeting of Baker and Tariq Aziz, the Iraqi foreign minister, in Geneva. His ground rules made the meeting pointless even before it happened: "No negotiations, no compromises, no attempts at face-saving and no rewards for aggression."[39]

The Tariq Aziz-Baker talks in Geneva went on for six hours on January 10, with no result. Baker was an Al Capone in striped pants; Tariq Aziz expressed himself with great dignity. Tariq Aziz had made clear that since Israel was in reality an integral part of Bush's Gulf coalition, it could not be exempt from retaliation if Iraq were to come under attack. For Bush, when millions of lives were at stake, the issue of greatest moment was a letter full of threats, written by Bush to Saddam Hussein, which Tariq Aziz had read, but refused to accept, and had left lying on the table in Geneva. (In this letter, which was later released, Bush warned Saddam, "we stand today at the brink of war between Iraq and the world," as if Bush were the chief executive of the entire planet.) Here was a new focus for Bush's apoplectic rage: He had been insulted by this Arab!

On January 9, the United Nations Security Council resolution, with its approaching artificial deadline which Bush had demanded, plus the failure of the Baker-Tariq Aziz meeting, became the tools of the White House in obtaining a congressional resolution for war. Bush was careful to stress his view that he could wage war without the Congress, but that he was magnanimously letting them express their support for him by approving such a motion. On this same day, the Kremlin dispatched troop contingents to seven Soviet republics where nationalist movements were gaining ground.

The congressional debate provided many eloquent pleas, generally from Democrats, for delaying military action in order to save Americans from useless slaughter. But these pleas were almost always vitiated by a failure to recognize the equal claim to humanity of the Iraqi population; the Democrats who urged continued reliance on sanctions were in effect calling for an equal or greater genocide prolonged over time.

Bush's war resolution passed the Senate by the narrow margin of 52–47. This vote reflects a deep ambivalence in the ruling elite about Bush's bellicose line, which was not as popular in U.S. ruling circles as it was in London. Bush's margin of victory was provided by a group of southern Bush Democrats (Gore, Graham, Breaux, Robb, Shelby). In the House, a similar Bush war resolution passed by 250 to 183. Many Congressmen from blue-collar districts being pounded by the economic depression reflected the disillusionment of their constituents by voting against Bush and the war. But the resistance was not enough.

Despite the extremely narrow mandate he had extorted from the Congress, Bush now appeared in a gloating press conference: He had his blank check for war and genocide. Now Bush was careful to create pretexts for attacking Iraq, even if Saddam were to order his forces out of Kuwait. Bush noted that "it would be, at this date, I would say impossible to comply fully with the United Nations resolutions," and he "would still worry about it, because it might not be in full compliance."[40] U.N. Resolution 242, calling for Israel to withdraw from the territories occupied in the 1967 war, had been flouted for almost a quarter-century, and the nation of Lebanon had just been snuffed out by Bush's friend Assad, but all of this paled into total irrelevance in comparison to the need to destroy Iraq.

The Mad Dog of War

The mad dog of war was now unleashed on the world.

According to the official account, Bush signed the National Security Directive ordering the attack against Iraq in the White House Oval Office at 10:30 A.M. on Tuesday morning, January 15, 1991. On Wednesday morning in Washington, when it was early evening in Baghdad, Bush ordered Scowcroft to call Cheney with a further instruction to implement the attack plan. The U.S. air attack on Iraq accordingly took place between 6:00 and 7:00 P.M. on Wednesday, January 16. The bombs began to fall during the first night in Baghdad after the expiration of Bush's deadline.[41] Within 24 hours, Iraq retaliated with Scud missiles against Israel and against U.S. bases in Saudi Arabia. One day after that, Bush described the Scud attacks as "purely an act of terror."

Day after day, Iraqi military and above all civilian targets were subjected to a hail of bombs. The centerpiece of Bush's personal self-justification remained the equation Saddam=Hitler. One party worker described Bush as "a man obsessed and possessed by his mission" in the Gulf war. There are indications that after a week to ten days of bombing, Bush was surprised and disappointed that all Iraqi resistance had not already collapsed. This is what some of his advisers were rumored in Washington to have promised him.

The 1991 State of the Union address was supposed to be the apotheosis of Bush as a warrior emperor. One of his themes was the "next American century," borrowed from Stimson and Luce. The apotheosis was somewhat dimmed by the economic difficulties the Gulf war had done nothing to assuage. Bush portrayed these problems as a mere ripple in "the largest peacetime economic expansion in history." "We will soon get this recession behind us," Bush promised. He conjured up "the long-held promise of a new world order—where brutality will go unrewarded, and aggression will meet collective resistance." He urged this country to take up "the burden of leadership." For many, the reference was clear:

Take up the White Man's burden—
Ye dare not stoop to less
Nor call too loud on Freedom
To cloak your weariness,

had written Rudyard Kipling in 1899 as part of a British campaign to convince the United States to set up a colonial administration in the Philippines. The racist jingo doggerel of imperialism caught Bush's mood precisely.

After the war, it would be shown that the U.S. bombers had concentrated their fire on the civilian infrastructure of Iraq, choosing targets of no immediate military relevance. The bombing was concentrated on systems providing potable water to cities, electrical generating facilities, bridges, highways and other transportation infrastructure. This was cynically called the "bomb now, die later" strategy, since the goal of the bombing was to destroy civilian infrastructure in order to lower the relative potential population density of the country below the actual level of the Iraqi population, thus producing an astronomical rise in infant mortality, plagues, and pestilence. It was, in short, a population war. It was a cowardly, despicable way to fight.

Bush had ordered all this, but he lied compulsively about it. After three weeks of bombing, he told a press conference that his bombers were going to "unprecedented lengths to avoid damage to civilians and holy places. We do not seek Iraq's destruction, nor do we seek to punish the Iraqi people for the decisions and policies of their leaders. In addition, we are doing everything possible and with great success to minimize collateral damage. . . ."[42]

The air war was designed to gut the economic infrastructure of Iraq; an additional objective was to kill at least 100,000 members of the Iraqi armed forces. This could only be accomplished by storming the Iraqi positions on the ground, and this is what Bush was determined to do. Published accounts suggested that the original executive order that started the war also contained instructions for a land battle to follow extensive bombing. This meant that all peace-feelers must be vigorously rebuffed, on the model of what Acheson and Stimson had done to Japan during July of 1945.

In those days, anti-war protesters had camped out in Lafayette Park, across Pennsylvania Avenue from the White House. They had been there since December 13. Bush had referred once to "those damned drums" and how they were keeping him awake at night. At his press conference of February 6, Bush told reporters that the drummers had been removed, not because he had ordered it, but because they were disturbing the guests at the posh Hay-Adams Hotel on the other side of the park.

But just as Bush was speaking, reporters could hear the thumping resume in the park outside. The drummers, much to Bush's chagrin, were at it again. Soon Lafayette Park was fenced in by the Bushmen.

On February 15, Radio Baghdad offered negotiations leading to the withdrawal of Iraqi forces from Kuwait. Bush, in tandem with the new British Prime Minister, John Major, rejected this overture with parallel rhetoric. For Bush, Saddam's peace bid was "a cruel hoax"; for Major, it was "a bogus sham." The Kremlin, seeking to save face with its Third World clients, found the proposal "encouraging." Iraq was now pulling key military units out of Kuwait, and Bush judged that the moment was ripe to call for an insurrection and military coup against Saddam Hussein and the Baath Party government. With this call, Bush triggered the simultaneous uprisings of the pro-Iranian Shiites in Iraq's southern provinces, and of the Kurds in the north, many of whom now foolishly concluded that U.S. military assistance would be forthcoming. It was a cynical ploy, since Bush can be seen in retrospect to have had no intention whatever of backing up these rebellions. During the month of March, tens of thousands of additional casualties and untold human misery would be the sole results of these insurrections, which led to the mass exodus of the hapless and wretched Kurds into Iran and Turkey.

The Soviets were still seeking to save half a face from a massacre which they had aided and abetted; diplomacy would also help take the mind of the world off the Baltic bloodshed of the Soviet special forces. During the week after Saddam Hussein's trial balloon for a pullout from Kuwait, Yevgeny Primakov attempted to assemble a cease-fire. Primakov's efforts were brushed aside with single-empire arrogance by Bush, who spoke off the cuff at a photo opportunity: "Very candidly . . . while expressing appreciation for his sending it to us, it falls well short of what would be required. As far as I am concerned, there are no negotiations. The goals have been set out. There will be no concessions." Diplomatically, the once mighty Soviet Union had ceased to exist; the collapse of the Soviet state had been accelerated by its seconding of the Anglo-American designs in the Gulf, and the opinions of the Kremlin now counted for nothing.

Primakov and Tariq Aziz then proceeded to transform the original Soviet eight-point plan into a more demanding six-point plan, including some of the demands of the Anglo-Americans on the timetable of withdrawal and other issues. Bush's answer to that, on the morning of Friday, February 22, was a 24-hour ultimatum to

Iraq to begin an "immediate and unconditional withdrawal from Kuwait" or face an immediate attack by coalition land forces. Many Iraqi units were now already in retreat; the essence of the U.S. demands was to make Iraq accept a pullout so rapid that all equipment and supplies must be left behind.

It is clear that, even if Iraq had accepted Bush's terms, he would have found reasons to continue the air bombardment. During the following days, the principal activity of U.S. planes was to bomb columns of Iraqi forces leaving Kuwait and retreating toward the north, toward Iraq, in exact compliance with the U.N. resolutions. But Bush now wanted to fulfill his quota of 100,000 dead Iraqi soldiers. During the evening of Saturday, February 23, Bush spoke from the White House announcing an order to General Schwarzkopf to "use all forces, including ground forces, to eject the Iraqi army from Kuwait."[43]

It emerged in retrospect that many Iraqi military units had left Kuwait weeks before the final land battle. Well-informed observers thought that the Iraqi Republican Guard had been reduced to less than three functioning combat divisions by Bush's air and ground assaults, but it shortly became clear that there were at least five Republican Guard divisions in the field at something approaching full strength. Finally, on February 27, after 41 days of war, Bush ordered a cease-fire. "Our military objectives are met," proclaimed Bush.[44]

The End of the War?

Because all reports on Operation Desert Shield and Operation Desert Storm were covered by the strictest military censorship, and because most news organizations of the U.S. and the other coalition states were more than willing to operate under these conditions, most of the details of these operations are still in the realm of Anglo-American mind war.

The coalition air fleets had carried out some 120,000 sorties against Iraq. If each sortie had claimed but a single Iraqi life, then 120,000 Iraqis had perished. In reality, total Iraqi casualties of killed, wounded and missing, plus the civilian losses from famine, disease and pestilence must have been in the neighborhood of 500,000 by the end of 1991.

In early March, Bush addressed a special session of the Congress on what he chose to call the end of the war. This time it was Bush's personal apotheosis; he was frequently interrupted by manic applause. Bush's mind war had succeeded. Resistance to the war had been driven virtually underground; bloodthirsty racism ruled most public discourse for a time. It was one of the most wretched moments of the American spirit. Bush, who was consciously preparing new wars, was careful not to promise peace: "Even the new world order cannot guarantee an era of perpetual peace."

Bush now turned his attention to "the domestic front," where he was quick to make clear that the new world order begins at home: His main proposal was the administration's omnibus crime bill. One of the main features of this monstrous legislation was an unprecedented expansion in the use of the death penalty for a long list of federal crimes. Bush had enjoyed giving international ultimata so much that he decided to try one on the Congress: "If our forces could win the ground war in 100 hours, then surely the Congress can pass this legislation in 100 days. Let that be a promise we make tonight to the American people."[45] Bring the killing back home, said Bush in effect.

Many commentators, especially Bush's own allies in the neoconservative, pro-Zionist camp, were greatly disappointed that Bush was terminating the hostilities without liquidating Saddam Hussein, and without guaranteeing the partition of Iraq. Bush was restrained by a series of considerations. Further penetration into Iraq would have necessitated the long-term occupation of large cities, exposing the occupiers to the dangers that the U.S. Marines had faced in Beirut in 1982. If Bush were determined to wipe out the government of Iraq, then he would have to provide an occupation government, or else let the country collapse into civil war and partition. Based on these and other considerations, Bush appears to have made a characteristic snap decision to end the war. Bush ended the war with a claim that the U.S. casualty list for the entire operation stood at 223 killed; but, in keeping with the mind-war censorship that had cloaked all the proceedings, no casualty list was ever published. The true number of those killed is therefore not known, and is likely to be much higher than that claimed by Bush.

On March 16, Bush met with British Prime Minister John Major on Bermuda. Bush's public line was that there could be no normalization of relations with Iraq as long as Saddam Hussein remained in power. Since the days of the Treaty of Sevres at the end of World War I, London had been toying with the idea of an independent Kurdish state in eastern Anatolia. The British were also anxious to use the aftermath of the war in order to establish precedents in international law to undermine the sovereignty of independent nations, and to create ethnic enclaves short of a complete partition of Iraq. British, Israeli and U.S. assets had combined to provoke a large-scale Kurdish uprising in northern Iraq, and this produced a civil war in the country.

During the latter half of March, calls were made for the creation of a Kurdish enclave in northern Iraq under the protection of the coalition. On April 2, the State Department restated the Bush administration line of non-intervention and "hands off" Iraqi internal affairs, and Bush himself repeated this line on April 3. But British pressure was about to create an extraordinary reversal, which showed the world that even after the departure of Thatcher, and while he was allegedly at the height of his glory, Bush was still taking orders from London. On April 5, Bush yielded partially to the clamor to intervene in favor of the Kurds, who had now been militarily defeated by the Iraqi Army and were seeking refuge in Iran and in the Turkish mountains of southeast Anatolia. On April 7, U.S. planes began air drops of supplies into these Turkish and Iraqi areas. Then, on April 8, Major repeated his demand for "safe zone" enclaves for the Kurds to be created and guaranteed by the coalition in territory carved out of northern Iraq. It was a clear interference in Iraqi internal affairs, and a clear violation of international law, but the British were backed up by the choplogic theorizing of French Foreign Minister Roland Dumas, who advanced the theory of the "humanitarian intervention" as a fig leaf for the sweeping power of wealthy imperialists to trample on the weak and the starving in the future.

British pressure was unrelenting; this was a chance to rewrite international law and to deal a crushing blow to previous concepts of sovereignty. Bush finally harkened to his master's voice. On April 16, he announced the total reversal of his own policy: ". . . I have directed the U.S. military to begin immediately to establish several encampments in northern Iraq where relief supplies for these refugees will be made available in large quantities and distributed in an orderly way."

This decision created an Anglo-American enclave in northern Iraq that expanded during a period of several weeks before stabilizing. U.S. forces left Iraqi territory by July 15, but some of them stayed behind as part of a very ominous rapid deployment force jointly created by the U.S., the U.K., France, Italy, Belgium and the Netherlands and based in southeast Turkey. This was called Operation Poised Hammer (in British parlance, Sword of Damocles), and was allegedly stationed to protect the Kurds from future attacks by Saddam. Many observers noted that this force was optimally positioned to go north and east as well as south and west, meaning that the Poised Hammer force had to be regarded as prepositioned for a possible move into the southern, Islamic belt of the crumbling Soviet empire.

On April 16 and April 29, Iraq, having complied with most of the cease-fire conditions imposed by Bush through the U.N. Security Council, requested that the economic embargo imposed in early August 1990 be finally lifted so as to permit the country to buy food, medicine and other basic goods on the world market, and to sell oil in order to pay for them.

But Bush's commitment to genocide was truly implacable. Bush first obstructed the Iraqi requests with a debate on the conditions for the payment of Iraqi reparations and the country's international financial debt, and then stated on May 20: "At this juncture, my view is we don't want to lift the sanctions as long as [Saddam Hussein] is in power." In the Congress, Rep. Tim Penny of Minnesota and Rep. Henry Gonzalez of Texas offered resolutions to relax the sanctions or to end them entirely, but the Bush machine blocked every move in that direction. Here Bush risked isolation in the court of world public opinion. On July 12, the Aga Khan returned from a visit to Iraq to propose that the sanctions be lifted. The lives of hundreds of thousands of Iraqi children were in danger because of the lack of clean water, food, medicine and basic health services; during the summer of 1991, infant mortality in Iraq rose almost 400 percent over the prewar period. An international effort launched by Mrs. Helga Zepp-LaRouche, the international Committee to Save the Children in Iraq, was able to send planeloads of medical supplies and infant formula into the country, and to focus international attention on Bush's ongoing high crime against humanity.

The spring of 1991 brought a political signal that was very ominous for Bush's future. This bad omen for George came in the form of a *New York Times* op-ed written by William G. Hyland, the well-known Kissinger clone serving as editor for the magazine *Foreign Affairs*, the quarterly organ of the New York Council on Foreign Relations, and one of the flagship publications of the Eastern Anglophile Liberal Establishment. The article was entitled "Downgrade Foreign Policy," and appeared on May 20, 1991. Hyland's thesis was that "the United States has never been less threatened by foreign forces than it is today. But the unfortunate corollary is that never since the Great Depression has the threat to domestic well-being been greater." Hyland demanded that Bush pay more attention to domestic policy, and his proposals for U.S. military disengagement abroad were radical enough to raise the eyebrows of the London *Financial Times*, which called attention to Hyland's catalogue of Bush's "disastrous domestic agenda: crime, drugs, education, urban crisis, federal budget deficits and a constant squeeze on the middle class, the backbone of our democracy."

What Hyland's backers had in mind as remedies for these problems boiled down to modern versions of the Mussolini fascist corporate state. Hyland's litany that Bush had to pay more attention to domestic crises and especially the battered U.S. economy soon became the stock rhetoric of Democratic presidential candidates, demanding a transition from Bush's voluntary corporatism (the "thousand points of light") to the compulsory corporatism of General Hugh Johnson's National Recovery Administration, with an economy organized into obligatory, state-controlled cartels to reduce wages and cut production. This was the reality that lurked behind the edifying rhetoric about poverty, joblessness and the decline of the middle class purveyed by the official Democratic presidential contenders who finally emerged by the end of 1991. But for Bush, the Hyland article was a clear indication that Wall Street was becoming disenchanted with his policies.

On to Free-Trade War

Bush was determined to exploit the momentum gained during the violence and extortion of the Gulf crisis to further the cause of Anglo-American economic war and trade war against Germany, Japan, the developing countries and the Soviet bloc. In mid-February, in the midst of the Gulf war, Bush's resident harpy at the Trade Representative's Office, Carla Hills, had virtually declared war against the Western European Airbus consortium, accusing this group of firms of protectionism, subsidies and violations of existing GATT regulations. On June 27, 1990, Bush had announced his "Enterprise for the Americas," in effect a plan for a free trade zone stretching from the North Pole to Tierra del Fuego, all to be subjected to unbridled looting by the U.S. dollar. At that time, Bush had stated that "the U.S. stands ready to enter into free trade agreements with other markets in Latin America and the Caribbean . . . and the first step in this process is a trade agreement with Mexico."

During the Gulf buildup, Bush had met with Mexican President Carlos Salinas de Gortari in Salinas's home town of Agualeguas in northern Mexico. The leading item on the agenda was the Wall Street demand for a U.S.-Mexico free trade agreement which, together with the existing U.S.-Canada free trade arrangement, would amount of a North American Free Trade Agreement (NAFTA). The negotiation of this deal would begin during 1991. The essence of

NAFTA was a wholly deregulated free trade zone in which remaining factories and other businesses in the United States would move their operations to Mexico, in order to take advantage of an average wage of 98 cents an hour as against $11 an hour in U.S. manufacturing. The legal minimum wage in Mexico was the equivalent of 59 cents an hour. It was a plan for runaway shops on an unprecedented scale; the Mexican sweat shops or "maquiladoras" were so brutal in their exploitative practices as to constitute an "Auschwitz below the border." Salinas visited Washington on April 7, 1991, and Bush once again called for free trade with Mexico.

Then there was the Uruguay Round of the General Agreement on Tariffs and Trade. The goal of the Bushmen in the GATT talks was to press forward toward what Bush called "global free trade"; all nations were to be coerced into giving up their inherent sovereign rights to intervene in favor of their own farmers, industrialists and other producers. An important aspect of this thrust was the Anglo-American demand that the European Community dismantle its system of payments to farmers. In October at the U.N., Bush would press for the completion of GATT.

Bush demanded from the U.S. Congress the ability to negotiate both GATT and NAFTA on a "fast track" basis. This meant that Bush wanted to be able to negotiate vital international trade agreements, and then submit them to Congress on an all-or-nothing, take-it-or-leave-it basis. The Congress could make no amendments nor add statements of clarification; such rubber-stamping would undermine the right of the Senate to provide advice and consent in treaties. There was considerable resistance in Congress to the fast track for NAFTA and GATT, and this was backed up by the rank and file of the AFL-CIO trade unions, who did not wish to see their jobs exported. But the chances for stopping the fast track in the summer of 1991 were ruined by the defection of Missouri Congressman Richard Gephardt, whose ties to organized labor were strong, but who nevertheless came out in favor of the fast track on May 9. The fast track cleared Congress on May 23.

Bush sought to extend the zone of "free trade" looting ever southward. In mid-June, Brazilian President Fernando Collor de Mello came to the White House, where Bush greeted him as "my kind of guy." Collor, like Salinas, was anxious to dissolve national sovereignty into a "free market." The discussion revolved around reducing trade barriers between the future NAFTA and the Southern Common Market of Brazil, Argentina, Paraguay and Uruguay. Collor also pledged to preserve the Amazon rain forest, a demand that was becoming the focus of the U.N.'s "Eco '92" conference set to

take place in Brazil. Shortly after this, Bush would hold a Rose
Garden ceremony to celebrate the triumphant progress of his Enterprise for the Americas free trade steamroller since its inception one
year before.

Continuing violence was the staple of the New World Order.
Elections in India were scheduled for late May, and the likely victor
was Rajiv Gandhi, whose mother had been assassinated by Anglo-
American intelligence in 1984. Rajiv Gandhi, during his time in
the opposition, had experienced a remarkable process of personal
maturation. During the Gulf crisis and the war against Iraq, he had
used his position as chief of the opposition to force the weak Chandra Shakar government to reject a U.S. demand for landing rights for
U.S. military aircraft transferring war materiel from the Philippines
toward Saudi Arabia. If reelected Prime Minister of India, Rajiv
Gandhi would very likely have assumed a position of leadership
among world forces determined to resist the Anglo-American New
World Order; he also would have offered the best hope of frustrating
London's gambit of a new Indo-Pakistani war according to the game
plan in which Bush had participated back in 1970. The Anglo-
American media did not conceal their venomous hatred of Rajiv.
He was assassinated while campaigning on May 21, and his death
was widely attributed in India to the CIA.

Launching Hot War in Europe

The Anglo-American approach to sabotaging and containing
continental Europe included doing everything possible to create a
new war on the Balkan flank of that continent. This was done as
openly as possible, through a visit to Belgrade by James Baker. On
June 22, 1991, Baker met with the Presidents of the two Yugoslav
federal republics which had been seeking either a loose confedera-
tion or else their own outright independence, Milan Kucan of Slovenia and Franjo Tudjman of Croatia. Baker warned both that they
would get no U.S. recognition and no U.S. economic aid if they
seceded from the Yugoslav federation. "The breakup of Yugoslavia
would have 'very tragic consequences,' " Baker said, adding very
ominously, "We worry, frankly, about history repeating itself."
Baker was talking about Sarajevo and how the conflict of Serbia
with Austria-Hungary had detonated a general war and devastated
Europe.

Also on June 22, Baker had a special meeting with the Serbian
fascist strongman, Slobodan Milosevic, in which Baker encouraged
the Serbian military to suppress any rebellion with military means.

The federal army assaults on Slovenia, and then on Croatia, can be dated from these exchanges, which succeeded in creating the first war and the first bombing of civilians in central Europe since 1945. Interviews during this same time frame by Undersecretary of State Lawrence Eagleburger, the Kissinger Associates veteran who had been on the board of the U.S. importer of Yugo automobiles, and on the board of a Yugoslav bank involved in drug money laundering, left no doubt of U.S. intent: in Eagleburger's babbling, every other word was "civil war."

U.S. brokerage houses waxed eloquent over how the incipient Yugoslav civil war would prevent investment in most countries of central Europe, and would ruin the economic hinterland of united Germany. Yugoslavia had been ravaged by the conditionalities of the IMF during the 1980s, and it was this regime that Bush was imposing in Poland, and which he wanted to extend to the rest of eastern Europe and the republics emerging from the former Soviet Union.

On the last two days of July, following the Group of Seven summit, Bush went to Moscow for a summit with Gorbachov that centered on the signing of a treaty on reducing strategic armaments. Erstwhile condominium partners Gorbachov and Primakov pressed for economic assistance and investments, but all that Bush was willing to offer was a vague commitment to forward to Congress the trade treaty of 1990, which would provide, if approved, for the extension of the Most Favored Nation treatment to Moscow. Soviet black beret special forces units deliberately massacred six Lithuanian border guards as Bush was arriving, but Bush maintained a pose of studied disinterest in the freedom of the Baltics. And not only of the Baltics: After the sessions with Gorbachov were over, Bush went to Kiev, the capital of Ukraine, where he rejected a private meeting with Ivan Drach, the leader of the Rukh, the main opposition movement. In the Ukrainian capital on August 1, "Chicken Kiev" Bush made his infamous speech in which he warned about the dangers inherent in nationalism.

Bush's Kiev speech stands out in retrospect as compelling evidence of his relentless opposition to anticommunist and anti-Soviet movements in the moribund Soviet empire: "Some people have urged the United States to choose between supporting President Gorbachov and supporting independence-minded leaders throughout the U.S.S.R. I consider this a false choice." And then, the crowning insult to the Ukrainians, who had been denied their nationhood for centuries: ". . . [F]reedom is not the same as independence. Americans will not support those who seek in order to replace a far-off tyranny with a local despotism. They will not aid those who promote a suicidal nationalism based upon ethnic hatred."[46] It was an insult the Ukrainians and other freedom fighters will not soon forget, and it had the benefit of opening the eyes of more than a few as to what kind of bird this Bush really was.

Again Bush's policy was a recipe for destabilization, starvation and war: He encouraged the Kremlin to crack down, but offered no economic cooperation, insisting instead on IMF superausterity. During the third week after Bush had left Moscow, the abortive putsch of the Group of 8 took place. In the wake of the failed putsch, Bush was one of the last world leaders to announce the restoration of diplomatic relations with the Baltic states through the sending of an ambassador; Bush had delayed for three additional days in response to an explicit request from Gorbachov. By the time Bush had accepted Baltic freedom, it was September 2. Bush clung to Gorbachov long after the latter had in fact ceased to exist. Gorbachov was gone by the end of 1991, and the alternative rejected by Bush in Kiev turned out to have been the real one.

Soviet policy led the agenda when Major visited Bush at Kennebunkport at the end of August. The two Anglo-Saxon champions proposed to offer the former Soviet republics "practical help in converting their economy into one that works," as Major put it. This translated into accelerating the "special association" of the Soviet Union (and/or its successor states) with the IMF, "with a view to full membership in due course for those who qualify" by virtue of their adoption of the disastrous Polish model. Bush urged Americans to wait "until the dust settles" and until "there are more cards on the table."[47]

But for George Bush, the essence of the postwar months of 1991 was a succession of personal triumphs, a succession which he hoped to extend all the way to the 1992 election. In mid-May, Queen Elizabeth II visited Washington in the context of a tour of several American cities. In an event which marked a new step in the moral degeneracy of the United States, Elizabeth Mountbatten-Windsor, lineal descendant of the hated George III of Hanover, became the first monarch of the United Kingdom ever to address a joint session of the Congress. Elizabeth spoke with the cynical hypocrisy which is the hallmark of Anglo-American propaganda. "Our views were identical and so were our responses," said Elizabeth, paying tribute to Bush. She also seemed to hint at open-ended commitments in the Gulf with her line that "unfortunately, experience shows that great enterprises seldom end with a tidy and satisfactory flourish."

One who preserved his honor by boycotting this session was

Illinois Congressman Gus Savage, who called Elizabeth "the Queen of colonialism," presiding over an exploited empire in the Third World.

In early June, there was the triumph accorded to General Schwarzkopf for the Gulf war. Bush viewed the parade and aircraft flyover from a reviewing stand set up in front of the White House, and met Schwarzkopf personally when he arrived. In the wake of the war, said Bush, "there is a new and wonderful feeling in America." In the Roman triumphs, the victorious general was crowned with bay leaves, and dressed in a purple toga embossed with golden stars. He also received the services of a slave who persistently reminded him that he was mortal, and that all glory was fleeting. Bush would have benefited from the services of such a slave on that June 8.[48]

The high tide of Bush's megalomania as the emperor of the New World Order was perhaps reached at the United Nations in September.

Bush's peroration reverted to the theme of the Single Empire, the Anglo-Saxon New World Order:

> Finally, you may wonder about America's role in the new world that I have described. Let me assure you, the United States has no intention of striving for a Pax Americana. However, we will remain engaged. We will not retreat and pull back into isolationism. We will offer friendship and leadership. And in short, we seek a Pax Universalis built upon shared responsibilities and aspirations.[49]

The emperor of the New World Order had spoken; now, woe to the vanquished!

Notes for Chapter XXIII

1. "Bush Hails 'Dramatic' Decision," *Washington Post*, Nov. 10, 1989.
2. "Bush: The Secret Presidency," *Newsweek*, Jan. 1, 1990.
3. "Berlin and Bush's Emotional Wall," *Washington Post*, Nov. 14, 1989.
4. "Text of President Bush's Address," *Washington Post*, Nov. 23, 1989.
5. *People*, April 9, 1990.
7. See "Tracking Thyroid Problems," *Washington Times*, May 29, 1991.
8. "Transcript of Bush-Gorbachov News Conference," *Washington Post*, June 4, 1990.
9. See Jim Hoagland, "The Deal Behind the Summit," *Washington Post*, June 5, 1990.
10. See "Marshall Says He Never Heard of Bush's Nominee," *New York Times*, July 27, 1990; "Marshall Slams Gavel on Souter," *Washington Times*, July 27, 1990. At about the same time that Marshall quit, Rep. William Gray of Philadelphia, the Democratic Majority Whip, announced his resignation from the House to become the president of the United Negro College Fund. Gray had been under heavy police state attack from the FBI, and was hounded from office. Within a few weeks, Bush had disposed of the top-ranking black officials of both the legislative and judicial branches of government.
11. Hobart Rowen, "A Near-Depression," *Washington Post*, Jan. 10, 1991.
12. "Bush Opens Door to Tax-Hike Talks," *Washington Post*, May 8, 1990.
13. In April 1991 federal regulators ended their 14-month inquiry into Neil Bush by directing

him to refrain from future conflicts of interest in his involvement with federally insured financial institutions. This was the mildest sanction in the official arsenal. In May 1991, the FDIC agreed to settle their negligence suit with Neil Bush and the other Silverado figures for $49.5 million. See the *New York Times,* June 9, 1991.

14. Webster G. Tarpley, "Is Bush Courting a Middle East War and New Oil Crisis?" *Executive Intelligence Review,* March 31, 1989. In early August 1989, after the pro-Iranian Organization of the Oppressed of the Earth had announced its execution of U.S. Marine Lt. Col. William R. Higgins, Bush did post a battleship and a carrier to the eastern Mediterranean, and a carrier in the northern Arabian Sea, thus threatening both Iran and Syria, whose forces went on alert in the Bekaa Valley and elsewhere.

15. "Stop Bush's Rush to World War III," *New Federalist,* Feb. 11, 1991.

16. "Administration Attempts to Blunt Israeli Criticism," *Washington Post,* March 6, 1990.

17. *EIR Special Report:* "Bush's Gulf Crisis: The Beginning of World War III?" (Washington: Sept. 1990), pp. 27–28.

18. Bob Woodward, *The Commanders* (New York: Simon and Schuster, 1991), pp. 205–06.

19. "Bush's Gulf Crisis: The Beginning of World War III?" *op. cit.,* pp. 28–29.

20. *Washington Post,* Aug. 3, 1990.

21. *New York Times,* Aug. 4, 1990.

22. See Maureen Dowd, "The Guns of August Make a Dervish Bush Whirl Even Faster," *New York Times,* Aug. 7, 1990; and "The Longest Week: How the President Decided to Draw the Line," *New York Times,* Aug. 9, 1990.

23. *New York Times,* Aug. 9, 1990.

24. *Washington Post,* Aug. 9, 1990.

25. "Bush's Talk of a 'New World Order': Foreign Policy Tool or Mere Slogan?" *Washington Post,* May 26, 1991.

26. *Washington Post,* Aug. 28, 1990.

27. "Bush: Out of These Troubled Times . . . a New World Order," *Washington Post,* Sept. 12, 1990

28. "Candidates Spurn Bush's Embrace," *Washington Post,* Oct. 24, 1990.

29. Kevin Phillips, "The Bush Blueprint Bombs," *Newsweek,* Nov. 19, 1990.

30. "Bush is Sharply Questioned By Lawmakers on Gulf Policy," *Washington Post,* Oct. 31, 1990.

31. *Washington Times,* Nov. 8, 1990.

32. *Washington Post,* Nov. 9, 1990.

33. James Reston, "Too Early for Bush to Dial 911," *New York Times,* Nov. 12, 1990.

34. *New York Times,* Nov. 16, 1990.

36. Lyndon LaRouche, "On Defining the Meaning and Necessity of the Concept of Psycho-Sexual Impotence," in *What Does Candidate LaRouche Think of Bush's Mental Health?* (Washington D.C.: Democrats for Economic Recovery-LaRouche in 92, 1991), pp. 4–6.

37. *Washington Post,* Dec. 1, 1990.

38. *New York Times,* Dec. 20, 1990.

39. *Washington Post,* Jan. 4, 1991.

40. *Washington Post,* Jan. 13, 1991.

41. *New York Times,* Jan. 18, 1991.

42. *Washington Post,* Feb. 6, 1991.

43. *Washington Post,* Feb. 24, 1991.

44. *Washington Post,* Feb. 28, 1991.

45. *New York Times,* March 7, 1991.

46. *New York Times,* Aug. 2, 1991.

47. *Washington Post,* Aug. 30, 1991.

48. *Washington Post,* June 9, 1991.

49. *Facts on File,* 1991.

XXIV

THYROID STORM

Caesar non super grammaticos*
—Marcus Pomponius Marcellus to Tiberius

When speaking in his capacity as an ideologue, George Bush has always expressed a great admiration for Theodore Roosevelt. When Bush moved into the Oval Office, he removed the portrait of Calvin Coolidge placed there by Reagan and replaced it with a likeness of the Rough Rider. Bush's references to his devotion to Theodore Roosevelt are strewn across his public career, and especially his White House years. They came thick and fast during the period of the Panama invasion, but were also prominent during the Gulf crisis. Here is one from late November 1990:

> Certainly I get inspiration from Teddy Roosevelt. Actually there's a parallel, not an exact parallel obviously, between San Juan Hill and Kuwait City. I've just been reading an interesting treatise on Teddy Roosevelt; his conviction and his determination and his leadership inspire me. All of those things inspire Presidents, I think.[1]

Bush's endorsement for Teddy Roosevelt is an endorsement for a world outlook and for a policy orientation. Inseparably from that, it is also a statement of affinity for a certain form of psychopathology that is associated with Teddy.

As one of the authors has shown,[2] Roosevelt's maternal uncle was

*The emperor cannot defy the grammarians.

Captain James D. Bulloch, the head of the Confederate intelligence services in Europe and the outfitter of the infamous Confederate raiders *Alabama, Shenandoah* and others. Theodore Roosevelt's elevation to the presidency represented a personal union between the New York-Boston patrician financiers and the secessionist slaveholders. First and foremost, Teddy Roosevelt was a political steward of the J.P. Morgan interests which dominated Wall Street. We see that Teddy Roosevelt's networks shared some essential features with those of George Bush. In many ways, these are the same networks.

In outlook and policy, Theodore Roosevelt was the President who elevated the solidarity of the white race, and especially of its alleged "Anglo-Saxon" component, above the ideas of the American Revolution. The argument was that shared "blood," language, culture, and the other bonds among the "English-speaking peoples" were far more important than the American System of Ben Franklin, George Washington, Alexander Hamilton, Henry Clay and Abraham Lincoln. Roosevelt marked the end of the sharp animosity toward the British crown which had been left in American public life in the wake of British support for the Confederacy during the Civil War. Roosevelt directed a wave of race hatred against Chinese and other yellow-skinned orientals; against Latin Americans and peoples of Mediterranean origin; against Germans; and against black- and brown-skinned people in general.

Teddy Roosevelt was of course a militant imperialist and empire-builder. The "Roosevelt corollary" to the Monroe Doctrine is no corollary, but rather a total reversal of the original anti-colonialist intent of James Monroe and his Secretary of State, John Quincy Adams. Teddy Roosevelt's claim to exercise international police powers over debtor nations launched a new imperialism, this time based in the United States.

Teddy Roosevelt was a dedicated Malthusian who did everything he could to abort the economic development of the United States west of the Mississippi. This Malthusian environmentalism lives on in the administration of the "environmental President." In order to enforce his alien policies, Teddy Roosevelt was in the vanguard of the creation of a U.S. domestic police state. He got his start by leading police-state attacks on the New York Tammany Democratic machine as New York City police commissioner, and later carried his assault to other constituency groupings, the kind Bush reviles today as "special interests." Roosevelt founded the centerpiece of the U.S. domestic police-state apparatus, the Federal Bureau of Investigation, and made Charles Bonaparte, a relation of the French imperial house, the first FBI director. Roosevelt's program of "trust-busting" (which wiped out industrial forces opposed to the Morgan interests), and his conservationism, led to the creation of a whole series of regulatory agencies, which are busily strangling U.S. economic activity today.

On a deeper level: If London had not been able to count on the United States as a future ally, it is doubtful that the British government would have encouraged Russia and France to go to war with Austria-Hungary and Germany in 1914. Without the short-term certainty of U.S. intervention on the British side, the Bolshevik Revolution would have been far less likely. Theodore Roosevelt's role as the first overtly and extravagantly Anglophile U.S. President after the Civil War thus helped to pave the way for some of the greatest disasters of the twentieth century.

Above and beyond all policy and strategic issues, Bush is attracted by the psychological gestalt of Theodore Roosevelt. Teddy Roosevelt suffered from a very limited attention span. He was vain, self-centered, unstable and tended toward exhibitionism. The most concise summary of Teddy's pathology can be found in a letter by Sir Cecil Spring-Rice of the British Foreign Office, certainly one of the most important influences on Roosevelt's life; some would call him Teddy's British controller. When another British diplomat, Valentine Chirol, complained about Teddy's wandering focus and intermittent attention span, Spring-Rice replied: "If you took an impetuous small boy on to a beach strewn with a great many exciting pebbles, you would not expect him to remain interested for long in one pebble. You must always remember that the President is about six."[3]

This restless and distracted inability to concentrate, this incapacity for the prolonged contemplation and examination of issues and problems, is one of the factors that made Teddy Roosevelt the psychological wreck that he was. Teddy could not think; the psychological background noise was far too loud. Instead, he was driven to undertake his legendary hunting exploits of killing vast quantities of birds and animals, his prodigious feats of physical exercise and, later, his hollow martial posturing as a "Rough Rider."

Bush's affinity for Teddy Roosevelt is based most profoundly on the shared cognitive impairment of these two political figures. In the case of Bush, the inability to think is expressed most demonstrably in the incoherence of verbal expression. Thanks in part to Dana Carvey, who has some insight into this side of Bush's character, the "Bushspeak" issue has been on the table at least since 1987–88. But Bush has been spewing out garbled verbiage for a very long time. The following sample was recorded by Elizabeth Drew in February

1980, during a ride from Worcester, Massachusetts to Boston. Ms. Drew commented that Bush seemed to enjoy campaigning. Bush replied in part:

> I do. Isn't that awful? I really enjoy it, and I say "awful" only because I'm just beginning to wonder what the hell's happening to me, you know, but I really do enjoy it. I loved going through that cafeteria, kidding with them and learning stuff and sitting and chatting and trying to be responsive to the person and yet have a concern for what concerns them. I mean it when I say I'm better. I'll be better, more sensitive, stronger, from things like that. And there *is* the smell of the greasepaint and that other crap; there's some of that. I mean, this is very different today. There was a time nobody'd stand out in even hot weather to see me. I was all alone four months ago, and here people are waiting. And there's a certain forward adrenaline that exists today. Hopefully, there will be more of them. Maybe not: maybe I'll be lousy and they'll go away, but that's part of the fun of it. Part of it is the process itself. It's a good process.[4]

Other aspects of Bush's outlook and mode of expression can be traced back to *Dink Stover at Yale*, a series of boy's novels by Owen Johnson which began coming out after the First World War, just after the Harriman brothers, Prescott Bush and Neil Mallon had graduated. Dink Stover was a preppy from Lawrenceville who talked about democracy and equality during his first three years at Yale. He always helped old ladies and did the right thing. When Tap Day rolled around, Dink Stover was tapped by Skull and Bones. Key elements of Bush's public mask, or persona, correspond to the community-service oriented do-gooder, Dink Stover, an early addition to the thousand points of light.

Some may claim that the most dissociated utterances by Bush are not his own responsibility, but result rather from Bush's attempt to regurgitate the contents of verbal briefings and briefing books. This assertion has a specious credibility. In hyper-prepared appearances like the debate with Dukakis, Bush does have a tendency to spout lines that mix up phrases and one-liners that he has drilled. In an answer on defense policy during the same debate with Dukakis, Bush stated: "We are going to make some changes and some tough choices before we go to the deployment on the Midgetman missile, or on the Minuteman, whatever it is. We're going to have to—the MX. We're going to have to do that." And then he added: "It's Christmas." And then, as the audience laughed, "Wouldn't it be nice to be the iceman so you never make a mistake?" The reference to Christmas was intended to be self-ironic; on September 7, 1988,

Bush had announced that it was Pearl Harbor Day; now, on September 25, he was announcing that it was Christmas.

But garbled incoherence is so much a staple of Bush's spoken discourse that it cannot be attributed solely to the pressure of his handlers; it is a life-long habit which has become more accentuated during the years of his presidency.

Bush once admitted that he had difficulty keeping the most elementary sense of direction in his mental life; he told a group of school children, "I read so much sometimes I start to read backwards, which is not very good."[5]

Bush is a bureaucrat and administrator at heart, with all the sinister overtones these have rightly acquired during the twentieth century. His discourse is highly bureaucratic, and is famous for being so. Bush's obsession with "things," as in the notorious "vision thing," reflects the essence of Aristotelian bureaucratic cataloguing. We saw the "adversary thing" back in 1976; since then we have seen the "Super Tuesday thing," "the vice-presidential thing," and a nostalgic glance at "this drilling thing," in reference to Bush's "experience in offshore drilling."[6] When Bush talked by telephone with the astronauts of the space shuttle Atlantis, he asked, "How was the actual deployment thing?"

Very often Bush's pronouncements are designed for self-defense against his detractors. In the spring of 1988, Bush was asked his reaction to Garry Trudeau's "Doonesbury" comic strip, and to the political satire of Dana Carvey of "Saturday Night Live." Bush answered:

> I used to get tense about that. My mother still does. She's 87. She doesn't like it when people say untrue and ugly things about her little boy. Having said that, it doesn't bother me any more. You know why, because we took a tremendous pounding, not just from elitists like Doonesbury, coming out of the elite of the elite, but untrue allegations, and you know I don't worry about it anymore, because the American people don't believe all this stuff. So I'm saying, why should I be all uptight?[7]

Many times the purpose of Bush's incoherence is to evade questions. He often refuses to talk about his role in Iran-Contra: "I forgot to tell you, I don't talk about what I told the President," was a favorite line. Who would be his running mate? "I forgot to tell you, I'm not in the speculation business." Would he purge the Reaganites? "I forgot to tell you, we're going to have wholesale change."[8]

Out of Control

Bush has called himself "a restrained kind of guy." He has often denied having "a rancor in there" against his opposition, but his rage states have become increasingly difficult to control over the years. He was unable to control his temper when defending his kowtow to Deng Xiaoping during 1989; after a ranting defense of his China policy he thanked the press for their questions, saying: "So, I'm glad you asked it because then I vented a spleen here."[9] Bush's rage episodes have often been associated with public criticism. Commenting once again on the "Doonesbury" comic strip, Bush once confessed: "Four years ago I'd go ballistic when I read some of this stuff. But hey, let him do his thing, and I'll do mine." "Ballistic" for Bush refers to a rage fit which might cause him to chew on the White House carpets; this is a not infrequent event. For lesser tantrums Bush has coined another expression, "semi-ballistic," as in an offhand remark during the 1988 campaign about his feelings when given speech drafts which he finds unsuitable: "Everybody on this airplane will have seen me semi-ballistic when people hand me things that I'm simply not going to say."

Another feeling state which, judging from the evidence of his statements, is meaningful for Bush is the state of being "frantic." During the 1988 campaign, Bush was asked about his tendency to assail Dukakis. Bush replied, "I don't feel frantic. I don't feel under any time constraints. There is a little bit of cholesterol rise, the frustration level going up. So I'm getting a little bit more combative."[10]

During 1989, Bush still faced grilling about Iran-Contra from a reporter. "You're burning up time. The meter is running through the sand on you, and I am now filibustering," taunted Bush.[11]

Bush's pattern of uncontrollable rage states became worse during 1990, in the interwar period between Panama and Iraq. During February 1990, Bush came under fire for duplicity, lying to the press, and excessive secret diplomacy. After a night's sleep on Air Force One on the way to an antidrug summit in Colombia, Bush came out of his quarters to confront the traveling press corps in a way that the *Washington Post* correspondent found "both testy and teasing." Bush, visibly furious, announced "a whole new relationship" with reporters. "From now on it's gonna be a little different. I think we have too many press conferences," ranted Bush. "It's not good. It's overexposure to the thing." Had he not slept well? asked one reporter. Bush replied, "I can't go into the details of that. Because someone will think it's too much sleep, someone will think it's too little. I'll give you a little insight into that. I had a very good night's sleep. And I've never—if I felt better it'd be a frame-up. There's something you can use."

Bush was incensed because he had denied that there was about to be a four-power conference on the future of Germany, and such a conference was announced the next day. Bush had been misleading about his plans for the Malta summit with Gorbachov, and he had kept secret the mission of Scowcroft and Eagleburger to Beijing on July 4, 1989. Various press accounts had noted these discrepancies, and Bush was now having a fit.

Q: Would he be signing a joint communiqué at the drug summit with Colombia, Peru and Bolivia?

Bush: I hate to be secretive, say nothing of deceptive. But I'm not going to tell you that.

Q: Would he discuss possible U.S. military interdiction of drug trafficking?

Bush: I'm not going to discuss what I'm gonna bring up.

Q: Would the drug summit bring any surprise proposals?

Bush: I'm not gonna discuss whether there are any surprises or not. This is a new thing. A new approach. Even if I don't discuss it. I'm not going to discuss it.

Q: Would the Colombian government now abandon its policy of extraditing drug traffickers?

Bush: I have no comment whatsoever on that.

Q: Did you know about it?

Bush: I have no comments on whether I knew about it.

Q: Is it true?

Bush: I can't comment on whether it's true or not.

Q: Did we turn you into this?

Bush: Yes. When I told you . . . that I didn't think there would be a deal [on the four-power conference on Germany], and then they shortly made a deal, and I'm hit for deceiving you. So from now on it's going to be a little different.

Q: Would he schedule a summit with Gorbachov for June 1990?

Bush again refused to answer, "Because I'm not gonna be burned for holding out or doing something deceptive."

Later the same afternoon, Marlin Fitzwater, the top White House spin doctor, attempted to interpret what had been an infantile fit of rage by assuring the reporters: "He was just kidding. He was having fun."[12] In retrospect, it is clear that Bush's thyroid was also on the warpath.

Later the same spring, Bush went semi-ballistic when reporters declined to join him for jogging at 7:15 A.M. in Columbia, South

Carolina. The White House reporters all got a wake-up call at 7:00 A.M. calling on them to join Bush for jogging in 15 minutes; usually the reporters watch Bush from the sidelines, but this time he was magnanimously inviting them to come running with him. There were no volunteers. Bush then bullied Rita Beamish of Associated Press into running with him, 13 laps around a football field for a total of 25 minutes. But even after that exertion, Bush was still full of fury. He proceeded to launch a diatribe at the press corps:

"The rest of you lazy guys, get out there and run. A fit America is a fine America. A fit America is a strong America. A fit America should include photo dogs [Bushspeak for photographers] as well as print reporters who slovenly sit back in the grandstands while some of us are out running."

When on vacation, Bush has always maintained a frenetic, hyperkinetic pace. After winning the 1988 election, Bush repaired to Delray Beach, Florida, to cavort with his plutocrat friend, William Stamps Farish III. Despite the exhausting rigors of the campaign, Bush "spent the bulk of his day exercising and resting: a quarter-mile swim, a 20-minute run, and a nap." He came back from a two-mile run in an "upbeat, almost giddy mood."[13]

Bush's hyperkinetic antics at Kennebunkport during September 1989 were described as follows by a first-hand observer:

> It was just an average day on President Bush's vacation.
> Hungering to catch a bluefish, he packed up his speedboat *Fidelity* and headed out to sea. But when he remembered that he had forgotten First Lady Barbara Bush, he turned the boat around and accidentally ran over a board, which broke a propeller.
> Undeterred by his disabled boat, the President took his party to the horseshoe pit, where they tossed several games for about 45 minutes as Mr. Bush exclaimed, "Mr. Smooth does it again" with each ringer. But soon that got old, and it was time to head to the golf course for 18 holes.
> This is President Bush, a man of nearly manic movement. All during his vacation, the last thing he did was relax. He's up at the crack of dawn for jogging, out on the tennis courts, teeing off for golf, pitching horseshoes, fishing, swimming, entertaining friends.

Bush, in sum, "can't sit still"; he even accepted a dare from his grandchildren and dove off a stone pier into the Atlantic Ocean, which is kept cold along the Maine coast by the frigid Labrador current.[14]

George Herbert Walker had reformed the rules of golf, eliminating the stymie; George Bush transformed the game into a manic exercise called "speed golf," whose object is to complete 18 holes in the briefest possible interval of time. According to one journalist, who attempted to match Bush's record of 1 hour 37 minutes for a threesome, as compared with almost four hours for leisurely golfers, speed golf may not be for everyone,

> but it is President Bush's game, however. He calls it cart polo. Bush has taken a leisurely game and turned it into what one reporter called a forced march—on wheels. "He barely gets out of the cart, whacks it, and he's gone," says Spike Heminway, Bush's longtime friend and frequent playing partner. Others have dubbed it aerobic golf, or golf in the fast lane. "Do you know who the winner is in speed golf?" a Portland, Maine doctor asked me. "The first one in the hole."[15]

During the summer of 1989, "Bush revealed himself to be a playful yet relentless exhibitionist," wrote another commentator. "He was forever restless and rarely alone." Out on the golf course, he called for silence: "All right, the crowd is hushed. They sense that Mr. Smooth is back." Later, when it came time to play tennis, Bush ordered a press aide to round up the photo dogs and reporters to "come see what Mr. Smooth is like on the courts."[16]

Bush's desire for frenetic movement, seeking in space what has been lost in time, carries over into his notorious penchant for foreign travel. By July 1991, he had logged 339,257 miles on Air Force One, and visited 32 countries, having surpassed in less than 30 months the previous record set by Nixon between 1969 and 1974.[17]

Bush has a history of psychosomatic illness. During the 1950s, when he was in his early thirties, he had been, according to his own account, a "chronic worrier." One morning during a "hectic business trip to London," Bush had fainted in his hotel room, and was unable to get to his feet. A hotel doctor thought he had food poisoning. Bush says he later sought treatment from Dr. Lillo Crain at the Texas Medical Center. Dr. Crain told Bush that he had a bleeding ulcer. "George, you're a classic ulcer type," Bush says he was told by Dr. Crain. "A young businessman with only one speed, all-out. You try to do too much and you worry too much." Bush says he expressed doubt there was any chance he could change his ways. The doctor replied, "There'd better be, or you won't be around in ten years, maybe five." Dr. Crain added: "If you want to keep this from happening again, it's up to you."[18] Bush claims he worked at "channeling my energies," and "never suffered a relapse."

After Bush's May 10, 1989 White House physical examination, a cyst was found on the third finger of Bush's right hand; this was

surgically removed in October 1989, and pronounced benign. This
was allegedly Bush's only problem. On April 12, 1990, White House
physician Dr. Burton Lee announced that Bush "is in truly excellent
health. . . . He continues to keep extremely fit through vigorous
physical activity." Bush was diagnosed with "early glaucoma" in
his left eye, a condition that was treated with Betagen eye drops. X-
rays of Bush's hips and back confirmed the presence of a "mild
degenerative osteoarthritis," which allegedly had been discovered
by previous examinations.[19] On March 27, 1991, Bush was given
another routine physical, and the White House doctors (and spin
doctors) announced once again that their charge was in "excellent
health."

On May 4, 1991, Bush delivered an address at the commencement
exercises of the University of Michigan at Ann Arbor. This campus
had been the site of the first antiwar teach-in of the Vietnam epoch,
in 1965, and the Ann Arbor campus had been the scene of significant
antiwar activity during Bush's Gulf adventure. Today Bar was also
present. His new speechwriter, Tony Snow, the former editorial
page editor of the *Washington Times*, had contributed to a speech
attacking the campus inquisition called "political correctness."

He was loudly heckled, with changes of "Bush lies." Bush's
temperature was rising from semi-ballistic to ballistic. He told the
students to ". . . fight back against the boring politics of division
and derision. Let's trust our friends and colleagues to respond to
reason. . . . And I remind myself a lot of this: We must conquer the
temptation to assign bad motives to people who disagree with us."[20]

After this speech, Bush flew to Andrews Air Force Base and
thence by helicopter to Camp David. Slightly after 3:30 P.M., Bush
gathered his retinue of Secret Service agents and announced that it
was time to go jogging. After about 30 minutes, he began complaining of fatigue and shortness of breath. He then proceeded to the
Camp David infirmary, where Michael Nash, one of his resident
team of doctors, determined that Bush was experiencing atrial fibrillation, an irregularity of the heartbeat. Nash recommended that
Bush go to Bethesda Medical Center for treatment. Bush arrived at
Bethesda at 6:00 P.M.

Thyroxin Attack

The news that Bush had entered the hospital at Bethesda was
flashed by wire services around the planet. Bush was exhibiting a
fast, irregular heart rhythm. The heart was working less efficiently,
producing a tendency for shortness of breath, light-headedness, and

even fainting. Sometimes atrial fibrillation is associated with a heart attack, or with damage to a heart valve. The first step in Bush's treatment was the attempt to slow the heart rate, and to restore the normal rhythm. After an hour of tests, doctors gave Bush digoxin, a drug used to restore the usual heart rhythm. When the digoxin proved unable to do the job alone, Bush's physicians began to administer another heart medication, procainamide. Though doctors claimed that Bush showed "some indications of a positive response" to this therapy, Bush's heart irregularity was resistant to the medicines and persisted through Sunday, May 5. Doctors also began to administer an anticoagulant drug, Coumadin, in addition to aspirin. Bush was thus being kept going with four different medications.

At this point, Bush's medical team was forced to contemplate resorting to electrocardioversion, a procedure in which an electric shock is administered to the heart, momentarily stopping the heart and resetting its rhythm. This prospect was enough to create a crisis of the entire regime, since electrocardioversion would have required Bush to undergo general anesthesia, which in turn would have mandated the transfer of presidential powers to Vice President Dan Quayle.

The specter of Acting President Dan Quayle brought forth a wave of public expressions of consternation and dismay. According to a *Washington Post*-ABC public opinion poll published May 7, 57 percent of those responding said that in their opinion Quayle was not qualified to take over as Acting President. In the night between Sunday, May 5 and Monday, May 6, Bush was still experiencing sporadic episodes of an irregular heartbeat. But on the morning of Monday, May 6, his doctors suddenly pronounced him fit to return to the Oval Office, where he was seated at his desk by 9:30 A.M., and resumed what was described as his normal work schedule. The doctors conceded only that they had asked Bush to curtail his usual frenetic schedule of recreational sports.

Bush returned to work wired with a portable heart monitor. This was a device about the size of a telephone pager, with white wires leading to patches on his chest which measured the rate of his heartbeat. Bush stated that he was "back to normal and the same old me." He declined to show off his heart monitor with the quip, "Do you think I'm Lyndon Johnson?" LBJ had pulled up his shirt to show reporters a scar on his stomach after a gall bladder operation.[21]

On May 7, Bush's chief attending physician, Dr. Burton Lee, gave a briefing at Bethesda in which he disclosed that Bush's bout with atrial fibrillation had been caused by an overactive thyroid gland.

Lee assured the press that the problem had been an overactive thyroid secreting too much of the hormone thyroxin, which helps to regulate the body's metabolic rate. This hormone goes into the circulatory system, and thus can disturb the proper functioning of the heart. Lower the rate of production of thyroid hormone, and everything would return to normal, was the message.

Lee said that Bush would undergo a thyroid scan and other tests to help determine the appropriate treatment. Contradicting earlier statements by Fitzwater that there had been no recent danger signals regarding Bush's health, Lee now revealed that Bush had experienced a small weight loss and episodes of unusual fatigue during jogging over the previous few weeks. The weight loss had been of eight or nine pounds during the month before Bush was hospitalized.[22] Some of Bush's symptoms appear to have emerged in February, during the time of the Iraq war. Lee claimed that Bush had never undergone tests of his thyroid functions because he had shown no symptoms of thyroid disturbance—a patent absurdity. According to Burton Lee, the first indication of a thyroid disturbance came on Monday morning, when a blood test showed that the level of thyroid hormone in Bush's blood was above normal. These results were then confirmed with repeated blood tests.

The official White House line was that this was good news, since thyroid disorders were easily treated. Fitzwater recounted that "the President was overjoyed. It means the problem was not a problem with his heart and that it is virtually 100 percent treatable." Burton Lee chimed in with his opinion that biochemical hyperthyroidism is "easily treatable."

On May 9, Bush's doctors announced that he was suffering from what they chose to call Graves' disease, a condition in which the thyroid gland becomes enlarged and produces excessive levels of hormone in response to "false messages" from other parts of the body about how much of the hormone is needed. Graves' disease is a disorder of the immune system in which the body produces an antibody which "mimics" the hormone that usually tells the thyroid how much thyroxin to produce. One decisive test was said to have involved Bush's swallowing of a small dose of radioactive iodine, followed by observation with a device resembling a geiger counter to obtain an image of the thyroid. This thyroid scan revealed a gland that was enlarged, and absorbing iodine at faster than the normal rate. During this press conference, Bush's medical team also conceded that Bush had experienced a renewed bout of atrial fibrillation in the form of a "rather brief episode" during the night of Tuesday, May 8.

During this press conference, Burton Lee once again repeated the story that Bush's thyroid had never been tested during his previous annual or other checkups. He offered the estimate that Bush's thyroid condition had developed after his last medical checkup, which had been conducted on March 27, 1991. According to Dr. Kenneth Burman, a thyroid specialist at Walter Reed Army Medical Center who had been assigned to Bush's case, the issue of whether thyroid tests should be a part of routine physical examination was controversial. Burman added that his personal opinion was that such tests were not cost-effective! Press reports reflected surprise on the part of outside experts about this alleged neglect of thyroid testing. Also joining in this press conference was Dr. Bruce K. Lloyd, the chief of cardiology at Bethesda Medical Center.

Bush's doctors announced that he had ingested a dose of radioactive iodine on the morning of May 9. Bush drank this iodine at Bethesda. One thyroid expert, Dr. Bruce D. Weintraub of the National Institutes of Health, told the *Washington Post* that as a result of this thyroid cocktail, which was designed to destroy a large part of Bush's thyroid, the public might henceforth see "a slower and less frenetic George Bush."[23]

On that same day, the White House announced the results of what was billed as Bush's first complete checkup since the day he swallowed radioactive iodine. The White House said that Bush had lost a total of 13 pounds since the onset of the crisis, but had managed to gain back a pound and a half. Tests showed that Bush's thyroid functions were now in the low-normal range, it was further alleged. Doctors tried to explain away Bush's fatigue by saying that it reflected the body's adjustment to a thyroid gland which was overactive less than two weeks before, but had now possibly become underactive as a result of the radioactive iodine therapy, which had destroyed many thyroxin-producing cells. By this point, Bush was still taking digoxin, procainamide, Coumadin, aspirin and non-radioactive iodine drops. These last, it was said, were designed to reduce the amounts of thyroxin entering the bloodstream.[24]

Bush was in Kennebunkport for Memorial Day, and the White House propaganda machine was churning out the line was that he was now well on his way to complete recovery. "I'm sleeping much better and I really do feel good and I wish I had about four more days here," Bush told the press. During this weekend, Bush tried fishing at nine of his favorite locations. On Sunday, May 26, Bush played a total of 27 holes of golf. Reporters found that he was back to his old ways as he "circled the golf course like a man on a merry-go-round." When he "passed the 18th hole once again on this vacation, he exuberantly flung a golf club at his cart and looked horrified when it nearly hit one of his Secret Service guards." On Monday, May 27, Bush traveled to New Haven to speak at the Yale commencement, and lost three pounds due to the rigors of the trip.[25]

Bush's speech at the Yale commencement was devoted to a pugnacious defense of his China policy, the policy of the kow-tow to the butchers of Beijing. In the words of one observer: "George Bush's address to the Yale graduating class was more like a tantrum than a speech. In it, he was defiant about renewing most-favored-nation trading status for the Chinese, and crushingly condescending to the opposition he faces. . . . The resolute commander-in-chief sounded like the querulous candidate of yesterday. He can do what he wants, talk out of both sides of his mouth and stage a preemptive strike on critics who say his position is immoral."[26]

On Wednesday, May 29, Bush proposed a freeze on the purchase and production of surface-to-surface missiles in the Middle East. On this day, Bush was again out on the golf course, and questions about his health were provoked once again by his ghastly personal appearance, which was best conveyed by a photograph appearing on the front page of the London *Financial Times* of Thursday, May 30.

After the beginning of June, references to Bush's atrial fibrillation and thyroid crisis become exceedingly rare, a tribute to the power of the Brown Brothers Harriman/Skull and Bones networks. On September 5, Burton Lee announced that he had halted Bush's daily doses of procainamide and digoxin shortly after the middle of August. But Bush continued to take daily doses of Coumadin to prevent blood clots, medication to replace lost thyroid hormone production, and aspirin every other day, also to prevent blood clots. This announcement came at the end of Bush's 29-day vacation in Kennebunkport. The White House spin was that Bush "appears to have overcome weight loss and fatigue associated with the thyroid condition, called Graves' disease, and treatment for it."[27]

Then, in mid-September, Bush underwent a two-hour medical examination designed to provide a "medical stamp of approval" for Bush's health as he prepared to run for reelection in 1992. "I gotta prove I'm well," said Bush as he went in for the checkup. According to Dr. Burman, "the President has been restored to his normal vigorous state of good health." Dr. Lee said that all tests had showed Bush's heart functions to be normal; he also claimed that there had been no recurrence of atrial fibrillation after May. Bush had commented in August that the only thing that could keep him from running for a second term would be a health problem. He now described his own condition as "100 percent. Perfect bill of health."[28] And that, as far as the regime was concerned, was that.

Despite the claims of Dr. Lee that political considerations played no role in his treatment, it is clear that all statements by White House physicians about Bush's physical and mental health must be regarded with the greatest skepticism; such pronouncements are likely to be as reliable as the censored war bulletins of Operation Desert Storm. Was there still a problem with Bush's health, including his mental health? The answer is an emphatic yes, a yes buttressed by the observation of continued paroxysms of obsessive rage on the part of Bush, who has not calmed down at all. Bush remains on an emotional roller coaster, complete with the snap decisions so typical of the hyperthyroid personality. In short, Bush's thyroid and mental disorders have the most devastating implications for his ability to govern.

What is Basedow's Disease?

The first question regards the nature and even the name of Bush's malady. According to a leading Baltimore psychiatrist who could not be described as politically hostile to Bush (but who understandably wishes to remain anonymous), it is clear that the man in the White House is suffering from the full-fledged symptoms of Basedow's disease. The difference between Graves' disease and Basedow's is more than a technical quibble: The term Graves' disease as used in the English-speaking world is misleading, in that it plays down the symptoms of mental disturbance which are more explicitly associated with Basedow's disease. According to this specialist, it is pointless to test the water in the White House, the Naval Observatory, Kennebunkport and Camp David, as was done following the diagnosis of Graves' disease, since it is well established that Basedow's disease is emotionally triggered. An emotional upheaval, psychic shock or other mental trauma stimulates the master endocrine gland of the body, the pituitary gland, into an overproduction of its hormone, which in turn provokes an overactivity of the thyroid, speeding up overall metabolism and further exacerbating the nervous and emotional crisis. This pattern of overstimulation of the mind, the pituitary, the thyroid, and so forth becomes a vicious, self-feeding cycle, which can be life-threatening if it is not effectively treated.

According to this Baltimore expert, the fact that Bush has experienced a pattern of atrial fibrillation is cause for concern, not so much because of what it portends for Bush's heart, but rather because it shows that Bush's case of Basedow's disease is already well advanced, with a significant excess of thyroid hormone. The overproduction of thyroid hormone can theoretically be brought under control through the administration of radioactive iodine, but this does not mean that the disease itself is easy to treat or to bring under control with any finality. Precisely because Basedow's disease is emotionally triggered, a sudden increase in emotional stress can result in a renewal of erratic behavior.

The good news, in the view of this expert, is that patients suffering from Basedow's disease do not have to be placed into a mental institution. Their symptoms can be managed, although they will continue to have their ups and downs. But such management requires a stress-free environment. The implications for Bush's further tenure in the White House are obvious enough: The Federal Aviation Administration will not grant a pilot's license of any kind to a person who has been diagnosed with Basedow's disease.

The Baltimore specialist also pointed out that although samples of Bush's blood, taken by his White House doctors and frozen over a period of months and years, might be tested for thyroid hormone in order to answer the all-important question of when Bush's case of Basedow's disease actually began, these findings might be fragmentary because of the significant day-to-day variations in the level of thyroid hormone. If a sample had been taken after Bush heard the news that Iraqi Foreign Minister Tariq Aziz had declined to accept Bush's threatening letter handed to him by Secretary of State James Baker, Bush's level of thyroid hormone that day might have been high enough to warrant immediate hospitalization.

In the opinion of this expert, these points all represent standard, well-known medical doctrine which is not subject to any controversy among physicians and specialists. Bush's White House medical team must therefore be keenly aware of all of them.

According to a California professor of radiology (who also spoke on condition of anonymity), hyperthyroidism is traditionally associated with patients who are irritable, restless, overactive and emotionally labile. They often lack the ability to concentrate, and have symptoms of anxiety. They also exhibit impulsive behavior. In addition, there are outright psychiatric disorders which are associated with hyperthyroidism. This professor pointed to Bush's decision to initiate hostilities against Iraq, in which he rejected the advice of eight out of nine Secretaries of Defense, three former Chairmen of the Joint Chiefs of Staff, and other prominent experts in order to wage war. Could this kind of decision-making process be associated with Bush's hyperthyroidism? In this specialist's opinion, it is difficult to say, because of the difficulty of determining with precision when Bush's hyperthyroid condition began. Bush's choice of Dan Quayle as a running mate might also fit into this type of pattern.

This California professor noted that there exists a literature on hyperthyroid patients who have developed schizophrenia. Sixty percent of patients with hyperthyroidism show intellectual impairment of some degree. What will Bush be like if and when he becomes euthyroid, or thyroid-normal? The California professor regarded this as a fascinating question to follow.

According to a leading international endocrinologist, hyperthyroidism must be regarded as a psychosomatic illness characterized by obsessive states. When the patient is unable to consummate his or her obsession, then cardiac arrhythmia results. When this happens, the condition of the patient deteriorates. This mechanism strongly suggests that such thyroid patients be disqualified for posts that involve stress and weighty responsibilities. According to this expert, it would be difficult for Bush to remain in office until January 1993, and it would be madness for him to attempt a second term. This specialist has a background of research in the psychological causes of thyroid disorders; one form of the etiology of hyperthyroidism he has studied involves the tendency of young children whose parents have died to develop thyroid problems as a result of grief and bereavement.

The question of the influence of Bush's hyperthyroid condition on his decision-making, especially his rageful and obsessive decisions to go to war in Panama and the Gulf, could not be avoided even by the pro-regime press. A *New York Times* article by Lawrence K. Altman, M.D. posed the question, "does an overactive thyroid gland affect mood and judgment?" According to this piece, experts interviewed admitted that they had "wondered about a theoretical link between [Bush's] Graves' disease and his presidential decisions. Most experts believe that people with hyperthyroidism do not make decisions as well as they would normally." "An important question," wrote Altman, "is when Mr. Bush's case of Graves' disease began." One way to shed light on this question would be to test stored blood samples that Bush's doctors would routinely keep. But the Secret Service has a policy of destroying all such specimens for security reasons! According to Dr. Andre Van Herle of UCLA, among patients suffering from hyperthyroidism, "some are not disturbed at all; others are basket cases." Altman elaborates:

> [P]eople with hyperthyroid conditions can exhibit uncharacteristic behavior like showing shortened attention spans, making snap deci-

sions, behaving frenetically, and tiring more easily than usual. People have been known to inexplicably get married or divorced when such important decisions are out of character. Students with overactive thyroids may be so jittery that they cannot sit through class or they do poorly on examinations.

The worst form of hyperthyroidism, known as thyroid storm, can be characterized by fever, marked weakness, muscle-wasting and psychosis. Mr. Bush's doctors have described his case as mild, and never near thyroid storm.

According to Dr. Peter C. Whybrow, head of the department of psychiatry at the University of Pennsylvania, also interviewed in the *Times* article, mild depression can be an initial symptom of hyperthyroid disorder. People with overactive thyroid glands "don't perform quite so well," in his view. "They feel, for reasons they cannot explain, a little agitated, a little preoccupied with themselves, jumpy. Their concentration is a little off." According to Altman, "some experts have raised the possibility that Mr. Bush could have had a mildly overactive thyroid in the 1988 Presidential campaign, or even earlier." Any normal medical checkup administered by a private doctor would have detected Bush's thyroid ailment through a $20 blood test that is done automatically unless it is specifically ruled out by the physician in advance.[29]

These views were supplemented by a piece in the *Washington Post* by Abigail Trafford, the editor of that newspaper's weekly health supplement, who was herself a victim of Graves' disease. Ms. Trafford warned her readers of "the bad news: It is difficult to live with and adjust to Graves's disease. What's missing in all the upbeat press releases from the White House is the powerful emotional impact the disease has on many patients and the effects of hyperthyroidism on mood, behavior, and judgment. And while Graves' is, indeed, curable, it can take months, sometimes years, for people to get their thyroid function back to normal." Joshua L. Cohen, assistant professor of medicine at George Washington University, told Ms. Trafford that "Graves' disease strikes on a psychological basis and it strikes a population that is not used to the concept of being sick." According to Washington endocrinologist James N. Ramey, "There's no question that the emotions are severely out of whack." Terry Taylor, acting chief of endocrinology at Georgetown University Medical Center, described Graves' patients: "Emotionally, they can be feeling very good and then very bad. There are a lot of ups and downs. . . . They cry at TV ads. . . . It takes several half-lives to get the thyroid level in the blood down." Therefore some patients take three months to feel like "their old selves," and some take a year.[30]

According to the *Textbook of Medical-Surgical Nursing* by Lillian Sholtis Brunner and Doris Smith Suddarth, hyperthyroidism "may appear after an emotional shock, nervous strain, or an infection—but the exact significance of these relationships is not understood." According to these authors, "patients with well-developed hyperthyroidism exhibit a characteristic group of symptoms and signs. Their presenting symptom is often nervousness. They are emotionally hyperexcitable; their state of mind is apt to be irritable and apprehensive; they cannot sit quietly; they suffer from palpitation; and their pulse is abnormally rapid at rest as well as on exertion." The disease "may progress relentlessly, the untreated patient becoming emaciated, intensely nervous, delirious—even disoriented—and the heart eventually 'racing itself to death.' " These authors also point out that "no treatment for hyperthyroidism has been discovered that combats its basic cause," even though a number of forms of treatment are available. Within the context of treatment, the following "overview of nursing management" is recommended:

> The objectives of nursing care are to assist the patient in overcoming his symptoms and to help him return to a euthyroid condition. The nurse maintains a calm manner and understands that much of his nervousness and anxiety is beyond his control. Activities to lessen the irritability of the nervous system may include the following: protecting the patient from stressful experiences, such as upsetting visitors or the presence of annoying or very ill patients; providing a cool and uncluttered environment; and encouraging the patient to enjoy pleasant music, light television entertainment, and interesting and relaxing hobbies.[31]

This is hardly a description of the White House situation room.

Operation Thyroid Storm?

On May 29, Bush's foremost political prisoner, Lyndon H. LaRouche commented on Bush's mental health:

> . . . In the past several days, particularly, there has been increasing discussion of President George Bush's state of mental health. At the same time, questions have been raised as to which of his decisions, beginning for example with the Panama decisions and the Iraqi decisions, might have been caused, or largely shaped, by the influence of a mental disorder. . . . I base myself primarily upon what I have

directly observed and have also reported since my observation of a press conference which President Bush delivered during the high point of the U.S. invasion of Panama, at the end of 1989. At that time, I observed, from what I saw on the television screen, that the President was in a dissociated state such that at least at that moment or in that context, the stresses of what he was doing had overwhelmed him, and he was to all intents and purposes virtually psychotic at that time.

LaRouche illustrated Bush's disorder with the following example:

Many of us know, some time, quasi-successful or successful business executives and others who are most unpleasant personalities to work with, precisely because they are given to obsessions, and can be set off into terrible states of rage if any of these irrational obsessions is disturbed. That is, if these obsessions are frustrated in any way, the obsession may erupt as a glower at work, on the job or elsewhere; it may take the form of the launching of a vendetta against some person on the slightest kinds of flimsy pretext; it may also take the form of kicking the wife, the children, the family dog on the weekend, at home, to compensate for the frustration that is experienced in the week before. We're all familiar with this type of personality; no one can go through life without knowing a number of close contacts whom one has closely observed who have a problem in this direction. We also know of cases, when extremely stressed, overloaded—shall we say, circuits overloaded—that the behavior we see is that which we would rightly associate with a psychotic or semi-psychotic state, as I observed in George Bush first in that press conference broadcast in the high point of the U.S. invasion of Panama.

There is no question, on the one hand, that if George Bush is such a personality—and there is no doubt that he is a disturbed personality who has great difficulty in coping rationally with the frustrations associated with his office under present conditions—there's no question that what he did in Panama, what he did in Iraq at some points must have been colored by psychosis, or this kind of psychosis.[32]

Was Operation Desert Storm really Operation Thyroid Storm? On May 20, one of the most fanatical supporters of war against Iraq had attempted to preempt the discussion of the role of hyperthyroid mental instability in Bush's military decisions. This was William Safire, who wrote:

Next, with more sinister intent, we can expect this question: To what extent was the President's uncharacteristically activist mindset after the Iraqi invasion affected by a hyperthyroid condition? Was he hyper last August 2? Did the overactive gland affect his decision to launch the air war or the ground war early this year?[33]

Bush himself had been asked to comment about this possibility. He replied that any idea that his warmongering in the Gulf had been facilitated by his thyroid disorder was "just plain, old-fashioned malarkey." Before leaving on a visit to St. Paul, Minnesota, Bush protested that his health was fine. "I'm not wary, you know, wondering what happens next," he said. "It makes me happy everything's okay. They diagnosed it right, treated it right, and there's nothing more serious to it." Just after he had boarded Air Force One at Andrews Air Force Base for his trip to the Twin Cities, Bush called reporters together and declared: "I just want to say everything's fine." Asked about any side effects of the five medicines he was then taking, Bush answered that his medication "affects my tummy."[34]

During June, there were hints from Bush and his retinue that he might not run for President again in 1992. This was largely a cynical public relations ploy, attempting to generate a story when it was clear that Bush was monomaniacally obsessed with holding onto power as long as he could and by any means. On a visit to Los Angeles, Bush alluded to this question, and tried to portray himself as a man whose sense of duty to the voters would only allow him to consider reelection if he were in perfect condition. Would he run again? "I haven't decided. It's too early. Don't push me." There was the testy note again. Any reasons why he might not? "Can't really think of a reason except, certainly, health."

Comparing the evidence adduced here so far about the etiology and symptoms of Basedow's disease with Bush's pattern of activity in 1988–91, three general conclusions are suggested:

1. Since 1987–88 at the latest, George Bush has exhibited a marked tendency toward obsessive rage states, often expressed by compulsive public displays of extreme anger and lack of self-control. These obsessive rage states and the quasi-psychotic impulses behind them may be regarded as the probable psychological trigger for Basedow's disease, a psychosomatic, autoimmune disorder.

2. There is much evidence that important decisions, including most notably Bush's decisions militarily to attack Panama and Iraq, were substantially facilitated by these obsessive rage states.

3. There are indications that Bush's inability to kill or capture Saddam Hussein, combined with his inability to destroy the Baath Party government of Iraq, frustrated one of Bush's obsessive compulsions and may thus have contributed to a hyperthyroid crisis and the emergence of atrial fibrillation in early May of 1991. Alterna-

tively, the accumulated tensions of the Gulf crisis, possibly in some combination with other events, may have been sufficient to precipitate Bush's hospitalization.

Is He Cured?

The question that remains to be considered is whether Bush can be considered cured of the mental and physiological disorders involved with his hyperthyroid crisis. The answer is that Bush demonstrably continues to exhibit those symptoms of rage, irritability, uncontrollable outbursts, compulsive and frenetic activity, and impulsive decisions, which we must conclude were part of the trigger for Basedow's disease in the first place. During the first six months after Bush drank his cocktail of radioactive iodine, he did not become any more tranquil. His agenda has remained packed, and his sports calendar frenetic. He still tends to make unpredictable snap decisions. He has often lost control of his emotions in public, most often through rage, but also through weeping and other forms of affective upheaval.

June 5: Bush addressed the annual meeting of the Southern Baptist Convention in Atlanta, Georgia, and recounted his tearful Camp David decision to launch war in the Gulf. As viewed by Andrew Rosenthal of the *New York Times*, the scene proceeded as follows:

> At that moment, Mr. Bush's voice broke, and tears filled his eyes. He brushed at them with a finger. Then he turned to one of the cameras near the lectern, flashed one of the incongruous grins that often appear in his moments of emotional discomfort, and pointed to his cheek. "Here we go," he said.
> Mr. Bush confessed to reporters afterward that he felt a little embarrassed by his display of emotion before the delegates. "I do that in church," he said. "Maybe in public it's a kind of a first, or maybe a third."[35]

June 16: Bush visited Los Angeles to attend a party thrown by Malibu producer Jerry Weintraub, who has been responsible for such films as "The Karate Kid" and "My Stepmother is an Alien." One press account suggests that Bush maintained his hyperthyroid pace:

> Apart from playing golf, Mr. Bush continued his usual mad dash of recreation. This morning, he was in such a hurry to get to a tennis game that his motorcade roared off without his personal aide, his

personal physician, and, more important, the military officer who carries codes for launching nuclear missiles. Unnerved by this omission, White House aides hurriedly rounded up transportation and sped the officer to the tennis courts.

July 12: Bush engaged in a question and answer session with reporters, while Senate hearings began on his nomination of Robert Gates to be head of the CIA. Bush was dressed in sporting togs, but today he was out of control. His first impulse was to escape from the reporters: "Hey, listen. I've got to go now. Heavy recreation coming up before we go abroad, so I've got to keep going."

He fought off some questions about Clarence Thomas allegedly smoking marijuana, commenting that this was not disqualifying. Then, there was a mention of Gates: "Has Gates told you about. . ."

That touched Bush's obsession of the day. Gates had been accused of complicity in Iran-Contra gun-running and drug-running; but Bush himself had once again come under attack for his role in the 1980 October Surprise conspiracy to delay the release of U.S. hostages held in Teheran. Several days before, the former director of Central American affairs for the CIA, Alan Fiers, had admitted lying to Congress. Special Prosecutor Lawrence Walsh was continuing his investigation, and it was now clear that the Senate would not vote on the Gates nomination until the autumn. At this point Bush broke in, and with a contorted face launched into an interminable enraged monologue, angrily brushing aside interruptions. His lengthy, contorted replies ended on this note:

> I'm seeing a man's character getting damaged, just as I feel mine was challenged when they said, hey, prove your innocence. You're guilty until innocent. Prove you weren't in Paris on—whatever the hell it was—October 20th. And here he went to the front yard at 10:22. He was at the so-and-so embassy at 10:27. He was so and so. And finally, well, that one just fades into the sunset and along comes a bunch of other allegations by unnamed people that you can't find and can't put your—like reaching out and touching a handful of whipped cream, you can't get ahold of it. I don't want to—I've been through a little bit—but I don't want to see Bob Gates, a man of honor and integrity, go through it anymore. That's all I'm trying to say.
> Thank you. Have a neat day.[36]

July 20: Bush was on a foreign trip that included a meeting with French President Mitterrand in Rambouillet, near Paris, the G-7 meeting in London, and a trip to Turkey and Greece. According to press accounts, he was examined every day by Dr. Burton Lee. As one journalist traveling with Bush's party tells it, "Toward the end of the trip, [Bush] looked tired. Last Saturday [July 20], he could not recall the details of a speech he was to give in two days. 'It's a speech in the Rose Garden to some special group,' he told a news conference. 'Don't ask me any more.' "

On Sunday, taking questions from reporters while posing for photographs with Suleyman Demirel, leader of a Turkish opposition party, Bush testily objected to the tone of an American radio reporter's question. "Now, wait a minute," Bush said. "You don't ask in that tone; just ask the question."[37]

July 23: At a White House meeting with GOP leaders, even the *New York Times* could not ignore Bush's "apparent irritation" on the Gates issue, a leading Bush obsession. Bush was still furious about Gates being left to twist in the wind all summer. "I think the man deserves to be confirmed, and I've seen nothing other than innuendo and reports that he must have known this or something. I don't want to get started. [Understandable, after his previous nonstop rage monologue.] I told the cabinet yesterday how strongly I feel about this and so I will stand by this man."[38]

August 2: One day after returning to Washington from the Moscow summit, Bush gave a news conference in the Rose Garden that was heavily colored by obsessive rage, as can be seen from a front-page photograph in the next day's *Washington Post*, which shows him snarling and gesticulating. Bush's main theme was an attack on the Congress, "a Congress that is frustratingly negative on everything." "I'm getting fired up thinking about it," Bush said.

After the long diatribes, it was perhaps not surprising that someone asked Bush how he was feeling. "Right now, I feel like a million bucks," he replied. But he was adamant that it was time for his vacation: "I'm history. . . . It's going to be a vacation. I think I've earned it, like a lot of Americans, and I'm looking forward to it. And it will not be denied."[39]

August 14: Bush's rage profile was once more on display as he called for an extension of the federal death penalty in a Pittsburgh speech that was also full of racist overtones. Addressing the National Convention of the Fraternal Order of Police, Bush ranted that "the time has come to show less compassion for the architects of crime and more compassion for its victims. Our citizens want and deserve to feel safe. . . . We must remember that the first obligation of a penal system is to punish those who break our laws. . . . You can't turn bad people into saints." Bush wanted courts to be able to use evidence that had been seized illegally: "There's no reason—none at all—that good police officers should be penalized and criminals freed because a judge or a lawyer bungled a search warrant." Journalists noted that the speech and the setting were typical of the standard campaign event of 1988, which was often a police group endorsing Bush, courtesy of the CIA Office of Security. The photo of Bush in the *Washington Post* is expressive of Bush's anger when making the speech.[40]

August 21: The Soviet putsch was a trying time for Bush, who staked a lot on his deal with Gorbachov. A remarkable flare-up by Bush came in response to the opinion expressed by Zviad Gamsakhurdia, the President of the Republic of Georgia, that Gorbachov was part of the conspiracy behind the coup. Bush, asked for a reaction, was incensed:

> Bush: . . . [S]ay to him he needs to get a little work done on the kind of statements he's making. I mean that's ridiculous. There's a man who has been also swimming against the tide, it seems to me, a little bit. And I don't want to go overboard on this, but he ought to get with it and understand what's happening around the world.

September 18: In a demagogic photo opportunity at the Grand Canyon, Bush again threatened to renew the bombing of Iraq. In remarks that recalled his psychotic rages against Saddam Hussein during the Gulf crisis, Bush raved that he was "fed up" with Saddam. Bush said that Saddam "may be testing and probing" his resolve, "but he knows better than to take on the United States of America. . . . I think the man will see that we are very serious about this, and he will do what he should have done in the first place: disclose and comply."[41]

October 11: Hoping that public attention was fixed on the Senate testimony of Anita Hill, Bush vetoed a bill to extend unemployment payments to more than 2 million Americans whose jobless benefits had run out. Bush had prepared this veto with a furious outburst against such an extension. At a $1,000-a-plate Republican fundraising dinner in New Brunswick, New Jersey, Bush had lashed out angrily at a Congress which was "doing nothing but griping— refusing to consider the new ideas and sending me a bunch of garbage I will not sign. I'll continue to veto the bad stuff until we get good bills." Bush's argument was that the prolonged unemployment benefits were not needed because the recession was over anyway. He stressed his responsibility not to break the October 1990 budget agreement, which by that time was producing a budget deficit officially admitted to be over $1 billion per day. Later, as the existence of the depression began to penetrate the public consciousness, Bush had to backtrack on this tirade.[42]

October 24: Attempting to focus public anger on Congress in the wake of the Clarence Thomas hearings, Bush attacked the lawmakers as "a privileged class of rulers." "When Congress exempts itself from the very laws it writes for others, it strikes at its own reputation and shatters public confidence in government," he said. This was a transparent bid to increase police-state attacks on the Congress by subjecting the legislative branch to the oversight of law enforcement agencies which are part of the executive, a favorite Bush obsession. Bush demanded a special prosecutor to investigate the leaks of FBI information during the Thomas hearings, and said that FBI reports would henceforth only be shown, not given to the Hill. As Bush read through his tirade, his face twisted and tightened into a mask of rage and hate. At one point, perhaps in response to signals from his handlers, he paused and apologized to the audience for getting so worked up, but the issue meant a lot to him.[43]

October 31: Bush held the first official event of his reelection campaign on Halloween; it was a $1,000-a-plate fundraiser at the Sheraton Astrodome in Houston. Bush offered an irate defense of his tenure in the presidency. But the audience of 800 GOP fat cats gave Bush only a tepid response. The heart of Bush's highly piqued performance was in these lines:

> Anyone who says we should retreat into an isolationistic cocoon is living in the last century, when we should be focused on the next century and the lives our children will lead. And they should know America's destiny has always been to lead. And if I have anything to do with it, lead we will. . . . I'm not going to let liberal Democratic carping keep me from leading.

When Bush said "carping," he seemed to spit and hiss at the same time. Then, with his bile and adrenaline building to a crescendo of rage, Bush recalled the Gulf war and how far Schwarzkopf would have gotten if Congress had been in command. "Thank God I didn't have to listen to these carpers telling me how to run that war," Bush exploded in a paroxysm of fury. The implication was also clear: To checkmate Congress, go to war.

November 5: This was election day, and exit polls in the late afternoon showed a decisive defeat of Thornburgh in Pennsylvania, reflecting rising popular resentment of the Bush regime. The next day, Bush was scheduled to depart for a NATO meeting and Rome and then for a meeting with the leaders of the European Community in The Hague. But, abruptly and in time for the evening news programs, Bush announced that he was canceling a later ten-day trip that was scheduled to have taken him to Japan, South Korea, Singapore and Australia. The rationale offered for this reversal was that Bush wanted to stay in Washington until the end of November and work on getting his "domestic legislative package" through Congress. This explanation was incongruous for at least two reasons: First, the congressional leadership clearly hoped to adjourn and go home for Thanksgiving recess by the time that Bush's scheduled trip to the Orient was to have begun; secondly, Bush had no domestic legislative package.

Some of Bush's closest associates were dismayed by his rapid collapse under pressure. "It makes it look like the Democrats have us on the total run," one senior administration official told the *Washington Post*. "This is ridiculous. We look like we're running around like chickens with our heads cut off," said a GOP official with close ties to the White House. The impression was that Bush had panicked when he became aware that the Democratic National Committee had produced a T-shirt celebrating Bush's "Anywhere but America Tour," listing trips completed and planned during 1991. Bush, who was watching his own support and popularity decline inexorably in the polls, had apparently been stampeded by the defeat of Thornburgh and wanted to propitiate public opinion by staying home. It looked very much like a hyperthyroid decision.

This impression was magnified by the chaotic way that Bush's cancellation became known. According to the *Washington Post*, "the shock of Bush's decision was intensified in Washington and Asia by the manner of its revelation. A White House official involved in trip planning said he heard of the postponement late Tuesday after a high-level meeting and just minutes before learning that NBC News had obtained the story, which was broadcast on its evening news program. Several Asian embassies in Washington heard the news from the press reports before receiving official word from the White House." On the way to Rome the next day, Bush was heard to complain about what he perhaps considered a leak: "You got the message oozed out of the White House before we had a chance to properly notify the parties," he berated the press on board Air Force One. "You guys are too good."[44]

Sometime during October, Bush had discussed with his handlers the possibility of canceling the Asia trip while simultaneously proposing a set of measures allegedly designed to improve economic conditions, and challenging the Congress to stay in town long enough to pass this package. But Bush had been unable to assemble any such set of measures. One GOP official complained that Bush's announcement late on election day, 1991 was "a cancellation without a purpose. This is nuts."[45] This Asian trip, featuring a stopover in Japan, was later rescheduled to start on December 30 and to extend through the first week of the New Year. It was during this trip that Bush vomited and collapsed to the floor during a state dinner with Japanese Prime Minister Kiichi Miyazawa.

November 7: During his address to the NATO summit of 16 heads of state and heads of government, Bush departed from his prepared text and inserted the following sentence off the cuff into his remarks: "If, my friends, your ultimate aim is to provide independently for your own defense, the time to tell us is today."

This was in many respects the most astounding threat ever made by an American President to the leaders of the North Atlantic Alliance, which had always been considered, since 1949, as the cornerstone of U.S. foreign policy. Bush now called the Atlantic Pact into question, apparently in a fit of rage. Press reports spoke of "clouds of suspicion" separating Bush from France and Germany; the State Department and the British were known to be hysterical about plans to expand the existing Franco-German brigade into a larger unit. U.S. officials told one reporter that Bush had become "exasperated" by the Byzantine tactics of "Tonton" Mitterrand. These frictions apparently had contributed to Bush's outburst. James Baker and other spin doctors tried to play down the importance of this shocking episode.[46]

November 8: At a press conference in Rome, Bush turned in yet another furious tantrum. The basic issues were that his travel obsession had been denied, and that he did not want to brook increasing criticism. Bush "complained bitterly" that he had been forced to abandon his prized trip to Asia owing to "some carping by people that don't understand" his awesome responsibilities as world leader. Bush angrily maintained that to be "driven away" from an Asia trip "by people holding up silly T-shirts is ridiculous." As one journalist saw the scene, "Bush, his voice rising and eyelids narrowing, talked at length about a President's responsibilities in foreign policy and the importance of Japan to American jobs. His passionate response contained an undercurrent of regret that he approved the cancellation that some Republicans said this week was precipitous and too reactive to the Democrats." Had calling off the trip somehow interfered with Bush's plans for unleashing the next war? Bush reverted to his favorite theme of his war leadership: "If I had had to listen to advice" of congressional Democrats "to do something about the Persian Gulf, we'd have still been sitting there in the United States, fat, dumb, and happy, with Saddam Hussein maybe in Saudi Arabia."

November 12: Bush's countenance was once more a mask of rage, venom and hatred as he stumbled through another $1,000-a-plate Republican fundraising dinner in Manhattan. He appeared thin and drawn. The take for Bush's campaign was estimated at $2.2 million, but press reports indicated that Bush's enraged monologue "prompted little applause or enthusiasm as the President moved from one topic to another, rarely devoting more than a few seconds to any theme." Bush's delivery was halting and confused, with signs of evident dissociation and a truncated attention span. The essence of the speech was a paranoid, self-righteous defense against critics named and unnamed. Bush labeled his tormenters as "tawdry," "phony" and "second-guessers." He pounded the lectern as he ranted: "I'm not going to be the javelin-catcher for the liberals in Congress anymore. . . . I am not going to apologize for one minute that I devote to advancing our economic principles aboard or working for world peace," postured the President of two wars and counting.

On the same day, Bush, speaking in New York and fumbling for bits of demagogy on the economic situation, expressed a vague desire to see lower interest rates for credit card holders. Many observers say that the two sentences on this topic uttered by Bush that day had been interpolated by Chief of Staff Sununu; Sununu later accused Bush of having ad-libbed the pronouncement on his own initiative. One day later, the Senate overwhelmingly approved a bill to cap credit card interest rates. With this, the secondary market in credit card debt collapsed, threatening to blow off the coverup of the bankruptcy of the largest U.S. banks. On Friday, November 15, the Dow Jones Industrial Average lost 4 percent of its value within a few hours, the biggest collapse since October 13, 1989. Bush, running for cover, hastily dispatched Treasury Secretary

Brady to denounce the interest cap as "wacky." It was yet another impulsive turnabout by the erratic and unstable Bush.

November 20: With Bush scheduled to sign a civil rights bill containing provisions which Bush had stigmatized as quotas and sworn he would resist to the death, the White House circulated a directive to federal agencies mandating the termination of all hiring policies designed to favor minority groups or women. Bush had not wanted any civil rights bill to be passed, preferring to keep the race issue in his quiver for the 1992 election, but he had been intimidated by the threat that Senator Danforth and other Republicans would support a Democrat-sponsored bill, leaving Bush painfully isolated.

Now Bush's attempted sleight of hand, signing a bill and simultaneously removing the hiring policies, caused a furor. "The President would have to lose his mind to make this statement," said Kerry Scanlon, a lawyer for the NAACP Legal Defense and Educational Fund. Within hours, the offending directive had been withdrawn, and blamed exclusively on Boy Gray, the White House resident racist who had indeed drafted the directive, but on instructions from Bush. It was yet another example of an impulsive snap decision made by Bush under pressure. Intriguingly, November 20 was also the day that Bush personally pronounced the much-tabooed word: *"DEPRESSION."* "I don't want to emphasize just the bad things, to talk us into a depression," he had told some television stations owned by NBC. It was a landmark: Presidents had made that word taboo for many decades.[47]

Toward the end of November, the pendulum of Bush's unpredictability had swing back: The Asia trip was being rescheduled for about a month later than originally planned. By now, the media was harping on the evident "disarray" in the White House, but none seemed to recall the thyroid episode of the springtime, nor the psychopathological trigger for the thyroid condition.

Changing the Profile

Sometime during November, just about the time his approval ratings were about to go below 50 percent, Bush apparently received urgent advice to moderate his "mad dog" public profile in favor of a more conciliatory and affable posture. This occurred during the same month. Whatever the details that led to the renovation of his image, he now began to exhibit concern for the victims of the Bush depression who, according to his litany, he now understood were "hurting." He began smiling more, and hissing somewhat less. Photo opportunities began to depict him fraternizing with the common people.

But that postponed Far East trip continued to loom as Bush's nemesis. Because of his desire to be seen doing something to improve the lot of the common man, Bush's handlers repackaged this trip as a crusade to open foreign markets to U.S. exports, thus helping to defend American jobs. Bush accordingly took along the widely discredited top executives of General Motors, Ford Motor Co. and Chrysler to symbolize his commitment to the moribund U.S. auto industry. These figures functioned like a Greek chorus of negative spin, pointing up Bush's misadventures and failures. The most outspoken of the Big Three bosses was predictably Chrysler's Lee Iacocca, of whom one reporter said that he would probably complain if the sun came up.

Bush displayed decided mental instability during this trip. In Canberra, Australia, he flashed a well-known obscene gesture to a group of farmers who were protesting his "free trade" farm policies. Bush told a luncheon cruise in Sydney harbor, "I'm a man that knows every hand gesture you've ever seen—and I haven't learned a new one since I've been here." As the *Washington Post* reported, "Down here, holding up the first two fingers to form a "V" with the back of the hand toward the subject is the same as holding up the middle finger in the United States. And that's just what Bush did from his limousine to a group of protesters as his motorcade passed through Canberra yesterday, apparently not knowing its significance. Or maybe he did."[48]

Then came Bush's visit to Japan, crowned by his seizure at a state dinner in the official residence of Prime Minister Miyazawa. Bush had vomited at least once before the dinner. "I got a preview in the receiving line. I turned to the prime minister and said, 'Would you please excuse me,' and I rushed into the men's room there. And I thought that had taken care of it, but back I came. It hadn't been halted. It was just the beginning."[49] According to Treasury Secretary Brady, Bush had been urged to skip the state dinner altogether by his personal physician, Dr. Burton Lee, but Bush had rejected this advice out of hand, saying that his absence would "disrupt" the proceedings.[50] After the vomiting and fainting scene was over, Bush was asked if he intended to slow down. "Nope," Bush retorted. "It's just a 24-hour flu."[51]

The truth about Bush's collapse in Tokyo has yet to be told; but it was clear that Bush had learned nothing, and was still determined to impose his will on the universe. Bush's first efforts at campaign oratory after his return from Japan indicated that rage was once again winning the upper hand, which was not a good sign for Bush's ability to function on the campaign trail.

In the light of the evidence reviewed here, it is evident that Bush's marked tendency toward rage episodes, public fits of anger, and obsessive fixations has not subsided. Indeed, Bush's uncontrollable temper tantrums became if anything more severe during October and November 1991, as his presidency began to buckle under the strain of the economic depression Bush was unable and unwilling to overcome.

We must therefore conclude, that the treatment received by Bush for his thyroid condition during May 1991 and the successive months has not remedied the mental and cognitive disturbances which were at the root of Bush's psychosomatic affliction, Basedow's disease. This means that Bush's health, and most especially his mental health, must be considered a decisive issue for his presidency—however long that lasts.

Notes for Chapter XXIV

1. "Tough and Tender Talk," *People,* Dec. 17, 1990, p. 53.
2. Anton Chaitkin, *Treason in America* (New York: New Benjamin Franklin House, 1985), pp. 476 ff.
3. Cited in Chaitkin, *ibid.,* p. 478.
4. Elizabeth Drew, *Portrait of an Election* (New York: Simon and Schuster, 1981), p. 106.
5. Maureen Dowd, "The Language Thing," *The New York Times Magazine,* July 29, 1990.
6. David Hoffman, "Reading Bush's Lips," *Washington Post,* Dec. 4, 1988.
7. *Ibid.*
8. *Ibid.*
9. Dowd, *op. cit.*
10. Hoffman, *op. cit.*
11. Dowd, *op. cit.*
12. "Bush to News Media: Mum's Going to Be the Word," *Washington Post,* Feb. 16, 1990.
13. "Transitioning in Florida," *Washington Post,* Nov. 12, 1988.
14. Gil Klein, "Bush Not Man to Sit Still," Media General Newspapers for the Sherman, Texas *Democrat,* Sept. 7, 1989.
15. Dan Balz, "The 18-Hole Drive to Play on Par with the President," *Washington Post,* Sept. 3, 1990.
16. David Hoffman, "See How He Plays," *Washington Post,* Sept. 3, 1989.
17. "Peripatetic Bush to Break Nixon Travel Record," *Washington Post,* July 27, 1991.
18. George Bush and Victor Gold, *Looking Forward* (New York: Doubleday, 1987), pp. 11–12.
19. "Bush Has 'Early Glaucoma' In Left Eye, Tests Disclose," *Washington Post,* April 13, 1990.
20. "President Assails Silencing of Unpopular Viewpoints," *Washington Post,* May 5, 1991.
21. "Bush Diagnosis: Thyroid Ailment," *Washington Post,* May 8, 1991.
22. "The Path to Diagnosis of the President's Ailment," *Washington Post,* May 11, 1991.
23. *Washington Post,* May 10, 1991.
24. *New York Times,* May 22, 1991.
25. *Washington Times,* May 29, 1991.
26. Mary McGrory, "China and an Imperial President," *Washington Post,* May 30, 1991.
27. *Washington Post,* Sept. 6, 1991.
28. "Bush Gets 'Medical Stamp of Approval' for '92," *Washington Post,* Sept. 14, 1991.
29. Lawrence K. Altman, M.D., "President's Thyroid: Questions of Mood," *New York Times,* May 21, 1991.
30. Abigail Trafford, "Me, Bush and Graves' Disease," *Washington Post,* May 21, 1991.

31. Lillian Sholtis Brunner and Doris Smith Suddarth, *Textbook of Medical-Surgical Nursing* (Philadelphia: Lippincott, 1964), pp. 796, 798.

32. Statement issued May 29, 1991, in *What Does Candidate LaRouche Think of Bush's Mental Health* (Washington: Democrats for Economic Recovery/LaRouche in 92, 1991), p. 3.

33. William Safire, "After the Flutter," *New York Times*, May 20, 1991.

34. "President is Bouyant About Health, Work," *Washington Post*, May 23, 1991.

35. Andrew Rosenthal, "Among Notables, Bush Plays One Tough Room," *New York Times*, June 17, 1991.

36. *Weekly Compilation of Presidential Documents*, July 15, 1991, pp. 941, 944–47.

37. "Peripatetic Bush to Break Travel Record," *Washington Post*, July 27, 1991.

38, *New York Times*, July 25, 1991.

39. "President Sounds Themes of Likely '92 Campaign," *Washington Post*, Aug. 3, 1991. Photos of a furious Bush are on pp. A1 and A4.

40. "Bush Anti-Crime Speech Echoes 1988 Campaign," *Washington Post*, Aug. 15, 1991.

41. *Washington Post*, Sept. 19, 1991.

42. "Bush Vetoes $6.4 Billion Bill to Extend Jobless Benefits," *Washington Post*, Oct. 12, 1991.

43. "Bush Launches Strike at Congress," *Washington Post*, Oct. 25, 1991.

44. "Deferral of Trip Raises Problems for U.S. Policy," *Washington Post*, Nov. 7, 1991.

45. "Bush Cancels Pacific Trip," *Washington Post*, Nov. 6, 1991.

46. "Bush Challenges Europeans To Define U.S. NATO Role," *Washington Post*, Nov. 8, 1991.

47. *Washington Post*, Nov. 21, 1991.

48. *Washington Post*, Jan. 3, 1992.

49. *Washington Post*, Jan. 9, 1992.

50. *Washington Post*, Jan. 11, 1992.

51. *Washington Post*, Jan. 9, 1992.

INDEX

Aaron, David 332
Aaron, Harold A. 333
Abrams, Elliott 528
Accius 479; *Atreus* 479
Acheson, Dean 71–72, 277, 588
à Court, Holmes 445
Acta Non Verba (Deeds Not Words) 397
Adams, John Quincy 96, 118–19, 524, 602
Addabbo, Joseph 313
Adenauer, Konrad 40
Aetna Co. 449
Aga Khan 593
Agca, Mehmet Ali 380–81, 383
Agnelli, Gianni 344
Agnew, Spiro 210, 261
Aikens, James 566
Ailes, Roger 489–91, 497
Ailes, Stephen 309
Ainsworth, Robert 376–77
Airline Pilots Association 457
Albert, Carl 313–14, 515
Alexander, Lamar 508
Alien Property Custodian 26, 28, 48
Allen, Charles E. 403, 405, 410
Allen, Richard 323, 356–57, 360, 365, 380
Allen, Robert H. 247
Allende Gossens, Salvador 316
Allied and Federated Stores 452
Allison, Jim 190, 211
Al-Shiraa 420
Alsop family 119
Altman, Lawrence K. 617–18
Aluminum Marine Products 466
American Airlines 457–58
American Broadcasting Corp. (ABC) 551, 611
American Eugenics Society 59, 74, 123

American Federation of Labor 41
American Jewish Committee 37, 41, 128
American Jewish Congress 41
American Museum of Natural History 48, 126, 130
American Ship and Commerce Corp. 22, 34–38, 42
America West Airline 458
Anderson, Clayton and Company 180
Anderson, Dillon 180
Anderson, Don 275
Anderson, Jack 250, 253, 458
Anderson, John 343, 346–47, 355
Anderson, Leland 180
Anderson, Ned 129–30, 132
Andover Theological Seminary 88–89
Andreas, Dwayne 247, 264, 508
Andreotti, Giulio 315
Andrews, Kurth, Campbell & Jones 331
Andropov, Yuri 381–82
Angelone, Oliver W. 255–57
Angleton, James Jesus 220, 251, 305, 323, 341, 433
Anti-Defamation League of B'nai B'rith 37, 41, 247, 365, 517
Antonov, Sergei 382
Aoun, Michel 583
Arafat, Yassir 558
Arbenz Guzman, Jacobo 148, 250
Archer Daniels Midland Corp. 247, 264, 508
Ardinger, Horace T. 329
Arias Calderon, Jaime 535
Arias Calderon, Ricardo 533, 535
Arizona Republic 132
Armitage, Richard 378
Arnold, Benedict 135
Arnold, Daniel C. 333

Arnold, Terry 403, 410
Arnold, Thurman 46, 97
Aronow, Don 462–67, 482, 521
Aronow, Lillian 465
Artamonov, Nikolai 323
Artim, Manuel 391
Ash Commission 215
Ash, Roy 215
Ashley, Thomas William Ludlow "Lud" 113, 132
Aspin, Les 301
Assad, Hafez al 462, 521, 583
Associated Press 608
Association for Voluntary Surgical Contraception 60
Astor, Lord 77
Atchison (Kansas) *Champion* 492
Atlantic Asset Trust 145
Atlantic Richfield Corp. 206, 331
Attlee, Clement 348
Atwater, Lee 159, 295, 480, 484–90, 494, 497–98, 516
A.U.V. 91–94, 97–98, 149
Augustus, Emperor 6–7
Austin, Stephen 183
Australian Channel Ten 474
Avvenimenti 471
Awami League 226, 229
Azcona, José Simón 408
Aziz, Tariq 585–86, 589, 616

Baker, Bobby 258
Baker & Botts 330–31, 442–43
Baker, Botts, Andrews & Shepherd 149, 162–63, 167, 180, 330–31
Baker family 330–31
Baker, Howard 209, 257–58, 260, 303, 311, 334, 336, 343, 346, 379
Baker, James A. 330–31
Baker, James A. III 11, 103, 160, 163, 169, 323, 330–33, 345–47, 352, 357, 364–69, 374, 378–79, 398, 484, 490–91, 501, 504–05, 508, 546–47, 549–50, 558, 569, 573, 580, 582, 585–86, 596, 616, 628
Bakhtiar, Shahpour 353
Bakker, Jim 488
Baldridge, Malcolm 378
Baldwin, Alfred C. 252

Balfour, Lord 220
Banaico 537
Banco Aleman 537
Banco Continental 535
Banco de Colombia 537
Banco del Istmo 537
Banco General 537
Bandar, Prince 567
Bani-Sadr, Abol Hassan 355, 358–59, 407
Bankers Trust 449
Bank for International Settlements 44
Bank für Handel und Schiff 31
Bank of Commerce and Credit International (BCCI) 378
Bank of England 31
Bank of New England 553
Bank voor Handel en Scheepvaart (BHS) 29, 31, 35
Barcella, Lawrence 318
Baring Bank 121
Barker, Bernard 245–46, 250, 252, 263, 297
Barletta, Nicky 527
Barnett, Frank 80, 389–90
Barr, William P. 508
Barrett, Bob 350
Barry, William Taylor Sullivan 122
Barthes, Roland 502
Bartholomew, Reginald 507
Bartlett, Charles 215, 300
Baruch, Bernard 15, 19
Basedow's disease 550, 615–16, 621–22, 632
Batista, Fulgencio 148, 391
Bay of Pigs invasion 80, 151, 250, 265–66, 306, 396, 419, 542
Beamish, Rita 608
Beardsley, Lehman F. "Lem" 93
Bear Stearns 248, 446
Bearsted, Lord 30
Beatrice Foods 449, 451
Bechtel, Stephen 338
Beck, Christian J. 37–38, 97
Beckington, Herbert 476
Beethoven, Ludwig van 518
Beheshti, Ayatollah 358, 360
Bellino, Carmine 253–60, 273
Bell Telephone Company 121

Beltrante, Nick, 253
Benjamin, Judah P. 122
Bennett, William 508, 510, 522
Benton, William 74
Bentsen, Lloyd 158, 181, 211–13, 215, 442
Bermudez, Enrique 404, 413
Bernhard, Prince 315
Bernstein, Carl 244, 246, 253
Bernstein, Dennis 493
Bertron, James A. 166
Best, Werner 385
Bhutto, Zulfikar Ali 219
Bickle, Travis 374
Biden, Joseph 303
Bierce, Ambrose 337
Biglow, Lucius Horatio Jr. 132–33
Billington, Michael 433, 435
Binder, David 326
Birely, William 253–54
Birth Control League 74–75
Birthright, Inc. 57
Bissell, Richard M. Sr. 126
Bissell, Richard M. Jr. 126–27
Bissell, William Truesdale 126
Blake, John 306
Blandón, Adolfo 420
Bloom, Allan 502
B'nai B'rith 37, 41, 128, 301
Boccaccio, Giovanni 12; *Genealogy of the Gods* 12
Boesky, Ivan 448, 450–52
Bohemian Club of San Francisco 238, 337, 454
Bohemian Grove 337, 454
Bonaparte, Charles 602
Bonhorst, Rainer 5–6; *George Bush: The New Man in the White House* 6
Bonnacci, Paul 471
Boren, David Lyle 129, 410
Bosch, Orlando 316
Boston Globe 322, 336
Botts, Benjamin 330
Botts, Walter Browne 330
Bowers, James 188
Bowie, Jim 183
Bowman, Steve 472
Boyd, Aquilino 525
Boys Town 473, 475–76
Brademas, John 313

Braden, Tom 291
Bradford, Amory Howe 128
Brady, James 364, 367
Brady, Nicholas 11, 56, 69–70, 199, 329, 415, 425, 439, 441, 454–55, 463–64, 486, 492, 504, 514, 523–24, 630–31
Brandi, Frederic 53, 56
Branstad, Terry 486
Brasco, Frank 249
Breaux, John B. 586
Breen, John 345, 347
Brenneke, Richard 359, 407, 411
Brezhnev, Leonid 102, 233, 381–82; *Malaya Zemlya* 102
Bricker, John W. 77
Brigade 2506 173
Briggs, Everett 527
Briscoe, Frank 188–89
British East India Company 120, 340, 501
British Eugenics Society 60, 331
British Imperial Tobacco 73
British Information Research Department 348
British Round Table 44
Brittain, Mike 466–67
Brokaw, Tom 337, 491
Brookings, Robert 19
Brooks, Jack 157
Broomfield, William 313
Brown Brothers 30–32, 48, 65, 69
Brown Brothers Harriman 2, 10, 14, 23, 26–27, 30–31, 34–35, 63, 66, 72–74, 76–77, 80, 91, 101, 107, 112, 117, 127, 139, 140, 148–49, 179, 192–93, 208–09, 220, 272–73, 277, 293, 307, 336, 352, 357, 363, 365, 446, 485, 494, 517, 614
Brown, George 309, 312
Brown, Jerry 339, 352
Brown, Moreau D. 69
Brown, Shipley 31
Brown, Thatcher M. 30–31, 69
Bruce, David K.E. 69, 223, 274, 280
Brumbaugh, Dan 557
Brunner, Lillian Sholtis 619; *Textbook of Medical-Surgical Nursing* 619

Bryan, Albert V. Jr. 435
Bryen, Steven 323
Brzezinski, Zbigniew 332, 342, 352–53, 367
Buchen, Philip 308
Buckeye Steel Castings Co. 15
Buckley, Jack 260
Buckley, James 317
Buckley, William F. 128, 317, 340–41, 485
Bulloch, James D. 602
Bundy, McGeorge 127, 277, 341
Bundy, William P. 127, 277, 341
Burch, Dean 262, 267, 274–75
Burdick, Thomas 465–67
Burman, Kenneth 613–14
Burr, Aaron Sr. 134–35
Burr, Aaron Jr. 119–21, 134–36
Bush, Barbara 5, 10, 85–86, 95–97, 102–04, 115–16, 142, 163, 165–66, 239, 275, 500, 550, 608
Bush, Dorothy Walker 13, 65, 83, 85, 565
Bush family 13, 21, 31, 33, 36–37, 39, 45–46, 48, 50, 52, 55, 57, 64–66, 68, 72, 77, 95, 98
Bush, Flora Sheldon 18
Bush, Fred 334, 378, 509
Bush, George Walker 25, 142, 373, 482, 494
Bush, Jeb 467
Bush, Jonathan 130, 132
Bush, Neil Mallon 113, 131, 141, 176, 199, 370–74, 513, 555–57, 565
Bush-Overbey Co. 139, 145
Bush, Prescott Jr. 83, 357
Bush, Prescott Sr. 2, 10, 13–18, 20–24, 26–28, 30–41, 48, 50–51, 54–55, 63–67, 69–80, 83–85, 97–98, 101–05, 115, 117, 124–26, 128, 130–32, 139–42, 145, 148–51, 161, 163, 165–66, 171, 178–80, 183, 192–93, 209, 215, 217, 220, 237, 296, 311, 348, 380, 444, 446–47, 454, 516, 524, 546, 604
Bush, Samuel P. 15–16, 30
Bush, Sharon 371–73
Butler, George A. 248

Buzhardt, J. Fred 267
Byrnes, John W. 192

Cabot family 119, 121
Caesar, Julius 7
Calero, Adolfo 411, 418
Calhoun, John C. 122
Cali Cartel 534–35
Caligula, Gaius Caesar 1, 7–9, 12, 479
Calvo, Escolastico 538
Camdessus, Michel 513
Camp, Sharon 205
Campaign to Check the Population Explosion 204
Campbell, Caroll 488
Campeau, Robert 452, 522
Canzeri, Joe 491
Capone, Al 586
Caradori, Gary 472, 477–78
Carener, Andrea L. 473
Carey, Hugh 313
Carlucci, Frank 380, 506
Carpenter, Walter S. Jr. 69
Carr, Fred 450
Carrel, Alexis 61; *Man the Unknown* 61
Carriles, Luis Posada 81, 404
Carter, Jimmy 159, 273, 314, 321–22, 324–25, 332–33, 335–36, 338–39, 343–45, 349, 352–61, 364, 367, 375, 385, 388, 501, 505, 538
Carvey, Dana 603, 605
Case, Clifford 303, 322
Casey, William 80, 302, 348, 352–60, 380, 390, 393, 398, 404, 407, 421
Casseb, Solomon 444
Cassin, William B. 167, 169
Castro, Fidel 81, 127, 148, 173, 250, 316, 320, 391, 435
Catto, Henry E. 378
Caulkins, John Erwin 132
Cavazo, Lauro 508
Cecchi, Albert 458
Center for Creative Leadership 78
Central Intelligence Agency (CIA) 11, 28, 55, 64, 67–69, 72, 76–81, 126–28, 130, 148, 173, 193, 220, 222, 245–47, 250–

52, 255, 263–69, 277, 286–
324, 332–33, 341, 343, 346,
348, 353–59, 365, 367, 382–
83, 388–426, 431, 433, 435,
466, 469, 471–72, 485, 490,
506, 508, 520, 525, 530, 534,
567–69, 596, 623, 625
Chafee, John H. 116
Ch'aio Kuan-hua 225
Chaitkin, Jacob 40–41
Chamberlain, Neville 520
Chambers, C. Fred 168–69
Chandra Shakar 596
Channell, Carl R. "Spitz" 430,
433
Chappell, William 249
Chardy, Alfonso 418
Chase Bank 345
Chatham House 219
Chauvenet, William 122
Cheney, Richard 350, 422, 505–
06, 531, 567–69, 585, 587
Cherne, Leo, 80, 301–02, 309,
321, 323, 325, 327, 349, 389–
90
Chernenko, Konstantin 381
Cheshire, Maxine 313
Chevron Corp. 441, 443
Chiang Kai-Shek 222–23
Chicago Tribune 475
Chin Shih Huang 285
Chirol, Valentine 603
Christian Science Monitor 382
Christic Institute 527
Chrysler Corp. 631
Church Committee 290, 301,
303–05, 308, 311
Church, Frank 289–93, 298–300,
303, 309–10, 312, 315
Churchill, Winston 2, 64, 151,
219, 517
Cisneros, Marc 533, 536
Citibank 14
City of London 11, 139, 145
Clairol Corp. 334
Clark Family Estate 147
Clark, Ramsey 157, 534
Clark, Tom 157
Clark, William Judkins 132
Clark, William P. 364, 380, 388–
89

Clarridge, Duane 410
Claudius, Emperor 7
Clay, Henry 602
Clayton, W.L. 180
Cleveland, Grover 68, 138
Clifford, Clark 71
Cline, Ray 332, 352, 356
Clines, Thomas 81, 307, 317, 378
Coakley, Jack 333
Cochran, Thomas 87, 89
Coelho, Tony 516
Coffin, Henry Sloane 128
Coffin, William Sloane 128, 341
Cohen, Herbert 357
Cohen, Joshua L. 618
Cohen, Peter 451
Colby, William 286–87, 291–92,
294, 301, 304–05, 312; Honor-
able Men 301
Cole, Albert L. 70, 171
Collins, James M. 293
Collor de Mello, Fernando 595
Colson, Charles W. 240
Columbia Broadcasting System
(CBS) 237, 292, 302, 310–11,
350, 420, 526
Columbia Savings and Loan 450
Columbia University 121
Combined Shipping Adjustment
Board 127
Commission on Population and
the American Future 202
Committee to Reelect the Presi-
dent (CRP) 208–10, 245–48,
259–60, 263, 266, 297, 334
Committee to Save the Children in
Iraq 593
Common Cause 516
Conable, Barber 261, 346
Confederate States of America 19,
122, 330
Connally, John 146, 157, 163,
169, 179, 181–82, 190, 209,
211, 214–17, 243, 343, 346,
379
Connelly, William James Jr. 132–
33
Connor, Bull 172
Connor, Jim 294
Connor, John T. 289
Conservation Foundation 508

Consolidated Silesian Steel Corp. 32–33
Continental Airlines 457–58
Continental Shelf Associates, Inc. (CSA) 396–97
Cook, George III 132
Coolidge, Archibald Cary 121
Coolidge, Calvin 90, 103, 601
Coolidge family 119
Coolidge, Joseph 121
Cooper, Gary 486
Copeland, Miles 485
Cornell University 123
Corr, Edwin 415
Cortiso, Captain (PDF) 526
Council on Foreign Relations (CFR) 121, 164, 179–80, 337, 339, 344–45
Counterspy magazine 301
Cox, Archibald 261
Cox, Jack 163, 179–81
Coy, Craig 403, 410
Craig, Earle 143
Craig, Larry 539
Crain, Lillo 609
Cramer, Richard Ben 4, 108
Crane, Philip 343, 346, 538–39
Cranston, Alan 423–26, 428, 430–32, 556
Crisis Management Center 386, 389, 410
Crocker family 337
Crockett, Davy 183
Cronkite, Walter 347, 350
Crossman, Gene 167
Crowe, William J. 531, 584
Crowley, Leo T. 28
Cruz, Rogelio 534
Cullen, Roy 169
Culver, John C. 300
Cuno, Wilhelm 35
Curlin, William Jr. 249
Cushing, Caleb 90
Cushing family 90, 119
Cushing, John Perkins 100

D'Amato, Alphonse M. 382–83
Dahlberg, Kenneth 246–47, 264–65
Daily Telegraph 567

Dallas Morning News 162, 179, 183
Danforth, John 490
Dardis, Martin 245
Darling, Arthur Burr 96; *Political Changes in Massachusetts, 1824 to 1848* 96; *The Central Intelligence Agency: An Instrument of Government, to 1950* 96
Darman, Richard 552–53
Dash, Sam 259
Davis, Milton 169, 179
Davison, Endicott Peabody 130, 132
Davison, F. Trubee 124–27, 130
Davison, Harry P. 125
Davison, Henry 125
Day family 119
Dean, John 242, 258, 263
Deaver, Michael 350, 364–66, 374, 378, 497
DeCamp, John W. 478
DeConcini, Dennis 556
Deep Throat 3, 254
de Gaulle, Charles 309
De Graffenreid, Kenneth 392
DelAmico, Mario 404
Delaney, John L. 104–08, 110–11, 113
Delaney, Mary Jane 113
Delano family 119
Delano, Warren Jr. 121
Delta Airlines 458
Delta Kappa Epsilon 117
Demirel, Suleyman 624
Demosthenes 340
Deng Xiaoping 274–76, 283, 342, 518–21, 606
Dent, Harry S. 207
Depew, Chauncey M. 123
Derwinski, Ed 507
Deterding, Sir Henri 47
Dewey, Thomas 496
Deyo, Harold 180
Diaz Serrano, Jorge 152–53
Diego, Felipe de 252
Diem, Ngo Dinh 277
Dillon, C. Douglas 54, 70, 75, 80, 289
Dillon, Clarence 15, 30, 53–54, 70
Dillon Read & Co. 30, 53–54, 56, 70–71, 454

Dilworth, J. Richardson 341
Dimitrov, Vassily 382
Dingell, John 440
Dinges, John 318
Diocletian, Emperor 541
Dirks, Leslie 306
Disraeli, Benjamin 220
Dole, Elizabeth Hanford 469, 490, 508
Dole, Robert 240, 324, 343, 345–47, 349, 480–81, 484–88, 490, 494, 505, 508, 575
Domenici, Pete 490
Donaldson, Sam 551
Donovan, John 466
Doubleday, Nelson 70
Douglas, Michael 446
Dowd, Maureen 568
Drach, Ivan 597
Drake, Ed 181
Draper Fund (See Population Crisis Committee) 55–56, 204–05
Draper, William H. Jr. 53–56, 70, 75, 200, 204–05
Draper, William H. III 56, 205, 378
Dresser Industries 6, 12, 48, 52, 140–43, 152
Dresser, Solomon R. 140
Drew, Elizabeth 603
Drexel Burnham Lambert 450, 452
Duarte, Napoleon 419
Duckett, Carl 306–07
Duckworth, Allan 183
Dukakis, Michael 3, 489–90, 495–97, 529, 604, 606
Duke family 73
Dulles, Allen 55, 73, 76–77, 80, 122, 127, 148, 274, 338
Dulles brothers 35, 39
Dulles, John Foster 38–41, 55, 59, 73, 75–76, 78–80, 87, 121–22, 127–28, 131
Dulles, Joseph Heatly 122
Dumas, Roland 592
Du Pont Corporation 69
DuPont family 56, 487
DuPont, Pierre 485
Duracell Corp. 451
Duval, Mike 308

Dwight, Theodore 119–20, 135
Dwight, Timothy 135
Dzerzhinsky, Feliks 22

Eagleburger, Lawrence 103, 393–94, 505, 520, 557, 597, 607
Earl of Oxford 455
Earl, Robert 403, 410
Eastern Airlines 457–58
Eastwood, Clint 486, 489
Economist magazine 512
Edwards family 119
Edwards, Henry W. 135
Edwards, Jonathan 121, 135–36
Edwards, Pierpont 135
Ehrlich, Paul 199–200
Ehrlichman, John 215–16, 239, 258, 260–61, 304
Eisenhower, Dwight D. 55, 70, 75–76, 78–81, 147, 156, 163–64, 181, 195, 208, 338, 523, 542
Eleta Almaran, Carlos 530, 534
Eli Lilly & Co. 329, 456–57
Elizabeth II, Queen 10, 46, 84, 248, 515, 559, 598
Ellenberg, Al 109
Ellsberg, Daniel 250
Elmhirst, Sir Thomas 68
Emerson, Ralph Waldo 121
Endara, Guillermo 530, 533–34, 536–38
Enders, Rudy 390, 397
English, Glenn 461
English Speaking Union 80
Ernst, Maurice 308
Ervin, Sam 242–44, 253–55, 257–60
Escalante, Jorge 153
Esquire magazine 108
Essex Junto 119, 135
Esso Corp. 396
Esterline, Jake 252
Estes, Billie Sol 169–70, 181
Eugenics Congress 49
Eugenics Federation 49
Eugenics Record Office 48
Evans and Novak 494
Evans, Rod 475
Evans, Rowland 291
Evans, Samuel M. 411

Evarts, William M. 123
Executive Intelligence Review (EIR) 353, 355, 360–61, 433, 476, 534, 557
Exner, Judith 253
Exxon Corp. 46, 331–34, 396

Fahd, King 327, 483, 569–70, 581
Fairbanks, Richard 378
Fairchild, Mark 433
Faisal, King 569
Falcon, Augusto 537
Falkiewicz, Andrew 333
Fallaci, Oriana 278
Family Planning Services and Population Research Act of 1970 198
Fang Lizhi 520
Farish, Mary 77
Farish, William Stamps Sr. 46–52, 54, 77
Farish, William Stamps Jr. 51
Farish, William Stamps III (Also see W.S. Farish & Co.) 46, 52, 77, 169, 248, 459, 514–15, 608
Farris, Anthony J.P. "Tough Tony" 443–44
Fascell, Dante 580
Federal Bureau of Investigation (FBI) 67, 103, 116, 130, 250–51, 253–54, 263–67, 293, 297, 303, 310, 312, 318–20, 353, 355, 370, 373, 375–76, 380, 400, 403, 410, 432–34, 466–67, 471, 475, 477, 525, 602, 626
Felt, Mark 264
Feltenstein, Harry D. Jr. 247
Fensterwald, Bud 254
FIAT Motor Company 344
Fidelity Printing Company 442
Fiers, Alan 623
Financial Times 593, 614
Finch, Robert 211
First Boston Bank 443, 451
First City National Bank 180
First Executive Corp. 450
First Executive Life 450
First Interamericas Bank 534–35
First International Bank 248

First International Bank of Houston 327, 332
First International Bankshares, Inc. ("Interfirst") 327–28
First International Bankshares Ltd. of London 327
First RepublicBank 328
Fisher, Irving 123
Fitzgerald, Jennifer 275, 334, 494
Fitzwater, Marlin 419, 431, 552, 554, 569–70, 607, 612
Flaherty, Victor A. 442
Flanigan, Peter 215
Fleming L. 180
Flick, Friedrich 32–33, 35
Foch, Ferdinand 17
Foley, Thomas 517, 553, 575
Forbes family 119
Forbes, John Murray 121
Ford, Betty 303
Ford Foundation 201
Ford, Gerald 80, 192, 209, 249, 262, 267, 272–73, 275, 281–83, 285–86, 289, 291, 293–96, 299–304, 308–13, 324, 334, 343, 349–51, 354, 454, 501, 505, 525
Ford, Guillermo "Billy" 533–34
Ford Motor Corp. 631
Foreign Affairs 593
Forrestal, James 71–72
Fortier, Donald 408
Fort Lauderdale News 291
Forum World Features 80, 348
Foster, Jodie 374–76
Fowler, Henry 323
Foxe, Fanny 193
Francis, David R. 19
Frandsen, G. Kent 492
Frank, John 255
Franklin, Benjamin 602
Franklin Committee 471, 473, 475–77
Franklin Community Credit Union 470, 473
Franks, Gary 579
Freed, Donald 320
Freedom House 389–90
Freeport Minerals 331
Frick, Wilhelm 49
Friedman, Milton 316

Frost, David 112
Fruehauf Corp. 452
Fuess, Claude Moore 89–91, 96, 98–99
Fuess, John Cushing 90
Fukuyama, Francis 502–03, 509
Fulbright, J. William 174
Fuller, Craig 414, 416, 509
Funk, Walter 43

Gallagher, Cornelius 313
Galton National Laboratory 48
Gambino, Robert 332, 352
Gamble, Clarence 58, 60
Gammell, James 145, 147, 149
Gamsakhurdia, Zviad 625
Gandhi, Indira 219, 228, 231
Gandhi, Rajiv 596
Garcia, Jesus 427
Garment, Leonard 489
Garrick, Robert 356
Gates, Artemus Lamb 99, 112, 125–26, 623–24
Gates, Robert 3, 506
Gaynor, Robert 251
Gelb, Leslie 292
General Motors Corp. 631
Genovese family 462
Gentleman's Quarterly (GQ) 472
Gephardt, Richard 517, 595
Gergen, David 378
German Atlantic Cable Company 39
German Credit and Investment Corp. 53–54, 204
German Steel Trust (United Steel Works Corp.) 27, 29–35, 40, 53, 56, 70, 201
Germany, E.B. 181
Germond, Jack 335, 351, 356
Geronimo 129–32
Gerry, Edward Harriman 50
Gerstein, Richard E. 245
Gesell, Gerhard 203
Getty, Gordon 442–44
Getty, J. Paul 140
Getty Museum 442–43
Getty Oil Co. 441–42
Getty Trust (Sarah) 442
G.H. Walker & Co. 30, 35, 128, 139, 145, 147, 516

Giancana, Sam 81
Gibbs, Lawrence 328, 445
Gilbert, Bob 187
Gilderhorn, Joseph B. 509
Gilman, Daniel Coit 123
Gingrich, Newt 516, 576
Giro Aviation Corp. 399
Glanville, James 442
Glaspie, April 562–63
Glenn, John 556
Global 2000 205
Godson, Roy 389
Goebbels, Josef 2, 102, 497
Gold, Victor 4; Looking Forward 4
Goldberg, Woody 369
Goldwater, Barry 155–56, 158–60, 167, 171, 173–74, 178–79, 181–83, 186–89, 222, 269, 296, 303
Goleniewski, Michael 220
Gomez, Max (see Felix Rodriguez) 306, 416, 418–20, 431
Gonzalez, Henry B. 157, 418, 582, 593
González, Virgilio 252
Good, Kenneth 555
Goodearle, Roy 164–67
Goodman, Robert 335
Gorbachov, Mikhail 518, 520, 532–33, 543, 546–50, 559–60, 573–74, 582, 597–98, 607, 625
Gore, Albert Jr. 511, 586
Göring, Hermann 55
Gorman, Dick 106
Gorman, Paul F. 400, 429
Graham, Daniel 321
Graham, Katharine Meyer 145
Graham, Phil 145, 586
Graves' disease 612, 614–15, 617–18
Graves, Henry Solon 123
Gray, Alice Shelton 58–59
Gray, Bob 191
Gray, Bowman 58
Gray, Bowman Jr. 73
Gray, Clayland Boyden "Boy" 57–58, 60, 379, 430, 434, 451–52, 492, 504, 630
Gray family 57–60, 78
Gray, Gordon 55, 58–59, 73, 78–79, 163, 379

Gray, L. Patrick 263–64, 266
Gray, Peter 330
Gray, Robert Keith 163
Gray, William 599
Great American Corp. 450
Green, Fitzhugh 4, 91, 107–08, 132, 182, 187; *George Bush: An Intimate Portrait* 4
Green, John Cleve 121
Green, Shirley M. 363, 373
Greene, Harold H. 493
Greenspan, Alan 350, 505
Gregg, Donald P. 274, 313, 356, 359, 386, 388, 390–91, 395, 397, 399, 401–02, 404, 408, 411, 414, 419, 423–32, 470, 506–07, 515, 527
Gregg, Hugh 345
Grimes, David Charles 132
Griswold, Erwin N. 289
Griswold family 119
Griswold, Sarah 121
Groeninger, Johann G. 27, 35
Grosvenor, Gilbert 510
Guaranty Trust Company 19, 22, 124
Gui, Luigi 315
Gulf Oil Co. 148, 151, 206, 441–42
Gulf Resources and Chemical Corp. 247–48
Gutfreund, John 451
Guttmacher, Alan 195

Habib, Philip 274, 283
Haggar Slacks 334
Haig, Al 3, 223, 229–30, 238, 262, 268, 364–70, 374, 378, 380
Haig, Sir Douglas 17
Hakim, Albert 307
Haldeman, H.R. 215–17, 239–40, 263–66, 304
Hall, Fawn 389
Hallowell, Norwood Penrose 93
Halper, Stephan 332, 352, 356, 360
Hamburg-Amerika Line 21–22, 31, 34–36, 38, 40, 42, 49–50, 61, 84, 97

Hamilton, Alexander 120, 135, 602
Hanes, James Gordon 58
Hanna, Marc 351
Hanna, Richard 249, 313–14
Hapag-Lloyd 37–38
Harkavy, Oscar 201
Harriman brothers 30, 604
Harriman Commission 127
Harriman, E.H. 14–15, 31, 330–31
Harriman, E. Roland "Bunny" 14, 20, 24, 26–27
Harriman family 14, 16, 19, 22–23, 27, 112, 123–24, 128, 141, 171
Harriman Fifteen Corp. 32–35
Harriman International Co. 38
Harriman, Pamela Churchill 517
Harriman Ripley & Co. 450
Harriman, Roland 125
Harriman, Wm. Averell (Also see W.A. Harriman & Co.) 2, 6, 14, 18–23, 27, 29–30, 32–35, 37–41, 48–50, 53, 55, 63–66, 68–80, 84, 93, 97, 112, 117, 123–28, 145, 151, 162, 180, 241, 277, 341, 517–18, 546
Harris, Lou 336
Hart, Gary 297–98, 300, 311, 494
Hart, Janice 433
Hart, Peter 152
Harvard University 88–89, 103, 119, 121–22, 143, 146, 490
Hasenfus, Eugene 415, 417–21, 425, 430, 432
Hashemi, Cyrus 353–55, 406, 411
Hashemi, Jamshid 355–56
Hassan, Prince 558
Hatfield, Mark 581
Havel, Vaclav 582
Hayes, Rutherford B. 122
Healy, Robert 336
Heard, Augustine 121
Hearst, William Randolph 24
Hegel, G.W.F. 502–04
Helfferich, Emil 38, 50
Helms, Richard 315
Heminway, Spike 609
Henry III, King 84, 95

Herman, George 292
Hermann, Albert B. "Ab" 255
Herndon, Claude Nash 58–59
Hersh, Seymour M. 289
Hess, Rudolf 55
Heymann, Hans 308
Higgins, William R. 600
Higginson, Stephen Jr. 88, 119, 121
Hill, Anita 625
Hilliard, Harry Talbot 143
Hills, Carla 501, 505, 594
Hillsborough Holdings 453
Himmler, Heinrich 32, 459, 515
Hinckley, John Warnock Sr. "Jack" 370, 372–73, 376
Hinckley, John Warnock Jr. 368, 370–76
Hinckley, Scott 370–74, 513, 555
Hitler, Adolf 13, 16, 26, 28, 30–41, 45–51, 53–55, 59, 64, 75, 77, 90, 93, 96–97, 102, 128, 335, 342, 489, 546, 570, 579, 581, 584, 587
Holdridge, John 275, 281–82
Hole, Legare 109–10
Holland-American Trading Corporation 27
Holloway, James L. III 403, 410
Holmes, Oliver Wendell Sr. 89
Holmes, Oliver Wendell Jr. 89
Honecker, Erich 547
Honegger, Barbara 360
Hoover, Herbert 103, 124
Hoover, J. Edgar 250, 312
Hopkins family 337
Hopkins, Harry 112
Horowitz, Herbert 275
Horton, Buster 435
Horton, Willie 196, 489–90
Hougan, James 250, 252, 254, 256
House, Edward M. 19, 330
Houston Chronicle 167–69, 187–88, 192, 211
Houston Oil and Minerals 334
Houston Post 210, 370, 372–73
Houston, Sam 183
Howard, Gary 342, 434
H. Smith Richardson Foundation 77, 80, 389–90

Hubbard family 119
Huddleston, Walter 311
Hughes, Charles Evans 24
Human Betterment League 58
Humble Oil Co. 48
Humphrey, Gordon 346
Humphrey, Hubert 215, 322
Hunt, E. Howard 81, 129, 250, 252, 255, 265–66, 306, 321, 391, 435
Hunt, H.L. 165, 179
Hunt, Ray 248
Huntington family 337
Hurt, Harry III 4, 245, 335
Hussein, King 463, 558, 586
Hussein, Saddam 542, 558, 561–63, 565–67, 569–72, 580, 585, 589, 591, 593, 621, 625, 629
Hutcheson, J.C. III 180
Hutcheson, Thad 163
Huxley, Julian 331
Hu Yaobang 518
Hyams, Joe 5, 102, 105–07, 112–13; Flight of the Avenger 5, 102, 112
Hyland, William G. 309, 593–94

Iacocca, Lee 631
Icahn, Carl 445, 450, 458
I.G. Farben Co. 46–47, 50–51, 54, 69
Ikle, Fred 356, 394
Iliescu, Ion 547
Iliopoulos, Nicolas 463
Ingalls, David S. 126–27
Inouye, Daniel K. 258–60
Inside News 473
Interarms Co. 435
International Derrick and Equipment Company (IDECO) 142–43
International Eugenics Congress 54, 123
International Federation of Eugenics Societies 48–49
International Herald Tribune 534
International Monetary Fund (IMF) 242, 285, 513–14, 527, 553, 597–98
International Rescue Committee (IRC) 302

Iran-Contra 3, 65, 69–70, 77, 81, 129, 151, 156–57, 255, 297, 306–07, 313, 358, 369, 385–438, 462, 467, 470–71, 486, 491, 505–07, 528, 605–06, 623
Ireland, Robert L. "Tim" 91
Italian State Oil Company 151

Jackson, Henry 79, 215
Jackson, Henry Rootes 122
Jamail, Joe "King of Torts" 443–44
James, Ellery S. 20, 131
Jardine Matheson 121
Jarring, Gunnar 236
Javits, Jacob 322
Jaworski, Leon 293, 314, 344, 379
Jefferson, Thomas 119, 136
Jeffords, James M. 578
Jenkins, Richard Elwood 132
Jensen, Arthur 52, 200
Jim Walker Co. 453
JM/WAVE 151, 404
John Birch Society 163–65, 167, 182–83, 187, 189
John Paul II, Pope 57, 380–81
Johnson, Hugh 594
Johnson, Loch K. 292
Johnson, Lyndon B. 56, 67, 80, 146, 156–57, 161, 170, 175, 181–83, 188, 210, 309, 542, 611
Johnson, Owen 604; *Dink Stover at Yale* 604
Johnson, Ross 451
Jones, David C. 369, 584
Jones, Edward Murray 256–57
Joyce, Mike 389
J.P. Morgan & Co. 19, 125
Juan Carlos, King 463
Juliana, Queen 315
Jupiter Island 64–66, 68, 70–71, 80, 126, 129, 171, 524
J. Walter Thompson Advertising Agency 190

Kahn, Otto 14
Kaiser Wilhelm Institute for Genealogy and Demography 49
Kalmbach, Herbert 259

Kampelman, Max 323
Karamessines, Thomas 252
Karrubi, Mehdi 356
Kayser, Paul 180
Keating Five 432, 556
Keene, David 334, 494
Keene, Thomas R. 111
Keeton, Robert E. 434
Kelley, Clarence 312
Kelley, Paul X. 406
Kemp, Jack 485, 487–88, 490, 508
Kempster, Norman 301
Kennan, George 502
Kennedy, David 207, 215–16
Kennedy, Edward "Ted" 339, 349, 352
Kennedy family 140
Kennedy, John F. 2, 80–81, 127, 156–57, 162–63, 172–73, 191, 250, 253, 256–57, 265, 277, 290, 309, 341, 368–69, 391, 479, 577
Kennedy, Joseph P. 47, 140
Kerr, Blaine 331, 441–42
Kerr, Robert 349
Kerrey, Robert 581
Kerr-McGee Corp. 331
Kerry, John F. 427–28
KGB 22, 220, 323, 381–82
Khan, Rao Farman Ali 229
Khmer Rouge 277–83
Khomeini, Ruhollah 352–61, 385, 408–09, 415, 421, 433
Kilpatrick, Martin E. 110
Kimberlin, Brett 493
Kimmitt, Robert 490
King, Dennis 390; *Lyndon LaRouche and the New American Fascism* 390
King, Lawrence E. Jr. 470–76
King, Martin Luther Jr. 200, 492
King, Nicholas 5; *George Bush: A Biography* 5
Kipling, Rudyard 588
Kirkland, Lane 289, 322
Kirkland, W.A. 180
Kirkpatrick, Jeane 393
Kissinger Associates 218, 504–05, 520, 597
Kissinger, Henry 11, 103, 214,

217–32, 234, 236–37, 239,
243–45, 249–51, 265, 267–69,
273–87, 290, 292, 302, 304,
308–09, 311, 313–14, 316–17,
320, 324, 337–38, 342–43,
348, 350, 360–61, 364–66,
380, 433, 454, 482, 485, 501,
504–05, 518–21, 542, 544,
557, 561, 567, 584, 593
Knaggs, John R. 192
Knoche, Enno Henry 305, 324
Knox, Frank 97
Koch, Noel 323, 403, 410
Kohl, Helmut 560, 582
Kohlberg, Jerome Jr. 248
Kohlberg, Kravis, Roberts (KKR)
445–53
Kohler, Foy 321
Kojeve, Alexandre 502
Korean Central Intelligence
Agency 249
Korth, Penne Percy 509
Kotany, Mildred 24
Kouwenhoven, H.J. 27, 29
Kozak, Michael G. 529
Kramer, Ben 465–66
Kramer, Jack J. 465–66
Kranish, Arthur 312
Kravis, Henry 11, 140, 248, 441,
446–53, 483, 492, 512, 515
Kravis, Ray 139–42, 146, 446
Kreuter, Alexander 53
Kucan, Milan 596
Kuhn Loeb and Co. 14, 40, 41

LaBoa, Monsignor 535–36
Lacaze, Jeannou 566
Laghi, Pio 381
Laird, Melvin 379
Lake Resources 413
Lamont, Thomas 62
Landau, George 317
Landau, Saul 318
Langehorne, Nancy 77
Lansky, Meyer 68, 81, 391, 461,
463, 465, 479, 517
Lapham, Anthony 307, 319–20,
466
Lapham, Lewis 307
LaRouche, Helga Zepp 593
LaRouche, Lyndon H. Jr. 11–12,

128, 164, 242–44, 286, 328,
337–43, 364, 390, 432–35,
483, 487, 495, 504, 539, 547–
48, 558, 583, 619–20
Lasell, Helen P. 180
Latchinian, Gerard 399
Lavi, Houshang 355
Lawn, John C. 527, 529
Laxalt, Paul 480
Lazard Freres 442
League of Nations 102
Leahy, Patrick 297, 300
Ledeen, Michael 348, 405
Le Duc Tho 223
Lee, Burton 610–15, 624, 631
Lee, Higginson & Co. 93
Lee, Ivy 50, 54
Leggett, Bob 313
Lehman, John 356
Lehman, Richard 322, 326
Lemnitzer, Lyman 289
Lenkowsky, Les 389
Lenzner, Terry 260
Leon, John 254–58
Leonard, Jerris 254–56
Leone, Giovanni 315
Letelier, Orlando 307, 316–20,
354, 466
Levi, Edward 308, 319
LeWinter, Oscar 359
Lewis, Anthony 301
Lewis, Drew 349, 351
Lewis, Fred 434
Liberty Broadcasting System 169
Liddy, G. Gordon 245, 251, 260,
265, 321; *Will* 251
Liedtke brothers 143, 146–50
Liedtke, J. Hugh 11, 143, 146–47,
149, 328, 441–46, 454
Liedtke, William C. Jr. 143, 149,
169, 245–47, 259, 263–64,
266, 297, 334
Liedtke & Liedtke 145
Lievense, Cornelis 27
Lilly, James 520
Liman, Arthur 442
Lincoln, Abraham 115, 123, 351,
554–55, 602
Lindemann, Karl 50
Lindner, Carl 450
Li Peng 274, 518

Lipton, Marty 442
Lithium Corporation of America 247
Liu Chieh 224
Livius, Titus 9
Lloyd, Bruce K. 613
Lockheed Corp. 312, 315
Lodge, Henry Cabot 277
Loeb, Nackey Scripps, 481–82
Loeb, William 343–44, 481–82
Lone Star Steel Co. 181
Long Boret 282
Long, Russell 207
Lon Nol 277–78, 281–82
Lord, Daniel 122, 124
Lord, Winston 274, 283–84
Lorenzo, Frank 441, 457–58
Los Angeles Times 529, 537
Louis IX (Saint Louis) 84
Lovett Committee 67
Lovett, Robert A. 2, 31, 66–68, 71–72, 80, 99, 112, 125–27, 277
Lovett, Robert S. 15, 24, 331
Low, Abiel Abbott 121
Low family 119
Low, Seth 121
Lowe, Jerry 476
Lowell family 119
Lowell, John Jr. 88
Luce, Henry 127, 336, 341, 451, 544, 587
Lugar, Richard G. 419
Lujan, Manuel 507

MacArthur, Douglas 67–68, 72, 124
MacGregor, Clark 209
Machiavelli, Niccolo 327; The Prince 327
Mack, Richard Gerstle 132
Mackin, B.J. 331
Madden, John B. Jr. 117
Magluta, Salvador 537
Magoon, Robert 467
Major, John 589, 591–92, 598
Malik, Yakov 228
Mallon, Henry Neil 48, 131, 140–42, 604
Manchester Union Leader 343–44, 481, 578

Mandel, Allan 151
Manley, Michael 314
Mansfield, Mike 174, 233
Manufacturers Hanover Trust 449
Mao Zedong 93, 221, 227, 275, 279, 283–85, 291, 518
Marcellus, Marcus Pomponius 601
Maritima BAM 391
Marsh, Jack O. 286, 308, 350
Marshall, George C. 72
Marshall Plan 71, 127
Marshall, Thurgood 551–52
Martella, Ilario 380–82
Martinez, Bob 508, 580
Martínez, Eugenio 250
Marx, Karl 503
Matamoros, Bosco 418
Mathews, Jessica 193
Mathias, Charles 311
Matson, Julius 320
Mattei, Enrico 151
Mayhew, Christopher 348
Mayor, James M. 188
Mazowiecki, Tadeusz 549
McAshan, Maurice 180
McCain, John III 131, 556
McCall Corporation 95
McCandless, Alfred A. 579
McCarthy, Joseph R. 74
McCloy, John J. 55
McClure, Frederick D. 457
McConnell, Mitch 430
McCord, James 250–52, 254, 258, 321
McCormick Oil and Gas Co. 334
McDonnell Douglas Corp. 334
McElroy, William 201
McFall, John 313
McFarlane, Robert "Bud" 356–57, 364, 380, 390, 392, 394, 398, 401, 403, 406, 413, 415, 421
McGee, William J. 19
McGovern, George 238, 249, 581
McGrory, Mary 546
McIntyre, Thomas 296, 300, 303
McKinley, John K. 444
McKinley, William 138, 351
McLaughlin, Father John 262
McLendon, Gordon 169–70, 181
McMahon, James O'Brien 76

McMichael, Dan 389
McNamara, Robert 277
Medina, Ramon 404, 420, 428
Meese, Edwin 344, 350, 352–53, 356, 364–69, 380, 393, 407, 516
Mellon, Andrew 69
Mellon family 69, 508
Mellon, Paul 69
Melvin, Don 105–10
Menarczik, E. Douglas 411–12
Mengdon, Walter 166, 187
Menges, Constantine 393–94
Menke, John Roger 247
Mental Hygiene Society 69, 126
Merck & Co. 70, 331
Merck, George W. 70
Merrill Lynch 452
Mesta, Perle 313
Metropolitan Life Insurance Company of New York 449
Metternich, Prince Klemens 503–04
Meyer, Cord 252, 307
Meyer, Eugene 145
Meyers, Willie 466
MI–6 565
Miami Herald 400
Michaux, Frank 180
Michel, Bob 575
Midway Airlines 458
Mierzejewski, Chester 105–06, 109–12
Mike Douglas Show 489
Milian Rodriguez, Ramon 399–400
Military Assistance Group-Special Operations Group (MAG-SOG) 391
Milken, Michael 446, 450–53, 512, 514
Mills, Wilbur D. 192–93, 206–07
Milner, Lord 44
Milosevic, Slobodan 596
Mitchell, George 511, 575
Mitchell, John 160, 249, 263, 265
Mitscher, Marc A. 104
Mitterrand, François 500, 573, 583, 623, 628
Miyazawa, Kiichi 628, 631
MK-Ultra 3, 77, 126, 250

M.M. Warburg Co. 35, 38
Mobil Oil Corp. 206, 331
Modrow, Hans 547
Moellering, John 403, 410
Moffitt, Ronnie 316, 318–19
Mondale, Walter 496
Monroe Doctrine 524, 602
Monroe, James 602
Moore, Milt 106
Moorer, Thomas 356
Moorhead, Jay 378
Mora, Gonzalo 534
Morgan Bank 41
Morgan family 19, 22, 125, 339, 351, 603
Morgan, John Pierpont (Also see J.P. Morgan & Co) 16, 22, 24, 70, 87, 89, 136, 138, 602
Morgan, Junius 136
Morgenthau, Henry 55
Morgenthau Plan 55
Moro, Aldo 219
Morris, Ray 27, 34
Morris, Robert 169, 211
Morse, Rev. Jedidiah 88–89, 96
Morton & Co. 22
Morton, Rogers C.B. 211, 239, 286
Mosbacher, Bus 265–66
Mosbacher Energy Corp. 483
Mosbacher, Robert 11, 139, 169, 245, 263–66, 274, 297, 334–35, 347, 483, 492, 504, 514
Moseley, Thomas Wilder 132
Mossad 359, 406–07
Moynihan, Daniel Patrick 216, 581
Mubarak, Hosni 463, 563
Mueller, Lawrence 110–12
Mullen, Francis Jr. 461
Mulligan, William 383
Murphy, Daniel J. 306, 368, 379, 392
Murphy, Robert D. 309
Muskie, Edmund 156, 343, 359, 422, 505
Mussolini, Benito 30, 90, 96, 102, 536, 594
Mutual Benefit Life Insurance Company of New Jersey 451
Mutual Security Corp. 127

Nadeau, Leo 104–05, 111
Napoleon Bonaparte 488
Nash, Michael 610
Nashua Telegraph 345–46, 349, 364, 480, 578
Nasser, Gamel Abdul 78
National Association for the Advancement of Colored People (NAACP) 630
National Biscuit Company 451
National Broadcasting Corp. (NBC) 233, 260, 263, 337, 627, 630
National City Bank 14–15
National Democratic Policy Committee 495
National Endowment for the Preservation of Liberty 433
National Geographic Society 510
National Law Journal 471
National Narcotics Border Interdiction Systm 460
National Review 160, 485
National Science Foundation 201
National Security Study Memorandum 200 (NSSM 200) 276, 283
National Socialists (Nazis) 16, 23, 26–44, 61, 64–65 69–70 73–74, 76–77, 84, 87, 93, 95, 97–98, 102, 124, 195, 200–01, 293–04, 331, 489, 546
National Strategy Information Center 80, 348, 390
National Taxpayers Union 512
Nazi Labor Front 37, 84
Nedzi, Lucien 290, 293
Negroponte, John 505
Nelson, William 306, 324
Nero, Emperor 7
Nessen, Ron 554
Neuhaus, Joseph R. 169
Neuro-Psychiatric Institute of the Hartford Retreat for the Insane 126
New Deal 157–59, 162
Newington, Barbara 433
Newman, Della M. 509
New Masses 41
New Solidarity 338
Newsweek 145, 320, 336, 482, 557

New York Air 457
New York Daily News 375
New York Post 109–11
New York Times 33, 37, 41, 104, 128, 190, 208–10, 289, 292, 301–02, 310, 313, 322–23, 336, 382–83, 418, 431, 471, 529, 563, 567–68, 581, 593, 617, 622, 624
Nichomachean Ethics 583
Nietzsche, Friedrich 583–84
Nir, Amiram 403, 405–07, 411, 415–16
Nitze, Paul 321–22, 502
Nixon, Richard M. 81, 142, 156–57, 159–60, 163, 190, 196–98, 202, 207–19, 221–33, 235–46, 248–50, 254, 256–69, 272, 278–79, 286, 290, 292–94, 296, 299–300, 302, 304–05, 310, 332, 338, 344, 354, 365, 379, 440, 443–44, 484–85, 489, 501, 505, 515, 554, 581
Noriega, Manuel Antonio 174, 306, 526–39, 542
Norman, Montagu Collet 31, 35, 40, 43, 47–48, 62, 69, 93
Norris, Bill 463
North Carolina National Bank 328
North German Lloyd Co. 37–38, 40, 97
North, Oliver 3, 309, 357, 388–89, 392–95, 398–99, 401, 403–18, 424, 429, 431, 433–35
Northwest Airlines 458
Northwestern Mutual 449
Nosenko 323
Novak, Robert 291
Nunn, Sam 581, 584
Nye, Gerald 15

Oakley, Robert 403, 410
Oberdorfer, Don 275
O'Brien, Larry 298–99
October Surprise 352–53, 356, 358, 360–61, 623
O'Donnell, Patrick 299
O'Donnell, Peter 163, 168, 215
Oden, Sydnor 180
Odom, William 584

ODRA 220
Office of Strategic Services (OSS) 68, 274
Ogarrio Daguerre, Manuel 246–47
Olin Foundation 389, 502
Oliver, Spencer 253
O'Neill, Tip 313
Operation Alliance 460–61
Operation Desert Shield 157, 576, 581, 590
Operation Desert Storm 590, 615, 620
Operation Just Cause 536
Operation Mongoose 250, 306
Operation Phoenix 127, 279, 392
Operation Poised Hammer 592
Operations Sub-Group 386, 410
Orejuela, Rodriguez 534
Osborne, Frederick 59
Osborne, Howard 250–51
Overbey, John 143–45, 147
Owen, Rob 491
Owens-Illinois Glass 451
Oxford University 129

Pacific Pumps 142
Packard, David 323
Paisley, John 251–52, 255, 321–23
Palestine Liberation Organization (PLO) 558
Paley, William 311
Pan American Airways 68, 126, 190, 458
Pan American Petroleum Corp. 152
Park Chung Hee 313
Parkinson, Paula 491
Park Thomson, Suzi 313
Park, Tongsun 306, 313–14
Passman, Otto 314
Paterculus, Gaius Velleius 6
Pathfinder Fund 60
Patman, Wright 157, 246–50
Patterson, Robert 67
Pauley, Edwin 152
Paul VI, Pope 194; *Humanae Vitae*
Paul, Weiss, Rifkind, Wharton & Garrison 442

Pax Christi 377
Payson, Charles 68
Payson, Joan Whitney 68–69
Pearson, Drew 75
Pell, Claiborne 217, 430, 432
Peltz, Nelson 450
Pemex Corp. 152
Pennington, Harold D. 27
Penny, Tim 593
Pennzoil Corp. 177, 245–46, 264, 266, 297, 328, 331, 334, 396, 441–45
Pennzoil-Getty-Texaco wars 149
Pentagon Papers 245, 250
People Express 457
People magazine 153
Peper, Craig 167
Peres, Shimon 403, 416
Perforaciones Marinas del Golfo (Permargo) 152–53
Perkins, John Jr. 122
Perkins, Thomas Handasyd 119
Perle, Richard 322–23
Pershing, John J. 17
Pettit, Tom 337
Pfau, George Harold Jr. 133
Philby, H. "Kim" 79, 341
Philip Morris Tobacco Co. 534
Philip of Macedonia 340
Philip, Prince 508
Phillips Academy in Andover 9, 86–99, 102, 136, 149, 329
Phillips, David Atlee 316, 333
Phillips, Kevin 160, 484, 523
Phillips, Samuel 88
Pickens, T. Boone 11, 441–42, 445, 450, 453–54
Pickering, Thomas R. 400–02, 507
Pico, Reinaldo 252
Pierce, Franklin 10, 95
Pierce, Marvin 95
Pierpont family 119
Pierpont, James 135–36
Pierpont, John 136
Pike, Albert 330, 517
Pike Committee 290, 294, 300, 302–05, 310–11
Pike, Otis 290, 303–04, 310–11
Pinchot, Gifford 123
Pinochet Ugarte, Augusto 316–17

Pipes, Richard 321–22
Planned Parenthood Federation 53, 60, 195–96, 198
Plecker, W.A. 48
Plötz, Alfred 49
Podell, Bertram 206
Poindexter, John 309, 380, 394, 403, 405–10, 415, 526–28
Pol Pot 276–77, 279, 282, 285, 341, 378
Population Council 59
Population Crisis Committee (PCC) (See Draper Fund) 53, 56, 204–05
Posada Carriles, Luis 404, 420, 428, 435
Posner, Victor 450
Post Oak Bank 248
Pottinger, John Stanley 318–20, 354–55
Pouliot, J. Herman 345–46
Powell, Colin L. 380, 409, 506, 567, 585
Presidential Task Force on Market Mechanisms 454
Primakov, Yevgeny 582, 589, 597
Primer Banco de Ahorros 537
Princeton University 121, 135, 143, 238, 331
Prior, Russell 167
Proctor and Gamble Co. 58
Proctor, Edward 306
Pronto 471
Propper, Eugene M. 318–20; Labrinth 319
Proxmire, William 233, 453
Prudential Insurance Company 67, 449
Pryor, Samuel F. 15, 22, 36, 65–66, 69
Psychical Research Society 123
Psychological Strategy Board 73, 78
Pulliam, Eugene C. 492
Pulliam family 457
Pung Peng Cheng 280–82
Purolator Oil Company 329

Qaddafi, Muammar 383
Qiao Guanhua 275–76, 280, 283

Quayle, J. Danforth 117, 457, 490–94, 611, 617
Quigley, Joan 377
Quinlan, J. Michael 493
Quintero, Rafael "Chi Chi" 81, 173, 412–13

Raab, Maxwell 383
Racine 101; Britannicus 101
Radcliffe, Donnie 5; Simply Barbara Bush: A Portrait of America's Candid First Lady 5
Rafsanjani, Hashemi 357–58, 405, 521
Rahman, Sheik Mujibur 226
Rajai, Ali 359–60
Ramey, James N. 618
RAND Corporation 230
Range, Rebecca 457
Rapid American Corp. 450
Rather, Dan 486, 491
Rayburn, Sam 157, 183
Raymond, Walter 389–90
Reader's Digest 70, 170–71, 489
Reagan, Nancy 331, 347, 377–78
Reagan, Ronald 3, 153, 157, 159, 164, 169, 205, 238, 244, 289, 296, 302, 306, 322–23, 328, 331–32, 335–38, 343–70, 374–75, 377–81, 385, 387–88, 392–95, 397–98, 400, 402, 405–10, 415–17, 420–22, 439–41, 445–46, 449, 453, 455–58, 460, 469, 479–85, 487–88, 491, 495, 497, 501–02, 505–06, 508–10, 512, 516, 522, 526, 529–30, 541, 543, 548–49, 553, 555, 570, 577, 605
Rebozo, Bebe 259, 515
Redbook Magazine 164
Reed, Joseph V. 65; Fun with Cryptograms 65
Reed, Joseph V. Jr. 66
Reed, Lawrence S. 180
Reed, Permelia Pryor 66
Rees, John Rawlings 69
Regan, Donald 156, 364, 369, 374, 404, 406–08, 415, 421–22, 456, 505
Reilly, William 507
Reimer, R.E. 142

Reliance Insurance Co. 450
Remington Arms 15, 22, 36, 65, 69
Republican Task Force on Earth Resources and Population 52, 199, 204
Resorts International 452
Reston, James 581
Reuther, Walter 176
Revco 452
Revell, Oliver "Buck" 403, 410, 434–35
Rhodes, Cecil 124
Rhodes, Donald 112
Rhodes, John 262, 267, 334
Rice University 331
Rice, William Marsh 331
Richardson, Elliot 223, 261, 379
Richardson, H. Smith (Also see H. Smith Richardson Foundation) 77–78
Ridley, Nicholas 544, 546
Riegle, Don 556
Riklis, Meshulam 450
R.J. Reynolds Tobacco Co. 58, 73, 451
RJR Nabisco 446–47, 451–53
Robb, Charles 432, 586
Roberts, George 447, 451
Robertson, Pat 486–88
Robinson, Pauline 95
Robson, John 458
Rockefeller Commission 289–90, 295, 305, 308, 312
Rockefeller, David 164, 338–39, 343–44, 530
Rockefeller family 49, 59, 69, 124, 180, 206, 345
Rockefeller Foundation 59
Rockefeller, Godfrey Anderson "Rocky" 93, 97–98
Rockefeller, Godfrey S. 93
Rockefeller, Happy 324
Rockefeller Institute 61
Rockefeller, John D. 14, 62
Rockefeller, John D. Jr. 50–51
Rockefeller, John D. III 51, 59, 202
Rockefeller, Nelson 158, 163, 179, 199, 223, 249, 272–73, 285–86, 300, 308, 504
Rockefeller, Percy A. 14–15, 20

Rockefeller, William 14
Rocky Mountain News 371–72
Rodino, Peter 244, 250
Rodriguez, Felix I. (See Max Gomez) 81, 178, 306, 388, 390–92, 395–96, 399–402, 404, 407, 409, 412–20, 423–26, 428–29, 431–32, 434–35, 507, 521; Shadow Warrior 391
Rogers, Samuel H. 247
Rogers, William 217, 222–23, 227–28
Rogovin, Mitchell 307, 355
Rohatyn, Felix 553
Roll, Sir Eric 219
Rollins, Ed 491, 553
Roman, Petre 547
Roosevelt, Franklin Delano 2, 8, 64, 97, 103, 112, 121, 151, 156, 159, 219, 490, 570
Roosevelt, Theodore 18, 89, 103, 121, 123, 138, 339, 351, 524–25, 529, 532, 552, 601–03
Root, Elihu 103
Roskens, Ronald 476–77
Rosselli, John 81
Rostenkowski, Dan 453
Rostow, Eugene V. 322
Roth, William V. 294
Rothschild, Carol Warburg 128
Rothschild, Evelyn 512
Rothschild, Lord Victor 219, 327
Rounds, Bruce 333
Roussel, Pete 3
Rowland, Tiny 327, 561
Royal Dutch Shell 151
Royal Institute of International Affairs 219
Ruckelshaus, William 261
Rüdin, Ernst 49, 54
Rumsfeld, Donald 286–87, 308–09, 505
Rupp, Heinrich 359
Ruppe, Loret Miller 378
Rusher, William 159
Rusk, Dean 277, 322
Russell family 118
Russell, John 135
Russell, Louis James 252–58
Russell Manufacturing Company 118–19, 121, 136

Russell, Matthew Talcott 135
Russell, Nodiah 135–36
Russell, Samuel 119–20, 135–36
Russell Trust Association (See
  Skull and Bones Society) 117–
  19, 123, 135, 340
Russell, William Huntington 118,
  120, 122, 135–36

Sabah family 11, 561
Sabah, Jabir al, Emir of Kuwait 1,
  177, 327, 561
Safeway Corp. 451
Safire, William 620
Salinas de Gortari, Carlos 594–95
Salomon Brothers 451
Sanders, Bernie 578
San Francisco Examiner 419
Sanford, Terry 432
Sanger, Margaret 195
Sar, Saloth (See Pol Pot) 278–79
Sarbanes, Paul 423–24, 426
Sargent, Frank 489
Saunders, Harold 354
Savage, Gus 599
SAVAK 354
Sawyer, Peter 472, 474
Saxbe, William 267–68
Scaife, Richard Mellon 389
Scali, John 526
Scanlon, Kerry 630
Schacht, Hjalmar 35, 38, 40, 44, 48
Scheuer, James 194, 197, 199
Schiff, Jacob 14
Schlembach, Anton 582
Schlesinger, James Rodney 286,
  289, 292, 584
Schlumberger family 332
Schmidt, Helmut 338
Schmitz, Hermann 50
Schneebeli, Herman 195
Schorr, Daniel 292, 302, 310
Schram, Martin 367
Schroeder family 35
Schroeder, Kurt von 35, 38, 44,
  50
Schroeder, Rudolph von 35
Schwarzkopf, Norman 566–67,
  590, 599, 626
Scoon, Paul N. 394
Scott, Hugh 239

Scottish Rite of Freemasonry 181,
  330
Scowcroft, Brent 156, 160, 268,
  275–76, 286, 308–09, 422,
  501, 505–06, 520, 550, 557,
  564, 567, 572, 574, 587, 607
Scranton, William 305
Seamans Furniture 453
Seamless Steel Equipment Corpo-
  ration 27
Sears, John 344–46
Sears Roebuck Co. 77
Secord, Richard 307, 392, 413–
  14, 434
Seiden, Elliott 458
Seidman, William 505
Sembler, Melvin 509
Seneca 363
Serrano, Diaz 152–53
Setoudeh, Siavash 354
Seven Sisters oil cartel 148, 151,
  176
Seymour, Charles 116
Shackley, Theodore G. "Ted" 81,
  127, 173, 279, 306–07, 317,
  333, 378, 383, 391–92, 396–
  97, 435
Shadrin, Nick (See Nikolai Arta-
  monov) 323
Shah of Iran 353–54, 356
Shakespeare, William 83; *Coriola-
  nus* 83
Shamir, Yitzak 235, 558
Shannon, Edgar F. Jr. 289
Sharp, Sarah 515
Shearson Lehman Hutton 451
Shelby, Richard C. 586
Shell Oil Co. 47
Shevardnadze, Eduard 549–50,
  569, 573
Sheymov, Viktor Ivanovich 381
Shimon, Joseph 256–57
Shivers, Allan 156–57, 161, 181
Shockley, William 52, 199–200
Short Bros. 413
Shultz, George P. 238–39, 392–
  94, 398, 404, 407, 411, 421,
  466, 507
Sick, Gary 355, 358
Sihanouk, Prince Norodom 278,
  280–83

Silberman, Laurence 357
Silesian-American Corporation 27, 34
Silesian Holding Co. 32
Silliman, Benjamin Jr. 122
Silverado Savings and Loan 513, 555–56
Silverman, Joy 509
Simmons Co. 20
Simmons, Wallace 18
Simmons, William R. 167
Simon, Paul 424–25
Simpson, Al 490
Singlaub, John K. 391, 416
Sisco, Joseph 218
Skadden, Arps, Slate, Meagher & Flom 443
Skull and Bones Society 9, 14, 17–18, 52, 65, 68, 70, 77, 89, 101, 103, 105, 107, 112–13, 115, 117–33, 135–36, 139, 141, 148, 161, 165, 168, 192, 209, 272–75, 277, 293, 307, 317, 336–37, 340–42, 352, 357, 363, 365, 451, 485, 490, 494, 497, 517, 544, 604, 614; History of Our Order 132
Sloat, Jack 334
Smith, Adam 158, 175, 364
Smith, Michel 360
Smith, Peter 578
Smith, Robert C. 578
Smith, William French 370
Sneed, Michael 494
Sneider, Richard 313
Snepp, Frank 359
Snow, Tony 610
Solomon, Richard 274
Somoza, Anastasio 316
Sorenson, Kathleen 474, 476
Souter, David 551
Southern Air Transport 415, 418
South Florida Task Force 460–61, 537
Southland Corp. 452
South Sea Company 455
Special Situation Group (SSG) 3, 366, 368, 386–89, 392–93, 397, 401
Spence, Craig 469–70, 472
Spencer, Stuart 350, 491, 497

Spiegel, Thomas 450
Spivak, John L. 41 A Man in His Time 41
Spring-Rice, Sir Cecil 603
Stalin, Josef 2, 96
Standard Brands 451
Standard Oil Co. of New Jersey (See Exxon Corp.) 46, 48, 50–52, 77, 93, 97, 179, 396, 514
Standard Oil Co. of California 151, 331
Standard Oil Co. of Indiana 331, 371
Standing Crisis Pre-Planning Group (CPPG) 386–89, 392–93, 401, 406
Stanford family 337
Stans, Maurice 245–46, 248, 260, 266, 334
Stearns, Alfred E. 89
Steel, Jack 165
Steele, James 401, 404, 409, 429, 431
Steinberg, Saul 450
Stennis, John 295–96, 299–300
Stephens, Roy 471
Sterilization League of America 57–58, 60
Stetson, Eugene Jr. 77
Stevens, John 187
Stevens, Robert "Stretch" 396
Stevens, Sayre 306
Stevenson, Adlai 156, 174
Stewart, Potter 341
Stewart, Robert H. III 327
Stillman, James 14
Stillwell, Richard 333
Stimson, Henry L. 97, 99, 102–03, 112, 124, 127, 277, 341, 587–88
Stoertz, Howard 321
Stone, Oliver 446; "Wall Street" 446
Stone, W. Clement 210
Storer Broadcasting 452
Strategic Bombing Survey 67
Strauss, Franz Josef 315
Strauss, Robert 332
Stroessner, Alfredo 316
Sturgis, Frank 81, 252, 435
Sturgis, Russell 119, 121

Suazo Cordova, Roberto 399, 402
Suda, Don 321
Sudameris 537
Suddarth, Doris Smith 619; *Textbook of Medical-Surgical Nursing* 619
Suetonius Tranquillus, Gaius 8, 479; *The Lives of the Twelve Caesars* 8
Sultan of Brunei 327–415
Sulzberger family 37, 128
Sununu, John 487, 505, 520, 551–53, 570, 629
Super Chief South Corporation 465–66
Superior Oil Co. 442
Sussman, Leonard 389
Sutsakhan, Sak 287
Swaggart, Jimmy 488
Symington, Stuart 217, 296

Tacitus, Publius Cornelius 7–8
Taft, Alphonso 122
Taft, Robert Alphonso 122, 345
Taft, William Howard 103, 122, 124, 141, 497
Talmadge, Herman Eugene 258–60
Tanaka, Kakuei 315
Tanassi, Mario 315
Task Force on Regulatory Relief 442, 446, 455–56
Tate, Sheila 495, 509
Tavistock Institute 565
Tavistock Psychiatric Clinic 67, 69
"Taxi Driver" 374
Taylor, Sid 511
Taylor, Terry 618
Teagle, Tommy 467
Team A 320–22
Team B 251, 320–23, 349
Teeley, Peter 346, 371, 373
Teeter, Bob 486, 490, 509
Tekoah, Yosef 236
Temple, William 466
Terpil, Frank 317, 380, 383
Terrorism Task Force 386, 402–03, 405, 408–10, 412, 416, 422, 434
Terrorist Incident Working Group 386, 397

Texaco Corp. 441, 443–46
Texas Air Corp. 457–58
Texas Commerce Bank 330
Texas Gulf, Inc. 329
Texas Gulf Producing Corp. 180
Texas Instruments 334
Texas Observer 188–89
Thatcher, Margaret 510–11, 544–46, 559–60, 564–68, 580–81, 583, 592
Thawley, Tom and Nancy 165
Third International Congress on Eugenics 48
Thomas, Bill 275
Thomas, Clarence 552, 623, 626
Thomas, Evan 482
Thomas, Gordon 382
Thomas, Jon R. 333
Thornburgh Doctrine 525
Thornburgh, Richard 157, 508, 525, 535, 627
Thurman, Maxwell Reid "Mad Max" 531, 533, 535
Thurmond, Strom 159, 295, 303, 484, 488, 497
Thyssen family 27–28
Thyssen, Fritz 27–32, 35, 40, 53–54, 65, 70, 84, 201; *I Paid Hitler* 28
Thyssen-Hütte foundry 35
Tiarks, Frank Cyril 43
Tiberius, Emperor 6–7, 9, 601
Tickell, Sir Crispin 510
Time magazine 128, 182, 336, 452, 523
Timmons, William 262
Tisch, Lawrence 450
"Titticut Follies" 78
Tolliver, Michael 412
Toombs, Robert 330
Torrijos, Omar 533, 538
Tower Commission 369, 407–08, 421, 505, 507
Tower, John 156, 207, 210–11, 216, 303, 380, 422, 505
Townhouse Fund 273, 290, 293, 344
Townley, Michael Vernon 316–17, 320
Tracy, Malin and Pottinger 354
Trafficante, Santos 81, 391

Trafford, Abigail 618
Traficant, James A. Jr. 575
Train, Russell 4, 507
Trajan, Emperior 7
Trans World Airlines (TWA) 457–58
Travis, Bill 183
Treleaven, Harry 190–91, 212
Trilateral Commission 164, 338–39, 343–45
Trotsky, Leon 22
Trott, Stephen 529
Trudeau, Garry 605; "Doonesbury" 605
Truman, Harry F. 46, 51, 64, 67, 71, 73, 157, 206, 496
Tsongas, Paul 365
Tucker, Carll 69
Tucker, Carll Jr. 70
Tucker, Marilyn 492
Tucker, Phillip C. 330
Tucker, Ron 342, 434
Tudjman, Franjo 596
Turner, Stansfield 388
Tutwiler, Margaret 490, 562
Twain, Mark 480
Twin City Sentinel 59
Tydings, Joseph 198–99, 204

Udahl, Morris 131
Union Banking Corporation 26, 28–29, 32–36, 38, 42, 48, 53, 63
Union Bank of Switzerland 537
Union Pacific Railroad 14–15, 31, 331
Union Theological Seminary 128
United Airlines 458, 514, 522
United Fruit Company 121
United Gas Co. 442
United Nations (U.N.) 56, 178, 180, 193, 205, 214–39, 273–75, 354, 359, 482, 525–26, 566, 568, 572–74, 581–84, 586–87, 590, 593, 595
United Nations Population Fund 56
United Negro College Fund 189
United Shareholders Association 453

University of Indiana Law School 492
Untermeyer, Charles G. "Chase" 371, 379, 509
Upper Silesian Coal and Steel Company 33
U.S.A. Advocate 453
U.S.A. Racing 466
U.S. Agency for International Development 56, 60
U.S. Golf Association 22
U.S. Information Agency 129
U.S. & International Securities Corp. 53
U.S. News and World Report 530
U.S. Rubber Co. 20
Usher, Joseph 466

Van Buren, Martin 501
Vance, Cyrus 354, 505
van Cleave, William 321
Vanderbilt Energy Corporation 371–72
Vanderbilt family 19, 124
Van Herle, Andre 617
Vanick, Charles 206
Vatican 381–82, 536
Veillot, Bernard 406
Vespasian, Emperor 138
Vessey, John W. 393–94
Vick Chemical Company 77
Vickers Co. 15
Victoria, Queen 523
Village Voice 302, 310, 359, 471
Vitro Corp. 68
Voegler, Albert 35
Vogt, John 321
Volcker, Paul 339
von Raab, William 378, 464
Vorys, John Martin 125

W.A. Harriman & Co. 20–23, 29–30, 34–35, 40, 65, 69, 83, 141, 274
Waite, Morris R. 123
Walker, Edwin 169, 179
Walker family 492
Walker, George Herbert "Bert" (Also see G.H. Walker & Co.) 10, 27, 29, 32–33, 42, 83, 608
Walker, George Herbert Jr. "Uncle

Herbie" 10, 25, 52, 139, 145, 147–50
Walker, George Herbert III 69
Walker, John 378
Walker, Samuel Sloane Jr. 133
Wallace, George C. 172, 370, 497
Wallace, Henry 497
Wallace, Mike 420, 526
Waller, Calvin A.H. 585
Waller, John 307
Wallison, Peter 308
Wall Street Journal 189, 395, 495
Walsh, Lawrence 434, 623
Walters, Julie 473–74, 476
Walters, Tracey 473
Walters, Vernon 263, 265–66, 304, 317, 320, 490
Walters, William 555
Warburg, Erich 37
Warburg family (Also see M.M. Warburg Co.) 38, 41, 69
Warburg, Felix 14, 40
Warburg, Frederick M. 37
Warburg, Max 36, 38
Warburg, S.G. 22, 219
War Industries Board 15, 19, 31
Warren Commission 80
Washington, Eulice "Lisa" 473–76
Washington, George 523, 602
Washington Post 132–33, 145, 209, 217, 223, 225, 236, 244, 246, 249, 291, 301, 303, 313, 315, 319–20, 332–33, 367, 373, 418, 471, 476, 480–81, 494–95, 563, 606, 611, 613, 618, 624–25, 627, 631
Washington Star 292, 300–01, 311
Washington Times 469–70, 581, 610
Wasserstein, Bruce 443
Watergate 3, 81, 159, 218, 229, 238–74, 278, 297–98, 306–07, 310, 312, 314, 324
Watson, Samuel J. III 409, 414, 417, 426, 429, 431, 527
Wayne, John 486
Weaver, Howard Sayre 133
Webb, Barbara 473
Webb, Jarrett 473

Webb, Tracey 476
Webster, Harry 333
Webster, William 506, 525
Wedtech Corporation 516
Weicker, Lowell 303
Weinberger, Caspar 369–70, 374, 378, 393–94, 404, 407, 409, 506
Weintraub, Bruce D. 613
Weintraub, Jerry 622
Weir, Benjamin 507
Weiss, Seymour 321
Weitzel, Bill 445
Welch, Jasper Jr. 321
Welch, Richard 300–01
Welch, Robert 163
Weld, William 128, 516
Wellington, Duke of 544
Wells, William 306
Westoff, Charles 202–03; *From Now to Zero* 203
Weyerhauser, Frederick E. 123
Weyrich, Paul 506
White, Andrew D. 123
White House Special Investigations Unit 245
White, Weld & Co. 128, 516
White, William Gardner "Ted" 105–09, 112–13
Whitney, Cornelius Vanderbilt "Sonny" 68
Whitney family 19, 124
Whitney, Gertrude Vanderbilt 68
Whitney, John Hay "Jock" 68, 80
Whitney, William C. 68
Whybrow, Peter C. 618
Wick, Charles Z. 389
Wicker, Tom 323
Wilkie, Valleau Jr. 133
Wilkins, Calvin Howard Jr. 509
Will, George 291, 480
William, Clayton 580
Williams and Connally 376
Williams, Edward Bennett 286, 376
Williams, Eugene F. Jr. 149
Williams, Harrison 380
Williams, Ted 103
Wilmer, Cutler, and Pickering 379
Wilson, Bob 211
Wilson, Edwin 317–18, 383, 431

Wilson, Joseph 569
Wilson, Sam V. 333
Wilson, Woodrow 19, 330
Winston-Salem Journal 59
Wirthlin, Richard 350, 352, 356
Witcover, Jules 335, 351, 356
Woerner, Frederick F. 531
Wolf, Lester 313
Wolfe, Thomas 321
Wolfowitz, Paul 321, 323
Wolper, Allan 109
Wood, Robert E. 77
Woodruff, George W. 123
Woodward, Bob 244, 253–54
Woolley, Knight 20, 141
World Council of Churches 128
World Federation of Mental
  Health 69
World Resources Institute 193
World Vision, Inc. 376–77
World Wildlife Fund 508
Wright, Jim 157, 516–17
W.S. Farish & Co. 459, 515
Wyatt, Oscar 6

Yahya Khan 221, 223, 226–29
Yale University 9, 13–14, 17–18,
  20–21, 48, 52, 59, 65, 69–70,
  72, 74–76, 89, 91, 93, 103,
  105, 115–19, 121–27, 129–30,
  132–33, 135–36, 139, 141,
  143, 189, 275, 306–08, 337,
  340–41, 375, 510, 604, 614
Yamani, Zaki 484
Yang Shankun 274
Yarborough, Ralph Webster 101,
  151, 155–56, 160–62, 168–71,
  176–79, 181–84, 186, 209–11
Yeutter, Clayton 508
Yost, Charles 216
Young, David 251

Zakem, Dov 323
Zapata de Mexico 152
Zapata International Corporation
  152, 331
Zapata Lining Corporation 152
Zapata Offshore 139, 150–53,
  162, 164, 177, 179
Zapata Oil Company 52
Zapata Overseas Corporation 152
Zapata Petroleum 139, 146, 149–
  50
Zappala, Joseph 509
Zavala Oil Company 152
Zeder, Fred M. 329, 509
Zero Population Growth (ZPG)
  199
Zhang Hanzghi 275
Zhou Enlai 221, 223, 225, 227,
  231, 275, 280, 285
Ziegler, Ron 225

Third edition of the explosive best seller

DOPE, INC.

Updated and expanded

The war on drugs could have been won ten years ago, if our politicians had heeded the warnings in *Dope, Inc.* The war can *still* be won, if we force them to listen now.

Order today
$16 plus $3 shipping and handling

Ben Franklin Booksellers
107 South King Street
Leesburg, Virginia 22075
Phone: (703) 777-3661
FAX: (703) 777-8287

Visa and MasterCard accepted.
Virginia residents please add 4.5% sales tax.

FED UP WITH WASHINGTON POLITICIANS?

Then Throw The Book At Them
(but read it first)

The Power of Reason:1988
an autobiography by Lyndon H. LaRouche, Jr.

THE POWER OF REASON: 1988

An Autobiography by Lyndon H. LaRouche, Jr.

Published by Executive Intelligence Review

Order from Ben Franklin Booksellers, 107 South King St., Leesburg, VA 22075. $10 plus shipping ($1.50 for first copy, .50 for each additional copy). Bulk rates available.

Where's The Recovery?

Hospitals shut down, industrial factories are turned into condominiums, farms are foreclosed—and the Harvard economists say this is the recovery, the "post-industrial society." Subscribe to the political intelligence weekly that knows better, and that knows what to do about the deepening crisis.

☐ 3 months for **$125**
☐ 6 months for **$225**
☐ 1 year for **$396**
☐ I would like more information; please have a representative telephone me.

EIR News Service, Inc.
P.O. Box 17390,
Washington, D.C. 20041-0390

SPEAK OF THE DEVIL

KISSINGER IS BACK!

THE NEW FEDERALIST

National Newspaper of the American System

The appointment of Kissinger Associates, Inc. officials Brent Scowcroft and Lawrence Eagleburger to high positions in the Bush administration signals the consolidation of a "Kissinger coup" in Washington. Kissinger's "New Yalta" deal is set to go. For more information, subscribe to

- - THE NEW FEDERALIST -

☐ $35 for 100 issues ☐ $20 for 50 issues ☐ $15 for 25 issues

Name _____

Address _____

Make checks payable to:
The New Federalist
P.O. Box 889
Leesburg, Va. 22075

City _____ State _____ Zipcode _____

Telephone _____

Allow about four weeks for delivery of first issue.

How did we get to the moon?
How will we get to Mars?

Find out. Subscribe to 21ˢᵗ CENTURY
SCIENCE & TECHNOLOGY

The magazine that brings you tomorrow's technologies today.

Special offer

Subscribe now and receive *21 Century's* beautiful 1990 Calendar
(8½" × 11" full color)

"A Grand Tour of the Solar System"

$8 each postpaid (regularly $10)

Enclosed is:
- ☐ $20 1 year (6 issues)   ☐ $38 2 years (12 issues)   ☐ $4 single issue
- ☐ $_____ for _____copies of 21 Century's 1990 Calendar (at $10 each; $8 each if ordered with a subscription)

Total enclosed: $ _____

Name _____

Address _____

City _____ State _____ Zip _____

Payment accepted in U.S. currency only. Gift cards available. Allow six weeks for delivery of calendar.

Make check or money order payable to:

21st Century Dept. R, P.O. Box 65473, Washington, D.C. 20035